THE UK TRAILWALKER'S HANDBOOK

edited by
Paul Lawrence, Les Maple and John Sparshatt

THE LONG DISTANCE WALKERS' ASSOCIATION
www.ldwa.org.uk

2 POLICE SQUARE, MILNTHORPE, CUMBRIA LA7 7PY
www.cicerone.co.uk

Eighth edition of the Handbook
First edition published by Cicerone 2009
ISBN: 978 1 85284 579 7

This directory was formerly published as *The Long Distance Walkers' Handbook* by A&C Black, the previous (seventh) edition under ISBN 0 7136 6096 1.

Printed by KHL Printing, Singapore
A catalogue record for this book is available from the British Library.

Acknowledgements

This book has been researched and compiled almost entirely by the Long Distance Walkers' Association (LDWA) Long Distance Paths (LDPs) Team, a group of enthusiastic volunteers with a common interest in communicating information about the UK LDPs network so that more people use, enjoy and benefit from it. In addition to the three editors many other LDWA members played significant roles. Particular thanks are due to regional researchers who covered parts of the UK: Peter Grayson, Edith Moran, Jeff Parr and Margaret Waller. Additional material and research was contributed by David Allen, Alan Castle, Geoff Crowder, Derek Ellis, Carol Engel, Katie Hunt, David Irons, Chris Kippin, John Knight, Laurence Main, Adrian Rayner, Ronald Turnbull and Mike Warner. Ann Sayer assembled many of the waymark logos and Tony Willey assisted with the map lists. The technical skills of Simon Leck were invaluable in creating the route maps. Thanks are also due to many members of the LDWA who contributed information or helped in other ways, along with individuals or organisations that have provided information or responded to enquiries. Since 2003, Paul Lawrence has led the development of the LDWA's LDPs services including their information web pages. He and Les Maple built the original database that was researched by Brian Smith and Sue Hazell and has since been implemented online. John Sparshatt updated a major part of the route information and prepared the mapping. The book also draws upon Natural England's landscape and natural areas classifications and their recent trails review. Numerous local authorities have given permission for reproduction of waymarks.

Photo credits

All photographs are by the editors, with the following exceptions: Fiona Barltrop: pages 15, 29, 44, 51, 169, 171, 182, 291, 295; Mick Birkinshaw, Barnsley Countryside Team: pages 12, 197–198; Steve Clark: page 263; Paddy Dillon: pages 2, 6, 8, 11, 19, 20, 21, 22, 27, 30, 33-39, 48, 52–56, 59, 88, 122, 133, 168, 214, 257, 317, 319, 322, 330, 345, 347–348, 351; Rodney Hart: pages 16 and 46; David Hunt: page 296; Terry Pilkington: pages 31 and 138; Mark Richards: pages 235–236. Tom Sinclair: pages 339 and 340; and Ronald Turnbull: pages 23–26, 91, 94, 113, 134–35, 137, 172, 237, 258, 272, 335–337.

Disclaimer

While every effort has been made to ensure that the information in this Handbook is accurate, no responsibility whatsoever can be accepted by the Long Distance Walkers' Association Limited, its directors, officers or authors, or the publishers, for any consequences arising from the contents of the Handbook. Inclusion of a route is in no way an indication of its quality in terms of scenery, attraction, usability or safety. Care has been taken to include routes that are on rights of way, or paths or access areas where permission exists, but inclusion of a route is no evidence of a right of way or permissive access. The content of this Handbook depends on information obtained from thousands of enquiries and from many publications, and reliance has had to be placed on the information providers. Every effort has been made to ensure correctness of detail but errors or omissions may have escaped notice. This Handbook does not attempt to provide advice on safety aspects of walking. There are inherent risks in any outdoor activity, and walkers should note the specific safety advice offered in the various publications available. Views expressed in this book are those of the editors.

Front cover: Walkers on the Cumbria Way in Great Langdale (Fiona Barltrop)

CONTENTS

FOREWORD

INTRODUCTION

THE TRAILS

LISTINGS

The Hadrian's Wall Path, seen here near Portgate, runs alongside the busy B6318

FOREWORD

The public footpath network in the United Kingdom is a national treasure and one of its most priceless recreational resources. Nowhere else in the world is there anything quite like this. We owe this network to our distant ancestors. Walking along it, for them, was an everyday necessity, not a leisure activity. It was about getting to the local market, going to work at the mill or transporting minerals to be smelted. The ancient drove roads, quite often covering long distances, were used to take cattle and sheep to the market sales.

As the canals, railways and motorised transport developed the use of this tangled web of local paths declined. Gradually, over the centuries, they faded into obscurity, left waiting to be rediscovered, like a watermark in the landscape.

Their rediscovery had to wait until the 19th-century, when working people, helped by a few visionary philanthropists, began to appreciate the benefits of escaping into the countryside from the smoky, crowded, polluted cities that had grown up from the industrial revolution. Although the rights to use the paths were mainly preserved, ramblers often had to fight for their rights of access on private uplands, for their 'right to roam' as the 1930s campaigner, Tom Stephenson, had put it. He also had a vision of a first 'National Trail', but it took until 1965 for it to bear fruit in the Pennine Way.

We have a remarkable range of inspiring, sometimes awe-inspiring, landscapes in the UK. Their origins lie in a rare combination of geology and human impact, a fascinating conjunction visible all along our trails. The peaks, ridges, rocky cwms, rounded hills, lakes, and river gorges that we see today were formed by fire, ice and the movement of the tectonic continental plates. We human beings have left our marks too: in scars of old mineral workings, in fishing coves, in field boundaries, and in our great cities.

Many trails have echoes of people from the past, shadowy groups like the Border Reivers and the Scottish caterans. Others recall great saints, monarchs, authors and scientists whose ideas changed the world. In Scotland and the Borders, you can walk in the footsteps of St Cuthbert, or along the Lothian shores where a young John Muir strode in his boyhood; or investigate the area frequented by the notorious Highland outlaw Rob Roy. You can see where Dylan Thomas took his inspiration in a Welsh coastal town; wander in meadows where an observant Darwin formed his radical ideas; or follow Charles II on his long escape route. There are routes that link neatly to major sites of importance – the world's first Iron Bridge, the Cornish tin mines, or the village of New Lanark where ideas of social welfare were born – all World Heritage Sites. Many trails visit National Parks and Areas of Natural Beauty, which have been designated in order to help protect many of the UK's important and beautiful areas. It could be said that the heritage of a nation is written along our paths, and themes can often bring a walk to life.

Growing numbers of people are looking for more ways to appreciate and enjoy the natural world. Walking trails and long distance routes can offer you that and, unlike many outdoor activities, trailwalking needs no expensive new facilities. The paths have long been there – abundant, free and widely accessible.

Finding information about the many hundreds of routes available can be a real barrier to tapping into this abundant resource. The LDWA has done an excellent job helping to fill this knowledge gap by researching all of these trails, explaining why they are there, what you will see en route, what publications are available, and how you can chose the right one for the experience that you are seeking. So let this book be your guide as you plan your next walking adventure. You will be spoilt for choice!

Sir John Johnson
President, Long Distance Walkers' Association

A pleasure barge noses its way carefully into Goring Lock on the River Thames while heading upstream

INTRODUCTION

The history of UK trails

In the UK we are fortunate, perhaps uniquely fortunate, to have such an extensive network of public rights of way that can be connected to make longer routes through our diverse landscape. This book is about these longer routes – Long Distance Paths (LDPs) – that now span the length and breadth of the nation. Walking is a valuable recreation from a purely physical point of view, but many of us find that a long journey along a trail is also an opportunity for mental and spiritual renewal as well.

This Handbook covers about 720 main trails and about 190 shorter routes, offering the walker a very wide range of experiences, but LDPs are in historical terms a comparatively recent introduction in the UK. In 1935 Tom Stephenson, a ramblers' campaigner, had the vision of 'a Long Green Trail, a Pennine Way from the Peak to the Cheviots'. Thirty years passed before his dream was realised in 1965 with the opening of the Pennine Way as the first UK National Trail. In 1969 the Cleveland Way followed and in 1970 Wales saw its first, the Pembrokeshire Coast Path. More national routes followed in the 1970s, and in 1980 Scotland's first, the West Highland Way, was designated as an official 'Scottish Long Distance Route'. Although still awaiting a 'national trail' of comparable pedigree, Northern Ireland has a small, growing and valuable collection of shorter walking routes, the Waymarked Ways, being designated as quality routes. At the moment, we list about ten totalling some 290 miles (460km).

These national trails soon grew in popularity with walkers, who appreciated their combination of some of the best countryside and high standards of trail maintenance and waymarking (where appropriate). They liked the interesting guidebooks, covering the trails' themes and the varied sites to be seen along the way. As trail usage grew, supporting services developed in parallel, with accommodation easily linked, complete guided holidays on offer, and baggage services opening the trails to those not wanting to backpack or 'rough it'. These trails now offer a reliable, easy-to-use 'package' to walkers who do not have the time or the skills, or perhaps the

Dorset, South West Coast Path, view towards Portland

inclination, to work out their own routes in unfamiliar areas far from home. On these well-used trails you will meet other walkers, making them less intimidating than less well-used trails and allowing the inexperienced to practise map reading and navigational skills. Britain now has some 3200 miles (5200km) of national trails in its 19 routes and they still have a vital role in setting benchmarks for subsequent route developers to follow. Coupled with their strong 'brand image' and wide public recognition, this has laid the essential foundations for the wider LDP network described in this book.

Inspired by the success of the national trails, keen walkers and ramblers, individually and through their clubs, soon started to develop their own informal trails and to write guidebooks, sometimes self-published, while in parallel, local authorities, seeing the benefits of providing their own networks, developed area routes, sometimes collaborating with their neighbouring areas to offer regional trails at standards sometimes not far short of those on the national routes.

It is a remarkable network. The LDWA has been documenting these trails since 1980 and since then the number of trails has increased from about 150 to the 720 main routes in this book. Tom Stephenson might be amazed to discover that we now cover some 60,000 miles of routes, right across the UK – a huge range of options. (The path network as a whole is close to 150,000 miles or 240,000km).

So what benefits do trails bring and how can their use best be fostered in the future?

The benefits of, and barriers to, trailwalking

As we have seen, the number of UK trails has been steadily growing. New trails are being developed all the time – since 2002, when the LDWA last published a similar Handbook, some 200 new routes have been added. Every new issue of the LDWA's *Strider* magazine includes many new routes.

However, only the successful routes continue long term – since 2002 over 100 routes have been lost. Only those offering a quality combination of a good theme, scenery, guidebook, mapping, funding, promotion, support and accessibility endure. Many routes established in a wave of enthusiasm last only a few years and some millennium routes (established with funding to mark the year 2000) have already been lost. Funding bodies need to consider these factors carefully when allocating initial capital.

It is evident from the number of commercial publishers involved in supporting LDPs (we list about 400 in our Directory of Suppliers), and the growing number of support services companies (currently over 60), that people walking trails generate substantial economic value. Local authorities developing new routes will first make an economic impact assessment and most have seen a positive value in having a route network in their area. Trail usage on the National Trails (NTs) is monitored and some 12 million people in England used at least one NT in 2005. Around half were out for a full day while a third aimed to complete the full trail, often over several trips.

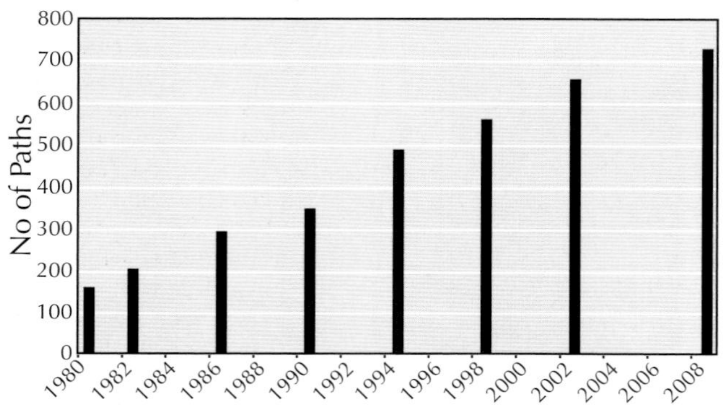

With no central management of the rest of the promoted routes network, until recently there has been little hard evidence of its use. In 2008, Natural England surveyed the adult public about use of the major promoted trails to produce a strategic review covering both the National Trails and the wider network. (Natural England's definition of a trail is broadly similar to this book's – a combination of rights of way, more than a day's walk in length – except that it excludes enthusiasts' routes.) The survey showed a wide appreciation that trails exist, and a very substantial level of use.

However, people said they found it hard to find information about routes – there are many more trails than people think there are. While people recognised the National Trails as an iconic 'brand' that they could trust to provide a 'high quality' route and a satisfying experience, they found it much harder to assess the experience they would get walking the other 'second rank' trails. Natural England concluded that there was a case for improved information provision, and also for an accreditation or recognition system to provide a form of 'quality mark' for 'the best trails'. At the time of researching this book they were reviewing detailed approaches to implementing these and various other changes to trail management.

Natural England's survey suggested that over the previous year (2007) almost two-thirds of the adult population (26 million) took part in leisure walking. Walking is the most popular outdoor activity. In the past year, some 16 million (38 per cent) had used a named LDP. Some 6.5 million (15 per cent) used a trail at least weekly, and a further 9 million (23 per cent) used them less often. These groups said they could be encouraged to use trails more, locally or on holiday. The survey identified a very substantial opportunity for even more people to become regular trailwalkers. Some 15 million more (36 per cent) could be encouraged to be more active generally to improve their health, and were interested in using trails, but had little awareness of them. The most commonly cited barrier to greater use of trails was lack of information (49 per cent), followed by path quality (35 per cent). Lack of promoted paths and need for better services were also perceived as significant barriers, but this may more often conceal a lack of information, rather than of actual trails or facilities – two thirds of local authorities believe there are now enough routes in England.

The survey also showed that the 15 million potential new users come from all age groups, income bands and cultural backgrounds, so trail walking is potentially a highly inclusive activity. Trails once established are a relatively cheap resource: while National Trails cost annually around £1000 a mile (about 20 pence per user per mile) – reflecting the often difficult or fragile terrain they cover (such as cliffs or peat areas) and their high and defined standards, typical rights of way cost

Walkers follow the South Downs Way along a clear track on the slopes of Linch Down

Leisure Activities in England – 2008

(Natural England survey of 1787 respondents)

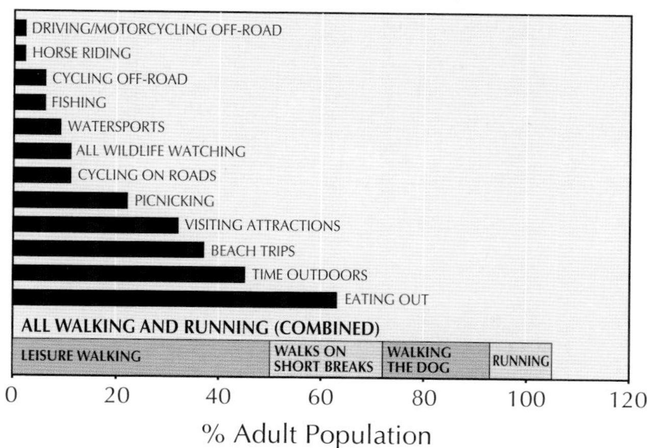

A tranquil spot in Canon Hall Country Park, Barnsley Boundary Walk

about £300 a mile. Promoted routes lie somewhere above the lower figure, depending on the needs for promotion, updated leaflets and fresh waymarking. In comparison just a single walker staying in the area may easily bring in £50 or more to the local economy daily (some flowing into taxes and duties) while leaving almost no trace on the ground and costing almost nothing at the margin.

For policy makers, the simple message from this evidence is that where there is already a good path network, a cheap and easy strategy is to promote, and to provide better information about, the established trails.

The way ahead for trails

Arguably there has never been a better time for trails and their future seems assured. They combine a potentially 'green' activity that should leave almost no trace and that, once the walker is on foot, has little or no carbon footprint, with a low cost and significant health benefits, both physical and mental. These benefits apply particularly to an ageing population often with fixed incomes and time to spare, that wants to remain fit and active while meeting new companions. In addition there is a substantial net benefit from 'trail tourism' to the rural economies often in poorer areas, where most paths run.

New trails will no doubt continue to be developed – with less than 60,000 miles of rights of way so far covered by trails out of about 144,000 miles. There is still much scope, while less successful routes will fall out of use.

A number of other trends are evident already or appear likely, with an overall policy shift towards providing an 'integrated access network' rather than a 'rights of way network'. The recent fresh approaches to managing rights of way and access, involving the rights of way improvement plans (ROWIPs) completed in 2007 by local authorities in England and Wales, have led to changes that emphasise making the best use of the whole network to benefit the public, through an integrated approach that looks at the health, sustainable transport, climate change and disabled access agendas together. For trails, this is likely to have most impact in urban areas with more linear and linking routes, making for a better-connected network. In rural areas major trail corridors will see developments around the mature core trails, such as shorter circular options, sometimes with the added benefit of reducing pressure on an over-used existing trail in a fragile landscape, and possibly calling on some agri-environment funding. However, the pressure for more short routes should not be to the detriment of the longer core route they rely on. Another issue is that, while walking itself is comparatively green, getting to and from a walk may not be, and efforts continue by local authorities to integrate public transport and trail access points better, and by walking groups to car share or use public transport more effectively.

There will also be developments in establishing new paths and local access, perhaps with permissive agreements, using green spaces such as canals, where they can augment or better link existing routes. Our network developed historically over the millennia for reasons of utility, driven by the needs of an ancient transport system that underpinned commerce. There is no reason why it should not now meet all the needs of recreational walkers, or even of those wishing to use it to get to their modern workplace. Some targeted trading of existing rights of way for new ones may provide benefits overall.

The recent wider changes in access legislation in Britain have opened up much new access land and some trails are already taking advantage, for example to access the source of a river previously 'out of bounds'. But in the main the trails we cover use rights of way and need to be marked, so this may not lead to much change, except in the case of enthusiasts' routes on access land. Of more significance is the enacting in England of

Access land sign in South Downs area

new legal rights to secure a continuous long-distance walking trail around the English coast. This will open up some new sections and complete the 'English Coastal Path', as a new National Trail incorporating the South West Coast Path, coastal sections of the Cleveland Way and many other existing promoted coastal routes.

While trails do have a positive future, great vigilance is still needed from walkers' campaigning organisations such as the Ramblers, to ensure that paths are not lost or the network eroded, and trailwalkers need to continue to support this work.

Routes in this Handbook

In this Handbook (and on the corresponding LDWA online database) we aim to include UK routes that have a name, that are mainly off-road and on public rights of way suitable for walkers, and that offer more than one day's walking for most users. In practice this means that most routes we list are over 15 miles and we aim to cover all those of 20 miles or more. Some shorter routes are included, where, for example, they provide useful links between longer routes, or have a particular significance for walkers: most of these we cover in summary only within the entry for the major route that they link to (their 'parent' route), but some warrant a full entry in their own right. Also included are many 'challenges' for which the detailed route is self-devised and for which navigational skills are required. All routes, major and minor, are included in the Index of Trails at the back of this Handbook.

The routes included all have some form of publication providing at least a basic route description or definition, and one that is readily available to the public, either free or at a reasonable cost. So we term all of these routes 'promoted routes', although they vary vastly in standard and in the experiences they provide. Walkers can chose anything from one of the easier national trails, walked as a tailored holiday package with full support, to an extreme unsupported challenge across moor and mountain between prescribed locations demanding endurance and navigational skills, rewarded perhaps by a certificate and a badge to mark the achievement.

We use the term 'trail' in this book as a catch-all shorthand. In the US the 'trail' may often be the only route in the landscape; in the UK trails are routes, combinations of the very many individual but linking 'rights of way', each often quite short. As you follow a trail, there will always be many paths on the ground to choose from, making it essential either to follow the waymarks, use a guidebook, or at least follow the line shown on Ordnance Survey maps (if your particular route is marked).

We also include some 200 'enthusiasts' routes' in this book, some suitable only for experienced and fit walkers. Of these, Anytime Challenges are normally unwaymarked routes, mostly devised by an individual or club, with a simple route description and often a certificate or a badge for successful completers available from a 'recorder' who may maintain a register. These challenges can be completed at any time. Some form the basis of annual challenge events, when there will be support, although the route may vary from the standard version. These challenges are mostly in the northern counties of England, where they are very popular. Kanters are a variant – a simple series of grid references to be linked by a self-devised route.

Selecting the right trail

Walking a long distance path is certainly a fulfilling experience: a fine route often through attractive countryside walked in good company, with the route planning taken care of, and, at the end, the satisfaction of having achieved a definite objective. But the nature of the experience people seek varies very widely indeed. Features that strongly attract one walker may not fit at all with another's objectives. The abilities and experience of your walking companions are also highly relevant. With so many routes available, it's difficult

View towards Woolacombe, Devon (South West Coast Path)

to know where to begin. In this book we aim to provide the information you will need to find a route that meets all your aspirations and criteria for a good walk.

First you need to decide where you plan to walk. Are you looking for a holiday trip to a new area, or a day walk nearer home, or perhaps a longer walk to see your local area from a new perspective? For each country and region we give a summary both of the area's geography and the defining landscapes that relate to the walking routes, and we summarise each of the routes, focusing on why they have been established. The locations of a selection of major mostly waymarked routes, excluding the National Trails, are included on the regional and national maps. The National Trails have a separate section, with its own introduction, overview map and a directory of routes by country. (A complete map of all the routes is available on the LDWA website at www.ldwa.org.uk.) The short letter code on each route marked can be used to identify it in the accompanying legend and there is a brief key to the regional maps on the front cover flap of this book. We also list some 'highlight' sections, which offer a taste of each area's defining features, if your time is limited. These sectional introductions should help you to shortlist some routes to consider.

The directory entries

To help you make your final selection we cover each route in a standardised format. For easy reference, there is a key to the layout of the directory entries on the back cover flap of this Handbook.

Each entry lists the basic trail information – its location, distance and whether it is waymarked and the symbol used if so. It also indicates where a trail is named on OS mapping and lists the relevant OS maps, both 1:50,000 and 1:25,000 scale. The locations of the start and finish of the paths is also given, with full grid references.

For each route, a brief thumbnail description aims to give a feel for the nature of the trail – its theme, why it is there at all, the terrain, and any particularly interesting sites or features en route. In addition the trails are graded for difficulty (see below) and any relevant user groups (eg the Pennine Way Association) or websites are listed.

There is also a list of relevant publications alongside details of any badges or certificates on offer to those who complete the route. Books or leaflets vary widely but usually have a route description or sketch map, and perhaps notes on local history and wildlife. The Directory of Suppliers at the back of the Handbook gives details of where these can be obtained, with full postal addresses and phone numbers for those not using the internet. (Many items are now available online.) Publication information is believed to be correct at the time of going to press, but it should be remembered that books go out of print, prices change, and some leaflets are revised regularly. Tourist Information Centres often stock publications relating to local paths.

For many walkers the degree of support available on a route is important. Increasing numbers of businesses now offer inclusive guided or self-guided holidays, or at least co-ordinated baggage carriage. These are listed as 'walking support providers' under each route, and their contact details are in the Directory of Suppliers. Their websites carry full information and often booking facilities.

Trail attributes

While walking is an exhilarating experience, physically and mentally, taking the walker away from the cares of everyday life into the open air often to enjoy fine views, trails also offer another dimension, which many walkers find attractive. Each has its own theme, that motivated its creators and that can be explored as you walk it. These themes vary widely, from following a geological line or a landscape feature, to the travels of a figure from history, the commemoration of a person, or a particular date or anniversary, such as the dawn of the third millennium. Others include a town's or borough's 'home route' that, following old UK traditions, 'beats the bounds' around it.

With this in mind, apart from the basic facts and figures for a trail, we also tag each trail with the key features that it offers – its 'attributes' – as a quick way to select the sort of experience you are seeking, or perhaps wanting to avoid, that apply to a significant part of the route. The categories into which potential attributes might fall are:

- **Trail Class:** National Routes, Quality Routes (in Northern Ireland), Anytime Challenges or Kanters
- **Trail Type:** such as multi-user trails, those designed mainly for horse-riders or cyclists or routes on former railway lines

Windsor Castle and the River Thames from Eton riverside (Thames Path)

- **Terrain:** such as mountain, moorland, coastal, lake/reservoir, river, canal, forest/woodland, downland, urban
- **Cultural:** such as World Heritage Site, other heritage interest (including industrial heritage or routes based on historical figures), military or literary routes, routes with religious themes or routes of pilgrimage, and paths with geological themes
- **Charity:** routes aiming to raise funds from sponsorship.

Trail gradings

To help you select routes of a suitable standard, some routes have been graded, on a rather subjective basis, as:

- **Very Challenging:** routes demanding considerable fitness and stamina, with support needed or sensible for many walkers, involving remote and rough upland terrain and self-navigation, usually unmarked and sometimes including off-path sections
- **Challenging:** routes featuring significant ascent and descent, some rough ground, often remote from habitations, with map-reading skills needed in bad weather or off-route, sometimes with extended distances between settlements
- **Easy:** routes on relatively undemanding terrain, often well-surfaced, well marked or easy to follow, with relatively good support services.

The majority of the trails – those of average difficulty – are not graded. We also assume average weather conditions for the region in question. However, it must be recognised that walking any trail over several days will be much more demanding than everyday walking at home and that the weather and the season can make what would otherwise be a simple route very challenging indeed. If you are just starting to walk trails, get experience first by day-walking with a similar size of pack to the one you will take on the trail.

As a very rough guide to the ease of following a trail, it will be easier to follow a waymarked route and one in lowland country. Waymarks may sometimes be missing, especially on older routes, and even on National Trails waymarking is deliberately less frequent in remote country to

A wooden fingerpost indicates the route of the South Downs Way

provide a wilder experience. If you are new to trailwalking start with a route near home, possibly an urban route, and go with a friend who has some experience, but try to do your own navigation. Better still, learn to navigate and to read a map using one of the many courses on offer.

Maps

Printed maps

A large-scale paper map should be carried when walking any LDP. Each directory entry lists the relevant Ordnance Survey (OS) map numbers. The Landranger 1:50,000 scale maps are good for initial planning and adequate for most route-finding purposes. For those who like more detail, including field boundaries and the like, the OS Explorer (1:25,000) series now covers all of Britain with rugged, waterproof versions available as the 'Active' series. The routes of many major LDPs are marked on these maps with red or green diamond lozenges.

Official guidebooks to the English National Trails contain extracts from OS maps, as do some other route guides, and these may suffice if detours from the route are not expected. Other publishers, in particular Harvey Maps, have produced dedicated maps for certain LDPs, while GEOProjects provide a range of waterways maps. A few routes are marked only on OS maps, their supporting paper publications having gone out of print. Maps are widely available through local book and outdoor shops. Some major stockists include Aqua3, Cordee Ltd, Dash4it, Elstead Maps, Guidepost, Map and Compass, National Map Centre, The Map Shop, Trident Maps and Stanfords.

Digital maps

Digital maps are becoming increasingly useful to trailwalkers. Full OS mapping is available for home use on a computer, enabling printing of tailored extracts, and a pre-plotted track can be added and transferred as waypoints to a GPS. A range of hand-held devices with varying battery life now support full-quality OS mapping, from PDAs through smart-phones to GPSs that take maps on memory cards. The main suppliers of digital maps are currently Anquet, Memory-Map and Tracklogs. Major suppliers of GPSs are Garmin and Satmap. For some routes, such as National Trails, tailored digital strip-mapping is also available for these devices.

Walking Long Distance Paths

There are many ways to walk an LDP, depending on time available, fitness, or whether the walk is to be combined with other local sightseeing. The most popular approach is to walk a path over several consecutive days, covering 10 to 20 miles each day and stopping at bed and breakfast accommodation en route, or perhaps camping. A number of commercial organisations offer guided holidays along LDPs, with accommodation and meals arranged. For some paths there is a central booking service that will arrange nightly accommodation along the route, and sometimes arrangements can be made to transport luggage between overnight stops. Longer paths can be completed in sections over several holidays or weekends. While many people walk an LDP near home as a series of day walks, this may be more difficult where transport back to the starting point is an issue. A shorter LDP can be an exhilarating challenge to complete in a single long day, and walking groups sometimes include a 20-mile route in their programme.

Careful planning is essential for any long-distance route and many of the publications listed in the directory entries give helpful advice tailored to the route. Hilly routes take much longer to walk than flatter routes and rough paths slow the pace. The distance to be walked each day requires thought: trying to walk too far carrying a heavy rucksack will detract from the enjoyment. Advice on safe walking may be found in many books, and specific local advice is contained in many of the path publications. The equipment, clothing and food to be carried will depend on the remoteness and terrain of the route.

Accommodation

Walking an LDP, especially for a group in summer, requires a very wide choice of accommodation to find a workable sequence. Some route publications include accommodation information, and the directory entries indicate this. National Trail websites increasingly list accommodation searchable by an interactive map. Local Tourist Information Centres (TICs) have extensive accommodation lists and their telephone numbers are online or obtainable from directory services. There are many other 'ungraded' rural bed and breakfasts that simply display a sign or rely on word of mouth. A web search can lead quickly to accommodation in many areas.

The various Youth Hostels Associations maintain networks of youth hostels and camping barns, and in some cases provide a booking service: in England and Wales, the Youth Hostels Association; in Scotland, the Scottish Youth Hostels Association, and for Northern Ireland, Hostelling International. There are increasing numbers of independent hostels and the Backpackers Press has an extensive website and publishes the *Independent Hostel Guide* annually. Those intending to camp may find it useful to join the *Backpackers Club* which lists campsites in remoter areas in its Long Distance Footpath Site and Pitch directory, covering many UK routes. Compiled and updated by its members, it is highly useful for the backpacker.

B&B sign for Old Water View on the Coast to Coast

Gritstone outcrops jut from the bleak moors around Gorple and Widdop on the Pennine Bridleway

Using the LDWA website

The LDWA has a comprehensive public website with trails information, corresponding to the structure of this book (visit www.ldwa.org.uk and follow 'Paths & Trails'). Frequently updated, it includes available information on major path diversions and news items on new and upgraded LDPs. It carries more detailed descriptions of routes, elevation profiles (to see how hilly a route is) and downloadable items such as GPS track files and some route leaflets. Many long distance paths, including national trails, have their own web pages, often well maintained, but not all information may be regularly updated.

Once you have used this book to select your route, you can use the LDWA site to link directly to a route's own web pages, often very hard to find on, say, a large local authority website, and we only list here the basic 'root' web address. The LDWA always welcomes information on new routes or publications and updates which should ideally be sent via the 'Contact Us' area of the website. The LDWA LDP web pages are free to use only by individuals (in keeping with the voluntary work to maintain them). If you wish to use them for business or professional purposes, the LDWA will provide a suitable licence, with higher levels of access and reporting than on the public site. The LDWA also provides consultancy services on the LDPs network.

Using this Handbook

The Handbook recognises two categories of routes: main routes (with their own entry) and sub-routes (mentioned within the 'parent' main route entries). Sub-routes are usually local, shorter or linking routes.

It is structured in three sections:

- **Introduction**
- **The Trails** – split into The National Trails (in England, Wales and Scotland), and Regional and Other Trails, organised into England (split into 8 English regions), Wales, Scotland, Northern Ireland and E-routes. Each section has an introduction and overview map, followed by an alphabetical directory of routes, with full information for each main path (outlined in 'The directory entries' on p15).
- **Listings** – Top 100 Trails by Distance – down to 100 miles (161 km); Index of Trails – an alphabetical index of all main routes and sub-routes listed in this Handbook; and Directory of Suppliers – full contact details of organisations that supply publications listed in the directory entries, walking support services and other useful postal addresses and websites.

How to find a named trail or path

- If you know the name of the route you are looking for, use the Index of Trails to find it

Descending from The Cheviot as the Pennine Way finally crosses the border into Scotland

(sub-routes are cross-referenced to the main route entry).

- If you are not sure of the name, look for similar names. If you know the names of nearby routes, read descriptions of those routes, in case the route you are looking for is mentioned there.
- Use the regional maps of major routes, if you are unsure of the name but know the area, in case your route is one of the ones shown.
- If you have access to the internet, check the LDWA website (www.ldwa.org.uk) and look at the full maps of the region that you are interested in.

How to find suitable routes in a particular area

- Read the regional summaries, covering most of the region's routes very briefly, and check the Key Facts boxes which highlight 'Don't Miss!' route sections and useful publications.
- Use the regional maps to find the major routes and see where they go.
- Check the directory entries with your shortlist to find which are suitable.

How to find more information on a route or get hold of a publication

- Use the Key to Trail Directory Entries, on the back cover flap, to help you navigate your directory entry. (See 'The directory entries' on p15 for more information explaining the terminology used.)
- If you are looking for a publication, identify the supplier shown in brackets after the entry, and find their full contact details in the Directory of Suppliers. (You may also be able to get publications from your local bookshop or over the internet.)
- If you have access to the internet, use the website address given for more, or more up-to-date, information and to contact any user group. Alternatively, use the online LDPs (Paths & Trails) pages on the LDWA website for route updates, more detailed information (especially on minor routes and challenges), elevation profiles, additional downloads and to connect directly to relevant third-party web pages for the route.

How to help us keep this Handbook and the LDWA online database up-to-date

- Please provide feedback, updates and new information to the LDWA by using the 'Contact Us' links online. This information will be published on the LDWA website as soon as practicable and incorporated into future editions of this Handbook.

LIGHTEN THAT LOAD

PADDY DILLON

Keen long-distance walkers are happiest walking day after day along trails that take weeks to complete, striding over the hills, spending every night in a different place. There is no better way to experience the rich variety of our landscapes, letting the spirit soar while enjoying the sights, sounds and scents of the countryside. If only it wasn't for the weight of the pack, the heavy load, slowing the footsteps, sapping fitness and energy, with shoulder straps gnawing into flesh. It's time to lighten up and offload excess baggage.

I heard about a man who walked the South West Coast Path with a huge pack. It contained five changes of clothing on top of all his camping gear, and it was a tremendous effort to carry it in the hot days of summer. He was overheating so much that he stripped almost naked, wearing only shorts and shoes. In effect, he was carrying his entire wardrobe on his back, without wearing any of it, so it would have been much better to leave it all at home!

The perils of over-packing

The temptation on any long-distance walk is to over-pack, as insurance against any eventuality on the trail. This may demonstrate that careful thought is going into the overall preparation, but when it doesn't all fit into your pack, or you can't lift the pack onto your back, it's a sure sign that you're packing too much and it's time to re-assess.

A heavy pack can cause pain, fatigue and misery, which simply isn't good enough when the idea is to have fun and revel in the freedom and

The food is lightweight, but everything else is heavyweight

The heavyweight says 'enough', while the lightweights keep going

joy of the great outdoors. Grossly overburdened backpackers shuffle slowly, with heads bowed, oblivious to the splendour and joys of the trail they came to enjoy. By the time they deal with the problem by posting excess baggage home, they are already sporting stresses, strains and injuries that should never have occurred. It seems a shame to spoil a walk with needless suffering.

A big, heavy, bulky pack is a tiresome and awkward burden. Big packs stick in narrow stiles, hit low branches, lodge in doorways, catch you off-balance and will probably clobber your mate at some point. Sometimes it may be funny, but more often it will be annoying, and if you're unlucky it could cause serious injury. Heavy packs cause the wearer to lean forward, stressing joints, restricting vision to the sight of feet shuffling monotonously onwards. A small, light pack leaves the wayfarer free to stand up, walk tall and enjoy the trail.

Aim low

Everyone who embarks on a long-distance walk for the first time makes the mistake of getting a big pack, and it is easy to pack more than you need. An average day sack is just about adequate for most trails, and a limit of 35 litres focuses the mind, but it takes time to pack properly. There is no room for bulky fleeces, spare shoes, three changes of clothes, a puffy sleeping bag and a big tent, but there is room for a carefully chosen selection of lightweight, low-bulk gear. If you need to pack food for several days, then a larger pack is required, but maybe five or ten litres of extra capacity will suffice.

The complete campsite, weighing 5 kilos. Just add food and water!

Lightweight tents and sleeping bags tip the scales at less than a kilo each and squash down very small. Modern fabrics mean that bulky clothing is a thing of the past, and no-one needs more than one change of clothing for the evening. All of a sudden that day sack is fine for a month outdoors, sacrificing little in comfort, but losing a lot of weight and bulk. An ultra-lightweight backpacker once lifted my pack and declared, 'Oh, you're carrying a little bit less than me!'

Clothing

Outdoor clothing comes in all shapes, sizes and colours, but your choice should be determined by performance. Will it keep you comfortable in the conditions you expect to experience? On one trail, you may need something that will keep you warm and dry in cold, wet weather. On another trail, you may need something that will keep you cool and protect you from the sun. If you can limit yourself to a single set of clothing for walking, and a lightweight change of clothes for the evening, then it should be possible to give the walking clothes an occasional wash and rinse at the close of a day's walk. Modern fabrics dry rapidly so should be ready to wear the following morning. Shop around until you find something that suits you and the conditions you expect to encounter.

Food

Packing food is the downfall of many. Too much food adds weight and consumes a lot of space. Water weighs a kilo a litre. The lightweight backpacker is easily seduced into packing lots of lightweight dehydrated meals, only to walk past delightful little shops selling wholesome food every day. The obvious thing is to buy food only when you need it, and pack just enough to get you to the next shop. On most trails in Britain, food can be bought on a daily basis and there is no need to carry excess weight. Buying food on the trail offers the chance to indulge in regional specialities, rather than boiling up the same old mush every evening. When following remote trails with little chance to buy food, dehydrated food becomes an attractive option. The choice is wide and prices vary enormously, so it is worth shopping around. Don't just look at the specialist 'trekker' fare, because supermarket shelves often carry a decent, more affordable selection.

Spare a thought for your companions. If you trek with someone else, a burden shared is a burden halved. A tent for two is lighter than two tents for one. You'll still need two sleeping bags, but you won't need two stoves, and with co-ordinated planning you can both carry much less than if you travel alone.

It's your choice how to shed the weight. Any amount of money can be spent on lightweight, low bulk, high performance kit but if finances are tight you may decide to replace items over several years, as they wear out. Read gear reviews and quiz retailers mercilessly. Ultra-lightweight backpackers say every item of gear should have two uses, so roll up your clothes to make a pillow and use a cooking pan as a mug. Some tents can be erected with trekking poles, so the tent poles can stay at home. Be critical of gear, even hyper-critical, but beware of getting to the stage where you peel the price labels off your soup packets!

Page 21–22 photographs © Paddy Dillon

The author packing light and standing tall on the Pennine Way

I DID IT MY WEST HIGHLAND, WEST ISLAND, WEST MENDIP, CUMBRIAN, CAMBRIAN, REIVERS, RIVERS, ROACH VALLEY WAY

RONALD TURNBULL

I would walk five hundred miles and I would
walk five hundred more
Just to be the man who walks a thousand miles
to fall down at your door

The Proclaimers

Dawn came grey, and awfully early. At 3am the spruce twigs started to show dark against the sky. The skylarks were scraping toast crumbs off their beaks, and heading blearily up into the sky to start their morning's twittering. I made my own breakfast of muesli and water, and headed north.

Behind me, Telford's stony road stretched in a straight line across the grey heather. Ahead, it did exactly the same. Above the mist rose the shadows of the mountains. The only sound was my boot on the rounded granite pebbles of Telford's roadway, followed, a second later, by the sound of the other boot. After 20 minutes and 1200 footfalls, the River Ba burbled in the darkness underneath its bridge, and bare rowan branches dripped onto the stone parapets. Across the moor, the sky took on a yellowish tinge like the stains in a urinal. Somewhere over there, it was being sunrise.

There's nothing new about this long-distance walking lark. After five days on the trail have rubbed off some of the tummy fat along with the urban attitudes, you learn that walking 15 or 20 miles a day, every day, is what human bodies are built for.

And so, as I strolled onwards through the Lairig Mor above Kinlochleven, I was recalling previous walkers. The Camerons of Lochaber used this path as a raiding route. A defeated army of Campbells passed by in 1645, their bloody bandages dripping into the snow. MacIain, the clan chieftain of Glencoe, came down the glen in the last days of 1691, an old man on a pony with a ghillie running alongside. He slipped four days off his long-distance schedule; his lateness

The West Highland Way uses Telford's road to cross Rannoch Moor

at Inveraray was made the excuse for the Glencoe Massacre two months later.

Or take the South West Coast Path. They call that a recreational footpath. It's not: it's a working walk. Its 600 miles were built and maintained by coastguards, who lurked along it with telescopes and pistols, trying to surprise the smugglers who were lurking along it in the opposite direction.

Fourteen hundred years ago, converting the UK to Christianity was serious long-distance business. From Iona to Canterbury, Augustine and Columba must have been 30-mile men, bothered about boots, and the weight of the pack, and finding the way, and the weather. We call it St Cuthbert's Way, but when St Cuthbert walked from Melrose down to Lindisfarne, he was on a road built by Roman soldiers. And it was probably old even when the Romans upgraded it, a path for Iron-age traders, a Bronze Age migration lane, a hunting trail when spears were tipped with flint.

The invention of the wheel was a bit of a mistake. Right into the 19th century, they never bothered with it in Borrowdale. It's fun in its way but you know, the pogo stick, the bouncy beachball, the wheel: not seriously for people who want to get across England. Until about 1850, you could walk anywhere you wanted on the roads. You'd walk up to Oxford University, or over to Wales to see the scenery, or to the Isle of Wight because you were Charles Dickens and

Crossing to Lindisfarne on the Pilgrim Path – St Cuthbert's Way, and Lakeland to Lindisfarne

you had a house there. The roads were sometimes stony, or muddy, and every hour or two you stepped aside into a thorn bush for a carriage to come past.

Even in 1938, when Alfred Wainwright walked from Settle to Hadrian's Wall and back, he did half of it on the roads. But from the 1950s the roads were just too nasty, and if you wanted to go to the other side of England you went there on wheels. Now, however, there's the UK Trailwalker's Handbook, and anywhere you want to go, you can go on foot, on a path. You might ask, do we need the Lambourn Valley Way from Newbury to Waylands Smithy? If you live in Reading and you want to visit your granny in Gloucester, then you do need the Lambourne Valley Way. So let's hope someone else needed it too and trampled it down so the nettles are less than neck high.

And when they see you heading up the Devil's Staircase when there's a perfectly good bus service to Fort William (you'd be there in forty minutes) they go: 'Oh, they're just doing the West Highland Way.'

Or the Cumbrian Way, or the Cambrian Way, or St Cuthbert's Way, or the Cateran Trail, or the Rivers Way, or the Reiver's Way, or even the Capital Ring for those who really like London. For who wants one long-distance path, when you can have 720 of them?

Despite the efforts of the NHS, a human lifetime is still too short for 720 long paths. So how to choose? Some questions are quickly answered. How far do I want to go? Where haven't I been already? (What a treat never to have been to the Lake District – you could walk the Cumbria Way.) Then I pull out the map and take a closer look. Some paths are special. And those ones tend to have:

- **upland:** mountains are the best sort of ground; and this is even truer if you don't go up the mountains (as the West Highland Way doesn't). Look for the paths around the bottoms of the tops, the paths passing through the passes.
- **downland:** fast grassy paths, at 300m, in country where 300m is as high as it gets: great walking, whether it's the Cheviot foothills or the Marlborough Downs.
- **lowland:** straths, vales and valleys linking one range to the next. Just so long as it isn't that dreary Vale of York on Wainwright's Coast to Coast.
- **riverside:** switch off the brain and let the ears enjoy the water noises. The Pennine Way goes up the Tees for a day and a bit. I say Tees, yes please!
- **footbridges:** dangly suspension ones, long white latticework ones, thrillingly over-engineered ones where somebody had some funding to use up: I love them all.
- **seaside:** all the advantages of riverside, scaled up, plus a salty smell. (Perhaps the South West Coast Path overdoes this aspect a tad.)
- **paths *across* steep hillsides:** folk in olden days didn't go up hills when they could go around. Contour-line paths are often old mine tracks, well-built but now grassy. And the views are great, even if one-sided.
- the small stone-built **market town**: you've heard about heather moorland and blanket bog, but this is the terrain that's really threatened today. Whether sandstone, limestone or granite, it has a pub with a silly name, plus a real bakery.

The Street, a Roman road giving access to the Cheviot section of the Pennine Way

- **silly little hills:** big hills and a big rucksack? Well yes if you've also got big legs. But climb for half an hour up a silly little hill. It's probably volcanic, so slightly rocky on top. It has views across the plains you just passed over. It even has a silly little name, such as the Skirrid (Ysgyryd Fawr) or Roseberry Topping, Crook Peak, Caer Caradoc, the Clwydians or Conic Hill.
- above all, **an idea**: paths may be walked on the feet but even more in the mind. Hadrian's Wall has field edges (see below), a bike path (see below), urban fringes and miles of roadside. But it's a coast-to-coast (almost), a Roman remain, and everybody's heard of it. Just divert it a little over the Winking Eye footbridge (see above).

Other paths are less than special. And their less-special features include:

- **field studies:** stile to stile across farmland. For the first two miles it's interesting navigation. More, and it's a bore. Then comes the field with the soaking-wet, neck-deep, oilseed rape.
- **forest roads:** wide, smooth-surfaced, and just great if you happen to be a 25-ton truck. The views are spruce, plus a whole lot more of the smooth track extending ahead.
- **old railway lines:** smooth, well graded, and no sharp bends – almost enjoyable. But you can see three miles ahead, and it's still smooth, and unsloped, and uninterestingly unbendy. Sometimes you're in a cutting, with hour-long opportunities to study brambles and willow herb. On the other hand, there will eventually be a viaduct.
- **bike paths:** bike paths or 'multi-use paths' are for bikes, plus wheelchairs. One Sustrans sculpture is not sufficient stimulation for the next five miles of tarmac and brambles.
- **beach pebbles:** stuck for a shoreline footpath, the path designer sends us along the shore. There might have been a seal but the seal's away today. What there *is* is slippery sea-rounded shingle; then sea-rounded slippery shingle with seaweed on.

Some like it high, and some like it low. But there's a long path anywhere you look. Somerset is an easy one. Somerset is a lovely county, and it's got seven ranges of hills, rising to a shaggy, heathery 519m at Dunkery Beacon. But attitude matters more than altitude. If I can't think how you would make something in Suffolk that was worth travelling to Suffolk for – this is just a failure of imagination on my part. The compilers of this book have found plenty of Suffolk stuff. I did walk the Weavers' Way in Norfolk. I got very excited because I hit some sand dunes and crossed the 10m contour line. Those sand dunes are demanding walking, they're quite steep, and the view is different from anything in the Scottish Highlands. You see 12 miles of sea, 15 miles of shingle and a huge windfarm.

If you want to be old-fashioned there's the Lairig Ghru (not featured here), there's the Lyke Wake Walk. There's the Derwent Valley Skyline, which middle-aged men from Manchester used to do between the wars. It's good to go in the footsteps of these old fellows, in their breeches so impregnated with peat they never needed to hang them up, they just stood them in the garden to dry. They tended to do these things at night and in the middle of winter. You still can, it's called the High Peak Marathon. The High Peak Marathon happens in March, and they start at 10pm so as to get the pleasure of the darkness. I spoilt it myself by doing it in midsummer; I even slept. I unrolled my bivvy bag on Kinder Scout, in some soft peaty heather, and I watched the orange streetlights of Manchester shine into the sky. All through the evening the jet planes circled and descended into the orange light, like an evil phoenix descending into the deadly flames.

Then there are the challenge events. There's the Across Wales Walk – an annual (rather than anytime) challenge so not in this book. Kind folk give you flapjack from the English border all the way across to the sea; and a bunch of fellow

West Mendip Way above Wells

walkers discuss every topic under the sun (or rather more likely, the rain). The first long distance walking book was Chaucer's *Canterbury Tales*. All these characters trekking from London to Canterbury, telling each other wonderful stories and having rows and encouraging each another. It's about 70 miles from London to Canterbury, you'd use the Darent Valley Path and a bit of the North Downs National Trail. Disappointingly Chaucer doesn't say how long and he doesn't give the crucial speed and time data.

Any journey demands a destination – a placename for when they say 'where you off to then?'. (Answers like 'the rest of my life' or 'because it's there' earn you a sad look and a well deserved nudge into the nettles.) Apart from speeds and distances, the important thing is the right lightweight gear. As I wrote this, Paddy Dillon hadn't yet sent in the useful piece included earlier in this introduction, so I asked a woman in the Long Distance Walkers' Association.

'Yes I *love* lightweight kit but only 'cos it's usually sexier than the heavy duty stuff and I'm a bit of a outdoor trendy. Also I must confess my secret to lightweight coast-to-coast walking is called a Sherpa Van, for trekking trips a yak or a mule and on LDWA outings my husband's rucksack.'

The fun often involves some suffering – Carreg Cennen Castle on the Beacons Way (Ffordd y Bannau)

St Cuthbert himself couldn't have said it better.

Some trendy kit, somewhere to say you're going; but the point of a long walk is the variety. Putting it at its simplest: to be somewhere and then, by means only of your own feet, to be somewhere else. After my grey, misty morning on Rannoch Moor, early afternoon saw me somewhere else. The Lairig Mor is a high glen running westwards below the stony slopes of the Mamores. The Lairig Mor was as dreary as dawn Rannoch, but dreary *in an altogether different way*. The brown heather now was varied with beige of winter grassland. The skylarks had fallen silent, and it was drizzling. Out of the brown and beige ground, there stuck up ruined shielings, grey lumpy mementos of the Highland Clearances. Between Rannoch and here, I'd crossed the head of Glen Coe; I'd crossed the Devil's Staircase, where, on their way back from the pub, the navvies of Blackwater used to perish in the snow. A long-distance walk, in late March, through one of the saddest parts of Scotland. It sounds a bit dismal. It is a bit dismal. I was just loving it.

But I loved it even more when the sky got those blue patches you sometimes see even in Scotland. And a sight still more unusual, poking above the spruce trees – the unclouded top bit of Ben Nevis. I diverted to the hill fort called Dun Deardail that's above the West Highland Way where it turns down to Glen Nevis. I couldn't see any of the vitrified stonework. What I could see was the high stony side of Ben Nevis, and a bit of snow like sugar frosting, and all going golden as the sun sank towards the hills. I lay in brown winter grasses, and enjoyed the tired feelings in my legs, the pine-scented cool breeze and the delicate flavour of a Mars bar garnished with rucksack fluff.

Glen Nevis was full of shadow, but orange lights of Fort William gleamed against the sea loch. Down in Fort William were bar meals, and beer, and a brand new pair of socks. But first I had to see the sun finish shining on Ben Nevis.

THE NATIONAL TRAILS

The Cleveland Way follows a roller-coaster route on its way to Hasty Bank

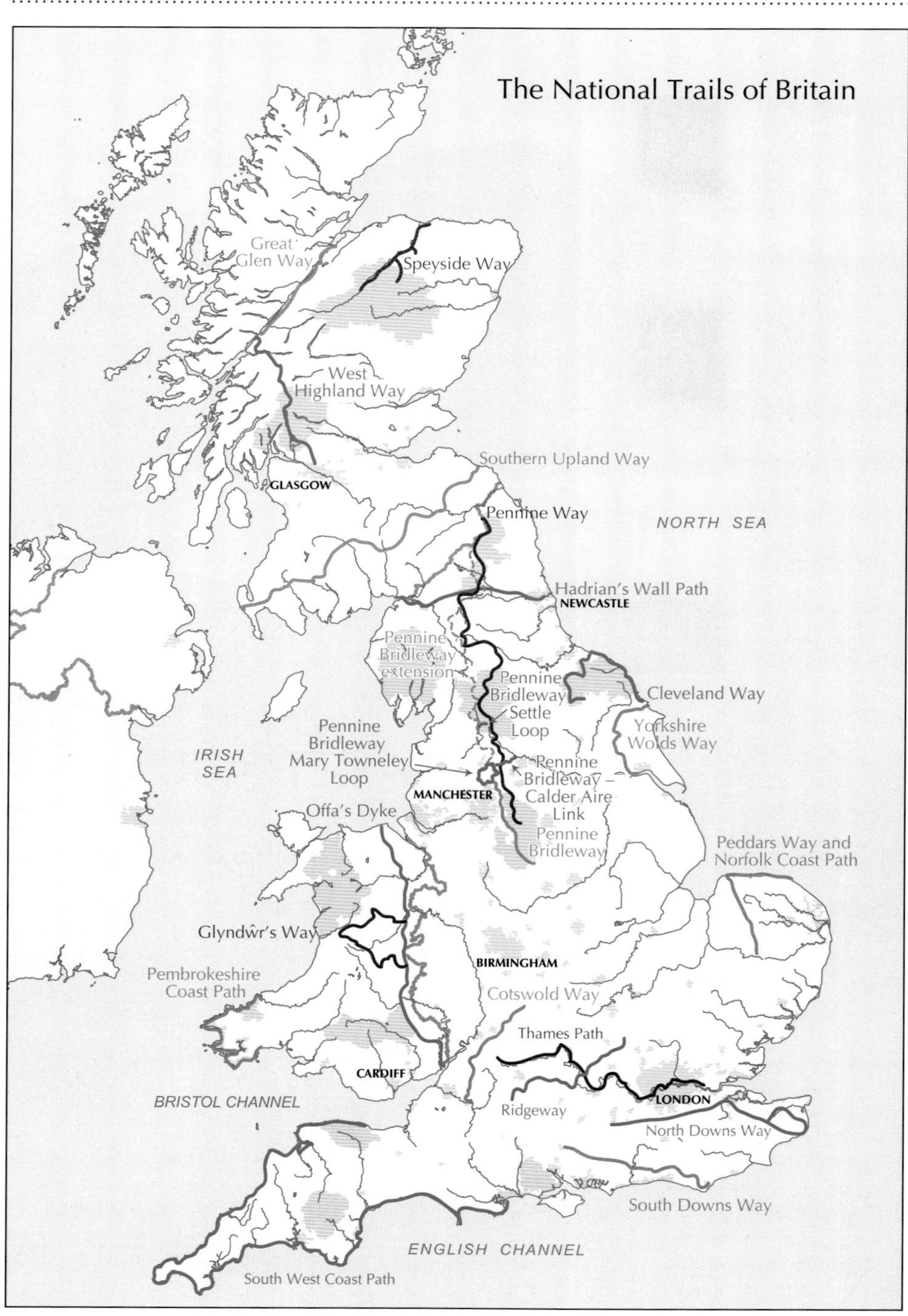
The National Trails of Britain
Great Glen Way
Speyside Way
West Highland Way
Southern Upland Way
GLASGOW
Pennine Way
NORTH SEA
Hadrian's Wall Path
NEWCASTLE
Pennine Bridleway extension
Pennine Bridleway
Settle Loop
Cleveland Way
Yorkshire Wolds Way
Pennine Bridleway Mary Towneley Loop
IRISH SEA
Pennine Bridleway – Calder Aire Link
MANCHESTER
Offa's Dyke
Pennine Bridleway
Peddars Way and Norfolk Coast Path
Glyndŵr's Way
BIRMINGHAM
Pembrokeshire Coast Path
Cotswold Way
Thames Path
CARDIFF
BRISTOL CHANNEL
LONDON
Ridgeway
North Downs Way
South Downs Way
ENGLISH CHANNEL
South West Coast Path

THE NATIONAL TRAILS

St Cuthbert's Way crosses the England–Scotland border near the Pennine Way

'National trails' are designated long distance routes for walking, cycling and horse riding through the finest landscapes. Britain (England, Wales and Scotland) now has 19 such trails. In England and Wales there are 15 National Trails (when complete two of these will be suitable for use by horse riders and cyclists along their entire length), of about 2500 miles (4000km), of which one is shared. In Scotland the equivalent trails are called Scottish Long Distance Routes (SLDRs), and they total about 470 miles (750km). The trails have been created by linking existing local footpaths, bridleways and minor roads and by developing new ones to fill gaps. The national trails in England and Wales are waymarked with the acorn logo and in Scotland with the white thistle waymark (a thistle within a hexagon).

In England and Wales, a National Trail Officer oversees their management and maintenance to nationally agreed standards. Funding for National Trails is provided by national government through Natural England (formerly the Countryside Agency) in England, and in Wales the Countryside Council for Wales (CCW), and also by local highway authorities and other funding partners. In Scotland, Scottish Natural Heritage (SNH) leads on proposals for official SLDRs, and after approval, ongoing management and maintenance transfers to the relevant local authorities along the routes, with SNH providing financial support towards their upkeep.

These national trails are listed below and the directory listings follow in the same, country by country, order.

England

- Cleveland Way National Trail – moorland on the North York Moors, then the Cleveland coast
- Cotswold Way National Trail – along the wooded limestone scarp of the Cotswold Hills
- Hadrian's Wall Path National Trail – along a Roman frontier that is a World Heritage Site
- North Downs Way National Trail – along the North Downs ridgeline south of London

A fine old railway trackbed is followed from Craigellachie to Ballindalloch on the Speyside Way

- Peddars Way & Norfolk Coast Path National Trail – a coastal and inland route in East Anglia
- Pennine Bridleway National Trail – a Pennine route, only partly open as yet, mainly for horseriders
- Pennine Way National Trail – Britain's first NT, keeping high along the moorland backbone of England
- Ridgeway National Trail – tracing an ancient ridgeway, the 'Oldest Road'
- South Downs Way National Trail – on the South Downs ridgeline with a coastal loop
- South West Coast Path National Trail – around the peninsula in spectacular coastal scenery
- Thames Path National Trail – the only national trail that follows a river from source to sea
- Yorkshire Wolds Way National Trail – across the wolds (downland), to the Cleveland Way

England and Wales (shared)

- Offa's Dyke Path National Trail – on the ancient border earthwork between England and Wales

Wales

- Pembrokeshire Coast Path National Trail – a coastal route around the peninsula
- Glyndwr's Way/Llwybr Glyndwr National Trail – a route commemorating Owain Glyndwr, a 15th-century warrior-statesman who tried to establish an independent Welsh nation

Scotland

- Great Glen Way – between mountains along the Great Glen fault line and its famous lochs
- Southern Upland Way – coast-to-coast across Scotland's southern hills
- Speyside Way – along a famous salmon river, linking the Moray Coast and Cairngorm fringes
- West Highland Way – between mountain groups from Loch Lomond to Fort William

Compendium books covering these Trails include: *The National Trails* by Paddy Dillon (Cicerone) 2007. ISBN: 978-1852845049. £17.95 and *Big Walks of Great Britain* by David Bathurst (Summersdale) 2007. ISBN: 978-1840245660. £9.99. **Digital stripmaps** for most of these trails are supplied by Memory Map and Satmap.

If you've walked a few of these trails and you'd like a certificate as a memento, the LDWA now maintains a public National Trails Register open to anyone completing several national trails, with a range from 'bronze' level (five trails) up to 'diamond' standard for those achieving all of the British Trails.

Cleveland Way CLWNT

CLEVELAND, N YORKS **177km/110 miles**

The Way climbs to the North York Moors at Sutton Bank passing the Kilburn White Horse, and then heads north along the western edge of the high heather moors to Osmotherley from where it follows tracks along the northern escarpment to Greenhow Moor. It turns over Kildale Moor, Roseberry Topping and Guisborough Moor to leave the North York Moors National Park and to reach the coast at Saltburn-by-the-Sea, then follows a varied and undulating coastal path southwards along clifftops and sands; passing several harbours and resorts. Other routes link the start and finish of this roughly horse-shoe shaped trail, including the waymarked Tabular Hills Link Walk (48 miles). The Cleveland Way and Yorkshire Wolds Way meet at Filey, enabling a longer continuous route on National Trails. Cleveland Circles enables the route of the Cleveland Way to be walked as circular day-walks. The waymarked Cleveland Street Walk (11 miles and on OS mapping) connects Guisborough with Loftus (and easy access to the coast/Cleveland Way National Trail), crossing it inland at Slapewath.

Attributes
Challenging; Coastal; Moorland
Start
Helmsley, N Yorks SE613837
Finish
Filey Brigg, N Yorks TA130815
Waymark
National Trail Acorn

Striding out towards Oakdale Reservoir and Osmotherly (Cleveland Way)

Cobles rest on the mud in Staithes Beck, Staithes (Cleveland Way)

Websites
www.nationaltrail.co.uk
Maps ◈
OS Landranger: 93, 94, 99, 100, 101
OS Explorer: 26, 27, 301, 306
Stripmap
Cleveland Way Map & Guide (Footprint)
Publications, badges and certificates
Paperbacks
Cleveland Way (National Trail Guides) by Ian Sampson (Aurum Press) 2007. ISBN 9781845132484. 144pp; 208 x 124. £12.99.
Cleveland Way and the Yorkshire Wolds Way with the Tabular Hills Walk by Paddy Dillon (Cicerone Press) 2005. ISBN 9781852844479. 192pp, laminated; 172 x 116. £12.00.
Booklets
Link Through the Tabular Hills Walk (North York Moors National Park) 1993. ISBN 9780907480440. 44pp; 120 x 170. £3.95 (+ 95p p&p).
Cleveland Way Accommodation and Information Guide (North York Moors National Park) Annual. Free.
Cleveland Way by John Merrill (John Merrill Foundation). ISBN 9780907496700. 80pp; A5 Wirebound. £8.95 (+ £1.00 p&p). Cheques to John Merrill Foundation.
Leaflets
Cleveland Way (Natural England). A4/3. Free.
Cleveland Street Walk (Redcar & Cleveland Borough Council) 1999. £0.50 (incs p&p).
Badges
Cleveland Way National Trail (North York Moors National Park). £0.99 (+ SAE).
Cleveland Way (Lyke Wake Club). £2.00 (+ SAE).
Badge & certificate
Cleveland Way National Trail (John Merrill Foundation). £5.00 (incs p&p).
Walking Support Providers
Brigantes; Coast to Coast Holidays; Contours; Discovery; HF; Mickledore; Sherpa Van

Cotswold Way COTSWNT

BATH NES, GLOS, S GLOS, WORCS **164km/102 miles**

This route is now upgraded to National Trail status, with some improvements to the previous line. The Trail meanders along the western edge of the Cotswold Hills, mainly following the often-wooded top of this limestone escarpment, from where there are extensive views over the Severn Vale to the Malverns and the distant hills of the Mendips and the Welsh borders. It descends from time to time to visit attractive villages nestling under the shelter of the edge. It crosses stone-walled farming countryside, passing villages and country houses built from the local limestone, and many sites of archaeological interest. The waymarked Frome Valley Walkway (18 miles and on OS mapping) provides a link from Old Sodbury, via Frenchay, to the confluence with the Avon in Bristol. The waymarked Jubilee Way (South Gloucestershire) (16 miles and on OS mapping) is another link from Old Sodbury, which ends at the Severn Bridge.

Attributes
Downland/Wolds; Heritage
Start
Chipping Campden, Glos SP152392
Finish
Bath, Bath NES ST751647
Waymark
National Trail Acorn

13 counties can be seen from Broadway Tower, on the Cotswold Way

Websites
www.nationaltrail.co.uk
Maps ◈
OS Landranger: 150, 151, 162, 163, 172
OS Explorer: 155, 167, 168, 179, 45
Harvey Map (Stripmap)
Cotswold Way (Harvey Maps)
Map (Other)
Cotswold Way: Illustrated Map (Reardon Publishing)
Publications, badges and certificates
Paperbacks
Cotswold Way: Two-way National Trail Route Description by Kev Reynolds (Cicerone Press) 2007. ISBN 9781852845520. 224pp; 116 x 172. £12.00.
Cotswold Way by Tricia & Bob Hayne (Trailblazer Publications) 2009. ISBN 9781905864164. 192pp; 120 x 176. £9.99.
Cotswold Way by Mark Richards (Reardon Publishing) 1995. ISBN 9781873877104. 64pp; A5. £5.95 (+ £1.00 p&p).
Cotswold Way National Trail Companion by Cotswold Way National Trail Office (Reardon Publishing) 2007. ISBN 9780955542206. 84pp; 204 x 146. £4.95.
(with full-colour OS maps)
Cotswold Way: National Trail Guides by Anthony Burton (Aurum Press) 2007. ISBN 9781854109149. 192pp; 210 x 130. £12.99.
Video
Cotswold Way by Nicholas Reardon, Mark Richards (actors) (Reardon Publishing) 1997. 60 minutes. £14.99 (+ £1.50 p&p). PAL or NTSC.
DVD
Cotswold Way: DVD by Anthony Burton (TV walks.com) 2007. National Trail Video Guide. £12.00 Mail Order; £6.00 Download from TVwalks.
CD ROM
Cotswold Way: Interactive Guide Book (Reardon Publishing) 1999. ISBN 9781873877388. £12.99 (+ £1.00 p&p).
Postcards
Six Scenes (Reardon Publishing). ISBN 9781873877340. £2.50 (+ 50p p&p).
Booklets
Frome Valley Walkway by South Gloucestershire Council (South Gloucestershire Council) 1999. 34pp; A4/3. Free. Free to download.
Jubilee Way by South Gloucestershire Council (South Gloucestershire Council) 1992. 28pp; 100 x 178. Free.
Walking Support Providers
Celtic; Contours; Cotswold; Discovery; Explore Britain; Footpath; HF; Instep; Let's Go Walking!; Ramblers; Sherpa Van; Wycheway

Milecastle 39 sits in a little gap and its north gate leads straight over a steep edge

Hadrian's Wall Path HWPNT

CUMBRIA, NORTHUMBERLAND, TYNE AND WEAR **137km/85 miles**

The Trail follows the line of the Wall built in the second century AD by order of Roman Emperor Hadrian as a defensive barrier that continued in use for most of the next 300 years until the Romans left our shores in the fifth century. Hadrian's Wall is part of the international World Heritage Site 'Frontiers of the Roman Empire'. The Trail provides a fine coast-to-coast walk and, if completed east to west, takes the walker from urban and riverside walking on the north bank of the Tyne to farmland above Tynedale. The upland sections along the wild and dramatic escarpments of Whin Sill give way to gentler pastures of Cumbria before the Solway estuary and its salt marshes bring the walker to Bowness.

Attributes
Moorland; World Heritage Site; Heritage
Start
Wallsend, Tyne & Wear NZ304660
Finish
Bowness-on-Solway, Cumbria NY225628
Waymark
National Trail Acorn
Websites
www.nationaltrail.co.uk, www.hadrians-wall.org, www.planyourinvasion.co.uk
Maps ◈
OS Landranger: 85, 86, 87, 88
OS Explorer: 43, 314, 315, 316
Harvey Map (Stripmap)
Hadrian's Wall Path: XT40 Map (Harvey Maps)

Publications, badges and certificates
Paperbacks
Hadrian's Wall Path: National Trail Guides by Anthony Burton (Aurum Press) 2007. ISBN 9781845132859. 144pp; 211 x 122. £12.99.
Walk Hadrian's Wall: The 84 Mile Route from Bowness-on-Solway to Wallsend by Brian Smailes (Challenge Publications) 2007. ISBN 9781903568408. 60pp; 185 x 125. £6.50 (incs p&p). Cheques to Brian Smailes.
Hadrian's Wall Path: Wallsend to Bowness-on-Stow by Henry Stedman (Trailblazer Publications) 2008. ISBN 9781905864140. 206pp; 120 x 180. £9.99.
(PVC)
Hadrian's Wall Path: Two-way National Trail Description by Helen Richards, Mark Richards (Cicerone Press) 2004. ISBN 9781852843922. 256pp; 118 x 178. £12.95.
Hardback
Spirit of Hadrian's Wall landscape photography by Mark Richards & Roger Clegg (Cicerone Press) 2008. ISBN 9781852845582. 192pp; 286 X 256. £20.00.
Packs
Hadrian's Wall Path: Walking Pack (Hadrian's Wall Heritage Ltd) 2007. £24.99 (+ £3.00 p&p). Harvey Map, Aurum Press Official Guidebook, Essential Companion.
Hadrian's Wall Path: National Trail User Information (Hadrian's Wall Heritage) 2007. Free. Order on NT websites/contacts, see User Information Pack 2.
Booklets
Hadrian's Wall Path: National Trail Accommodation Guide (Hadrian's Wall Heritage Ltd) 2007. Free. Free download from NT websites.
Essential Companion to Hadrian's Wall Path National Trail by David McGlade (National Trail Manager) (Hadrian's Wall Heritage Ltd) 2007. ISBN 9780954734213. £3.95.
Walking in Hadrian's Wall Country (Hadrian's Wall Heritage Ltd) 2007. Free. Free download from NT websites.
Certificate
Certificate & Summer Passport for Hadrian's Wall Path National Trail (Hadrian's Wall Heritage). £2.95 for certificate with completed Passport. Order Passport on NT websites/contacts, see User Information Pack 2.
DVD
Hadrian's Wall Path: DVD by Anthony Burton (TV walks.com) 2007. National Trail Video Guide. 27 minutes. £12.00 Mail Order; £6.00 Download from TVwalks.
Walking Support Providers
Brigantes; Celtic; Contours; Discovery; Explore Britain; Footpath; HF; Instep; Macs; Mickledore; Northwestwalks; Ramblers; Shepherd's Walks; Sherpa Van; Trek-Inn; Walkers Bags; Walking Support; Wycheway

North Downs Way National Trail — NDWNT

KENT, SURREY — **250km/155 miles**

The North Downs Way National Trail broadly follows the historic Pilgrims Way along the Downs to Canterbury. The first 14 miles are over sandy countryside to the south of the Downs. They are first reached at Newlands Corner, east of Guildford and from there on the Trail follows the crest of the southern escarpment of the North Downs or footpaths and tracks along their lower slopes. There are views over the Weald to the South Downs and several steepish ascents where the ridge is cut by valleys, notably those of the Mole at Box Hill, the Darent at Otford, the Medway at Rochester, and the Stour near Wye. Generally the route provides comparatively easy walking through woods, over chalk grassland and, especially in Kent, through orchards and farmland. At Boughton Lees there is a choice of routes. The direct one goes through Wye, over the Downs to Folkestone and along the cliffs to Dover. The alternative follows hills to the west of the river Stour and passes through orchards and the picturesque village of Chilham to Canterbury. From the cathedral city it heads south-east via Barham Downs, Shepherdswell and Waldershare Park to Dover. Canterbury Cathedral is part of a World Heritage Site. The waymarked Thames Down Link (15 miles and on OS mapping) connects the Thames Path at Kingston with the North Downs Way near Westhumble, following a green corridor through Maldon Manor, Horton Country Park, the Commons of Epsom and Ashstead, and Mickleham Downs. The Pilgrims' Way, which ran between Winchester and Canterbury, is not itself a single promoted long distance path, it is, however, approximated by the St Swithun's and North Downs Ways.

A field path climbs over a gentle rise on the way to the village of Otford

Chalk cliffs above Samphire Hoe Country Park between Folkestone and Dover

Attributes
Downland/Wolds; World Heritage Site

Start
Farnham, Surrey SU844468

Finish
Dover, Kent TR308399

Waymark
National Trail Acorn

Websites
www.nationaltrail.co.uk

Maps ◈
OS Landranger: 177, 178, 179, 186, 187, 188, 189
OS Explorer: 137, 138, 145, 146, 147, 148, 149, 150, 163

Harvey Map (Stripmap)
North Downs Way (West), North Downs Way (East): Dover to Medway (Harvey Maps)

Publications, badges and certificates

Paperbacks

North Downs Way: National Trail Guides by Neil Curtis, Jim Walker (Aurum Press) 2007. ISBN 9781845132729. 168pp; 210 x 130. £12.99.

North Downs Way by Kev Reynolds (Cicerone Press) 2001. ISBN 9781852843168. 128pp; 174 x 116. £8.00.

North Downs Way: Farnham to Dover by John Curtin (Trailblazer Publications) 2006. ISBN 9781873756966. 208pp; 176 x 120. £9.99. 80 maps, includes town plans.

Leaflets

North Downs Way National Trail (North Downs Way National Trail Officer) 2007. 3 Leaflets. Free. Also downloads from Trail websites, General, Transport & Accommodation.

Lost Landscapes: North Downs Way Circular Walks (North Downs Way National Trail Officer) 2007. Free.

Thames Down Link (Lower Mole Project) 2001. A4/3. Free (+ SAE).

Accommodation list

Accommodation Information (North Downs Way National Trail Officer) 2007. Planned to be online on Trail websites.

Walking Support Providers
Contours; Explore Britain; Orchard; Walk Awhile

Peddars Way & Norfolk Coast Path — PDWNT

NORFOLK, SUFFOLK — **150km/93 miles**

This easy-access National Trail provides both inland and coastal walking. The Peddars Way is one of the links in a prehistoric route, often called the Greater Ridgeway, from The Wash to the Dorset Coast, and it reaches the coast at Holme-next-the-Sea, from where the Trail follows the Norfolk Coast Path east. The first part of this National Trail follows tracks, footpaths and minor roads along, or as near as possible to, the Peddars Way (a Romanised section of the prehistoric Icknield Way, the extant sections of which are a scheduled ancient monument). From the wooded, sandy Breckland heaths, it passes Castle Acre (linking with the Nar Valley Way) and the ruins of the priory and castle to reach the North Norfolk coast at Holme-next-the-Sea. Here a short section of the original Norfolk Coast Path leads west to Hunstanton, while the main Trail heads east along or near to the shoreline over low cliffs, sand dunes, coastal defences enclosing marshes and mud flats, passing woodland, bird sanctuaries and harbours. Near to Great Hockham, the Great Eastern Pingo Trail (8 miles) provides a circular route through an SSSI in the Thompson Common area. Pingos are glacial features.

Attributes
Easy; Forest/Woodland; Coastal; Heath
Start
Knettishall Heath, Suffolk TL944807
Finish
Cromer, Norfolk TG218424
Waymark
National Trail Acorn

Websites
www.countrysideaccess.norfolk.gov.uk, www.nationaltrail.co.uk
Maps ◈
OS Landranger: 132, 133, 144
OS Explorer: 229, 230, 236, 237, 238, 250, 251, 252
Publications, badges and certificates
Paperbacks
Peddars Way & Norfolk Coast Path: National Trail Guides by Bruce Robinson (Aurum Press) 2007. ISBN 9781845132071. 144pp; 210 x 130. £12.99.
Peddars Way: Footprints of History by Dennis Dear (Pathway Publishing) 2006. ISBN 9780952662860. 28pp.
Greater Ridgeway: A walk from Lyme Regis to Hunstanton by Ray Quinlan (Cicerone Press) 2003. ISBN 9781852843465. 256pp; 172 x 116. £12.95.
Booklets
Peddars Way & North Norfolk Coast Path with the Weavers Way Guide by Ian Mitchell (Editor), Sheila Smith (Editor) (RA Norfolk Area) 2006. ISBN 9781906494148. 28pp; A5. £3.70 (incs p&p). Cheques to Ramblers Association (Norfolk Area). Includes accommodation list.
Peddars Way: Pocket Companion (Peddars Way National Trail Office) 2009. Free on email request on Trail websites. Accommodation, travel, tourist information.
Leaflets
Peddars Way & Norfolk Coast Path (Peddars Way National Trail Office) 2000. A4/2. Free.
Great Eastern Pingo Trail (Diss Tourist Information Centre). A5. Free (+ SAE). Downloadable.
Walking Support Providers
Celtic; Contours; Explore Britain; HF

A prominent landmark windmill rises above reedbeds at Cley next the Sea

A dusting of snow picks out a moorland track on the slopes of Brown Wardle Hill

Pennine Bridleway PBWNT

CUMBRIA, DERBYS, LANCS, N YORKS, NORTHUMBERLAND, W YORKS **558km/347 miles**

Opening in stages over several years, the Pennine Bridleway is a new National Trail that has been designed specifically for horse riders and mountain bikers and will also form a major new route for walkers. Broadly parallel to the Pennine Way National Trail, the full route from Middleton Top in Derbyshire to Byrness in Northumberland travels through some of the finest scenery in England passing through the Peak District, Yorkshire Dales and Northumberland National Parks, using old tracks and quiet roads, taking a generally lower line in valleys and on hillsides and across moorland. In 2008, 130 miles of waymarked route were open from Derbyshire to the top of the Mary Towneley Loop, plus the 10-mile Settle Loop in the Yorkshire Dales east of the town. The section north of the Mary Towneley Loop to Ravenstonedale, Cumbria is due to open in 2010 providing 206 miles of route. Funding is currently being looked at for the northern section through Cumbria and Northumberland. A feeder route from West Yorkshire, the Calder–Aire link, is open and two more are under construction from the West Pennines and the Northern Peak District.

A row of old cottages between Uppermill and Diggle on the way to Standedge

Attributes
Horse Ride (Multi User); Moorland
Start
Middleton Top, near Carsington Reservoir, Derbys SK275551
Finish
Fat Lamb Inn, Ravenstonedale, Kirkby Stephen, Cumbria NY739023
Waymark
National Trail Acorn
Websites
www.nationaltrail.co.uk
Maps ◈
OS Landranger: 91, 98, 103, 109, 110, 119
OS Explorer: 1, 2, 19, 21, 24

Harvey Map (Stripmap)

Pennine Bridleway: Derbyshire to South Pennines (Harvey Maps)

Publications, badges and certificates

Paperback

Middleton Top to Matley Moors – Walking the Pennine Bridleway in Derbyshire by John Merrill (John Merrill Foundation) 2006. ISBN 9781903627617. 84pp, wire bound; 206 x 154. £8.95 (+ £1.00 p&p). Cheques to John Merrill Foundation.

(spiral bound)

Mary Towneley Loop: A Pocket Guide to the 48 Mile Loop of the Pennine Bridleway for Horseriders, Cyclists and Walkers by Chris Peat (Forest of Rossendale Bridleways Association) 2004. ISBN 9780954781309. 72pp; 116 x 170. £4.95 (+ £1.00 p&p).

Hardback

Pennine Bridleway (South): Derbyshire to the South Pennines (National Trail Guides) by Sue Viccars (Aurum Press) 2004. ISBN 9781854109576. 168pp; 205 x 130. £12.99.

Leaflets

Pennine Bridleway – An Adventure on Horse, Bike or Foot (Natural England) 1995. A4/3. Free.

Pennine Bridleway – Mary Towneley Loop Guide by Natural England (Natural England). 1pp; A2 (A5 folded). Free. From Pennine Bridleway Team Tel: 0161 237 1061 and local TICs.

Pennine Bridleway – Settle Loop Guide (Natural England) 2007. 1pp; A3 (A5 folded). Free. From Pennine Bridleway Team Tel: 0161 237 1061 and local TICs. Download free from Trail websites.

The Pennine Bridleway runs below Stoodley Pike, while the Pennine Way runs past it

Pennine Bridleway – Calder Aire Link

W YORKS **27km/17 miles**

Attributes

National Trail/National Route; Horse Ride (Multi User); Moorland

Start

St Ives, Bingley, W Yorks SE098390

Finish

Clough Foot, near Widdop Reservoir, W Yorks SD945324

Waymark

National Trail Acorn

Websites

www.bradford.gov.uk

Maps ◈

OS Landranger: 103, 104

OS Explorer: 21, 288

Pennine Bridleway – Mary Towneley Loop

DERBYS **72km/45 miles**

Attributes

Challenging; National Trail/National Route; Horse Ride (Multi User); Moorland

Start and Finish

Charlestown, Hebden Bridge, West Yorkshire SD969262

Websites

www.nationaltrail.co.uk

Maps ◈

OS Landranger: 103, 109

OS Explorer: 21

Pennine Bridleway – Settle Loop

N YORKS **16km/10 miles**

Attributes

National Trail/National Route; Horse Ride (Multi User); Moorland

Start and Finish

Settle, N Yorks SD820637

Websites

www.nationaltrail.co.uk

Maps ◈

OS Landranger: 98

OS Explorer: 2

A stone-flagged path wanders through pastures as it climbs away from Edale

Pennine Way **PWNT**

CUMBRIA, DERBYS, DURHAM, GTR MAN, N YORKS, NORTHUMBERLAND, BORDERS, W YORKS **404km/251 miles**

This first National Trail was formally opened after a 30-year campaign led by Tom Stephenson of the Ramblers. It follows the central upland spine of England from Derbyshire to the Scottish Borders, crossing a wide variety of terrain. The Way crosses the expanse of the gritstone moorlands of the Kinder Plateau, the Bronte country and the predominantly limestone areas of the Yorkshire Dales National Park which is traversed via Malham, Pen-y-ghent, Great Shunner Fell and Keld. The Way then descends from the high fells to reach the River Tees which is followed past High Force and Cauldron Snout waterfalls, crossing the fells to High Cup, Great Dun Fell and Cross Fell and descending to Alston to reach the Northumberland National Park and Hadrian's Wall. The Wall is followed to Housesteads Fort before turning north across the Kielder Forest to Redesdale and the uplands of the Cheviot Hills. Here the English-Scottish border fence is followed before gradually descending to Kirk Yetholm, where it can be linked with the St Cuthbert's Way. A register is maintained at the Pen-y-ghent Café, Horton-in-Ribblesdale for signature/comments from those involved in walking the Way. Practical advice on attempting the Pennine Way is available from the Pennine Way Association (9 x 4 SAE required). At Alston the Way links with the South Tyne Trail (10 miles), providing a low level alternative up the valley towards Hadrian's Wall. See also E-Routes (E2).

Attributes
Challenging; Moorland
Start
Edale, Derbys SK122859
Finish
Kirk Yetholm, Borders NT827281
Waymark
National Trail Acorn
Websites
www.nationaltrail.co.uk
Maps ◈
OS Landranger: 74, 75, 80, 86, 87, 91, 92, 98, 103, 109, 110
OS Explorer: 1, 2, 16, 19, 21, 30, 31, 41, 42, 43, 288

Moorland slopes are always in view as the Pennine Way runs though South Tynedale

Stripmaps

Pennine Way South, Pennine Way Central, Pennine Way North (Harvey Maps)

Pennine Way, Part One: South – Edale to Teesdale, Map & Guide, Pennine Way, Part Two: North – Teesdale to Kirk Yetholm, Map & Guide (Footprint)

Publications, badges and certificates

Paperbacks

Circular Walks Along the Pennine Way by Kevin Donkin (Frances Lincoln) 2006. ISBN 9780711226654. 368pp. £12.99.

Pennine Way by Keith Carter, Edward De La Biliere (Trailblazer Publications) 2008. ISBN 9781905864027. 270pp; 174 x 120. £9.99.

Pennine Way North: National Trail Guides by Tony Hopkins (Aurum Press) 2007. ISBN 9781845132675. 168pp; 210 x 130. £12.99.

Pennine Way South: National Trail Guides by Tony Hopkins (Aurum Press) 2007. ISBN 9781845132682. 144pp; 210 x 130. £12.99.

Guide to the Pennine Way by Christopher John Wright (Constable and Robinson Ltd) 1991. ISBN 9780094706408. 240pp; 171 x 114. £10.95.

(PVC)

Pennine Way National Trail From Edale to Kirk Yetholm by Martin Collins (Cicerone Press) 2003. ISBN 9781852843861. 160pp; 172 x 116. £10.00.

Leaflets

Pennine Way: Accommodation & Service (Pennine Way Project Officer). A3/6. Free (+ 9 x 4 SAE).

Pennine Way (Natural England). A4/3. Free.

(waterproof)

South Tyne Trail (Carlisle City Council). A2 folded. £2.00. Also available from TICs in Alston & Haltwhistle.

CD ROM

Running the Pennine Way by Roy McKee (Mind Technology Limited). £12.00 – buy on supplier's websites. CD version. Includes a full photograph gallery.

Badge & certificate

Pennine Way National Trail (John Merrill Foundation). £5.00 (incs p&p).

Certificate

Pennine Way National Trail by Pennine Way Project (Peak National Park Information Centre). £4.50 (incs p&p).

Completion Memento

Selection of sketches on A3 Poster by John Needham (John Needham). 1pp; A3 Poster. £3.00. An A3-sized parchment-like poster of 15 prominent and well-known features along the Way.

Walking Support Providers

Brigantes; Discovery; Footpath; HF; Sherpa Van; UK Exploratory

A tall pillar cairn near the summit of Cross Fell on the highest part of the Pennines

The heavily rutted Ridgeway stretches across the arable (Berks/Oxon) Downs

Ridgeway RNT

BUCKS, HERTS, OXON, SWINDON, W BERKSHIRE, WILTS 136km/85 miles

One of the links in a prehistoric route, often called the Greater Ridgeway, from The Wash to the Dorset Coast, comprising the Wessex Ridgeway (Lyme Regis to Overton), Ridgeway National Trail (Overton to Ivinghoe), Icknield Way (Ivinghoe to Thetford) and Peddars Way (Knettishall to Hunstanton). The Ridgeway is a trail of two contrasting halves, separated by the Thames. The western part of this National Trail largely follows the route of a prehistoric ridge track along the crest of the North Wessex Downs and passes many historic sites, including Barbury, Liddington, Uffington and Segsbury Castles (hill forts), Wayland's Smithy (long barrow) and Uffington White Horse. The *Oldest Road* publication explores this ancient heritage in words and pictures. Much of the Trail here is along a broad track which used to be rutted, but it has been resurfaced and protected against motorised traffic by regulations. Near the start of the route, that is at the Sanctuary, is the Avebury World Heritage Site (a joint Site with Stonehenge). The eastern part at Streatley crosses, and then follows, the River Thames for five miles before heading east into the Chiltern Hills, mainly along the north-western escarpment. The walking on the eastern half is more varied, along tracks and paths, across open downland, and through farm and woodland, passing Nuffield, Watlington, Chinnor, Princes Risborough (see Swan's Way), Wendover and Tring. The waymarked Ridgeway Link (7.5 miles and coincident with the Icknield Way Path on OS mapping) is a linking route from the Chilterns Gateway Visitor Centre near Dunstable to the finish of the Ridgeway National Trail at Ivinghoe Beacon, where there are no visitor facilites. The Link uses the route of the existing Icknield Way Path that has been upgraded to make it stile-free. Steps have been added on a steep section. At Wendover the waymarked Chiltern Link (8 miles and on OS mapping) leads to Chesham (see Colne Valley Routes). The Ridgeway is linked at Ivinghoe Beacon with the Greensand Ridge Walk, and by the Two Ridges Link (8 miles and included on OS mapping) that in turn also connects with the Icknield Way Path. The Ashridge Estate Boundary Trail (16 miles) is a waymarked circular route coincident in part with the east end of the Ridgeway. The Beacon View Walk (5 miles) provides a link between the Ridgeway and the Grand Union Canal Walk.

Attributes
Downland/Wolds; World Heritage Site
Start
Overton Hill, Wilts SU118681
Finish
Ivinghoe Beacon, Bucks SP960168
Waymark
National Trail Acorn
Websites
www.nationaltrail.co.uk
Maps ◈
OS Landranger: 164, 165, 173, 174, 175
OS Explorer: 157, 169, 170, 171, 181
Harvey Map (Stripmap)
Ridgeway (Harvey Maps)
Publications, badges and certificates
Paperbacks
Greater Ridgeway: A walk from Lyme Regis to Hunstanton by Ray Quinlan (Cicerone Press) 2003. ISBN 9781852843465. 256pp; 172 x 116. £12.95.
Ridgeway: Avebury to Ivinghoe Beacon by Nick Hill (Trailblazer Publications) 2009. ISBN 9781905864171. 192pp; 180 x 120. £9.99 (incs p&p).
Discovering the Ridgeway by Howard Clarke, Vera Burden (Shire Publications) 2002. ISBN 9780747805342. 80pp; 112 x 177. £3.95 (+ £1.00 p&p).
Oldest Road: Exploration of the Ridgeway by J.R.L. Anderson, Fay Godwin (Whittet Books) 1987. ISBN 9780905483528. 200pp.
Hardback
Ridgeway: National Trail Guides by Anthony Burton (Aurum Press) 2008. ISBN 9781845133092. 144pp; 206 x 130. £12.99.
Leaflets
Beacon View Walk (Chiltern Society Office). Free (+ SAE).
Chiltern Link (Buckinghamshire County Council). A4/3. Free (+ SAE). Downloadable.
Ridgeway Link by Chilterns Conservation Board (Chilterns AONB) 2007. A4/3. Free. Download only from websites, or free from local TICs/libraries.
(history, natural history)
Ridgeway: Information (Heritage) Pack (Ridgeway National Trail Officer) 2006. A4/3. £3.30 (incs p&p).
Booklets
Ridgeway: Public Transport Guide (Ridgeway National Trail Officer) Annual. 36pp; A5. Free (+ 9 x 6 1st class SAE).
Badge
Ridgeway National Trail (Ridgeway National Trail Officer). £2.75 (+ 60p SAE). Sweat and T-shirts also available; order form on websites.
Video
Along the Ridgeway (Ridgeway National Trail Officer). 118 minutes. £14.99 (+ £1.60 p&p).
DVD
Ridgeway: DVD by Anthony Burton (TV walks.com) 2007. National Trail Video Guide £12.00 Mail Order; £6.00 Download from TVwalks.
Pack
Pack 1: Vale of Aylesbury Countryside Pack (Buckinghamshire County Council). £3 per pack or £5 for both. 19 recreational routes from Westbury in the north to Stoke Mandeville and Bishopstone in the south.
Walking Support Providers
Contours; Explore Britain

Distant views over the Oxfordshire plain are seen from the Ridgeway

A panoramic view of the South Downs, now a National Park

South Downs Way SDWNT

E SUSSEX, HANTS, W SUSSEX 161km/100 miles

This National Trail follows the northern escarpment of the chalk Downs from where there are extensive views across the Weald to the north and over the rounded hills and dry valleys to the sea in the south. There are several steep ascents when crossing the valleys of the Rivers Cuckmere at Alfriston, Ouse at Southease, Adur south of Bramber and Arun at Amberley. It visits Jevington and passes Iron Age hillforts and barrows. Between Eastbourne and Alfriston there is a coastal alternative to the inland route, running along the scenic cliff tops to Beachy Head and the Seven Sisters and turning inland at Cuckmere Haven along the Cuckmere Valley to rejoin the inland Way route at Alfriston. Here there is a connection to the 1066 Country Walk that leads in turn to the Saxon Shore Way – see E-Routes (E9).

Attributes
Downland/Wolds
Start
Eastbourne (Holywell), E Sussex TV600972
Finish
Winchester, Hants SU483293
Waymark
National Trail Acorn
Websites
www.nationaltrail.co.uk, www.visitsouthdowns.com
Maps ◈
OS Landranger: 185, 197, 198, 199
OS Explorer: 119, 120, 121, 122, 123, 132
Harvey Map (Stripmap)
South Downs Way, South Downs Way: DVD & Stripmap (with Saxon Shore Way) (Harvey Maps)

Publications, badges and certificates
Paperbacks
South Downs Way: National Trail Guides by Paul Millmore (Aurum Press) 2008. ISBN 9781845133115. 168pp; 208 x 124. £12.99.
South Downs Way: Eastbourne to Winchester by Kev Reynolds (Cicerone Press) 2005. ISBN 9781852844295. 192pp; 118 x 178. £10.00. Route described in both directions.
South Downs Way by Jim Manthorpe (Trailblazer Publications) 2009. ISBN 9781905864188. 192pp; 120 x 180. £9.99.
Companion on the South Downs Way (Per-Rambulations) 2006. ISBN 9780954965419. 96pp; 208 x 156. £8.95 (+ £1.55 p&p).
Hardback
South Downs Way by Belinda Knox (Frances Lincoln) 2008. Illustrated guide. ISBN 9780711228535. 112pp. £14.99.
Booklets
Accommodation Guide to the South Downs Way (South Downs Way National Trail Officer). Free (+ 3 x 2nd class stamps). Accommodation information on Trail websites with download.
South Downs Way: Public Transport Guide (South Downs Way National Trail Officer). Free. Free PDF download on Trail websites.
Leaflets
South Downs Way (South Downs Way National Trail Officer). Free. Free PDF download on Trail websites.
DVD National Trail Video Guide
South Downs Way: DVD by Anthony Burton (TV walks.com) 2007. £12.00 Mail Order; £6.00 Download from TVwalks.
Walking Support Providers
Bobs; Contours; Explore Britain; Footprints; HF; Instep

South West Coast Path SWCP

CORNWALL, DEVON, DORSET, PLYMOUTH, SOMERS, TORBAY **1014km/630 miles**

Our longest National Trail gives the opportunity to enjoy some of Britain's finest coastal landscapes. These are extremely varied, from rugged and remote clifftops to sheltered estuaries, busy harbours and resorts. Moorland stretches contrast with plateaux incised by steep coastal valleys and intimate coves with long pebbly or sandy beaches. South Cornwall and Devon offer spectacular 'drowned' estuaries, while in East Devon and Dorset there are extensive 'undercliffs' resulting from landslips. Ferries operate across most of the larger estuaries but some offer a reduced service, or cease altogether, out of the holiday season. Details are available in the South West Coast Path Association's Annual Guide. Two World Heritage Sites cover sections of the coastline. Mining was a major industry during the 18th and 19th centuries and transformed the Cornwall and West Devon Mining Landscape. This Site comprises ten separate areas both along the coast and inland. The Jurassic Coast is England's only natural World Heritage Site and includes 95 miles of unspoilt cliffs and beaches from Exmouth in East Devon to Old Harry Rocks near Studland Bay in Dorset. In 2002, Plymouth City Council created a continuous walking route along its coastline and appointed a team of artists to mark the route and interpret the many stories along it. Promoted as Plymouth's Waterfront Walkway (10 miles) this is now part of the South West Coast Path National Trail and is not separately named on OS mapping. For the E9 route that runs between Plymouth and Dover, Exploring the Bournemouth Coast Path covers the 37-mile stretch between Swanage and Lymington and includes the E9 route through Bournemouth. See E-Routes (E9). East of Lulworth army ranges restrict access at certain times (for details telephone 24 hour answering service 01929 462721 x4819). The St Michael's Way (12 miles), which is included on OS mapping, links Lelant (north coast of Cornwall) with Penzance/Marazion/St Michael's Mount on the south coast. It can be extended into a much longer circular route when combined with the National Trail. The Coast-to-Coast Trail (Cornwall Mineral Tramways) (11 miles) traverses from the north to south coasts from Portreath to Devoran via Cambrose and Scorrier down the Poldice Valley and the Carnon riverside, passing through old mining landscapes. The circular waymarked Dart Valley Trail (17 miles and on OS mapping) connects to the National Trail and has the

Descending from Swyre Head towards Durdle Door, with St Oswald's Bay just beyond

Main picture: Trewavas Cliff, Porthleven in distance, Cornwall
Inset: SWCP start point marker at Minehead, Devon

ferry between Dartmouth and Kingswear in common. It also links to the national rail network at Totnes. The Templer Way (18 miles and on OS mapping), which is waymarked, except on open moorland, starts at Haytor Quarry and meets the National Trail at Teignmouth. It uses the ferry from Shaldon to Teignmouth. As an alternative to the large number of OS maps, six Harvey stripmaps cover the full route. GPS track files may be downloaded from the National Trail's Websites.

Attributes
Challenging; Coastal; World Heritage Site; Geological
Start
Minehead, Somers SS972467
Finish
South Haven Point, Dorset SZ036866
Waymark
National Trail Acorn
Websites
www.southwestcoastpath.com, www.cornish-mining.org.uk, www.jurassiccoast.com
Maps ◈
OS Landranger: 180, 181, 190, 192, 193, 194, 195, 200, 201, 202, 203, 204
OS Explorer: 101, 102, 103, 104, 105, 106, 107, 108, 109, 110, 111, 114, 115, 116, 126, 139, 9, 15, 20
Harvey Map (Stripmap)
South West Coast Path: Map 1, South West Coast Path: Map 2, South West Coast Path: Map 3, South West Coast Path: Map 4, South West Coast Path: Map 5, South West Coast Path: Map 6, South West Coast Path: Set of 6 Maps, South West Coast Path: Set of 6 Maps & DVD (Harvey Maps)
Publications, badges and certificates
Paperbacks
South West Coast Path: Minehead to Padstow (Official Guide) by Roland Tarr (Aurum Press) 2007. ISBN 9781845132699. 168pp; 210 x 130. £12.99.
South West Coast Path: Padstow to Falmouth (Official Guide) by John Macadam (Aurum Press) 2007. ISBN 9781845132705. 144pp; 210 x 130. £12.99.
South West Coast Path: Falmouth to Exmouth (Official Guide) by Brian Le Messurier (Aurum Press) 2008. ISBN 9781845133139. 168pp; 206 x 130. £12.99.
South West Coast Path: Exmouth to Poole (Official Guide) by Roland Tarr (Aurum Press) 2007. ISBN 9781845132712. 168pp; 210 x 130. £12.99.
Complete Guide to the South West Coast Path (South West Coast Path Association) Annual. ISBN 9780907055150. 168pp; 208 x 148. £8.50 (+ £2.00 p&p). Free to SWCPA members. Reverse guide available.
South West Coast Path: Reverse Guide (South West Coast Path Association) 2006. £3.50 (SWCPA members), £4.50 (non-members).
Cornwall Coast Path by Edith Schofield, revised by Jim Manthorpe (Trailblazer Publications) 2009. ISBN 9781905864195. 256pp; 120 x 180. £9.99.
Exploring the Bournemouth Coast Path by Leigh Hatts (Countryside Books) 2005. ISBN 9781853069086. 96pp; 150 x 210. £7.99. Includes Solent Way first section.
Exploring Cornwall's Tramway Trails Coast-to-Coast Trail: Portreath to Devoran by Bob Acton (Landfall Publications) 2000. Volume 2. ISBN 9781873443378. 240pp; 204 x 148. £7.50.
(PVC)
South West Coast Path: Minehead to South Haven Point by Paddy Dillon (Cicerone Press) 2003. ISBN 9781852843793. 288pp; 172 x 116. £12.95.
Hardbacks
Exploring the South West Coast Path by Philip Carter (Halsgrove Press) 2009. ISBN 9781841148519. 144pp. £14.99.
Jurassic Coast (Halsgrove Press) 2007. ISBN 9781841146737. 144pp; 230 X 214. £12.99.
Certificate
South West Coast Path National Trail (South West Coast Path Association). £3.50 (incs p&p) – free to SWCPA members.
Badge (cloth)
South West Coast Path National Trail (South West Coast Path Association). 100 x 80. £2.70 (incs p&p).
Booklets
South West Coast Path: Through Torbay by John Risdon (Torbay Coast & Countryside Trust). 35pp; A5. £2.50 (+ 50p p&p).
Plymouth's Waterfront Walkway (Plymouth City Council) 2000. 32pp; A5. £2.50 (+ 50p p&p). Downloadable.
Leaflets
South West Coast Path (South West Coast Path Team) 2007. A4/3. Free. Promotional Leaflets with contact details.
South West Coast Path Association by South West Coast Path Association (South West Coast Path Association). Free.
English Riviera Geopark Trail (Torbay Coast & Countryside Trust).
DVD
South West Coast Path (Striding Edge Limited) 2008. 62 minutes. PAL. £12.99 (+ £2.95 p&p).
South West Coast Path: Virtual Book One (Virtual Book Company) 2008. £19.95 (+ £1.95 p&p). Multi-media planning guide.
Walking Support Providers
Bobs; Celtic; Contours; Encounter; Explore Britain; HF; Instep; Let's Go Walking!; Ramblers; Westcountry

Thames Path TPNT

BUCKS, GLOS, GTR LONDON, OXON, READING, SLOUGH, SURREY, SWINDON, W BERKSHIRE, WILTS, WINDSOR M, WOKINGHAM **296km/184 miles**

This National Trail, unique insofar as it is the only one mainly following a river, was officially opened in 1996. From the source the Trail meanders through Cricklade, Lechlade, Oxford, Abingdon, Reading, Henley, Marlow, Maidenhead and Windsor, passing Windsor Castle and the palaces of Hampton Court, Kew, and Richmond. It then traverses central London with options on either bank, to reach the Thames Barrier. Kew Gardens, sites at Westminster, the Tower and Maritime Greenwich, all close to the route, are World Heritage Sites. There is extensive public transport availability along the route by way of rail, bus and river boat. The websites provide tide times and other downloads useful for walkers: a users' guide and camping leaflets. For the sections in London, leaflets can be downloaded from the Walk London link below or ordered online or by phone or post. The waymarked Thames Path Extension (10 miles), which extends the national trail east from the Thames Barrier to Crayford Ness, does not have National Trail status. It follows the south bank downstream from the Thames Barrier to Crayford Ness along east London's working river to link the Thames Path National Trail with the London LOOP at Erith, after which these two routes run together, joining with the Cray Riverway, to the Ness. The waymarked Thames Down Link (15 miles and on OS mapping) provides a link from Kingston upon Thames to Westhumble on the North Downs Way National Trail. The waymarked Beeches Way (16 miles and on OS mapping) makes a link with the Grand Union Canal at West Drayton. The Green Trail (Richmond) (15 miles) links with the Thames Path at Hammersmith Bridge and Hampton, going via Barnes Common, Richmond Park, Ham Common, Bushey Park and Home Park.

Marlow church is seen, looking upstream across the Thames

Windsor Castle and the River Thames from Eton riverside

Attributes
River; Urban; World Heritage Site; Heritage
Start
Thames Source near Kemble, Glos ST981994
Finish
Thames Barrier, Gtr London TQ417794
Waymark
National Trail Acorn
Websites
www.nationaltrail.co.uk, www.portoflondon.co.uk, www.visitthames.co.uk, www.thamespath.org.uk, ww.walklondon.org.uk
Maps ◈
OS Landranger: 163, 164, 173, 174, 175, 176, 177
OS Explorer: 45, 159, 160, 161, 162, 168, 169, 170, 171, 172, 173, 180
Stripmap
Thames, the River and the Path (GEOprojects)
Map (Other)
London Docklands & Greenwich (GEOprojects), London Street Atlas (Geographer's A-Z Map Company), Thames Ring Atlas (Inland Waterways Maps) (GEOprojects)
Publications, badges and certificates
Paperbacks
Thames Path: Sea to the Source by Leigh Hatts (Cicerone Press) 2005. ISBN 9781852844363. 224pp; 172 x 116. £12.00.
Thames Path: National Trail Guides by David Sharp (Aurum Press) 2007. ISBN 9781845132668. 168pp; 210 x 130. £12.99.
Thames Path: Companion (Thames Path National Trail Officer). ISBN 9780953520787. 134pp; A5. £5.75 (incs p&p). Order form on websites; cheques only.
Leaflets
Thames Path: Public Transport Leaflets (Thames Path National Trail Officer) Annual. A5. Free (+ 30p p&p). Order form on websites; cheques only.
From Source to West London *Thames Path: Walks Pack 1* (Thames Path National Trail Officer). £1.10 (+ £1.60 p&p). London area in separate Leaflets.
Hampton Court to Crayford Ness *Thames Path: In Greater London* (Walk London – Strategic Walks Information Service) 2006. 4 Leaflets; A4/3. Free. Downloads, local TICs or Tel: 0870 608 2000 or 01322 558676; also as Pack 2 from Trail Office.
Thames Down Link (Lower Mole Project) 2001. A4/3. Free (+ SAE).
Cray Riverway (Bexley Council). 2pp. Free. Downloadable.
Booklets
Rural Walks around Richmond (RA Richmond) 2004. £2.25 (incs p&p).
Walking Support Providers
Explore Britain; HF; Instep

Yorkshire Wolds Way YWNT

E YORKS, N YORKS **127km/79 miles**

A journey from the Humber estuary to the dramatic Cleveland coast through the gentle chalk hills of the Yorkshire Wolds in typical downland scenery, with chalk grassland peppered with poppies, patches of woodlands and dry valleys. The trail was originally an initiative of the Ramblers Association and went on to become the tenth National Trail launched by the then Countryside Commission. The Trail first goes west along the River Humber and then north around the western edge of the Yorkshire Wolds, in woods and across arable land through Thixendale, and along the northern escarpment of the Wolds that rises to over 600ft. It travels on ridges and through dry valleys and sheep pasture to reach the coast at Filey and the fine headland of Filey Brigg. At Filey Brigg it meets the Cleveland Way National Trail, enabling walkers to take a longer continuous route on these two National Trails.

Attributes
River; Downland/Wolds
Start
Hessle (Haven), E Yorks TA035256
Finish
Filey Brigg, N Yorks TA126817
Waymark
National Trail Acorn

Websites
www.nationaltrail.co.uk
Maps ◈
OS Landranger: 100, 101, 106, 107
OS Explorer: 281, 291, 293, 294, 300, 301
Publications, badges and certificates
Paperbacks
Cleveland Way and the Yorkshire Wolds Way With the Tabular Hills Walk by Paddy Dillon (Cicerone Press) 2005. ISBN 9781852844479. 192pp; 172 x 116. £12.00.
Yorkshire Wolds Way: National Trail Guides by Roger Ratcliffe (Aurum Press) 2007. ISBN 9781845132736. 144pp; 206 x 130. £12.99.
Booklets
Yorkshire Wolds Way: National Trail Accommodation & Information Guide (Yorkshire Wolds Way Project) Annual. 30pp. Free.
Leaflets
Yorkshire Wolds Way Leaflets (Yorkshire Wolds Way Project). 1pp; A3 folded. Free. Tel: 01439 770657 for details.
CD ROM
Running the Wolds Way (Mind Technology Limited). £6.00 (buy on supplier's websites). Includes a full photograph gallery.
Badge
Wolds Way National Trail (RA East Yorkshire & Derwent Area). £1.00 (+ SAE).
Walking Support Providers
Brigantes; Contours; Discovery

The Wolds Way runs along the brow of a grassy dale as it heads for Huggate

Sheep gently graze as walkers approach along Offa's Dyke NT

Offa's Dyke Path ODPNT

DENBIGHS, FLINTS, GLOS, MONS, POWYS, SHROPS, WORCS, WREXHAM **284km/176 miles**

For over 60 miles the route of this National Trail runs along or close to the 8th century dyke passing many historical sites. The Trail meanders along the east side of the Wye Valley to Monmouth, crosses lowland farmland to Pandy and Hatterrall Ridge which is then followed to Hay-on-Wye. The Radnorshire Hills are crossed to Knighton, as is the hill country of Clun. The next part of the route is across the plain of Montgomery, along the Severn Valley and across the Vale of Llangollen to the Clwydian Hills. The waymarked Three Castles Walk (Mons) (19 miles and on OS mapping) is a circular walk from Offa's Dyke visiting Skenfrith, White and Grosmont castles. The St Winefride's Way is a 14-mile pilgrim's trail that links St Asaph's Cathedral, Denbighshire, with St Winefride's Well in Holywell, Flintshire.

Attributes
Moorland; Heritage
Start
Sedbury Cliff, Chepstow, Monmouthshire ST552929
Finish
Prestatyn, Denbighs SJ060837
Waymark
National Trail Acorn
Websites
www.nationaltrail.co.uk, www.offasdyke.demon.co.uk, www.tourism.powys.gov.uk
Maps ◈
OS Landranger: 116, 117, 126, 137, 148, 161, 162, 172
OS Explorer: 13, 14, 155, 167, 177, 201, 216, 240, 255, 256, 264, 265, 285
Harvey Map (Stripmap)
Offa's Dyke Path North (Harvey Route Map), Offa's Dyke Path South (Harvey Route Map) (Harvey Maps)
Stripmap
Strip Maps of Offa's Dyke Path (Offa's Dyke Association)
Publications, badges and certificates
Paperbacks
Offa's Dyke Path by David Hunter (Cicerone Press) 2008. ISBN 9781852845490. 288pp; 115 x 175. £12.95.
Offa's Dyke Path North: Knighton to Prestatyn (National Trail Guides) by Ernie Kay, Kathy Kay, Mark Richards (Aurum Press) 2008. ISBN 9781845133122. 144pp; 206 x 128. £12.99.
Offa's Dyke Path South: Chepstow to Knighton (National Trail Guides) by Ernie Kay, Kathy Kay, Mark Richards (Aurum Press) 2007. ISBN 9781845132743. 144pp; 206 x 130. £12.99.
Offa's Dyke Path by Keith Carter, Tricia Hayne, Bob Hayne (Trailblazer Publications) 2007. ISBN 9781905864065. 208pp; 176 x 120. £9.99.

Special Offa: Walking the Offa's Dyke Path by Bob Bibby (Eye Books) 2004. ISBN 9781903070284. 256pp; 194 x 130. £9.99.

Langton's Guide to the Offa's Dyke Path: A Coast to Coast Walk (Langton's Guides) by Andrew Durham (Andrew Durham) 1996. ISBN 9781899242023. 224pp; 210 x 130. £12.99 (incs p&p).

St Winefride's Way: St. Asaph to Holywell by John Merrill (John Merrill Foundation). ISBN 9781903627662. 40pp; 208 x 142. £4.95 (+ £1.00 p&p). Cheques to John Merrill Foundation.

(spiral bound)

Three Castles Walk: Skenfrith, White & Grosmont by Monmouthshire County Council (Offa's Dyke Association). 32pp. £3.95 (+ p&p).

Hardback

Offa's Dyke: A journey in words & pictures by Jim Saunders (Offa's Dyke Association) 2006. ISBN 9781843236993. 144pp; 248 x 220. £19.99.

Booklets

Offa's Dyke Path: South to North (Offa's Dyke Association) 2000. £2.00 (+ £3.75 p&p).

Offa's Dyke Path & Glyndwyr's Way: Accommodation Guide (Offa's Dyke Association) Annual. A6. £4.50 (+ £0.50 p&p).

Looseleaf

Backpackers & Camping List for Offa's Dyke Path and Glyndwyr's Way (Offa's Dyke Association) Annual. £1.50 (+ £0.50 p&p).

Leaflets

Offa's Dyke Path/Llwybr Clawdd Offa by Countryside Council for Wales (Countryside Council for Wales). A4/3. Free (+ SAE). Downloadable.

Beyond the Offa's Dyke Path: Circular walks (Denbighshire County Council). 9 Leaflets; A4/3. Free (+ SAE). Downloadable.

Badge & certificate

St. Winefride's Way by John Merrill (John Merrill Foundation). £5.00 (incs p&p).

Walking Support Providers

Byways; Celtic; Contours; Discovery; Explore Britain; Instep; Marches Walks; Wycheway

A good section of Offa's Dyke is seen on the ascent north of Kington

Dylife Gorge, view from near Glyndwr's Way

Glyndwr's Way/ Llwybr Glyndwr — GWNT

POWYS — **217km/135 miles**

The route, named after Owain Glyndwr, the 15th century warrior/statesman who attempted to establish an independent Welsh nation, passes close to many sites and places associated with his rebellion, including Abbey-cwm-hir, Llanidloes, Machynlleth, Llangadfan, Lake Vyrnwy and Meifod. It links with Offa's Dyke Path National Trail at both start and finish, hence providing an opportunity to make a circular walk. The route became a National Trail in 2000 and part of the upgrade significantly reduced the amount of road walking. The Ann Griffiths Walk (7 miles) between Pont Llogel and Pontrobert, along the Afon Efyrnwy, links with Glyndwr's Way National Trail at each end, creating a circular route of about 16 miles.

Attributes
Challenging; Downland/Wolds; Moorland
Start
Knighton, Powys SO283724
Finish
Welshpool, Powys SJ227074
Waymark
National Trail Acorn and Welsh Dragon
Websites
www.nationaltrail.co.uk, www.tourism.powys.gov.uk
Maps ◈
OS Landranger: 125, 126, 135, 136, 137, 147, 148
OS Explorer: 23, 200, 201, 214, 215, 216, 239

Publications, badges and certificates
Paperbacks
Glyndwr's Way by C. & R. Catling (Cicerone Press) 2005. ISBN 9781852842994. 128pp. £10.00.
Glyndwr's Way: National Trail Guides by David Perrott (Aurum Press) 2004. ISBN 9781854109682. 168pp; 210 x 124. £12.99.
Owain Glyndwr's Way by Richard Sale (Gwasg Carreg Gwalch) 2001. ISBN 9780863816901. 148pp; 183 x 121. £4.95 (+ £1.50 p&p).
Leaflets
Glyndwr's Way/Llwybr Glyndwr by Countryside Council for Wales (Machynlleth Tourist Information Centre). A4/3. Free (+ SAE).
Booklets
Ann Griffiths Walk (Powys County Council). 20pp; A5. £2.80 (incs p&p). Cheques to Powys County Council.
Offa's Dyke Path & Glyndwyr's Way: Accommodation Guide (Offa's Dyke Association) Annual. A6. £4.50 (+ £0.50 p&p).
Looseleaf
Backpackers & Camping List for Offa's Dyke Path and Glyndwyr's Way (Offa's Dyke Association) Annual. £1.50 (+ £0.50 p&p).
Accommodation list
Walking in Mid Wales & Brecon Beacons (Powys County Council) 2005. A4/3. Free (+ SAE).
Badge (cloth)
Glyndwr's Way (Offa's Dyke Association). £1.30 (+ 26p p&p).
Walking Support Providers
Celtic; Contours

Pembrokeshire Coast Path PEMBCP

CEREDIGION, PEMBROKES 299km/186 miles

The route of this walk, the first National Trail in Wales, lies mainly within the Pembrokeshire Coast National Park. With the exception of the Milford Haven Waterway and three MOD establishments it follows the coastline around the county of Pembrokeshire. The scenery provides an ever-changing contrast between the softer sedimentary rocks of the south coast, with its fine beaches, and the more rugged rocks of the northern coast. The area is rich in prehistoric remains and is noted for its sea birds and seals. Towns and villages visited include Newport, Fishguard, St David's, Broad Haven, Marloes Sands, Bosherston, Manobier, Tenby and Saundersfoot.

Attributes
Challenging; Coastal; Heritage
Start
St Dogmaels, Pembrokes SN163469
Finish
Amroth, Pembrokes SN172072
Waymark
National Trail Acorn
Websites
www.nt.pcnpa.org.uk
Maps ◈
OS Landranger: 145, 157, 158
OS Explorer: 198, 35, 36
Map (Other)
Memory-Map V5 Brecon Beacons & Pembrokeshire Coast OS (Memory-Map Europe)
Publications, badges and certificates
Paperbacks
Pembrokeshire Coast Path: Official Guide by Brian John (Aurum Press) 2008. ISBN 9781845133108. 168pp; 210 x 130. £12.99.

Pembroke Castle reflected in the natural moat formed by the Pembroke River

The Strumble Head lighthouse sits on a small island connected to the mainland by a bridge

Pembrokeshire Coast Path by Jim Manthorpe (Trailblazer Publications) 2007. ISBN 9781905864034. 210pp. £9.99. 2nd Revised Edition.
(PVC)
Pembrokeshire Coastal Path: A Practical Guide for Walkers by Dennis Kelsall, Jan Kelsall (Cicerone Press) 2005. ISBN 9781852843786. 256pp; 172 x 116. £12.95.
Booklets
Pembrokeshire Coast Path by John Merrill (John Merrill Foundation). ISBN 9780907496694. 84pp; A5. £4.95 (+ £1.00 p&p). Cheques to John Merrill Foundation.
Leaflets
Llwybr Arfordir Sir Benfro/The Pembrokeshire Coast Path by Countryside Council for Wales (Pembrokeshire Coast National Park). A4/3. Free (+ SAE).
Video
Great Walks From The Air: Pembrokeshire Coast Path (Pembrokeshire Coast National Park). £12.99 (+ £1.50 p&p).
Badge & certificate
Pembrokeshire Coast Path National Trail (John Merrill Foundation). £5.00 (incs p&p).
Pembrokeshire Coast Path National Trail (Pembrokeshire Coast National Park). £5.00.
Walking Support Providers
Celtic; Contours; Explore Britain; Greenways; HF; Instep; Tony's Taxis; Wycheway

Great Glen Way GGW

HIGHLANDS **117km/73 miles**

The fourth and indeed last of the official Long Distance Routes in Scotland links the west coast at Fort William, the end of the West Highland Way, with the east coast at Inverness via the Great Glen and Loch Ness. Use is made of forestry tracks, the towpath of the Caledonian Canal and various minor lanes and tracks with very little use made of the main A82.

Attributes
Forest/Woodland; Lake/Reservoir; Canal
Start
Fort William, Highland NN104743
Finish
Inverness, Highland NH667452
Waymark
Thistle within hexagon
Websites
www.greatglenway.com
Maps ◈
OS Landranger: 26, 34, 41
OS Explorer: 392, 400, 401, 416, 431
Stripmap
Caledonian Canal & the Great Glen (GEOprojects), Great Glen Way & Great Glen Cycle Route (Footprint)

Publications, badges and certificates
Paperbacks
Great Glen Way: Two-way Trail Guide by Paddy Dillon (Cicerone Press) 2007. ISBN 9781852845032. 160pp; 172 x 116. £10.00.
Great Glen Way: Paperbacks by Brian Smailes (Challenge Publications) 2003. ISBN 9781903568132. 180 x 124. £5.95.
Scottish Glens – Book 6: The Great Glen by Peter D. Koch-Osbourne (Cicerone Press) 1997. ISBN 9781852842369. 144pp; 116 x 176. £6.99.
(spiral/laminated)
Great Glen Way & Map: The Official Guide by Jacquetta Megarry, Sandra Bardwell (Rucksack Readers) 2005. ISBN 9781898481249. 64pp + 5pp map flap; 145 x 215. £10.99.
Grid Reference List
Great Glen Way Grid: Reference List (Walking Support). £2.50 + VAT. Available from Walking Support website.
Walking Support Providers
Aberchalder; Absolute Escapes; Celtic; Contours; Discovery; Easyways; Explore Britain; Great Glen Baggage Transfer; Great Glen Travel; Let's Go Walking!; Macs; Make Tracks; Mickledore; North-West Frontiers; Sherpa Van; Transcotland; Walking Support; Wilderness Scotland

A whitewashed lighthouse overlooks Loch Lochy near Gairlochy on the Great Glen Way

A view of Loch Trool, close to the site of Robert the Bruce's famous ambush site

Southern Upland Way SUW

DUMFRIES & GALLOWAY, BORDERS, S LANARK **343km/213 miles**

This official Long Distance Route provides a coast-to-coast traverse of southern Scotland by a varied path through sparsely populated terrain, generally avoiding the high tops but with the highest point at The Merrick (843m). Across the Rhinns of Galloway and Glen Trool Forest Park to Sanquhar, the open, heather-clad Lowther Hills, it reaches St Mary's Loch near Broad Law. From here the Way passes through Melrose (where it can be linked with the St Cuthbert's Way), Lauder and over the foot hills of the Lammermuir Hills to reach the east coast. West from Melrose, where the St Cuthbert's Way joins, the route is part of the E2 E-Route. See also E-Routes (E2).

Attributes
Moorland
Start
Portpatrick, Dumfries and Galloway NX000542
Finish
Cockburnspath, Borders NT775711
Waymark
Thistle within hexagon
Websites
www.southernuplandway.gov.uk
Maps ◈
OS Landranger: 82, 67, 71, 73, 74, 76, 77, 78, 79
OS Explorer: 330, 309, 310, 317, 318, 319, 320, 322, 328, 329, 337, 338, 345, 346, 351
Publications, badges and certificates
Paperbacks
Southern Upland Way: Official Guide by Roger Smith (Mercat Press) 2005. ISBN 9781841830773. 218pp; 218 x 136. £17.99.
Southern Upland Way: Recreational Path Guides by Anthony Burton (Aurum Press) 1997. ISBN 9781854104557. 168pp; 210 x 130. £12.99.
Southern Upland Way & St Cuthbert's Way by Mike Salter (Mike Salter) 2007. 47pp; OS map size. £3.95 (+ 50p p&p). Only available direct from author.
(PVC)
Southern Upland Way: Scotland's Coast to Coast Trail by Alan Castle (Cicerone Press) 2007. ISBN 9781852844097. 224pp; 172 x 116. £12.00.
Booklets
Short Walks on the Eastern Section of the Southern Upland Way (Scottish Borders Tourist Board). £2.50.
Writing the Way by Dumfries and Galloway Council (Dumfries and Galloway Council). 64pp. £5.00. A Collection of Journeys along the Southern Upland Way.
Leaflets
Southern Upland Way (Dumfries and Galloway Council). A4/3. Free (+ 9 x 4 SAE).
Southern Upland Way: Accommodation List (Dumfries and Galloway Council) Annual. A4/3. Free (+ 9 x 4 SAE). Free PDF download on SUW websites.
Southern Upland Way: Wildlife Guide – various wildlife/history/trees/geology etc (Dumfries and Galloway Council) 2007. A4/3. Free (+ 9 x 4 SAE) for set. Free PDF download on SUW websites.
Southern Upland Wayfarer (Famedram Publishing Ltd) Annual. Free (+ A5 SAE).
Certificate
Southern Upland Way (Dumfries and Galloway Council). Free. Request button on websites.
Walking Support Providers
Celtic; Make Tracks; Southern Upland Way

Speyside Way SPEYSW

HIGHLANDS, MORAY 135km/84 miles

One of the officially designated Long Distance Routes in Scotland, it traces the River Spey, a renowned salmon river, linking the Moray Coast with Aviemore in Strathspey and the Cairngorm fringes over some 65 miles, but with spurs added from Craigellachie to Dufftown (4 miles) and from Ballindalloch to Tomintoul (15 miles). Although it generally offers easy walking on level ground, much on past railway tracks, before Craigellachie there are climbs to over 900ft on Ben Aigan to Red Sheugh, and the extension into Tomintoul contains two more climbs on Cairnacay and Carn Daimhup to over 1,800ft. After Craigellachie it rises gently on the old trackbeds and, after Ballindalloch, a little more steeply in forest to cross the Spey at Cromdale to reach Grantown. The final stages offer views south to the Cairngorms massif and the Lairig Ghru cleft and west to the Monadhliath Mountains. Numerous whisky distilleries are sited along the route, including Glenfiddich. There are proposals to extend the route beyond Aviemore to Badenoch and Newtonmore. The Dava Way (23 miles and on OS mapping) is a multi-user trail across the ancient Celtic province of Morayshire linking the historic towns of Forres and Grantown-on-Spey (itself now in Highland), following the past Highland Railway line across Dava Moor.

Attributes

Former Railway; Forest/Woodland; Coastal; River; Moorland

Start

Buckie, Moray NJ418655

Finish

Aviemore, Highland NH892125

Waymark

Thistle within hexagon

Websites

www.moray.org

Maps ◈

OS Landranger: 27, 28, 35, 36

OS Explorer: 403, 404, 418, 419, 424

Harvey Map (Stripmap)

Speyside Way (Harvey Maps)

Stripmap

Speyside Way (Footprint)

Publications, badges and certificates

Paperbacks

Speyside Way & Map by Jacquetta Megarry, Jim Strachan (Rucksack Readers) 2007. ISBN 9781898481270. 64pp + 5pp map flap, spiral bound and laminated; A5. £10.99.

Leaflets

Speyside Way Accommodation & General Information Guide (Speyside Way Ranger Service). Free. Accommodation list online on Way websites; DVD also sold.

Dava Way (Dava Way Association) 2005. A4/3. Free. From local TICs and downloadable.

Walking Support Providers

Absolute Escapes; Celtic; Contours; Easyways; Explore Britain; HF; Macs; Make Tracks; Wilderness Scotland

A grassy track climbs into the hills to cross the slopes of Cairnacay

Bridge near Bà Cottage on General Caulfeild's military road across Rannoch Moor

West Highland Way WHW

ARGYLL AND BUTE, E DUNBARTON, HIGHLANDS, STIRLING 153km/95 miles

Scotland's first official Long Distance Route crosses a variety of terrain which becomes more rugged as it moves northwards and between the major mountain groups. The Way follows the eastern side of Loch Lomond, crossing the slopes of Ben Lomond to Crianlarich and Bridge of Orchy, the western edge of Rannoch Moor and the entrances to Glen Etive and Glen Coe, and up and over the Devil's Staircase and the highest point of the route at 550m, to reach Kinlochleven. The final section follows General Caulfield's military road over the slopes of the Mamores, crossing wild country with extensive views of the Ben Nevis range to reach Fort William. The waymarked Kelvin Walkway (9 miles and on OS mapping) connects Milngavie with the Glasgow Heliport on the north bank of the River Clyde, providing a link into central Glasgow, and this Walkway is included in the Trailblazer guide.

Attributes
Challenging; Lake/Reservoir; Moorland; Mountain
Start
Milngavie, East Dunbartonshire NS555745
Finish
Fort William, Highland NN105742
Waymark
Thistle within hexagon
Websites
www.west-highland-way.co.uk
Maps ◈
OS Landranger: 41, 50, 56, 57, 64
OS Explorer: 347, 348, 364, 377, 384, 392
Harvey Map (Stripmap)
West Highland Way, West Highland Way: DVD & Stripmap (Harvey Maps)
Stripmap
West Highland Way: Map & Guide (Footprint)
Publications, badges and certificates
Paperbacks
West Highland Way by Charlie Loram (Trailblazer Publications) 2008. ISBN 9781905864133. 192pp; 120 x 180. £9.99.
West Highland Way & Map: Official Guide by Bob Aitken, Roger Smith (Mercat Press) 2006. ISBN 9781841831022. 180pp. £16.99.
West Highland Way by Dan Bailey (Pocket Mountains) 2008. ISBN 9780955454851. 80pp; 150 x 102. £7.99.
West Highland Way: Recreational Path Guides by Anthony Burton (Aurum Press) 1996. ISBN 9781854103918. 144pp; 210 x 130. £12.99.
(PVC)
West Highland Way: Milngavie to Fort William by Terry Marsh (Cicerone Press) 2007. ISBN 9781852843694. 128pp; 172 x 116. £10.00.
(spiral/laminated)
West Highland Way & Map by Jacquetta Megarry (Rucksack Readers) 2007. ISBN 9781898481300. 64pp + 6pp map flap; 145 x 210. £10.99.
Booklets
Official West Highland Way Pocket Companion (West Highland Way Ranger) Annual. Free (+ 9 x 4 SAE).
Leaflets
West Highland Wayfarer (Famedram Publishing Ltd). Free (+ A5 SAE).
Walking Support Providers
Absolute Escapes; AMS; Caledonia; Celtic; Contours; Discovery; Easyways; Explore Britain; Footpath; Great Glen Travel; HF; Let's Go Walking!; Macs; Make Tracks; Mickledore; North-West Frontiers; Sherpa Van; Transcotland; Travel-Lite; UK Exploratory; Wilderness Scotland

ENGLAND

England has a wide range of landscapes and good access for walkers, both on rights of way and Access Land which includes large areas of its uplands. England is the largest of the four countries that make up the UK, with a land area about 50,000 square miles (130,000km^2) and a population of over 50 million.

Walking traditions in England are very strong and trailwalking is very popular, so England has close to 600 promoted routes, many of which are waymarked. Included among these are its 15 National Trails, one shared with Wales, and these are covered in the National Trails section. Anytime Challenge routes abound in England, with some 200, mostly in the north.

With so many trails and such a variety of distinctive landscapes we cover England as eight regions. Heading clockwise from the south-east and the capital these are as follows.

South East England is the most populous and it includes the walker-friendly capital city of London. The North and South Downs offer good ridge walking and the Thames a fine easy riverside trail. There is some countryside that feels surprisingly remote and some interesting coastal walking on Saxon shores and along high and undulating chalk cliffs.

South West England is remarkable for its sustained and spectacular coastal walking and for its moorlands, especially wild Dartmoor with its tors, and there is much industrial heritage in its past mining industries.

West Midlands & the South Welsh Borders offers many fine hill ranges including the dramatic Malvern Hills and the fringes of the Cotswolds, along with some scenic river gorges where the Wye cuts the Forest of Dean. It is also a commercial heartland, with England's second, and just as walker-friendly, city of Birmingham.

North West England includes, to the south of the Mersey river, the moorland Shropshire hills and the Cheshire ridge, and to its north the Lancashire moorlands and the west Pennine fringes, while along the Mersey's populous estuary and its valley are its principal cities of Liverpool and Manchester, both with good urban trails. We also include here the coastal and inland trails on the Isle of Man, a UK Crown Protectorate.

Cumbria & Northumberland includes the Lake District, a gem for hill walkers packed with ridge walking above its famous lakes but with fewer major trails, while Northumberland offers the lonely rolling north Pennine moorlands and the Cheviot Hills, as well as an atmospheric coastline with dramatic headland castles.

Northern England includes some great walking country, with much of the Pennines, the Dales, the heather-covered North York Moors and the gentler Yorkshire Wolds chalk downlands, and it is home to myriad challenge walks.

East Central England has the Peak District as its main lure for walkers, with fine moorland edges, while nearer the coast are the gentler Lincolnshire Wolds.

East of England has gentle hills and wide skies in East Anglia alongside flat fenlands and the Broads, all contrasting with the inland greensand ridgeline, rising westwards towards the undulating Chiltern Hills and their glowing autumn beechwoods.

England's Regions
GLASGOW
Cumbria and
Northumberland
NORTH SEA
NEWCASTLE
Northern England
IRISH SEA
MANCHESTER
North
West England
East
Central England
East
of England
BIRMINGHAM
West Midlands and
South Welsh
Borders
CARDIFF
LONDON
BRISTOL CHANNEL
South East
England
South West
England
ENGLISH CHANNEL

SOUTH EAST ENGLAND

A footbridge spans a narrow River Thames near Inglesham (Thames Path)

KEY FACTS	
Areas	Berkshire, Greater London, Hampshire (including Isle of Wight), Kent, Surrey, Sussex (East & West)
National Parks	New Forest, South Downs
Principal AONBs	North Wessex Downs, Isle of Wight, Chichester Harbour, Sussex Downs, Surrey Hills, High Weald, Kent Downs
World Heritage Sites	Maritime Greenwich; London: Tower, Westminster (Abbey, Palace, Church); Canterbury (Cathedral, Abbey, Church); Kew Gardens; 'Darwin at Downe' (under designation)
Heritage Coast	Isle of Wight (SW – Tennyson; NW - Hamstead), Sussex (Seven Sisters), Kent: Dover-Folkestone, South Foreland
E-Routes	E2 (Eastern Variant: Dover – Stranraer); E9 (Dover – Plymouth)
National Trails (England)	North Downs Way, South Downs Way, Thames Path (part), Ridgeway (part)
Walking Routes	67 main routes (4360 miles); 44 waymarked (2460 miles)
Resident population	16 million, 8 million in Greater London

DON'T MISS! TRAIL SECTIONS (CHALLENGING/REMOTE MARKED WITH *)	
South Downs Way	from Eastbourne to Alfriston the Seven Sisters, dramatic cliff-top switchback* (17km, 1828ft ascent)
White Cliffs Trail	from Dover atop the classic 'white cliffs' of the South Foreland* (18km, 1376ft ascent)
Saxon Shore Way	Rye to Hastings, canalside, then across the gorse 'firehills' cliffs* (19km, 1634ft ascent)
Isle of Wight – Tennyson Trail	Carisbrooke Castle to the Needles and Alum Bay along an island's spine* (23km, 1997ft ascent)
Thames Path – Henley to Maidenhead	easy riverside walking, locks, boats, gracious houses (26km, 398ft ascent)
Jubilee Walkway	for London first-timers, great sites linked on foot (on pavement!) (19km, 688ft ascent)
Capital Ring (Section 6) – Wimbledon Park to Richmond	easy park and riverside walking, 'wombles', a City view and grand Thames river frontages (11km, 481ft ascent)
Bromley Circular Walks – Leaves Green	views, Darwin's Downe and a historic airfield (7km, 645ft ascent)
Greensand Way	Wescott to Shamley Green, across Leith Hill and the Surrey tops* (20km, 1877ft ascent)
North Downs Way	Guildford to Dorking along the chalk ridge* (21km, 1478ft ascent)
Wealdway	Buxted to Ashurst across Ashdown Forest's remote crown (* and navigation) (22km, 1302ft ascent)

REFERENCE AND COMPENDIUM BOOKS INCLUDING MANY REGIONAL ROUTES	
Paperback	*London: The Definitive Walking Guide* by Colin Saunders (Cicerone Press) 2002. ISBN 978-1852843397. 312pp; 137 x 215. £12.99. The London walkers' 'bible'.
Paperback	*Big Walks of London* by John Merrill (John Merrill Foundation) 2008. ISBN 978-0955651137. 184pp. £12.95 (+ p&p).
Paperback	*Walking the Riversides of Sussex* by David Bathhurst (S B Publications) 2008. ISBN 978-1857703375. 160pp; 208 x146. £8.50.

SOUTH EAST ENGLAND

Seven Sisters, the cottages, on the Vanguard Way

A quarter of the English population, some 16 million, lives in the south east of England, the UK's most densely populated and developed region, with some 8 million of them in Greater London, but this region has many attractions for the walker. There are fine stretches of coastline, varied inland scenery, many rivers and waterways, and a network of easy urban walking routes in and around London linking parkland and waterside corridors with interesting heritage sites. Away from the main population centres, in Greater London and along the south coast's urban stretches, there is comparatively deserted countryside and coast with sustained ridges and dramatic cliffs, mixed with easy walks on quiet canals and green riversides.

Geology and history

The region's northern limits lie in the gentler terrain of the London Basin and the North Kent Plain, drained by The Thames and its tributaries. Four main hill ranges shape the rest of the region, all with a common origin in its distant geological past. Long ago much of the region was a vast towering dome of rock – an inverted saucer-shape of layers of strata rising to several thousand feet and centred on the area now known as the High Weald in Kent and Sussex. Erosion and the action of the ice sheets that extended here cut the top off this dome and left the harder layers projecting as what we now see as the North and South Downs chalk ridges and between them the High Weald, now centred on Ashdown Forest.

Between the High Weald and the North Downs lies the gentler Low Weald made of softer rocks, but another higher ridge also intervenes here, formed of the resistant greensand, a stone that now forms the Surrey 'tops' including Leith Hill, the region's highest point. This ridge of sandstone then arcs around west forming the lower Hampshire and Sussex heaths. Inland, the western limits of the region are the Berkshire and the Hampshire Downs, hills locally called 'hangers', that give way south to the gently undulating New Forest, leading in turn to the Hampshire coastline, a haven for boaters. Offshore, just across the Solent, the Isle of Wight, an extension of the Purbeck geology in Dorset, provides more chalk ridges and cliffs.

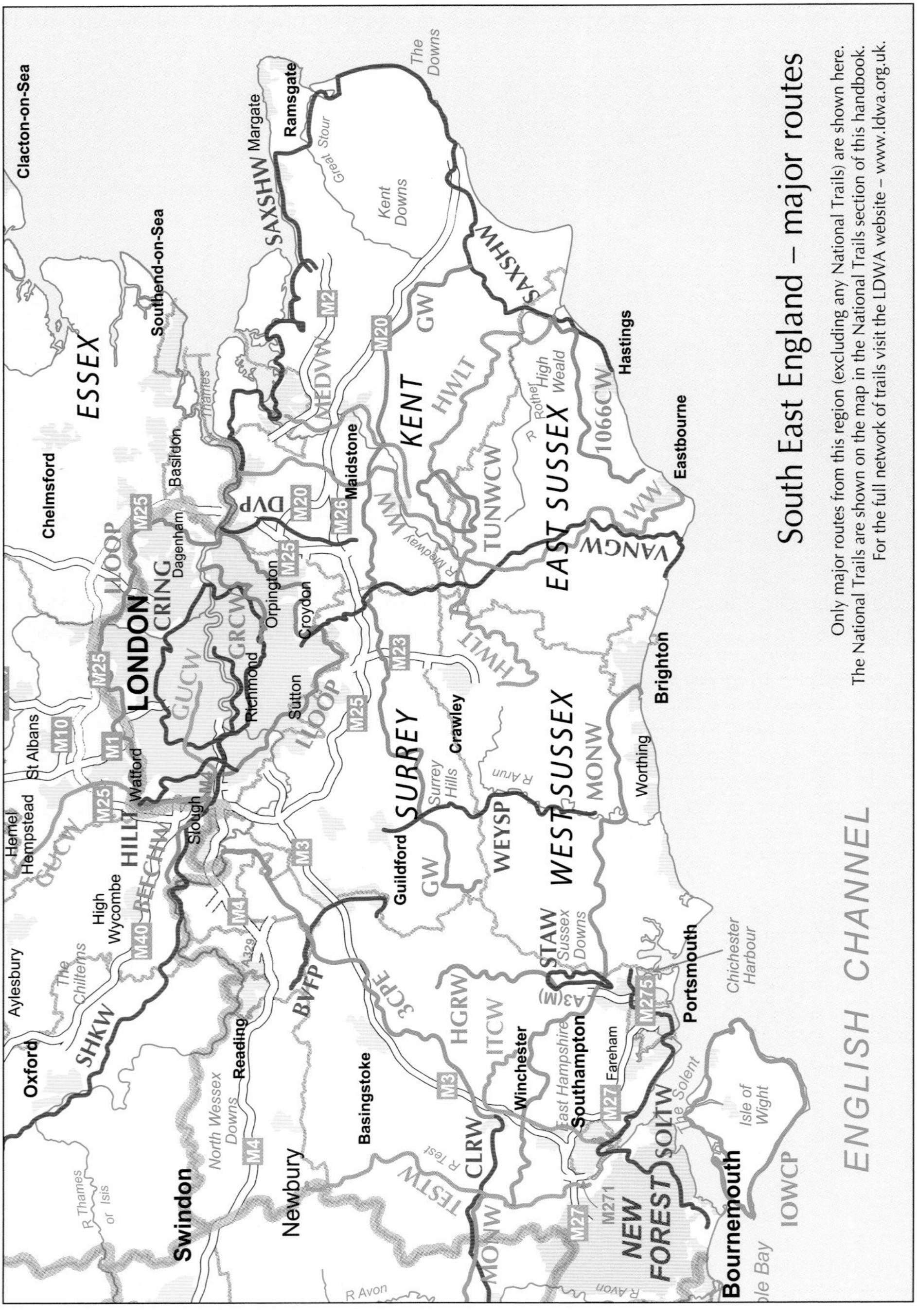

South East England – major routes

Only major routes from this region (excluding any National Trails) are shown here.
The National Trails are shown on the map in the National Trails section of this handbook.
For the full network of trails visit the LDWA website – www.ldwa.org.uk.

Hartfield church, Sussex, on the High Weald Landscape Trail

Within this region, the New Forest and the newly defined South Downs are designated National Parks.

Britain's heritage is well represented in the region with World Heritage Sites at Maritime Greenwich, the Tower of London, Westminster (Abbey, Palace, Church), Canterbury (Cathedral, Abbey, Church), Kew Gardens, while 'Darwin at Downe' is awaiting designation as the first such site connected with the 'workplace' of a renowned naturalist. London's other heritage sites are almost too numerous to mention, and in its eastern fringes a new city is rising on the old docklands at Canary Wharf, with a spectacular urban skyline – London's new 'Manhattan' – while just a little further east the Olympic Park is rapidly growing from dereliction, regenerating a significant area east of the Lea River.

The region's terrain and its history, represented by the inheritance of its past industries and its famous sons, provide a rich source of inspiration for the trail developers who have provided the region's long distance path network.

ROUTE CODES

1066	1066 Country Walk
3CPE	Three Castles Path (England)
BEECHW	Beeches Way
BVFP	Blackwater Valley Footpath
CLRW	Clarendon Way
CRING	Capital Ring
DVP	Darent Valley Path
GRCW	Green Chain Walk
GUCW	Grand Union Canal Walk
GW	Greensand Way
HGRW	Hangers Way
HILLT	Hillingdon Trail
HWLT	High Weald Landscape Trail
IOWCP	Isle of Wight Coastal Path
ITCW	Itchen Way
LLOOP	London Loop
MEDVW	Medway Valley Walk
MONW	Monarch's Way
SAXSHW	Saxon Shore Way
SHKW	Shakespeare's Way
SOLTW	Solent Way
STAW	Staunton Way
TESTW	Test Way
TUNWCW	Tunbridge Wells Circular Walk
VANGW	Vanguard Way
WEYSP	Wey South Path
WW	Wealdway

The Trails

The most densely populated area – **Greater London –** has six major trails, maintained to high standards, which form the capital's core Strategic Walks Network. These comprise two orbital routes, an outer, the London Loop, fringing the suburbs, and another closer in, the Capital Ring, plus a third, inner route, the Jubilee Walkway, linking major tourist sites, while there is riverside walking on The Thames and along the Lea Valley (on respectively the London section of the Thames Path National Trail and Lea Valley Walk). The Green Chain Walk, a daisy-chain network in south-east London, completes the six. A Jubilee Greenway route is being developed marking the 2012 Games and Diamond Jubilee of the Royal Accession.

The region's lengthy **coastline** provides some memorable cliff-top walking as well as gentler options. From Kent the Saxon Shore Way traces the former Saxon coastline round into Sussex and includes the iconic 'White Cliffs'. The South Downs Way includes at its eastern end the challenging roller-coaster Seven Sisters cliffs, while the Isle of Wight Coast Path encircles the island.

Two **downland ridges** provide the setting of the North Downs Way and the South Downs Way, the two English National Trails that run wholly within this region. The **greensand ridges** are traced first by the Greensand Way across Kent and Surrey, then the Serpent Trail snakes among the heathland outcrops out into Hampshire and Sussex. The Hampshire Downs are home to the Hangers Way, Staunton Way and the Oxdrove Way.

Two trails **traverse** these landscapes making a north-to-south journey from London's river and suburbs to the south coast – the Wealdway and the Vanguard Way, sometimes interweaving, while a third, the High Weald Landscape Trail, crosses from west to east.

Saxon Shore Way Waymarker

The region has a wealth of **waterside** walking along both rivers and canals, often gentle. The Thames Path crosses the region from its Cotswold source with many rewarding rural sections before London is reached. There are more again on its South Eastern Extension out towards the estuary. The Thames' tributaries in the Colne Valley west of London offer a range of routes. Many other regional rivers and estuaries offer mostly easy walking: the Sussex Ouse, the Wey and its 'Navigations', the Solent, Itchen, Test and Meon in Hampshire, and the eastern Yar on the Isle of Wight, while Kent offers its Darent, Stour, Len, Elham and Medway rivers and the Wantsum channels. In Berkshire there is the Blackwater. Canal. Towpath walking is extensive and easy, including the Grand Union, Regent's, Kennet and Avon, Basingstoke and Royal Military Canals, and even an aqueduct into London in the form of the New River.

Heritage themes – historic, religious, scientific and literary – are also well represented. The Three Castles Path (England) leads off from Windsor Castle to the famous 'Long Walk', while there are compendium books on walking the castles in Sussex and Kent. The Normans landed at Pevensey, an event marked by the 1066 Country Walk. The Greenwich Meridian Trail marks the 150th anniversary in 2009 of the Prime Meridian line. The St Swithun's and North Downs Ways approximate or parallel the ancient Pilgrim's Way, the latter keeping to the ridge above the spring-line of the pilgrims' route. The West Sussex Literary Trail remembers several past authors living there while Shakespeare's Way reaches the Globe from his birthplace at Stratford upon Avon. The Bromley Circular Walks visit Charles Darwin's Downe where he wrote his seminal works.

Finally there are **enthusiasts' routes** too, some of them challenging and requiring navigational skills. The Founders' Footpaths remembers the LDWA's own founders; the Horsham Round encircles the town; the Fox Way encircles Guildford and there is also the Chairman's Walk in Reading. Two walks remember former county boundaries: the Middlesex Greenway and North to South Surrey Walk.

1066 Country Walk 1/1066CW

E SUSSEX **50km/31 miles**

In September 1066, William, Duke of Normandy brought his army to Pevensey, Sussex and went on to defeat King Harold in the town of Battle in what many people know as the Battle of Hastings. You can follow in the steps of William the Conqueror taking in historical sites on a generally low level walk through ancient towns and villages, over hillsides and through woodland, and passing oast houses and windmills. The route includes the Normans' landing point at Pevensey, the battle site, and the castles at Pevensey and Herstmonceux.There are links from the main route between Battle and Bexhill and between Doleham and Hastings. From Pevensey Castle there are further links to two points on the South Downs Way National Trail near to Jevington. In essence a link is created between the Saxon Shore Way (at Rye) and the South Downs Way. From Rye to Jevington, the route is part of the E9 E-Route.

Attributes
Heritage; Monarchy
Start
Pevensey Castle, Pevensey, E Sussex TQ644048
Finish
Rye, E Sussex TQ921204
Waymark
Red & white named discs with arrow logo
Website
www.1066country.com
Maps ◈
OS Landranger: 189, 199
OS Explorer: 123, 124, 125
Publications, badges and certificates
Paperbacks
1066 Country Walk by Brian Smailes (Challenge Publications) 2000. ISBN 9781903568002. 57pp; 125 x 185. £4.95 (incs p&p). Also sold from publisher's website.
Badge
1066 Country Walk (Challenge Publications). £2.50 (incs p&p).
Certificate
1066 Country Walk (Challenge Publications). £1.20 (incs p&p).
Leaflet
1066 Country Walk by Rother District Council (Battle & Bexhill Tourist Information Centre) 2000. A4/3. Free (+ 9 x 4 SAE).
Walking Support Providers
Orchard

Allan King's Way KINGW

HANTS **68km/42 miles**

Devised by the Hampshire Area RA in memory of Allan King, one of their early members, the route links the old Roman strongholds of Portchester and Winchester. From Porchester Castle the route heads west along the foreshore before turning north to reach Fort Nelson and Nelson's Monument. Still meandering northwards the route takes in World's End, Soberton, the River Meon, the ruined Bishop's Palace at Bishop's Waltham, a section of the old Roman road from Porchester to Winchester, Upham, Cheesefoot Head and Ovington. From here the walk turns west along the Itchen Way before finally following the Nun's Walk in to Winchester. On OS mapping the route is shown as 'King's Way'.

Attributes
Coastal; River; Downland/Wolds; Military
Start
Portchester, Hants SU626044
Finish
Winchester, Hants SU487293
Waymark
Yellow arrow with name
Maps ◈
OS Landranger: 185, 196
OS Explorer: 119, 132, 29
Publications, badges and certificates
Booklets
King's Way by Pat Miles (RA Meon Group) 1995. ISBN 9780861460915. 48pp; A5. £3.25 (+ £1.00 p&p). Cheques to Ramblers Association (Meon Group).

Ashdown Forest Perambulation ASHFP

E SUSSEX **64km/40 miles**

This is basically a clockwise figure-of eight walk centred on Gills Lap, but with a convenient start from the Forest Visitor Centre. The full route could be walked as two 20-mile circuits using nearby car parks, or by links from stations at Crowborough, Eridge, Ashurst and East Grinstead to make longer day-walks. Ashdown Forest derives its name from a royal hunting 'forest' and lies on a sandstone ridge comprising the High Weald AONB, surrounded by the lower Weald, providing consistently fine views and some apparently remote terrain so near to London. It is the largest area of 'lowland heath' in south east England. Well-known locations visited en route include Hartfield with 'Pooh Corner', Pooh

Sticks bridge, and Gills Lap – the 'enchanted place' (all associated with Winnie the Pooh); the Four Counties viewpoint (car park) at the highest point of the Forest at 229 metres, Camp Hill Clump, the Airman's Grave and Nutley windmill.

Attributes
Heath; Heritage; Industrial History; Literary
Start and Finish
Ashdown Forest Centre, Wych Cross, Forest Row, E Sussex TQ431323
Website
www.per-rambulations.co.uk
Maps
OS Landranger: 187, 188, 198, 199
OS Explorer: 135
Publications, badges and certificates
Booklets
Ashdown Forest Perambulation by Terry Owen, Peter Anderson (Per-Rambulations) 2006. ISBN 9780954965426. 24pp; A5. £2.95 (+ 55p p&p).

Basingstoke Canal Walk BASCW

HANTS, SURREY 53km/33 miles

A permissive trail on the restored tree-lined towpath that extends from Penny Bridge, Up Nately, 3½ miles from Basingstoke, to the 200-year-old Basingstoke Canal's junction with the Wey Navigation at Woodham, Surrey. The route passes through woodland, wetland, heathland and pasture, and takes in Odiham Castle, aqueducts, the Deepcut flight of locks, scenic villages and historic buildings.

Attributes
Canal; Heritage; Industrial History
Start
Penny Bridge, Up Nately, Basingstoke, Hants SU693521
Finish
Woodham, Surrey TQ054621
Website
www3.hants.gov.uk, www.basingstoke-canal.co.uk
Maps
OS Landranger: 186
OS Explorer: 144, 145, 160
Stripmap
Basingstoke Canal and the River Wey Navigations (GEOprojects)
Publications, badges and certificates
Paperbacks
Basingstoke Canal by Dieter Jebens (NPI Media Group) 2007. ISBN 9780752431031. 128pp; 234 x 160. £12.99.

Leaflet
Basingstoke Canal (Basingstoke Canal Authority) 2004. A4/3. Free.

Blackwater Valley Footpath BVFP

BRACKNELL F, HANTS, SURREY, WOKINGHAM 37km/23 miles

A route of contrasting halves, the river first flows through the suburban areas of Aldershot, Farnborough, Frimley and Blackwater, looping east and north to reach Sandhurst, after which it takes a westerly course in much more rural surroundings between a series of flooded gravel pits with interesting birdlife, across quiet meadows and sometimes on recent new permissive paths, to reach the confluence with the Loddon. It crosses the Basingstoke Canal Walk at the aqueduct near Aldershot (SU887513).

Attributes
Easy; River
Start
Rowhill Nature Reserve, Aldershot, Hants SU848500
Finish
Swallowfield, Wokingham SU727648
Waymark
Coot and reed logo in blue, footprint in green arrow
Website
www.blackwater-valley.org.uk
Maps ◈
OS Landranger: 175, 186
OS Explorer: 145, 159, 160
Publications, badges and certificates
Booklets
Blackwater Valley Path (Blackwater Valley Countryside Partnership) 2004. £3.00 (incs p&p). Cheques to Blackwater Valley.
Leaflet
Explore the Blackwater Valley (Blackwater Valley Countryside Partnership). A4/3. Free.

Brighton Way BRNW

BRIGHTON H, E SUSSEX, SURREY, W SUSSEX 84km/52 miles

This route, through farmland, villages and over the South Downs, is comprised of seven connecting walks from Horley to the Palace Pier at Brighton. Each walk of between 6 and 10 miles starts at a station and ends at one or two stations down the line. It links with the South Downs Way National Trail at Buckland Bank.

Attributes
Easy
Start
Horley, Surrey TQ286426
Finish
Brighton H TQ313038
Maps
OS Landranger: 187, 198
OS Explorer: 122, 134, 135, 146
Publications, badges and certificates
Guidebook (waterproof cover)
Brighton Way by Norman Willis (John Merrill Foundation) 2002. ISBN 9781903627235. 40pp; A5. £4.50 (+ £1.00 p&p). Cheques to John Merrill Foundation.
Badge & certificate
Brighton Way (John Merrill Foundation). £5.00 (incs p&p); certificate £1.95 (incs p&p).

Bromley Circular Walks BROMCW

GTR LONDON, KENT **125km/78 miles**

A series of inter-linking circular walks in the rural southern fringes of the London Borough of Bromley in two sets based on (Pack One): Nash (5.2 miles), Leaves Green (6.5 miles), Farnborough (4.5 miles), Cudham (7.5 miles), Berrys Green (7.5 miles), Biggin Hill (7 miles), and Green Street Green (7.5 miles) and (Pack Two): Jubilee Park (1.4 miles), St Mary Cray (2.2 miles), Bromley Common (4 miles), Petts Wood (4 miles), St Pauls Cray (4 miles), Three Commons (5 miles), Chelsfield (5.5 miles) and Cray Riverway (Bromley) (6 miles). The village of Downe, visited on some of the routes, was the home of Charles Darwin, where he wrote *On the Origin of Species*. World Heritage Site status is being sought for this area, with full details, mapping, audio trails and podscrolls on the 'Darwin at Downe' website. The London Loop passes through High Elms Country Park nearby.

Attributes
Easy; World Heritage Site; Heritage
Start and Finish
Various
Waymark
Name on green/yellow disc; oak leaf/ acorn logo
Website
www.tfl.gov.uk, www.darwinatdowne.co.uk
Maps
OS Landranger: 177, 187, 188
OS Explorer: 147, 148, 162

Publications, badges and certificates
Folders
Bromley Circular Walks & Trails: Pack One (Bromley Countryside Ranger Service) 2000. 7 laminated route cards; A5. £2.60 (+ 50p p&p).
Bromley Circular Walks & Trails: Pack Two (Bromley Countryside Ranger Service) 2000. 8 laminated route cards; A5. £2.60 (+ 50p p&p).

Capital Ring CRING

GTR LONDON **126km/78 miles**

An inner London circular orbital route linking parks, commons and open spaces, and very well served by public transport. While there is a significant proportion of hard surface and pavement on the route, there are many sections that seem quite rural, in green parks and woods, round lakes and reservoirs and along rivers and canals, and long parkland sections such as in Richmond Park, and many fine views across the distant City from the higher sections. There are numerous points of interest along the way, highlighted in the well-researched guidebook and leaflets. Leaving the Thames Path at Woolwich, the route includes Maryon Park, Woolwich Commons, Oxleas Wood, Eltham Palace, Crystal Palace, Wimbledon Park, Richmond Park, crossing of the Thames at Richmond, Syon Park, Brent River Park, Grand Union Canal, Horsenden Hill, Harrow on the Hill, Fryent Park, Brent Reservoir, Queens Wood, Parkland Walk, Finsbury Park, the New River, Clissold Park, the Lea river, the Olympic Park site at Stratford, the Greenway, and finally the Woolwich foot tunnel under the Thames. From the start the route soon coincides with the Green Chain Walk to Crystal Palace. The Dollis Valley Greenwalk (10 miles and included on OS mapping) provides a link between the London Loop and the Capital Ring as does the Thames Path South East Extension to Erith.

Attributes
Easy; Forest/Woodland; Lake/ Reservoir; River; Canal; Urban; Heritage; Industrial History
Start and Finish
Woolwich Foot Tunnel TQ432793
Waymark
Name with Big Ben in arrow ring on green disc
Website
www.tfl.gov.uk, www.walklondon.org.uk
Maps ◈
OS Landranger: 176, 177
OS Explorer: 161, 162, 173, 174

Map (Other)
London Street Atlas (Geographer's A-Z Map Company)
Publications, badges and certificates
Guidebook
Capital Ring by Colin Saunders (Aurum Press) 2006. ISBN 9781845130756. 168pp; 130 x 210. £12.99.
Leaflets
Walk the Capital Ring (Walk London – Strategic Walks Information Service). 15 leaflets; A4/3. Free (+ SAE). Downloads or order leaflets free from Walk London website.

Chairman's Walk CHMW

READING, W BERKSHIRE 161km/100 miles

Hugging the boundary of West Berkshire, in a clockwise direction, the route takes in sections of the Thames Path, the Ridgeway, the Kennet & Avon Canal, and visits Mapledurham, Silchester (Roman Calleva), the River Enborne, Greenham Common, Walbury Hill, Combe Gibbet, Hungerford, and Lambourn Downs.

Attributes
River; Canal; Downland/Wolds
Start and Finish
Pangbourne, W Berkshire SU636768
Website
www.wberksramblers.org.uk
Maps
OS Landranger: 174, 175
OS Explorer: 158, 159, 170
Publications, badges and certificates
Paperbacks (spiral bound)
Chairman's Walk: Around the Perimeter of West Berkshire by Patricia Cooper, Fred Burke (RA West Berkshire). ISBN 9781901184594. 64pp. £3.00 (+£1 p&p). Special price to LDWA members available from West Berkshire Ramblers.

Colne Valley Routes COLNEV

BUCKS, HERTS, GTR LONDON, SLOUGH, SURREY, WINDSOR M 72km/45 miles

To the west of London the Colne valley is the first major countryside corridor heading north of the Thames; beginning at Staines it includes the Colne Valley Regional Park. This group of linked walking routes explores the River Colne and some of its tributaries, extending to the north beyond St Albans and west into the Chiltern hills and becoming generally more rural as it goes. The separate Colne Brook, flowing parallel to the Colne river a little further west, initially has no promoted routes until the South Bucks Way is reached; the Brook eventually becomes the Misbourne, reaching Great Missenden. The Grand Union Canal section between Yiewsley and Rickmansworth is close to the Colne and its tributaries, taking its water supply from them. The southern part of the Colne valley up to Rickmansworth has a number of major reservoirs and many flooded gravel pits, havens to wildlife. Initially the Colne flows close to Heathrow airport and the M25, but beyond Uxbridge it has gained some separation. Between Yiewsley and Rickmansworth the Colne is paralleled by the Grand Union Canal. Also at Yiewsley the River Pinn joins the Colne. After Rickmansworth the Chess first leaves north west to Chesham and the Chilterns. The Gade next leaves to the north initially along with the Grand Union Canal, passing west of Watford and Cassiobury Park, while after the canal heads west the Gade's final course is north to Gaddesden. Beyond Watford the Ver runs north past St Alban's (Roman name Verulanium) to Redbourn while the Colne's final course is past London Colney to Colney Heath and Hatfield. The Colne Valley Way covers the southern end of the Valley whilst the Colne Valley Trail covers the north. The Colne Valley Way starts at the Thames Path National Trail and connects with the Colne Valley Trail (14 miles) which then goes on to Rickmansworth, coincident for much of its length with both the London Loop and the Grand Union Canal Walk. From Rickmansworth a short link leads to the Ebury Way (3 miles; on OS maps as a cycleway) and to Oxhey Park. From Oxhey Park it is a short distance to the waymarked Ver-Colne Valley Walk (15 miles between Watford and Redbourn and on OS mapping). Also at Rickmansworth the waymarked Chess Valley Walk (10 miles and on OS mapping) goes to Chesham to join to the Chiltern Link, providing a link to the Ridgeway National Trail. From Yiewsley the waymarked Celandine Route (12 miles) heads along the River Pinn to Pinner.

Attributes
Easy; Lake/Reservoir; River
Start
Staines, Surrey TQ028717
Finish
Oxhey Park, Herts TQ111953
Waymark
Named discs with walker/cyclist graphic (Trail)
Website
www.colnevalleypark.org.uk,
www.discover-colnevalley.org.uk
Maps ◈
OS Landranger: 166, 176
OS Explorer: 160, 172, 173, 182

Publications, badges and certificates
Leaflets
Colne Valley Trail (Sections 1 & 2) (Groundwork Thames Valley) 2004. Free (+ SAE).
Chess Valley Walk (Buckinghamshire County Council) 1996. A4/3. Free (+ SAE). Detailed walk leaflet from Rights of Way Team on (01296) 382171/email row@ buckscc.gov.uk.
Celandine Route (Hillingdon LB) 2000. A4/3. Free.

Darent Valley Path DVP

KENT **31km/19 miles**

The River Darent flows from its source in the Greensand hills, south of Westerham, to join the Thames, north of Dartford. The walk is through a varied landscape of riverside fringed with ancient willows, hop gardens and cornfields, secretive woodlands, downland carpeted with wild flowers, and expanses of marshland. It also has the added attractions of Roman remains, majestic viaducts, historic houses, old mills, and picturesque villages with beautiful churches. The 2007 guidebook covers the route only in outline, concentrating on shorter walks. An older edition, which may still be obtainable, will be useful to those walking the full route. There is an alternative start point at Chipstead (TQ500561).

DARENT VALLEY PATH

Attributes
Easy; River; Downland/Wolds; Heritage; Industrial History
Start
Sevenoaks, Kent TQ522554
Finish
Confluence of Rivers Darent (east bank) and Thames, Kent TQ542779
Waymark
Stylised tree and river with name
Maps ◈
OS Landranger: 177, 188
OS Explorer: 147, 162
Publications, badges and certificates
Leaflet
Darent Valley Path (North West Kent Countryside Project) 2004. A4/3. Free.
Guidebook
Darent Valley Path/Short Walks (Kent County Council) 2007. ISBN 9781901509779. 50pp. £4.99. Overview only; focus on four shorter walks.

Diamond Way (Sussex) SUSDIW

E SUSSEX, W SUSSEX **97km/60 miles**

A gently undulating route in the Low Weald passing through farmland, heath and woodland, and visiting Heathfield where it joins the waymarked Cuckoo Trail (14 miles and on OS mapping) which follows a disused railway south to Hampden Park, via Polegate and Hailsham.

Attributes
Downland/Wolds
Start
Midhurst, W Sussex SU885213
Finish
Heathfield, E Sussex TQ578213
Maps
OS Landranger: 197, 198, 199
OS Explorer: 133, 134, 135
Publications, badges and certificates
Booklets
Sussex Diamond Way (RA Sussex Area). 46pp; A5. Free (+ £1.00 p&p). Cheques to Ramblers Associaton (Heathfield & District Group).
Leaflet
Cuckoo Trail (Wealden District Council) 2000. A4/3. Free. Download available on route website.

Founders Footpaths FF

SURREY **42km/26 miles**

A Surrey Hills classic over both downland and greensand ridges, visiting five sites linked to the LDWA's Founders, including Steer's Field and Blatchford Down. The route involves over 3000ft of ascent.

Attributes
Challenging; Anytime Challenge; Downland/Wolds
Start and Finish
Steer's Field, Surrey TQ141504
Maps
OS Landranger: 186, 187
OS Explorer: 145, 146
Publications, badges and certificates
Booklets
Founders Footpaths (Ann Sayer) 1998. 12pp; A5. Free (+ 9 x 6 SAE).
Certificate
Founders Footpaths (Ann Sayer). £1.00 (incs p&p).

Fox Way FOXW

SURREY 63km/39 miles

Devised by Win King and Richard Fox, this is a circular walk around Guildford. The walk can be divided into seven stages (between Ripley Green, Clandon, Shere, Bramley, Godalming, Wanborough and Worpleston), using four railway stations around Guildford. The walk passes through a range of habitats including ancient woodlands, chalk downland, heathland, meadows and waterways. Participants are invited to report unusual finds to the Surrey Wildlife Trust (info@surreywt.org.uk – mention Fox Way).

Attributes
Heath; Downland/Wolds
Start and Finish
Ripley Village Green, Surrey
TQ054569
Waymark
Yellow disc with fox head, crown and route name
Website
www.thefoxway.com, www.surreywildlifetrust.co.uk
Maps
OS Landranger: 186, 187
OS Explorer: 145
Publications, badges and certificates
Booklets (illustrated)
Fox Way by Richard Fox, illustrated by Win King (Richard Fox) 2005. ISBN 9780955086700. 28pp; A5. £6.95 (incs p&p). Cheques to Richard Fox.

Grand Union Canal Walk GUCW

BUCKS, HERTS, GTR LONDON, NORTHANTS, WARKS, W MIDLANDS 234km/145 miles

This first National Waterways walk was created as part of the 200th anniversary celebrations of the creation of the canal companies that later formed the Grand Union Canal. Being mainly towpath walking it provides much for those interested in canal history. From the centre of London, at Little Venice, the canal heads to Slough and then through Hertfordshire and the Chilterns to Tring. Apart from the stretch through Milton Keynes the route is then largely rural, passing the Canal Museum at Stoke Bruerne, to Leamington Spa and Warwick. The final stretch is through the suburbs of Birmingham. From Little Venice the Regent's Canal (8½ miles) takes the walker to Limehouse Basin and the Thames Path National Trail. On the way the Hertford Union Canal (1½ miles) provides a link to the Lea Valley Walk. At Startop's End, near Marsworth, the Aylesbury Arm (6 miles) provides a link to that town. Similarly, at Bulbourne the Wendover Arm (6 miles) links to Wendover. The Two Ridges Link (8 miles and on OS mapping) at Leighton Buzzard gives access to the Ridgeway National Trail and the Greensand Ridge Walk.

Attributes
Canal
Start
Little Venice, Paddington, Gtr London
TQ260818

Finish
Birmingham, Gas Street Basin, W Midlands SP062867
Waymark
Named black discs
Maps ◈
OS Landranger: 139, 151, 152, 165, 166, 175, 176
OS Explorer: 160, 161, 172, 173, 181, 182, 192, 207, 220, 221, 222, 223
Stripmap
Grand Union Canal map 1: Birmingham to Fenny Stratford, Grand Union Canal map 2: Braunston to Kings Langley, Grand Union Canal map 3: Fenny Stratford to the Thames, Grand Union Canal map 4: Leicester Line, Soar Navigation and Erewash Canal (GEOprojects)
Map (Other)
Thames Ring Atlas (Inland Waterways Maps) (GEOprojects)
Publications, badges and certificates
Paperbacks
Grand Union Canal (South): A Towpath Guide by Nick Corble (Tempus Publishing Ltd) 2005. ISBN 9780752435398. 240pp; 124 x 258. £12.99.
Grand Union Canal (North): Towpath Guide by Nick Corble (Tempus Publishing Ltd) 2006. ISBN 9780752438030. 240pp; 124 x 258. £12.99.
Exploring the Regent's Canal by Michael Essex-Lopresti (Brewin Books Ltd) 1994. ISBN 9781858580173. 101pp; 148 x 209. £8.95 (+ £2.00 p&p).
(wire bound)
Walking the Canals of London: Regent Canal, Grand Union Canal & River Thames Walks by John Merrill (John Merrill Foundation) 2006. ISBN 9780955369124. 108pp. £9.95 (+ £1.00 p&p). Cheques to John Merrill Foundation.
Leaflets
Aylesbury Arm (Buckinghamshire County Council). A4/3. Free (+ SAE).
Wendover Arm (Buckinghamshire County Council). A4/3. Free (+ SAE).
Grand Union Canal an Explorers Guide (British Waterways – Fazeley) 2000. A5. Free (+ SAE).

Green Chain Walk GRCW

GTR LONDON **64km/40 miles**

The Green Chain Walk provides a link between the River Thames and many of the open spaces in South-East London. The walk, which can also be started from the Thames Barrier or Erith riverside, caters for several variations of route as it passes through Oxleas Wood and Mottingham to terminate at either Crystal Palace or Chislehurst. Though there is inevitably some street walking, there is a surprising amount of woodland, grassland, park and garden and some interesting heritage sites are passed, such as Eltham Palace. The 'daisy chain' layout of the route enables many options for circular and linear walks. Between Maryon Park, Charlton and Crystal Palace the route is coincident with the Capital Ring, and at the Thames riverside it links to the Thames Path and the Thames Path South East Extension.

Attributes
Easy; Forest/Woodland; River; Urban; Heritage
Start
Thamesmead, Gtr London TQ472813
Finish
Crystal Palace, Gtr London TQ343705
Waymark
Named signs with logo
Website
www.greenchain.com, www.walklondon.org.uk
Maps ◈
OS Landranger: 176, 177
OS Explorer: 161, 162
Map (Other)
Poster map of Green Chain Walk (SE London Green Chain Project), London Street Atlas (Geographer's A-Z Map Company)
Publications, badges and certificates
Folder
Explore South East London's Green Chain (SE London Green Chain Project) 1999. Set of ten cards; A4/2. £3.50 (incs p&p). Cheques to Greenwich Council.
Leaflets
Explore South East London's Green Chain (Overview) (SE London Green Chain Project). A4/3. Free.
(laminated)
Green Chain Walk (Walk London – Strategic Walks Information Service). 10 sectional; A4/2. Free. Downloads or order leaflets free from Walk London website.

Greensand Way GW

KENT, SURREY **173km/107 miles**

The Greensand Way follows the ridge of greensand rock across Surrey and Kent, to the edges of Romney Marsh and almost to the Kent coast. The Way takes its name from the layers of sandstone in each of which is found the green coloured mineral glauconite. The greensand ridge runs broadly parallel to, and south of, the North Downs ridge. Excellent views can be obtained of the North Downs and across to the Weald to the South. It traverses two areas designated as Areas of Outstanding Natural Beauty: Hindhead to Leith Hill in Surrey and the Sevenoaks ridge from the Kent-Surrey Border to Borough Green in Kent. The former well produced guidebook is out of print. A new edition was planned for 2009. In Surrey the Way passes the Devil's Punch Bowl and crosses Hascombe Hill and Winterfold Heath then traverses the main Surrey tops of Pitch, Holmbury and Leith Hills, where Leith Hill's tower reaches 1000ft, before descending north to Dorking. In Kent it crosses Toys and Ide Hills, descends to Sevenoaks Weald and crosses the Medway Valley to Yalding. Then ascending the ridge it passes through villages, orchards and hop gardens and views over the Weald are achieved. The ridge becomes indistinct beyond Great Chart but the route crosses a rolling landscape of farmland and woodland. There are a number of link routes with the North Downs Way National Trail. A further link is provided by the waymarked Reigate and Banstead Millennium Trail (18 miles), a route between Banstead Downs and Horley. The Way meets the Saxon Shore Way at Hamstreet near to the Royal Military Canal. At its start, the Serpent Trail provides a 64-mile route on the Sussex greensand hills and heaths. The Four Stations Way (12 miles) links Haslemere to Godalming.

Attributes
Downland/Wolds
Start
Haslemere, Surrey SU905328
Finish
Hamstreet, Kent TR002334
Waymark
Disc with letters GW in Surrey; oast-house in Kent
Website
www.kent.gov.uk
Maps ◈
OS Landranger: 186, 187, 188, 189
OS Explorer: 125, 133, 134, 136, 137, 145, 146, 147, 148

Publications, badges and certificates
Booklets
Along and Around the Greensand Way by Bea Cowan (Surrey County Council) 1997. ISBN 9781873010914. 128pp; 212 x 204. £6.00.
Leaflets
Reigate & Banstead Borough Council Millennium Trail (Reigate and Banstead Borough Council) 2000. 8 leaflets; A4/3. Free.
Route cards
Four Stations Way (RA Godalming and Haslemere) 2000. 2 cards; A4/2. £2.00 (incs p&p).
Walking Support Providers
Orchard

Greenwich Meridian Trail GMT

CAMBS, E YORKS, E SUSSEX, ESSEX, HERTS, GTR LONDON, LINCS, SURREY, W SUSSEX 444km/276 miles

Using public footpaths and bridleways, the route follows as closely as practical the line of the Prime Meridian. It traverses south to north across eastern England between Sussex (English Channel) and East Yorkshire (North Sea). The route visits the origin of the Meridian at Greenwich (at TQ388773). Maritime Greenwich is recognised as a World Heritage Site. Other places include Lewes, Oxted, Chingford, Cambridge (via an optional loop), Holbeach, Boston, Cleethorpes and Hull. A wide variety of rural landscapes include downlands, The Weald and fenland.

Attributes
River; Canal; World Heritage Site; Heritage
Start
Meridian Monument, Peacehaven, E Sussex TQ410008
Finish
Meridian coast crossing, near Tunstall, E Yorks TA318313
Maps
OS Landranger: 107, 113, 122, 131, 142, 154, 166, 167, 177, 187, 198
OS Explorer: 122, 135, 146, 161, 162, 174, 194, 209, 225, 227, 235, 249, 261, 273, 283, 292
Publications, badges and certificates
Guidebook
Greenwich Meridian Trail: South & North (Hilda & Graham Heap) 2009. Book in preparation, part of route description available from supplier.

Hangers Way HGRW

HANTS 34km/21 miles

Named after the series of steep-sided hills, the Hampshire Hangers, the route goes through both wooded and grassed areas and visits the village of Selborne, home of past naturalist Gilbert White. At Queen Elizabeth Country Park it meets with the South Downs Way National Trail, and links with the Staunton Way which heads south to reach the coast at Langstone Harbour.

Attributes
Downland/Wolds
Start
Alton, Hants SU723397
Finish
Queen Elizabeth Country Park, Hants SU718182
Waymark
Green and white named discs with tree on hill
Website
www3.hants.gov.uk
Maps ◈
OS Landranger: 186, 197
OS Explorer: 120, 133, 144
Publications, badges and certificates
Leaflet
Hangers Way (Hampshire County Council). A4/3. Free (+ SAE).

HAMPSHIRE COUNTY COUNCIL
HANGERS WAY

Haslemere Circular Walk HASCW

HANTS, SURREY, W SUSSEX 36km/22 miles

A circuit around Haslemere, much of it through National Trust woodland and heathland, visiting Gibbet Hill, Blackdown, Marley Common, Waggoners Wells and the Devil's Punchbowl.

Attributes
Anytime Challenge; Heath
Start and Finish
Devil's Punchbowl, Surrey SU890358
Maps
OS Landranger: 186
OS Explorer: 133
Publications, badges and certificates
Looseleaf
Haslemere Circular Walk by Elizabeth Pamplin (Elizabeth Pamplin). 3pp; A4. Free (+ SAE).
Route cards
Four Stations Way (RA Godalming and Haslemere) 2000. 2 cards; A4/2. £2.00 (incs p&p).

High Weald Landscape Trail HWLT

E SUSSEX, KENT, W SUSSEX **151km/94 miles**

A walking route through the unique landscape of the High Weald, the centre of the 16th Century iron industry and still the most wooded area of England. The Trail takes in hop gardens, orchards, villages and historic gardens. Only a leaflet is still available but the route is on OS maps and waymarked.

Attributes
Downland/Wolds; Heritage
Start
Horsham Station, W Sussex TQ178310
Finish
Strand Quay, Rye, E Sussex TQ918202
Waymark
Green named signs and discs with tree and church
Website
www.highweald.org
Maps ◈
OS Landranger: 187, 188, 189, 198, 199
OS Explorer: 125, 134, 135, 136, 124
Publications, badges and certificates
Leaflet
High Weald: Landscape Heritage Trails in West Sussex (West Sussex County Council) 1997. A5. Free.
Walking Support Providers
Orchard

Hillingdon Trail HILLT

GTR LONDON **32km/20 miles**

This route spans the London Borough of Hillingdon from Cranford Park in the south to Springwell Lock, on the Grand Union Canal, in the north.

Attributes
Easy; River; Canal
Start
Cranford Park, Gtr London TQ103782
Finish
Springwell Lock, Gtr London TQ043929
Waymark
Fingerposts and trail logo
Website
www.hillingdon.gov.uk
Maps ◈
OS Landranger: 176
OS Explorer: 161, 172, 173

Horsham Round HORD

W SUSSEX **45km/28 miles**

A route, created by Horsham Joggers, which uses rural paths through the undulating Wealden countryside as it encircles the town. It offers views of the Surrey hills and Sussex downs.

Attributes
Anytime Challenge
Start and Finish
Horsham Town Hall, Horsham, W Sussex TQ173305
Maps
OS Landranger: 187
OS Explorer: 134
Publications, badges and certificates
Booklets
Horsham Round by Andy Mallpress (Andy Mallpress) 2004. A5. £1.00 (+ 9 x 6 SAE). Cheques to Horsham Joggers.

Isle of Wight Coast Path IOWCP

IOW **113km/70 miles**

The coastal path encircles the island and, with the exception of detours to the west of Thorness Bay and round the Osborne Crown Property at Osborne Bay, stays close to the coast. It is a very varied walk over chalk and sandstone cliffs, through popular holiday resorts and the less crowded inlets, bays, marshes and saltings. Coastal links from north (Cowes) to south (St Catherine's Lighthouse) and from east (Bembridge) to the Needles (west) add further route options. The bus service allows it to be split over several days and the route can be joined at many convenient places. The sections from Ryde to Bembridge and from the Needles to Yarmouth form part of the E9 E-Route, see E-Routes, (E9). There are seven other trails on the island which are all included on OS mapping and some of which are connecting to the Vectis Trail and the Isle of Wight Coast Path. These are: Bembridge Trail (12 miles) – Newport (Shide) to Bembridge; Nunwell Trail (10 miles) – Ryde St Johns to Sandown; Hamstead Trail (8 miles) – Brooke Bay to Hamstead Ledge; Shepherds Trail (10 miles) – Carisbrooke to Atherfield; Stenbury Trail (10 miles) – Blackwater to Week Down; Tennyson Trail (15 miles) – Carisbrooke to Alum Bay; Worsley Trail (15 miles) – Shanklin to Brightstone. These trails are covered on the website below and the *Inland Trails* booklet.

Attributes
Coastal; Downland/Wolds
Start and Finish
Cowes, IoW SZ500956
Waymark
Named signs, blue with white gull motif
Website
www.islandbreaks.co.uk
Maps ◈
OS Landranger: 196
OS Explorer: 22, 29
Publications, badges and certificates
Paperbacks
Complete Isle of Wight Coastal Footpath by Brian Smailes (Challenge Publications). ISBN 9780952690061. 33pp; 140 x 202. £3.75.
Isle of Wight North to South & East to West by Brian Smailes (Challenge Publications) 2002. ISBN 9781903568071. £3.75 (incs p&p).
Walkers Guide to the Isle of Wight by Martin Collins, Norman Birch (Cicerone Press) 2004. ISBN 9781852842215. 216pp; 172 x 114. £10.00.
Isle of Wight Coastal Path: Notebook by Russell Mills, Suzanne Mills (Ottakars) 1993. ISBN 9780953578917. 63pp; A5. £4.99 (+ £1.00 p&p).
Booklets
Isle of Wight Coast Path by John Merrill (John Merrill Foundation). ISBN 9780907496687. 56pp; A5. £6.95 (+ £1.00 p&p). Cheques to John Merrill Foundation.
Isle of Wight Coastal Path & Inland Trails (Isle of Wight Tourism). A4/3. £3.00 (+ £1.00 p&p). Cheques to Isle of Wight Council.
Badge & certificate
Isle of Wight Coast Path (John Merrill Foundation). £5.00 (incs p&p).
Walking Support Providers
Bag Tag; Celtic; Contours; HF; Step by Step

Itchen Way — ITCW

HANTS — **50km/31 miles**

Following the River Itchen from the mouth to the source this varied route leads from the chalk downland through Winchester to water meadows and nature reserves and the downs.

Attributes
Easy; River; Downland/Wolds; Urban
Start
Sholing Station, Southampton, Hants SU447110
Finish
Hinton Ampner, Hants SU596272
Waymark
Named standard arrows
Website
www.eastleighramblers.hampshire.org.uk
Maps ◈
OS Landranger:185, 196
OS Explorer: 22, 132
Publications, badges and certificates
Book
Itchen Way: Guide Book by Richard C. Kenchington FRICS IRRV (Eastleigh Ramblers) 2008. 40pp. £6.00 (+ £1.00 p&p). Cheques to Walk the World Limited.

Jubilee Greenway — JUBGW

GTR LONDON — **97km/60 miles**

In 2012 Her Majesty The Queen will, it is hoped, celebrate 60 years as Sovereign and London will host the Olympic Games for the first time since 1948. To celebrate this conjunction the Jubilee Walkway Trust has developed the concept of a Jubilee Greenway circling inner London. The aim of the route, announced in November 2007, is to provide continuous, green and attractive walking and cycling to all nine London venues which will host the Olympic Games, while connecting many of London's main visitor attractions, historic places, parks, open spaces, waterways and views and many major public transport hubs. It is already walkable. Sites at Westminster and Greenwich form World Heritage Sites.

Attributes
Easy; River; Canal; Urban; World Heritage Site; Heritage; Monarchy
Start and Finish
Buckingham Palace, Gtr London TQ291797
Waymark
Crown, laurel and diamond symbols and name in green disc
Website
www.jubileegreenway.com
Maps
OS Landranger: 176, 177
OS Explorer: 161, 173
Map (Other)
London Street Atlas (Geographer's A-Z Map Company)
Publications, badges and certificates
Booklets
Jubilee Greenway (Jubilee Walkway Trust) 2008. 34pp. Free. Downloadable.

Jubilee Walkway JUBWW

GTR LONDON 23km/14 miles

The Jubilee Walkway is the capital's most popular walking trail and one of six walking routes of the Strategic Walks Network. The Walkway was first developed for The Queen's Silver Jubilee in 1977 and extensively refurbished in the Queen's Golden Jubilee year. It is designed to link the majority of London's key attractions. Highlights include: National Gallery, Trafalgar Square, Admiralty Arch, The Mall, Buckingham Palace, St James Park, Westminster Abbey, Houses of Parliament, Thames Path National Trail, Aquarium, London Eye, South Bank Centre, Tate Modern, Millennium Bridge, Shakespeare Globe Theatre, Southwark Cathedral, HMS Belfast, Tower Bridge, St Katherine's Docks, Tower of London, Bank of England, Guildhall Art Gallery, Barbican, Museum of London, St Paul's Cathedral, Fleet Street, British Library, British Museum, John Soanes Museum, Royal Opera House, London Transport Museum and the National Portrait Gallery. Sites at Westminster and the Tower are World Heritage Sites. In 2012, it is hoped that the Queen will celebrate her Diamond Jubilee and a second linked trail, the Jubilee Greenway, is walkable.

Attributes
Easy; River; Urban; World Heritage Site; Heritage; Monarchy
Start and Finish
Leicester Square, Westminster, Gtr London TQ298807
Waymark
Name and crown symbol in direction of travel, on pavement plaques
Website
www.jubileewalkway.org.uk, www.walklondon.org.uk
Maps
OS Landranger: 176, 177
OS Explorer: 161, 173
Map (Other)
London Street Atlas (Geographer's A-Z Map Company)
Publications, badges and certificates
Leaflet
Jubilee Walkway (Walk London – Strategic Walks Information Service). Free. Downloads, local TICs or Tel: 0870 240 6094 (normal call charges will apply).
Booklets
Jubilee Greenway (Jubilee Walkway Trust) 2008. 34pp. Free. Downloadable.

Kennet and Avon Walk KTAW

BATH NES, BRISTOL, N SOMERS, READING, W BERKSHIRE, WILTS 135km/84 miles

Linking the Thames at Reading with the west coast and also the Thames Path to the Cotswold Way National Trails, it follows the canal through Thatcham, Hungerford, Pewsey, Devizes, Bradford-on-Avon and Bath where advantage is then taken of the waymarked River Avon Trail (25 miles and included on OS mapping) through the spectacular Avon Gorge to Bristol.

Attributes
River; Canal
Start
Reading SU730739
Finish
Pill, N Somers ST525759
Waymark
Barge/name on blue disc on River Avon Trail section
Website
www.waterscape.com, www.visitkanda.com
Maps
OS Landranger: 172, 173, 174, 175
OS Explorer: 154, 155, 156, 157, 158, 159
Stripmap
Kennet & Avon Canal (GEOprojects)
Publications, badges and certificates
Leaflet
Kennet & Avon Canal by British Waterways (British Waterways). A2 folded. Free.
Booklets
River Avon Trail Guide by Forest of Avon (Forest of Avon) 2007. 32pp; A4/3. Free. For your free copy Tel: 0117 953 2141, or download on Route's Website.
Walking Support Providers
Explore Britain; Instep

Kent Coastline Walk KENTCW

KENT 286km/178 miles

An end-to-end traverse of the diverse Kent coastline rich with maritime and wartime history. From Dungeness and Romney Marsh the route takes in Hythe, Folkestone, Dover, Deal, Sandwich, Ramsgate, Broadstairs, Margate, Herne Bay, the Isle of Sheppey, then on to the Medway towns, and finally past the Dartford QEII river bridge crossing. The many estuarine and mudflat areas abound in birdlife. Care should be taken to check the tides on the low-lying parts of the route. An optional detour visits the Isle of Grain.

Attributes
Coastal; Urban
Start
Kent border, Broomhill Sands, Dungeness, Kent TR007177
Finish
Kent border, Darent river, Kent TQ541779
Maps
OS Landranger: 177, 178, 179, 189
OS Explorer: 162, 163, 149, 150, 138, 125
Publications, badges and certificates
Paperbacks
Walking the Kent Coast from End to End by David Bathurst (S B Publications) 2007. ISBN 9781857703269. 144pp; 206 x 148. £8.50 (+ £1.00 p&p).

London Loop — LLOOP

BUCKS, ESSEX, HERTS, GTR LONDON, SURREY — 241km/150 miles

Pioneered by the London Walking Forum, it provides a green ring route around London generally towards the outer edges of the suburbs or in countryside. Starting at the Thames at Erith and finishing on the opposite bank at Coldharbour it passes through numerous woods, commons and parks, and uses waterside paths alongside the Grand Union Canal and London rivers such as the Colne, Crane, Cray, Darent and Ingrebourne. The Dollis Valley Greenwalk (10 miles and included on OS mapping) provides a link between the London Loop and the Capital Ring. The waymarked Watling Chase Timberland Trail (10 miles) from Elstree to near Hatfield is coincident with the Loop at its start. From Hatfield there is a described link to St Albans: the Alban Way.

Attributes
River; Canal; Downland/Wolds
Start
Erith Riverside TQ511781
Finish
Coldharbour Point TQ519789
Waymark
Named discs with hovering kestrel and ring motif
Website
www.walklondon.org.uk
Maps ◈
OS Landranger: 166, 167, 176, 177, 187
OS Explorer: 146, 147, 160, 161, 162, 172, 173, 174, 175
Publications, badges and certificates
Paperbacks
London Loop: Recreational Path Guides by David Sharp (Aurum Press) 2006. ISBN 9781845131999. 168pp; 210 x 130. £12.99.
Leaflets
London Loop (Walk London – Strategic Walks Information Service) 2006. 24 leaflets (one for each section); A4/3. Free. Downloads or order leaflets free from Walk London website.
Dollis Valley Greenwalk (Barnet Council). 2 leaflets; A4/3. Free (+ SAE). North and South leaflets.
Watling Chase Timberland Trail (Hertfordshire County Council) 2005. A4/3. Free. Free PDF download on weblink on path page.
LOOP Walks South London (Downlands Project) 1999. 8 leaflets; A4/3. Free. Ring 01737 737 700.

Medway Valley Walk — MEDVW

KENT, MEDWAY — 45km/28 miles

A valley walk in west Kent, with interesting landscape, natural history and archaeology. It passes through a varied landscape of downland, woodland, orchards, hop gardens, meadows and farmland, lakes and marshland, unspoilt villages and historic towns. Kent County Council plan to produce a new guidebook containing shorter circular walks along the route. The full route is shown on OS mapping. The start of the walk is linked by the waymarked Eden Valley Walk (15 miles and on OS mapping) to the Vanguard Way at Haxted. The Len Valley Walk (12 miles) connects with the Medway Valley Walk at Maidstone following the course of the River Len.

Attributes
Easy; River; Downland/Wolds; Heritage
Start
Tonbridge, Kent TQ590465
Finish
Rochester, Medway TQ741688
Waymark
Kingfisher logo & walk name
Website
www.kent.gov.uk, www.environment-agency.gov.uk
Maps ◈
OS Landranger: 178, 188
OS Explorer: 136, 147, 148, 163
Publications, badges and certificates
Booklets
Len Valley Walk by Tim Pitt (Maidstone Borough Council) 1999. 24pp; A5. £3.50 (incs p&p). Cheques to Maidstone Borough Council.
Eden Valley Walk by Caroline Wing (Kent County Council) 1991. ISBN 9781873010068. 28pp; 210 x 210. £2.95 (post free).

Meon Valley Churches Walk MVCW

HANTS **34km/21 miles**

This countryside walk connects all the Churches in the Meon river valley between East Meon and Titchfield.

Attributes
Easy; Former Railway; Religious
Start
All Saints, East Meon, East Meon, Hants SU680223
Finish
St Peters Church, Titchfield, Fareham, Hants SU540058
Website
www.winchester.gov.uk
Maps
OS Landranger: 196, 185
OS Explorer: 119
Publications, badges and certificates
Leaflet
Meon Valley Churches (Winchester City Council) 2006. 1pp; A2 Folded. Free. Winchester TIC Tel: 01962 840 500.

Middlesex Greenway MIDDG

ESSEX, HERTS, GTR LONDON, SURREY **69km/43 miles**

Crossing almost all of the old county of Middlesex through West Drayton, Uxbridge, Ruislip, Pinner, Mill Hill, Finchley and Enfield, it was designed to heighten public awareness of the former county and to help safeguard the Green Belt. It makes an arc across north west and north London, between Surrey and Essex, spanning between the Thames and the Lea valleys, via a mixture of green corridors, suburbs and waterside walking. There are many public transport links from the central area of London. The Greenway publication with schematic maps can be downloaded from the link below.

Attributes
River; Canal; Urban
Start
Middlesex former county boundary, Staines, Surrey TQ031715
Finish
Waltham Abbey, Essex TL376005
Website
www.redgoblin.infinites.net
Maps
OS Landranger: 166, 176, 177
OS Explorer: 160, 172, 173, 174
Map (Other)
London Street Atlas (Geographer's A-Z Map Company)
Publications, badges and certificates
Looseleaf
Middlesex Greenway by Stephen J. Collins (Stephen J. Collins) 1990. 16pp; A4. £1.00 (+ A4 SAE). Remaining stock only.

Miner's Way Trail MINWT

KENT **43km/27 miles**

The Miner's Way Trail winds its way through the picturesque countryside of East Kent, linking together pretty villages, small farmsteads, grand country estates and the remains of this area's industrial and mining heritage. From Sholden it explores the lower slopes of the North Downs between Deal and Shepherdswell, past what remains of old coal mines opened in the 1920's rush for 'black gold'.

Attributes
Cycle Route; Downland/Wolds; Heritage; Industrial History
Start and Finish
Sholden, Deal, Kent TR355524
Waymark
Miners lamp, train and leaf
Website
www.whitecliffscountryside.org.uk
Maps
OS Landranger: 179
OS Explorer: 138, 150
Publications, badges and certificates
Booklets
Travelling the Miner's Way Guidebook with Pull-out Map Sections (White Cliffs Countryside Project) 2007. ISBN 9780951757727. 120pp. £10.99.
Leaflets
Miners Way Trail (White Cliffs Countryside Project). £3.95 (incs p&p). 9 laminated leaflets describing circular walks. Also available from Dover TIC Tel: 01304 205108.

New Lipchis Way NLIPW

HANTS, W SUSSEX **61km/38 miles**

A route across the heaths, woods and farmland of the western Weald over Older Hill and Woolbeding Common to Midhurst and Heyshott and then across the South Downs via The Trundle to Lavant and Chichester and finally to Chichester Harbour, with an optional visit around East Head. It crosses the rivers Rother and Lavant en route.

Attributes
Easy; Forest/Woodland; Heath; Downland/Wolds
Start
Liphook, Hants SU842309
Finish
West Wittering, W Sussex SZ778982
Waymark
Downs, river and yatch logo, named disc
Website
www2.westsussex.gov.uk
Maps
OS Landranger: 186, 197
OS Explorer: 120, 133
Publications, badges and certificates
Leaflets
Lipchis Way (West Sussex County Council) 2008. A4/3. £1.00. Downloadable.

North to South Surrey Walk NSSW

SLOUGH, SURREY 66km/41 miles

A north-south traverse of the 'old county' of Surrey via Runnymede, Windsor Park, Chobham Common and Gibbet Hill.

Attributes
Challenging; Anytime Challenge
Start
Colnbrook, Slough TQ030771
Finish
Haslemere Edge, Surrey SU914312
Maps
OS Landranger: 176, 186
OS Explorer: 133, 145, 160
Publications, badges and certificates
Looseleaf
North-South Surrey (Keith Chesterton) 2002. 2pp; A4. Free (+ SAE).

Oxdrove Way OXD

HANTS 40km/25 miles

The Ox Drove itself is part of an old cross-country route on the Downs to the northeast of Winchester called the Lunway, a name recalled in the former Lunways Inn at Itchen Wood. The Ox Drove was once a drove route for cattle. Promoted as an off-road cycle and horse-riding route, it forms a figure of eight using the Ox Drove, initially heading north and visiting Preston Down, Bradley, Upper Wield, and Old Alresford. At Itchen Down, near Abbotstone, there is a westward loop to Itchen Wood, returning to Itchen Down, the route then passing through Abbotstone to reach the finish. It is coincident in parts with the Three Castles Path. The route takes in rolling downland, woods and farmland, and with a detour village facilities are available at New Alresford. Also, by using a short link on the Three Castles Path, at Itchen Abbas there are links to the Itchen valley routes: Itchen Way, St Swithun's Way, and King's Way. A free Oxdrove leaflet can be downloaded from the link below.

Attributes
Cycle Route; Horse Ride (Multi User); Downland/Wolds
Start and Finish
Abbotstone Down, Hants SU585361
Waymark
White arrows with green ox logo
Website
www3.hants.gov.uk
Maps ◈
OS Landranger: 185
OS Explorer: 132, 144
Publications, badges and certificates
Leaflets
Ox Drove (Hampshire County Council). 2pp; A4/3. Free (+ SAE). Download free on Hampshire CC website.

Pilgrims' Trail PILGT

HANTS, PORTSMOUTH 45km/28 miles

The Trail, also called the Hampshire Millennium Pilgrims' Trail, forms part of a longer route St Michael's Way between Winchester and Mont Saint Michel in Normandy, France. It follows a route dating from medieval times when pilgrims visited Winchester Cathedral from the country, and abroad, to worship at the shrine of St Swithun, a former teacher of the young Alfred the Great. In Hampshire, the Trail follows the course of a Roman Road to Bishop's Waltham and from there via Kingsmead to the finish.

Attributes
Pilgrimage
Start
Winchester Cathedral, Hants SU481293
Finish
Ferry Port, Portsmouth SU639018
Waymark
Silhouette of Mont Saint Michel/sea shell/walking stick

Website
www3.hants.gov.uk
Maps ◈
OS Landranger: 185, 196
OS Explorer: 119, 132
Publications, badges and certificates
Folder
Pilgrims' Trail (Hampshire County Council). 4 leaflets; A4/3. £2.99 (+ 54p p&p). Available from Hampshire TICs.

Rother Valley Walks RVW

HANTS, W SUSSEX **Various**

There are fourteen linked circular walks providing many options of traversing the Rother Valley. The scenery is varied and interesting and road walking has been kept to a minimum.

Attributes
Easy; River
Start
Selborne, Hants SU742336
Finish
Pulborough, W Sussex TQ043187
Website
www.visitsouthdowns.com
Maps ◈
OS Landranger: 186, 197
OS Explorer: 120, 121, 133
Publications, badges and certificates
Booklets
Rother Valley Walks (Sussex Downs Joint Commitee HQ) 2000. 34pp; A5. Free.

Royal Military Canal Path RMCP

E SUSSEX, KENT **43km/27 miles**

The Royal Military Canal Path mainly follows a canal-side path, which fringes the northern edge of Romney Marsh and which was built in the early 19th century as a defence against a possible invasion by Napoleon. The Canal is a Scheduled Ancient Monument and an SSSI. In addition to its historical and archaeological interest it is a valuable wetland habitat for a variety of species of flora and fauna. Links are made with the Saxon Shore Way at various points providing for circular options.

Attributes
Canal; Heritage; Industrial History; Military
Start
Pett Level, E Sussex TQ888134
Finish
Seabrook, Kent TR188349
Waymark
Reeds and canal
Website
www.royalmilitarycanal.com, www.waterscape.com
Maps ◈
OS Landranger: 179, 189, 199
OS Explorer: 124, 125, 138
Publications, badges and certificates
Pack
Royal Military Canal Walks Pack (Romney Marsh Countryside Project). £3.95. Cheques to Dover District Council.

Saxon Shore Way SAXSHW

E SUSSEX, KENT, MEDWAY **262km/163 miles**

The Way, around the ancient coastline, offers a diversity of scenery, from wide expanses of marshland bordering the Thames and Medway estuaries to the White Cliffs of Dover. There are views over Romney Marsh from the escarpment that marks the ancient coastline between Folkestone and Rye and from the cliffs of the High Weald at Hastings. It was here that the Romans invaded Britain and, later, built the Saxon Shore forts to defend the island against a new wave of invaders. St Augustine also landed here to bring the Gospel to the Anglo-Saxon Kingdom, which would later fall to the Normans who, in their turn, erected great fortresses like Dover Castle to defend their conquests. Two linking walks (included on OS mapping) are the Swale Heritage Trail – from Murston to Goodnestone (12 miles, covered by OS LR 178 and 179 and Ex 149 maps) which caters for circular walks of up to 20 miles when incorporated with the Saxon Shore route between Murston and Faversham; and the waymarked Wantsum Walks (30 miles, covered by OS LR 179 and Ex 150 maps) between Herne Bay and Birchington, around the Wantsum river, which can be incorporated to provide extended circular routes, as the Way skirts west of the Wantsum. From Dover to Rye it is coincident with the E9 – see E-Routes (E9). At Rye the route connects with the 1066 Country Walk. The waymarked Maritime Heritage Trail (total 32 miles) is a series of four connecting circular walks between Hastings and Rye. Based on Hastings (7 miles), Fairlight (8 miles), Winchelsea (10 miles) and Rye (7 miles) they provide alternative routes for the 20 miles between the two towns.

Attributes
Coastal; Heritage
Start
Gravesend, Kent TQ647745
Finish
Hastings, E Sussex TQ825094
Waymark
Red Viking helmet
Maps ◈
OS Landranger: 177, 178, 179, 189, 199
OS Explorer: 124, 125, 137, 138, 148, 149, 150, 162, 163
Harvey Map (Stripmap)
South Downs Way: DVD & Stripmap (with Saxon Shore Way) (Harvey Maps)
Publications, badges and certificates
Guidebook
Saxon Shore Way (Kent County Council) 2006. ISBN 9781901509915. 68pp; 206 x 216. £4.99.
Booklets
Swale Heritage Trail (Kent County Council) 1995. ISBN 9781873010501. 28pp; 210 x 148. £2.45.
Folder
Rye Bay Countryside Pack – includes Maritime Heritage Trail by East Sussex County Council (Rye Bay Countryside Service). A5. £1.50 (incs p&p). 5 route cards and 9 leafets. Cheques to E Sussex County Council.
Walking Support Providers
Orchard; Walk Awhile

Serpent Trail SERPT

HANTS, SURREY, W SUSSEX 103km/64 miles

The Serpent Trail is designed to highlight some of the finest heathland and woodland landscapes in the South East. It follows a rough "S" shape along the hills of the Sussex Greensand – snaking between Haslemere, Petworth, Midhurst and Petersfield in a habitat of snakes. It is part of the Sussex Wealden Greensand Heaths Project (SWGHP). The project sets out to restore heathland in West Sussex, more than 80% of which has been lost in the last 200 years due to forestry, agriculture and development and, more recently, a lack of management, whilst conserving existing areas. At Haslemere, the Greensand Way provides a 108-mile route east across greensand ridges almost as far as the Kent coast.

Attributes
Heath
Start
Haslemere High Street, Surrey (near station) SU905331
Finish
Petersfield Heath, Petersfield, Hants SU754226
Waymark
White disc/serpent in purple triangle/encircling name
Website
www.surreywildlifetrust.co.uk,
www.visitsouthdowns.com
Maps
OS Landranger: 186, 197
OS Explorer: 120, 121, 133, 134
Publications, badges and certificates
Booklets (water resistant)
Serpent Trail: Official Guide (Sussex Downs Joint Commitee Northern Area Office) 2007. ISBN 9781900543422. 36pp; A5. Free.
Leaflets
Serpent Trail (Petersfield TIC). Free.

Socratic Trail SOCT

BRIGHTON H, E SUSSEX, GTR LONDON, SURREY, W SUSSEX 76km/47 miles

Following paths and quiet country lanes across the rolling Surrey hills and the Sussex Weald, the route makes use of short stretches of the North Downs Way, Greensand Way and the South Downs Way.

Attributes
Downland/Wolds
Start
Old Coulsdon, Gtr London TQ312582
Finish
Brighton TQ333034
Maps
OS Landranger: 177, 187, 198
OS Explorer: 122, 135, 146
Publications, badges and certificates
Booklets
Socratic Trail Guide (Socratic Walker's Club) 2007. 30pp; A5. £2.95 (+ A5 SAE). Cheques to WE Gilbert; profits to cancer charities.

Solent Way SOLTW

HANTS, PORTSMOUTH, SOTON 96km/60 miles

Crossing coastal marshes to Lymington before going inland and past the heaths, woods and the New Forest villages of Bucklers Hard and Beaulieu, it reaches Hythe on the Test Estuary. The ferry is taken to Southampton where it then follows the Solent shoreline, crossing the

River Hamble, to reach Portsmouth via the Gosport ferry. Heading along the historic waterfront of Portsmouth and Southsea it passes the coastal marshes and quays around Langstone Harbour. Between Broadmarsh and Portsmouth it forms part of the E9 E-Route. The first 7 miles of the Solent Way between Milford-on-Sea and Lymington are described in the book by Leigh Hatts (Countryside Books). Route details are on the website below.

Attributes
Coastal; Heath; Urban
Start
Milford-on-Sea, Hants SZ291918
Finish
Emsworth, Hants SU753055
Waymark
Tern on named green arrow
Website
www3.hants.gov.uk
Maps ◈
OS Landranger: 196, 197
OS Explorer: 119, 120, 22, 29
Publications, badges and certificates
Leaflets
Solent Way (Hampshire County Council). A4/3. Free (+ SAE).
Paperbacks
Exploring the Bournemouth Coast Path by Leigh Hatts (Countryside Books) 2005. ISBN 9781853069086. 96pp; 150 x 210. £7.99. Includes Solent Way first section.
Walking Support Providers
Let's Go Walking!

St Swithun's Way — STSWW

HANTS, SURREY — **55km/34 miles**

This historic walk takes a rural path from Winchester, the capital of Saxon England, where Swithun was bishop in the ninth century. It can be considered as the first part of a modern Pilgrim's Way since at Farnham it joins the North Downs Way National Trail that takes the walker on to Canterbury. With its shrine to St Swithun and tomb of Alfred the Great, Winchester was the first principal place of pilgrimage. Later Becket's shrine at Canterbury became more important and pilgrims would have visited both. Much of the original Pilgrim's Way here follows the busy A31 road so this walking route uses rural paths and some lanes or minor roads along the same broad line. From Winchester it passes through the Itchen river valley, with attractive villages and interesting churches, then passes the market towns of Alresford and Alton, and Chawton, home of Jane Austen. The final section along the River Wey leads to Farnham. The route also links with the South Downs Way at Winchester. Some six miles are coincident with the King's Way in the stretch between Winchester and Ovington.

Attributes
River; Downland/Wolds; Heritage; Pilgrimage
Start
Winchester Cathedral, Hants SU481293
Finish
Farnham, Surrey SU844466
Waymark
Named green and white discs with shell/two croziers
Website
www3.hants.gov.uk
Maps ◈
OS Landranger: 185, 186
OS Explorer: 132, 144, 145
Publications, badges and certificates
Folder
St Swithun's Way (Hampshire County Council) 2002. 5 leaflets; A4/3. £3.99 (incs p&p). Includes transport/accommodation information.
Walking Support Providers
Wycheway

Staunton Way — STAW

HANTS — **34km/21 miles**

The Staunton Way is a combination of routes, connecting Queen Elizabeth Country Park with Staunton Country Park, Havant, which together can make a circular route of 21 miles. It roughly follows the Hampshire/Sussex border south through Chalton and Finchdean. After visiting Staunton Country Park it returns via Stansted Forest and Ditcham Park School, and along the undulating ridge of the downs above Buriton. It is named after Sir George Staunton, an early 19th century Portsmouth MP who created a country estate, now the Staunton Country Park.

Attributes
Forest/Woodland; Downland/Wolds
Start and Finish
Queen Elizabeth Country Park, Hants SU718187
Waymark
Deer's head on named green arrow
Website
www3.hants.gov.uk

Maps ◈
OS Landranger: 197
OS Explorer: 120
Publications, badges and certificates
Leaflets
Staunton Way (Hampshire County Council) 2004. A4/3. Free (+ SAE).

Strawberry Trail — STRAWT

HANTS — **24km/15 miles**

A walk in the Hamble river valley, visiting its attractive villages and providing distance options for mostly easy riverside, coastal, country park and rural walking. Essentially a figure-of-eight route from Botley, its first smaller loop goes around Manor Farm Country Park. Its larger loop from Bursledon visits Netley and Hamble-le-Rice with a section on Southampton Water (coincident with the Solent Way). This was an important strawberry growing area and Bursledon was where horse-drawn carts would load their baskets of strawberries from the fields of the 'Strawberry Coast' to load onto the Strawberry Special trains to London. The Hamble riverside has a history of boatbuilding and includes salt marsh and mudflat habitats with a variety of wildlife, as does Southampton Water. There are marinas and boating activity to add interest. From Eastleigh, Portsmouth and Southampton there are good public transport links. Rail, bus, ferry and local summer riverbus options, along with the ferry link across the River Hamble from Hamble-le-Rice to Warash, are covered in a leaflet along with pubs and tea-rooms.

Attributes
Easy; Coastal; River
Start and Finish
Botley, Hampshire SU514130
Waymark
Strawberry logo on red markers/riverside information panels
Website
www.hamblevalley.com
Maps
OS Landranger: 196
OS Explorer: 119, 22
Map (Other)
Hamble Valley Official Map (Walking Distance (Maps) Ltd)
Publications, badges and certificates
Leaflets
Strawberry Coast: Hamble Valley – Coast to Countryside (Hampshire County Council) 2005. 1pp; A4/3. Free. From Hampshire CC Information Centre Tel: 0800 028 0888.

Sussex Ouse Valley Way — SOVW

E SUSSEX, W SUSSEX — **68km/42 miles**

The route broadly traces the course of the River Ouse from close to its source to the sea, running from Lower Beeding, near Horsham, through the Low Weald to Newhaven and Seaford Bay.

Attributes
Easy; River
Start
Lower Beeding Village Hall, W Sussex TQ220265
Finish
Seaford Bay, E Sussex TV468997
Waymark
Blue/grey disc with viaduct, river and path name
Website
www.sussexousevalleyway.co.uk, www.per-rambulations.co.uk
Maps
OS Landranger: 198
OS Explorer: 122, 134, 135
Publications, badges and certificates
Guidebook
Sussex Ouse Valley Way (Per-Rambulations) 2007. 72pp; A5. £7.95 (+ £1.55 p&p).
Badge
Sussex Ouse Valley Way (Per-Rambulations). £3.00 (incs p&p). Cloth, embroidered.
Walking Support Providers
HF

Tandridge Border Path — TANBP

E SUSSEX, GTR LONDON, KENT, SURREY, W SUSSEX — **80km/50 miles**

Following the boundary of Tandridge District with Kent, Sussex and Greater London, it links the villages and hamlets of East Surrey.

Attributes
No significant attribute
Start and Finish
Tatsfield Village Green, Surrey TQ413568
Waymark
Named green and white discs

Website
www.per-rambulations.co.uk
Maps
OS Landranger: 187
OS Explorer: 146, 147
Publications, badges and certificates
Booklets
Tandridge Border Path (Per-Rambulations). A5. Free (+ £2.00 p&p in UK).

Test Way — TESTW

HANTS, W BERKSHIRE, WILTS — 72km/45 miles

It follows the Test Valley from Eling Wharf on the outskirts of Southampton, where the Test flows into Southampton Water. After lowland farmland and woodland paths it continues along a disused railway line past Romsey, Mottisfont Abbey, Stockbridge, Wherwell and St Mary Bourne, before gradually climbing to Inkpen Beacon on the crest of the chalk downs.

Attributes
Easy; Former Railway; River
Start
Eling Wharf, Hants SU366126
Finish
Inkpen Beacon, W Berkshire SU365622
Waymark
Letters TW on named green arrow
Website
www3.hants.gov.uk
Maps ◈
OS Landranger: 174, 185, 196
OS Explorer: 131, 144, 158, 22
Publications, badges and certificates
Leaflets
Test Way (Hampshire County Council) 2004. A4/3. Free (+ SAE).
Booklets
Walks Along the Test Way by Peter Radburn (Peter Radburn). 48pp. £3.00 (+ 40p p&p).
Walking Support Providers
Let's Go Walking!

Three Castles Path (England) — 3CPE

BRACKNELL F, HANTS, WINDSOR M — 96km/60 miles

The route takes in Windsor Great Park, Ascot, the Crown Estate south of Bracknell, the Blackwater Valley, the Basingstoke Canal, the Whitewater River, then follows the River Itchen from Itchen Abbas to Winchester. It is mainly easy walking and, apart from Hartley Witney and Odiham/North Warnborough, only small villages are passed en route.

Attributes
River; Canal; Heath; Heritage; Monarchy
Start
Windsor Castle, Windsor M SU968770
Finish
Winchester Castle Hall, Hants SU483293
Maps ◈
OS Landranger: 175, 176, 185, 186
OS Explorer: 132, 144, 159, 160
Map (Other)
Windsor & The Great Park (RA East Berkshire Group)
Publications, badges and certificates
Booklets
Three Castles Path by David Bounds (RA East Berkshire Group) 1998. ISBN 9781874258087. 48pp; 128 x 210. £2.95 (+ 60p p&p). Cheques to East Berks RA Publications.
Three Castles Path Guide to Bed & Breakfast Accommodation by Dave Ramm (Bracknell Tourist Information Centre). A4. Free. Also from Ramblers' Central Office.

Three Downs Link — 3DL

HANTS, W BERKSHIRE, WILTS — 164km/102 miles

A multi-user pan-handle shaped route connecting the national trails of the South Downs Way and Ridgeway. It provides fine views from the open chalk downland ridges, crosses Watership Down and passes many iron age hill-forts. The valley sections offer rivers, canals and small villages. From Exton in Hampshire it follows the South Downs Way northeast towards Malborough, turning north and taking a large sweeping circle back towards Newbury before rejoining the outward route to the southeast of Hungerford.

Attributes
Challenging; Horse Ride (Multi User); Heath; Downland/Wolds
Start and Finish
Exton, Hants SU611210
Waymark
Name on BHS blue bridleway sign
Website
www.ride-uk.org.uk
Maps
OS Landranger: 174, 185
OS Explorer: 132, 144, 157, 158, 170

Publications, badges and certificates
Leaflets
Three Downs Link by British Horse Society (British Horse Society). With accommodation list and schematic map.1pp; A2 Folded. Free. £2 donation requested. Cheques to British Horse Society.

Tunbridge Wells Circular Walk TUNWCW

E SUSSEX, KENT 44km/27 miles

Formerly named the High Weald Walk, it explores the variety of countryside around Royal Tunbridge Wells and along the borders of Kent and East Sussex within the High Weald AONB. It passes through a rolling landscape of ridges and valleys with a patchwork of small fields, hedges and broadleaved woodland. On the route are Groombridge Place, High Rocks, Eridge Rocks and Harrison's Rocks, all sandstone outcrops popular with climbers; and Eridge Park, a remarkably unpopulated area for south east England. In addition to the long distance path there are four marked linked routes from the centre of Royal Tunbridge Wells enabling shorter options. On older editions of OS maps the route is shown as the High Weald Walk. Parts of the route coincide with the Wealdway and High Weald Landscape Trail. Using the marked linked routes and the stations at Southborough (High Brooms), Tunbridge Wells, Frant and Eridge, shorter circular and linear walking options are possible. Its origins go back to 1989 when Tunbridge Wells Borough Council asked Mike Smith of Kent LDWA Group to organise a 25-mile circular walk to mark the Centenary of the Granting of the Borough Charter and this event took place from 1989-1991. Sadly Mike died shortly after this. The original Kent County Council guidebook was dedicated to his memory.

Attributes
Downland/Wolds
Start and Finish
Southborough Common, Kent TQ575427
Waymark
Named green squares with hill, path and trees
Website
www.kent.gov.uk, www.khwp.org.uk
Maps ◈
OS Landranger: 188
OS Explorer: 135, 136, 147

Publications, badges and certificates
Guidebook
Along and Around the Tunbridge Wells Circular Walk (Kent County Council) 2002. ISBN 9781901509625. 56pp; 206 x 202. £4.00. Also available from Kent High Weald Project at £5.00 (+75p p&p).
Badge & certificate
Tunbridge Wells Circular Walk (Kent High Weald Project). Free. If walk completed in three days or less. Details in guidebook.

Vanguard Way VANGW

E SUSSEX, GTR LONDON, KENT, SURREY
106km/66 miles

A walk from the London suburbs to the sea originated by the Vanguards Rambling Club. It passes the Selsdon Nature Reserve, the woods and heaths of Ashdown Forest, Alfriston village and finally follows the scenic coast through Seaford to the finish. As the guidebooks are now out of date, a route description is available for free download on the website below. The Wandle Trail (11 miles) provides a link to the Thames Path National Trail at Wandsworth, completing a route from the Thames to the sea.

Attributes
Coastal; Heath
Start
East Croydon Railway Station, Gtr London TQ328658
Finish
Newhaven Harbour, E Sussex TQ449009
Waymark
Named discs
Website
www.vanguardway.org.uk
Maps ◈
OS Landranger: 176, 177, 187, 188, 198, 199
OS Explorer: 122, 123, 135, 146, 147, 161
Publications, badges and certificates
Booklets
Vanguard Way (Graham Butler (Vanguards Rambling Club)) 1997. 68pp; A5. £1.00 (incs p&p) or free online. Cheques to Vanguards Rambling Club. While stocks last.
Badge
Vanguard Way (Vanguards Rambling Club). £2.50 (+ SAE). Cheques to Vanguards Rambling Club.
Paperbacks
Wandle Guide by Wandle Group (Sutton London Borough) 1997. ISBN 9780907335337. 78pp; 210 x 145. £4.95 (+ £1.50 p&p).

Leaflets
Wandle Trail (Wandle Industrial Museum). £1.50 (+ SAE).

Vectis Trail VT

IOW 120km/75 miles

This is a figure-of-eight route. From Yarmouth it heads south towards Alum Bay, then turns east over Tennyson Down towards Freshwater Bay. After Brook the route follows the downland ridges to Brighstone Down. It passes Carisbrook Castle and continues east to Brading, where it turns to pass through Whitwell, Walpen Chine near Chale, and Shorwell before returning to Yarmouth.

Attributes
Coastal; Downland/Wolds
Start and Finish
Yarmouth, IoW SZ355897
Website
www.islandbreaks.co.uk,
www.catbells.streamlinenettrial.co.uk
Maps
OS Landranger: 196
OS Explorer: 29
Publications, badges and certificates
Booklets
Vectis Trail by Iris Evans, Barbara Aze, Mike Marchant (RA Isle of Wight) 2006. 32pp; 210 x 149. £2.50 (incs p&p). Cheques to Isle of Wight Ramblers Association.
Paperbacks
Walkers Guide to the Isle of Wight by Martin Collins, Norman Birch (Cicerone Press) 2004. ISBN 9781852842215. 216pp; 172 x 114. £10.00.
Walking Support Providers
Step by Step

Viking Coastal Trail VIKCT

KENT 47km/29 miles

The Viking Coastal Trail is a multi-user route around the Isle of Thanet, the point where Vikings first landed in Britain. It keeps as close as possible to the coast from Reculver, passing through Margate, Broadstairs and Ramsgate to reach Pegwell Bay. From here the Trail uses an inland loop, along quiet lanes, through pretty Kentish villages with ancient churches, and passes Minster Abbey, one of England's oldest inhabited buildings founded in 670. A downloadable leaflet is available from the website below. The waymarked Thanet Coastal Path (20 miles and on OS mapping but no separate publication) is an often coincident linear route on the coastal section between the Thanet boundary near Reculver and Pegwell Bay. It winds its way past sandy beaches and bays, often against a backdrop of spectacular chalk cliffs. Ramsgate and Margate are lively seaside resorts and Broadstairs has nostalgic charm. For walkers the obvious inland return is on the Saxon Shore Way but the nearest footpath link to Pegwell Bay is at Sandwich, making a much longer route. Both the Trail and Path link with the Saxon Shore Way (and Wantsum Walks) at Reculver.

Attributes
Easy; Cycle Route; Coastal
Start and Finish
Pegwell Bay, Kent TR337627
Waymark
Named logo with bird/fish/sandcastle (Thanet Coastal Path)
Website
www.kent.gov.uk
Maps ◈
OS Landranger: 179
OS Explorer: 150
Publications, badges and certificates
Leaflets
Viking Coastal Trail (Ramsgate Tourist Information Centre) 2001. A4/3. Free (+ SAE).

Walk Around Hayling Island HAYI

HANTS 32km/20 miles

A John Merrill challenge walk around Hayling Island along or near the coastline, visiting North Hayling, Fleet, Mengham, Eastoke and West Town.

Attributes
Easy; Anytime Challenge; Coastal
Start and Finish
Ship Inn, Langstone, Havant, Portsmouth SU719048
Maps
OS Landranger: 197
OS Explorer: 120
Publications, badges and certificates
Booklets
Walk Around Hayling Island by John Merrill (John Merrill Foundation). ISBN 9780955651168. 44pp; A5. £5.95.
Certificate
Walk Around Hayling Island by John Merrill (John Merrill Foundation) 2008. £2.00 (incs p&p).

Walking the Castles of Kent CASK

KENT **311km/193 miles**

A walk connecting 25 castles in beautiful or interesting locations in Kent. The book has architectural and historical studies of the castles.

Attributes
Heritage; Monarchy
Start
Richborough Castle, Kent TR323602
Finish
Canterbury Castle, Kent TR144575
Maps
OS Landranger: 178, 179, 188, 189
OS Explorer: 125, 137, 138, 148, 149, 150
Publications, badges and certificates
Paperbacks
Walking the Castles of Kent by David Harrison (S B Publications) 2007. ISBN 9781857703276. 133pp; 208 x 146. £8.50.

Walking the Castles of Sussex WCASS

E SUSSEX, W SUSSEX **291km/181 miles**

From Pevensey Castle the route visits Herstmonceux Castle, Crowhurst, Battle, Hastings Castle, Winchelsea, Camber Castle, Rye, Bodiam Castle, Wadhurst, Eridge Park, Bolebroke Castle, Hartfield, Isfield, Lewes Castle, Edburton Hill, Bamber Castle, Knepp Castle, Petworth, Cowdray, Amberley Castle, and Arundel Castle.

Attributes
Easy; Heritage
Start
Pevensey Castle TQ645048
Finish
Arundel Castle TQ017073
Maps
OS Landranger: 187, 197, 198, 199
OS Explorer:
121, 122, 123, 124, 133, 134, 135, 136
Publications, badges and certificates
Paperbacks
Walking the Castles of Sussex by David Harrison (S B Publications) 2008. ISBN 9781857703351. 130pp; 208 x 146. £8.50.

Walking the Disused Railways of Sussex WDRS

SURREY, W SUSSEX **55km/34 miles**

Walking the Disused Railways of Sussex includes a 34-mile route (and 12 other shorter routes) from Shoreham-by-Sea to Shalford, via Christ's Hospital, linking the Adur and Wey river valleys. From Shoreham an old railway route, now a multi-user track, is used. The route goes along the Adur valley, through a gap in the South Downs, to Steyning then across the Sussex weald, via Henfield and Partridge Green, to Southwater and Christ's Hospital. Continuing on to Rudgwick and reaching the Wey river valley after Cranleigh; passing Bramley on its way to the finish. The route is partly coincident with the Downs Link, and the Wey-South Path.

Attributes
Easy; Former Railway; Cycle Route
Start
Shoreham-by-Sea, W Sussex TQ217054
Finish
Shalford Station, Surrey TQ001471
Maps
OS Landranger: 186, 187, 198
OS Explorer: 122, 134, 145
Publications, badges and certificates
Paperbacks
Walking the Disused Railways of Sussex by David Bathurst (S B Publications) 2004. ISBN 9781857702927. 208 x 146. £8.50.

Walking the Riversides of Sussex WRIVS

E SUSSEX, W SUSSEX **404km/251 miles**

A series of 16 walks, ranging from 5 to 42 miles long, in East and West Sussex, each following a riverside where possible. Sussex has many varied rivers, from the wide and imposing Arun and Ouse to the more modest but enchanting Lavant and Brede. The walks visits historic towns and beautiful country churches. Other rivers include the Cuckmere, Dudwell, Ems, Kird, Limden, Medway, Mole, Rother, Tillingham and Uck.

Attributes
Easy; Forest/Woodland; River
Start and Finish
Various
Maps
OS Landranger: 189, 197, 198, 199
OS Explorer: 120, 121, 122, 123, 124, 133, 135, 136

Publications, badges and certificates

Paperbacks

Walking the Riversides of Sussex by David Bathhurst (S B Publications) 2008. ISBN 9781857703375. 160pp; 208 x146. £8.50.

Wealdway WW

E SUSSEX, KENT **132km/82 miles**

This route, through three AONBs, connects the Thames Estuary with the English Channel. Passing through the Weald of Kent and Sussex it takes in chalk downlands, river valleys and wooded farmland in often remote country, including a full traverse of Ashdown Forest. It links the North Downs Way at Trottiscliffe with the South Downs Way near Eastbourne. No publication is available but Kent County Council plan to produce a book of circular walks. The route is on OS mapping and waymarked.

Attributes

Downland/Wolds

Start

Gordon Promenade, Gravesend, Kent TQ654744

Finish

Pier, Eastbourne, E Sussex TV617989

Waymark

Letters WW on standard arrows

Website

www.kent.gov.uk

Maps ◈

OS Landranger: 177, 178, 188, 198, 199

OS Explorer: 123, 135, 136, 147, 148, 162, 163

Walking Support Providers

Orchard

West Sussex Literary Trail WSLIT

W SUSSEX **89km/55 miles**

Linking Horsham in West Sussex with Chichester Cathedral, this is a route rich in literary associations. Percy Bysshe Shelley's millennium fountain marks the start of the trail. John Galsworthy would have crossed the River Arun by ferry from his house in Bury; whilst Bob Copper wrote a wonderful anecdote about the ferryman. Hilaire Belloc was everywhere, and part of the route follows in the footsteps of his Four Men, before reaching Chichester and its strong ties with William Blake and John Keats.

Attributes

Easy; River; Downland/Wolds; Literary

Start

Horsham station, Horsham, West Sussex TQ178309

Finish

Chichester cathedral, West Sussex SU859048

Waymark

Pen and book on blue with black ring and name

Website

www.westsussexliterarytrail.co.uk, www.per-rambulations.co.uk

Maps

OS Landranger: 197, 198

OS Explorer: 120, 122, 134

Publications, badges and certificates

Guidebook (full colour)

West Sussex Literary Trail (Per-Rambulations) 2007. ISBN 9780954965433. 112pp; 206 x 148. £8.95 (+ £1.55 p&p).

Badge (cloth)

West Sussex Literary Trail (Per-Rambulations). £3.00 (incs p&p). Mail order only from 'Per-Rambulations'.

Wey Navigations RWEYN

SURREY **32km/20 miles**

The River Wey Navigations, which includes the Godalming and Wey Navigations, provide a canal towpath walk that connects Godalming with the River Thames at Weybridge. It passes through the centre of Guildford, with remnants of its past canalside industries, crosses water meadows, then along green waterside corridors through the Surrey suburbs to reach the River Thames. The route is coincident with the E2 E-Route up to the Thames.

Attributes

Easy; River; Canal; Urban; Industrial History

Start

Godalming Town Bridge, Surrey SU973441

Finish

Thames Lock, Weybridge, Surrey TQ072655

Website

www.weyriver.co.uk

Maps ◈

OS Landranger: 176, 186

OS Explorer: 160, 145

Stripmap

Basingstoke Canal and the River Wey Navigations (GEOprojects)

Publications, badges and certificates

Paperbacks

River Wey Navigations (National Trust: River Wey & Godalming Navigations) 1990. 33pp; A5. £3.50 (+ A5 Large Letter SAE). Includes fold-out map.

Leaflets

River Wey Navigations (National Trust: River Wey & Godalming Navigations) 2006. A4/3. Free (+DL SAE). Includes schematic stripmap.

Wey-South Path — WEYSP

SURREY, W SUSSEX — **58km/36 miles**

The Path mainly follows the towpath of the Godalming Navigation along the River Wey to its confluence with the Wey & Arun Junction Canal, crossing the North Downs Way National Trail near the start. The route continues beside the Arun Navigation to the River Arun and then on to meet the South Downs Way National Trail above Amberley. The Wey-South Path, along with the Wey Navigations, form part of the E2 E-Route up to the Thames.

Attributes

Easy; River; Canal

Start

Millmead Lock, Guildford, Surrey SU995491

Finish

Near Amberley, W Sussex TQ033125

Website

www.weyriver.co.uk

Maps ◈

OS Landranger: 186, 187, 197

OS Explorer: 121, 134, 145

Publications, badges and certificates

Booklets

Wey-South Path by Aeneas Mackintosh, Geoff Perks, Ken Bacon (W & A Enterprises Ltd) 2006. 68pp; A5. £3.60 (incs p&p). New edition due 2009.

Paperbacks

River Wey Navigations (National Trust: River Wey & Godalming Navigations) 1990. 33pp; A5. £3.50 (+ A5 Large Letter SAE). Includes fold-out map.

Yar River Trail — YARRT

IOW — **31km/19 miles**

The route follows the island's longest river across the south east of the island from its source, a spring near Niton, to the sea at Bembridge harbour. This is the Eastern Yar; the Isle's other Yar, the Western Yar, meets the sea at Yarmouth. The Trail features stone-carved milestones and six sculptures by local artist Paul Mason and is waymarked. It uses a variety of surfaces mainly paths and the course of a dismantled railway. Alverstone, Newchurch, Godshill and Whitwell are passed en route. There are a number of shorter linking trails that are described in leaflets and downloads; including the separately waymarked Godshill Trail (4 miles) around this picturesque village.

Attributes

Easy; Former Railway; River

Start

Source of Yar, Niton, IoW SZ503766

Finish

Bembridge Harbour, IoW SZ636893

Waymark

Blue logo based on letters YAR; stone mile posts/six sculptures

Website

www.island2000.org.uk

Maps ◈

OS Landranger: 196

OS Explorer: 29

Publications, badges and certificates

Booklets

Yar River Trail (Island 2000 Trust) 2002. 28pp; A5. £1.99 (incs p&p). Cheques to Island 2000 Trust.

Walking Support Providers

Step by Step

SOUTH WEST ENGLAND

Deckchairs arranged on the promenade alongside The Den at Teignmouth (South West Coast Path)

KEY FACTS	
Areas	Avon, Cornwall & Isles of Scilly, Devon, Dorset, Somerset, Wiltshire
National Parks	Dartmoor, Exmoor
Principal AONBs	The Cotswolds (part), Mendip Hills, Quantock Hills, Cranborne Chase & West Wiltshire Downs, Blackdown Hills, Dorset, East Devon, North Devon, South Devon, Tamar Valley, Cornwall, Isles Of Scilly
World Heritage Sites	Stonehenge, Avebury and Associated Sites; City of Bath; Dorset and East Devon Coast; Cornwall and West Devon Mining Landscape
Heritage Coast	Cornwall: Godrevy-Portreath, Gribben Head-Polperro, Isles of Scilly, Pentire Point-Widemouth, Penwith, St Agnes, The Lizard, The Roseland, Trevrose Head, Devon: East Devon, Exmoor, Hartland, Lundy, Rame Head, South Devon, North Devon, Dorset: Purbeck, West Dorset
E-Routes	E9 Plymouth – Dover
National Trails (England)	Cotswold Way (part), Ridgeway (part), South West Coast Path
Walking Routes	59 main routes (4767 miles); 37 waymarked (2686 miles)
Resident population	5 million

Devon, footpath sign

DON'T MISS! TRAIL SECTIONS (CHALLENGING/REMOTE MARKED WITH *)	
South West Coast Path:	Minehead to Porlock Weir, the more exposed alternative* 'Rugged Coast Path' has better views (14km, 1226ft ascent); Clovelly to Hartland Quay, quaint Clovelly, wooded slopes, high cliffs, fine views and a lighthouse* (15km, 2500ft ascent); Zennor to Cape Cornwall, scenic cliff-top walking in a past mining landscape* (17km, 2341ft ascent); Mullion to Lizard, coves, seabirds, rugged serpentine cliffs once part of an ocean floor (12km, 1410ft ascent); Plymouth's Waterfront Walkway, maritime history, the Hoe, good access, hard surface, audio available (13km, 765ft ascent); Lulworth to Kimmeridge, a cove, and cliff-top walking on the Jurassic Coast (check Army Ranges are open)* (7km, 1719ft ascent)
Dart Valley Trail:	Dartmouth to Totnes, waterside and valley walking, boat return option (20km, 2316ft ascent)
Two Moors Way/Tarka Trail:	Lynmouth to Hillsford Bridge above East Lyn river, return along river via Watersmeet, optional visit to Valley of Rocks from Lynton (on Coast Path) (8km, 1447ft ascent)
Two Moors Way:	Widecombe to Holne, wooded valleys, the Dart, moorland and tors* (12km, 1242ft ascent)
West Mendip Way:	Wells to Cheddar, Wells Cathedral (West Front), Wookey Hole, Mendip plateaus and Cheddar Gorge* (12km, 2111ft ascent)

REFERENCE SOURCE INCLUDING MANY REGIONAL ROUTES	
Booklet	*Walking Trails in Devon* (Devon County Council). A5 booklet. Free.

SOUTH WEST ENGLAND

West Mendip Way on Wavering Down, Somerset

The south west of England offers a vast range of landscapes, many spectacular or unusual, reflecting its highly varied geological past. Coastal walking is the highlight of this region. The coastal scenery is outstanding and, for walkers, is accessible from Poole Bay all the way to Minehead on the South West Coast Path that extends a full 630 miles along a coast of quite remarkable and sustained scenic quality.

There is great variety, from sheltered chalk bays such as Studland in the south east, rock arches at Durdle Door, perfectly formed bays as at Lulworth Cove, shingle ridges at Chesil Beach, dunes, brackish lagoons as at Fleet, the highest seacliff on the southern coast at Golden Cap, all then giving way beyond the Lizard to wilder and rockier coasts and former fishing coves, while on the north coasts there are yet more rocky headlands and high and dramatic cliffs.

There are 16 mainland coast sections designated as Heritage Coasts, while the 'Jurassic Coast', running 95 coastal miles between Exmouth and Swanage, is recognised as the Dorset and East Devon Coast World Heritage Site and offers, literally, a 'walk through time' following the geological sequence of Jurassic rocks from the oldest in the west. East from Poole, the Bournemouth Coast Path provides a promoted route around Bournemouth to join with the Solent Way. These three routes together make up the course of the coastal E-9 E-Route, the 'European Coastal Path', as it makes its way to Plymouth from Dover.

Geology and history

Several ranges of hills and upland moorland areas form the inland scenery. Extending from the north into the region, the limestone Cotswold Hills head south-westward to Bath. Then, south of the Avon, the Mendip Hills rise before falling away to the Somerset Levels. To the south in Wiltshire, running parallel to the Cotswolds, are the gently undulating chalk hills of the Marlborough and Wessex Downs and the broad open area of Salisbury Plain. The chalk ridge continues through Cranbourne Chase and the North Dorset Downs and is broadly followed by The Ridgeway and the Wessex Ridgeway trails to reach Lyme Regis and the sea. The region's south-eastern limits are the Isles of Portland and of Purbeck, with active and also past limestone quarrying and a temperate climate.

West into Devon, near its north coast, the Quantocks rise from the Levels, followed by the Brendon Hills. The most striking inland features for walkers in Devon, however, are the higher moorland massifs of Exmoor and Dartmoor. Both are National Parks. These moors have quite different geological origins: Exmoor's lies

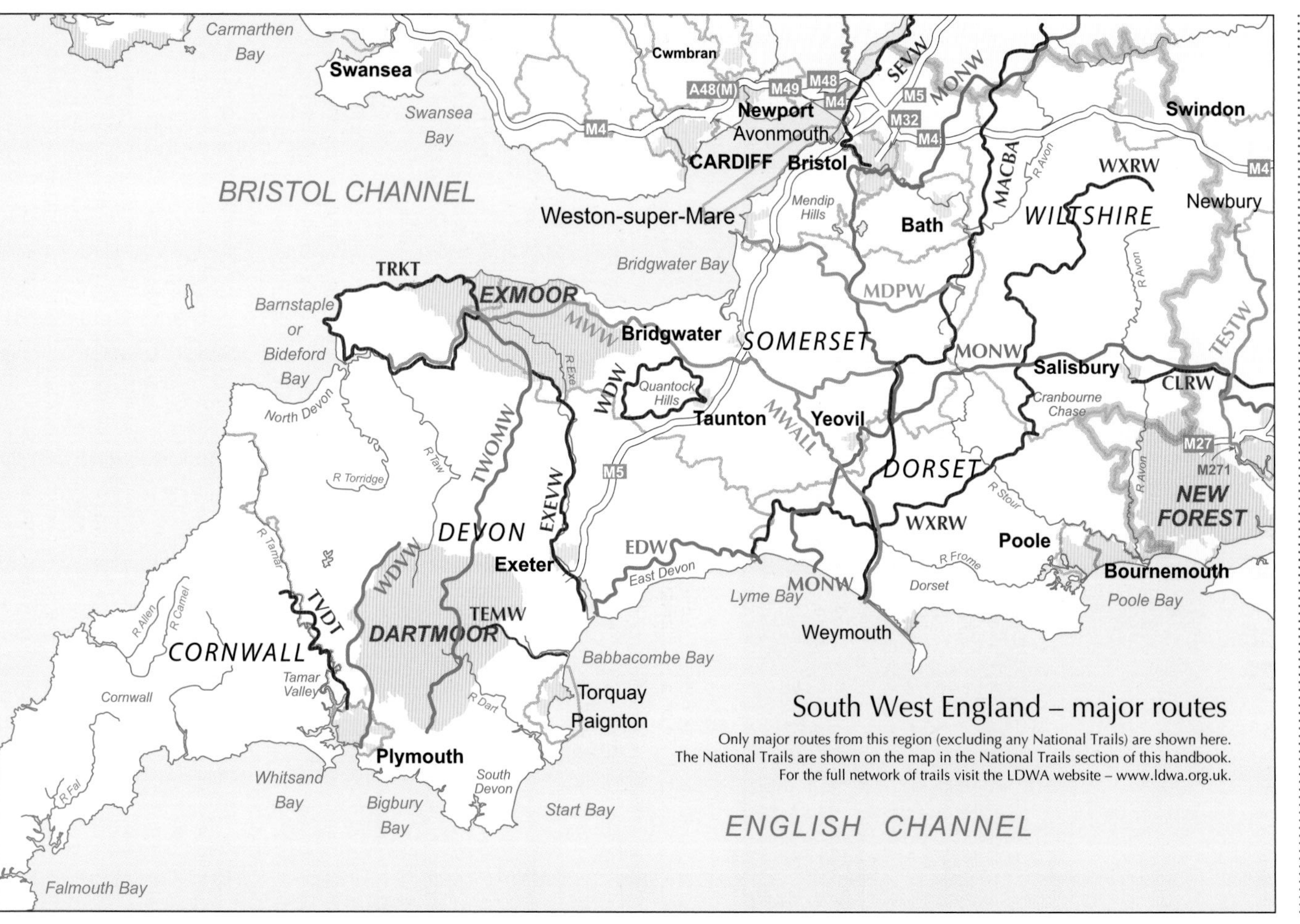
Carmarthen Bay
Swansea
Cwmbran
A48(M)
M49
M48
M4
M5
M32
Newport
Avonmouth
CARDIFF
Bristol
SEVW
MONW
Swindon
Swansea Bay
BRISTOL CHANNEL
Weston-super-Mare
Mendip Hills
Bath
MACBA
R Avon
WXRW
WILTSHIRE
Newbury
Bridgwater Bay
TRKT
EXMOOR
MDPW
Barnstaple or Bideford Bay
MWW
Bridgwater
SOMERSET
TESTW
MONW
Salisbury
CLRW
R Exe
WDW
Quantock Hills
Taunton
MWALL
Yeovil
Cranbourne Chase
North Devon
R Taw
R Torridge
TWOMW
EXEVW
M5
DORSET
M27
M271
NEW FOREST
R Stour
DEVON
WXRW
Poole
EDW
R Frome
Exeter
WDVW
East Devon
Bournemouth
R Tamar
Lyme Bay
MONW
Dorset
Poole Bay
TVDT
TEMW
R Allen
R Camel
DARTMOOR
Weymouth
CORNWALL
Babbacombe Bay
Tamar Valley
Torquay
Cornwall
R Dart
Paignton
South West England – major routes
Only major routes from this region (excluding any National Trails) are shown here.
The National Trails are shown on the map in the National Trails section of this handbook.
For the full network of trails visit the LDWA website – www.ldwa.org.uk.
Plymouth
R Fal
Whitsand Bay
South Devon
Bigbury Bay
Start Bay
ENGLISH CHANNEL
Falmouth Bay

in sedimentary rocks, while Dartmoor's lies in an igneous, volcanic past, with granite intrusions underlying the moor. Weathering of these Dartmoor granite outcrops has produced the famous 'tors' so characteristic of the moors.

Further to the west in Cornwall, Bodmin Moor has similar origins and its own tors. Igneous activity has also formed the Penwith (Land's End) peninsula and, offshore, the Isles of Scilly. The region's former mining industry is linked with the minerals associated with its igneous past: in the early 19th century, almost half of the world's copper came from here, recognised in the Cornwall and West Devon Mining Landscape World Heritage Site. By contrast, the Lizard peninsula includes outcrops of serpentine rocks, once part of an ancient ocean floor. The fertile, rolling lowlands forming much of the rest of the region are very different in feel from these high moorlands. They include the 'red soils' of Devon, notable in the Exeter area and in the 'red cliffs' at Budleigh Salterton. The colour here is caused by iron in the sandstones and mudstones left from a past desert era.

For walkers, in bad weather or in poor visibility, the moorland can be a hostile, trackless environment, despite being so far south in England. The coastline is also very exposed and, especially as the peninsula narrows to the west, the climate, although still temperate, is increasingly maritime, with high rainfall and strong winds.

A head to head confrontation on Tarr Steps, Devon (Two Moors Way)

Britain's heritage is well represented elsewhere in the region with World Heritage Sites at Stonehenge, Avebury and its associated sites, in the City of Bath, as well as the Dorset and East Devon Coast and the Cornwall and West Devon Mining Landscape.

The Trails

This often-narrow peninsula invites **coast-to-coast** walking variants and there are several on offer. The 102-mile Two Moors Way, promoted as Devon's own coast-to-coast, links Exmoor's coast with the southern coastline near Plymouth via a full traverse of Dartmoor. The Saint's Way links Padstow and Fowey, the Channel to Channel (Devon to Somerset) links the Bristol and English Channels and the Coast to Coast (Southern England) links the same channels from Somerset to Kent.

Walking on the three main **moorland massifs** and around their fringes, forms the basis for several routes. Dartmoor offers the Dartmoor Way and is circuited by the Dartmoor Ancient Boundary Perambulation. The Templer Way traces the route taken by granite quarried on the moor at Haytor transported to the coast at Teignmouth. The West Devon Way keeps close to the western moorland fringes on its way from Okehampton to Plymouth while the Two Castles Trail heads west from the shadow of the moor as it links Okehampton and Launceston castles. Inland Exmoor has the Tarka Trail and Two Moors Way and along its scenic coastline the South West Coast Path. Bodmin Moor is traversed by the Smugglers' Way while more honest past occupations in its mining industry inspire the Copper Trail's circuit.

ROUTE CODES

Code	Route	Code	Route
CLRW	Clarendon Way	**SEVW**	Severn Way
EDW	East Devon Way	**TEMW**	Templer Way
EXEVW	Exe Valley Way	**TESTW**	Test Way
MACBA	Macmillan Way (Boston to Abbotsbury)	**TRKT**	Tarka Trail
MDPW	Mendip Ways	**TVDT**	Tamar Valley Discovery Trail
MWW	Macmillan Way West (Castle Cary to Barnstaple)	**TWOMW**	Two Moors Way (Devon Coast to Coast)
MONW	Monarch's Way	**WDVW**	West Devon Way
MWALL	Macmillan Abbotsbury–Langport Link	**WDW**	West Deane Way
		WXRW	Wessex Ridgeway

Cadbury Castle on the Macmillan Way, southeast Somerset

There are trails on the region's several other **hill ranges**, including the Mendips (the two Mendip Ways), the Quantocks (Quantock Greenway and Quantock Way while the West Deane Way visits these hills en route to Taunton) and in Dorset the Purbeck Hills (the two Purbeck Ways). The Limestone Link from the southern end of the Cotswold Way joins the Cotswolds and the Mendips. The rolling Wiltshire downland and historic Wessex is the setting for the Wessex Ridgeway, the Wessex Heights Walk, and for the westerly conclusion of the Ridgeway National Trail near Marlborough.

The region has a wealth of often easy **waterside** walking along its numerous attractive and interesting rivers. There are routes on the Avon, Axe, Dart, Erme, Parrett, Plym, Tamar, Teign and Wylye, while the Tarka Trail, based on the fictional otter, includes sections on the Torridge/Okement, Taw and Bray and above the East Lyn River. The Two Rivers Way links the Yeo and the Avon in an arc south of Bristol. Canal walking is provided along the course of the Great Western Canal.

Routes making a **traverse** or **circuit** in the region include the Devonshire Heartland Way linking Okehampton to the Exe valley, in Dorset the Jubilee Trail (Dorset) makes a west-east traverse and the Round Dorset Walk keeps close to the county borders. The Mid-Wilts Way makes a traverse of Wiltshire, while the Salisbury Country Way encircles that city, and the Clarendon Way links it to Winchester. The Two Counties Way links Taunton in Somerset to the south Devon coast. From Bristol the Bristol to Brecon Walk begins its journey into Wales, going across the old Severn Bridge, while the Community Forest Path encircles the city. The Gordano Round includes estuary walking in its circuit of Gordano. Land's End provides a start of the epic End-to-End walking route to John O'Groats (covered here as Land's End to John O'Groats (LEJOG)).

Historical themes underpin several routes: the Leland Trail in Somerset aims to follow John Leland's 16th-century survey, while the linking Liberty Trail follows the 1685 walk to join the Protestant rebellion at Lyme Regis, and the Orange Way traces the long march of Prince William in 1688 from Brixham to London.

In the region's main **urban** areas, the Bristol City Triangular Walk and the South Bristol Circular Walk provide walking on longer trails, while in Plymouth the city's historic Waterfront Walkway forms part of the South West Coast Path. The John Musgrave Heritage Trail remembers a keen Rambler in circuiting the fringes of Torbay.Walks based on old **railway lines** include the Bristol & Bath Railway Path and the Camel Trail.

Charity routes include parts of the Macmillan network, the Macmillan Way West (Castle Cary–Barnstaple) and the Abotsbury–Langport Link, along with the Samaritan's Way South West (Bristol–Lynton). Two **enthusiasts' routes** requiring navigational skills complete the picture: the Old Sarum Challenge heads from Amesbury over downland, while the Sidmouth Saunter includes both coastal and inland scenery and has a shorter variant.

Avon Valley Path (Hampshire to Dorset) AVPHD

DORSET, HANTS, WILTS **55km/34 miles**

The Path follows the lower reaches of one of England's best-known chalk rivers, through a valley much of which is designated as an SSSI and of great botanical interest besides being known for its salmon. Much of the Path does not follow the riverbank itself, but aims to keep as close as possible. The route visits Downton, Fordingbridge and Ringwood.

Attributes
Easy; River
Start
Salisbury Cathedral, Wilts SU142295
Finish
Christchurch Priory, Dorset SZ160925
Waymark
Green signs with bridge logo
Websites
www3.hants.gov.uk
Maps ◈
OS Landranger: 184, 195
OS Explorer: 130, 22
Publications, badges and certificates
Paperbacks
Avon Valley Path by Marjorie Kerr (Editor) (RA New Forest Group) 1994. ISBN 9780861460885. 64pp; A5. £2.99 (+ A5 SAE). Cheques to Ramblers Association (New Forest Group).
Leaflets
Avon Valley Path (Hampshire County Council). A4/3. Free (+ SAE).
Walking Support Providers
Bobs; Let's Go Walking!

Bournemouth Coast Path BCP

DORSET, HANTS **60km/37 miles**

A route of varied interest with two natural harbours, ferries, woods, high cliffs and some of the finest views on the south coast. It links the Dorset Coast Path, the most easterly section of the South West Coast Path National Trail, with the Solent Way running from Milford-on-Sea to Emsworth. This creates a continuous route from Minehead to Emsworth on the Hampshire-Surrey border. The Bournemouth Coast Path forms part of the E9 E-Route (see E-Routes: E9).

Attributes
Challenging; Coastal; Urban
Start
Swanage, Dorset SZ031789
Finish
Lymington, Hants SZ325958
Waymark
E9 symbol (EU stars on blue)

Websites
www.bournemouthcoastpath.org.uk
Maps
OS Landranger: 195, 196
OS Explorer: 15, 22
Publications, badges and certificates
Paperbacks
Exploring the Bournemouth Coast Path by Leigh Hatts (Countryside Books) 2005. ISBN 9781853069086. 96pp; 150 x 210. £7.99. Includes Solent Way first section.

Bristol & Bath Railway Path BBRP

BATH NES, BRISTOL, N SOMERS **26km/16 miles**

This leisure path is an off road route providing a wildlife corridor between the cities of Bristol and Bath. The path is open to walkers and cyclists and access is provided for disabled users.

Attributes
Easy; Former Railway; Urban
Start
Old Market Area, Bristol ST601731
Finish
Pulteney Bridge, Bath NES ST751649
Website
www.bristolbathrailwaypath.org.uk, www.cobr.co.uk
Maps ◈
OS Landranger: 172
OS Explorer: 155
Publications, badges and certificates
Leaflet
Bristol and Bath Railway Path by Avon Valley Partnership (Forest of Avon). Ring Avon Valley Partnership on 0117 922 4325 or the Forest of Avon 0117 953 2141.

Bristol City Triangular Walk BTW

BRISTOL, S GLOS **29km/18 miles**

This circular walk offers attractive views within and across the city of Bristol, taking in the Clifton Suspension Bridge, Clifton Downs, Sea Mills, Blaise Hamlet (NT), Henbury Church, Henleaze and Redland.

Attributes
Easy; Urban; Heritage; Industrial History

Start and Finish
Temple Meads Station, Bristol ST595723
Websites
www.bristolramblers.org.uk
Maps
OS Landranger: 172
OS Explorer: 155
Publications, badges and certificates
Leaflets
Bristol City Triangular Walk (Bristol Tourist Information Centre). Free (or SAE).

Bristol to Brecon Walk BRBRW

BRISTOL, MONS, POWYS, S GLOS **137km/85 miles**

This tough but scenic route takes in Blaise Castle, Spaniorum Hill, Severn Beach and the old Severn Bridge. Continuing through Wales it visits Chepstow Castle, Gray Hill, Wentwood Forest, Usk, the Blorenge ridge and Abergavenny. From here the route ascends the Sugar Loaf and stays at fairly high level to Table Mountain before making the descent to Crickhowell. A low level stretch is followed before climbing Tor y Foel, with panoramic views of the Brecon Beacons. The traverse of this classic mountain range between Talybont and Brecon includes the ascent of Pen y Fan, the high point of the walk. The route can be enjoyed either as a progressive series of day walks or by creating shorter circular walks.

Attributes
Challenging; River; Moorland
Start
Blaise Castle Estate, Henbury, Bristol ST559786
Finish
Brecon, Powys SO044287
Websites
www.bristolramblers.org.uk
Maps
OS Landranger: 160, 161, 171, 172
OS Explorer: 12, 13, 14, 152, 155, 167
Publications, badges and certificates
Paperbacks
Bristol to Brecon Walk by Nigel Andrews (Nigel Andrews). £6.75 (incs p&p). Cheques to Nigel Andrews.

Camel Trail CT

CORNWALL **29km/18 miles**

A multi-user trail based on two sections of disused railway line from Padstow via Wadebridge and Boscarne Junction to Bodmin (11 miles), and from Boscarne Junction to Poley's Bridge on the edge of Bodmin Moor (7 miles). The Padstow to Wadebridge section is along the Camel estuary, the rest through densely wooded landscapes. A further system of linking multi-user trails, creating a distance of over 160 miles, based on Mineral Tramways are being developed across Cornwall. Including the Camel Trail these will be known as 'The Cornish Way'.

Attributes
Easy; Former Railway; Cycle Route; World Heritage Site
Start
Padstow, Cornwall SW920754
Finish
Poley's Bridge, Cornwall SX082742
Waymark
Named signs
Websites
www.destination-cornwall.co.uk,
www.cornwall.gov.uk,
www.explorecornwall.com,
www.cornish-mining.org.uk,
www.sustransshop.org.uk
Maps ◈
OS Landranger: 200
OS Explorer: 106, 107, 109
Publications, badges and certificates
Leaflets
Camel Trail (Cornwall County Council) 1993. A4/3. Free (+ SAE). North Cornwall Information, tel: 01872 327310.

Channel to Channel (Devon – Somerset) CCDS

DEVON, SOMERS **80km/50 miles**

A route that links the English and Bristol Channels, it passes through or close to Axminster, Taunton and Wilton as it crosses the narrow waist of the south west peninsula and over the Quantocks. It connects with the South West Coast Path National Trail at Seaton, and with the West Deane Way at Taunton.

Attributes
No significant attribute
Start
Seaton, Devon ST245899
Finish
Watchet, Somers ST073435
Maps
OS Landranger: 181, 193
OS Explorer: 116, 128, 9

Publications, badges and certificates
Booklets
Channel to Channel (Ken Young). 28pp; A5. £2.00 (+ 50p p&p).

Clarendon Way — CLRW

HANTS, WILTS — **39km/24 miles**

Named after Clarendon Park on the eastern edge of Salisbury, the Way links the city, on the River Avon, with Winchester, on the River Itchen. Crossing the River Test at Kings Somborne, the scenery ranges from the water meadows of the valleys, with their charming villages; woodlands; and chalk downs with fine views.

Attributes
Downland/Wolds
Start
Salisbury, Wilts SU143297
Finish
Winchester, Hants SU483293
Waymark
Bishop's mitre on green and white discs
Websites
www3.hants.gov.uk
Maps ◈
OS Landranger: 184, 185
OS Explorer: 130, 131, 132
Publications, badges and certificates
Leaflets
Clarendon Way by Hampshire County Council (Hampshire County Council). Free (+ SAE).
Booklets
Clarendon Way by Peter Radburn (Peter Radburn) 2004. £2.50 (+ 30p p&p).
Walking Support Providers
Let's Go Walking!

Community Forest Path — CFP

BATH NES, BRISTOL, N SOMERS, S GLOS — **72km/45 miles**

A route around Bristol using footpaths, tracks and some sections of rural lanes around the Forest of Avon, providing a variety of landscapes with views of the Mendip Hills, Severn Estuary and the Severn road bridges. It takes in Ashton Court, Blaise Castle and the Clifton Suspension Bridge.

Attributes
River; Heritage
Start and Finish
Keynsham, Bath NES ST656690
Waymark
Named disc with Forest of Avon logo

Websites
www.forestofavon.org.uk
Maps ◈
OS Landranger: 172
OS Explorer: 154, 155, 167
Publications, badges and certificates
Leaflets
Community Forest Path by Forest of Avon (Forest of Avon) 1998. A5. Free.

Copper Trail — COPT

CORNWALL — **97km/60 miles**

A circular route around Bodmin Moor where Minions and Caradon Hill were once the centre of a great copper mining boom. It takes in many historical and archaeological features such as the Iron Age hillfort of Berry Castle, Trethevy Quoit a tomb dating back to 4500 BC, and the villages of St Neot and St Cleer. There are scenic granite tors and wooded valleys, home to many species of birds and other wildlife. Good map reading and navigation skills are required.

Attributes
Challenging; Moorland; Heritage; Industrial History
Start and Finish
Minions, Cornwall SX260711
Websites
www.coppertrail.co.uk
Maps
OS Landranger: 200, 201
OS Explorer: 109
Publications, badges and certificates
Paperbacks
Copper Trail: Once Around Bodmin Moor by Mark Camp (Best of Bodmin Moor) 2005. ISBN 9780954491239. 48pp. £4.95 (+ £1.00 p&p). Cheques to B G Shears.
Walking Support Providers
Let's Go Walking!

Dart Valley Trail — DART

DEVON — **27km/17 miles**

Classic river and estuary landscapes of one of the county's most beautiful valleys provide a route linking Totnes with the South Devon Coast Path. It follows the east and west banks of the Dart between Dartmouth and Greenway, and a west bank route to Totnes. Ferries at Dartmouth, Dittisham and Totnes enable a circular route with a difference.

Attributes
River
Start
Dartmouth, Devon SX879514
Finish
Totnes, Devon SX806603
Waymark
Stylised river and castles
Maps ◈
OS Landranger: 202
OS Explorer: 20, 110
Publications, badges and certificates
Booklets
Dart Valley Trail by Devon County Council (Devon County Council) 2007. £3.50 Quote Ref. DP42. Cheques to Devon County Council.
Walking Support Providers
Let's Go Walking!

Dartmoor Way DARTW

DEVON **138km/86 miles**

A route around Dartmoor's scenic upland and valleys, linking towns, hamlets and villages. It is coincident with the Tarka Trail between Sticklepath and Okehampton and with the West Devon Way between Okehampton and Tavistock.

Attributes
Challenging; Moorland
Start and Finish
Buckfastleigh, Devon SX736661
Maps ◈
OS Landranger: 191, 201, 202
OS Explorer: 28, 108, 110, 112, 113
Publications, badges and certificates
Paperbacks
Walking the Dartmoor Way: A Guide to 24 Walks That Cover the Whole of the Dartmoor Way by Michael Bennie (Peninsula Press) 2007. ISBN 9781872640549. 96pp. £5.99.
Illustrated map guide (with Booklets, map)
Dartmoor Way: Map Pack by The Dartmoor Way (Dartmoor Towns Ltd) 1999. ISBN 9780953587209. 56pp; 132 x 210. £7.95 (incs p&p). Accommodation list included.
Leaflets
Dartmoor Way: Escapes on foot (Ashburton Tourist Information Centre). A4. Free (+ A4 SAE).

Walking Support Providers
Contours; Let's Go Walking!

Dartmoor's Ancient Boundary Perambulation DABP

DEVON **80km/50 miles**

One of the oldest walks on Dartmoor, the route visits Great Mis Tor, Yes Tor, King's Oven, Dartmeet, Ryder's Hill, Eastern White Barrow and Siward's Cross. It is necessary to check times of military firing in the area – the ranges website has a link.

Attributes
Challenging; Anytime Challenge; Moorland
Start and Finish
Rundlestone, Devon SX574750
Websites
www.ian.kirkpatrick2.btinternet.co.uk, www.dartmoor-ranges.co.uk
Maps
OS Landranger: 191, 202
OS Explorer: 20, 28
Publications, badges and certificates
Looseleaf
Dartmoor's Ancient Boundary Walk (Ian & Caroline Kirkpatrick). 1pp; A4. Free (+ SAE).
Badge & certificate
Dartmoor's Ancient Boundary Perambulation (Ian & Caroline Kirkpatrick). £2.00 (+ SAE) & £0.30 (+ A4 SAE). Car stickers are 35p.

Devonshire Heartland Way DHW

DEVON **69km/43 miles**

A west-to-east route across pastoral Devon, starting with Dartmoor backdrops. Using ancient footpaths, bridleways and some minor roads, the route visits Sampford Courtenay; North Tawton where it links with the Tarka Trail; Down St Mary where it links with the Two Moors Way; Colebrooke, Yeoford and Crediton, before ending just north of Exeter.

Attributes
No significant attribute
Start
Okehampton, Devon SX587952
Finish
Stoke Canon, Exeter, Devon SX936980
Waymark
Spindle Berry Flower

Maps
OS Landranger: 191, 192
OS Explorer: 28, 113, 114
Publications, badges and certificates
Booklets
Devon Heartland Way (Devon County Council). 32pp.
Walking Support Providers
Let's Go Walking!

East Devon Way **EDW**

DEVON **64km/40 miles**

Following the River Exe estuary to Lympstone, the route then turns east over the commons and rolling hills of the East Devon AONB via Harpford, Sidbury, Farway and Colyton. It can be combined with part of the South West Coast Path National Trail to form a circular walk.

Attributes
River; Moorland
Start
Exmouth, Devon SX999814
Finish
Uplyme, Devon SY333933
Waymark
Foxglove (logo of AONB) and name
Maps ◈
OS Landranger: 192, 193
OS Explorer: 110, 115, 116
Publications, badges and certificates
Booklets
East Devon Way by Norman Barns (Devon County Council). 60pp. £6.45 (incs p&p) Quote Ref. DP17. Cheques to Devon County Council.

Exe Valley Way **EXEVW**

DEVON, SOMERS **72km/45 miles**

From the Exe Estuary to the steeply wooded valleys on Exmoor it follows, for the most part, quiet country lanes and footpaths along the Exe valley through Bickleigh, Tiverton and Bampton. The scenery varies from the broad river estuary, through pastoral land and then steeper, wooded valleys to open moorland.

Attributes
River; Moorland
Start
Starcross, Devon SX977817
Finish
Hawkridge, Somers SS861307

Waymark
Named discs with stylised V symbol (not on moorland section)
Maps ◈
OS Landranger: 181, 192
OS Explorer: 110, 114, 9
Publications, badges and certificates
Booklets
Exe Valley Way (Devon County Council). 24pp; 210 x 98. Free (+SAE) Quote Ref. DP14.
Walking Support Providers
Let's Go Walking!

Gordano Round **GORR**

N SOMERS **42km/26 miles**

Initially a figure-of-eight walk following the coast path of the Severn Estuary past the Black Nore Lighthouse to Clevedon. Turning inland, through the town, it then follows wooded countryside to Clapton in Gordano. More farmland and woods lead to the eastern limit of the walk at Abbots Leigh. Here the route circles back to Clapton, finishing in open countryside. The guidebook includes four links that can be used to make short circular walks.

Attributes
Coastal
Start and Finish
Roath Road, Portishead ST466762
Waymark
Green named discs with lapwing
Websites
www.gordano-footpath-group.org.uk
Maps ◈
OS Landranger: 171, 172
OS Explorer: 153, 154, 155
Publications, badges and certificates
Booklets
Gordano Round (Gordano Footpath Group) 2001. 56pp; A5. £3.99 (+ £1.00 p&p).

Grand Western Canal **GWC**

DEVON, SOMERS **38km/24 miles**

A route along the course of the Grand Western Canal which is partly water-filled, between Tiverton and Greenham, and partly dry. The area is noted for its flora and fauna.

Attributes
Easy; Canal

Start
Tiverton, Devon SS963124
Finish
Taunton, Somers ST228255
Maps ◈
OS Landranger: 181
OS Explorer: 114, 128
Publications, badges and certificates
Leaflets
Grand Western Canal Country Park: Devon Section (Devon County Council). A3/4. Free (+ SAE) Quote Ref. DP37.

John Musgrave Heritage Trail JMUSHT

DEVON, TORBAY **56km/35 miles**

A varied walking route around the fringes of Torbay, created from a legacy left by John Musgrove who was a keen walker. It links the Dart Valley Trail, Torbay Totnes Trail (T3), Torbay Dart Link and South West Coast Path with new sections of path to make a route through Teignbridge, Torbay and South Hams. The trail is divided into four individual sections, ending at Cockington, Totnes, Dittisham, and Brixham, each is accompanied by a series of interpretation boards. A longer, complete circuit could be made by returning along the Coast Path through Torbay.

Attributes
Coastal; Urban; Heritage
Start
Maidencombe, Torbay SX926684
Finish
Brixham Harbour, Torbay SX925562
Waymark
Yellow boot print on black arrow with name
Websites
www.countryside-trust.org.uk,
www.southdevonramblers.com
Maps ◈
OS Landranger: 202
OS Explorer: 20, 110
Publications, badges and certificates
Booklets
John Musgrave Heritage: Trail Guide Pack by John Risdon (Devon County Council) 2006. £3.99 (incs p&p) Quote Ref. DP 107. Cheques to Devon County Council. Also from Trust website: About Us/Publications; or South Devon RA.
Leaflets
John Musgrave Heritage Trail (Devon County Council) 2006. Free (+ SAE) Quote Ref. DP106.

Jubilee Trail (Dorset) DJT

DORSET **142km/88 miles**

A trail created to celebrate the RA Diamond Jubilee crossing Dorset from border to border. The route takes in quiet villages, old churches, historic sites and stately homes, and offers extensive views of the rolling downs and secret valleys.

Attributes
Downland/Wolds; Heritage
Start
Forde Abbey, Dorset ST361053
Finish
Bokerley Dyke, Dorset SU049188
Waymark
Combined tree, arrow and name on green background
Maps ◈
OS Landranger: 183, 184, 193, 194, 195
OS Explorer: 116, 117, 118, 15
Publications, badges and certificates
Paperbacks
Dorset Jubilee Trail (RA Dorset) 2008. ISBN 9781906494100. 54pp; A5. £5.50 (+ £1.00 p&p). Cheques to Ramblers Association (Dorset Area).
Badge
Dorset Jubilee Trail (RA Dorset). £2.50 (+ SAE). Cheques to Ramblers Association (Dorset Area).
Walking Support Providers
Let's Go Walking!

Land's End to John O'Groats LEJOG

NUMEROUS **1368km/850 miles**

There is no set route for this, one of the ultimate walking challenges in the UK, and whatever the chosen route, it will not be less than 850 miles. There are inherent dangers in using lanes/roads but there are various established long distance routes of which advantage can be taken to avoid these hazards. The Cicerone guide for example is divided into six sections: Land's End–Barnstaple–Knighton–Hebden Bridge–Jedburgh–Fort William–John O'Groats, then sub-divided further to create 61 day walks in total. The LDWA/Harvey Maps Long Distance Paths Chart is another useful aid in planning the overall routing if long distance paths are to be used. Creating one's own route is almost a challenge in itself. A comprehensive bibliography can be found on the website listed below ('longwalks') and this includes reviews. The Moxon and Blease books are recent personal accounts.

Attributes
Challenging; Moorland
Start
Land's End, Cornwall SW343251
Finish
John O'Groats, Highland ND379734
Websites
www.landsendjohnogroats.info, www.longwalks.org.uk
Maps
Map (Other)
Long Distance Paths Chart (Harvey Maps)
Publications, badges and certificates
Paperbacks

End to End Trail: Land's End to John O'Groats on Foot by Andy Robinson (Cicerone Press) 2007. ISBN 9781852845124. 416pp; 172 x 116. £15.00.

Land's End to John O'Groats Walk by Andrew McCloy (Cordee Ltd) 2001. ISBN 9781871890594. 192pp; 220 x 124. £11.99.

John O'Groats to Land's End: The Official Challenge Guide by Brian Smailes (Editor) (Challenge Publications) 2004. ISBN 9781903568187. 66pp. £6.95 (incs p&p). Cheques to Brian Smailes.

Lands End to John O'Groats Cycle Guide by Brian Smailes (Challenge Publications) 2004. ISBN 9781903568118. 180 x 118. £6.95. Log books also available for both directions.

When I Walk, I Bounce: Walking from Land's End to John O'Groats by Mark Moxon (Mark Moxon) 2007. ISBN 9781846855559. 236pp. £9.95. Also available as a free download at http://www.longwalks.org.uk/index.html.

End to End by Steve Blease (Book Guild Publishing Ltd) 2008. ISBN 9781846242014. 240pp; 211 x 137. £9.99.

Certificate

Trophy for Land's End to John O'Groats (Land's End to John O'Groats Association). See application details on website or with membership.

Land's End Trail — LENDTR

CORNWALL, DEVON, SOMERS, WILTS — **480km/298 miles**

A route from the Ridgeway at Avebury, connecting with other long distance routes, as it takes an inland, generally high-level line through the South West peninsula. It provides an alternative option to those routes often used in linking Land's End with England's central ways.

Attributes
Challenging; Moorland
Start
Avebury, Wilts SU102699
Finish
Land's End, Cornwall SW343251
Waymark
Yellow chevron – sparingly and not on moorland (Dartmoor, Exmoor, Bodmin, Penwith)
Websites
www.oliverscornwall.co.uk
Maps
OS Landranger: 173, 180, 181, 182, 183, 185, 191, 200, 201, 203, 204
OS Explorer: 102, 104, 106, 108, 109, 113, 127, 128, 130, 140, 141, 142, 143, 157, 9, 28
Publications, badges and certificates
Looseleaf

Land's End Trail: South to North (R. Preston) 1998. 29pp; A4. £7.00 (incs p&p & accomodation list). Cheques to Robert Preston.

Land's End Trail: North to South (R. Preston) 1998. 25pp; A4. £7.00 (incs p&p & accomodation list). Cheques to Robert Preston.

Leland Trail — LELT

SOMERS — **45km/28 miles**

A route through the rolling hills of Somerset from near Stourhead to near Stoke-sub-Hamdon following the route traversed by John Leland during his 16th century survey of Britain. It connects with the Liberty Trail at Ham Hill.

Attributes
Easy; Heritage
Start
Alfred's Tower, Somers ST745352
Finish
Ham Hill, Somers ST478172
Waymark
Bust of John Leland
Maps ◈
OS Landranger: 183, 193
OS Explorer: 129, 142
Publications, badges and certificates
Folder

Leland Trail (Yeovil Heritage and Visitor Information Centre) 1997. 14pp; A5. £4.25 (+ 75p p&p).

Walking Support Providers
Let's Go Walking!

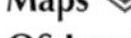

Liberty Trail LIBT

DORSET, SOMERS **45km/28 miles**

Linking the Leland Trail with the South West Coast Path National Trail, this route follows the footsteps of people who, in 1685, walked to join the protestant Monmouth rebellion at Lyme; taking in Crewkerne and Forde Abbey. For the last stretch through Dorset, via the Iron Age hillforts of Lamberts and Coneys Castles, into Lyme Regis it is coincident with the Wessex Ridgeway.

Attributes
Heritage
Start
Ham Hill, Somers ST478172
Finish
Lyme Regis, Dorset SY347922
Waymark
Name in script on square green signs
Maps ◈
OS Landranger: 193
OS Explorer: 116, 129
Publications, badges and certificates
Folder
Liberty Trail (Yeovil Heritage and Visitor Information Centre) 1996. A5. £4.25 (+ 75p p&p).
Walking Support Providers
Let's Go Walking!

Limestone Link (Cotswolds to Mendips) LLCM

BATH NES, SOMERS, S GLOS **58km/36 miles**

A route joining the limestone of the Cotswolds to that of the Mendip Hills through the valleys and villages south of Bath. It heads from the Cotswold Way National Trail, through St Catherine's Valley, along the Kennet and Avon Canal to Dundas Viaduct, and then to the Mendip escarpment past Burrington Combe and Dolebury Warren to the finish. It also links with the West Mendip Way (Mendip Ways).

Attributes
Easy
Start
Cold Ashton, S Glos ST751728
Finish
Shipham, Somerset ST443572
Waymark
Ammonite logo
Websites
www.mendiphillsaonb.org.uk
Maps ◈
OS Landranger: 172, 182
OS Explorer: 141, 142, 155
Publications, badges and certificates
Leaflets
Limestone Link: Somerset (Mendip Hills AONB Service) 2007. Free. Section in the Mendips AONB from Hinton Blewett only.
Booklets
Limestone Link by Yatton Ramblers (Yatton Ramblers) 1995. 66pp; A5. £3.45 (incs p&p).

Macmillan Abbotsbury–Langport Link MWALL

DORSET, SOMERS **64km/40 miles**

The route goes north from Abbotsbury through Compton Valence, Maiden Newton, Cattistock, Evershot, Halstock, Hardington Manderville, East Chinnock and Martock to reach Langport. The Macmillan Abbotsbury-Langport Link allows walkers to traverse 126 miles coast-to-coast from Abbotsbury to Barnstaple, using the Macmillan Way West from Langport onwards.

Attributes
Charity
Start
Abbotsbury, Dorset SY560845
Finish
Langport, Somerset ST419268
Waymark
Green bow, walk name and the words – Across Country for Cancer Care (both directions)
Websites
www.macmillanway.org
Maps ◈
OS Landranger: 193, 194
OS Explorer: 15, 117, 119
Publications, badges and certificates
Booklets
Macmillan Abbotsbury: Langport Link by Macmillian Way Association (Macmillan Way Association). 28pp. £3.50.

Macmillan Way West – Castle Cary to Barnstaple MWW

DEVON, SOMERS **164km/102 miles**

A branch of the main Macmillan Way, parting at Castle Cary, it crosses the Somerset Levels and the Quantocks and can be linked with the South West Coast Path National Trail at Minehead. It then crosses Exmoor and follows the Tarka Trail to Barnstaple, where it again links with the South West Coast Path. Using Macmillan routes thus creates a 346-mile walk across England from Boston to Barnstaple.

Attributes
Downland/Wolds; Charity
Start
Castle Cary, Somers ST640323
Finish
Barnstaple, Devon SS558328
Waymark
Green bow, walk name and 'Across Country for Cancer Care'. Both directions.
Websites
www.macmillanway.org,
www.somerset.gov.uk
Maps ◈
OS Landranger: 180, 181, 182, 183, 193
OS Explorer: 128, 129, 140, 141, 142, 9
Publications, badges and certificates
Booklets
Macmillan Way West: Guidebook by Peter Titchmarsh (Macmillan Way Association) 2001. ISBN 9780952685135. 56pp; A5. £6.75 (incs p&p).
Macmillan Way West: Planner (Macmillan Way Association). 8pp; A4. £2.50 (incs p&p).
Leaflets
Macmillan Way West (Macmillan Way Association). A4/3. Free.
Badge
Macmillan Way (Macmillan Way Association). £2.50 (incs p&p).
Walking Support Providers
Let's Go Walking!

Mendip Ways MDPW

N SOMERS, SOMERS **79km/49 miles**

Comprising the West Mendip (30 miles) and the East Mendip (19 miles) Ways, the first section runs from the Bristol Channel at Uphill and, in places, affords fine views over the Somerset Levels. It crosses the central Mendip plateau, leading down to the spectacular Cheddar Gorge, before eventually taking in the beautiful city of Wells. Between Wells and Frome open hilltops are replaced by deep secluded valleys. The Strawberry Line (10 miles and on OS mapping) follows the Cheddar Valley Railway from Yatton to Cheddar built in 1869 to carry strawberries from Cheddar.

Attributes
Downland/Wolds
Start
Uphill, N Somers ST315585
Finish
Frome, Somers ST777481
Waymark
Mendip Way West – Rotary International logo;
Mendip Way East – Ash key logo in green
Websites
www.somerset.gov.uk
Maps ◈
OS Landranger: 172, 182, 183
OS Explorer: 141, 142, 153
Publications, badges and certificates
Paperbacks
Uphill to Frome: A Guide to the Mendip Way by David Wright (David Wright) 2000. ISBN 9780953923700. 75pp; 212 x 144. £6.99.
West Mendip Way by Derick Moyes (Ex Libris Press) 1999. ISBN 9780948578458. 111pp; 212 x 138. £5.95.
Booklets
West Mendip Way by Andrew Eddy (Weston-super-Mare Heritage Centre). £3.50 (+ 50p p&p).
Leaflets
Strawberry Line (Forest of Avon).
Walking Support Providers
Contours; Footpath; Ramblers

Mid-Wilts Way MDWW

WILTS **109km/68 miles**

This east to south-west traverse of the county of Wiltshire provides varied walking with extended open downland stretches on the ancient ridgeways of the Wansdyke over Tan Hill, passing burial mounds and white horses. Easier terrain follows along the Kennett and Avon Canal with the interesting Caen Hill lock flight, and then some lovely vale walking skirting below the western fringes of Salisbury Plain. The book covers the original 55-mile route from Wootton Rivers to Mere, but the extension starting at Ham, that takes the route to the Berkshire border, is waymarked and future OS map editions will show the full route. Twelve villages lie on the full route: Ham, Wilton, Wootton Rivers, Oare, Seend Cleeve, Keevil, Steeple Ashton, Bratton, Upton Scudamore, Horningsham, Kingston Deverill and Mere.

Attributes
Canal; Downland/Wolds; Heritage
Start
Ham, Wilts SU330630
Finish
Mere, Wilts ST812323

Waymark
MWW in green on white arrow discs
Websites
www.visitwiltshire.co.uk
Maps ◈
OS Landranger: 173, 174, 183, 184
OS Explorer: 143, 156, 157, 158
Paperbacks
Mid-Wilts Way by James Alsop (Ex Libris Press) 2007. ISBN 9781903341421. 80pp; A5. £5.95 (incs p&p). Post free from publisher. Or at local TICs.

Old Sarum Challenge OSC

WILTS **40km/25 miles**

A route from Amesbury over chalk downland linking Old Sarum and intervening villages.

Attributes
Challenging; Anytime Challenge; Downland/Wolds
Start and Finish
Amesbury Sports Centre, Wilts SU161418
Maps
OS Landranger: 184
OS Explorer: 130
Publications, badges and certificates
Looseleaf
Old Sarum Challenge (Richard Archard). £1.00 (inc p&p).
Badge (cloth)
Old Sarum Challenge (Richard Archard). £2.00 (+ SAE).

Orange Way ORW

DEVON, DORSET, HANTS, GTR LONDON, READING, SOMERS, W BERKSHIRE, WILTS **563km/350 miles**

An historic walk tracing the route taken by Prince William of Orange in 1688 when he led his army from Devon across the countryside to London. It covers the story of the 'Glorious Revolution' and highlights events that took place on or near the route.

Attributes
Heritage; Monarchy
Start
Brixham Harbour, Devon SX926564
Finish
St James's Palace, London TQ293800
Maps
OS Landranger: 164, 174, 175, 176, 183, 184, 192, 193, 194, 202
OS Explorer: 20, 110, 114, 115, 116, 129, 130, 131, 143, 157, 159, 160, 161, 170, 172, 158, 171
Publications, badges and certificates
Paperbacks
Orange Way: A Long Distance Walk Following the March of William of Orange from Brixham to London by Les Ham (Meridian Books) 2003. ISBN 9781869922474. 176pp; 226 x 144. £9.95 (+ £1.00 p&p).

Purbeck Way PBKW

DORSET **24km/15 miles**

A route with varied scenery – riverside, heathland, woodland and downland – taking in Corfe Castle, the Purbeck Hills and the dramatic Dorset coast. The Purbeck Way West (12½ miles and waymarked) leads from the Purbeck Way at Wareham to Coombe Keynes with a loop to Lulworth. At Wareham, both link with the Wareham Forest Way (13 miles and waymarked).

Attributes
Coastal; Downland/Wolds
Start
Wareham, Dorset SY924871
Finish
Swanage, Dorset SZ040786
Waymark
Name and cliff scene logo on green disc
Websites
www.purbeck.gov.uk
Maps ◈
OS Landranger: 195
OS Explorer: 15
Publications, badges and certificates
Leaflets
Purbeck Way (Purbeck Information & Heritage Centre). A5. £0.40 (+ SAE).
Four Walks in Purbeck by Purbeck District Council (Purbeck Information & Heritage Centre). £1.50 (+ SAE).
Wareham Forest Way (Purbeck Information & Heritage Centre). A5. £0.40 (+ SAE).
Walking Support Providers
Let's Go Walking!

Quantock Greenway QG

SOMERS **58km/36 miles**

This figure-of-eight walk visits the villages around the hills with only the crossover route ascending to land above 300 metres. There are plans to develop the route for multi-use.

Attributes
Downland/Wolds
Start and Finish
Fyne Court Visitor Centre, Broomfield, Somers ST221322
Waymark
Named discs
Websites
www.somerset.gov.uk
Maps
OS Landranger: 181
OS Explorer: 140
Publications, badges and certificates
Leaflets
Quantock Greenway by Quantock Hills AONB Team (Quantock Hills AONB Team) 1992. A5. Free.

Quantock Way QW

SOMERS **53km/33 miles**

The Way visits Kingston St Mary, Timbercombe, Bicknoller Combe, West Quantoxhead and Watchet. An alternative route beyond Bicknoller Combe, through the Brendon Hills, extends the distance to over 40 miles.

Attributes
Anytime Challenge; Downland/Wolds
Start
Taunton, Somers ST231254
Finish
Minehead, Somers SS979462
Maps
OS Landranger: 181, 182, 193
OS Explorer: 128, 140, 9
Publications, badges and certificates
Booklets
Quantock Way by John Merrill (John Merrill Foundation) 1999. ISBN 9781841730042. 60pp; A5. £5.95 (+ £1.00 p&p). Cheques to John Merrill Foundation.
Badge & certificate
Quantock Way (John Merrill Foundation). £5.00 (incs p&p).

River Axe Walk RIVAW

DEVON, DORSET, SOMERS **45km/28 miles**

A walk following, as closely as possible, the course of the River Axe from source to sea, using minor roads only where necessary. The former Cistercian Monastery of Forde Abbey is passed on the way and alternative routes are described at Axminster.

Attributes
River; Heritage
Start
Beaminster, Dorset ST480013
Finish
Axmouth Harbour, Devon SY256897
Maps
OS Landranger: 193
OS Explorer: 116
Publications, badges and certificates
Booklets
River Axe Walk by Richard Easterbrook, Geoff Broadhurst (Easterhurst Publications Ltd) 2000. ISBN 9780953827206. 56pp; A5. £3.95 (incs p&p).

River Otter Walk ROTW

DEVON, SOMERS **55km/34 miles**

A walk following, as closely as possible, the course of the River Otter from its source at Otterhead Lakes to the sea. It uses minor roads only where necessary.

Attributes
River
Start
Churchinford, Somers ST213126
Finish
Budleigh Salterton, Devon SY072820
Maps
OS Landranger: 192, 193
OS Explorer: 115, 116, 128
Publications, badges and certificates
Booklets
River Otter Walk by Richard Easterbrook, Geoff Broadhurst (Easterhurst Publications Ltd) 2002. ISBN 9780953827213. 56pp; A5. £4.95 (incs p&p).

River Parrett Trail RPRT

DORSET, SOMERS **80km/50 miles**

A route which follows the River Parrett from source to mouth, winding through the Somerset Levels, moors, ecologically sensitive areas and some of England's richest pasture land where there is an abundance of history and wildlife. The Trail crosses the Liberty Trail near Haselbury and Ham Hill, where it also meets up with the Leland Trail. The waymarked Brit Valley Way (11 miles) follows the River Brit from West Bay to Chedington.

Attributes
River
Start
Chedington, Dorset ST490059
Finish
Steart, Somers ST281469
Waymark
Disc with curved line depicting river
Websites
www.riverparrett-trail.org.uk
Maps ◈
OS Landranger: 182, 193
OS Explorer: 116, 117, 128, 129, 140, 153
Publications, badges and certificates
Booklets
River Parrett Trail (Yeovil Heritage and Visitor Information Centre). ISBN 9781899983308. 12pp; 208 x 156. £5.95 (+ 85p p&p).
Folder
Brit Valley Way & Circular Routes by Dorset County Council (Dorset County Council). 8 route cards; 152 x 215. £3.95 (+ 9 x 6 SAE).
Walking Support Providers
Let's Go Walking!

River Teign Walk RIVTW

DEVON **71km/44 miles**

A walk following, as closely as possible, the course of the River Teign from its source on Dartmoor to the sea, using minor roads only where necessary. The end of the walk is on the tidal foreshore.

Attributes
River
Start
Postbridge Car Park, Devon SX647789
Finish
The Ness, Shaldon, Devon SX940719
Maps
OS Landranger: 191, 202
OS Explorer: 110, 28
Publications, badges and certificates
Booklets
River Teign Walk by Richard Easterbrook, Geoff Broadhurst (Easterhurst Publications Ltd) 2005. ISBN 9780953827220. 56pp; A5. £4.95 (incs p&p).

Round Dorset Walk RDORW

BOURNEMOUTH, DORSET, POOLE **291km/181 miles**

The route does not adhere faithfully to the county boundary but, instead, seeks out ridges and high places and avoids road walking wherever possible. From Poole Harbour, beneath the Purbeck Hills, it visits the peaceful downs of Cranborne Chase and crosses the rolling hills of Blackmore Vale and Marshwood Vale. The journey is completed along the Jurassic Coast. There are two memorable ridge walks. The first begins at Abbotsbury Castle and looks down on the coast at Weymouth and Portland. The second travels into the heart of the Isle of Purbeck before turning back to the coast at Corfe Castle.

Attributes
River; Downland/Wolds
Start
Sandbanks Ferry, North Haven Point, Poole SZ038871
Finish
South Haven Point, Sandbanks, Dorset SZ036867
Websites
http://arounddorsetwalk.co.uk
Maps
OS Landranger: 183, 184, 194, 195, 193
OS Explorer: 15, 22, 116, 117, 118, 120
Publications, badges and certificates
Booklets
Round Dorset Walk: Long Distance Footpath, the Illustrated Guide by Steven Crockford (Hobnob Press) 2006. ISBN 9780946418497. 112pp. £8.95.

Saints' Way/Forth an Syns STSW

CORNWALL **47km/29 miles**

The Way follows a route thought to have been taken by the ancient Cornish and Welsh Saints across mid-Cornwall, through valleys, woodland, moors and villages. From the north coast, it crosses St Breock Downs to reach Helman Tor Gate where there are options through either St Blazey or Milltown to the south coast.

Attributes
Pilgrimage; Religious
Start
Padstow, Cornwall SW920754
Finish
Fowey, Cornwall SX127522

Waymark
Celtic Cross on named signs
Websites
www.cornwall.gov.uk
Maps ◈
OS Landranger: 200, 204
OS Explorer: 106, 107, 109
Publications, badges and certificates
Folder
Saints' Way: Forth an Syns (Cornwall County Council) 1999. 12 laminated cards; A5. £3.99 (incs p&p). Includes accommodation leaflet.
Walking Support Providers
Celtic; Contours; Encounter; Let's Go Walking!

Salisbury Country Way SALCW

HANTS, WILTS 96km/60 miles

A varied downland route, from Stonehenge, around Salisbury through ancient woodlands and a number of chalk stream valleys following age-old tracks. Public transport access into Salisbury is available at a number of points.

Attributes
Downland/Wolds; Heritage
Start and Finish
Stonehenge, Wilts SU122423
Maps
OS Landranger: 184
OS Explorer: 118, 130, 131, 22
Publications, badges and certificates
Booklets
Salisbury Country Way (Bill Brown) 1998. 24pp; A5. £2.95 (incs p&p).
Certificate
Salisbury Country Way (Bill Brown). Free (+ A5 SAE).

Samaritans Way South West, Bristol to Lynton SWSW

BATH NES, BRISTOL, DEVON, N SOMERS, SOMERS 166km/103 miles

From the Avon Gorge, the route takes in the Chew Valley, the Mendip, Polden, Quantock and Brendon Hills, the Somerset Levels and Exmoor. There is a suggested extension of 30 miles along the coast path from Lynton to Croyde. The River Avon Trail could be used to link the Cotswold Way National Trail at Bath with the start of this route. All funds raised from sales go to the Samaritans.

Attributes
Lake/Reservoir; Downland/Wolds; Moorland; Charity
Start
Clifton Suspension Bridge, Bristol ST565731
Finish
Lynton, Devon SS721495
Maps ◈
OS Landranger: 172, 180, 181, 182, 183
OS Explorer: 9, 139, 140, 141, 154, 155
Publications, badges and certificates
Paperback
Walk from Bristol to Lynton by Graham Hoyle (Samaritans Way SW) 2000. ISBN 9780953776702. 96pp; 142 x 104. £4.95 (+ 50p p&p). Cheques to Samaritans Way SW.

Sidmouth Saunter SIDSR

DEVON 40km/25 miles

A circuit combining coastal footpath and picturesque East Devon scenery. There is also a 13-mile route.

Attributes
Challenging; Anytime Challenge; Coastal
Start and Finish
The Ham, Sidmouth, Devon SY129873
Maps
OS Landranger: 192
OS Explorer: 115
Publications, badges and certificates
Looseleaf
Sidmouth Saunter (Terry Bound). 3pp; A4. Free (+ SAE).
Badge & certificate
Sidmouth Saunter (Terry Bound). £1.00 (+ SAE) & free (+ A4 SAE).

Smugglers' Way SMGW

CORNWALL 59km/37 miles

A route across Bodmin Moor visiting Jamaica Inn, Dobwalls, Herodsfoot and Sowden's Bridge. Good navigation skills are essential.

Attributes
Challenging; Anytime Challenge; Moorland
Start
Boscastle, Cornwall SX094914
Finish
Looe, Cornwall SX257530
Websites
www.smugglersway.co.uk

Maps
OS Landranger: 190, 201
OS Explorer: 107, 109, 111
Publications, badges and certificates
Booklets
Smugglers' Way by Frank Squibb (Frank Squibb) 1997. 32pp; A5. £2.50 (incs p&p). Accommodation/public transport information free online or on request with booklet.
Certificates
Smugglers' Way (Frank Squibb). £2.00 (+ stamp).
Saints and Smugglers' 100 (Frank Squibb). £2.00 (+ stamp).

South Bristol Circular Walk SBCW

BRISTOL, N SOMERS 37km/23 miles

A city walk, devised by Bristol RA Group, offering good views within and across the city; exploring the Avon Valley; crossing the Clifton Suspension Bridge, and taking in Stockwood Nature Reserve, Dundry Hill, Ashton Court and the Waterfront.

Attributes
Downland/Wolds; Heritage
Start and Finish
Temple Meads Station, Bristol. ST596724
Websites
www.bristolramblers.org.uk
Maps
OS Landranger: 172
OS Explorer: 155
Publications, badges and certificates
Booklets
South Bristol Circular Walk (Bristol Tourist Information Centre). Free.

Tamar Valley Discovery Trail TVDT

CORNWALL, DEVON 48km/30 miles

A route along the valley of the River Tamar, through Bere Ferrers, Bere Alston, Gunnislake and Milton Abbot and crossing two rivers at Lopwell Dam (by foot) and Calstock (by train or ferry). The Trail links with the West Devon Way and Two Castles Trail to form a circuit of approximately 90 miles, dubbed as the 'West Devon Triangle'.

Attributes
River
Start
Tamerton Foliot, Devon SX470611

Finish
Launceston, Cornwall SX330846
Waymark
Outline of apple
Maps ◈
OS Landranger: 201
OS Explorer: 108, 112
Publications, badges and certificates
Brochure
Tamar Valley Discovery Trail (Devon County Council). A5. £4.50 (incs p&p) Quote Ref. DP19. Cheques to Devon County Council.

Tarka Trail TRKT

DEVON, SOMERS 291km/181 miles

The Trail traces the journeys of Tarka the Otter, taking in locations featured in the book. In effect, the Trail comprises two routes based on Barnstaple. The northern section takes an easterly line to, and over, Exmoor to reach the sea at Lynmouth. It then follows the coastline west through Braunton to the finish. The southern section goes through Bideford and Great Torrington to Okehampton and Sticklepath, returning north and terminating at Eggesford where advantage can be taken of a rail link back to Barnstaple. Both routes include sections in river valleys, including the Torridge, Taw, Bray, and above the East Lyn. The Taw-Teign Link (6 miles and on OS mapping) links the Tarka Trail at Sticklepath with the Two Moors Way at Chagford, on the northern fringe of Dartmoor. A second link, by way of the Little Dart Ridge & Valley Walk (11 miles and included on OS mapping), is available in connecting Eggesford with Witheridge, which is also on the Two Moors Way.

Attributes
Challenging; Coastal; River; Moorland
Start and Finish
Barnstaple, Devon SS558331
Waymark
Otter pawmark
Maps ◈
OS Landranger: 180, 190, 191
OS Explorer: 113, 126, 127, 139, 9, 28
Publications, badges and certificates
Leaflets
Tarka Trail: An Introduction by Devon County Council (Devon County Council). Free (+ SAE) Quote Ref. DP101.
Taw-Teign Link (Devon County Council). 6pp; A4. Free (+ SAE) Quote Ref. DP36.
Ridge & Valley Walk (Devon County Council). 12pp; A4. Free (+ SAE) Quote Ref. DP35.

Guidebook
Tarka Trail: Guide Pack (Devon County Council) 1995. 88pp; 150 x 230. £3.50 (incs p&p) Quote Ref. DP102. Cheques to Devon County Council.
Walking Support Providers
Celtic; Contours; Explore Britain; Let's Go Walking!; Westcountry

Templer Way — TEMW

DEVON — **29km/18 miles**

Named after the Templer family, who constructed the Stover Canal and Tramway which brought granite quarried at Haytor on Dartmoor to the coast at Teignmouth, the Way provides interest for ecological reasons as well as for the locks and buildings. The terrain ranges from open moor to woodland and estuary foreshore. The Way connects to the South West Coast Path having the ferry between Shaldon and Teignmouth in common.

Attributes
Moorland; Heritage
Start
Haytor Quarry, Devon SX760776
Finish
Teignmouth, Devon SX943731
Waymark
White logo on brown (not on open moorland)
Maps ◈
OS Landranger: 191, 192, 202
OS Explorer: 28, 110
Publications, badges and certificates
Leaflets
Templer Way by Devon County Council (Devon County Council). Free (+ SAE) Quote Ref. DP38.

Two Castles Trail — TCST

CORNWALL, DEVON — **38km/24 miles**

The Trail follows river valleys, ridge roads, open downland and woods away from the northern edges of Dartmoor, linking the imposing Norman castles at Okehampton and Launceston. The Trail is coincident with the West Devon Way between Okehampton and Bridestowe. The Trail links with the Tamar Valley Discovery Trail and the West Devon Way to form a circuit of approximately 90 miles, dubbed the 'West Devon Triangle'.

Attributes
River; Downland/Wolds; Heritage
Start
Okehampton, Devon SX589952
Finish
Launceston, Cornwall SX331848
Waymark
Named logo
Maps ◈
OS Landranger: 190, 191, 201
OS Explorer: 112, 113, 28
Publications, badges and certificates
Paperbacks
Two Castles Trail (Devon County Council) 1997. A5. £3.50 Quote Ref. DP41. Cheques to Devon County Council.

Two Counties Way — TCOW

DEVON, SOMERS — **90km/56 miles**

The path follows the route of the Grand Western Canal to Tiverton and then down the Exe Valley, via Bickleigh, Silverton, Killerton and Broad Clyst to Exeter. The final section takes in the towpath of the Exeter Ship Canal, and Powderham (with its Castle), to reach the end at Starcross. Passing through, or near to, Bradford on Tone, Wellington, Tiverton, Bickleigh, Exeter and Kenton, the route is coincident in short sections with the West Deane Way, Grand Western Canal walk and the Exe Valley Walk. In essence it provides a link from Taunton to the South West Coast Path National Trail.

Attributes
River; Canal
Start
French Weir, Taunton, Somers ST220249
Finish
Starcross, Devon SX973817
Waymark
Named signs with coot logo
Websites
www.tauntonramblers.org.uk
Maps
OS Landranger: 181, 192, 193
OS Explorer: 110, 114, 128
Publications, badges and certificates
Leaflets
Two Counties Way (Taunton TIC). A4/3. Free (+ 9 x 6 SAE). Schematic maps on route website.
Certificate
Two Counties Way (Gary Broom). Free (+ A4 SAE).

Two Moors Way (Devon Coast to Coast) TWOMW

DEVON, SOMERS **145km/90 miles**

A route across Dartmoor, over exposed moorland, to Teigncombe from where the River Teign is followed to Castle Drogo. Exmoor National Park is reached at Tarr Steps and the Way then climbs to Exe Head and through Cheriton to the finish. Access to Ivybridge from the South Devon coast can be achieved by way of waymarked trails, both included on OS mapping. These are the Erme-Plym Trail (10 miles) which provides a route from each of Plymouth and Wembury to Brixton, and then a single route to Sequer's Bridge near Ermington. From here the Erme Valley Trail (3 miles) can be taken to Ivybridge. Devon County Council are supporting and promoting this route together with the Erme-Plym Trail as a 'Coast to Coast' route from Lynmouth to Wembury. They have produced a new publication covering the whole route. See below for details. The Taw-Teign Link (6 miles and on OS mapping) links the Tarka Trail at Sticklepath and the Two Moors Way at Chagford, on the northern fringe of Dartmoor.

Attributes
Challenging; River; Moorland
Start
Ivybridge, Devon SX636563
Finish
Lynmouth, Devon SS721497
Waymark
Letters MW on standard waymarks
Maps ◈
OS Landranger: 180, 181, 191, 202
OS Explorer: 9, 20, 28, 113, 114, 127
Publications, badges and certificates
Paperbacks
Two Moors Way/Devon Coast to Coast incorporating Erme-Plym Trail (Devon County Council). A5. £4.99 Quote Ref. DP15. Cheques to Devon County Council.
Two Moors Way by James Roberts (Cicerone Press) 1994. ISBN 9781852841591. 96pp. £5.99.
Booklets
Two Moors Way/Coast to Coast Walk incorporating the Erme-Plym Trail (Two Moors Way Association) 1996. ISBN 9780900613432. 48pp; A5. £4.95 (incs p&p). Cheques to Two Moors Way Association.
Looseleaf
Two Moors Way: Accommodation List (Two Moors Way Association). A5. £2.00 (+ SAE). Cheques to Two Moors Way Association.
Badge & certificate
Two Moors Way (Two Moors Way Association). £1.00 each (+ SAE). Cheques to Two Moors Way Association.
Leaflets
Two Moors Way: Introductory Leaflet by Devon County Council (Devon County Council). Free (+ SAE) Quote Ref. DP34.
CD ROM
Running the Two Moors Way by Roy McKee (Mind Technology Limited). £8.00. CD version. Includes a full photograph gallery.
Illustrated map guide
Two Moors Way: Illustrated Map (Two Moors Way Association). 620 x 210. £1.50 (incs p&p). Cheques to Two Moors Way Association.
Walking Support Providers
Celtic; Contours; Let's Go Walking!; Westcountry

Two Rivers Way TRW

BATH NES, N SOMERS **32km/20 miles**

This route from Congresbury, in the River Yeo valley, to Keynsham, on the River Avon, where it meets the River Avon Trail (25 miles and on OS mapping), passes through farmland and historic villages, such as Chew Stoke, Chew Magna and Compton Dando. The Three Peaks Circular Walk (17 miles and on OS mapping) which takes in the gentle tops of Maes Knoll, Knowle Hill and Blackberry Hill crosses the Way at Pensford and Chew Magna.

Attributes
Lake/Reservoir; River
Start
Congresbury, N Somers ST438639
Finish
Keynsham, Bath NES ST658690

Waymark
Named discs with wave motif
Maps ◈
OS Landranger: 172, 182
OS Explorer: 154, 155
Publications, badges and certificates
Booklets
Two Rivers Way by Marian Barraclough (Yatton Ramblers) 1992. ISBN 9780951134269. 42pp; A5. £3.15 (incs p&p). Used copies only.
Leaflets
Two Rivers: Congresbury to Keynsham (Bath & North East Somerset Council). A4/3. Free.
Three Peaks Circular Walk (Forest of Avon). A4/3. Free (+ 9 x 4 SAE).

Wessex Heights Walk WXHW

DORSET, WILTS **124km/77 miles**

Devised to use some less-walked paths over hills and with a minimum of road walking. It passes several hill forts with views across eastern Dorset and south Wiltshire. The route also visits Salisbury.

Attributes
Downland/Wolds; Heritage
Start
Maiden Castle, Dorchester, Dorset SY667885
Finish
Old Sarum, Salisbury, Wilts SU137328
Maps
OS Landranger: 184, 194
OS Explorer: 117, 118, 130
Publications, badges and certificates
Booklets
Walking the Wessex Heights (Marjorie Kerr). 64pp; A5. £1.50 (incs p&p).

Wessex Ridgeway WXRW

DEVON, DORSET, WILTS **221km/137 miles**

One of the links of a prehistoric route, often called the Greater Ridgeway, from The Wash to the Dorset Coast, it extends from the Ridgeway National Trail to the south-west. On its way through Wiltshire it takes in the stone circles at Avebury (a World Heritage Site jointly with Stonehenge), the Vale of Pewsey, the northern edge of Salisbury Plain, the Wylye Valley and Win Greene Hill. Then, in Dorset, it visits Cranbourne Chase, Cerne Abbas with the 180ft high Cerne Giant, and Pilsden Pen, before a short route through Devon leads to the finish, back in Dorset. At Marlborough, a five-mile link leads to the waymarked Wansdyke Path (14 miles and on OS mapping). The publication for this walk includes the Tan Hill Way (7 miles, waymarked and on OS mapping).

Attributes
Horse Ride (Multi User); Downland/Wolds; Heritage
Start
Marlborough, Wilts SU187685
Finish
Lyme Regis, Dorset SY347922
Waymark
Wessex wyvern on named green discs (Dorset only)
Websites
www.dorsetforyou.com
Maps ◈
OS Landranger: 173, 183, 184, 193, 194, 195
OS Explorer: 116, 117, 118, 129, 130, 143, 157
Publications, badges and certificates
Paperbacks
Greater Ridgeway: A walk from Lyme Regis to Hunstanton by Ray Quinlan (Cicerone Press) 2003. ISBN 9781852843465. 256pp; 172 x 116. £12.95.
Leaflets
Wessex Ridgeway Trail (Dorset County Council) 2006. A4/3. Free.
Folder
Wansdyke Path & Tan Hill Way (Kennet District Council). 7 leaflets. £2.00 (+ 50p p&p). Cheques to Kennet District Council.
Walking Support Providers
Explore Britain

West Deane Way WDW

SOMERS **72km/45 miles**

Providing a variety of landscapes, including the flood plain and wooded valley of the River Tone, and the Quantock Hills AONB, the route visits Appley, Waterrow, Wiveliscombe, Lydiard St Lawrence and Kingston St Mary. There are industrial remains, historic houses and gardens on or near to the route. It is coincident with the Somerset section of the Grand Western Canal walk between Greenham and Taunton.

Attributes
River; Canal; Downland/Wolds; Heritage; Industrial History
Start and Finish
Taunton, Somers ST226248
Waymark
Named dark green discs
Websites
www.somerset.gov.uk
Maps ◈
OS Landranger:181, 182, 193
OS Explorer: 9, 128, 140
Publications, badges and certificates
Softback (spiral bound)
West Deane Way (Taunton Tourist Information Centre) 1999. 57pp; A5. £5.00 (+ £1.00 p&p).

West Devon Way WDVW

DEVON, PLYMOUTH **57km/35 miles**

The Way explores the rugged and spectacular countryside on the western fringe of the Dartmoor National

Park along the 18 miles between Okehampton, where it links with the Tarka Trail, and Tavistock. From there it continues a further 17 miles mainly in river valleys to Plymouth where it connects with the Erme-Plym Trail – see Two Moors Way. After Tavistock the River Walkham is crossed and below Yelverton the valleys of the Meavy and Plym are followed. The Way links with the Tamar Valley Discovery Trail and the Two Castles Trail to form a circuit of approximately 90 miles, dubbed the 'West Devon Triangle'.

Attributes
Challenging; Cycle Route; Moorland
Start
Okehampton, Devon SX589953
Finish
Plymouth SX503529
Waymark
Stylised walker/church on hilltop
Maps ◈
OS Landranger: 191, 201, 202
OS Explorer: 20, 28, 108, 112, 113
Publications, badges and certificates
Folder
West Devon Way (Devon County Council) 1999. 16pp; A5. £4.50 (incs p&p) Quote Ref. DP16. Cheques to Devon County Council.

Wylye Way — WYW

WILTS — **50km/31 miles**

A walk along the River Wylye linking the great Wiltshire estates of Stourhead, Longleat and Wilton through a mixture of scenery including chalk downland and watermeadows. The guide features numerous public houses.

Attributes
River; Downland/Wolds; Heritage
Start
Stourhead Visitor Car Park, Wilts ST777340
Finish
Wilton House Park, Wilts SU104308
Maps
OS Landranger: 183, 184
OS Explorer: 130, 142, 143
Publications, badges and certificates
Booklets
Wylye Way by Bill Brown (Bill Brown) 2002. 24pp; A5. £2.95 (incs p&p).
Certificate
Wylye Way (Bill Brown). Free (+ A5 SAE).

WEST MIDLANDS & SOUTHERN WELSH BORDERS

Hereford Cathedral, corner point on the Three Choirs Way, and start of Wye to the Thames

KEY FACTS	
Areas	Gloucestershire, Herefordshire, Warwickshire, Worcestershire, West Midlands
Principal AONBs	Malvern Hills, The Cotswolds (part), Wye Valley (part)
E-Routes	E2 (Eastern Variant: Dover – Stranraer)
National Trails	(England) part of each of Offa's Dyke Path, Cotswold Way, Thames Path
Walking Routes	51 main routes (3594 miles); 22 waymarked (2031 miles)
Resident population	3.75 million

DON'T MISS! TRAIL SECTIONS (CHALLENGING/REMOTE MARKED WITH *)	
Wysis/Gloucestershire Ways	Mitcheldean to Bream, across Forest of Dean in mixed woods, sculpture trail/visitor centre option halfway* (16kms, 1200ft, navigation in forests!)
Wye Valley Walk	Walford/Kerne Bridge to Symonds Yat (East) Rock, waterside walking, gorge views (13kms, or extend west on river)
Cotswold Way	Leckhampton Hill to Cooper's Hill/A46, high along wooded Cotswold scarps (14km, 1500ft, passes Crickley Hill Country Park with visitor centre)
Cotswold Way	Painswick to Stonehouse/A46, more wooded Cotswold scarps, (14km, 1400ft up/1600ft down)
Wysis Way	Mitcheldean to Symonds Yat (East), across Forest of Dean in mixed woods* (16kms, 1400ft, navigation in forests!)
North Worcestershire Path	Clent Hills to Lickey Hills Country Parks, peaks near Birmingham (13kms, 1500ft up, 1300ft down, three visitor centres via Windmill Hill CP)
Worcestershire Way	near Martley (just off route) across Suckley Hills/Ankerdine Hill/Malverns to Great Malvern (22km, 2500ft ascent); extra Malverns tops options (North Hill or Worcestershire Beacon)
Mortimer Trail	Ludlow to Asymestry (21km, 2400ft ascent), with three hills – Mary Knoll, High Vinnals, Yatton Hill

The path meanders as it traverses the main ridge of the Malvern Hills

WEST MIDLANDS & SOUTHERN WELSH BORDERS

The West Midlands and southern Welsh borders is a region with varied terrain from productive, gentle, rolling farmland to steep ridges and fine riverside walking. It also has distinctive villages and cathedral cities of distinction.

Geography

While it has no true coastline, the River Severn flows south, bisecting it through Gloucestershire and Worcestershire to reach its wide, funnel-shaped estuary with the world's second largest tidal range. Here there are sandbanks, wide mudflats and marshes, home to waterfowl. To the west of the Severn the higher Dean Plateau, with the extensive mixed woodlands of the Forest of Dean, is cut by the dramatic limestone gorge of the River Wye. To reach here the Wye has traversed the fertile lowlands of Herefordshire from its source in the Welsh mountains beyond, crossing Offa's Dyke Path National Trail that traces some of the Welsh border.

To the east of the Severn, now in Gloucestershire, the wooded Cotswold Hills scarp rises sharply. These limestone hills extend north east to the Warwickshire border, making the line for the Cotswold Way National Trail. East of the Cotswolds the infant Thames rises, to start the Thames Path National Trail. The Wysis Way links Offa's Dyke Path to the Thames Path, crossing the three distinctive areas of the Forest of Dean, Severn Vale and Cotswolds.

The northern extent of this region is in the densely populated West Midlands, where the terrain is gentler. This is now an industrial heartland with its roots in the coal seams and mineral wealth that once underlay it and its prosperity – when its smoking chimneys earned it its name, the 'Black Country'.

The Trails

Many walking routes trace the region's **rivers**. The Severn Way follows this principal river while the Wye, the other major river flowing into the Severn estuary, is traced by the Wye Valley Walk. The Wye to the Thames route links these two rivers. The Ross Round is an undulating circuit around Ross including the Wye. The walkable Monnow forms part of Herefordshire's border, and the Dore in turn flows down the fertile Golden Valley, traversed by the Herefordshire Trail, to join the Monnow. The Avon crosses Warwickshire through Stratford-upon-Avon, marked by Shakespeare's Avon Way. The Leadon Valley Walks cover a Severn tributary known as a 'secret river' as it avoids any significant settlements, and a shorter linked walk, the Daffodil Way–Dymock is popular in spring. The hilly Mortimer Trail crosses the Teme, Lugg and Arrow on its way from Ludlow (in Shropshire) to Kington. The Riversides Way, in the Welsh Marches, joins the valleys and hills of the Teme and Lugg, while the Teme Valley Walk follows this rural river.

Canal walking fans are also well supplied. The Navigation Way, Oxford Canal Walk, Worcester & Birmingham Canal Walk and Cotswold Canals Walk, all offer miles of easy towpath. The long Grand Union Canal Walk has its northern terminus in Birmingham, from where the Birmingham to Aberystwyth Walk heads for Wales along Black Country canals. The Elan Valley Way broadly follows an aqueduct supplying water to Birmingham.

Viewed from the east, the ridge of the **Malvern Hills** rises dramatically from the surrounding Worcestershire lowlands. Its roots are a resistant granitic intrusion, the oldest such rocks in Britain, running south to north. Several smaller ranges continue this trend northwards, including the Suckley and Abberley Hills and, below Birmingham, the Clent Hills. This ridge line is taken by the Worcestershire Way. The Geopark Way highlights geology and landscape by linking geological sites in the Abberley and Malvern Hills Global Geopark, and in the Wyre Forest coalfield. Bredon Hill is an outlier west of the Cotswolds and its Saxon ridgeway is visited by several routes: the Wychavon Way, linking the Severn and Costwolds, St Kenelm's Way and the Bredon Climber.

West Midlands and South Welsh Borders – major routes

Only major routes from this region (excluding any National Trails) are shown here. The National Trails are shown on the map in the National Trails section of this handbook. For the full network of trails visit the LDWA website – www.ldwa.org.uk.

Bourton on the Water in the Cotswolds

City and **town** routes are not forgotten, with Birmingham a walker-friendly city. There are good trails leading from these centres and other routes nearby, all with good transport links. For long routes the Birmingham Greenway provides an urban traverse linking green spaces. The Beacon Way is a green route from Sandwell at the heart of the West Midlands conurbation with lakes, nature reserves, woods, and the banks of canals, while the linking waymarked Forest of Mercia Timberland Trail lies in this Community Forest north of Walsall. The North Worcestershire Path links four country parks on the southern edge of the Birmingham conurbation. The Arden Way is a route with a historic theme in the Forest of Arden. Several routes encircle other cities, such as 'A Coventry Way' (that mimics Wainwright's naming!), the Nuneaton Rotary Walk, Southam Circular Walk, Bromsgrove Circular Walk and Cheltenham Circular Footpath, while the Glevum Way is a Ramblers' Jubilee route around Gloucester. The Herefordshire Trail visits all eight of the county's market towns. The aptly named 'The WaLK' links Warwick, Leamington Spa and Kenilworth. The Seven Shires Way counties tour visits Warwickshire and Gloucestershire at its westerly limits.

Among the **themed** routes, monarchy is remembered with the start of the very long Monarch's Way, first taken by Charles II. Literary figures are led by the Bard from Stratford, with Shakespeare's Way following in his footsteps to London. The Three Choirs Way links the festival cities of Gloucester, Hereford and Worcester with a musical theme. The Black and White Villages Trail features this unusual Herefordshire architectural style. The Warwickshire Villages Trail links 71 villages. The Donnington Way has a distinctly hoppy flavour, based on the Cotswold brewery of Donnington in Stow-on-the-Wold and its 15 pubs. The D'Arcy Dalton Way starts in Warwickshire, a CPRE route, it is named after the late Colonel WP d'Arcy Dalton who worked for over half a century to preserve rights of way in Oxfordshire and it is mainly in that county. The Centenary Way (Warwickshire) marks that county's anniversary year. The Cotswold Diamond Way is another Ramblers' Jubilee walk visiting many small villages using quiet footpaths. Religious themes are featured in the St Kenelm's Way and Trail, that join the two places linked with the legend of St Kenelm, grandson of King Offa, going from the Clent Hills south-west of Birmingham, the scene of his death, to his Cotswolds burial place at Winchcombe.

There are many **enthusiasts' routes** on offer, for those seeking a greater challenge. Two developers account for most of these. Eric Perks' many charity challenges here include the Abberley Amble, Carpet Bagger's 50, Chaddesley Chase, Crooked Spire Walk, Kinver Clamber, Mini Alps, Robert's Romp and the Wyre Forest Alpine Walk. David Irons is the creator of the Black Pear Marathon, Bredon Climber, Malvern Link, North Worcestershire Hills Marathon, Severn Valley Marathon and Wychavon Marathon. In addition, John Merrill provides the Malvern Hill Challenge Walk.

ROUTE CODES

GLOUCSW	Gloucestershire Way
GUCW	Grand Union Canal Walk
HOEW	Heart of England Way
NWORP	North Worcestershire Path
MACBA	Macmillan Way
MONW	Monarch's Way
OXCW	Oxford Canal Walk
OXFW	Oxfordshire Way
SEVW	Severn Way
SHKW	Shakespeare's Way
STFW	Staffordshire Way
WORCW	Worcestershire Way
WYEVW	Wye Valley Walk

Abberley Amble — ABAM

WORCS — **32km/20 miles**

An undulating route through woods and valleys, it passes Glasshampton Monastery, the Burf (a cider house) and Grubbers Alley. Profits go to a local club catering for disabled youngsters.

Attributes
Challenging; Anytime Challenge; Charity
Start and Finish
Bewdley, Worcs SO788754
Maps
OS Landranger: 138
OS Explorer: 204, 218
Publications, badges and certificates
Looseleaf
Abberley Amble by Eric Perks (Eric Perks). 4pp; A4. £1.00 (+ 9 x 6 SAE). Cheques to Blakebrook Gym Club.
Badge & certificate
Abberley Amble (Eric Perks). £2.00 & £1.00 (+ SAE). Cheques to Blakebrook Gym Club.

Arden Way — ARDW

WARKS — **42km/26 miles**

Developed by the Heart of England Way Association, this Forest of Arden route visits Henley in Arden, Alcester, and Ullenhall. It is coincident, in parts, with the Heart of England Way between Henley and south of Alcester.

Attributes
Heritage
Start and Finish
Henley-in-Arden, Warks SP151658
Waymark
White arrow on green background, motif on the arrow and named
Websites
http://ardenway.org, www.heartofenglandway.org
Maps ◈
OS Landranger: 150, 151
OS Explorer: 205, 220
Publications, badges and certificates
Booklets
Arden Way Guide (Heart of England Way Association). £3.00 (+ 50p p&p). Cheques to Heart of England Way Association to S. Cross, 20 Ridgeley Close, Warwick, CV34 5FD.
Badge
Arden Way (Heart of England Way Association). £1.65 (incs p&p).

Beacon Way — BEAW

STAFFS, W MIDLANDS — **40km/25 miles**

A green route from Sandwell, at the heart of the West Midlands conurbation, via the outskirts of Birmingham through the countryside of Walsall and into Staffordshire. It takes in the Forest of Mercia, lakes, nature reserves, woods, and canal banks. The northern end links with the Heart of England Way on Gentleshaw Common. Only the section from Sandwell to Chasewater is shown on OS maps. The linking way-marked Forest of Mercia Timberland Trail (9 miles and on OS mapping) is a circular walk in the Forest of Mercia north of Walsall.

Attributes
Easy; Cycle Route; Lake/Reservoir; Canal; Urban
Start
Sandwell Park Farm, W Midlands SP019914
Finish
Gentleshaw Common, Staffs SK050119
Waymark
Horseshoe and name on black disc
Maps ◈
OS Landranger: 139
OS Explorer: 220, 244
Publications, badges and certificates
Binder (weatherproof route cards)
Roots & Leaves: Walks for all in the Forest of Mercia by Staffordshire County Council (Forest of Mercia). £10.00 (+ £2.00 p&p). Beacon Way and other routes, includes updates service.

Birmingham and Aberystwyth Walk — BIRABW

CEREDIGION, HEREFS, POWYS, SHROPS, STAFFS, W MIDLANDS, WORCS — **238km/148 miles**

It follows canals through the Black Country to Stourbridge, crosses rural Shropshire, visiting the high point of Titterstone Clee before entering Wales at Knighton. It then goes over wild hilly country to reach Rhaeadr. After skirting the Elan Valley reservoirs, more desolate moorland is crossed to Devil's Bridge before it meets the coast.

Attributes
Lake/Reservoir; Canal; Moorland
Start
Gas Street Canal Basin, Birmingham, W Midlands SP062866
Finish
Bridge Street, Aberystwyth, Ceredigion SN583813
Maps
OS Landranger: 135, 138, 139, 147, 148
OS Explorer: 187, 200, 201, 203, 213, 218, 219, 220
Publications, badges and certificates
Paperbacks
Birmingham & Aberystwyth Walk by John Roberts (Walkways) 2001. ISBN 9780947708375. 128pp; A5. £7.50 (incs p&p).

Birmingham Greenway — BGW

W MIDLANDS — **37km/23 miles**

Across Birmingham from the north east to the south western edges using many of the city's green spaces, ending less than half a mile from the North Worcestershire Path.

Attributes
Easy; Urban
Start
Camp Farm, Watford Gap, W Midlands SK117003
Finish
Ten Ashes Lane, Cofton Hackett, W Midlands SP001758
Maps
OS Landranger: 139
OS Explorer: 220
Map (Other)
Cycling and Walking Map Birmingham (Birmingham City Council)
Publications, badges and certificates
Paperbacks
Birmingham Greenway by Fred Willits (Meridian Books) 2000. ISBN 9781869922405. 64pp; A5. £4.95 (+ £1.00 p&p).

Black Pear Marathon — BLPM

WORCS — **42km/26 miles**

A walk including some of the finest hill walking encountered along the Worcestershire Way.

Attributes
Challenging; Anytime Challenge
Start and Finish
New Inn, Noutards Green, Stourport, Glos SO799663
Maps
OS Landranger: 138
OS Explorer: 218
Publications, badges and certificates
Looseleaf
Black Pear Marathon by Dave Irons (Dave Irons). £1.00 (incs p&p).

Bredon Climber — BRC

WORCS — **35km/22 miles**

An intricate circuit and exploration of Bredon Hill in south-east Worcestershire. To complete the tour, all the checkpoints must be visited in the correct order.

Attributes
Challenging; Anytime Challenge
Start and Finish
Elmley Castle, Worcs SO983414
Maps
OS Landranger: 150
OS Explorer: 190
Publications, badges and certificates
Looseleaf
Bredon Climber by Dave Irons (Dave Irons). 5pp. £1.00 (incs p&p).

Bromsgrove Circular Walk — BGCW

WORCS — **48km/30 miles**

Devised by Bromsgrove Ramblers to celebrate their 30th anniversary, it starts at Wychbold and visits Chaddesley Corbett, the Lickey Hills, Alvechurch and Tardebigge.

Attributes
Easy; Canal
Start and Finish
Wychbold, Worcestershire SO928668
Maps
OS Landranger: 139, 150
OS Explorer: 204, 219, 220
Publications, badges and certificates
Booklets
Circular Walk around Bromsgrove by Bromsgrove Ramblers (Bromsgrove Ramblers) 2003. 16pp; A5. £1.50. Cheques to Ramblers Association Bromsgrove Group.

Carpet Baggers 50 CB50

SHROPS, STAFFS, WORCS **80km/50 miles**

The route passes through Bewdley, along the Severn Valley, taking in Seckley Wood, the Wyre Forest, Arley, Alverley, Claverley, Seisdon, Trysul, Abbot's Hill, Staffordshire Way and Kinver Edge.

Attributes
Challenging; Anytime Challenge; River; Moorland; Charity
Start and Finish
Stourport-on-Severn, Worcs SO815736
Maps
OS Landranger: 138, 139
OS Explorer: 218, 219
Publications, badges and certificates
Looseleaf
Carpet Baggers 50 (Eric Perks). 4pp; A4. £1.00 (+ 9 x 6 SAE). Cheques to Blakebrook Gym Club.
Badge & certificate
Carpet Baggers 50 (Eric Perks). £2.00 & 50p (+ large SAE). Cheques to Blakebrook Gym Club.

Centenary Way (Warwickshire) CWW

WARKS **158km/98 miles**

Celebrating one hundred years of Warwickshire County Council, it passes the Tame Valley, Atherstone Ridge, the George Eliot country around Nuneaton, before passing to the east of Coventry to Kenilworth, Warwick and Leamington Spa. From here it heads to the Burton Dassett Hills, Edge Hill, Shipston-on-Stour and Ilmington Downs.

Attributes
Literary
Start
Kingsbury Water Park, Warks SP204959
Finish
Upper Quinton, Warks SP177464
Waymark
Bear and ragged staff in green on white disc
Maps ◈
OS Landranger: 139, 140, 151
OS Explorer: 191, 205, 206, 221, 222, 232, 45
Publications, badges and certificates
Paperbacks
Centenary Way by Geoff Allen, John Roberts (Walkways) 1996. ISBN 9780947708337. 124pp; 210 x 145. £7.50 (incs p&p).

Chaddesley Chase CHDC

WORCS **35km/22 miles**

A route on open fields and following streams and lanes taking in Chaddesley, Santery Hill, Pepper Wood and Hillpool Mill.

Attributes
Anytime Challenge; Charity
Start and Finish
Chaddesley Corbett, Worcs SO892736
Maps
OS Landranger: 138, 139
OS Explorer: 218, 219
Publications, badges and certificates
Looseleaf
Chaddesley Chase by Eric Perks (Eric Perks). 4pp; A4. £1.00 (+ 9 x 6 SAE). Cheques to Blakebrook Gym Club.
Badge & certificate
Chaddesley Chase (Eric Perks). £2.00 (+ SAE) & £1.00 (+ 9 x 6 SAE). Cheques to Blakebrook Gym Club.

Cheltenham Circular Footpath CHCF

GLOS **40km/25 miles**

A route around Cheltenham with views of the Cotswold escarpment and the Severn Vale.

Attributes
No significant attribute
Start and Finish
Cheltenham, Glos SO955237
Waymark
Walk name under a green tree
Maps
OS Landranger: 162, 163
OS Explorer: 179
Publications, badges and certificates
Booklets
Cheltenham Circular Footpath (Reardon Publishing) 1996. ISBN 9781873877173. 40pp; 206 x 144. £4.95 (+ 50p p&p).

Cotswold Canals Walk COTCW

GLOS, WILTS **76km/47 miles**

From the Severn to the Thames it follows the line of old canals through scenic countryside, sometimes passing interesting industrial archaeology sites.

Attributes
Canal; Industrial History
Start
Framilode, Glos SO750104
Finish
Lechlade, Glos SU214994
Websites
www.countryside-matters.co.uk
Maps
OS Landranger: 162, 163
OS Explorer: 168, 169, 170, 14
Publications, badges and certificates
Paperbacks
Cotswold Canals Walk: Stroudwater, Thames and Severn by Gerry Stewart, Genny Proctor (Countryside Matters) 2000. ISBN 9780952787037. 96pp; A5. £5.95 (incs p&p).

Cotswold Ring COTSR

GLOS, WORCS **89km/55 miles**

This route takes in many Cotswold villages, including Bourton-on-the-Water, Stow-on-the-Wold and Moreton-in-Marsh. It has links with the Cotswold Way National Trail & Heart of England Way.

Attributes
No significant attribute
Start and Finish
Cheltenham, Glos SO237955
Maps
OS Landranger: 150, 151, 163
OS Explorer: 179, 45
Publications, badges and certificates
Booklets
Cotswold Ring by Christopher Knowles (Reardon Publishing) 1996. ISBN 9781873877166. 40pp; 210 x 150. £2.95 (+ 50p p&p).

Coventry Way COVW

WARKS, W MIDLANDS **64km/40 miles**

A circuit never more than five miles or so from the centre of Coventry. It is partly coincident with the Heart of England and Centenary (Warwickshire) Ways and visits a number of villages and hamlets including Stoneleigh, Bubbenhall, Ryton, Wolston, Bretford, Brinklow, Ansty, Barnacle and Corley Moor. The route is fully named 'A Coventry Way', in Wainwright's footsteps.

Attributes
No significant attribute
Start and Finish
Queens Head, Old Road, Meriden, Warks SP252820
Waymark
Named disc with three white spires on green background
Websites
www.acoventryway.org.uk
Maps ◈
OS Landranger: 140
OS Explorer: 221, 222
Publications, badges and certificates
Booklets
Coventry Way by Cyril J. Bean (A Coventry Way Association) 2000. 20pp; A5. £1.00 (+ 50p p&p). Cheques to ACWA.
Certificate
Coventry Way (A Coventry Way Association). Free (+ A5 SAE). Includes 40 miler club card.

Crooked Spire Walk CSPW

SHROPS, WORCS **35km/22 miles**

A route taking in Wyre Forest, Buckridge, Bayton, Cleobury Mortimer (which has a church with a crooked spire) and Shakenhurst.

Attributes
Anytime Challenge; Religious; Charity
Start and Finish
Bewdley, Worcs SO752740
Maps
OS Landranger: 138
OS Explorer: 218
Publications, badges and certificates
Looseleaf
Crooked Spire Walk by Eric Perks (Eric Perks). 4pp; A4. £1.00 (+ 9 x 6 SAE). Cheques to Blakebrook Gym Club.
Certificate
Crooked Spire Walk (Eric Perks). £1.00 (+A4 SAE).

d'Arcy Dalton Way DRDW

GLOS, OXON, WARKS **107km/66 miles**

Devised, with involvement from the CPRE, to mark the Oxford Footpaths Society Diamond Jubilee. It is named after the late Col. W. P. d'Arcy Dalton who worked for over half a century to preserve rights of way in Oxfordshire. It links four major paths that cross Oxfordshire: Oxford Canal Walk, Oxfordshire Way, Thames Path and Ridgeway, following roughly the western boundary of Oxfordshire in unspoilt

The drum towers of White Castle reflect in a moat near Llantilio Crossenny

countryside. It takes a meandering route, crossing ironstone hills to Epwell and Hook Norton, and following footpaths and tracks across the limestone uplands of the eastern Cotswolds via Great and Little Rollright, Churchill, Fifield, Great Barrington and Holwell. The route crosses the River Thames at Radcot Bridge and continues across the flatter farmland of the Vale of the White Horse, finally climbing to the crest of the chalk ridge of the Oxfordshire Downs, along which the Ridgeway runs. The guidebook includes eight circular walks.

Attributes
Downland/Wolds; Heritage
Start
Wormleighton, Warks SP448518
Finish
Wayland's Smithy, Oxon SU281853
Waymark
Named signs
Maps
OS Landranger: 151, 163, 164, 174
OS Explorer: 170, 191, 206, 45
Publications, badges and certificates
Paperback
d'Arcy Dalton Way across the Oxfordshire Cotswolds and Thames Valley by Nick Moon (Book Castle) 1999. ISBN 9781871199345. 128pp; A5. £6.99.
Leaflets
Walk the d'Arcy Dalton Way (Abingdon Information). A4/3. Free to personal callers. Tourist information and schematic map only.

Diamond Way (North Cotswold) NCDW

GLOS **105km/65 miles**

This imaginative and scenic route through rural Gloucestershire was created by the RA's North Cotswold Group to celebrate the 60th Jubilee in 1995. Using quiet footpaths the roughly diamond shaped walk visits many small villages and stretches from Northleach in the south to near Chipping Campden in the north, and from Guiting Power in the west to near Bourton-on-the-Water in the east.

Attributes
Easy
Start and Finish
Moreton-in-Marsh, Glos SP205324
Waymark
Blue diamond

Maps ◈
OS Landranger: 150, 151, 163, 164
OS Explorer: 205, 45
Publications, badges and certificates
Paperback
North Cotswold Diamond Way by Elizabeth Bell (RA Gloucestershire Area) 2001. ISBN 9781901184372. 100pp; A5. £6.99 (+ £2.00 p&p). Cheques to Ramblers Association (North Cotswold Group).
Walking Support Providers
HF

Donnington Way DONW

GLOS, OXON, WARKS, WORCS **99km/62 miles**

Based on the Cotswold brewery of Donnington in Stow-on-the-Wold, the Way's theme is the brewery and its 15 pubs. It visits Bourton-on-the-Water, Naunton, Guiting Power, Broadway, Chipping Campden and Moreton-in-Marsh.

Attributes
Easy; River
Start and Finish
Stow-on-the-Wold, Glos SP192258
Waymark
Beer mug in brown and name
Maps
OS Landranger: 150, 151, 163
OS Explorer: 45
Publications, badges and certificates
Paperbacks
Donnington Way by Colin Handy (Reardon Publishing) 1991. ISBN 9781874192008. 44pp; A5. £4.95 (+ 50p p&p).

Elan Valley Way EVW

HEREFS, POWYS, SHROPS, WORCS **206km/128 miles**

The route keeps within three miles of the Elan Valley aqueduct, a Birmingham water supply, and passes through Cookley, Bewdley, Ludlow, Knighton and Rhayader.

Attributes
River
Start
Frankley, Worcs SO999804
Finish
Elan Valley Visitor Centre, Powys SN935645

Maps
OS Landranger: 138, 139, 147, 148
OS Explorer: 200, 201, 203, 218, 219
Publications, badges and certificates
Paperback
Elan Valley Way by David Milton (Meridian Books). ISBN 9781869922399. 160pp; 232 x 150. £7.95 (+ £1.00 p&p).

Glevum Way — GLV

GLOS — **42km/26 miles**

A route around the outskirts of the City of Gloucester devised by Gloucester Ramblers Group to mark the RA Diamond Jubilee.

Attributes
No significant attribute
Start and Finish
Castle Meads, Glos SO826185
Waymark
Named discs with letters GW
Maps
OS Landranger: 162
OS Explorer: 179
Publications, badges and certificates
Illustrated map guide
Glevum Way (RA Gloucester) 2001. A3/6. £0.50 (+ 40p p&p). Also from Gloucester TIC at £1.00.

Herefordshire Trail — HRT

HEREFS — **248km/154 miles**

A circuit of fertile Herefordshire between the Malvern Hills and the Black Mountains. It includes the Golden Valley, watered by the River Dore, a tributary of the Monnow; black and white villages, and visits the five market towns of Leominster, Bromyard, Ledbury, Ross-on-Wye and Kington. The Monnow is walkable but its route guide is out of print.

Attributes
Easy; Heritage
Start and Finish
Heritage Centre, Ledbury, Herefs SO712477
Waymark
Tree outline in black and path name on white disc
Websites
www.herefordshiretrail.com
Maps
OS Landranger: 148, 149, 161, 162
OS Explorer: 13, 14, 189, 190, 201, 202, 203
Publications, badges and certificates
Guidebook
Herefordshire Trail (Spiral-bound) by RA Hereford Group (Hereford Ramblers) 2005. ISBN 9781901184730. 96pp; 208 x 152. £5.95 (+ £2.00 p&p). Cheques to Hereford Group of the Ramblers' Association.

Kinver Clamber — KINVC

WORCS — **32km/20 miles**

Using forestry tracks, canal paths, open field-paths, ridge paths and a Roman Road, this walk passes Enville Hall, Kinver Edge rock dwellings, Caunsall and Whittingham.

Attributes
Forest/Woodland; Canal; Charity
Start and Finish
Stourbridge, Worcs SO882840
Maps
OS Landranger: 138, 139
OS Explorer: 219
Publications, badges and certificates
Looseleaf
Kinver Clamber by Eric Perks (Eric Perks). 4pp; A4. £1.00 (+ 9 x 6 SAE). Cheques to Blakebrook Gym Club.
Badge & certificate
Kinver Clamber by Eric Perks (Eric Perks). £2.00 (+ SAE) & £1.00 (+ 9 x 6 SAE). Cheques to Blakebrook Gym Club.

Leadon Valley Walks — LVW

GLOS, HEREFS — **48km/30 miles**

Walks providing ways of traversing the Leadon Valley from the source of the river to its confluence with the Severn, all but one are circular and most are linked. The 'Secret River' publication is so named as it avoids towns and villages of any size. At Dymock three additional circular walks are met: Poets' Paths I and II (both 8 miles) and the Daffodil Way–Dymock (10 miles).

Attributes
River
Start
Evesbatch, Herefs SO686482
Finish
Over, Glos SO817199
Maps
OS Landranger: 149, 150, 162
OS Explorer: 14, 179, 190, 202

Publications, badges and certificates
Paperbacks
Secret River by Roy Palmer, Pat Palmer (Green Branch Press) 1998. ISBN 9780952603122. 76pp; 152 x 210. £6.95 (post free).
Leaflets
Dymock Daffodil Way by Windcross Public Paths Group (Ledbury TIC). A6. £1.00 (+ p&p). Cheques to Herefordshire Council.
Poets' Path I by Windcross Public Paths Group (Ledbury TIC) 1998. A6. £0.50 (+ p&p). Cheques to Herefordshire Council.
Poets' Path II by Windcross Public Paths Group (Ledbury TIC) 1994. A6. £1.00 (+ p&p). Cheques to Herefordshire Council.

Malvern Hills Challenge Walk MHCW

HEREFS, WORCS 32km/20 miles

This walk around the Malvern Hills, involving 3,000ft of ascent, heads south via Little Malvern on the lower slopes and returns north along the ridge.

Attributes
Challenging; Anytime Challenge; Heritage
Start and Finish
Old Wyche, Malvern, Worcs SO773442
Maps
OS Landranger: 150
OS Explorer: 190
Publications, badges and certificates
Booklets
Malvern Hills Challenge Walk by John Merrill (John Merrill Foundation). ISBN 9780907496953. 32pp; A5. £4.95 (+ £1.00 p&p). Cheques to John Merrill Foundation.
Badge & certificate
Malvern Hills Challenge Walk (John Merrill Foundation). £5.00 (incs p&p).

Malvern Link MALL

WORCS 72km/45 miles

This route links the North Worcestershire Path with the Worcestershire Way and visits the city of Worcester. It is part of a future hundred miles route called 'A Worcestershire Round'.

Attributes
Anytime Challenge; River; Canal; Heritage; Monarchy
Start
Forhill, Worcs SP055755
Finish
The Gullet, Worcs SO756380
Maps
OS Landranger: 139, 150
OS Explorer: 190, 204, 220
Publications, badges and certificates
Looseleaf
Malvern Link by Dave Irons (Dave Irons) 2001. 9pp; A4. £1.50 (incs p&p).

Mini-Alps MINA

WORCS 32km/20 miles

The route takes in Worcestershire Beacon, Old Hollow, Whithams Hill, Hatfield Coppice and Herefordshire Beacon, where it follows the ridge path.

Attributes
Anytime Challenge; Downland/Wolds; Charity
Start and Finish
Old Wyche, Malvern, Worcs SO773442
Maps
OS Landranger: 150
OS Explorer: 190
Publications, badges and certificates
Looseleaf
Mini-Alps by Eric Perks (Eric Perks). 4pp; A4. £1.00 (+ 9 x 6 SAE). Cheques to Blakebrook Gym Club.
Badge & certificate
Mini-Alps (Eric Perks). £2.00 (+ SAE) & £1.00 (+ 9 x 6 SAE). Cheques to Blakebrook Gym Club.

Monarch's Way MONW

BATH NES, BRIGHTON H, BRISTOL, DEVON, DORSET, E SUSSEX, GLOS, HANTS, N SOMERS, SHROPS, SOMERS, S GLOS, STAFFS, WARKS, W MIDLANDS, W SUSSEX, WILTS, WORCS 990km/615 miles

The Way is based on the lengthy route taken by King Charles II during his escape after his defeat by Cromwell at the final battle of the Civil Wars at Worcester in 1651, when for six weeks the 21-year-old was hotly pursued by Parliamentary troops. It takes in Boscobel (**the** Royal Oak Tree), Stratford upon Avon, the Cotswolds, Mendips and the South Coast from Charmouth to Shoreham. There are many historic buildings, features of interest and antiquity, with connections to numerous other long distance routes. The whole route is now 615 miles in length, following the battlefield paths (5 miles) in Worcester becoming definitive, and is the longest trail across inland England.

Attributes
Heritage; Monarchy
Start
Powick Bridge, Worcester, Worcs SO835525
Finish
Shoreham-by-Sea, W Sussex TQ237046
Waymark
Name and crown in oak tree surmounted by ship
Websites
www.monarchsway.50megs.com
Maps ◈
OS Landranger: 127, 138, 139, 150, 151, 163, 172, 173, 183, 184, 185, 193, 194, 196, 197, 22, 162
OS Explorer: 116, 117, 119, 120, 121, 122, 129, 130, 132, 141, 142, 143, 154, 155, 167, 168, 204, 205, 218, 220, 221, 242, 244, 45, 131
Publications, badges and certificates
Paperbacks
Monarch's Way Book 1: Worcester to Stratford-upon-Avon by Trevor Antill (Meridian Books) 2005. ISBN 9781869922528. 112pp; 229 x 145. £6.95 (+ £1.00 p&p).
Monarch's Way Book 2: Stratford-upon-Avon to Charmouth by Trevor Antill (Meridian Books) 1995. ISBN 9781869922283. 136pp; 229 x 145. £6.95 (+ £1.00 p&p).
Monarch's Way Book 3: Charmouth to Shoreham by Trevor Antill (Meridian Books) 1996. ISBN 9781869922290. 136pp; 229 x 145. £6.95 (+ £1.00 p&p).
Leaflets
Monarch's Way: Accommodation List (B&B) (Monarch's Way Association). Free (+ SAE).
Certificates
Monarch's Way (Monarch's Way Association). Free (+ 9 x 6 SAE). Available for each book section.
Badge
Monarch's Way by Monarch's Way (Monarch's Way Association). £5.00 (incs p&p).
Walking Support Providers
Wycheway

Navigation Way NAVW

W MIDLANDS **161km/100 miles**

A meandering towpath walk passing through a mixture of urban and rural areas. The first loop follows the Birmingham and Fazeley, Grand Union, Stratford-upon-Avon, and Worcester and Birmingham Canals, returning to Gas Street Basin. The second loop follows the Birmingham, Dudley, Stourbridge, Staffordshire and Worcestershire, Tame Valley, Rushall and Wyrley, and Essington canals.

Attributes
Easy; Canal; Urban
Start
Gas Street Basin, Birmingham, W Midlands SP062867
Finish
Chasewater, W Midlands SK040070
Maps
OS Landranger: 138, 139
OS Explorer: 219, 220
Publications, badges and certificates
Paperbacks
Navigation Way by Peter Groves, Trevor Antill (Meridian Books) 1998. ISBN 9781869922351. 112pp; A5. £5.95.

North Worcestershire Hills Marathon NWHM

WORCS **42km/26 miles**

The route passes through Burcot, Linthurst and Lickey Beacon to the Clent Hills, and returns via Belbroughton, Pepper Wood, Dodford, Park Gate and Sanders Park.

Attributes
Challenging; Anytime Challenge
Start and Finish
Bromsgrove, Worcs SO960707
Maps
OS Landranger: 139
OS Explorer: 219
Publications, badges and certificates
Looseleaf
North Worcestershire Hills Marathon (Dave Irons) 1994. 6pp; A4. £1.00 (incs p&p).

North Worcestershire Path NWORP

WARKS, W MIDLANDS, WORCS **56km/35 miles**

The North Worcestershire Path, shown on OS mapping, now starts at Bewdley and terminates at Major's Green, on the south edge of the Birmingham conurbation. This mainly rural route meets with the Staffordshire Way at the sandstone Kinver Edge. It links four country parks providing contrasting views of Birmingham and the Black Country in the north and the Vale of Worcester and Severn Valley to the south. The Midland Link (partly on OS maps) starts at Forhill, then visits Earlswood, Tanworth in Arden, Kingswood, where a link is achieved with the Heart of England Way, Wroxhall, and Kenilworth, where it links with the Centenary Way (Warwickshire).

Start
Town Centre, Bewdley, Worcs SO785753
Finish
Majors Green, Birmingham, W Midlands SP100781
Waymark
Pine cone logo and name
Maps ◈
OS Landranger: 138, 139
OS Explorer: 218, 219, 220
Publications, badges and certificates
Paperbacks
North Worcestershire Path & Midland Link by John Roberts (Walkways). 76pp; A5. £5.95 (incs p&p).
North Worcestershire Path Walkers Guide (Worcestershire County Council) 1997. ISBN 9781853010224. 38pp. £3.95 (+ p&p).

Nuneaton Rotary Walk NRW

LEICS, WARKS **34km/21 miles**

A route around Nuneaton with shorter variants, devised by, and intended to raise funds for, the Nuneaton Rotary Club's projects. It visits Chapel End, Bermuda and the Lime Kilns, linking with the Heart of England Way to the west.

Attributes
Easy; Charity
Start and Finish
Sandon Park, Warks SP358932
Waymark
Rotary International Wheel logo
Maps
OS Landranger: 140
OS Explorer: 221, 232
Publications, badges and certificates
Leaflets
Nuneaton Rotary Walk by Bob Bacon, Chris Mountford (Rotary Club of Nuneaton) 1999. A4/3. £1.00 (incs p&p).
Certificate
Nuneaton Rotary Walk (Rotary Club of Nuneaton). £1.00 (incs p&p).

Oxford Canal Walk OXCW

NORTHANTS, OXON, WARKS, W MIDLANDS
133km/83 miles

A walk connecting the cathedral cities of Oxford and Coventry using the continuous canal towpath, passing 43 locks, many bridges, one tunnel and crossing only one road. See also E-Routes (E2) of which it is part. A series of shorter walks, the North Oxfordshire Circular Walks, with distances varying up to 14 miles, have links to the Canal walk.

Attributes
Easy; Canal
Start
Coventry, W Midlands SP332796
Finish
Oxford, Oxon SP508064
Waymark
Multi-coloured diamond, named squares
Websites
www.waterscape.com, www.cherwell-dc.gov.uk
Maps ◈
OS Landranger: 140, 151, 152, 164
OS Explorer: 180, 191, 206, 221, 222
Stripmap
Oxford Canal: Map (GEOprojects)
Map (Other)
Thames Ring Atlas (Inland Waterways Maps) (GEOprojects)
Publications, badges and certificates
Leaflets
North Oxfordshire Circular Walks (Cherwell District Council). 11 leaflets; A4/3. £5.00 (+ £1.00 p&p) from Banbury TIC. Downloadable.
The Oxford Canal: An Explorers Guide (British Waterways – Tring) 1996. A5. Free (+ SAE).

Oxfordshire Way OXFW

GLOS, OXON **108km/67 miles**

The Way, a traverse of Oxfordshire from the Cotswolds to the Chilterns, links the Heart of England Way with the Thames Path National Trail. It takes in the rolling limestone countryside of the Cotswold Hills, passing through Shipton-under-Wychwood, Charlbury and other villages before crossing Otmoor to Studley, north of Oxford. Here it turns to Tetsworth and Pyrton, and crosses the open farmland and woods of the chalk hills of the Chilterns to reach the Thames. The Way connects to Blenheim Park (a World Heritage Site) – see Wychwood Way. The waymarked Thame Valley

Walk (15 miles and on OS mapping), which starts near Aylesbury, ends at Albury on the Oxfordshire Way forming connections with the North Bucks Way and the Aylesbury Ring. See also E-Routes (E2).

Attributes
Downland/Wolds; World Heritage Site
Start
Bourton-on-the-Water, Glos SP167207
Finish
Henley-on-Thames, Oxon SU763827
Waymark
Letters OW on standard waymarks
Websites
www.oxfordshire.gov.uk
Maps ◈
OS Landranger: 163, 164, 165, 175
OS Explorer: 171, 180, 191, 45
Publications, badges and certificates
Paperbacks
Oxfordshire Way: A Walker's Guide by Faith Cooke, Keith Wheal (Oxfordshire County Council) 2004. ISBN 9781900478014. 90pp; A5. £5.99 (+ 95p p&p).
Looseleaf
Oxfordshire Way: Accommodation list & Refreshment information (Oxfordshire County Council). 3pp; A4. Free. Downloadable.
Leaflets
Thame Valley Walk (Buckinghamshire County Council). A4/3. Free (+ SAE). Downloadable.

Riversides Way RIVW

HEREFS, POWYS, SHROPS 115km/71 miles

A walk in the Welsh Marches centered on Aymestrey and taking in the valleys and hills of the rivers Teme and Lugg.

Attributes
River; Moorland
Start and Finish
Aymestrey, Herefs SO425655
Maps
OS Landranger: 137
OS Explorer: 201, 203
Publications, badges and certificates
Paperbacks
Riversides Way by David Milton (Meridian Books) 2001. ISBN 9781869922436. 160pp; 145 x 230. £8.95 (+ £1.00 p&p).

Robert's Romp ROBR

WORCS 48km/30 miles

This remembrance walk includes views of Glasshampton Monastery, Abberley Clock Tower and the picturesque Teme and Severn valleys.

Attributes
Challenging; Anytime Challenge; Charity
Start and Finish
Dunley, Worcestershire SO789693
Maps
OS Landranger: 138
OS Explorer: 204, 218, 219
Publications, badges and certificates
Looseleaf
Robert's Romp by Eric Perks (Eric Perks). £1.00 (+ 9 x 6 SAE). Cheques to Blakebrook Gym Club.
Certificate
Robert's Romp by Eric Perks (Eric Perks). £1.00 (+ A4 SAE). Cheques to Blakebrook Gym Club.

Ross Round ROSSRD

GLOS, HEREFS 29km/18 miles

An undulating circuit around Ross-on-Wye, including the River Wye to 'Hole in the Wall', then up across Eaton Park to reach the 'Burnt House' with its Civil War connections, Crow Hill, Upton Bishop, Upton Crews, Weston Under Penyard, an old Roman town called 'Ariconium', Howle Hill and Cubberley, with an easier alternative from Weston.

Attributes
Former Railway; Forest/Woodland; River; Heritage
Start and Finish
near Riverside Inn, east bank, River Wye, Herefs SO595241
Waymark
Green ring with name and yellow centre/green arrow
Maps
OS Landranger: 149, 162
OS Explorer: 14
Publications, badges and certificates
Booklets (spiral bound)
Ross Round: Exploring Old Border Country by Guy Vowles (Chelwood Publications) 2004. ISBN 9780954820503. 34pp. £3.50. Or from TICs in the area.

Seven Shires Way SVSW

BUCKS, GLOS, NORTHANTS, OXON, WARKS, W BERKSHIRE, WILTS **377km/234 miles**

As it circles the county boundary of Oxfordshire, the Way encroaches into six other counties thus making up the Seven Shires. A wide variation of countryside includes the stone villages of the Cotswolds, the ironstone villages of North Oxfordshire, the marlstone scarp slopes of Warwickshire, the clay Vale of Aylesbury, the beech woods of the Chilterns, the Thames riverbank and the downland of Berkshire.

Attributes
River; Downland/Wolds
Start and Finish
A44 out of Moreton-in-Marsh, Glos SP213324
Websites
www.sevenshiresway.co.uk
Maps
OS Landranger: 151, 152, 163, 164, 165, 174, 175
OS Explorer: 159, 170, 171, 180, 181, 191, 192, 206, 45
Publications, badges and certificates
Paperbacks
Seven Shires Way by Elaine Steane (Reardon Publishing) 2002. ISBN 9781873877517. 208pp; 148 x 210. £12.95.

Severn Valley Marathon SVM

WORCS **42km/26 miles**

Based on the Severn Way, the route takes in the Wyre Forest, Eymore Woodlands, Stourport, Upper Arley and Bewdley.

Attributes
Challenging; Anytime Challenge; River; Moorland
Start and Finish
Blackstone CP and Picnic Site, Bewdley by-pass, Worcs SO796744
Maps
OS Landranger: 138
OS Explorer: 218
Publications, badges and certificates
Looseleaf
Severn Valley Marathon by Dave Irons (Dave Irons). 4pp; A4. £1.00 (incs p&p).

Shakespeare's Way SHKW

BUCKS, GTR LONDON, OXON, WARKS **235km/146 miles**

A further scenic cross-country route from the Macmillan Way stable, offering the optional opportunity to raise funds for the Shakespeare Hospice. It follows closely a route Shakespeare may have taken between his home-town of Stratford-upon-Avon and London, the city where he spent his productive years. From the Birthplace, this 'journey of imagination' passes through Blenheim Park (a World Heritage Site), Oxford, Stonor, Marlow, Cookham, Burnham Beeches, then continues on the Grand Union Canal and the Thames to its end at Shakespeare's Globe (Theatre), London. It is planned that the route will be shown on OS maps, up to the intersection with the Grand Union Canal Walk (TQ057805). The *Walking with William Shakespeare* paperback links his works with some of the locations and landscapes and covers Warwickshire and London, but it is not a guide to this route.

Attributes
Challenging; River; Canal; Urban; World Heritage Site; Heritage; Literary; Charity
Start
Shakespeare's Birthplace, Stratford-upon-Avon, Warks SP201551
Finish
Shakespeare's Globe (Theatre), Southwark, London TQ322805
Waymark
Shakespeare's Head logo within named green circle/disc
Websites
www.shakespearesway.org
Maps ◈
OS Landranger: 151, 163, 164, 165, 175, 176
OS Explorer: 45, 160, 161, 170, 171, 172, 173, 180, 191, 205
Publications, badges and certificates
Guidebook (full colour)
Shakespeare's Way by Peter Titchmarsh (Shakespeare's Way Association) 2006. ISBN 9780952685166. 80pp; A5. £7.75 (incs p&p). Cheques to Shakespeare's Way Association.
Accommodation list
Shakespeare's Way: Planner by Peter Titchmarsh (Shakespeare's Way Association) 2006. A4/3. £3.25 (incs p&p). Cheques to Shakespeare's Way Association.

Guidebook and guide to the reverse route

East-West Supplement to Shakespeare's Way by Peter Titchmarsh (Shakespeare's Way Association) 2006. 32pp. £5.75 (incs p&p). Cheques to Shakespeare's Way Association.

Leaflets

Shakespeare's Way by Peter Titchmarsh (Shakespeare's Way Association) 2008. 1pp; A4 folded. Free.

Paperbacks

Walking with William Shakespeare by Anne-Marie Edwards (Jones Books) 2005. ISBN 9780976353904. 224pp; 212 x 140. £9.95.

Walking Support Providers

Contours; Let's Go Walking!

St Kenelm's Routes — STKN

GLOS, WORCS — **97km/60 miles**

Two distinct routes, respectively St Kenelm's Way and Trail, joining the two places often linked with the legend of St Kenelm, grandson of King Offa, making walks from the Clent Hills south-west of Birmingham, the scene of his death, south to his burial place, Winchcombe, in the Cotswolds. The routes intertwine, sometimes in common, as on the Worcester-Birmingham canal. The Way has more canal towpath and runs nearer to Evesham, while the Trail takes a Saxon ridgeway over Bredon Hill. At 60 miles the Trail is the longer by 10 miles and has more ascent (5200ft versus 3700ft).

Attributes

Canal; Heritage; Pilgrimage; Religious

Start

Romsley Church, Clent Hills, Worcs SP944807

Finish

Abbey Terrace, Winchcombe, Glos SP024284

Websites

www.countryside-matters.co.uk,
www.pricejb.pwp.blueyonder.co.uk

Maps

OS Landranger: 139, 150

OS Explorer: 45, 204, 190, 219

Publications, badges and certificates

Paperbacks

St Kenelm's Trail by John Price (John Merrill Foundation) 2007. ISBN 9780955369162. 60pp; 208 x 142. £6.95 (+ £1.00 p&p).

St Kenelm's Way: Clent to Cotswold by Gerry Stewart (Countryside Matters) 2003. ISBN 9780952787044. 80pp; 210 x 136. £5.95 (incs p&p).

Teme Valley Walk — TEVW

HEREFS, POWYS, SHROPS, WORCS — **150km/93 miles**

A walk tracing the Teme, as close to this often-secretive, fast-flowing and rural river as is possible, from its confluence with the River Severn and visiting its source on Cilfaesty Hill (SO124845), just south of Newtown in Mid Wales. Significant towns on the Teme are Tenbury Wells, Ludlow and Knighton.

Attributes

River

Start

Worcester, Worcs SO846547

Finish

Newtown, Powys SO107918

Maps

OS Landranger: 136, 137, 138, 149, 150

OS Explorer: 214, 201, 203, 204

Publications, badges and certificates

Paperbacks

Teme Valley Walk by David Milton (Meridian Books) 2002. ISBN 9781869922450. 176pp. £8.95 (+ £1.00 p&p).

Three Choirs Way — TCHW

GLOS, HEREFS, WORCS — **161km/100 miles**

A route between Gloucester, Hereford and Worcester through countryside of hop-yards, vineyards and orchard; with a theme linking the walk to the ancient music festivals celebrated annually in the three Cathedrals. The rivers Severn, Wye, Teme and Lugg are crossed, as are the Marcle and Malvern Ridges and the Suckley Hills.

Attributes

Religious

Start and Finish

Gloucester, Glos SO830190

Waymark

Treble clef, name and 'Blessed is the eye between Severn and Wye' in black on white disc

Websites

www.countryside-matters.co.uk

Maps

OS Landranger: 149, 150, 162

OS Explorer: 179, 189, 190, 14

Publications, badges and certificates

Paperbacks

Three Choirs Way: Gloucester, Worcester, Hereford by Gerry Stewart, Genny Proctor (Countryside Matters) 1999. ISBN 9780952787020. 108pp; A5. £5.95 (post free).

Worcester & Birmingham Canal Walk WBC

W MIDLANDS, WORCS **48km/30 miles**

A towpath walk linking the Severn Way in the south to the Grand Union Canal Walk at Birmingham.

Attributes
Easy; Canal
Start
Diglis Basin, Worcester, Worcs SO849538
Finish
Gas Street Basin, Birmingham SP062867
Websites
www.waterscape.com
Maps
OS Landranger: 139, 150
OS Explorer: 204, 220
Stripmap
Worcester & Birmingham Canal (GEOprojects)
Publications, badges and certificates
Booklets
Canals Guide Birmingham & Black Country by waterscape.com (British Waterways – Tamworth). Free (+A5 SAE).
Discovering Birminghams Canals by waterscape.com (British Waterways – Tamworth). Free (+ A5 SAE).

Worcestershire Way WORCW

WORCS **50km/31 miles**

Starting along the River Severn in the Georgian town of Bewdley, it crosses rolling farmland to reach the Abberley Hills. It continues over the hills of Penny and Ankerdine to cross the River Teme. The Suckley Hills are also traversed and from Cowleigh it crosses the northern main Malvern Hills to the Victorian spa town of Great Malvern.

Attributes
Challenging; River; Heritage
Start
Bewdley, Worcs SO785755
Finish
Great Malvern, Worcs SO775459
Waymark
Green pear logo on named discs
Websites
http://worcestershire.whub.org.uk
Maps ◈
OS Landranger: 138, 149, 150
OS Explorer: 190, 204, 218
Publications, badges and certificates
Paperbacks
Worcestershire Way Walker's Guide (Worcestershire County Council) 2004. ISBN 9781902999098. 42pp; 200 x 160. £5.00 (+ 66p p&p).

Wychavon Marathon WYCHM

WORCS **42km/26 miles**

A country walk visiting some of Worcestershire's most attractive villages. The route includes short sections of the Wychavon Way.

Attributes
Challenging; Anytime Challenge
Start and Finish
Pipers Hill, Worcs SO957653
Maps
OS Landranger: 150
OS Explorer: 204, 205
Publications, badges and certificates
Looseleaf
Wychavon Marathon by Dave Irons (Dave Irons) 2001. 12pp; A4. £1.00 (incs p&p).

Wychavon Way WYCW

GLOS, WORCS **67km/42 miles**

The Way provides a link from the River Severn to the Cotswolds. It was opened to commemorate the Royal Silver Jubilee in 1977 and takes in Ombersley, Droitwich, The Lenches and Fladbury. Just after Netherton there is an optional detour via the summit of Bredon Hill, then on to Ashton under Hill, Gretton and the finish at Winchcombe.

Attributes
River
Start
Holt Fleet, Worcs SO824633
Finish
Winchcombe, Glos SP025283
Waymark
Crown symbol as letter W on named discs
Maps ◈
OS Landranger: 138, 150, 163
OS Explorer: 45, 190, 204, 205
Publications, badges and certificates
Paperbacks
Wychavon Way An illustrated guide by Mark Richards (Wychavon District Council) 1993. ISBN 9780950809908. 80pp; A5. £2.95 (+ 65p p&p).

Wye to the Thames WY2TH

GLOS, HEREFS, OXON, WORCS 192km/119 miles

Devised by railway enthusiasts, to encourage walkers to use the train when planning walks between Hereford and Oxford, it meanders across the Malverns and the Cotswolds taking in Ledbury, Great Malvern, Evesham and Moreton-in-Marsh.

Attributes
Downland/Wolds
Start
Hereford, Herefs SO515406
Finish
Oxford, Oxon SP503063
Websites
www.clpg.co.uk
Maps
OS Landranger: 149, 150, 151, 163, 164
OS Explorer: 189, 190, 204, 205, 180, 45
Publications, badges and certificates
Booklets
From the Wye to the Thames (Cotswold Line Promotion Group) 1996. ISBN 9780952539704. 60pp; A5. £2.50 (incs p&p). Includes updated addendum sheet, also online.

Wyre Forest Alpine Walk WYRFAW

WORCS 32km/20 miles

A demanding walk in the Wyre Forest area encircling the Severn Valley and always within sound of the Severn Valley Railway.

Attributes
Challenging; Anytime Challenge; Moorland; Charity
Start and Finish
Bewdley, Worcs SO788754
Maps
OS Landranger: 138
OS Explorer: 218
Publications, badges and certificates
Looseleaf
Wyre Forest Alpine Walk by Eric Perks (Eric Perks). 4pp; A4. £1.00 (+ 9 x 6 SAE). Cheques to Blakebrook Gym Club.
Badge & certificate
Wyre Forest Alpine Walk (Eric Perks). £2.00 (+ SAE) & £1.00 (+ 9 x 6 SAE). Cheques to Blakebrook Gym Club.

NORTH WEST ENGLAND

A path drops steeply to a gap, with Moel Arthur rising steeply on the other side (Offa's Dyke Path)

KEY FACTS

Laxey Wheel, Isle of Man

Areas	Cheshire, Isle of Man, Lancashire (including unitaries), Greater Manchester, Merseyside (unitaries), Shropshire, Staffordshire
National Park	Peak District (part)
Principal AONBs	Shropshire Hills, Cannock Chase, Forest of Bowland
World Heritage Sites	Ironbridge Gorge, Liverpool – Maritime Mercantile City
E-Routes	E2 variants Dover – Stranraer; and E8
National Trails (England)	Offa's Dyke Path (part), Pennine Bridleway (part), Pennine Way (part)
Walking Routes (trail miles)	93 main routes (4172 miles); 42 waymarked (2045 miles)
Resident population	7.75 million

DON'T MISS! TRAIL SECTIONS (CHALLENGING/REMOTE MARKED WITH *)

Sandstone Trail	Tarporley to Larkton Hill car park, sandstone ridges, Beeston Castle, Peckforton Hills (17km, 1400ft ascent)
Ironbridge Way	Apley Castle Park to Ironbridge, easy, accessible, interesting approach to the World Heritage Site for the first iron bridge, steam railway, old trackbeds (15km, 750ft ascent)
Shropshire Way	Bridges (pub) circular over the remote Long Mynd*, Betchcott Hills, via Ratlinghope (19km, 1500ft ascent)
Jack Mytton Way	Much Wenlock to Roman Bank, multi-user route, via Wenlock Edge (15km, 1000ft ascent), or continue on the Edge to Craven Arms
Staffordshire Way	Mow Cop to Horse Bridge, Congleton Edge, The Cloud, Churnet Valley (28km, 1940ft ascent)
Manifold Way	Waterhouses to Hulme End, easy multi-user route, attractive river valley, moorland (13km, 1200ft ascent/descent)
Heart of England Way	Milford to Lichfield over Cannock Chase in mixed forest (25km, 1400ft ascent)
Gritstone Trail	Disley to Tegg's Nose Country Park, Lyme Park, gritstone edges, views* (20km, 2400ft ascent)
Cown Edge Way	Marple to Gee Cross, Cown Edge Rocks, Werneth Low, moorland, Goyt and Etherow valleys (24km, 2270ft ascent)
Mersey Valley Timberland Trail	Lymm to Murdishaw (Runcorn), easy, Mersey valley views, canal history – Bridgewater Canal (26km, 930ft ascent)
Trans Pennine Trail	from Sefton Park, Liverpool City section with a World Heritage Site historic urban waterfront, easy (11km)
Sefton Coastal Footpath/ Trans Pennine Trail	Southport/Hillside to Hightown over coastal dunes, easy, train links (18km)
Lancashire Trail	Rivington to Tockholes Abbey Village, Anglezarke Moor, reservoirs (15km, 1250ft ascent)
Ribble Way	Clitheroe to Hurst Green, riverside, with optional literary Tolkein Trail (circular), easy (15kms, Tolkein Trail an extra 8kms)
Pendle's Three Peaks	from Pendle Heritage Centre, Nelson, two of these walks climb Pendle Hill (SD796418, 1840ft, 8km) and Weets Hill* (SD857448, 1300ft, 10km)
Pendle Way	Higham to Barrowford/Pendle Heritage Centre via Pendle Hill (16km, 2000ft ascent)

NORTH WEST ENGLAND

North west England includes landscapes as contrasting as the often-remote moorlands of the Pennine fringes, traversed by the Pennine Way and Bridleway National Trails, extensive coastal dunes and major estuaries, home of much birdlife. Along the Mersey valley are the industrial and commercial areas of Merseyside and Greater Manchester, where the Trail originators have created interesting urban and waterside walking as well as paths in secret countryside, not far from populated areas. Offshore is the scenic Isle of Man.

Geography and history

South of the Mersey, this is a largely land-locked region apart from stretches of the wide estuaries of the Mersey and the Dee on either side of the Wirral, but with a variety of attractive landscapes for the walker. The sandstone ridge of Cheshire crosses the elevated Cheshire Plain. There are the gritstone edges of the Peak District's western fringes, where the limits of the Peak District – the South West Peak – extend into Cheshire and Staffordshire with its moorlands and isolated gritstone ridges. Close to the Welsh border the Shropshire Hills and intervening valleys provide some excellent walking. There is much industrial history, accessed by trails, with the birthplace of the canal system here in the Bridgewater Canal and the world's first iron bridge at Ironbridge, celebrated in a World Heritage Site.

The Merseyside and Lancashire coastlines, although also much developed with resorts and for residential commuter use, offer some fine walking, including England's largest undeveloped dune system near Formby. Further north are the vast sandflats of Morecambe Bay exposed by the tides, with views across to the distant Lakeland fells. For those seeking challenging walking, there are fine moorlands on the Pennine fringes and several other upland masses apart from these Pennine borders: a number of the area's Anytime Challenges are set on these moors.

The Anglezarke and Turton Moors lie north of Bolton, and near Clitheroe is the whaleback ridge of Pendle Hill, topped by resistant millstone grit sandstone. North across the broad valley of the Ribble and its tributaries are the larger moorland masses of the Forest of Bowland also with hard grit cores. Gentler lowland walks are provided on the Ribble and the many other rivers and on canals. Several other rivers run off the Bowland moors, to the south the Hodder, to the north the Wenning and the Hindburn, tributaries of the Lune, and to the west the Wyre and Calder.

Lhiattee ny Beinnee, Isle of Man Coast Path

North West England – major routes

Only major routes from this region (excluding any National Trails) are shown here.
The National Trails are shown on the map in the National Trails section of this handbook.
For the full network of trails visit the LDWA website – www.ldwa.org.uk.

The view west from Stiperstones, Shropshire

The Trails

Walkers know that the **hills of Shropshire** can provide a strenuous day out with fine views. Here the five main ranges run generally south-west to north-east. Starting in the west they begin with Stiperstones, moving east through The Long Mynd, the Caradoc Hills, Wenlock Edge (these are separated from The Wrekin by the Severn) and the Clee Hills, with the main summits of Titterstone Clee and Brown Clee. Several routes visit these hills: The Jack Mytton Way follows Wenlock Edge and climbs the Long Mynd, the Shropshire Way includes Wenlock Edge, the Wrekin, and also the Clee Hills, the latter being the theme of the Clee Climber challenge walk. The Shropshire Cakes and Ale Trail visits Titterstone Clee, Wenlock Edge, Stiperstones and The Long Mynd. In the borderlands to the south, Offa's Dyke Path traverses the lower Clun hills.

The region's **geology** and its landforms are the themes of many other routes. The Gritstone Trail follows the elevated gritstone edges on the Peak District's western fringe, with views both to its higher hills and the Cheshire Plain. The partly urban, mostly rural, Mersey Valley Timberland Trail follows the northern sandstone edge of the Cheshire Plain and descends to the Mersey valley itself, with sections along the Bridgewater Canal. The Sandstone Trail follows the sandstone ridge of central Cheshire that forms the county's backbone. The Cown Edge Way on the eastern fringes of Manchester includes this 'edge'. The Staffordshire Way traverses the county, and not only follows several more edges, but also travels along canals and in the river valleys of the Churnet and Dove. The Geopark Way starts its long journey through geological time in Bridgnorth, then goes south to the Abberley and Malvern Hills Global Geopark.

The region's **river valleys** provide the theme for the Bollin Valley Way, Etherow–Goyt Valley Way and the Irwell Sculpture Trail, while the Medlock Valley Walk (not currently promoted) follows the river to its confluence with the Irwell. The Tame Valley Way traces this populous, but wooded, valley along both canalside and

ROUTE CODES

Code	Route	Code	Route
BRTW	Bronte Way	**MONW**	Monarch's Way
CCUCW	Cumbria Coastal Way	**OLDW**	Oldham Way
EGVW	Etherow–Goyt Valley Way	**RIBW**	Ribble Way
GT	Gritstone Trail	**SANDT**	Sandstone Trail
HOEW	Heart of England Way	**SEVW**	Severn Way
IOMCP	Isle of Man Coastal Path	**SHRW**	Shropshire Way
LCCW	Lancashire Coastal Way	**STFW**	Staffordshire Way
MAELW	Maelor Way	**TPT**	Trans Pennine Trail
MDSW	Midshires Way	**TSDT**	Tameside Trail

Coming off Larkton Hill near Maiden Castle, on the Sandstone Trail in Cheshire

riverside paths while the Tameside Trail includes the Etherow, Tame and Medlock Valleys. The Manifold Way (one of the White Peak Trails) follows the Manifold valley through the Staffordshire Moorlands. The Wirral Shore Way follows the old coastline of Wirral, bordering the Dee Estuary. Further north, the river routes include the Hodder Way, Lune Valley Ramble and Lunesdale Walk, the Ribble Way (and Ribble villages are explored by Villages of the Valley), the Tidewater Way (Lune and Wenning) and the Wyre Way. The Ribble Valley arguably includes the centre of the British Isles, marked by the Centre of the Kingdom Walk.

Canal walks include: the Cheshire Ring Canal along six historic canals, including the Bridgewater Canal, Britain's first; the Llangollen Canal Walk; the Middlewich Challenge Walk; and the Trent & Mersey Canal Walk, that initially also takes the Bridgewater Canal, on its way to Derwents Mouth. Further north are the Lancashire Lakeland Link and the Lancaster Canal (also followed by the Lunesdale Walk). Walkers may use two major multi-user routes designed primarily for horse-riders, the Bishop Bennet Way and the Jack Mytton Way, Shropshire's long distance bridleway.

City, borough and **town circuits** are provided by the Bolton Rotary Way Footpath, the Burnley Way, the Oldham Way, the Rochdale Way, the Rossendale Way and the West Craven Way. The Millennium Way (Staffordshire) spans the width of the county. The three interlinked Telford and Wrekin Walks span urban open spaces and countryside, and include the Ironbridge Way, that visits the World Heritage Site. There is good walking in and near urban areas. The Trans Pennine Trail provides interesting routes across developed Merseyside, with an option to visit the City of Liverpool and its fine waterfront, now recognised in a World Heritage Site, then finally taking the shoreline to Southport. The Witton Weavers Way network to the west of Blackburn and Darwen includes Jumbles Reservoir.

There are routes providing county **traverses** and longer distance links. The lengthy Shropshire Way makes a county circuit visiting many of its notable hills. The Mortimer Trail sets off south from Ludlow into Herefordshire. The Newcastle Way (Staffordshire) traverses north-west Staffordshire to link the Staffordshire Way at Mow Cop with the Shropshire Union Canal. The North Cheshire Way heads across from the Wirral to the Peak District. The South Cheshire Way links the Sandstone Trail and Staffordshire Way. The Maelor Way is a useful route linking several others, such as the Sandstone Trail and Offa's Dyke Path.

A number of **long routes** start from, or extend into, the region. The Heart of England Way starts its 100-mile journey in Staffordshire, heads south for Cannock Chase and the Arden countryside, and ends in the Cotswolds. The Midshires Way links the Ridgeway National Trail with the Trans Pennine Trail, crossing the shires of Middle England and going through the Goyt Valley, to reach its end at Stockport. The Trans Pennine Trail traverses along the Mersey valley, often close to the river, on its journey between the coasts. Paul Hannon's Trans Pennine Way is a long distance link between the Forest of Bowland and Nidderdale AONBs and Brian Smailes' Lancashire Trail joins St Helens and the Pennine Way via Pendle Hill.

The Hope House Way is a 335-mile **charity route**, extending into Wales, ranging widely over areas served by a Children's Respite Hospice. **Local personalities** are recognised in the Simon Evans Way, created to remember Cleobury Mortimer's postman writer, and taking in the River Rea valley in the South Shropshire countryside. The **urban** Fred Perry Way visits a sportsman's roots in Stockport in the Bollin Valley. Past **literary figures** are represented in the Bronte Way, linking Bronte sites across the Pennines, and the short Tolkien Trail off the Ribble Way marks a workplace of the author of *Lord of the Rings*.

Some 37 **enthusiasts' routes** across the region come from 20 route developers. John Merrill, who was based in the Peak District, leads the way with eight, each with interesting features or presenting a challenge. They include: the Llangollen Canal Walk; Middlewich Challenge Walk; the Salter's Way that follows an old salt track across lowland Cheshire; the Staffordshire Moorlands Challenge Walk; the Sweet Pea Challenge Walk that heads from Wem, the birthplace of the sweet pea; the Three Counties Challenge Walk that visits Cheshire, Staffordshire's 'The Roaches', and Derbyshire via Peak District tops; and the Trent & Mersey Canal Walk.

Other promoters include Eric Perks who provides the Applecake Hill 20 (a Shropshire charity route) and David Irons has the Clee Climber in Shropshire's Clee Hills. Alan Edwards offers the Churnet Valley Challenge Walk and White Peak Rollercoaster. Four routes explore the area of Saddleworth Moor, west of Manchester on the fringes of the Dark Peak: Carole Engel has three – the New Five Trig Points Walk, Saddleworth Five Trig Points Walk and the Ten Reservoirs Walk that makes a watery circuit; and Sam Taylor has the fourth, the Saddleworth Skyline.

The historic Pioneers Round (Derek Magnall) was devised to mark the Co-operative Movement's 150th anniversary. It starts from Rochdale. The Salt & Sails Trail (David Burkhill) traces the Weaver Navigation. The Spanners Round (Norman Thomas) links six reservoirs, and there are two routes from the LDWA East Lancashire Group – the Three Towers Circuit join the towers of Peel, Rivington and Darwen, and the Two Crosses Circuit includes both a Roman and Pilgrim's Cross.

North of Manchester the Crowthorn Crawl, Crowthorn Rose and Crowthorn Star (Margaret Griffiths) have a charity element and include watersides. The Four Pikes Hike (Norman Thomas) from Horwich visits separate major regional tops, and his Ramsbottom Round includes the Irwell valley. Tony Wimbush provides the Hebden Valleys Heritage Trek. Ramblers NE Lancashire offers the Hyndburn Clog near Accrington, Anton Citiris the Twin Valley 20 Walks in Calderdale and Rossendale, and Max Tattersall the Weavers Shuttle from Worsthorne. The Anglezarke Moors are visited by the Anglezarke Amble (LDWA West Lancs) and Anglezarke Anguish (Norman Thomas). The Pendle and Ribble area has the Pendle and Ribble Round (Derek Magnall) and Witches Way (Jim Ashton). Ramblers Clitheroe provides the Clitheroe 60K. Several routes also cover the Forest of Bowland area: John Merrill's eighth is the Forest of Bowland Challenge Walk; LDWA West Lancashire has the Heart of Bowland Walk; and David Johnson has the North Bowland Traverse.

Offshore, the **Isle of Man** offers a long coastline and some impressive moorland scenery inland, rising to over 2000ft (621m) on Snaefell. The main promoted trail is the coastal path, the Raad ny Foillan in Manx or Way of the Gull, created for the Island's 'Heritage Year' celebrations in 1986. Three other significant Manx walking trails cross the island, the Millennium Way (Isle of Man) celebrates the Manx Millennium in 1979 and covers the western slopes of Snaefell, the Herring Road (Bayr ny Skeddan in Manx) is an old fishermen's route from Castletown that visits the Round Table, and the Heritage Trail uses the old Douglas to Peel railway from east to west, parallel to the TT course.

Anglezarke Amble — ANAM

LANCS — **34km/21 miles**

Devised by the West Lancs Group of the LDWA, the route goes over Rivington Pike, Winter Hill and passes several reservoirs along the way.

Attributes
Challenging; Anytime Challenge; Moorland
Start and Finish
Rivington Hall Barn, Lancs SD633144
Maps
OS Landranger: 109
OS Explorer: 287
Publications, badges and certificates
Looseleaf
Anglezarke Amble (LDWA West Lancashire Group). Free (+ 9 x 4 SAE).
Badge & certificate
Anglezarke Amble (LDWA West Lancashire Group). £1.50 (+ A4 SAE).

Anglezarke Anguish — ANAN

LANCS — **32km/20 miles**

This walk takes in Leverhulme Park, Pidgeon Tower, Rivington Pike, the village of White Coppice and three reservoirs. There is an alternative 10-mile route.

Attributes
Challenging; Anytime Challenge; Moorland
Start and Finish
Rivington Hall Barn, Lancs SD633144
Maps
OS Landranger: 109
OS Explorer: 287
Publications, badges and certificates
Looseleaf
Anglezarke Anguish Walk (Norman Thomas). Free (+ SAE).
Badge & certificate
Anglezarke Anguish (Norman Thomas). £1.50 (+ SAE).

Applecake Hill 20 — AH20

SHROPS — **32km/20 miles**

A figure-of-eight walk taking in woodland, brookland, fields and hills and visiting the villages of Bayton, Mamble, Neen Sollars and Shakenhurst. Profits go to a local club catering for disabled youngsters.

Attributes
Challenging; Anytime Challenge; Moorland; Religious; Charity
Start and Finish
Cleobury Mortimer, Shrops SO674758
Maps
OS Landranger: 138
OS Explorer: 203, 218
Publications, badges and certificates
Looseleaf
Applecake Hill 20 (Eric Perks) 2003. 7pp; A4. £1.00 (+ 9 x 6 SAE). Cheques to Blakebrook Gym Club.
Badge & certificate
Applecake Hill 20 (Eric Perks). £2.00 & £1.00 (+ large SAE). Cheques to Blakebrook Gym Club.

Bishop Bennet Way — BPBW

CHESHIRE, SHROPS — **55km/34 miles**

Named after an 18th century traveller, the Way was primarily devised for use by horse riders. Whilst part of the route is along minor roads, most of this can be avoided by walkers using other rights of way. The route also takes in green lanes, bridleways and field paths as it passes through Milton Green, Coddington, Shocklach and Grindley Brook.

Attributes
Easy; Horse Ride (Multi User)
Start
Beeston, Cheshire SJ526596
Finish
Wirswall, Shrops SJ537448
Waymark
Horseshoe and name on black disc
Maps ◈
OS Landranger: 117
OS Explorer: 257, 266, 267
Publications, badges and certificates
Booklets
Bishop Bennet Way by Discover Cheshire (Cheshire County Council). Free (+ 9 x 6 SAE).

Bollin Valley Way — BVW

CHESHIRE, GTR MAN — **40km/25 miles**

The River Bollin rises in the Pennine Foothills and flows through Macclesfield, Prestbury, Wilmslow, Hale and Bowdon, eventually joining the Manchester Ship Canal/Mersey at Bollin Point. The Way follows the river and is also a spine route giving access to a wider footpath network. The waymarked Fred Perry Way (14 miles; route maps online on Stockport website) spans urban Stockport Borough from Woodford in the south to Reddish in the north, commemorating this legendary tennis ace.

Attributes
Easy; River
Start
Macclesfield, Cheshire SJ915746
Finish
Partington, Gtr Man SJ706912
Waymark
River and leaf logo on yellow named discs
Websites
www.bollinvalley.org.uk, www.stockport.gov.uk
Maps
OS Landranger: 109, 118
OS Explorer: 268, 276
Publications, badges and certificates
Folder
Bollin Valley Way (Bollin Valley Partnership) 2004. Set of 5; A4/3. Free (+ A5 SAE). Downloadable.

Bolton Rotary Way Footpath BRW

GTR MAN **80km/50 miles**

Following the borough boundary of Bolton MBC, in most places through countryside, the route includes industrial heritage, reservoirs, sections of the Manchester to Bury Canal and the Leeds and Liverpool Canal towpaths, the river Irwell, historic estates, memorials and country parks and some inevitable motorway crossings. Every section affords views of the route's highest point – Winter Hill.

Attributes
Moorland; Heritage
Start and Finish
Affetside Millenium Green, Bolton, Gtr Man SD757136
Waymark
White disc/yellow Rotary symbol/green arrrow
Maps
OS Landranger: 109
OS Explorer: 276, 277, 287
Publications, badges and certificates
Guidebook
Rotary Way Footpath – Over 50 miles Around Bolton by Rotary Clubs of Bolton (Rotary Club of Westhoughton) 2005. 36pp; A5. £5.00 (+ 75p p&p). Cheques to Rotary Club of Westhoughton.

Bronte Way BRTW

LANCS, W YORKS **71km/44 miles**

The Way provides a cross-Pennine route linking various places associated with the lives and works of the Bronte sisters. It takes in the Thursden Valley to link with the Pendle Way at Wycoller Hall (Ferndean Manor in the novel *Jane Eyre*), the moors to Top Withins (*Wuthering Heights*), Haworth Parsonage, where the Brontes lived and now a Bronte Museum, the Brontes' birthplace at Thornton, and the hills west of Bradford to the Spen Valley (Shirley country), before finishing at Oakwell Hall (Fieldhead in the novel *Shirley*).

Attributes
Challenging; Moorland; Heritage; Literary
Start
Gawthorpe Hall, Lancs SD806341
Finish
Oakwell Hall, W Yorks SE217271
Waymark
Named posts
Maps ◈
OS Landranger: 103, 104
OS Explorer: 288, 21
Publications, badges and certificates
Paperbacks
Bronte Way by Paul Hannon (Hillside Publications) 2002. ISBN 9781870141567. 56pp; 115 x 178. £4.50 (+ 60p p&p).
Bronte Way by Marje Wilson (RA West Riding Area) 1997. ISBN 9781901184051. 64pp; A5. £4.50 (+ £1.00 p&p).
Folder
Bronte Way (Haworth Tourist Information Centre) 1997. 4pp; A5. £2.00 (+ 54p p&p).

Burnley Way BURNW

LANCS **64km/40 miles**

A varied route around Burnley with a wide range of terrain, from the town centre and Calder riverside and the Leeds and Liverpool Canal towpath it passes a number of reservoirs, but it also climbs onto high moorland. It includes Forest of Burnley woodlands and the wilder South Pennine Moors with the route's highest point at Thieveley Pike, and industrial heritage such as from past limestone extraction at Shedden Clough contrasted with the nearby windfarm at Coal Clough.

Attributes
Challenging; Forest/Woodland; Lake/Reservoir; River; Canal; Moorland; Urban; Industrial History

Start and Finish
Weavers' Triangle Visitor Centre, Burnley, Lancs SD838322
Waymark
Stylised B and bird logo in yellow on green disc
Websites
www.visitburnley.com
Maps ◈
OS Landranger: 103
OS Explorer: 287, 21

Publications, badges and certificates
Leaflets
Burnley Way (Visit Burnley) 2008. 6 sectional leaflets; A4/3. Free.

Centre of the Kingdom Walk COTKW

LANCS **77km/48 miles**

A route visiting many historical sites in the Ribble Valley taking in Chatburn, Bolton by Bowland, Slaidburn, Dunsop Bridge, Whitewell, Chipping and Bashall Eaves. Dunsop Bridge is located near to the centre of the British Isles. Route descriptions can be downloaded from the website below.

Attributes
River; Heritage
Start and Finish
Clitheroe Castle, Lancashire SD741416
Websites
www.visitlancashire.com
Maps
OS Landranger: 103
OS Explorer: 41
Publications, badges and certificates
Folder
Journey Through the Centre of the Kingdom (Ribble Valley Borough Council). 8 leaflets. £1.00. With accommodation list.

Cheshire Ring Canal Walk CRC

CHESHIRE, GTR MAN, STAFFS **158km/98 miles**

A route following towpaths along six historic canals of various ages and character. This Walk offers views of the Cheshire Plain and Peak District hills and the solitude of quiet countryside away from the hustle and bustle of city streets. It includes the Bridgewater Canal, the first in Britain built separately from an existing watercourse. The waymarked Middlewood Way (11 miles and on OS mapping) offers a mostly level and traffic-free route, for walkers, cyclists and horseriders, on the former Macclesfield, Bollington and Marple Railway between historic mill towns. It runs parallel with the Macclesfield Canal and provides easy circular walk options.

Attributes
Easy; Canal; Heritage; Industrial History
Start and Finish
Marple, Gtr Man SJ962884
Waymark
Metal plaque with bridge and barge
Websites
www.manchester2002-uk.com, www.macclesfield.gov.uk
Maps ◈
OS Landranger: 108, 109, 117, 118
OS Explorer: 1, 24, 257, 258, 267, 268, 275, 276, 277
Map (Other)
Cheshire Ring (GEOprojects)
Publications, badges and certificates
Booklets
Walking the Cheshire Ring by John Merrill (John Merrill Foundation) 1990. ISBN 9780907496632. 80pp; A5. £8.95 (+ £1.00 p&p). Cheques to John Merrill Foundation.
Exploring the Cheshire Ring by British Waterways, Manchester Ship Canal Company (British Waterways). £1.00. From local TICs.
Leaflets
Middlewood Way (Stockport Metropolitan Borough Council) 2004. A4/3. Free.

Cheshire Ways CRW

CHESHIRE, WARRINGTON **Various**

A group of routes, lying mostly north-west of Chester, up to the Mersey valley, including Delamere Forest. The Ways comprise the Baker Way (13 miles) Chester – Delamere; Delamere Way (22 miles) Stockton Heath – Frodsham; Eddisbury Way (18 miles) Frodsham – Burwardsley; Longster Trail (11 miles) Helsby – Pipers Ash. They provide links with the Sandstone Trail at Frodsham.

Attributes
Easy
Start and Finish
Various

Waymark
Named discs
Maps ◈
OS Landranger: 109, 117, 118
OS Explorer: 257, 266, 267

Publications, badges and certificates
Booklets
Baker Way (Christleton to Brine's Brow (Delamere Forest)) (Mid Cheshire Footpath Society). 16pp; 100 x 223. £1.00 (incs p&p). Cheques to Mid Cheshire Footpath Society.
Baker Way (Brine's Brow (Delamere Forest) to Christleton) (Mid Cheshire Footpath Society). 16pp; 100 x 223. £1.00 (incs p&p). Cheques to Mid Cheshire Footpath Society.
Delamere Way (Frodsham – Stockton Heath) (Mid Cheshire Footpath Society). 100 x 223. £1.50 (incs p&p). Cheques to Mid Cheshire Footpath Society.
Delamere Way (Stockton Heath – Frodsham) (Mid Cheshire Footpath Society). 16pp; 100 x 223. £1.50 (incs p&p). Cheques to Mid Cheshire Footpath Society.
Eddisbury Way (Frodsham – Burwardsley) (Mid Cheshire Footpath Society). £1.00 (incs p&p). Cheques to Mid Cheshire Footpath Society.
Eddisbury Way (Burwardsley – Frodsham) (Mid Cheshire Footpath Society). £1.00 (incs p&p). Cheques to Mid Cheshire Footpath Society.
Longster Trail: Helsby to Pipers Ash (Mid Cheshire Footpath Society). 8pp; 100 x 223. £1.00 (incs p&p). Cheques to Mid Cheshire Footpath Society.
Longster Trail: Pipers Ash to Helsby (Mid Cheshire Footpath Society). 8pp; 100 x 223. £1.00 (incs p&p). Cheques to Mid Cheshire Footpath Society.

Churnet Valley Challenge Walk — CVCW

STAFFS — **39km/24 miles**

The route takes in several villages in the Churnet Valley, a section of the Caldon Canal and part of the Staffordshire Way. There is 2,600ft of ascent.

Attributes
Challenging; Anytime Challenge; Canal
Start and Finish
Froghall, Staffs SK027476
Maps
OS Landranger: 119
OS Explorer: 259, 24
Publications, badges and certificates
Looseleaf
Churnet Valley Challenge Walk (Alan S. Edwards). 2pp. Free (+ SAE).
Certificate
Churnet Valley Challenge Walk (Alan S. Edwards). A5. £0.50 (+ A5 SAE).

Clee Climber — CLEEC

SHROPS — **34km/21 miles**

Using field paths and bridleways, the route circles the Clee summits of Abdon Burf, Titterstone Clee Hill and Clee Burf.

Attributes
Challenging; Anytime Challenge
Start and Finish
Cleobury North, Shropshire SO623869
Maps
OS Landranger: 138
OS Explorer: 218, 217
Publications, badges and certificates
Looseleaf
Clee Climber by Dave Irons (Dave Irons). £1.00 (incs p&p). Bredon Climber + Clee Climber, £1.25 (incs p&p).

Clitheroe 60K — CL160

LANCS — **60km/37 miles**

From the Ribble Valley the route takes in Longridge Fell, the Hoddle Valley, Newton, skirts Grindleton Fell to Sawley and Downham, finally traversing Pendle Hill. It links with the Pendle Way (on Pendle Hill) and Ribble Way (at Sawley Bridge).

Attributes
Challenging; Anytime Challenge; Moorland
Start and Finish
Clitheroe, Lancs SD741420
Maps
OS Landranger: 103
OS Explorer: 287, 41
Publications, badges and certificates
Leaflets
Clitheroe 60k route card by Eddie Ross (RA Clitheroe Group) 1995. 2pp; A5. Free (+ 9 x 6 SAE).
Certificate
Clitheroe 60K (RA Clitheroe Group). Free (+ 9 x 6 SAE).

Cown Edge Way — CEW

DERBYS, GTR MAN — **30km/19 miles**

This generally U-shaped and hilly route on the eastern edge of Greater Manchester rises to Cown Edge Rocks via Strines and Mellor, returning via Charlesworth and Werneth Low. There is a mixture of terrain from urban to moorland.

Attributes
Moorland; Urban
Start
Hazel Grove, Gtr Man SJ925875
Finish
Gee Cross, Gtr Man SJ945930
Waymark
Named posts and amber discs and arrows
Maps ◈
OS Landranger: 109, 110
OS Explorer: 1, 268, 277
Publications, badges and certificates
Booklets
Cown Edge Way (RA Manchester Area). 29pp; A5. £1.00 (incs p&p). Cheques to RA Manchester Area.

Crowthorn Crawl CRCRAWL

LANCS **43km/27 miles**

A walk in the country north of Bolton taking in Darwen Tower, Snig Hole, Irwell Vale and Stubbins Wood. Proceeds from sales of badges are donated to the National Children's Homes Charity.

Attributes
Challenging; Anytime Challenge; Lake/Reservoir; Moorland
Start and Finish
Clough Head Information Centre, Lancs SD752232
Maps
OS Landranger: 103, 109
OS Explorer: 287
Publications, badges and certificates
Looseleaf
Crowthorn Crawl (Margaret Griffiths). Free (+ 9 x 4 SAE).
Badge
Crowthorn Crawl (Margaret Griffiths). £1.50 (+ SAE).

Crowthorn Rose CRROSE

LANCS **64km/40 miles**

Two separate walks, one based on Crowthorn School and the other on Baxenden Church, the routes take in country near Accrington, Haslingden and Ramsbottom. Proceeds from the badge sales are donated to the National Children's Homes Charity.

Attributes
Challenging; Anytime Challenge; Lake/Reservoir; Moorland

Start and Finish
Stage 1: Crowthorn School, Lancs SD746183;
Stage 2: Baxenden Church, Lancs SD773265
Maps
OS Landranger: 103
OS Explorer: 287, 21
Publications, badges and certificates
Looseleaf
Crowthorn Rose (Margaret Griffiths). 2pp; A4. Free (+ 9 x 4 SAE).
Badge
Crowthorn Rose (Margaret Griffiths). £1.50 (+ SAE).

Crowthorn Star CRSTAR

LANCS **63km/39 miles**

A series of five walks, varying in distance, based on Crowthorn School. The walks explore the countryside around the school. Proceeds from badge sales are donated to National Children's Homes.

Attributes
Anytime Challenge; Lake/Reservoir
Start and Finish
Crowthorn School, Lancs SD746183
Maps
OS Landranger: 103
OS Explorer: 287
Publications, badges and certificates
Looseleaf
Crowthorn Star (Margaret Griffiths). 2pp; A4. Free (+ 9 x 4 SAE).
Badge
Crowthorn Star (Margaret Griffiths). £1.50 (+ SAE).

Cumbria Coastal Way CCUCW

CUMBRIA, DUMFRIES & GALLOWAY, LANCS **293km/182 miles**

From Silverdale on Morecambe Bay, the route follows the fascinating Cumbria coast from the boundary with Lancashire, around the southern Cumbrian peninsulas with their vast stretches of estuarine sands, through the Lake District National Park and the industrial heritage of the west coast, along the Solway Firth and through rough border country with glimpses of Hadrian's Wall and along the River Eden to the historic city of Carlisle, then first on the Eden's other bank into Scotland to the official finish at the famous border town of Gretna. The M6 motorway has been extended across the River Esk, where OS mapping shows the route ending. A minor road running alongside the motorway provides a route across the river and on to Gretna. Alternatively a 2.5 mile road walk back to Rockcliffe links to an infrequent bus service to Carlisle.

Attributes
Easy; Coastal; Industrial History
Start
Silverdale Station, Cumbria SD475752
Finish
River Esk south bank, Metal Bridge, Cumbria NY356649
Waymark
Named posts on green disc: Milnthorpe – Carlisle
Maps ◈
OS Landranger: 85, 89, 96, 97
OS Explorer: 7, 6, 303, 4, 314, 315, 323
Publications, badges and certificates
Paperbacks
Cumbria Coastal Way by Ian O. Brodie, Krysia Brodie (Cicerone Press) 2007. ISBN 9781852844301. 256pp; 172 x 116. £12.00. 1st Edition.
Leaflets
Cumbria Coastal Way: Morecambe Bay estuaries – Milnthorpe to Barrow-in-Furness (South Lakeland District Council). A4/3. Free (+ 9 x 4 SAE).

Etherow – Goyt Valley Way EGVW

CHESHIRE, DERBYS **24km/15 miles**

A route linking Stockport with Longdendale on the western edge of the Peak District. It follows the River Goyt upstream to the confluence with the River Etherow north of Marple which it then follows to Broadbottom, continuing through Woolley Bridge and Hollingworth to Bottoms Reservoir and the Longdendale Trail. There is a link to the Trans Pennine Trail walking route at Bottoms Reservoir. From Compstall to Broadbottom, the E2 E-Route uses the Etherow – Goyt Valley Way.

Attributes
Lake/Reservoir; River
Start
Vernon Park, Stockport, Cheshire SJ907905
Finish
Hadfield, Derbys SK024960
Waymark
Stylised heron and name on green disc
Websites
www.tameside.gov.uk
Maps ◈
OS Landranger: 109, 110
OS Explorer: 1, 268, 277
Publications, badges and certificates
Booklets
Etherow: Goyt Valley Way (Tameside Countryside Warden Service). 24pp; A5. £2.40 (incs p&p).

Forest of Bowland Challenge Walk FOBCW

LANCS **43km/27 miles**

A route through remote countryside in the Forest of Bowland taking in Beacon Fell, Parlick and Fair Snape. With over 3,000 feet of ascent it is important to note that there are no facilities available.

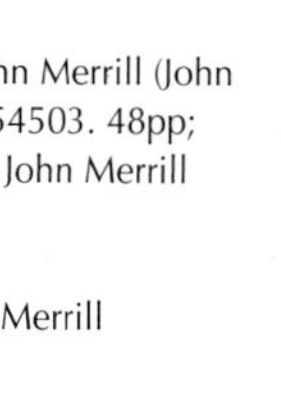

Attributes
Challenging; Anytime Challenge; Moorland
Start and Finish
Beacon Fell, Lancs SD565426
Maps
OS Landranger: 103
OS Explorer: 41
Publications, badges and certificates
Booklets
Forest of Bowland Challenge Walk by John Merrill (John Merrill Foundation). ISBN 9781874754503. 48pp; A5. £4.95 (+ £1.00 p&p). Cheques to John Merrill Foundation.
Badge & certificate
Forest of Bowland Challenge Walk (John Merrill Foundation). £5.00 (incs p&p).

Four Pikes Hike FPH

GTR MAN, LANCS, W YORKS **72km/45 miles**

A route over contrasting countryside taking in the Pikes of Rivington, Howlow, Thieveley and Stoodley.

Attributes
Challenging; Anytime Challenge; Moorland
Start
Great House Barn, Horwich, Lancs SD628138
Finish
Hebden Bridge, W Yorks SD992273
Maps
OS Landranger: 103, 109
OS Explorer: 287, 21
Publications, badges and certificates
Looseleaf
Four Pikes Hike (Norman Thomas). Free (+ 9 x 4 SAE).

Badge & certificate
Four Pikes Hike (Norman Thomas). £2.00 (+ SAE).

Geopark Way GPW

GLOS, HEREFS, SHROPS, WORCS **175km/109 miles**

A route devised to highlight geology, landscape and associated heritage by linking geological sites in the Abberley and Malvern Hills Global Geopark. It makes a sinuous north-south traverse from the Severn in Shropshire through Wyre Forest coalfield to the wind-blown sands of Hartlebury Common near Stourport. Crossing to the Abberley Hills, it then goes along the crests of the ancient Malvern Hills, which have volcanic origins. In Gloucestershire it traverses the Leadon valley, visits May Hill and Huntley Quarry Geological Reserve before crossing the Vale of Gloucester and Severn where the Cotswold Hills come into full view.

Attributes
River; Downland/Wolds; Heritage; Geological; Industrial History
Start
Bridgnorth Castle, Shropshire SO717927
Finish
Gloucester Cathedral, Glos SO831188
Waymark
Fossil (dalmanites tribolite)/route name, logo on posts
Websites
www.earthheritagetrust.org, www.geopark.org.uk
Maps
OS Landranger: 138, 149, 150, 162
OS Explorer: 14, 179, 189, 190, 204, 218, 219
Publications, badges and certificates
Paperbacks (spiral bound)
Geopark Way Trail Guide (Herefordshire & Worcestershire Earth Heritage Trust) 2009. ISBN 9789558390097. 136pp; A5. £9.95 (+£2.00 p&p).
Leaflets (download only)
Geopark Way – Visitor Guide by Hereford and Worcestershire Earth Heritage Trust (Herefordshire & Worcestershire Earth Heritage Trust) 2009. Free to Download.

Gritstone Trail GT

CHESHIRE, STAFFS **56km/35 miles**

The Trail, which now includes the former Mow Cop Trail, follows the gritstone edge providing views of the Peak District and Cheshire Plain, with much of the upland walking above 1,000ft. The route takes in Lyme Park, Sponds Hill, Tegg's Nose Country Park, Croker Hill and Mow Cop. It links with the Staffordshire Way near to Rushton Spencer and the South Cheshire Way at Mow Cop. The Trail section from Rushton Spencer to Disley is part of the E2 E-Route. At Lyme Park the Trail connects with the Ladybrook Interest Trail Walk (10 miles and on OS mapping but no publication).

Attributes
Moorland
Start
Disley Station, Disley, Cheshire SJ972846
Finish
Kidsgrove, Staffs SJ837542
Waymark
Black bootmark & yellow letter G
Websites
www.cheshire.gov.uk
Maps ◈
OS Landranger: 109, 118
OS Explorer: 1, 24, 258, 268
Publications, badges and certificates
Paperbacks
Gritstone Trail & Mow Cop Trail by Carl Rogers (Northern Eye Books Limited (Mara)) 1995. ISBN 9780952240945. 68pp; 135 x 210. £4.25 (+ £2.00 p&p).
Leaflets
Gritstone Trail (Cheshire County Council) 2001. A2/3. Free (+ 9 x 6 SAE). Includes Mow Cop Trail; downloadable.
Walking Support Providers
Byways

Heart of Bowland Walk HBOWW

LANCS, N YORKS **29km/18 miles**

A varied circuit that includes steep-sided valleys, rivers and forests in the picturesque Forest of Bowland

Attributes
Challenging; Anytime Challenge; Moorland
Start and Finish
Slaidburn, Lancs SD714523

Maps
OS Landranger: 103
OS Explorer: 41
Publications, badges and certificates
Looseleaf
Heart of Bowland Challenge Walk (LDWA West Lancashire Group). 1pp; A4. Free (+ 9 x 4 SAE).

Badge & certificate
Heart of Bowland Walk (LDWA West Lancashire Group). £1.50 (+ A4 SAE).

Heart of England Way HOEW

GLOS, STAFFS, WARKS, W MIDLANDS 163km/101 miles

The Way follows a curving route through gently undulating farmland, lowland heath, woodland and along riverside paths. It takes in Cannock Chase, Lichfield, Kingsbury Water Park, the Arden countryside (see Arden Way), the Avon Valley, and the northern aspects of the Cotswolds to Chipping Campden, Swell and Lower Slaughter. The Heart of England Way Association provides a volunteer warden service. See also E-Routes (E2). The waymarked Avon Valley Footpath (10 miles and included on OS mapping but no publication) provides a link from Stratford-upon-Avon to the Way near Bidford-on-Avon.

Attributes
River
Start
Milford, Staffs SJ973209
Finish
Bourton-on-the-Water, Glos SP170209
Waymark
Named green and white discs with oak trees
Websites
www.heartofenglandway.org
Maps ◈
OS Landranger: 127, 128, 139, 140, 150, 151, 163
OS Explorer: 45, 205, 220, 221, 232, 244
Publications, badges and certificates
Paperbacks
Heart of England Way by John Roberts (Walkways) 2000. ISBN 9780947708405. 124pp; 206 x 146. £7.50 (incs p&p). Includes sketch maps and accommodation list. Also available from the HOEW Association.
Booklets
Heart of England Way: Chipping Camden to Bourton-on-the-Water by Cotswold Wardens (Cotswold District Council) 1992. 22pp; A5. £1.25 (+ 33p p&p).

Hebden Valleys Heritage Trek HVHT

LANCS, W YORKS 31km/19 miles

A roller-coaster route encircling Hebden Bridge and visting High Town, Hardcastle Crags, Jumble Hole Clough, Stoodley Pike, Broadhead Nature Reserve and the Rochdale Canal towpath. With the Manorlands Meander, it makes up the South Pennines Twin Challenge.

Attributes
Challenging; Anytime Challenge; Moorland
Start and Finish
Hebden Bridge Tourist Information Centre, W Yorks SD992272
Maps
OS Landranger: 103, 104
OS Explorer: 21
Publications, badges and certificates
Booklets
Hebden Valleys Heritage Trek (Tony Wimbush). £2.00 (+ SAE). Cheques to W. A. Wimbush.
Badge & certificate
Hebden Valleys Heritage Trek (Tony Wimbush). £1.50 (+ SAE). Cheques to W. A .Wimbush.

Hodder Way HODW

LANCS 43km/27 miles

From the river's source on Access Land near the Cross of Greet to Hodder Foot, where it joins the River Ribble, the route passes through the attractive villages of Slaidburn, Newton, Dunsop Bridge, Whitewell, Bashall Eaves and Great Mitton.

Attributes
River
Start
Cross of Greet, north of Slaidburn, Lancs SD682608
Finish
Confluence of Hodder and Ribble, near Hurst Green, Lancs SD709382
Maps
OS Landranger: 103
OS Explorer: 41
Publications, badges and certificates
Booklets
Hodder Way With Circular Walks Along The Hodder by Clitheroe Ramblers (RA Clitheroe Group). £4.50. Cheques to RA Clitheroe Group Social Account.

Hope House Way HHW

CEREDIGION, DENBIGHS, GWYNEDD, HEREFS, POWYS, SHROPS, TELFORD W, WREXHAM 539km/335 miles

The route, both varied in terrain and rich in history, takes in Ironbridge, Wenlock Edge Ludlow, Presteigne,

Kington, Hay on Wye, Builth Wells, Rhayader, Elan Valley, Devil's Bridge, Machynlleth, Dinas Mawddwy, Bala, Llangollen, Craignant, Montgomery, All Streetton and Cressage before returning to Wellington. It was devised to cover areas served by Hope House Children's Respite Hospice.

Attributes
Heritage; Charity
Start and Finish
Millennium Clock, Market Square, Wellington, Shropshire SJ650116
Websites
www.hopehouse.org.uk
Maps
OS Landranger: 117, 125, 127, 135, 138, 147, 148
OS Explorer: 13, 18, 23, 188, 200, 201, 202, 203, 213, 215, 216, 217, 240, 241, 242, 255, 256
Publications, badges and certificates
Paperbacks (spiral bound)
Hope House Way (Hope House Hospices) 2004. ISBN 9780954814601. 128pp; 190 x 120. £9.95 (+ £1.00 p&p). Proceeds to Hope House Children's Hospices.
Walking Support Providers
Bobs

Hyndburn Clog — HYC

LANCS — 50km/31 miles

A route that circumscribes Accrington, passing through pastures, villages and reservoirs. The booklet includes details of two other routes: the Canal Clog (20 miles) and the Moorland Heights Clog (18 miles).

Attributes
Challenging; Anytime Challenge; Moorland
Start and Finish
Stanhill Village, Accrington, Lancs SD723277
Waymark
Clog logo on brown disc
Websites
www.hyndburnramblers.co.uk
Maps
OS Landranger: 103
OS Explorer: 287
Publications, badges and certificates
Leaflets
Hyndburn Clog (RA North East Lancashire Area). A5. £0.20 (+ 9 x 6 SAE).
Badge & certificate
Hyndburn Clog (RA North East Lancashire Area). £1.00 & £0.50 (+ SAE). Cheques to Ramblers Association (Hyndburn Group).

Irwell Sculpture Trail — IST

GTR MAN, LANCS — 48km/30 miles

The Trail links the centre of Manchester with the moors above Bacup. It makes use of a former railway line and follows the former Bolton – Bury Canal, and goes through Bury, Ramsbottom and Rawtenstall to the finish, near Irwell Spring, where it links with the Rossendale Way. Since 1987, various sculptures have been sited along the Trail, the intention being that, on completion, there will be 50 in place. A major re-development will provide GPS and mobile phone technology for onsite interpretation and new routes linking other tourist attractions such as Salford Quays and Rossendale Adrenaline Gateway.

Attributes
Easy; Former Railway; Cycle Route; River; Canal; Moorland
Start
Salford Quays, Gtr Man SJ833976

Finish
Deerplay Moor, Lancs SD866264
Waymark
Dragonfly on fawn square
Maps ◈
OS Landranger: 103, 109
OS Explorer: 277, 21, 287
Publications, badges and certificates
Folder
Irwell Sculpture Trail (Rossendale Borough Council). 12 leaflets. £1.00 (+ 50p p&p).

Jack Mytton Way — JMYW

SHROPS — 117km/73 miles

From the northern edge of Wyre Forest, it follows a disused railway to Highley and the Severn Valley, then goes across rolling farmland to Much Wenlock where it follows the escarpment of Wenlock Edge, to cross Ape Dale and descend to Church Stretton. It climbs to The Long Mynd, via the Cardingmill Valley, to reach Plowden and Clun Forest. It runs for a stretch alongside Offa's Dyke before finishing on the Shropshire/Powys border. An additional circa-25 mile loop from the start at Billingsley runs down to Cleobury Mortimer and on to Rushbury, where it rejoins with the main route.

Attributes
Former Railway; Horse Ride (Multi User); Moorland
Start
Cleobury Mortimer, Shrops SO670759
Finish
Llanfair Waterdine, Shrops SO245761
Waymark
Horseshoe motif with horse and rider

Websites
www.shropshire.gov.uk
Maps ◈
OS Landranger: 127, 137, 138, 148
OS Explorer: 201, 216, 217, 218, 242
Publications, badges and certificates
Leaflets
Jack Mytton Way: Shropshire's Long Distance Bridleway (Shropshire County Council) 2004. Free. Downloadable.

Lancashire Coastal Way LCCW

LANCS **106km/66 miles**

It follows the coastline between Merseyside and Cumbria, diverting inland where necessary. Lancashire's coast has a variety of landscapes from the distinctive limestone scenery of Arnside and Silverdale to salt-marshes and agricultural land and the seaside resorts of Morecambe, Blackpool and the Fylde coast. Lancaster and Carnforth are passed en route. There are major river estuaries of the Lune, Wyre and Ribble, with much birdlife. There is evidence of past industries based on iron, salt and limestone, alongside many modern businesses and the busy harbours at Fleetwood, Heysham and Glasson Dock. There are views of Morecambe Bay, the Bowland Fells and the Lake District.

Attributes
Easy; Coastal; River
Start
Silverdale, Lancs SD456755
Finish
Freckleton, Lancs SD434288
Waymark
Gull & wave logo
Websites
www.lancashire.gov.uk
Maps ◈
OS Landranger: 97, 102
OS Explorer: 286, 296, 41
Publications, badges and certificates
Leaflets
Lancashire Coastal Way (Lancashire County Council). A5. Free.
Paperbacks
Lancashire Coastal Way & the Wyre Way: Fleetwood and Knott End to Lancaster by Ian O. Brodie, Krysia Brodie (Lancashire County Books) 1993. ISBN 9781871236200. 64pp; 140 x 96. £2.95.

Lancashire Trail LANCT

GTR MAN, LANCS, MERSEYSIDE, N YORKS **116km/72 miles**

A route linking industrial Lancashire with the Pennine Way National Trail, taking in Billinge, Abbey Lakes, Ashurst's Beacon, Harrock Hill, Coppull Moor, Blackrod, Rivington Pike, Abbey village, Mellor, Whalley, Pendle Hill and Barley. Links to Wigan, Bolton, Burnley, to the the Ribble Way at Sawley, and to the Sandstone Trail are also described.

Attributes
Lake/Reservoir; Moorland; Urban
Start
St Helens, Merseyside SJ512956
Finish
Thornton-in-Craven, N Yorks SD906484
Maps
OS Landranger: 102, 103, 108, 109
OS Explorer: 21, 41, 275, 276, 285, 287
Publications, badges and certificates
Paperbacks
Lancashire Trail by Brian Smailes (Challenge Publications) 2003. ISBN 9781903568101. 68pp; 125 x 185. £5.95.

Lancashire–Lakeland Link LLLINK

CUMBRIA, LANCS **114km/71 miles**

Using former railway lines, parkland, canal towpath and riverside, the route visits Garstang, Galgate, Lancaster, Carnforth, Silverdale, Milnthorpe, Levens and Kendal. Easy access to castles, pele towers and mansions is also available. It links with the Dales Way at Burneside.

Attributes
Former Railway; River; Canal
Start
Preston, Lancs SD542297
Finish
Windermere, Cumbria SD414986
Maps
OS Landranger: 97, 102
OS Explorer: 286, 7, 41

Publications, badges and certificates
Paperbacks
Lancashire-Lakeland Link (Jack Jowett) 1994. ISBN 9781873888605. 96pp; 122 x 182. £4.99 (+ 50p p&p).

Lancaster Canal LANCC

CUMBRIA, LANCS **91km/57 miles**

A towpath walk from the Ribble across the Fylde and through Lancaster and Carnforth to the Lake District.

Attributes
Easy; Canal
Start
Preston, Lancs SD526303
Finish
Kendal, Cumbria SD520931
Websites
www.citycoastcountryside.co.uk
Maps
OS Landranger: 97, 102
OS Explorer: 286, 7, 41
Map (Other)
Lancaster Canal (GEOprojects)
Publications, badges and certificates
Paperbacks
Walker's Guide to the Lancaster Canal by Robert Swain (Cicerone Press) 1998. ISBN 9781852840556. 116pp; 116 x 176. £5.99.
Leaflets
Lancaster Canal: Lancaster to Kendal (South Lakeland District Council). 12pp; A4/3. Free (+ 9 x 4 SAE).

Llangollen Canal Walk LLANCW

CHESHIRE, DENBIGHS, WREXHAM **82km/51 miles**

This walk follows the Shropshire Union Canal to Hurleston Junction where it joins the Llangollen Canal, visiting Whitchurch, Ellesmere, Chirk, Trevor, the Pontcysyllte Aqueduct and Llangollen.

Attributes
Anytime Challenge; Canal; Heritage; Industrial History
Start
Nantwich, Cheshire SJ650524
Finish
Horseshoe Falls, Llangollen, Denbighs SJ203434
Websites
www.canaljunction.com, www.waterscape.com
Maps
OS Landranger: 117, 118, 125
OS Explorer: 256, 257
Map (Other)
Llangollen & Montgomery Canals (GEOprojects)
Publications, badges and certificates
Booklets
Walker's Guide to the Llangollen Canal by John Merrill (John Merrill Foundation) 1999. ISBN 9781841730172. 56pp; A5. £4.95 (+ £1.00 p&p).
Badge & certificate
Llangollen Canal Walk (John Merrill Foundation). £5.00 (incs p&p).
Walking Support Providers
Byways

Lune Valley Ramble LVR

LANCS **27km/17 miles**

It traces the course of the River Lune's lower reaches through lowland countryside, bounded by high moors, limestone hills and shadowed by the distant peaks of Ingleborough, Whernside and Leck Fell.

Attributes
Easy; River
Start
Lancaster Railway Station, Lancs SD471617
Finish
Kirkby Lonsdale, Cumbria SD615783
Waymark
Named signposts
Websites
www.citycoastcountryside.co.uk
Maps ◈
OS Landranger: 97
OS Explorer: 2, 41, 296, 7
Publications, badges and certificates
Booklets
Lune Valley Ramble (Lancaster City Council). 16pp; A5. Free (+ SAE).

Lunesdale Walk LUW

LANCS **59km/37 miles**

From Carnforth the Lancaster Canal is followed to Capernwray, where the route traces a figure-of-eight line through Swarthdale, Melling, Roeburndale, Hornby, Arkholme and back to Capernwray and the finish. The crossing-over point is at Loyn Bridge on the River Lune near to Hornby. The Carnforth Canal Walks publication describes three short circular walks between Carnforth and Capernway providing alternative routes between those locations.

Attributes
River; Canal
Start and Finish
Carnforth Railway Station, Lancs SD497708
Waymark
Named discs (yellow/green)

Websites
www.citycoastcountryside.co.uk
Maps
OS Landranger: 97
OS Explorer: 41
Publications, badges and certificates
Booklets
Lunesdale Walk (Lancaster City Council). 20pp; A5. Free.
Carnforth Canal Walks (Lancaster City Council). 16pp; A5. Free.

Maelor Way MAELW

CHESHIRE, SHROPS, WREXHAM **38km/24 miles**

The Way links the Sandstone Trail, South Cheshire Way, Marches Way and Shropshire Way at Grindley Brook, to the Offa's Dyke Path National Trail at Chirk. It crosses farmland to Hanmer Mere and Overton, then follows woodland trails alongside the Rivers Dee and Ceiriog to Chirk. It uses public footpaths, bridleways, quiet lanes and canal towpath to reach Bronygarth in the shadow of Chirk Castle.

Attributes
River; Canal
Start
Grindley Brook, Cheshire SJ522433
Finish
Bronygarth, Shrops SJ263375
Waymark
MW monogram as yellow arrow/name on green disc
Websites
www.wrexham.gov.uk
Maps ◈
OS Landranger: 117, 126
OS Explorer: 240, 241, 255, 256, 257
Publications, badges and certificates
Paperbacks
Guide to the Maelor Way by Gordon Emery (Wrexham Tourist Information Centre) 2008. ISBN 9781872265988. 126pp; A5. £1.00 (+ p&p). Updates are free online.

Mersey Valley Timberland Trail MVTT

CHESHIRE **35km/22 miles**

Passing through Lymm, the route connects with the towpath of the Bridgewater Canal and passes Lymm Dam, Grappenhall Wood, Appleton Dingle, Daresbury Firs, Windmill Hill and Halton Village. It is partly urban, mostly rural, taking in low-lying hills, woodland, parkland, farmland and sections of the Bridgewater Canal. It broadly follows the sandstone edge of the Cheshire Plain or drops to the Mersey valley below it, giving views from both levels.

Attributes
Easy; Forest/Woodland; Canal; Urban; Literary
Start
Spud Wood, Oughtrington, Lymm, Cheshire SJ702875
Finish
Runcorn Hill, Runcorn, Cheshire SJ507816
Waymark
Named signs, black stylised tree, white background
Websites
www.discovercheshire.co.uk,
www.discoverthemerseyforest.co.uk
Maps ◈
OS Landranger: 108, 109
OS Explorer: 267, 275, 276
Publications, badges and certificates
Leaflets
Walking the Mersey Valley Timberland Trail (Mersey Valley Partnership) 2001. A3/8. Free (+ 9 x 6 SAE).

Middlewich Challenge Walk MIDDCW

CHESHIRE **35km/22 miles**

A figure-of-eight route taking in the Middlewich Canal which links the Trent & Mersey and Shropshire Union Canals.

Attributes
Challenging; Anytime Challenge; Canal
Start and Finish
Church Minshull, Cheshire SJ667606

Maps
OS Landranger: 118
OS Explorer: 257, 267
Publications, badges and certificates
Booklets
Middlewich Challenge Walk by John Merrill (John Merrill Foundation) 1996. ISBN 9781874754633. 32pp;

A5. £4.50 (+ £1.00 p&p). Cheques to John Merrill Foundation.

Badge & certificate

Middlewich Challenge Walk (John Merrill Foundation). £5.00 (incs p&p).

Millennium Way – Staffordshire MLWS

STAFFS **66km/41 miles**

Spanning the width of the county, the route makes use of the Stafford – Newport Greenway, farmland paths and canal towpaths as it passes through or close to Stafford, Colwich, Rugeley, Yoxall and Barton Under Needwood.

Attributes
Easy; Former Railway; Canal
Start
Outwoods, Staffs SJ786187
Finish
Burton upon Trent, Staffs SK234234
Waymark
Red arrowhead on white background with rope knot and WMM
Websites
www.staffordshire.gov.uk
Maps
OS Landranger: 127, 128
OS Explorer: 242, 244, 245
Publications, badges and certificates
Booklets (spiral bound)
Way for the Millennium (Staffordshire County Council). 52pp; A5. £3.50 (+ 50p p&p). Cheques to Staffordshire County Council.
Leaflets
Staffordshire Way & Millennium Way: Information & Accommodation guide (Staffordshire County Council). A5/4. Free (+ 9 x 6 SAE).

Mortimer Trail MORT

HEREFS, SHROPS **48km/30 miles**

A walk through the Marches of England, with extensive forests, limestone tops and gentle pastures, in an area dominated in mediæval times by the Mortimer family, one of the most powerful Norman earldoms. It follows a succession of hills and ridges, with some strenuous climbs, and crosses the valleys of the rivers Teme, Lugg and Arrow. The route also takes in the Mary Knoll Valley, the High Vinnals, Orleton Common, Croft Ambrey and Wapley hill fort.

Attributes
Challenging; Forest/Woodland; Moorland; Heritage
Start
Ludlow, Shrops SO510746
Finish
Kington, Herefs SO296566
Waymark
Green/brown/yellow named disc with crown and shield logo
Websites
www.royalforestofdean.info
Maps ◈
OS Landranger: 137, 138, 148, 149
OS Explorer: 201, 203
Publications, badges and certificates
Paperbacks
Mortimer Trail: Walker's Guide (Leominster TIC) 2002. ISBN 9780953698318. 48pp; 210 x 117. £6.60 (incs p&p). Cheques to Herefordshire County Council.
Walking Support Providers
Contours; Marches Walks

New Five Trig Points Walk NFTPW

GTR MAN, W YORKS **29km/18 miles**

This circular walk, over the Pennine moors, visits the trig points on Bishop Park, Tame Scout, Blackstone Edge, White Hill and Standedge. It is partly coincident with the Pennine Way National Trail.

Attributes
Challenging; Anytime Challenge; Moorland
Start and Finish
Delph, Gtr Man SD985079
Maps
OS Landranger: 109, 110
OS Explorer: 1, 21
Publications, badges and certificates
Looseleaf
New Five Trig Points Walk (Carole E. Engel). A4. Free (+ 9 x 4 SAE).
Badge & certificate
New Five Trig Points Walk (Carole E. Engel). £1.50 (+ SAE) & £0.20 (+ 9 x 6 SAE).

Newcastle Way (Staffordshire) NCWST

STAFFS **40km/25 miles**

A traverse across the Borough of Newcastle under Lyme, from Mow Cop to the Shropshire border near Market Drayton, visiting Kidsgrove Bank, Red Street, Black Bank, Madeley, Black Brook and Loggerheads. There is varied terrain, from moorland scenery through industrial relics of coal mining, iron furnaces and brick making, to farming country and the sandstone ridges of Maer and Ashley. The idea for such a route originated from a Newcastle Councillor, Nigel Jones. It links with the Staffordshire Way at Mow Cop and with the Shropshire Union Canal at Market Drayton.

Attributes
Moorland; Industrial History
Start
Mow Cop, Staffordshire SJ858576
Finish
Market Drayton, Staffordshire SJ685343
Waymark
Blue Pit Wheel with yellow arrow.
Websites
www.staffordshire.gov.uk
Maps
OS Landranger: 118, 127
OS Explorer: 243, 257, 258
Publications, badges and certificates
Booklets
Newcastle Way (Staffordshire County Council) 2007. 20pp; A5. Free.

North Bowland Traverse NBOWT

LANCS, N YORKS **50km/31 miles**

A mainly low-level walk through the north eastern Bowland Fells crossing farmland and meadowland. It links with the Witches Way and Ribble Way at Slaidburn. Note that much of the route is well away from any good roads and conditions can change rapidly.

Attributes
Easy; Anytime Challenge
Start
Slaidburn, Lancs SD712524
Finish
Stainforth, N Yorks SD821673
Maps
OS Landranger: 97, 98, 103
OS Explorer: 41
Publications, badges and certificates
Looseleaf
North Bowland Traverse (David Johnson). Free (+ 9 x 4 SAE). Route outline, grid refs, accommodation/transport details.
Badge & certificate
North Bowland Traverse (David Johnson). £1.50 (+ 6 x 4 SAE).

North Cheshire Way NCW

CHESHIRE **113km/70 miles**

Developed by the Mid-Cheshire Footpath Society, the route has been designed to run close to the major urban areas of Merseyside, north Cheshire and Manchester with easy access by car or public transport. It heads from the Wirral to the Peak District across some of Cheshire's most beautiful countryside. Places of interest along the way include Chester and the Wirral, Helsby Hill, Frodsham Hill, Weaver Valley, the Anderton Boat Lift, Marbury Country Park, Manchester Airport, Styal Quarry Bank Mill and Country Park, The Edge at Alderley, Adlington Hall, Lyme Park and Disley.

Attributes
Moorland; Heritage; Industrial History
Start
Hooton Station, Cheshire SJ350782
Finish
Disley Station, Cheshire SJ972846
Waymark
Yellow arrow on black with NCW in bold
Websites
www.mcfs.org.uk
Maps
OS Landranger: 117, 118, 109
OS Explorer: 266, 267, 268, 1
Publications, badges and certificates
Paperbacks (spiral bound)
North Cheshire Way by Mid Cheshire Footpath Society (Mid Cheshire Footpath Society) 2006. ISBN 9780955357305. 112pp; 216 x 150. £8.95 (+ 90p p&p). Cheques to Mid Cheshire Footpath Society.

Oldham Way OLDW

GTR MAN **64km/40 miles**

A walk around the borough, where the landscape varies from moorland to urban canal. It starts at Dove Stone Reservoir near Greenfield, and continues over Saddleworth Moor to Diggle and Castleshaw Moor and then to Denshaw. It skirts to the north of Shaw and Royton to meet the Rochdale Canal at Chadderton Hall Park. It follows the canal south through Chadderton to Failsworth, after which it joins the Medlock Valley to Daisy Nook and Park Bridge before climbing over Hartshead Pike to Quick. See also E-Routes (E2). The overlapping circular Standedge Trail (12 miles and on OS mapping) is a moorland walk across the Pennines linking both ends of Standedge Tunnel, where remains from the canal, rail and turnpike eras may be seen.

Attributes
Challenging; Lake/Reservoir; Canal; Moorland; Urban
Start and Finish
Dove Stone Reservoir, Gtr Man SE017044
Waymark
Owl disc
Maps ◈
OS Landranger: 109, 110
OS Explorer: 1, 21, 277
Publications, badges and certificates
Folder
Oldham Way (Oldham Metropolitan Borough Council). 9 leaflets; A4/3. £3.49 (incs p&p).
Leaflets
Standedge Trail by Kirklees Countryside Unit (Kirklees Metropolitan Council). £1.30 (+ 50 p&p). or £4.20 with a Marsden centred OS map.

Pendle and Ribble Round — PARR

LANCS — **32km/20 miles**

A route crossing Pendle Hill and visiting Downham before returning by riverside and farm paths.

Attributes
Anytime Challenge; River; Moorland
Start and Finish
Whalley, Lancs SD732362
Maps
OS Landranger: 103
OS Explorer: 287, 41
Publications, badges and certificates
Booklets
Bronte Round/Pendle & Ribble Round by Derek Magnall (Norman Thomas) 1994. 36pp; A5. £1.85 (incs p&p).
Badge & certificate
Pendle and Ribble Round (Norman Thomas). £2.00 (+ SAE).

Pendle Way — PDW

LANCS — **72km/45 miles**

A route through contrasting scenery, ranging from moorland to river valleys visiting Barnoldswick, Thornton-in-Craven, Wycoller, Reedley, Newchurch and Pendle Hill. The latter part of the route has associations with the Pendle Witches, the theme of the 7.5 mile Pendle Witches Walking Trail. The three principal summits in the area, Pendle Hill, Weets Hill and Boulsworth Hill can be climbed as 'Pendle's Three Peaks'.

Attributes
Challenging; Moorland
Start and Finish
Pendle Heritage Centre, Park Hill, Barrowford, Nelson, Lancs SD863398
Waymark
Black witch logo
Maps ◈
OS Landranger: 103
OS Explorer: 287, 21, 41
Publications, badges and certificates
Paperbacks
Pendle Way by Paul Hannon (Hillside Publications) 1998. ISBN 9781870141574. 48pp; 175 x 115. £3.50 (+ 60p p&p).
Folder
Pendle Way (Pendle Borough Council) 2001. 8 leaflets; A4/3. £3.00. Cheques to Pendle Borough Council.
Booklets
Pendle's Three Peaks (Pendle Borough Council). £0.50.
Leaflets
Witches Walking Trail (Pendle Borough Council) 2005. Free. DVD also available from TICs/Heritage Centre Tel: 01282 661701.
Walking Support Providers
Northwestwalks

Pioneers Round — PIONR

GTR MAN, LANCS — **32km/20 miles**

A route starting from Toad Lane, the birthplace of the Co-operative Movement, taking in Healey Dell, Watergrove Reservoir, Hollingworth Lake, Milnrow and the Rochdale Canal.

Attributes
Anytime Challenge; Lake/Reservoir; Canal
Start and Finish
Rochdale, Gtr Man SD894136

Maps
OS Landranger: 109
OS Explorer: 21, 277
Publications, badges and certificates
Booklets
Pioneers Round by Derek Magnall (Rochdale Pioneers Museum) 1994. 34pp; A5. £2.00 (incs p&p).
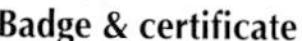
Badge & certificate
Pioneers Round (Rochdale Pioneers Museum). £1.50 (+ SAE).

Raad ny Foillan (Isle of Man Coastal Path) IOMCP

IOM 153km/95 miles

The Raad ny Foillan or Way of the Gull is a footpath around the Manx coast created to mark the island's 'Heritage Year' celebrations in 1986. It follows the coast wherever it can and traverses terrain which varies from shingle beaches at the Ayres in the north, hills of over 600ft and cliffs above the Sloc (Stacks) in the west, and the coastal sward at Scarlett near Castletown. There are spectacular clifftop views with much birdlife and contrasting sections on resort promenades. Using public roads only when necessary, it can easily be walked in sections between towns and villages using public transport. Three other significant routes provide for traverses of the island. The Millennium Way – Isle of Man – celebrates the Manx Millennium, the 1000th anniversary in 1979 of the establishment of Tynwald, the Island's Parliament. This 28-mile walk (waymarked and on OS mapping) uses an ancient ridgeway route, "Via Regia" or the Royal Way, on which the former Kings of Man travelled to its former capital, Castletown. From near Ramsey it goes south over the island, climbing to open heather moorland on the western slopes of Snaefell to reach the Way's highest point at 1,500ft, descending to Crosby and following paths, roads and the banks of the Silverburn river through Ballasalla to the medieval castle of Rushen. The 10-mile waymarked Herring Road ('Bayr ny Skeddan' in Manx, an old fishermens' route) goes north from the coast at Castletown via South Barrule and Glen Maye to Peel, rising to 1000ft at the Round Table. The Heritage Trail (10 miles, waymarked and on OS mapping but no publication) follows the old Douglas to Peel railway line across the island from east to west parallel to the TT course as far as St John's, with branches to Sulby (15 miles). The Cicerone book by Terry Marsh is a general guide to walking on the island.

Attributes
Coastal; Heritage
Start and Finish
Douglas, IoM SC384754
Waymark
White gull on blue sign with name
Websites
www.visitisleofman.com, www.gov.im
Maps ◈
OS Landranger: 95
Isle of Man Map
Isle of Man: North & South – 1:25000 (Isle of Man Department of Tourism & Leisure)
Harvey Map (Sheet Map)
Isle of Man (Superwalker) (Harvey Maps)
Publications, badges and certificates
Paperbacks
Isle of Man Coastal Path: Raad ny Foillan – The Way of the Gull – The Millenium and Herring Ways by Aileen Evans (Cicerone Press) 2004. ISBN 9781852844004. 160pp; 116 x 170. £10.00.
Walking on the Isle of Man: 40 Walks Around the Island by Terry Marsh (Cicerone Press) 2004. ISBN 9781852843991. 160pp; 170 x 114. £10.00.
Booklets
Walking the Isle of Man Coastal Path by John Merrill (John Merrill Foundation). ISBN 9781874754534. 48pp; A5. £5.50 (+ £1.00 p&p). Cheques to John Merrill Foundation.
Looseleaf
Raad ny Foillan (Coastal Path) & Bayr ny Skeddan (Herring Road) Information/Accommodation List (Isle of Man Department of Tourism & Leisure) 2006. 2pp; A4. Free.
Millennium Way: Information Sheet (Isle of Man Department of Tourism & Leisure). 2pp; A4. Free.
Leaflets
Walks on the Isle of Man: Visitors Pocket Guide (Isle of Man Department of Tourism & Leisure) 2001. A5/8. Free.
Badge & certificate
Isle of Man Coast Path (John Merrill Foundation). £5.00 (incs p&p).
Walking Support Providers
Celtic

Ramsbottom Round RAMR

LANCS 32km/20 miles

A route around Ramsbottom taking in the Irwell Valley, Irwell Vale and Summerseat.

Attributes
Challenging; Anytime Challenge; River; Moorland
Start and Finish
Ramsbottom, Lancs SD792168
Maps
OS Landranger: 103, 109
OS Explorer: 287
Publications, badges and certificates
Booklets
Ramsbottom Round/Spanners Round (Norman Thomas) 1992. 36pp; A5. £1.85 (incs p&p).
Badge & certificate
Ramsbottom Round (Norman Thomas). £2.00 (+ SAE).

Ribble Way — RIBW

LANCS, N YORKS — **105km/65 miles**

It traces the valley of the River Ribble from the mouth to the source near to the Pennine Way National Trail on Gayle Moor. From the tidal marshes, the route passes Preston, Ribchester, Clitheroe, with views of Pendle Hill, Settle and Horton-in-Ribblesdale to finish in moorland terrain below the three peaks of Ingleborough, Whernside and Pen-y-Ghent. At Horton, the Pen-y-Ghent Café maintains a register for signature/comments by those taking part in the walk. The Tolkien Trail (5.5 miles) starting from Hurst Green passes Stonyhurst College, associated with J. R. R. Tolkien, and its river section coincides with the Ribble Way.

Attributes
River; Moorland; Literary
Start
Longton, Lancs SD458255
Finish
Gayle Moor, N Yorks SD813832
Waymark
Blue and white letters RW/wave logo
Websites
www.lancashire.gov.uk, www.ribblevalley.gov.uk
Maps ◈
OS Landranger: 98, 102, 103
OS Explorer: 2, 21, 41, 286, 287
Publications, badges and certificates
Paperbacks
Ribble Way: A Northern England Trail by Dennis Kelsall, Jan Kelsall (Cicerone Press) 2005. ISBN 9781852844561. 144pp; 172 x 116. £10.00.
Leaflets
Tolkien Trail (Ribble Valley Borough Council). A3/6. Free. Downloadable.
Walking Support Providers
Byways

Rochdale Way — ROCHW

GTR MAN — **72km/45 miles**

A route around the Borough of Rochdale over moorland and through wooded valleys and passing historic urban sites. Blackstone Edge, Healey Dell, Knowl Hill, Queens Park, Tandle Hill and Piethorne Valley are visited along the Way.

Attributes
Moorland; Heritage
Start and Finish
Hollingworth Lake Visitor Centre, Littleborough, Rochdale, Gtr Man SD939152
Waymark
Clogs and cobble logo
Maps ◈
OS Landranger: 103, 109
OS Explorer: 21, 277
Publications, badges and certificates
Paperbacks
Rochdale Way (Hollingworth Lake Visitor Centre). 34pp; A5. £2.50 (+ 9 x 6 SAE + 2 x 2nd class stamps). Includes local history information.

Rossendale Way — RSW

GTR MAN, LANCS — **66km/41 miles**

A high-level route around Bacup, Rawtenstall, Haslingden and Whitworth in the Rossendale Valley, crossing the open moors and farmland of the South Pennines which roughly follows the Rossendale Borough boundary. Although easy to follow, it does need care in poor conditions. The waymarked Weighver's Way (9 miles and on OS mapping) is a linear route from Hollingworth Lake, Littleborough, which connects with the Rossendale Way at Healey Dell.

Attributes
Challenging; Moorland; Industrial History
Start and Finish
Sharneyford, Lancs SD889246
Waymark
Letters RW, green on yellow arrows

Maps ◈
OS Landranger: 103, 109
OS Explorer: 287, 21
Publications, badges and certificates
Folder
Rossendale Way (Rossendale Borough Council). 8pp; A4/3. Set of 8 leaflets. £1.00 (+ 50p p&p).

Leaflets
Weighver's Way (Hollingworth Lake Visitor Centre). A4/3. Free if ordered with Rochdale Way booklet.

Saddleworth Five Trig Points Walk — SFTPW

GTR MAN — **32km/20 miles**

A tough circuit linking five trig points on the Saddleworth Moors: Alphin Pike, Black Hill, Featherbed Moss, West Nab and Broadstone Hill. Navigational skills are recommended.

Attributes
Challenging; Anytime Challenge; Moorland
Start and Finish
Greenfield, Gtr Man SE002040
Maps
OS Landranger: 109, 110
OS Explorer: 1
Publications, badges and certificates
Looseleaf
Saddleworth Five Trig Points Walk (Carole E. Engel). A4. Free (+ 9 x 4 SAE).
Badge & certificate
Saddleworth Five Trig Points Walk (Carole E. Engel). £1.50 (+ SAE) & £0.20 (+ 9 x 6 SAE).

Saddleworth Skyline — SWSKY

GTR MAN — **45km/28 miles**

A high-level route east of Manchester, linking the tops of Saddleworth Moor, over moorland, hills and valleys.

Attributes
Challenging; Anytime Challenge; Moorland
Start and Finish
Dovestones Reservoir, Gtr Man SE013034
Maps
OS Landranger: 109, 110
OS Explorer: 1, 21
Publications, badges and certificates
Looseleaf
Saddleworth Skyline (Sam R. Taylor). Free (+ 9 x 4 SAE).
Badge & certificate
Saddleworth Skyline (Sam R. Taylor). £1.80 & £0.20 (+ SAE).

Salt & Sails Trail — SAST

CHESHIRE — **32km/20 miles**

A route following the Weaver Navigation from the River Mersey, passing a number of locks and the Anderton Lift.

Attributes
Easy; Anytime Challenge; Canal
Start
Weston Point, Cheshire SJ494816
Finish
Winsford, Cheshire SJ655663
Maps
OS Landranger: 117, 118
OS Explorer: 267, 268
Publications, badges and certificates
Booklets
Salt & Sails Trail by David Burkhill-Howarth (John Merrill Foundation) 1995. ISBN 9781874754589. 44pp; A5. £4.50 (+ £1.00 p&p). Cheques to John Merrill Foundation.
Badge & certificate
Salt & Sails Trail (John Merrill Foundation). £5.00 (incs p&p).

Salter's Way — SALTW

CHESHIRE — **38km/24 miles**

Following an old salt track across lowland Cheshire, from the salt area around Northwich to the moors above Macclesfield. It passes still-working brine pumps, Jodrell Bank, and the raised lowland bog of Danes Moss.

Attributes a
Anytime Challenge; Moorland; Industrial History
Start
Broken Cross, Cheshire SJ682732
Finish
Salterford, Cheshire SJ983763
Maps
OS Landranger: 118
OS Explorer: 267, 268, 24
Publications, badges and certificates
Booklets
Salter's Way by John Merrill (John Merrill Foundation). ISBN 9780907496977. 32pp; A5. £4.50 (+ £1.00 p&p). Cheques to John Merrill Foundation.
Badge & certificate
Salter's Way (John Merrill Foundation). £5.00 (incs p&p).

Sandstone Trail SANDT

CHESHIRE, SHROPS **51km/32 miles**

The Trail follows the dissected central Cheshire sandstone ridge, which rises to heights of over 700ft, and takes in Delamere Plain, Beeston Gap, the wooded Peckforton Hills and Bickerton Hills, to reach the Shropshire Union Canal, where it links with the South Cheshire Way. Lowland heath and undulating farmland complete the Trail's wide range of terrain.

Attributes
Forest/Woodland; Canal; Heath
Start
Frodsham Town Centre, Cheshire SJ517779
Finish
Jubliee Park, Whitchurch, Shrops SJ537415
Waymark
Black bootmark and yellow letter S
Websites
www.cheshire.gov.uk, www.discovercheshire.co.uk
Maps ◈
OS Landranger: 117
OS Explorer: 257, 267
Publications, badges and certificates
Paperbacks
Walking Cheshire's Sandstone Trail: Official Guide by Tony Bowerman (Northern Eye Books Limited (Mara)) 2008. Laminated cover. ISBN 9780955355714. 224pp; 210 x 130. £11.99 (+ £2.00 p&p) from publisher.
Circular Walks along the Sandstone Trail (Northern Eye Books Limited (Mara)) 2006. Laminated cover. ISBN 9781902512105. 104pp; 208 x 134. £4.99 (+ £2.00 p&p).
Leaflets
Sandstone Trail (Cheshire County Council). A2/3. Free (+ 9 x 6 SAE).
Walking Support Providers
Byways

Sefton Coastal Footpath SEFTCF

MERSEYSIDE **34km/21 miles**

From the northern outskirts of Liverpool this route through dunes, marshes and the towns of Southport and Crosby passes the Ainsdale Nature and Formby National Trust Reserves. Sefton's Natural Coast, as it is now known, is the largest undeveloped dune system in England, extending from Southport and the Ribble Estuary to Seaforth at the mouth of the River Mersey.

Attributes
Easy; Cycle Route; Coastal; River; Heath
Start
Waterloo Station, Merseyside SJ321981
Finish
Crossens, Merseyside SD374205
Waymark
Natterjack toad logo
Websites
www.seftonsnaturalcoast.com, www.sefton.gov.uk, www.seftoncoast.org.uk
Maps ◈
OS Landranger: 102, 108
OS Explorer: 266, 275, 285
Publications, badges and certificates
Booklets
Walking & Cycling Guide to Sefton's Natural Coast (Sefton Metropolitan Borough Council). 68pp; A4/3. Free.

Shropshire Cakes and Ale Trail SCALET

SHROPS **177km/110 miles**

A seven-section walk around the Shropshire hills and countryside. From the Italianate hill-town of Bridgnorth it heads along the River Severn to Cleobury Mortimer, following in the steps of the poet-postman, Simon Evans. It next takes in Titterstone Clee and Ludlow, then goes via Aldon Gutter and Bury Ditches hillfort to Clun. A climb on to Offa's Dyke leads to Bishop's Castle (micro-breweries), then over Stiperstones and The Long Mynd into Church Stretton. After climbs of Caer Caradoc and Wenlock Edge it visits Much Wenlock before the final stretch leads back, through history, to Bridgnorth.
Start and Finish
Bridgnorth, Shrops SO716931
Websites
www.penninepens.co.uk
Maps
OS Landranger: 127, 137, 138, 148
OS Explorer: 201, 203, 216, 217, 218, 242
Publications, badges and certificates
Paperbacks
Shropshire Cakes and Ale Trail by Bob Bibby (Pierrepoint Press) 2007. ISBN 9780953319640. 116pp; 196 x 124. £10.00.

Shropshire Way SHRW

SHROPS **224km/139 miles**

A varied route crossing lowland farmland and many of the notable hills of Shropshire. It passes through Shrewsbury, Clun and Ludlow (the most southerly point), and on the return takes in the Clee Hills, Wenlock Edge, Ironbridge and the Wrekin. An 11 mile spur runs north from Wem to meet the Sandstone Trail, the Marches, Maelor and South Cheshire Ways at Grindley Brook. 'The Shropshire Way' publication is to be revised by the local authority and there may be changes to the route. The Kerry Ridgeway (16 miles on OS mapping) follows a ridgetop, overlooking Wales on the one side and England on the other, between Bishop's Castle on the Shropshire Way and Kerry Hill in Powys.

Attributes
Downland/Wolds; Moorland
Start and Finish
Wem, Shrops SJ513289
Waymark
Buzzard on named black discs
Maps ◈
OS Landranger: 117, 126, 127, 137, 138, 148
OS Explorer: 201, 203, 216, 217, 241, 242, 257
Publications, badges and certificates
Paperbacks
Rambler's Guide to the Shropshire Way by R. W. Moore, I. R. Jones (Pengwern Books) 2004. ISBN 9780946679447. 70pp; A5. £6.99 (+ £1.00 p&p). Online from Pengwern websites.
Booklets
Kerry Ridgeway (Powys County Council). £1.80 (incs p&p). Cheques to Powys County Council.
Walking Support Providers
Bobs; Byways

Simon Evans Way SIEW

SHROPS **29km/18 miles**

A figure of eight walk around the South Shropshire countryside, visiting both sides of the River Rea and taking in the villages of Neen Savage, Oreton and Stottesdon. It links with the Jack Mytton Way near Detton Hall.

Attributes
No significant attribute
Start and Finish
Cleobury Mortimer, Shrops SO670759
Websites
www.cmfa.co.uk
Maps
OS Landranger: 138
OS Explorer: 217, 218
Publications, badges and certificates
Paperbacks
Simon Evans Way (Cleobury Mortimer Footpath Association) 2006. ISBN 9780947712457. 32pp. £3.50 (+ £1.00 p&p). Cheques to Cleobury Mortimer Footpath Association.

South Cheshire Way SCHW

CHESHIRE, SHROPS **55km/34 miles**

A bi-directional route linking the Sandstone Trail with the Staffordshire Way running through lowland farmland and low hills, passing Crewe and Alsager, before climbing to the finish.

Attributes
No significant attribute
Start
Grindley Brook, Shrops SJ522433
Finish
Mow Cop, Cheshire SJ856573
Waymark
Letters SCW on black/yellow waymarks
Websites
www.mcfs.org.uk
Maps ◈
OS Landranger: 117, 118
OS Explorer: 257, 258, 268
Publications, badges and certificates
Booklets (for each direction)
Guide to the South Cheshire Way by Justin McCarthy (Mid Cheshire Footpath Society) 2003. £2.00 each (incs p&p). Cheques to Mid Cheshire Footpath Society.

Spanners Round SPANR

GTR MAN, LANCS **32km/20 miles**

A circuit linking three reservoirs of the old Bolton Water Authority with three reservoirs of the former Irwell Valley Water Board.

Attributes
Challenging; Anytime Challenge; Moorland
Start and Finish
Jumbles Reservoir, Gtr Man SD736139

Maps
OS Landranger: 103, 109
OS Explorer: 287, 21
Publications, badges and certificates
Booklets
Ramsbottom Round/Spanners Round (Norman Thomas) 1992. 36pp; A5. £1.85 (incs p&p).
Badge & certificate
Spanners Round (Norman Thomas). £2.00 (+ SAE).

Staffordshire Moorlands Challenge Walk SMCW

STAFFS **38km/24 miles**

A walk from the Churnet Valley, involving 2,000ft of ascent. The route takes in Froghall Wharf, the Weaver Hills, Ordley Dale, Alton and Ousal Dale.

Attributes
Challenging; Anytime Challenge; Moorland
Start and Finish
Oakamoor, Staffs SK053448
Maps
OS Landranger: 128
OS Explorer: 259
Publications, badges and certificates
Booklets
Staffordshire Moorlands Challenge Walk by John Merrill (John Merrill Foundation). ISBN 9780907496670. 32pp; A5. £4.50 (+ £1.00 p&p). Cheques to John Merrill Foundation.
Badge & certificate
Staffordshire Moorlands Challenge Walk (John Merrill Foundation). £5.00 (incs p&p).

Staffordshire Way STFW

CHESHIRE, DERBYS, STAFFS, WORCS **153km/95 miles**

The route initially goes along Congleton Edge to The Cloud, where it links with the southern end of the Gritstone Trail. It continues along the towpath of the Caldon Canal, through the Churnet Valley (see Churnet Valley Challenge Walk) and follows the River Dove to Uttoxeter. The Trent and Mersey Canal is then followed to Shugborough Hall with Cannock Chase and Highgate Common visited before reaching the sandstone Kinver Edge. See also E-Routes (E2).

Attributes
Canal; Moorland
Start
Mow Cop, Cheshire SJ856573
Finish
Kingsford Country Park, Worcs SO829822
Waymark
Staffordshire knot
Websites
www.staffordshire.gov.uk
Maps ◈
OS Landranger: 118, 119, 127, 128, 138, 139
OS Explorer: 24, 218, 219, 242, 244, 258, 259, 268
Publications, badges and certificates
Paperback
Staffordshire Way: Official Guide (Staffordshire County Council). 102pp; A5. £5.00 (+ £1.00 p&p). Cheques to Staffordshire County Council.
Leaflets
Staffordshire Way & Millennium Way: Information & Accommodation guide (Staffordshire County Council). A5/4. Free (+ 9 x 6 SAE).

Sweet Pea Challenge Walk SPCW

SHROPS **43km/27 miles**

A route from the birthplace of the sweet pea through Grinshill and Prees, and along the Llangollen Canal.

Attributes
Challenging; Anytime Challenge; Canal
Start and Finish
Wem, Shrops SJ514289
Maps
OS Landranger: 126
OS Explorer: 241
Publications, badges and certificates
Booklets
Sweet Pea Challenge Walk by John Merrill (John Merrill Foundation) 1995. ISBN 9781874754497. 44pp; A5. £4.95 (+ £1.00 p&p). Cheques to John Merrill Foundation.
Badge & certificate
Sweet Pea Challenge Walk (John Merrill Foundation). £5.00 (incs p&p).

Tame Valley Way TAVW

GTR MAN **37km/23 miles**

The Way runs from central Stockport to Reddish Vale and Hyde from where canal towpaths are followed through Ashton-under-Lyne, Stalybridge and Mossley. From Uppermill, the route leaves the canal, following riverside paths to Delph and Denshaw. Though the route goes through densely populated areas, there is much woodland.

Attributes
Forest/Woodland; Canal; Urban
Start
Stockport, Gtr Man SJ893903
Finish
Denshaw, Gtr Man SD975105
Waymark
Named green discs
Websites
www.tameside.gov.uk
Maps ◈
OS Landranger: 109
OS Explorer: 277, 1, 21
Publications, badges and certificates
Folder
Tame Valley Way (Tameside Countryside Warden Service). 10 leaflets; A4/3. £2.60 (incs p&p).

Tameside Trail — TSDT

GTR MAN — **64km/40 miles**

A walk along the Etherow Valley and Tame Valley to Stockport, where it turns through Audenshaw and Droylsden and picks up the Medlock Valley to Park Bridge. From Mossley it returns via the Swineshaw Valley and Hollingworth. From Broadbottom to Mossley, the E2 E-Route uses the Tameside Trail.

Attributes
Forest/Woodland; River; Canal; Moorland; Urban; Heritage; Industrial History
Start and Finish
Broadbottom, Gtr Man SJ996936
Waymark
River graphic on named brown discs
Websites
www.tameside.gov.uk
Maps ◈
OS Landranger: 109, 110
OS Explorer: 1, 277
Publications, badges and certificates
Folder
Tameside Trail (Tameside Countryside Warden Service) 1994. ISBN 9781871324112. 27pp; A5. £3.00 (incs p&p).

Telford and Wrekin Walks — TWW

TELFORD W — **Various**

These three interlinked walks use the open spaces and countryside of the area. The Hutchison Way (18½ miles) goes from Wellington via Telford to Newport. The Silkin Way (14 miles) winds from Bratton to Coalport along dry canal beds and abandoned railway lines. The Ironbridge Way (10 miles) starts at Leegomery to end at Ironbridge, a World Heritage Site on the river Severn at Ironbridge Gorge, site of the world's first iron smelting industry and the famous 1781 bridge. Both Coalport and Ironbridge are on the Severn Way.

Attributes
Easy; Former Railway; Canal; Heritage
Start
Various
Finish
Various
Waymark
Discs with named walks
Websites
www.telford.gov.uk
Maps
OS Landranger: 127
OS Explorer: 242
Publications, badges and certificates
Leaflets
Hutchison Way (Telford & Wrekin Countryside Service) 2008. A4/3. Free (+ SAE).
Silkin Way (Telford & Wrekin Countryside Service). A4/3. Free (+ SAE).
Ironbridge Way (Telford & Wrekin Countryside Service). A4/3. Free (+ SAE).

Ten Reservoirs Walk — TENRW

DERBYS, GTR MAN — **35km/22 miles**

A tough circuit over the Saddleworth Moors. It visits Yeoman, Hey, Greenfield, Black Moss, Swellands, Blakeley, Wessenden, Wessenden Head, Torside and Chew Reservoirs.

Attributes
Challenging; Anytime Challenge; Lake/Reservoir; Moorland
Start and Finish
Dovestone Reservoir, Gtr Man SE014034
Maps
OS Landranger: 110
OS Explorer: 1

Publications, badges and certificates
Looseleaf
Ten Reservoirs Walk (Carole E. Engel). A4. Free (+ 9 x 4 SAE).
Badge & certificate
Ten Reservoirs Walk (Carole E. Engel). £1.50 & £0.20 (+ 9 x 6 SAE).

Three Counties Challenge Walk 3CCW

CHESHIRE, DERBYS, STAFFS **45km/28 miles**

A tough route straddling the borders of Cheshire, Staffordshire and Derbyshire, taking in The Roaches, Shutlingsloe, Tegg's Nose, Shining Edge and Three Shires Head.

Attributes
Challenging; Anytime Challenge; Moorland
Start and Finish
Tittesworth Reservoir, Staffs SJ994605
Maps
OS Landranger: 118, 119
OS Explorer: 24
Publications, badges and certificates
Booklets
Three Counties Challenge Walk by John Merrill (John Merrill Foundation) 1993. ISBN 9781874754152. 36pp; A5. £4.50 (+ £1.00 p&p). Cheques to John Merrill Foundation.
Badge & certificate
Three Counties Challenge Walk (John Merrill Foundation). £5.00 (incs p&p).

Three Towers Circuit TTCIRC

GTR MAN, LANCS **56km/35 miles**

A route through the West Pennine Moors taking in the towers of Peel, Rivington and Darwen. Navigational skills are appropriate.

Attributes
Challenging; Anytime Challenge; Moorland
Start and Finish
Tottington, Gtr Man SD776129
Maps
OS Landranger: 103, 109
OS Explorer: 287
Publications, badges and certificates
Looseleaf
Three Towers Circuit (LDWA East Lancs). Free (+ 9 x 4 SAE).
Badge & certificate
Three Towers Circuit (LDWA East Lancs). £1.50 (+ 9 x 6 SAE).
Booklets
Three Towers Challenge Walk (Kenneth Fields) 2003. 16pp; A5. £1.30 (incs p&p).

Tidewater Way TIDEW

LANCS, N YORKS, W YORKS **145km/90 miles**

The route follows the Rivers Lune and Wenning, crossing the Pennine Way National Trail near Malham, the Dales Way in Wharfedale and it also uses parts of the Ebor Way. A percentage of the proceeds from sales are donated to Christian Aid.

Attributes
River; Moorland
Start
Skerton Weir, Lancaster, Lancs SD482632
Finish
Ulleskelf, N Yorks SE525401
Maps
OS Landranger: 97, 98, 104, 105
OS Explorer: 289, 290, 297, 2, 41
Publications, badges and certificates
Paperbacks (spiral-bound)
Tidewater Way (Spiral-bound) by Tony Rablen (Mark Comer) 1996. ISBN 9781871125276. 32pp; 210 x 148. £4.50 (+ £1.00 p&p). Cheques to Christian Aid.

Trans Pennine Way TPW

LANCS, N YORKS, W YORKS **161km/100 miles**

The route links the Forest of Bowland and Nidderdale AONB's, taking a line through Pendle Country, Haworth, Ilkley Moor, Washburn Valley, Pateley Bridge and the area of Brimham Rocks.

Attributes
Challenging; Moorland
Start
Garstang, Lancs SD496460
Finish
Ripon, N Yorks SE315711
Maps
OS Landranger: 99, 102, 103, 104
OS Explorer: 287, 297, 298, 21, 41

Publications, badges and certificates
Paperbacks
Trans Pennine Way by Paul Hannon (Hillside Publications) 1999. ISBN 9781870141666. 112pp; 175 x 115. £6.99 (+ 70p p&p).

Trent & Mersey Canal Walk TMCW

CHESHIRE, DERBYS, STAFFS 161km/100 miles

This route, from the River Mersey to Derwents Mouth on the River Trent, follows the Bridgewater Canal and the Trent & Mersey Canal. A diversion is currently in place at Shardlow. For details refer to entry on the LDWA website.

Attributes
Easy; Anytime Challenge; Canal; Heritage; Industrial History
Start
Runcorn, Cheshire SJ504823
Finish
Shardlow, Derbys SK458308
Maps
OS Landranger: 108, 117, 118, 127, 128, 129
OS Explorer: 243, 244, 245, 258, 260, 267, 268
Stripmap
Trent & Mersey Canal – Map 1 – Preston Brook to Fradley Junction, Trent & Mersey Canal – Map 2 – Great Haywood Junction to Cromwell Lock (GEOprojects)
Publications, badges and certificates
Booklets
Walking the Trent & Mersey Canal by John Merrill (John Merrill Foundation) 1999. ISBN 9781874754190. 68pp; A5. £6.95 (+ £1.00 p&p). Cheques to John Merrill Foundation.
Badge & certificate
Trent & Mersey Canal Walk (John Merrill Foundation). £5.00 (incs p&p).

Trevine Trail TREVT

LANCS 87km/54 miles

A walk through the countryside of the lower Ribble Valley, based on Whalley heading to Hurst Green and Clitheroe and returning over Pendle Hill and Sabden.

Attributes
River
Start and Finish
Whalley Abbey, Whalley, Lancs SD729361
Maps
OS Landranger: 102, 103
OS Explorer: 41, 287
Publications, badges and certificates
Booklets
Trevine Trail by Trevor Headley (Trevor Headley) 2005. 36pp; A5. £5.00 (incs p&p). Cheques to Trevor Headley. Also from TICs in the Ribble Valley.
Pack
Two Days in the Valley by Trevor Headley (Trevor Headley) 2006. 12 booklets, one on each village. £8.00 (incs p&p). Cheques to Trevor Headley.

Twin Valley 20 Walks TV20W

LANCS, W YORKS 97km/60 miles

Two separate self designed walks: the Twin Valley 20 (Calderdale – 33 miles) and the Twin Valley 20 (Rossendale – 27 miles). On each you must visit 10 provided trig points.

Attributes
Challenging; Anytime Challenge; Moorland
Start and Finish
Various
Maps
OS Landranger: 103, 104
OS Explorer: 287, 21
Publications, badges and certificates
Looseleaf
Twin Valley 20 (Anton Ciritis). A4. Free (+ 9 x 4 SAE).
Badge & certificate
Twin Valley 20 Walks (Anton Ciritis). £2.00. On completion of both walks.

Two Crosses Circuit TWOCC

GTR MAN, LANCS 40km/25 miles

A route through the West Pennine Moors taking in the Roman Cross at Affetside; the Pilgrim's Cross at Bull Hill, and passing Turton Tower and the Turton & Entwistle Reservoir.

Attributes
Challenging; Anytime Challenge; Lake/Reservoir; Moorland
Start and Finish
Tottington, Gtr Man SD776129
Maps
OS Landranger: 109
OS Explorer: 287

Publications, badges and certificates
Looseleaf
Two Crosses Circuit (LDWA East Lancs). Free (+ 9 x 4 SAE).
Badge & certificate
Two Crosses Circuit (LDWA East Lancs). £1.50 (+ 9 x 6 SAE).

Villages of the Ribble Valley VORV

LANCS **39km/24 miles**

A walk through the cental areas of the Ribble Valley countryside encircling Clitheroe. It visits 12 valley villages: Whalley, Mitten, the outskirts of Clitheroe, Waddington, West Bradford, Grindleton, Chatburn, Sawley, and returning under Pendle Hill via Downham, Worston, Pendleton and Wiswell.

Attributes
River
Start and Finish
Whalley Abbey, Whalley, Lancs SD729361
Maps
OS Landranger: 103
OS Explorer: 41, 287
Publications, badges and certificates
Booklets
Villages of the Valley by Trevor Headley (Trevor Headley) 2005. 32pp; A5. £4.00 (incs p&p). Cheques to Trevor Headley. Also from TICs in the Ribble Valley.
Pack
Two Days in the Valley by Trevor Headley (Trevor Headley) 2006. 12 booklets, one on each village. £8.00 (incs p&p). Cheques to Trevor Headley.

Weaver Way (Cheshire) WEW

CHESHIRE **64km/40 miles**

Taking you deep into some of Cheshire's finest countryside, it follows meandering waterways along the county's spine. With heritage sites, including the Salt Museum in Northwich, telling the story of Cheshire's exploitation of this valuable mineral; and the restored Anderson Boat Lift that raises boats up 50ft from the River Weaver to the Trent and Mersey Canal. The Whitegate Way (7 miles) links from Winsford to Cuddington, near Delamere Forest Park, using the former Whitegate railway line that carried salt for almost 100 years.

Attributes
Easy; River; Canal; Urban; Heritage; Industrial History
Start
Audlem Locks, near Bagley Lane Bridge, Cheshire SJ658420
Finish
A56 Bridge, Frodsham, Cheshire SJ529785
Waymark
W and river emblem
Websites
www.discovercheshire.co.uk
Maps
OS Landranger: 117, 118
OS Explorer: 257, 267
Publications, badges and certificates
Leaflets
Weaver Way (Cheshire County Council). A4/3. Free. Downloadable.
Whitegate Way by Cheshire County Council (Cheshire County Council). A4/3. Free (+ 9 x 4 SAE).

Weavers Shuttle WEAVSH

LANCS **64km/40 miles**

This interesting and historical walk makes a circuit around the urban areas of Burnley, Nelson and Colne in the Rossendale, Burnley and Pendle Districts. There is 5000ft of ascent.

Attributes
Challenging; Anytime Challenge; Moorland; Heritage; Industrial History; Literary
Start and Finish
Worsthorne, Lancs SD876324
Maps
OS Landranger: 103
OS Explorer: 21
Publications, badges and certificates
Booklets
Weavers Shuttle (Max Tattersall). Free (+ 9 x 6 SAE).
Badge & certificate
Weavers Shuttle (Max Tattersall). £1.00 (+ A4 SAE). Please submit start/finish time and summary of walk.

West Craven Way WCW

LANCS, N YORKS **39km/24 miles**

A circular route in the West Craven area visiting interesting villages and ancient houses. It takes in Great Edge, the Copy House notable for links with the 'Dissenters', a section of the Pendle Way, and Thornton in Craven where it links with the Pennine Way. A second leg starts from the Cross Keys pub at East Marton and visits Gledstone Hall, the drumlin area, Horton,

Stock, Bracewell, and Weets Hill, passing below the summit, where the Pendle Way is again encountered. Shorter circular routes are an option at Barnoldswick on the the Leeds & Liverpool Canal.

Attributes
Heritage
Start and Finish
Anchor Inn, Salterforth, Earby, Lancs SD889453
Maps
OS Landranger: 103
OS Explorer: 21, 41
Publications, badges and certificates
Leaflets
West Craven Way (Pendle Borough Council) 2006. 3 leaflets; A5 folded. Free.

White Peak Rollercoaster WPROLL

DERBYS, STAFFS **38km/24 miles**

A scenic circular walk set in the southern part of the Peak District National Park based on the Dove, Hamps and Manifold valleys. There is 4,500ft of ascent.

Attributes
Challenging; Anytime Challenge; Moorland
Start and Finish
Alstonefield, Staffs SK131556
Maps
OS Landranger: 119
OS Explorer: 24
Publications, badges and certificates
Looseleaf
White Peak Rollercoaster by Alan S. Edwards (Alan S. Edwards) 2007. 4pp; A4. Free (+ 9 x 6 SAE).
Badge & certificate
White Peak Rollercoaster (Alan S. Edwards). £2.75 (incs p&p).

Wirral Coastal Walk WIRCW

MERSEYSIDE **24km/15 miles**

The route follows the Egremont Promenade towards New Brighton, with views across the River Mersey to the famous Liverpool waterfront, then along the coast of the Wirral Peninsula, through the North Wirral Coastal Park, to Hoylake and then to Red Rocks, where the Dee Estuary meets the Irish Sea, continuing past West Kirby Marine Lake onto the Wirral Way to finish.

Attributes
Easy; Coastal; Lake/Reservoir
Start
Seacombe Ferry Terminal, Wirral, Merseyside SJ325908
Finish
Thurstaston Country Park, Wirral, Merseyside SJ238834
Maps
OS Landranger: 108
OS Explorer: 266
Publications, badges and certificates
Leaflets
North Wirral Coastal Park: Wirral Coastal Walk (Thurstaston Visitor Centre). A5. Free (+ 9 x 6 SAE).

Wirral Shore Way WIRSW

CHESHIRE, MERSEYSIDE **36km/22 miles**

The route is dictated by the old coastline of the Wirral bordering the Dee Estuary. From historic Chester the path passes the remains of a Norman fortress; a line of dried out Elizabethan sea ports; and a host of villages and seaside resorts. Along the Dee Estuary, the Way briefly links into the Wirral Way, and from Hoylake, the Wirral Coastal Walk provides a 10-mile extension to Seacombe. The Wirral Way itself (12 miles) uses the track of an old railway that goes from West Kirby to Hooton in mid-Wirral, offering superb views over the Dee Estuary to Wales. Originally the railways formed a circuit of Wirral and this is the missing link.

Attributes
Coastal; Heritage
Start
Chester Cathedral, Chester, Cheshire SJ406665
Finish
West Kirby, Wirral, Merseyside SJ204886
Maps
OS Landranger: 108, 117
OS Explorer: 265, 266
Publications, badges and certificates
Paperbacks
Walker's Guide to the Wirral Shore Way by Carl Rogers (Northern Eye Books Limited (Mara)). ISBN 9781902512051. 48pp; 135 x 210. £3.95 (+ £2.00 p&p).
Leaflets
Wirral Country Park: Wirral Way (Thurstaston Visitor Centre). A5. Free (+ 9 x 6 SAE).
North Wirral Coastal Park: Wirral Coastal Walk (Thurstaston Visitor Centre). A5. Free (+ 9 x 6 SAE).

Witches Way WITW

LANCS **50km/31 miles**

From the heart of industrial Lancashire, the route goes over the moors between Blackburn and Accrington, then across lowland to Read before climbing to the summit of Pendle Hill. It descends to Downham and crosses the Ribble valley before going over Standridge Hill to Slaidburn.

Attributes
Anytime Challenge; Moorland
Start
Rawtenstall, Lancs SD809230
Finish
Slaidburn, Lancs SD712524
Maps
OS Landranger: 103
OS Explorer: 287, 21, 41
Publications, badges and certificates
Looseleaf
Witches Way (Jim Ashton) 1997. A4. Free (+ 9 x 4 SAE). Route outline, grid refs, local and transport information.
Badge & certificate
Witches Way (Jim Ashton). £1.50 & £0.15 (+ SAE).

Witton Weavers Way WITTWW

LANCS **51km/32 miles**

The Way is a network of four circular routes (named the Beamers, Reelers, Tacklers and Warpers Trails, respectively 6, 8, 11 and 9 miles), linked together with further sections of trail to form a large loop to the west of Blackburn and Darwen. The route takes in Abbey Village, Darwen Moor and Jumbles Reservoir on the northern outskirts of Bolton. There is a link into Darwen itself.

Attributes
Lake/Reservoir; Moorland
Start and Finish
Witton Park, Lancs SD659273
Waymark
Mill logo in brown on named discs
Websites
www.blackburn.gov.uk
Maps ◈
OS Landranger: 102, 103, 109
OS Explorer: 287
Publications, badges and certificates
Leaflets
Witton Weavers Way: Blackburn & Darwen Borough-wide Walk (Blackburn with Darwen Borough Council) 1994. 6pp each; A5. £2.00. Five colour leaflets (Beamers, Reelers, Tacklers. Warpers) and linking description.

Wyre Way WYREW

LANCS **72km/45 miles**

A walk exploring the history and wildlife of the Wyre estuary from the estuary mouth as the river snakes to its source in the Forest of Bowland. The Way comprises three routes: from Fleetwood to Knott End via Shard Bridge (16 miles), from Shard Bridge to Garstang (11 miles) and from Garstang to the finish at Abbeystead Reservoir (18 miles). Both sides of the estuary are visited – the ferry between Fleetwood and Knott End is seasonal and the route is subject to flooding at Spring tides.

Attributes
Coastal; River
Start
Fleetwood, Lancs SD339484
Finish
Abbeystead Reservoir, Lancs SD555537
Waymark
Named discs
Maps ◈
OS Landranger: 102
OS Explorer: 286, 296
Publications, badges and certificates
Leaflets
Wyre Way: Fleetwood to Knott End & Shard Bridge to Garstang (Wyreside Ecology Centre) 1999. A5/8. Free (+ A5 SAE). Photocopies only available.
Wyre Way: Garstang to Marshaw/Tarnbrook (Wyreside Ecology Centre) 1999. A5/8. Free (+ A5 SAE). Photocopies only available.
Badge & certificate
Wyre Way (Wyreside Ecology Centre). Details from Wyreside Ecology Centre.
Paperbacks
Lancashire Coastal Way & the Wyre Way: Fleetwood and Knott End to Lancaster by Ian O. Brodie, Krysia Brodie (Lancashire County Books) 1993. ISBN 9781871236200. 64pp; 140 x 96. £2.95.

CUMBRIA & NORTHUMBERLAND

Skiddaw, crossed by the Allerdale Ramble, from Castlerigg stone circle

KEY FACTS

Areas	Cumbria, Northumberland
National Parks	Northumberland, Lake District
Principal AONBs	Arnside & Silverdale, North Pennines, Northumberland Coast, Solway Coast
Heritage Coast	Northumberland: North Northumberland; Cumbria: St Bees Head
E-Routes	E2 variants Dover – Stranraer, E2 variant Harwich – Stranraer
National Trails (England)	Pennine Way (part), Pennine Bridleway (part), Hadrian's Wall (part)
Walking Routes (trail miles)	65 main routes (3618 miles); 11 waymarked (513 miles)
Resident population	0.8 million

DON'T MISS! TRAIL SECTIONS (CHALLENGING/REMOTE MARKED WITH *)

Allerdale Ramble	Portinscale, various circuits on Skiddaw*, with summit and Derwent River options (20km, 3500–4000ft ascent).
Cumbria Way	Rosthwaite to Keswick, Borrowdale, Derwent River and Derwent Water (14km, 800ft ascent)
Cumbria Way	Skelwith Bridge to Stake Pass, Langdale, Stake Pass, Borrowdale (20km, 2150ft ascent)
Coast to Coast (Wainwright)	Grasmere to Patterdale, Grisedale Hause, Tarn and dale (14km, 2500ft ascent), options to Helvellyn or St Sunday Crag
Hadrian's Wall Path	Walwick to Cavoran (for Greenhead), museums, milecastles, Housesteads Fort (halfway) is an alternative start (28km, 2000ft ascent)
Pennine Way	Middleton in Teesdale to Dufton, Teesdale, High Force, Cauldron Spout, High Cup Nick* (32km, 2000ft ascent, shorter 20km option from Forest in Teesdale omits High Force)
Reiver's Way	Alwinton to Wooler, includes the Cheviot* (32km, 3570ft ascent); Alnmouth to Embleton Bay, coastal, Dunstanburgh Castle (18kms, 500ft ascent)
St Cuthbert's Way	Wooler to Holy Island, Kyloe Hills, coastal, causeway (29kms, 1500ft ascent)

REFERENCE SOURCES

While not LDP books, keen Lakeland fellwalkers have long valued the classic Alfred Wainwright *Pictorial Guides to the Fells*. Now over 50 years old, they cover the 214 'Wainwrights' tops (seven volumes, from Frances Lincoln, reprinted 2007). Mark Richards' new *Lakeland Fellranger* series provides a modern alternative (eight volumes, four published, from Cicerone Press).

Hadrian's Wall snakes along a rocky crest, with a view of Crag Lough in the distance

CUMBRIA & NORTHUMBERLAND

Skiddaw from Ashness Bridge, near Watendlath, the Lake District

With some of England's best walking country and two major National Parks, Cumbria and Northumberland have contrasting inland scenery and interesting coastlines.

For walkers, the gem of Cumbria (and maybe of England) is the Lake District National Park, whose intoxicating offer of sustained ridge routes high above its many lakes is an irresistible attraction to day walkers. Frequented perhaps more by the peakbagger counting his or her 'Wainwrights' completions (there are 214 in all), there are still some fine trails, although in keeping with traditions in the Park most are not waymarked, and so Anytime Challenges abound.

In the Lake District you may rarely walk for long alone, but Northumberland, with its own sparsely populated National Park, can offer solitude in plenty, deep among its miles of rolling hills and on the remoter Cheviot tops. The Irish Sea and North Sea coastlines also contrast – Northumberland's long strands have an austere beauty, while Cumbria offers wide estuaries, with much birdlife and views to distant hills.

Geology

The varied geology of the Cumbrian Lake District includes the Skiddaw slates and the Borrowdale volcanics, and there is much evidence of past mineral industries. The Lakeland peaks rise to over 3000ft and include England's highest, Scafell Pike. The landscape that we see today has been shaped by glacial erosion during several ice ages over the last half a million years, carving out corries and lake basins, and leaving eroded material to form the hummocky lower ground. Surrounding the Lake District's central core of high fells is limestone country providing fine karst scenery that includes the limestone pavements of the many 'Scars'. Between the Lakeland fells and the Pennines are the pastoral, wooded lowlands

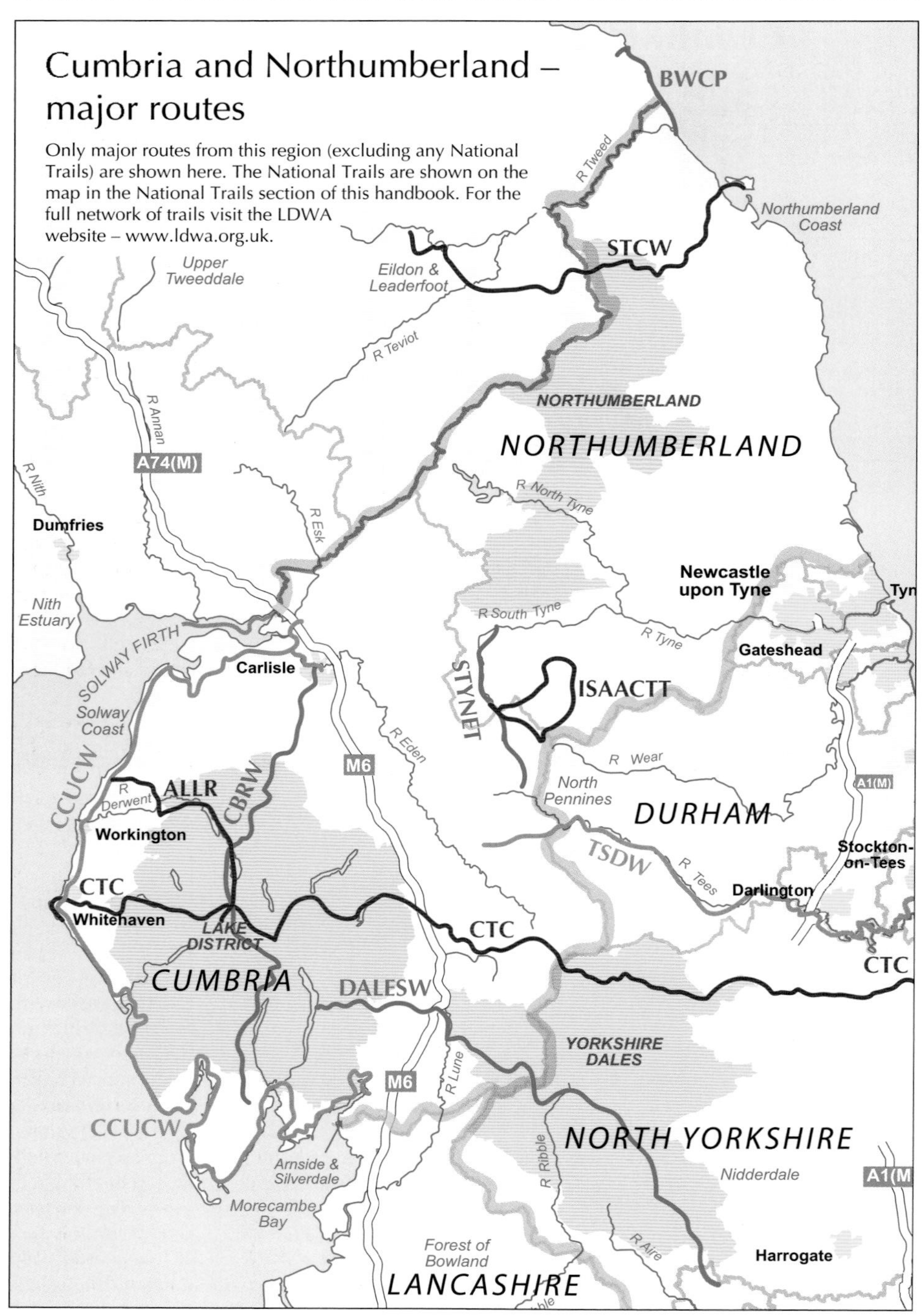
Cumbria and Northumberland – major routes
Only major routes from this region (excluding any National Trails) are shown here. The National Trails are shown on the map in the National Trails section of this handbook. For the full network of trails visit the LDWA website – www.ldwa.org.uk.
BWCP
R Tweed
Northumberland Coast
STCW
Upper Tweeddale
Eildon & Leaderfoot
R Teviot
NORTHUMBERLAND
NORTHUMBERLAND
R Annan
A74(M)
R Nith
Dumfries
R Esk
R North Tyne
Newcastle upon Tyne
Nith Estuary
R South Tyne
R Tyne
SOLWAY FIRTH
Gateshead
Carlisle
STYNET
ISAACTT
Solway Coast
R Eden
CCUCW
M6
R Wear
ALLR
R Derwent
CBRW
North Pennines
A1(M)
DURHAM
Workington
TSDW
R Tees
Stockton-on-Tees
CTC
Darlington
Whitehaven
LAKE DISTRICT
CTC
CTC
CUMBRIA
DALESW
YORKSHIRE DALES
R Lune
M6
CCUCW
NORTH YORKSHIRE
R Ribble
Arnside & Silverdale
Nidderdale
A1(M)
Morecambe Bay
R Aire
Forest of Bowland
Harrogate
LANCASHIRE

Dunstanburgh Castle on the Inn Way...to Northumberland

of the Eden valley, with sandstone gorge exposures along the river.

Much of the Northumbrian borderlands are rolling hills covered by peat moorlands and commercial forestry, home to the major Kielder Water reservoir, and drained by the North Tyne and other Tyne tributaries. In the north these Border uplands culminate with the higher granite peaks of the Cheviot massif, remnants of an ancient volcano. The Pennines extend up into the southern part of Northumberland, with its exposed moorlands, and sheltered dales coloured by spring flower meadows. The dramatic north-facing escarpment of Whin Sill that traverses much of this area is an igneous intrusion, and Hadrian's Wall often follows this line. Whin Sill provides the remarkable features of High Cup Nick, Cauldron Snout, and England's largest waterfall, High Force (all on the Pennine Way).

ROUTE CODES	
ALLR	Allerdale Ramble
BWCP	Berwickshire Coastal Path
CBRW	Cumbria Way
CCUCW	Cumbria Coastal Way
CTC	Coast to Coast
DALESW	Dales Way
ISAACTT	Isaac's Tea Trail
STCW	St Cuthbert's Way
STYNET	South Tyne Trail
TSDW	Teesdale Way

Geography

The Cumbrian coastal plain provides dairy pasture in the south and rougher sheep grazing further north. It is also home to major industries including the Sellafield nuclear facility. Across the Solway Firth – the Eden's estuary – are the distant Galloway hills in Scotland, while from the Lakeland tops both the Isle of Man and Northern Ireland may also be seen.

The mostly low, soft cliffs of the Cumbian coast, with their dune grassland relics, are punctuated by the resistant red sandstone headland cliffs at St Bees. To the south are the intertidal flats of Morecambe Bay, the estuary for the Wyre, Lune, Keer, Kent and Leven, and an important habitat for birdlife. The Northumbrian coast offers long sandy beaches, dunes, tidal flats, cliffs, and headlands topped with characteristic ruined castles.

The Trails

Much of the region's two **coastlines** have a walking route. On the Cumbrian coast the Cumbria Coastal Way that starts in Lancashire extends to the Solway Firth. Also on this coast Hadrian's Coastal Route traces the line of Roman coastal defences that extended Hadrian's Wall south. The Smugglers Route links sites associated with that infamous occupation. On the Northumbrian coast the Northumberland Coast Path extends inland before returning seawards to Holy Island; further north the Berwickshire Coastal Path extends from Berwick across the Borders.

River valley routes include, in Northumberland, several on the Tyne rivers. These include the South Tyne Trail, the Tyne – Estuary to Source, Walking the North Tyne, while the Tyne Valley Train Trails links former stations in the Tyne valley. The Teesdale Way starts in Cumbria, and three main routes include parts of the Eden valley: the Miller's Way, the Ravenber Way and the Cumbria Coastal Way that follows the Eden's lower reaches. The Allerdale Ramble includes part of the Derwent.

Three **National Trails** pass through these counties (see National Trails section). Hadrian's Wall Path traverses from the Tyne estuary to the Solway Firth on a scenic Roman frontier that is now a World Heritage Site. A fragile environment, the heavy tourist use here is a major concern. Thus, to encourage walkers to venture out into the rewarding surrounding landscapes other trails are being developed, including the Roman Ring and the Moss Troopers' Trail. The intersecting Pennine Way wends its way northwards to cross the Scottish Borders, taking in some of Whin Sill's sites, and the Cheviots. The developing multi-user Pennine Bridleway will provide for lower level alternatives.

While Hadrian may take credit for the first of the major **coast-to-coast** walking routes, another iconic path that needs no introduction links the west and east coasts. Pioneered by Alfred Wainwright, the classic 'A Coast to Coast Walk' from St Bees crosses the Lakes, the Eden valley, the Dales and the Vale of York, to reach the Cleveland Hills and coast. 'AW' intended its modest, singular name to encourage other 'CTC' routes; it has succeeded and the Alternative Coast to Coast, the Bay to Bay Walks starting from Grassington, the One Week Coast to Coast Trek and the Ravenber Way are all examples. 'AW' is also remembered in the Wainwright Memorial Walk and Wainwright's Remote Lakeland.

In the Lakes, the Cumbria Way is a popular Lakeland passes route that **traverses** the District from Ulverston to Carlisle. The Westmorland Way also crosses the Lake District and this old county. The Limestone Link traverses the limestone country of south Cumbria around Arnside. Two routes make a circuit of Windermere, the Windermere Way and Windermere – Walking Around the Lake. Both the Tour of the Lake District and the High Street Stroll provide lengthy Lakeland walking circuits. Covering both Cumbria and Northumbria, the Lake to Lake Walk links Windermere with Kielder Water, where a new Lakeside Way will circuit this reservoir. The Great English Walk finally comes to rest at Berwick after an epic 600-mile journey from Chepstow.

Figures from **history** are represented in the the Reiver's Way – commemorating the raiders who operated along the Anglo-Scottish border for many centuries. It heads from the Tyne

Berwick Old Bridge, where the Northumbria Coast Path hands over to the Berwickshire Coastal Path

Borrowdale fellsides in evening light

Valley past Hadrian's Wall, through the rolling Northumberland hills and over the Cheviots to end on the north coast. The Miller's Way remembers a Kendal-born quaker who started a biscuit industry in Carlisle. In Northumberland, Isaac's Tea Trail remembers Isaac Holden, an Allendale Methodist and itinerant tea seller.

There is a **borough** circuit in the Berwick Borough Boundary Walk, remembering Berwick's past as a (frequent) part of Scotland. Linking many hostelries, author Mark Reid offers two more Inn Way... routes, these heading to the Lakes and to Northumberland. The past mining industries of Furness are explored by the Haematite Trail. Three routes have **religious** or pilgrimage associations. St Oswald's Way in Northumbria links Holy Island with Hadrian's Wall Path; St Bega's Way, in Cumbria, links two churches dedicated to this saint; and St Cuthbert's Way crosses the border from Scotland, heading over the Cheviot Hills to the Northumbrian coast at Lindisfarne.

The challenging, and often remote, terrain of these two counties' is mirrored in a good crop of 26 **Anytime Challenges**, with nine rated as very challenging. The prolific Brian Richmond offers 11. These cover much of the Lake District and its environs: the Coniston Water Circuit, then, all in Furness, the Crake Valley Round, Furness Five Trigs Walk and Kirkby Moor Round & Burney. There are the Duddon Triangle Walk, the Duddon Horseshoe and the Dunnerdale Horseshoe and Burney Challenge and also in the Duddon area is the Whicham Valley Five Trigs Walk. Near Ulverston there is the Pennington Round. The Thirlmere Round and the Grasmere Skyline Classic Walk circuit these lakes.

In the Howgills Brian provides the Howgills 2000ft Tops. Other Howgill challenges are the Great Cautley Challenge (Simon Townson) and Tony Wimbush provides Over the Hill. Tony also ventures to the Derwent fells with his Lakeland Mountain Heritage Trail. John Merrill's contribution is the Lakeland Challenge Walk taking in ten major peaks. In the northern Lakes are Back o' Skidda (Joyce Sidebottom), the Old Crown Round (Mick Cooper) and the North Western Fells (George Foot). Over on the Shap side is the Three Rings of Shap and across on the Pennines is the Helm Wind Walk (both LDWA Cumbria).

In the Cheviots in Northumberland are the Cheviot Hills 2,000ft Summits, the Three Peaks of Cheviot Walk and, for those interested in ancient earthworks, the Hillfort Round (all three from LDWA Northumbria). Richard Sewell offers the Falklands Way/The Yomp, linking the Coast to Coast and Pennine Way. Arnold Underwood's Trans-Dales Trail – 3 links Cumbria and the Yorkshire Dales.

Allerdale Ramble — ALLR

CUMBRIA — **87km/54 miles**

From central Lakeland the route heads northwards along the western side of Borrowdale and Derwent Water to Keswick. Here there is a choice of route, either across the foothills of Skiddaw or over its summit, before heading along the Derwent valley to Cockermouth. The Ramble then crosses the agricultural land of mid-Allerdale to reach the coast at Maryport, where it turns along the flat coastline providing extensive views across the Solway Firth.

Attributes
Challenging; Coastal; Lake/Reservoir; River; Moorland; Mountain
Start
Seathwaite, Cumbria NY235119
Finish
Grune Point, Cumbria NY145569
Waymark
Named posts
Maps ◈
OS Landranger: 85, 89, 90
OS Explorer: 4, 303, 314
Publications, badges and certificates
Paperbacks
Cumbria Way & The Allerdale Ramble by Jim Watson (Cicerone Press) 2001. ISBN 9781852842420. 144pp. £6.99.

Back 'O' Skidda — BOS

CUMBRIA — **45km/28 miles**

A high-level circuit across some of the mountains of the northern Lake District. With over 7,600ft of ascent it includes the summits of High Pike, Calva, Skiddaw, Blencathra and Bannerdale Crags.

Attributes
Very Challenging; Anytime Challenge; Moorland; Mountain
Start and Finish
Mosedale, Cumbria NY357323
Maps
OS Landranger: 90
OS Explorer: 4, 5
Publications, badges and certificates
Looseleaf
Back 'O' Skidda (Joyce Sidebottom). Free (+ 9 x 4 SAE).
Badge & certificate
Back 'O' Skidda (Joyce Sidebottom). £2.50 (+ 9 x 7 SAE).

Berwick Borough Boundary Walk — BERBBW

NORTHUMBERLAND, BORDERS — **193km/120 miles**

A varied route across farmland, tougher sections through the Cheviots, and some coast and beach to finish. A ten mile detour to visit Lindisfarne (Holy Island) is an option if tides allow.

Attributes
Challenging; Coastal; Moorland; Religious
Start and Finish
Town Hall, Berwick on Tweed, Northumberland NT998528
Maps
OS Landranger: 67, 74, 75
OS Explorer: 16, 332, 339, 340, 346
Publications, badges and certificates
Paperbacks
Walk Round Berwick Borough: Five Castles, a Palace & a Mountain by Arthur Wood (RA Berwick on Tweed) 2006. ISBN 9870954533113. 128pp; A6. £4.95 (incs p&p). Cheques to Berwick Ramblers.

Berwickshire Coastal Path — BWCP

NORTHUMBERLAND, BORDERS — **24km/15 miles**

The Path crosses farmland and cliff tops as it passes through Burnmouth, Eyemouth and St Abbs. Some of the cliff walking is very exposed and reaches a maximum height of 340ft. A short extension to the route can be gained by taking advantage of the paths of the National Nature Reserve of St Abbs Head.

Attributes
Coastal
Start
Berwick on Tweed, Northumberland NU005528
Finish
Coldingham, Borders NT904660
Waymark
Named 'Scottish Border Walks' signs
Maps ◈
OS Landranger: 67, 75
OS Explorer: 346
Publications, badges and certificates
Leaflets
Berwickshire Coastal Path (Berwick-upon-Tweed Tourist Information Centre) 2006. A4/3. Free (+ 9 x 4 SAE).
Walking Support Providers
Footpath

Cheviot Hills 2,000ft Summits — C2KS

NORTHUMBERLAND — **40km/25 miles**

This walk, involving 5,000ft of ascent, links the Cheviot, Windy Gyle, Bloodybush Edge, Cushat Law, Comb Fell and Hedgehope, each over 2,000ft. Good navigation skills are required. An alternative route from Wooler is also described.

Attributes
Very Challenging; Anytime Challenge; Moorland; Mountain
Start and Finish
Hawsen Burn, near Wooler, Northumberland NT954225
Websites
www.walknortheast.org.uk
Maps
OS Landranger: 74, 75, 80
OS Explorer: 16
Publications, badges and certificates
Looseleaf
Cheviot Hills 2,000 foot Summits (LDWA Northumbria Group). Free (+ 9 x 4 SAE) or download from website.
Certificate
Cheviot Hills 2,000 foot Summits (LDWA Northumbria Group). Free (+ 9 x 6 SAE & loose 1st class stamp).

Coast to Coast (Wainwright) — CTC

CUMBRIA, N YORKS — **294km/183 miles**

Linking three National Parks – the Lake District, Yorkshire Dales and the North Yorkshire Moors – this classic Alfred Wainwright walk crosses England from the Irish Sea to the North Sea. After leaving the coastal plain it takes a high level route through the Lake District to Shap; crosses the Westmorland limestone plateau to Kirkby Stephen; then climbs over the Pennines to Keld. Between Keld and Reeth you have the choice of a high level route over Gunnerside Moor and Melbeck Moor, or a low level route through Swaledale. Easier walking follows to Richmond and through the Vale of Mowbray before gaining height again as it crosses the North York Moors to reach the North Sea coast a few miles north of Robin Hood's Bay. The revised edition of Wainwright's original guidebook includes marked alternatives to his original route where there was no public right of way or where erosion issues have required seasonal route options. These are clearly identified in the text. The original maps have been updated by Chris Jesty. Alfred Wainwright intended to encourage others to devise their own coast to coast walking routes so the route is modestly named 'A Coast to Coast Walk'.

Details of route publications for alternative routes are listed below marked by an *.

Attributes
Challenging; Lake/Reservoir; Moorland
Start
St Bees, Cumbria NX959119
Finish
Robin Hood's Bay, N Yorks NZ953048
Maps
OS Landranger: 89, 90, 91, 92, 93, 94, 98, 99, 100
OS Explorer: 303, 304, 4, 5, 7, 19, 26, 27, 30
Stripmaps
Coast to Coast – West: St Bees to Keld, Coast to Coast – East: Keld to Robin Hood's Bay, Coast to Coast Maps (East & West) and DVD Package (Harvey Maps)
Coast to Coast: Part 1: St Bees Head to Swaledale – map & guide, Coast to Coast: Part 2: Swaledale to Robin Hood's Bay – map & guide (Footprint)
Publications, badges and certificates
Hardbacks
Coast to Coast Walk by A. Wainwright (map revisions by Chris Jesty) (Frances Lincoln) 2007. ISBN 9780711222366. 208pp; 161 x 132. £12.99.
Coast to Coast with Wainwright by A Wainwright, Derry Brabbs (images) (Frances Lincoln) 2009. ISBN 9780711229341. 256pp; 272 x 229. £25. New edition, updated text, improved photography.
Paperbacks
Northern Coast to Coast Walk: From St Bees to Robin Hood's Bay by Terry Marsh (Cicerone Press) 2006. ISBN 9781852845056. 240pp; 118 x 172. £12.95.
Coast to Coast Walk: Recreational Path Guide by Martin Wainwright (Aurum Press) 2007. ISBN 9781845132224. 168pp; 210 x 130. £12.99.
Coast to Coast Walk by Paul Hannon (Hillside Publications) 1999. ISBN 9781870141550. 152pp; 172 x 112. £8.99 (+ 90p p&p).
Coast to Coast Bed & Breakfast Accommodation Guide by Doreen Whitehead (Coast to Coast Guides) Annual. 80pp; 100 x 150. £5.00 (+ £1.00 p&p).
* *Coast to Coast on the Ravenber Way* by Ron Scholes (Landscape Heritage) 2003. ISBN 9781858211855. 292pp; 116 x 176. £7.50 (incs p&p). LDWA members price £6.50 (incs p&p).
* *Grassington to West Coast Walk* by John White (Fractal Press) 2008. ISBN 9781870735353. 96pp; 206 x 178. £9.95.
* *Grassington to East Coast Walk* by John White (Fractal Press) 2003. ISBN 9781870735308. 96pp; 206 x 178. £9.95.

* *Lakeland to Lindisfarne: Ravenglass to Holy Island* (190 miles) by John Gillham (Crowood Press) 1996. ISBN 9781852239756. 96pp; 178 x 114. £7.99.

Coast to Coast Path by Henry Stedman (Trailblazer Publications) 2008. ISBN 9781905864096. 240pp; 178 x 120. £9.99.

Booklets

Coast to Coast: In the Middle Ages by Lesley Bell (P3 Publications) 2002. ISBN 9780953720330. 64pp; A5. £4.99 (+ £1.50 p&p). Cheques to David Ramshaw.

DVD

Coast to Coast Walk: DVD by John Woodvine (narrator) (Striding Edge Limited). 55 minutes. £12.99.

Certificate (board mounted)

Coast to Coast Walk (Instep Walking Holidays). £3.50. Order form online.

Walking Support Providers

Brigantes; Coast to Coast Holidays; Coast to Coast Packhorse; Contours; Discovery; Explore Britain; Footpath; HF; Instep; Knobbly Stick; Macs; Mickledore; Northwestwalks; Sherpa Van; UK Exploratory

Coniston Water Circuit — CWC

CUMBRIA — **35km/22 miles**

A route around Coniston Water taking in Nibthwaite, Brockbarrow, Tilberthwaite, Coniston and Beacon Fell. It is coincident with the Cumbria Way in parts.

Attributes

Anytime Challenge; Lake/Reservoir; Moorland

Start and Finish

Wateryeat, Cumbria SD288891

Maps

OS Landranger: 96

OS Explorer: 6, 7

Publications, badges and certificates

Looseleaf

Coniston Water Circuit (Brian Richmond). Free (+ 9 x 4 SAE).

Badge & certificate

Coniston Water Circuit (Brian Richmond). £1.50 (+ SAE).

Crake Valley Round — CVR

CUMBRIA — **37km/23 miles**

The route passes through the villages of Spark Bridge, Broughton Beck and Nibthwaite and takes in Brockbarrow and small sections of the Cumbria Way and Furness Way.

Attributes

Challenging; Anytime Challenge; Moorland

Start and Finish

Kirkby in Furness, Cumbria SD235822

Maps

OS Landranger: 96

OS Explorer: 6, 7

Publications, badges and certificates

Looseleaf

Crake Valley Round (Brian Richmond). Free (+ 9 x 4 SAE).

Badge & certificate

Crake Valley Round (Brian Richmond). £1.50 (+ SAE).

Cumbria Way — CBRW

CUMBRIA — **112km/70 miles**

The Way provides a relatively low-level crossing of the Lake District National Park, following tracks and paths along valleys and over passes in the midst of splendid and varied scenery. It passes Coniston Water, Tarn Hows and Dungeon Ghyll and crosses the Stake Pass to Borrowdale, Derwent Water and Keswick. The Way continues to Caldbeck either via Dash Falls or over High Pike, and then follows the Caldew valley to Carlisle. The Ramblers have been involved in waymarking and route upgrades. There is 10,000ft of ascent.

Attributes

Challenging; Lake/Reservoir; Moorland; Mountain

Start

Ulverston, Cumbria SD285785

Finish

Carlisle, Cumbria NY401560

Waymark

Name on green disc, including in National Park

Maps ◈

OS Landranger: 85, 89, 90, 96, 97

OS Explorer: 4, 5, 6, 7, 315

Stripmap

Cumbria Way (Harvey Maps)

Publications, badges and certificates

Paperbacks

Cumbria Way: 72 Miles Through the Lake District by Paul Hannon (Hillside Publications) 2005. ISBN 9781870141765. 80pp; 117 x 175. £5.99.

Cumbria Way: Official Ramblers Guidebook by John Trevelyan (Dalesman Publishing Co Ltd) 2000. ISBN 9781855681972. 32pp; 120 x 185. £2.99. For sale on Dalesman website or from A Rogers, Lakeing, Grasmere, Cumbria LA22 9RW or bookshops.

Cumbria Way & The Allerdale Ramble by Jim Watson (Cicerone Press) 2001. ISBN 9781852842420. 144pp. £6.99.

Leaflets

Cumbria Way (Ulverston TIC) 2002. Free. Also Coniston or Carlisle TICs.

DVD

Cumbria Way by Eric Robson (Striding Edge Limited) 2008. 68 mins. £14.99 + £2.95 p&p. Mail order: 0800 027 2527.

Walking Support Providers

Aengus; Brigantes; Celtic; Contours; Discovery; Explore Britain; HF; Knobbly Stick; Mickledore; Northwestwalks; Ramblers; Sherpa Van; Trek-Inn

Duddon Horseshoe — DUDH

CUMBRIA — **32km/20 miles**

An undulating route around the Duddon Valley, visiting the summits of Harter Fell, Hardknott, Little Stand, Cold Pike, Swirl How, Dow Crag, White Pike and Caw.

Attributes

Very Challenging; Anytime Challenge; Moorland; Mountain

Start and Finish

Seathwaite, Cumbria NY235121

Maps

OS Landranger: 96

OS Explorer: 6

Publications, badges and certificates

Looseleaf

Duddon Horseshoe (Brian Richmond). Free (+ 9 x 4 SAE).

Badge & certificate

Duddon Horseshoe (Brian Richmond). £1.00 (+ SAE).

Duddon Triangle Walk — DUDTW

CUMBRIA — **32km/20 miles**

A tough mountain walk encircling the Duddon Valley and taking in Whitfell, Harter Fell and Caw.

Attributes

Challenging; Anytime Challenge; Moorland

Start and Finish

Ulpha Bridge, Cumbria SD196930

Maps

OS Landranger: 96

OS Explorer: 6

Publications, badges and certificates

Looseleaf

Duddon Triangle Walk (Brian Richmond). Free (+ 9 x 4 SAE).

Badge & certificate

Duddon Triangle Walk (Brian Richmond). £1.00 (+ SAE).

Dunnerdale Horseshoe and Burney Challenge — DUNHBC

CUMBRIA — **32km/20 miles**

Three connecting loops walking through Grizebeck, Broughton Mills, The Knott, Stickle Pike and Thornthwaite; taking in the Dunnerdale Fells.

Attributes

Challenging; Anytime Challenge; Moorland; Mountain

Start and Finish

Beckside, Cumbria SD235822

Maps

OS Landranger: 96

OS Explorer: 6

Publications, badges and certificates

Looseleaf

Dunnerdale Horseshoe & Burney Challenge (Brian Richmond). Free (+ 9 x 4 SAE).

Badge & certificate

Dunnerdale Horseshoe and Burney Challenge (Brian Richmond). £1.50 (+ SAE).

Falklands Way/The Yomp — FWTY

CUMBRIA — **72km/45 miles**

A route linking part of the Coast to Coast Walk with the Pennine Way National Trail, visiting Tan Hill, Keld, Muker, Great Shunner Fell, Cotterdale, Swarth Fell Pike and Wild Boar Fell. The Yomp is an annual event usually run at the end of May.

Attributes

Challenging; Anytime Challenge; Moorland

Start and Finish

Kirkby Stephen, Cumbria NY774086

Maps

OS Landranger: 91, 98

OS Explorer: 19, 30

Publications, badges and certificates

Booklets

Falklands Way: Mallerstang Horseshoe & Nine Standards Yomp by Richard Sewell (Mark Petefield). 20pp; 150 x 210. £1.95 (+ 9 x 6 SAE).

Furness Five Trigs Walk FUFTW

CUMBRIA **40km/25 miles**

The route visits the trig points at Bank House Moor, High Haume, Yarlside, Birkrigg Common and the Hoad Monument.

Attributes
Challenging; Anytime Challenge; Moorland
Start
Gillbanks, Ulverston, Cumbria SD285787
Finish
Hoad Monument, Ulverston, Cumbria SD294791
Maps
OS Landranger: 96
OS Explorer: 6, 7
Publications, badges and certificates
Looseleaf
Furness Five Trigs Walk (Brian Richmond). Free (+ 9 x 4 SAE).
Badge & certificate
Furness Five Trigs Walk (Brian Richmond). £1.00 (+ SAE).

Furness Way FUW

CUMBRIA **121km/75 miles**

A route across southern Lakeland from coast to coast, beginning at the eastern side of Morecambe Bay and traversing much of the old county of Lancashire, north of the Sands, to its finish on the Irish Sea.

Attributes
Moorland
Start
Arnside, Cumbria SD455787
Finish
Ravenglass, Cumbria SD083963
Maps
OS Landranger: 89, 96, 97
OS Explorer: 6, 7
Publications, badges and certificates
Paperbacks
Furness Way by Paul Hannon (Hillside Publications) 1994. ISBN 9781870141277. 104pp; 175 x 115. £5.99 (+ 60p p&p).
Walking Support Providers
Contours; HF

Grasmere Skyline Classic Walk GSCW

CUMBRIA **32km/20 miles**

A high level route taking in Heron Pike, Fairfield, Seat Sandal, Steel Fell, Calf Crag, Sergeant Man, Blea Rigg, Silver How and Loughrigg Fell.

Attributes
Anytime Challenge; Moorland; Mountain
Start and Finish
White Moss Common, Cumbria NY348065
Maps
OS Landranger: 90
OS Explorer: 5, 6, 7
Publications, badges and certificates
Looseleaf
Grasmere Skyline Classic Walk (Brian Richmond). Free (+ 9 x 4 SAE).
Badge & certificate
Grasmere Skyline Classic Walk (Brian Richmond). £1.00 (+ SAE).

Great Cautley Challenge GCC

CUMBRIA **45km/28 miles**

A tough circuit on the southern edge of the Howgills visiting Winder, Calders and Calf and returning via Uldale and Dentdale.

Attributes
Very Challenging; Anytime Challenge; River; Moorland
Start and Finish
People's Hall, Sedbergh, Cumbria SD655922
Maps
OS Landranger: 98
OS Explorer: 19, 2
Publications, badges and certificates
Looseleaf
Great Cautley Challenge by Simon Townson (Simon Townson) 2007. 1pp; A4. Free (+ SAE).

Hadrian's Coastal Route HDCR

CUMBRIA **169km/105 miles**

A walk along the little-known Roman western coastal defences that stretched between Ravenglass and Bowness-on-Solway, where it links with Hadrian's Wall Path. Most of the walk is on tracks and minor roads and visits Maryport and other sites linked with this period of Roman history. There are good train and bus connections between Maryport and Bowness. A related route, Hadrian's Eastern Way, goes from Ravenglass over Hardknott (with its Roman fort – Mediobogdum) and Wrynose, to Ambleside with the fort of Galleva nearby.

Attributes
Easy; Cycle Route; Coastal; Heritage
Start
Mite viaduct, Ravenglass, Cumbria SD083966
Finish
Bowness-on-Solway, Cumbria NY225628
Maps
OS Landranger: 85, 89, 96
OS Explorer: 6, 303, 4, 314
Publications, badges and certificates
Paperbacks
Hadrian's Coastal Route: Ravenglass to Bowness-on-Solway by Clifford Jones (Tempus Publishing Ltd) 2008. ISBN 9780752446103. 144pp; 224 x 122. £9.99.
Hadrian's Eastern Way: Ravenglass to Ambleside by Clifford Jones (Striding Edge Limited) 2009. ISBN 9780956222909. 147pp; 224 x 122. £9.99.

Haematite Trail HAET

CUMBRIA **29km/18 miles**

The Trail was devised to explore some of the remains of the iron mining industry which brought about the industrial expansion of Furness and the subsequent emergence of Barrow. In its heyday the Furness mining industry was an equivalent to the American Gold Rush and provided some of the richest iron ore worked in Britain. The route passes Newton, Little Urswick, Lindal, Marton and Askam.

Attributes
Industrial History
Start and Finish
Barrow-in-Furness, Cumbria SD202699
Waymark
Pithead logo and named posts
Maps
OS Landranger: 96
OS Explorer: 6
Publications, badges and certificates
Leaflets
Haematite Trail (Barrow Tourist Information Centre). A3/6. Free.

Helm Wind Walk HELMWW

CUMBRIA **32km/20 miles**

The Walk traverses Cross Fell and Great Dun Fell with its radar station golf ball and passes through the Moor House National Nature Reserve. Good navigation skills are required.

Attributes
Anytime Challenge; Moorland
Start and Finish
Garrigill, Cumbria NY744417
Maps
OS Landranger: 87, 91
OS Explorer: 31
Publications, badges and certificates
Looseleaf
Helm Wind Walk (LDWA Cumbria Group). Free (+ 9 x 4 SAE).
Badge & certificate
Helm Wind Walk (LDWA Cumbria Group). £1.50 & £0.50 (+ SAE).

High Street Stroll HISTS

CUMBRIA **48km/30 miles**

A scenic high-level route over the mountains of the central and eastern Lake District, avoiding tourist spots and visiting Harter Fell, Nabs Moor, Swindale, Mardale and High Street.

Attributes
Challenging; Moorland; Mountain
Start and Finish
Ambleside, Cumbria NY376045
Maps
OS Landranger: 90
OS Explorer: 5, 7
Publications, badges and certificates
Looseleaf
High Street Stroll (Joyce Sidebottom). Free (+ 9 x 4 SAE).
Badge & certificate
High Street Stroll (Joyce Sidebottom). £2.50 (+ 9 x 7 SAE).

Hillfort Round HFR

NORTHUMBERLAND **42km/26 miles**

This tough walk, involving some 7,000ft of ascent, visits thirteen Iron Age Hillforts in the Cheviot Hills. Good navigation skills are required.

Attributes
Challenging; Anytime Challenge; Moorland; Heritage
Start and Finish
Hethpool, Northumberland NT894281
Websites
www.walknortheast.org.uk
Maps
OS Landranger: 74, 75
OS Explorer: 16, 339
Publications, badges and certificates
Looseleaf
Hillfort Round (LDWA Northumbria Group). Free (+ 9 x 4 SAE) or download from website.
Certificate
Hillfort Round (LDWA Northumbria Group). Free (+ 9 x 6 SAE & loose 1st class stamp).

Howgills 2000ft Tops H2000T

CUMBRIA **24km/15 miles**

The route visits the 2000ft tops in the Howgills with over 5000ft of ascent within a time limit of 9 hours. Navigational skills are essential for this walk.

Attributes
Challenging; Anytime Challenge; Moorland
Start and Finish
Cross Keys, Sedbergh, Cumbria SD697970
Maps
OS Landranger: 97, 98
OS Explorer: 19
Publications, badges and certificates
Looseleaf
Howgills 2000ft Tops Route Sheet Grid References by Brian Richmond (Brian Richmond) 2008. Free.
Certificates
Howgills 2000ft Tops Completion Certificate by Brian Richmond (Brian Richmond) 2008. £1.50 (+A5 SAE). 50p donated to Motor Neurone Disease.

Inn Way...to Northumberland IWTN

NORTHUMBERLAND **151km/94 miles**

This walk from Mark Reid follows the course of the River Coquet down to the North Sea at Warkworth, then visits Alnmouth, Craster, Dunstanburgh, Beadnell, Seahouses and Bamburgh before turning west to visit Chatton and Wooler. It then crosses the Cheviot Hills to reach Alwinton and the River Coquet, which is then followed back to Rothbury. Some 48 pubs are passed along the way, although there are none on the Cheviot Hills section.

Attributes
Coastal; River; Moorland
Start and Finish
Rothbury, Northumberland NU057017
Websites
www.innway.co.uk
Maps
OS Landranger: 81, 75, 80
OS Explorer: 42, 16, 332, 325, 340
Publications, badges and certificates
Paperbacks
Inn Way...to Northumberland by Mark Reid (Inn Way Publications) 2004. ISBN 9781902001081. 216pp; A5. £8.95 (+ £1.00 p&p).
Badge & certificate
Inn Way...to Northumberland (Inn Way Publications). £2.50 & £1.75 (both + 50p p&p).
Walking Support Providers
Brigantes

Inn Way...to the Lake District IWTLD

CUMBRIA **145km/90 miles**

A walk taking in the attractions of the Lake District including Rydal Water, Braithwaite, Boot and Coniston. 44 traditional inns are passed along the route.

Attributes
Challenging; Lake/Reservoir; Moorland
Start and Finish
Ambleside, Cumbria NY376045
Websites
www.innway.co.uk
Maps
OS Landranger: 89, 90, 96, 97
OS Explorer: 4, 6, 7
Publications, badges and certificates
Paperbacks
Inn Way...to the Lake District by Mark Reid (Inn Way Publications) 2006. ISBN 9781902001012. 200pp; A5. £8.95 (+ £1.00 p&p).
Badge & certificate
Inn Way...to the Lake District (Inn Way Publications). £2.50 & £1.75 (both + 50p p&p).
Walking Support Providers
Brigantes

Isaac's Tea Trail ISAACTT

NORTHUMBERLAND 58km/36 miles

A tough circuit around Allendale Common with over 4500ft of ascent, passing Methodist Chapels and sites linked with the Holden family. Isaac worked as a travelling tea seller and money raiser.

Attributes
River; Moorland; Heritage; Religious
Start and Finish
Ninebanks Youth Hostel, Northumbria NY771514
Waymark
Isaac logo on green disc
Websites
www.teatrail.info, www.northumberlandlife.org
Maps ◈
OS Landranger: 87
OS Explorer: 31, 43
Publications, badges and certificates
Booklets
Isaac's Tea Trail (Ninebanks Youth Hostel). 28pp; A5. £2.00 (+ 9 x 6 SAE).
Badge & certificate
Isaac Holden Tea Trail (Ninebanks Youth Hostel). £1.50 (+ 50p p&p).
Leaflets
Isaac's Tea Trail (Ninebanks Youth Hostel). 1pp; A3 folded.

Kirkby Moor Round & Burney KIRMRB

CUMBRIA 29km/18 miles

A route in the Furness Fells visiting Bank House Moor, Winnow, Gray Crags, Cocklakes, Shooting House Hill and Great Burney.

Attributes
Challenging; Anytime Challenge; Moorland
Start and Finish
Kirkby Community Centre, Kirkby-in-Furness, Cumbria SD232822
Maps
OS Landranger: 96
OS Explorer: 6
Publications, badges and certificates
Looseleaf
Kirkby Moor Round & Burney (Brian Richmond). Free (+ 9 x 4 SAE).
Badge & certificate
Kirkby Moor Round & Burney (Brian Richmond). £1.00 (+ SAE).

Lake to Lake Walk LTOLW

CUMBRIA, DURHAM, NORTHUMBERLAND 267km/166 miles

The route, which links Lake Windermere with Kielder Water, takes a line through Appleby and Brough to the Pennines then heads north through Middleton in Teesdale, Allenheads, Allendale and Bellingham. It crosses Hadrian's Wall near to Chester's Fort.

Attributes
Challenging; Lake/Reservoir; Moorland
Start
Bowness, Cumbria SD403967
Finish
Kielder Water, Northumbria NY707882
Maps
OS Landranger: 80, 87, 90, 91, 92, 97
OS Explorer: 5, 7, 31, 42, 43
Publications, badges and certificates
Paperbacks
Lake to Lake Walk by Alistair Wallace (MC Publications) 1999. ISBN 9781841040066. 156pp; 150 x 210. £7.50 (+ £1.00 p&p).

Lakeland Challenge Walk LAKCW

CUMBRIA 29km/18 miles

A tough circular walk, with 6,000ft of ascent, of ten Lakeland peaks including the Langdale Pikes, Esk Hause, Scafell Pike, Bowfell, Crinkle Crags and Pike of Blisco.

Attributes
Very Challenging; Anytime Challenge; Moorland; Mountain
Start and Finish
Dungeon Ghyll, Langdale, Cumbria NY294065
Maps
OS Landranger: 89, 90
OS Explorer: 4, 6
Publications, badges and certificates
Booklets
Lakeland Challenge Walk by John Merrill (John Merrill Foundation). ISBN 9780907496502. 32pp; A5. £4.50 (+ £1.00 p&p). Cheques to John Merrill Foundation.
Badge & certificate
Lakeland Challenge Walk (John Merrill Foundation). £5.00 (incs p&p).

Northumberland, Lindisfarne sunset

Lakeland Heritage Trail LAKHT

CUMBRIA **27km/17 miles**

A route designed to be completed in stages, following paths and fells, and visiting Grange in Borrowdale, Castle Crag, Ashness Bridge and Surprise View.

Attributes
Moorland; Heritage
Start and Finish
Moot Hall, Keswick, Cumbria NY266235
Maps
OS Landranger: 89
OS Explorer: 4
Publications, badges and certificates
Looseleaf
Lakeland Heritage Trail (Tony Wimbush). Free (+ 9 x 4 SAE).
Certificate
Lakeland Heritage Trail (Tony Wimbush). £0.50 (+ 9 x 4 SAE). Cheques to WA Wimbush – proceeds go to charity.
Book
Lakeland Trails by Tony Wimbush (Tony Wimbush) 1998. 88pp; A5. £5.95 (incs p&p). Cheques to WA Wimbush.

Lakeland Mountain Heritage Trail LAKMHT

CUMBRIA **40km/25 miles**

A circuit of the Derwent Fells including Causey Pike, Cragg Hill, Buttermere, Robinson and Hindscarth, with 8000ft of ascent.

Attributes
Very Challenging; Anytime Challenge; Moorland; Mountain
Start and Finish
Keswick Moot Hall, Cumbria NY266235
Maps
OS Landranger: 89
OS Explorer: 4
Publications, badges and certificates
Book
Lakeland Trails by Tony Wimbush (Tony Wimbush) 1998. 88pp; A5. £5.95 (incs p&p). Cheques to WA Wimbush.
Looseleaf
Lakeland Mountain Heritage Trail (Tony Wimbush). Free (+ 9 x 4 SAE).
Certificate
Lakeland Mountain Heritage Trail (Tony Wimbush). £0.50 (+ 9 x 4 SAE). Cheques to WA Wimbush – proceeds go to charity.

Lakeland Tour LAKTOUR

CUMBRIA **167km/104 miles**

A route taking in Patterdale, Derwentwater, Ennerdale, Eskdale, Borrowdale and Dunnerdale. A low level alternative (98 miles) is also described.

Attributes
Moorland; Mountain
Start
Staveley, Cumbria SD469982
Finish
Ambleside, Cumbria NY376045
Maps
OS Landranger: 89, 90, 97
OS Explorer: 4, 5, 6, 7
Publications, badges and certificates
Paperbacks
Walking Tour of Lakeland (Paul Buttle) 1997. ISBN 9780951934517. 96pp; 198 x 128. Free (+ SAE). Free with SAE while stocks last.

Limestone Link (Cumbria) LMLC

CUMBRIA **21km/13 miles**

The Link runs across the limestone country of South Cumbria with its nationally important flora, through the low wooded hills of the Arnside area, across the flat open mosses between Hale and Holme, and over the rocky fells of Clawthorpe and Hutton Roof.

Attributes
Easy; Moorland
Start
Arnside, Cumbria SD461788
Finish
Kirkby Lonsdale, Cumbria SD615782
Waymark
Named discs
Maps ◈
OS Landranger: 97
OS Explorer: 2, 7
Publications, badges and certificates
Leaflets
Limestone Link (South Lakeland District Council) 1994. 12pp; A4/3. Free (+ 9 x 4 SAE).

Miller's Way MILLW

CUMBRIA 82km/51 miles

Jonathan Dodgson Carr (1806–1884) left Kendal in 1831 and moved to Carlisle where he set up his own flour mill and bakery. A successful Quaker visionary, from selling bread to the local population he soon diversified into biscuit production, with a flour mill at Silloth and a biscuit factory (Carr's) in Carlisle, both still in production. This tribute route basically follows the trek that he took in 1831, by foot and horse drawn carriage, from Kendal to Carlisle. It gives a taste of the Shap Fells, the Howgills, the Pennines and the tranquil Eden Valley and is a generally low-level route (total ascent 1418m). A further 30-mile route, Miller's Way 2, is planned to symbolically link the Carr's biscuit works in Caldewgate, Carlisle and its existing flour mill at Silloth on the west coast of Cumbria.

Attributes
Easy; River; Heritage
Start
Market Place, Kendal, Cumbria SD515928
Finish
Mercat Cross, Carlisle, Cumbria NY401560
Waymark
White disc with green symbol and walk name
Websites
www.carrsbreadmaker.info
Maps
OS Landranger: 85, 86, 90, 91, 97
OS Explorer: 5, 7, 315
Publications, badges and certificates
Booklets
Miller's Way: A Journey of Destiny (Carrs Breadmaker) 2006. 32pp; 125 x 210. £2.99 (incs p&p). Cheques to Carr's Flour.

Moss Troopers' Trail MOSSTT

NORTHUMBERLAND 32km/20 miles

This walk takes in the wild country immediately north of the Whin Sill, between Carvoran and Newbrough. By combining several link routes, a number of shorter circular options are possible.

Attributes
Moorland
Start
Carvoran, Northumberland NY667659
Finish
Newbrough, Northumberland NY874679
Websites
www.markrichards.info, www.planyourinvasion.co.uk
Maps
OS Landranger: 86, 87
OS Explorer: 43
Publications, badges and certificates
Paperbacks
Roman Ring and Moss Troopers' Trail by Mark Richards (Shepherd's Walks) 2006. ISBN 9780955262401. 128pp. £9.99.
Leaflets
Roman Ring and Moss Troopers' Trail (Shepherd's Walks). 1pp; A4 folded. Free.
Walking Support Providers
Shepherd's Walks

North Western Fells NWF

CUMBRIA 80km/50 miles

A route visiting all the peaks described in A. Wainwright's book: *North Western Fells* and which involves 18,000ft of ascent.

Attributes
Very Challenging; Anytime Challenge; Moorland; Mountain
Start and Finish
Rannerdale Knotts, Cumbria NY162182
Maps
OS Landranger: 89
OS Explorer: 4
Publications, badges and certificates
Looseleaf
North Western Fells (A. G. Foot). Free (+ 9 x 4 SAE).
Certificate
North Western Fells (A. G. Foot). £1.50 (incs p&p). Cheques to A. G. Foot.

Northumberland Coast Path NORDCP

NORTHUMBERLAND 103km/64 miles

Part of the North Sea Trail; from Cresswell it hugs the coast as far as Bamburgh before heading inland to Belford and the Kyloe Hills. From here it joins St. Cuthbert's Way and returns to the coast at Holy Island causeway before continuing to Berwick. Good views.

Attributes
Coastal

Start
Cresswell, Northumberland NZ293936
Finish
Berwick upon Tweed, Northumberland NT995527
Maps
OS Landranger: 81, 75
OS Explorer: 325, 332, 340, 346
Publications, badges and certificates
Booklets
Northumberland Coast Path (Berwick-upon-Tweed Tourist Information Centre). 44pp; A5. £4.50.
Walking Support Providers
CarryLite; Footpath; Mickledore

Old Crown Round OCR

CUMBRIA **29km/18 miles**

A route over the tops of Skiddaw, Blencathra, Carrock Fell and Great Cockup, which can be achieved in any order. The same location must be used for the start and finish of the walk and be completed within 20 hours. Navigational skills are essential.

Attributes
Challenging; Anytime Challenge; Moorland
Start and Finish
Hesket Newmarket, Cumbria NY343386
Maps
OS Landranger: 90
OS Explorer: 4, 5
Publications, badges and certificates
Looseleaf
Old Crown Round (Mick Cooper). 1pp. Free (+ 9 x 4 SAE).
Badge & certificate
Old Crown Round (Mick Cooper). £1.50 for both (+ 9 x 4 SAE). Cheques to M. Cooper.

One Week Coast to Coast Trek OWCTCT

CUMBRIA, LANCS, N YORKS, REDCAR AND CLEVELAND **193km/120 miles**

This is an Irish Sea to North Sea coast to coast route designed to be walked in eight days. The route follows The Limestone Link from Arnside to Kirkby Lonsdale, then via Ribblehead, Bainbridge, Askrigg, Leyburn, Hunton, Hackforth, Yafforth, and Brompton to Osmotherley before following the Cleveland Way to Saltburn-by-the-Sea.

Attributes
Moorland
Start
Arnside, Lancs SD456789
Finish
Saltburn-by-the-Sea NZ666217
Maps
OS Landranger: 97, 98, 99, 93
OS Explorer: 7, 2, 30, 302, 26
Publications, badges and certificates
Paperbacks
One Week Coast to Coast Trek by Dick French (Expedition North) 1994. 24pp; 150 x 105. £3.00 (+ 9 x 6 SAE).

Over the Hill OTHC

CUMBRIA, N YORKS **72km/45 miles**

An undulating self-devised route linking seven summits in the Howgill area: Baugh Fell, Green Bell, Winder, Great Shunner Fell, Middleton, Wild Boar Fell and The Calf. There is a 24-hour time limit.

Attributes
Very Challenging; Anytime Challenge; Moorland
Start and Finish
Church Gates, Sedbergh, Cumbria SD657920
Websites
www.gofar.org.uk
Maps
OS Landranger: 97, 98
OS Explorer: 19
Publications, badges and certificates
Looseleaf and registration form with certificate
Over the Hill Club routes (Tony Wimbush). Free or download from website. Quality colour certificate: £1:50 with registration form.

Pennington Round PENR

CUMBRIA **40km/25 miles**

A countryside walk visiting the John Barrow monument, which overlooks the delightful market town of Ulverston. It is partly coincident with the Cumbria Way.

Attributes
Challenging; Anytime Challenge; Moorland
Start and Finish
Beck Side, Cumbria SD235822
Maps
OS Landranger: 96
OS Explorer: 6

Publications, badges and certificates
Looseleaf
Pennington Round (Brian Richmond). Free (+ 9 x 4 SAE).
Badge & certificate
Pennington Round (Brian Richmond). £1.00 (+ SAE).

Ravenber Way RAVNBR

CUMBRIA, NORTHUMBERLAND 338km/210 miles

This coast-to-coast walk from Cumbria to Northumberland heads through the mountain heart of Lakeland and over the High Street Range. It crosses the pastoral Eden Valley and climbs the high Pennines towards the remote fell country of Northumberland. The forested and rounded heights of the Cheviot Hills give way to the leafy River Till valley and then the River Tweed to the North Sea. En route there are charming villages and towns and much history.

Attributes
Lake/Reservoir; Moorland
Start
Ravenglass, Cumbria SD084964
Finish
Berwick-upon-Tweed, Northumberland NT991534
Websites
www.landscapeheritage.co.uk
Maps
OS Landranger: 67, 75, 80, 81, 87, 89, 90, 91, 96
OS Explorer: 5, 6, 7, 31, 16, 42, 43, 339, 346
Publications, badges and certificates
Paperbacks
Coast to Coast on the Ravenber Way by Ron Scholes (Landscape Heritage) 2003. ISBN 9781858211855. 292pp; 116 x 176. £7.50 (incs p&p). LDWA members price £6.50 (incs p&p).

Reiver's Way REIVW

NORTHUMBERLAND 242km/150 miles

A meandering route recently updated by Paddy Dillon, across Northumberland in the footsteps of the notorious border reivers, starting in the Tyne Valley passing the finest remains of Hadrian's Wall, and then heading northwest to Rothbury, over the Cheviots to Wooler, and finishing with the coast path from Budle Bay to Alnmouth. Reivers were raiders along the Anglo-Scottish Border country between the 13th and 16th centuries, with their heyday in the last hundred years during the Tudor dynasty in England.

Attributes
Coastal; Moorland; Heritage
Start
Corbridge Town Centre, Northumberland NY988644
Finish
Alnmouth Station, Northumberland NU230111
Maps
OS Landranger: 75, 80, 81, 87
OS Explorer: 16, 42, 43, 307, 332, 340
Publications, badges and certificates
Paperbacks
Reiver's Way by Paddy Dillon (Cicerone Press) 2009. ISBN 9781852844981. 128pp; 172 x 116. £10.00.
Walking Support Providers
Sherpa Van

Roman Ring ROMRG

CUMBRIA, NORTHUMBERLAND 84km/52 miles

The Roman Ring runs parallel to, and to the south of, Hadrian's Wall between Lanercost Priory and Halton Chesters. When walked in conjunction with the National Trial it makes a round walk equal in distance to the entire coast-to-coast trail. A 20-mile Moss Troopers' Trail, in the same publication, strides out into wilder country immediately north of the Whin Sill, from Carvoran to Newbrough. By combining several north/south link routes, a number of shorter circular options are possible.

Attributes
Moorland
Start
Haytongate, Cumbria NY557647
Finish
Halton Chesters, Northumberland NY996685
Websites
www.markrichards.info, www.planyourinvasion.co.uk
Maps
OS Landranger: 86, 87
OS Explorer: 43
Publications, badges and certificates
Paperbacks
Roman Ring and Moss Troopers' Trail by Mark Richards (Shepherd's Walks) 2006. ISBN 9780955262401. 128pp. £9.99.
Leaflets
Roman Ring and Moss Troopers' Trail (Shepherd's Walks). 1pp; A4 folded. Free.
Walking Support Providers
Shepherd's Walks

Rucksack and Rail RUCKAR

CUMBRIA **35km/22 miles**

Four themed walks linking the railway stations of Arnside, Silverdale and Carnforth. They can be walked individually, as a pair, or in total to make a figure of eight walk.

Attributes
Easy
Start and Finish
Silverdale Station, Cumbria SD475752
Maps
OS Landranger: 97
OS Explorer: 7, 41
Publications, badges and certificates
Leaflets
Rucksack and Rail (Arnside/Silverdale AONB and Countryside Management Service). 4 leaflets. £1.00 (+50p p&p).

Smugglers Route (Cumbria) SRCUMB

CUMBRIA **45km/28 miles**

Initially the route follows the coastline to Allonby then to Hayton, Aspatria and Mealsgate. Certain locations along the way have some smuggling history. Other sites of interest includes old churches, Roman settlements and nature reserves.

Attributes
Coastal; Heritage
Start and Finish
Maryport, Cumbria NY038361
Websites
www.solwaycoastaonb.org.uk
Maps
OS Landranger: 85, 89
OS Explorer: 4
Publications, badges and certificates
Paperbacks
Smugglers Route by Ben Brinnicombe (Solway Coast Heritage Centre) 2000. 90pp; A5. £6.00 (+ 70p p&p).

South Tyne Trail STYNET

CUMBRIA, NORTHUMBERLAND **37km/23 miles**

A multi-user route using paths, bridleways, quiet roads, or along the former South Tynedale Railway, through the remote and less-visited countryside of East Cumbria and the North Pennines, and along the South Tyne from its source, through Alston, and on to Haltwhistle near Hadrian's Wall.

Attributes
Former Railway; Horse Ride (Multi User); River; Moorland
Start
Tynehead, Garrigill, Cumbria NY752351
Finish
Haltwhistle Railway Station, Northumberland NY704638
Waymark
Blue stylised 'S' and trail name
Maps ◈
OS Landranger: 86, 91
OS Explorer: 31, 43
Publications, badges and certificates
Leaflets (waterproof)
South Tyne Trail (Carlisle City Council). A2 folded. £2.00. Also available from TICs in Alston & Haltwhistle.

St Bega's Way STBEW

CUMBRIA **58km/36 miles**

A walk linking the Norman Priory Church of St Mary and St Bega at St Bees, on the Irish Sea coast, to the pre-Norman church of St Bega by the shores of Bassenthwaite Lake. The route takes in Dent hill, Ennerdale Bridge, the north shore of Ennerdale Water, the flank of Brandreth, Honister Pass, Borrowdale, the River Derwent, Derwentwater, Portinscale, and Bassenthwaite Lake. Proceeds from book sales are donated to the two churches.

Attributes
Lake/Reservoir; River; Moorland; Heritage; Pilgrimage; Charity
Start
St Bees Priory, St Bees, Cumbria NX969121
Finish
St Bega Church, Bassenthwaite Lake, Cumbria NY226287
Websites
www.stbegasway.org.uk
Maps
OS Landranger: 89
OS Explorer: 4, 303
Publications, badges and certificates
Booklets
St Bega's Way by Rosalinde Downing (Rosalinde Downing) 2008. £4.50 (incs p&p). Local stockists on website, or mail order.

St Oswald's Way — STOSW

NORTHUMBERLAND — **156km/97 miles**

Linking St Cuthbert's Way at Holy Island with Hadrian's Wall Path at Heavenfield, this route recalls King Oswald (Saint Oswald) who ruled and travelled this part of the countryside during the 7th century, playing a major part in bringing Christianity to the United Kingdom.

Attributes
Coastal; Heritage; Pilgrimage; Religious
Start
Holy Island, Northumberland NU136417
Finish
Heavenfield, Northumberland NY936694
Waymark
Named discs/flying bird logo
Websites
www.stoswaldsway.com
Maps
OS Landranger: 75, 81, 87
OS Explorer: 42, 43, 113, 125, 332, 340
Map (Other)
St Oswald's Way: Maps for Walkers (Alnwick Tourist Information Centre)
Publications, badges and certificates
Paperbacks
St Oswald's Way by Martin Parminter (Alnwick Tourist Information Centre) 2007. ISBN 9780955380617. 128pp. £11.95.
Certificate Pack
St Oswald's Way Certificate Pack (Alnwick Tourist Information Centre). £2.50. Also from the St Oswald's Way website.
Walking Support Providers
CarryLite; Shepherd's Walks; Walking Support

Stepping Over Stone — STEPOS

CUMBRIA — **21km/13 miles**

Using minor roads, tracks, part of a former railway track through a nature reserve and footpaths, the route visits Winton, Soulby, Crosby Garrett, Smardale, and Waitby. There are links with the Yoredale Way and the Coast to Coast Walk.

Attributes
Former Railway; Heritage; Industrial History
Start and Finish
Kirkby Stephen, Cumbria NY775087
Maps
OS Landranger: 91
OS Explorer: 19
Publications, badges and certificates
Leaflets
Stepping Over Stone (Kirkby Stephen Tourist Information Centre). 1pp; A4 extended/5. Free (+ 9 x 4 SAE).

Teesdale Way — TSDW

CLEVELAND, CUMBRIA, DURHAM — **148km/92 miles**

The Way largely follows the banks of the River Tees as it passes from the remote high moorlands of Cumbria and Durham to the industrial landscapes of Teeside and the coast. From Dufton it coincides with the Pennine Way National Trail, visiting High Cup Nick, Cauldron Snout and High Force before separating at Middleton-in-Teesdale. It passes through Barnard Castle and runs south of Darlington to the North-East coast at Warrenby, Redcar. There are rail links at, and east of, Darlington. From Middlesbrough Dock, the Tees Link (11 miles), which is waymarked and included on OS mapping, provides a connection to the Cleveland Way National Trail at High Cliff Nab. See also E-Routes (E2), which uses the Way's section from Middleton to Middlesbrough and then the Link to Guisborough, in all some 77 miles.

Attributes
River; Moorland
Start
Dufton, Cumbria NY689250
Finish
South Gare Breakwater, Warrenby, Redcar, Cleveland NZ556279
Waymark
Named green discs with dipper (Durham), salmon (Cleveland)
Maps ◈
OS Landranger: 91, 92, 93
OS Explorer: 26, 31, 304, 306
Publications, badges and certificates
Paperbacks
Teesdale Way: Dufton to the North Sea by Martin Collins, updated by Paddy Dillon (Cicerone Press) 2005. ISBN 9781852844615. 160pp; 172 x 116. £10.00.
Leaflets
Teesdale Way: Piercebridge to Hurworth Place (Darlington Borough Council). A4/3. Free (+ 9 x 4 SAE).

Teesdale Way: Hurworth Place to Low Middleton (Darlington Borough Council). A4/3. Free (+ 9 x 4 SAE).
Teesdale Way (Darlington Borough Council). A5. Free (+ 9 x 6 SAE).
Tees Link (Tees Forest). A3/4 (A5 folded). Free (+ 9 x 6 SAE).
Walking Support Providers
Contours

Thirlmere Round THIRLR

CUMBRIA 35km/22 miles

A tough high level walk around Thirlmere visiting Helm Crag, Calf Crag, Ullscarf, High Seat, Sticks Pass, Helvellyn and Seat Sandal.

Attributes
Challenging; Anytime Challenge; Moorland; Mountain
Start and Finish
Grasmere, Cumbria NY339072
Maps
OS Landranger: 90
OS Explorer: 4, 5, 7
Publications, badges and certificates
Looseleaf
Thirlmere Round (Brian Richmond). Free (+ 9 x 4 SAE).
Certificate
Thirlmere Round (Brian Richmond). £0.30 (+ SAE).

Three Peaks of Cheviot Walk TPOCW

NORTHUMBERLAND 48km/30 miles

This tough walk in the Cheviot Hills encircling the Cheviot involves 5,700ft of ascent and requires good navigational skills. It links the Schil, Windy Gyle and Hedgehope.

Attributes
Challenging; Anytime Challenge; Moorland
Start and Finish
Hawsen Burn, near Wooler, Northumberland NT954225
Websites
www.walknortheast.org.uk
Maps
OS Landranger: 74, 75, 80, 81
OS Explorer: 16
Publications, badges and certificates
Looseleaf
Three Peaks of Cheviot (LDWA Northumbria Group). A4. Free (+ 9 x 4 SAE) or download from website.
Certificate
Three Peaks of Cheviot Walk (LDWA Northumbria Group). Free (+ 9 x 6 SAE & loose 1st class stamp).

Three Rings of Shap TROS

CUMBRIA 100km/62 miles

The Three Rings of Shap consists of three circular routes all from Shap. Badges and certificates are available on the completion of 1, 2 or all 3 Rings. A route description may be downloaded from the LDWA Cumbria Group website, via the main LDWA site.

Attributes
Very Challenging; Anytime Challenge; Moorland; Mountain
Start and Finish
Shap, Cumbria NY563151
Websites
www.ldwa.org.uk
Maps
OS Landranger: 90, 91
OS Explorer: 5, 19
Publications, badges and certificates
Badge & certificate
Three Rings of Shap (Barrie Blenkinship). £1.50 & £0.50 (+ SAE). Cheques to Cumbria LDWA.

Tour of the Lake District TLAKED

CUMBRIA 150km/93 miles

The circular route starts at Windermere and passes through Ambleside, Coniston, and Eskdale before heading north to Keswick. It then heads south, through Rosthwaite to Grasmere; across to Patterdale and thence back to Windermere. Five alternative high-level routes are available.

Attributes
Challenging; Lake/Reservoir; Moorland
Start and Finish
Windermere, Cumbria SD413986
Maps
OS Landranger: 89, 90
OS Explorer: 4, 5, 6, 7
Publications, badges and certificates
Paperbacks
Tour of the Lake District by Jim Reid (Cicerone Press) 2007. ISBN 9781852844967. 224pp; 170 x 120.

Trans-Dales Trail – 3 TRANDT3

CUMBRIA, N YORKS 91km/57 miles

This strenuous route takes in Mallerstang, Garsdale Head, Wensleydale, Askrigg, Thoralby, Carlton-in-Coverdale, West Scrafton Moor, Nidderdale and Masham. It intersects the related routes, Trans-Dales Trail 1 at Middlesmoor and Trail 2 at Askrigg.

Attributes
Challenging; Anytime Challenge; Moorland; Heritage
Start
Kirkby Stephen Railway Station, Cumbria NY761067
Finish
Masham, N Yorks SE225807
Websites
www.dalestrails.co.uk
Maps
OS Landranger: 92, 98, 99
OS Explorer: 19, 30, 298
Publications, badges and certificates
Paperbacks
Trans-Dales Trail 3 (Arnold Underwood) 1999. 42pp; A5. £2.50 (incs p&p). Cheques to Arnold Underwood.

Tyne – Estuary to Source TETS

CUMBRIA, NORTHUMBERLAND 133km/83 miles

A route following the Tyne and South Tyne Valleys through North Shields, Newcastle, Hexham, Haltwhistle, Slaggyford, Alston and Garrigill.

Attributes
River; Moorland
Start
Tynemouth, Northumberland NZ370698
Finish
Tynehead, Garrigill, Cumbria NY753351
Maps
OS Landranger: 87, 88, 91
OS Explorer: 316, 31, 43
Publications, badges and certificates
Paperbacks
Walking the Tyne by J. B. Jonas (RA Northumbria) 2004. ISBN 9781901184709. 68pp; A5. £5.50. Cheques to J B Jonas; profits to Ramblers Association.

Tyne Valley Train Trails TVTT

NORTHUMBERLAND 69km/43 miles

A series of short walks south of Hadrian's Wall and based on the Tyne Valley railway which passes through the station towns/villages of Prudhoe, Stocksfield, Riding Mill, Corbridge, Hexham, Haydon Bridge and Bardon Mill, all of which can be linked to provide a linear route of at least 43 miles through woodlands, farmland, across open fells and along riverside paths.

Attributes
Moorland; World Heritage Site; Heritage
Start
Wylam, Northumberland NZ120642
Finish
Haltwhistle, Northumberland NY704637
Maps
OS Landranger: 86, 87, 88
OS Explorer: 316, 43
Publications, badges and certificates
Folders
Tyne Valley Train Trails – West (Northumberland County Council). 6pp. £3.95. Downloadable from Hadrian's Wall website.
Tyne Valley Train Trails – East (Northumberland County Council). 6pp. £3.95. Downloadable from Hadrian's Wall website.

Wainwright Memorial Walk WAINMW

CUMBRIA 164km/102 miles

Following in the footsteps of Alfred Wainwright and three of his friends on a walk they took between Windermere and Ambleside. Their devised route promises that the walker should be able to see 'Every lake, Every valley, and Every mountain, even if not actually visited'.

Attributes
Challenging; Lake/Reservoir; Moorland; Mountain
Start
Windermere, Cumbria SD409988
Finish
Ambleside, Cumbria NY375044
Maps
OS Landranger: 89, 90, 96, 97
OS Explorer: 4, 5, 6, 7

Publications, badges and certificates

Book

Wainwright Memorial Walk by A. Wainwright (Striding Edge Limited) 2004. ISBN 9780711224025. 192pp; 168 x 120. £10.99 (+£2.95 p&p).

DVD

Wainwright's Memorial Walk by Eric Robson (Striding Edge Limited) 2004. 105 minutes.

Walking Support Providers

Ramblers

Wainwright's Remote Lakeland WWTRL

CUMBRIA **306km/190 miles**

This is an adventure through the remote mountains of Lakeland. It is a walk that should not be underestimated and it is essential that the walker should have good navigation skills.

Attributes

Challenging; Moorland; Mountain

Start and Finish

Penrith, Cumbria NY513304

Maps

OS Landranger: 89, 90, 96, 97

OS Explorer: 4, 5, 6, 7

Publications, badges and certificates

Book

After Wainwright (Wainwright's Remote Lakeland) by Eric Robson (Striding Edge Limited) 2003. ISBN 9780946812035. 205pp; 170 x 116. £9.99 (+£2.95 p&p).

DVD

Wainwright's Remote Lakeland DVD by Eric Robson (Striding Edge Limited).

Walking the North Tyne WNTYNE

NORTHUMBERLAND **76km/47 miles**

The route explores the northern branch of the River Tyne from Hexham to the source near Deadwater in the Kielder Forest area, including a walk alongside Kielder Water. The Lakeside Way is a Forestry Commission project to encircle Kielder Water, with a 15 mile (24km) stretch from the south corner of Kielder Dam to Kielder Village. Information is available online.

Attributes

Lake/Reservoir; River

Start

Hexham, Northumberland NY941650

Finish

Deadwater, Kielder Forest, Northumberland NY605968

Websites

www.forestry.gov.uk

Maps

OS Landranger: 80, 87

OS Explorer: 42, 43

Publications, badges and certificates

Paperbacks

Walking the North Tyne by J. B. Jonas (RA Northumbria) 2005. ISBN 9781901184822. 52pp; 202 x 144. £5.00. Cheques to J B Jonas; profits to Ramblers Association.

Westmorland Way WMDW

CUMBRIA **153km/95 miles**

A relatively low-level route across the historic county of Westmorland and the Lake District National Park using footpaths, tracks and country lanes. It takes in Shap, Pooley Bridge, Patterdale, Grasmere, Troutbeck, Kendal and Morecambe Bay.

Attributes

River; Moorland

Start

Appleby-in-Westmorland, Cumbria NY683204

Finish

Arnside, Cumbria SD461788

Websites

www.mickledore.co.uk

Maps

OS Landranger: 90, 91, 97

OS Explorer: 5, 7, 19

Publications, badges and certificates

Paperbacks

Westmorland Way by Paul Hannon (Hillside Publications) 1998. ISBN 9781870141581. 88pp; 175 x 115. £5.99 (+ 60p p&p). From publisher's website.

Walking Support Providers

Brigantes; Contours; Discovery; Mickledore

Whicham Valley Five Trigs Walk WVFTW

CUMBRIA **32km/20 miles**

A tough walk taking in Knott Hill, Black Combe, Whitfell and Stickle Pike. Good map reading and compass skills are essential.

Attributes

Challenging; Anytime Challenge; Moorland; Mountain

Start and Finish
Duddon Bridge, Cumbria SD199882
Maps
OS Landranger: 96
OS Explorer: 6
Publications, badges and certificates
Looseleaf
Whicham Valley Five Trigs Walk (Brian Richmond). Free (+ 9 x 4 SAE).
Badge
Whicham Valley Five Trigs Walk (Brian Richmond). £0.85 (+ SAE).

Windermere – Walking Around the Lake WINDWAL

CUMBRIA **48km/30 miles**

A circuit of Windermere, England's longest and largest natural lake. The route keeps as close to the lake as possible, though at times can be up to a mile from it. This is compensated with some good views of the lake and the more distant Howgills, Pennines and Morecambe Bay. Among the points of interest are Jenkin's Crag, Holehird with its gardens, Townend house, Orrest Head, Bowness, Gummer's How – the highest point, Fell Foot, Stott Park Heights, Rawlinson Nab, Ferry House opposite Bowness, Claife Heights and Wray Castle. There is about 4700ft (1435m) of ascent, mostly gradual.

Attributes
Lake/Reservoir; Moorland; Charity
Start and Finish
Waterhead Pier, Waterhead, Cumbria NY375031
Maps
OS Landranger: 90, 97
OS Explorer: 7
Publications, badges and certificates
Hardback
Windermere: Walking Around the Lake by Duncan Turner (Palatine Books) 2006. ISBN 9781874181347. 128pp; 180 x 122. £6.95. Proceeds to Leonard Cheshire Home.

Windermere Way WMRW

CUMBRIA **72km/45 miles**

A route around Lake Windermere, taking in Ferry House, Lakeside, Bowness Bay and Bowness, with good vantage points. Through use of the various public transport facilities available, namely bus, ferry and steamer, it is possible to complete the Way via a series of short walks.

Attributes
Lake/Reservoir; Moorland
Start and Finish
Bowness-on-Windermere SD400968
Waymark
Name enclircling yellow arrow
Websites
www.windermere-way.co.uk
Maps
OS Landranger: 90, 97
OS Explorer: 7
Publications, badges and certificates
Booklets
Windermere Way by Phil Kirby (Mozaic) 2003. A2 (A4/3 folded). £2.47 (incs p&p).

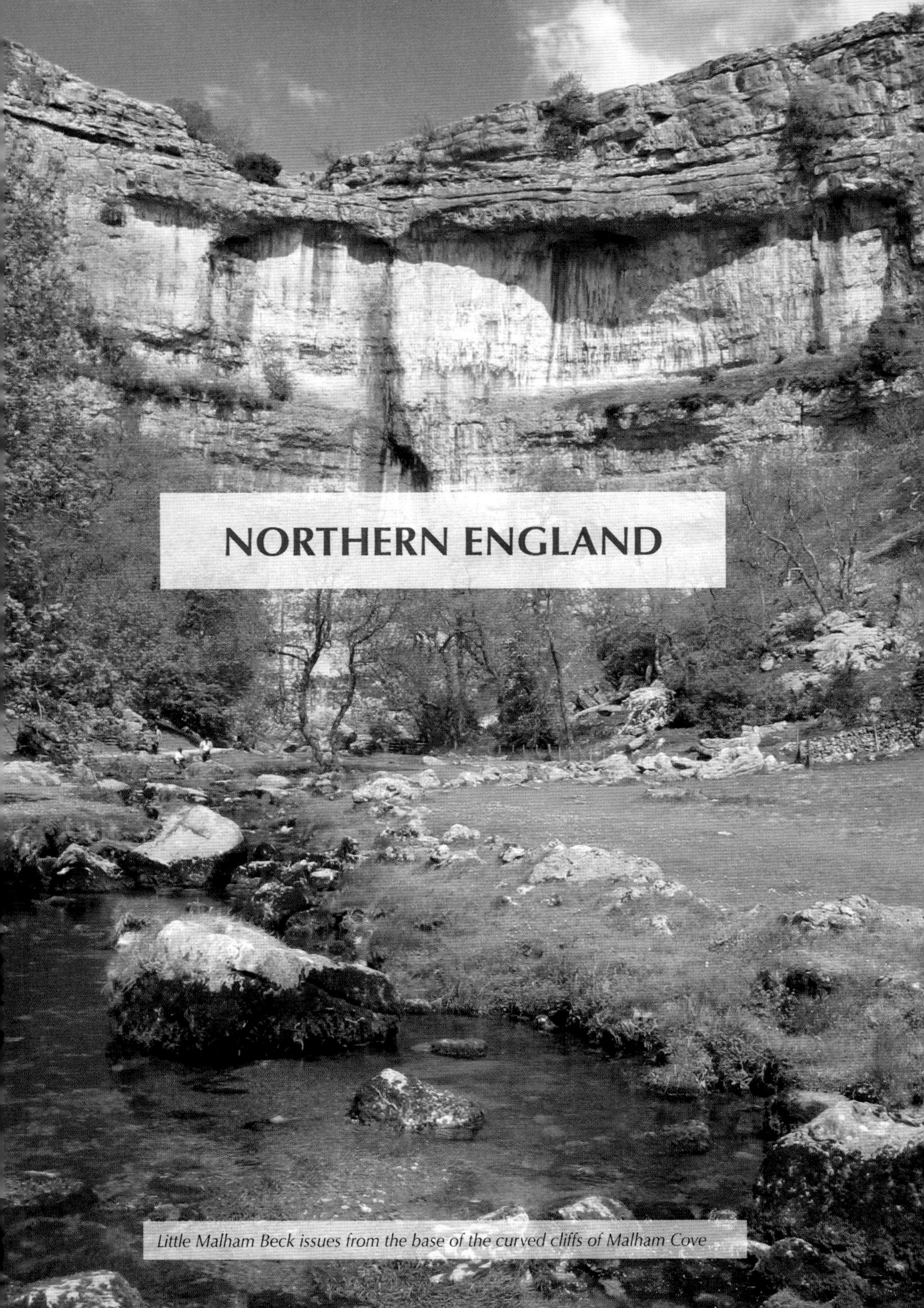

NORTHERN ENGLAND

Little Malham Beck issues from the base of the curved cliffs of Malham Cove

KEY FACTS	
Areas	Cleveland, Durham, North Lincolnshire, Yorkshire (North, East; South & West), Tyne & Wear – areas include unitaries
National Parks	Yorkshire Dales, North York Moors
Principal AONBs	Nidderdale, Howardian Hills, North Pennines
World Heritage Sites	Durham Castle & Cathedral, Saltaire, Studley Royal Park including the ruins of Fountains Abbey, Hadrian's Wall
Heritage Coast	Yorkshire: North Yorkshire and Cleveland, Flamborough Headland, Spurn
E-Routes	E2 variants Dover – Stranraer , E2 variant Harwich – Stranraer, E8 Hull – Liverpool
National Trails (England)	Cleveland Way, Hadrian's Wall (part), Pennine Way (part), Pennine Bridleway (part), Yorkshire Wolds Way
Walking Routes (trail miles)	132 main routes (6507 miles); 33 waymarked (2317 miles); 70 Anytime Challenges (2474 miles)
Resident population	7 million

DON'T MISS! TRAIL SECTIONS (CHALLENGING/REMOTE MARKED WITH *)	
Yorkshire Wolds Way	Fridaythorpe to Pocklington (just off route), Holm, Pasture and Warren Dales (17.5km, 1600ft ascent)
Nidderdale Way	Circular from Lofthouse, moors, Nidd valley, Scar House Reservoir (16km, 1600ft ascent/descent)
Pennine Way	Malham Tarn to Horton in Ribblesdale* (over Fountains Fell and Pen-y-Ghent top) (19km, 2100ft ascent, 2500ft descent)
Airedale Way	Skipton to Malham (from Gargrave to Malham is also Pennine Way) (17km, 700ft ascent), option to Malham Cove extra 2/3 km
Ripon Rowel	Masham to North Stainley along the River Ure, easy (13km, 500ft ascent)
Lady Anne's Way	Hawes to Kirkby Stephen in the Eden valley, the High Way, Pendragon Castle (26km, 1800ft ascent)
Dales Way	Kettlewell to Beckermonds in Upper Wharfedale and Langstrothdale, classic barns (15km, 800ft ascent)
Dales Way	Cavendish Pavilion at Bolton Abbey to Grassington, past The Strid (Dales Bus return) (15km, 900ft ascent)
Coast to Coast	Reeth to Richmond, Swaledale and historic Richmond (16km, 1300ft ascent)
Cleveland Way	Slapewath to Kildale, over Roseberry Topping, visiting Captain Cook's Monument (16km, 1600ft ascent)
Newtondale Trail	Pickering to Newtondale Halt, Newton Dale (either way and train to start/finish) (15km, 1500ft ascent)

Tees river, Teesdale

NORTHERN ENGLAND

A remote farmhouse is passed on the Dales Way, near Ribblehead

Northern England has some of the scenic jewels of England's crown. It is home to two major National Parks: the Yorkshire Dales National Park with its many long dales cutting through limestone uplands; and the North York Moors National Park that includes the moorland masses of the Cleveland Hills and the North York Moors themselves, with some of the most extensive heather moors in Europe extending across to the Cleveland coast. Here the Cleveland coastline provides fine cliff scenery, while further south, on the Holderness coast, lower cliffs of softer, eroding boulder-clay extend to Spurn Point where the Humber estuary divides Yorkshire from North Lincolnshire.

Geography

From the chalk cliffs at Flamborough Head on the East Yorkshire coast a crescent-shaped range of gentler hills, the Yorkshire Wolds, arcs around south towards the Humber, offering typical chalk downland landscapes. There is a similar lower range – the Lincolnshire Wolds – south of the Humber. Away from these hills much of this area has a flatter, agricultural landscape, crossed by the Trent as it flows to the Humber estuary. Thorne and Hatfield Moors are part of the largest complex of lowland raised bogs in Britain.

Bounding the region to the west is the sweep of the Pennines – the famous backbone of England – that together with the North York Moors form the watershed for many of Yorkshire's great rivers, that flow eventually to the Humber estuary. From the Pennines the Swale, Ure, Nidd and Wharfe join the Ouse, while the Calder joins the Aire. From the North York Moors the Derwent flows south to the Humber. Between the Pennines and the Moors lies the Vale of York, with its pastoral lowland landscapes and the historic City of York. Further north the estuaries of the Tees, Wear and Tyne are home to much industry, providing employment for the large urban populations in Teeside, Wearside and Tyneside.

The Trails

With such varied attractions for walkers, there are strong walking traditions and not surprisingly a large choice of routes, with about 6500 miles of trails in all. There are almost 2300 miles of waymarked trails, some offering easy-to-follow routes suitable for the less experienced.

This is also a great area for those seeking a challenge, with over half of the routes rated

Northern England – major routes
Only major routes from this region (excluding any National Trails) are shown here. The National Trails are shown on the map in the National Trails section of this handbook. For the full network of trails visit the LDWA website – www.ldwa.org.uk.
NORTH SEA
R North Tyne
Newcastle upon Tyne
Tynemouth
South Shields
R Tyne
Gateshead
Sunderland
R South Tyne
DUCP
WEARW
R Wear
A1(M)
North Pennines
DURHAM
TSDW
Hartlepool
Stockton-on-Tees
R Eden
R Tees
Darlington
Middlesbrough
R Esk
LYKEWW
NORTH YORK MOORS
DALESW
NORTH YORKSHIRE
YORKSHIRE DALES
NIDW
RIPR
Howardian Hills
Nidderdale
A1(M)
RIBW
R Derwent
R Ouse
Bridlington Bay
Forest of Bowland
Harrogate
York
CASHIRE
R Ribble
R Aire
EAST YORKSHIRE
Leeds
LCW
BRTW
M65
Burnley
Bradford
M62
TPT
Kingston upon Hull
Blackburn
CALW
Halifax
M62
R Humber
M62
KLW
Rochdale
BBW
Scunthorpe
Bolton
M66
Huddersfield
Grimsby
M180
M60
Oldham
Barnsley
M1
Doncaster
MANCHESTER
Ashton-under-Lyne
Lincolnshire Wolds
M18
Warrington
M67
Stockport
Sheffield
A1(M)
R Trent
RTRW
TPT
SHCYW
M6
PEAK DISTRICT
Lincoln
Chesterfield
R Witham
CHESHIRE
M1
NOTTINGHAMSHIRE
Stoke-on-Trent
LINCOLNS
Newcastle-under-Lyme
DERBYSHIRE
Nottingham

as 'challenging'. There are about 70 Anytime Challenges on offer, totalling some 2400 miles, each offering a completion certificate and often a badge.

With distinctive landscapes on display there are four contrasting **National Trails** to choose from, the Cleveland Way, with sections both on the North York Moors and along the coastline, reaching at Filey the linking Yorkshire Wolds Way, that runs through softer, rolling downland. From Tyneside Hadrian's Wall Path starts its scenic coast-to-coast traverse along a Roman frontier, now the Hadrian's Wall World Heritage Site. The Pennine Way meanders from dale to dale as it passes through the north Pennines, while the broadly parallel Pennine Bridleway, designed mainly for horse riders and mountain bikers, forms a major new route for walkers through the Yorkshire Dales, usually taking a lower line. (For more details of these, see the National Trails section.) Routes related to the Cleveland Way include the Tabular Hills Link Walk that provides a missing link to complete the main route's horseshoe shape. Cleveland Circles provides a daisy-chain of options for circular walks based on the main trail, while the Cleveland Street Walk links Guisborough with Loftus.

Several routes **traverse** one or more of the dales. The major Dales Way journeys from Ilkley across the Yorkshire Dales to Cumbria and it is a very popular route. The Denby Way explores Denby Dale with its famous pie while the Eskdale Way, Newtondale Trail and the Nidderdale Way explore their own dales and rivers. An alternative route aimed mainly at horse-riders is the Newtondale Horse Trail. High-level dales routes include the Dales High Way and the Barningham Trail that links Teesdale with Arkengarthdale. Other routes with **landscape** themes include the Chalkland Way in the chalk hills of the Yorkshire Wolds and the Peatlands Way on the Hatfield peat moors. Forestry routes include the Blue Man Walk, in coniferous woodland in the North York Moors, and the Great North Forest Heritage Trail.

River routes include the Airedale Way, Colne Valley Circular Walk, Dearne Way, Ebor Way (Foss and Ouse), Foss Walk, River Wear Trail and Weardale Way, and the Swale Way. The Lake Pickering Circuit goes around the Vale of Pickering, the likely site of a glacial lake at one time. The Calderdale Way encircles the Calder river valley's towns.

There are some **coast-to-coast** variants originating in the region: the Trans Pennine Trail is now a major network of multi-user trails spanning the country from Hull to Liverpool with several spur routes. The two Bay to Bay Walks link Barrow to Robin Hood's Bay via Grassington. Coastal footpaths include the Durham Coastal Footpath.

'Beating the bounds' is a strong English tradition, nowhere more manifest than in the north. Many routes **circuit** a borough, town or city: the

Royd Moor windmills (Spicer Hill)

ROUTE CODES

Code	Route	Code	Route
BBW	Barnsley Boundary Walk	NIDW	Nidderdale Way
BRTW	Bronte Way	RIBW	Ribble Way
CALW	Calderdale Way	RIPR	Ripon Rowel
DALESW	Dales Way	RTRW	Rotherham Round Walk
DUCP	Durham Coastal Footpath	SHCYW	Sheffield Country Walk
KLW	Kirklees Way	TPT	Trans Pennine Trail
LCW	Leeds Country Way	TSDW	Teesdale Way
LYKEWW	Lyke Wake Walk	WEARW	Weardale Way

Poppies add a dash of colour to a field above Woolley Colliery Village

Barnsley Boundary Walk, Brighouse Boundary Walk, Doncastrian Way, Harrogate Ringway, Kirklees Way, Leeds Country Way, Maltby Circular Walk, Penistone Boundary Walk, Ripon Rowel, Rotherham Ring Route, Rotherham Round Walk and Wakefield Way. The Heron Way offers many options near Doncaster. The Holme Valley Circular Walk visits the heights above the valley. There are millennium routes for Bradford and York: Millennium Way – Bradford and Millennium Way – York, while the Todmorden Centenary Way marks a town's anniversary. The Jorvic Way – Jorvic is the Viking name for York – celebrates the City's Viking history. The Silver Lincs Way is a Ramblers' route linking Grimsby and Louth, while both the South Tyneside Heritage Trail and the Spen Way Heritage Trail (in the former Spenborough) include heritage sites.

Literary figures are marked in the Herriot Way in James Herriott's Yorkshire country and the Bronte Round (an Anytime Challenge) links Bronte sites, as does the Bronte Way that starts in Yorkshire. The Hambleton Hillside Mosaic Walk includes many mosaics en route. **Heritage** is represented by the Lady Anne's Way that remembers Lady Ann Clifford, member of a famous family. The Wilberforce Way marks the Hull-born campaigner against the slave trade, William Wilberforce. Other World Heritage Sites are visited by several routes, including Fountains Abbey (Abbey Trail and Ripon Rowel), while Durham Castle and Cathedral are passed by the Weardale Way. There is a Christian theme for the Abbey Trail that visits seven historic abbeys and for the Abbeys Amble that also includes three castles, while Tyneside's Bede's Way remembers the Venerable Bede. The Minster Way links famous Minsters at Beverley and York. The Whitby Way visits several pilgrimage sites. At Shipley, the Saltaire Village World Heritage Site, a complete 19th-century industrial village, lies on the Dales Way – Shipley Link. Other industrial heritage includes former railway routes on the Durham Railway Paths and Penistone Line Trail. The mineral industries in Durham are remembered by the Lead Mining Trail.

Mark Reid provides two routes themed on the Black Sheep pubs: the Inn Way...to the North

York Moors and the Inn Way...to the Yorkshire Dales link hostelries, and a third of his many routes, the Yorkshire Water Way, supported by Yorkshire Water, links their reservoirs.

The best known of the **Anytime Challenges** in this region are the classic Lyke Wake Walk on a traditional coffin-route across the North York Moors, and the Three Peaks Walk (Yorkshire) above Ribblesdale, climbing over 5000ft on Pen-y-ghent, Whernside and Ingleborough. Brian Smailes provides a guidebook for both, along with his own Yorkshire Dales Top Ten. (The Shepherd's Round provides an alternative to the overused and eroded Lyke Wake Walk.)

Significant route developers and recorders include two with four routes: Louise Mallinson (Almscliffe Amble, Sting in the Tail, Two Beacons Challenge and Wharfedale–Washburn Challenge) and Ian Parker (Settle Scramble, Skipton Double Trigger, Skipton Saunter and Skipton–Settle Link). There are three routes each from Peter Bayer (Three Crags, Three Moors and Three Rivers Walks), John Eckersley (Nidd Valley Link, Rezzy Rush and Yorkshire Dales Challenge Walk) and Simon Townson (Ainsty Bounds Walk, Dales Traverse and Seahorse Saunter). Two routes each come from Ben Booth, Derek Haller, John Merrill, Kim Peacock, John Sparshatt and Arnold Underwood. Several LDWA Groups act as route Recorders for Calderdale, Cleveland, East Yorkshire and Nidderdale.

ANYTIME CHALLENGES	
Cleveland	Langbaurgh Loop, Samaritan Way
Durham	Trans-Dales Trail – 2
East Yorkshire	East Riding Heritage Way, East Thriding Treble Ten, High Hunsley Circuit, Howden 20, Howdenshire Way, Humber Bridge Link Walk, North Wolds Walk
North Yorkshire	Afoot in Two Dales, Ainsty Bounds Walk, Beacon Banks Challenge, Bilsdale Circuit, Cavendish 27 Circuit, Dales Traverse, Hambleton Hobble, Harrogate & Knaresborough Heritage Trail, Hovingham Hobble, Knaresborough Round, Loaves & Fishes Walk, Lyke Wake Walk, Nidd Vale Circuit, Nidd Valley Link, North York Moors Wobble, North Yorkshire Moors Challenge Walk, Rezzy Rush, Ribskip Challenge, Rosedale Circuit, Scarborough Rock Challenge, Seahorse Saunter, Settle Scramble, Skipton Double Trigger, Skipton Saunter, Skipton–Settle Link, Tan Hill to Kirkstone Inn, Three Crags Walk, Three Peaks Walk (Yorkshire), Trans-Dales Trail – 1, Trollers Trot, Walden Round, White Rose Challenge Walk, Yorkshire Dales Challenge Walk, Yorkshire Dales Top Ten
South Yorkshire	Compo's Way, Dunford Round, Gritstone Edge Walk, Hope Valley Line Challenge, Newlands Way, Penistone Loop-D-Loop
West Yorkshire	Abbott's Hike, Aiggin Stone Amble Anytime Challenge, Almscliffe Amble, Apostles Walk, Bog Dodgers Way, Bronte Round, Burley Bridge Hike, Cal-Der-Went Walk, Cuckoo Walk, Harden Hike, Manorlands Meander, Myrtle Meander, Otley Nine Leagues, Sting in the Tail, Three Moors Walk, Three Rivers Walk, Two Beacons Challenge, Wadsworth Millennium Walk, Wharfedale Washburn Challenge, Yorkshire Ridings 200 Furlongs

Abbey Trail ABBT

N YORKS, W YORKS 187km/116 miles

The Trail links seven of England's greatest abbeys, at Kirkstall, Fountains, Byland, Rievaulx, Lastingham, Rosedale and Whitby, as it winds its way across the beautiful Yorkshire countryside.

Attributes
World Heritage Site; Heritage; Pilgrimage
Start
Kirkstall Abbey, Leeds SE259361
Finish
Whitby Abbey, North Yorks NZ901113
Maps
OS Landranger: 104, 99, 100, 101
OS Explorer: 26, 27, 288, 297, 299, 302
Publications, badges and certificates
Paperbacks
Abbey Trail: Over 100 Miles of Walks Through Yorkshire's Finest Countryside by Clive Newsome (Sigma Leisure) 2003. ISBN 9781850588030. 132pp; 206 x 148. £6.95.
Walking Support Providers
Bobs

Abbeys Amble ABBAM

N YORKS 166km/103 miles

A walk that links three Yorkshire Abbeys (Fountains, Bolton and Jervaulx) and three Yorkshire castles (Ripley, Bolton and Middleham), and uses sections of established routes – Harrogate Ringway, Dales Way, Yoredale Way and Ripon Rowel.

Attributes
Heritage; Religious; Charity
Start and Finish
Ripon, N Yorks SE315710
Maps
OS Landranger: 98, 99, 104
OS Explorer: 297, 298, 302, 30, 2, 289, 299
Publications, badges and certificates
Paperbacks
Abbeys Amble (John Eckersley) 1999. ISBN 9780953586202. 88pp; 248 x 170. £7.99 (+ £1.00 p&p). Profits to Christian Aid.
Certificate
Abbeys Amble (John Eckersley). £1.00 (incs p&p). Profits to Christian Aid.

Abbott's Hike ABBH

CUMBRIA, N YORKS, W YORKS 172km/107 miles

Named after its originator, this route from Yorkshire to the Lake District includes 25 miles of the Dales Way, 14 miles of the Three Peaks Walk and 3 miles of the Pennine Way National Trail.

Attributes
Challenging; Anytime Challenge; Moorland
Start
Ilkley, W Yorks SE117476
Finish
Pooley Bridge, Cumbria NY470247
Maps
OS Landranger: 90, 91, 97, 98, 104
OS Explorer: 297, 2, 5, 7, 19, 30
Publications, badges and certificates
Paperbacks
Abbott's Hike by Peter Abbott (Peter Abbott) 1980. 64pp; 210 x 149. £2.00 (incs p&p).

Afoot in Two Dales AFTD

N YORKS 80km/50 miles

A tough circular walk with over 5,500ft of ascent using footpaths, bridleways and quiet roads through scenic Wensleydale and Swaledale including an ascent of Great Shunner Fell. The walk can be done over two or three days using local accommodation.

Attributes
Challenging; Anytime Challenge; River; Moorland
Start and Finish
Car Park, Harmby Village Hall, Leyburn, N Yorks SE127895
Maps
OS Landranger: 98, 99
OS Explorer: 30
Publications, badges and certificates
Looseleaf
Afoot in Two Dales Route Description (Jill King). 4pp. Free (+A5 SAE). Free to download from LDWA website.
Badge & certificate
Afoot in Two Dales (Jill King). £2.00 (+A4 SAE). Cheques to Cleveland LDWA.

Aiggin Stone Amble Anytime Challenge AIGSA

LANCS, W YORKS **45km/28 miles**

A route on the Lancashire/Yorkshire border visiting Shore, Littleborough, Hollingworth, Withens Clough Reservoir and the Aiggin Stone, an ancient waymarker on the Roman road at Blackstone Edge Moor.

Attributes
Challenging; Anytime Challenge; Moorland
Start and Finish
Todmorden, W Yorks SD934245
Maps
OS Landranger: 103, 104, 109, 110
OS Explorer: 21
Publications, badges and certificates
Leaflets
Aiggin Stone Amble Anytime Challenge (LDWA Calderdale Group). 2pp; A4. Free (+ 9 x 4 SAE). Free to download from LDWA website.
Badge & certificate
Aiggin Stone Amble Anytime Challenge (LDWA Calderdale Group). £1.50 & £1.00 (+ SAE).

Ainsty Bounds Walk AINSBW

N YORKS **71km/44 miles**

This walk in the Ainsty area, mainly along the banks of the Rivers Wharf, Nidd and Ouse, passes through Boston Spa, Wetherby, Moor Monkton, the outskirts of York, and Bolton Percy. It is coincident in parts with the Jorvic Way. Proceeds from the sales of the publication are donated to a local hospice.

Attributes
Anytime Challenge; River
Start and Finish
River Bridge, Tadcaster, N Yorks SE488434
Maps
OS Landranger: 105
OS Explorer: 289, 290
Publications, badges and certificates
Looseleaf
Ainsty Bounds Walk (Simon Townson) 2007. 4pp; A4. £1.50 (incs p&p). Free to download from LDWA website.

Airedale Way AIREW

N YORKS, W YORKS **80km/50 miles**

A largely rural route from Leeds to the heart of the Yorkshire Dales, following as far as possible paths by the River Aire and passing through the small industrial towns of Shipley, Bingley and Keighley.

Attributes
Easy; River; Moorland
Start
Leeds, W Yorks SE298333
Finish
Malham Tarn, N Yorks SD894661
Maps
OS Landranger: 98, 103, 104
OS Explorer: 2, 21, 41, 288, 289, 297
Publications, badges and certificates
Paperbacks
Airedale Way by Douglas Cossar (RA West Riding Area) 1996. ISBN 9780900613951. 80pp; A5. £4.50 (+ £1.00 p&p). Cheques to Ramblers Association (West Riding).
Badge
Airedale Way (RA West Riding Area). £1.50. Cheques to Ramblers Association (West Riding).

Almscliffe Amble ALMSA

N YORKS, W YORKS **48km/30 miles**

A tough walk from Otley RUFC, visiting Otley Chevin, Bramhope, Harewood House, Almscliffe Crag and Farnley. A 20-miles alternative route is also available.

Attributes
Challenging; Anytime Challenge
Start and Finish
Otley, W Yorks SE217457
Maps
OS Landranger: 104
OS Explorer: 297
Publications, badges and certificates
Looseleaf
Almscliffe Amble (Louise Mallinson). Free (+ 9 x 4 SAE). Free to download from LDWA website.
Certificate
Almscliffe Amble (Louise Mallinson). £0.50 (+ SAE). Badge no longer available.

Apostles Walk APW

LANCS, W YORKS **129km/80 miles**

A walk in aid of church funds for St. Matthews Church, Wilsden taking in parts of the Dales Way, Pennine Way, the Leeds – Liverpool Canal and visiting Ilkley, Grassington, Malham and Skipton.

Attributes
Challenging; Anytime Challenge; Canal; Moorland; Religious
Start and Finish
Wilsden, W Yorks SE094362
Maps
OS Landranger: 98, 103, 104
OS Explorer: 297, 2
Publications, badges and certificates
Looseleaf
Apostles Walk by A. T. Ashworth (A. T. Ashworth) 1971. 1pp; A4. Free (+ 9 x 4 SAE). Free to download from LDWA website.
Badge
Apostles Walk (A. T. Ashworth). £1.00 (+ SAE).

Barningham Trail BARNT

DURHAM **39km/24 miles**

This is a circular route linking the southern slopes of Teesdale with Arkengarthdale, taking in Barningham Moor and Stang Forest, providing good views and hidden valleys.

Attributes
Challenging; Moorland
Start and Finish
Barningham village green, Durham NZ085104
Maps
OS Landranger: 92
OS Explorer: 30
Publications, badges and certificates
Paperbacks
Barningham Trail by Ed Coles (Trailguides Ltd) 2007. ISBN 9781905444182. 48pp. £4.99. Also from local TICs.

Barnsley Boundary Walk BBW

S YORKS, W YORKS **117km/73 miles**

The walk provides a view of the varied countryside, industrial heritage and other points of interest in the Borough. Included are Langsett Reservoir, the former salt road to Dunford Bridge, several reservoirs, and the Country Parks at Cannon and Bretton Halls.

Attributes
Challenging; Heritage; Industrial History
Start and Finish
A629 Huddersfield Road, Ingbirchworth, Barnsley, W Yorks SE225058
Waymark
'B' logo in yellow on green square
Maps ◈
OS Landranger: 110, 111
OS Explorer: 278, 288, 1
Publications, badges and certificates
Pack
Barnsley Boundary Walk (Barnsley Metropolitan Borough Council). 6 leaflets. £2.00 (incs p&p). Other short walks are available for the Barnsley area.

Bay to Bay Walks BTBW

CUMBRIA, LANCS, N YORKS **307km/191 miles**

Two 100-mile, 7 day, walks centred on Grassington, one heading east and one west. Each starts from Grassington and are named: Grassington to East Coast and Grassington to West Coast Walks. The Grassington to East Coast Walk goes via Upper Nidderdale, Masham, the Vale of Mowbray, Hutton-le-Hole and Fylingdales Moor to the North Sea coast. The Grassington to West Coast Walk crosses the heart of the Yorkshire Dales via Malham, Ingleborough and Kirkby Lonsdale to Morecambe Bay and the South Lakes peninsula. Together they provide a coast-to-coast traverse.

Attributes
Challenging; Moorland
Start
Village Square, Grassington, N Yorks SE002640
Finish
Slipway, Robin Hood's Bay, N Yorks NZ953049, or Piel Island, Barrow, Cumbria SD233638
Websites
www.bay2bay.co.uk
Maps
OS Landranger: 96, 97, 98, 99, 100, 101
OS Explorer: 2, 6, 7, 26, 27, 30, 298, 299
Publications, badges and certificates
Paperbacks
Grassington to East Coast Walk by John White (Fractal Press) 2003. ISBN 9781870735308. 96pp; 206 x 178. £9.95.

Grassington to West Coast Walk by John White (Fractal Press) 2008. ISBN 9781870735353. 96pp; 206 x 178. £9.95.

Beacon Banks Challenge BBC

N YORKS 40km/25 miles

This route, through a scenic and little walked area of Yorkshire, provides views of the Howardian Hills and the White Horse of Kilburn. It passes Byland Abbey and visits Husthwaite and Kilburn.

Attributes
Challenging; Anytime Challenge
Start and Finish
Easingwold, N Yorks SE528696
Maps
OS Landranger: 100
OS Explorer: 300
Publications, badges and certificates
Looseleaf
Beacon Banks Challenge (Ben Booth). 5pp; A4. Free (+ 9 x 4 SAE). Free to download from LDWA website.
Badge & certificate
Beacon Banks Challenge (Ben Booth). £2.00 (+ 9 x 6 SAE).

Bilsdale Circuit BIC

N YORKS 48km/30 miles

A strenuous circuit in the North York Moors National Park with over 4,000ft of ascent. The route goes across high moors within sight of the Bilsdale TV mast, mainly along tracks, and takes in Roppa Edge, West Moor, and Urra Moor where it is coincident with the Lyke Wake Walk and Cleveland Way National Trail.

Attributes
Challenging; Anytime Challenge; Moorland
Start and Finish
Newgate Bank Top, N Yorks SE564890
Maps
OS Landranger: 93, 100
OS Explorer: 26
Publications, badges and certificates
Looseleaf
Bilsdale Circuit (LDWA Cleveland Group). Free (+ 9 x 4 SAE). Free to download from LDWA website.
Badge & certificate
Bilsdale Circuit (LDWA Cleveland Group). £1.70 & £0.30 (+ SAE).

Blue Man Walk BMW

N YORKS 26km/16 miles

A Forestry Commission route through the upland coniferous forests on the east side of the North York Moors.

Attributes
Forest/Woodland
Start
Reasty Bank Top, N Yorks SE964945
Finish
Allerston, N Yorks SE876830
Waymark
Blue man logo
Websites
www.forestry.gov.uk
Maps
OS Landranger: 101
OS Explorer: 27
Publications, badges and certificates
Looseleaf
Blue Man Walk Route (Forest Enterprise North Yorkshire). 1pp; A4. Free (+ 9 x 4 SAE).
Badge
Blue Man Walk (Forest Enterprise North Yorkshire). £0.75 (+ SAE).

Bog Dodgers Way BDW

LANCS, W YORKS 37km/23 miles

A demanding route, partly coincident with the Pennine Way National Trail, taking in Wessenden Moor, Black Hill and Standedge.

Attributes
Challenging; Anytime Challenge; Moorland
Start and Finish
Marsden Church, West Yorks SE047116
Maps
OS Landranger: 110
OS Explorer: 1, 21
Publications, badges and certificates
Looseleaf
Bog Dodgers Way (LDWA Vermuyden Group). 1pp. Free (+ 9 x 4 SAE).
Badge & certificate
Bog Dodgers Way (LDWA Vermuyden Group). £2.00 (+ 9 x 6 SAE).

Brighouse Boundary Walk BRBW

W YORKS **29km/18 miles**

A walk encircling the town, gaining access to the moors and crossing the Calder Valley.

Attributes
Moorland; Heritage
Start and Finish
Wellholme Park, Brighouse, W Yorks SE147237
Waymark
Letter B with arrow protruding from base
Websites
www.calderdale.gov.uk
Maps
OS Landranger: 104, 110
OS Explorer: 288
Publications, badges and certificates
Folder
Brighouse Boundary Walk (Hebden Bridge Visitor and Canal Centre). 5 leaflets. £1.75 (+ 1st class stamp).

Bronte Round BROR

W YORKS **37km/23 miles**

The route links places associated with the Bronte Family, visiting Haworth (home of the Bronte family and the Bronte Museum) and Top Withins before returning to Hebden Bridge.

Attributes
Anytime Challenge; Moorland; Heritage; Literary
Start and Finish
Hebden Bridge, W Yorks SD992272
Maps
OS Landranger: 103, 104
OS Explorer: 21
Publications, badges and certificates
Booklets
Bronte Round/Pendle & Ribble Round by Derek Magnall (Norman Thomas) 1994. 36pp; A5. £1.85 (incs p&p).
Badge & certificate
Bronte Round (Norman Thomas). £2.00 (+ SAE).

Burley Bridge Hike BBRH

W YORKS **34km/21 miles**

A stenuous walk, with 2669ft of climb, around Rombalds Moor taking in Cow & Calf Rocks, Swastika Stone, Windgate Nick, Leeds & Liverpool Canal before returning via Hawksworth Moor and Burley. The Burley Bridge Hike is also run as an annual challenge event on the second Saturday in November each year.

Attributes
Challenging; Anytime Challenge; Canal; Moorland
Start and Finish
Burley-in-Wharefdale, W Yorks SE164458
Maps
OS Landranger: 104
OS Explorer: 297
Publications, badges and certificates
Badge & certificate
Burley Bridge Hike by John Sparshatt (John Sparshatt) 2007. £2.00 (+ A5 SAE).
Looseleaf
Burley Bridge Hike by John Sparshatt (John Sparshatt) 2007. 3pp; A4. Free (+ A5 SAE). Free to download from LDWA website.

Cal-Der-Went Walk CADWW

DERBYS, S YORKS, W YORKS **48km/30 miles**

A route taking in Bretton Park, High Hoyland and Penistone; and crossing the watersheds and valleys of the Calder, Dearne, Don and Derwent.

Attributes
Challenging; Anytime Challenge; Moorland
Start
Horbury Bridge, W Yorks SE281179
Finish
Ladybower Reservoir, Derbys SK195865
Maps
OS Landranger: 110
OS Explorer: 278, 1
Publications, badges and certificates
Booklets
Cal-Der-Went Walk by Geoffrey Carr (John Merrill Foundation) 1995. ISBN 9781874754268. 40pp; A5. £4.95 (+ £1.00 p&p). Cheques to John Merrill Foundation.
Badge & certificate
Cal-Der-Went Walk (Geoffrey Carr). £2.00 (+ A5 SAE).

Calderdale Way — CALW

W YORKS — **80km/50 miles**

A tough route around Calderdale encircling Halifax, Hebden Bridge and Todmorden, following old pack-horse ways across the open gritstone hillsides with sections of traditional stone causeway, passing through hillside villages and old mill towns on the banks of the River Calder.

Attributes
Challenging; Moorland; Industrial History
Start and Finish
Greetland, W Yorks SE097214
Waymark
Letters CW/trefoil
Maps ◈
OS Landranger: 103, 104, 110
OS Explorer: 21, 288
Publications, badges and certificates
Paperbacks
Calderdale Way by Paul Hannon (Hillside Publications) 2001. ISBN 9781870141710. 48pp; 115 x 178. £3.99 (+ 60p p&p).
(spiral bound)
Calderdale Way Guide by Calderdale Way Association (Calderdale Way Association). ISBN 9780950632919. 72pp; A5. £4.99 (+ 70p p&p).

Cavendish 27 Circuit — C27

N YORKS — **43km/27 miles**

A route following the river Wharfe to Bolton Bridge, then taking in the villages of Draughton, Eastby, Embsay, Flasby, Rylstone, Cracoe, Thorpe, Burnsall and Howgill before climbing Simon's Seat and returning via the Valley of Desolation.

Attributes
Challenging; Anytime Challenge; Moorland
Start
Cavendish Pavilion car park, Bolton Abbey, N Yorks SE077552
Finish
Cavendish Pavilion car park, Bolton Abbey, N Yorks SE077552
Waymark
Some waymarks (C27C)
Maps
OS Landranger: 98, 103, 104
OS Explorer: 2
Publications, badges and certificates
Looseleaf
Cavendish 27 Circuit by Alec Bottomley (Alec Bottomley) 1984. 2pp; A4. Free (+ A5 SAE). Free to download from LDWA website.
Badge & certificate
Cavendish 27 Circuit by Alec Bottomley (Alec Bottomley). £2.00 (+ A5 SAE). Walker to provide short summary and comments.

Chalkland Way — CHALKW

E YORKS — **64km/40 miles**

A tour around the Yorkshire Wolds, noted for its green, dry valleys, including the villages of Great Givendale, Bishop Wilton, Bugthorpe, Thixendale, Fimber, Wetwang and Huggate.

Attributes
Downland/Wolds
Start and Finish
Pocklington, E Yorks SE802488
Waymark
Black swan encircled by name on green
Websites
www.beehive.thisishull.co.uk
Maps ◈
OS Landranger: 100, 101, 106
OS Explorer: 294, 300
Publications, badges and certificates
Looseleaf
Chalkland Way (Ray Wallis) 1994. Free (+ A5 SAE).
Badge
Chalkland Way (Ray Wallis). £1.00 (+ SAE).

Cleveland Circles — CLVCIRC

CLEVELAND, N YORKS — **Various**

Dividing the Cleveland Way National Trail into 30 separate but interconnected routes, these circular walks provide an opportunity to explore the foothills of the Hambleton Hills and parts of the North York Moors. A total of 318 miles are mapped and described and the itineraries visit a number of famous abbeys and historic churches.

Attributes
Downland/Wolds; Moorland; Heritage; Pilgrimage; Religious

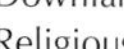

Start
Numerous
Finish
Numerous
Maps
OS Landranger: 93, 94
Publications, badges and certificates
Paperbacks
Cleveland Circles by John Eckersley (John Eckersley) 2006. 108pp; 248 x 170. £9.00 (+ £1.00 p&p). All proceeds to Christian Aid.

Compo's Way — COMPW

S YORKS, W YORKS — 61km/38 miles

A route through country associated with the television series – 'Last of the Summer Wine'.

Attributes
Challenging; Anytime Challenge; Moorland
Start
Hunter's Bar, Sheffield, S Yorks SK333857
Finish
Sid's Cafe, Holmfirth, W Yorks SE142082
Maps
OS Landranger: 110
OS Explorer: 1
Publications, badges and certificates
Booklets
Compo's Way by Alan Hiley (John Merrill Foundation). ISBN 9781874754732. 44pp; A5. £5.50 (+ £1.00 p&p). Cheques to John Merrill Foundation.
Badge & certificate
Compo's Way (John Merrill Foundation). £5.00 (incs p&p).

Cuckoo Walk — CUCKWK

GTR MAN, W YORKS — 29km/18 miles

An upland circuit via Wessenden Reservoir, Black Hill and White Moss; it is partly coincident with the Pennine Way National Trail.

Attributes
Challenging; Anytime Challenge; Lake/Reservoir; Moorland
Start and Finish
Marsden Station, W Yorks SE046118
Maps
OS Landranger: 110
OS Explorer: 1, 21
Publications, badges and certificates
Looseleaf
Cuckoo Walk by D. E. Wilkins (D. E. Wilkins) 2007. 5pp; A4. Free (+ A5 SAE).
Badge & certificate
Cuckoo Walk (D. E. Wilkins). £1.35 (+ SAE) & £0.15 (+ 9 x 4 SAE).

Dales High Way — DALHW

CUMBRIA, N YORKS, W YORKS — 145km/90 miles

An exhilarating 90 mile route across the glorious high country of the Yorkshire Dales exploring its rich history, geology and culture. With over 13,900ft of ascent, this spectacular walk takes in Rombalds Moor, Malhamdale, Ingleborough, the flanks of Whernside, the Howgill Fells and the Eden Valley.

Attributes
Challenging; River; Moorland; World Heritage Site; Geological
Start
Saltaire Station, W Yorks SE138381
Finish
Appleby-in-Westmorland, Cumbria NY686207
Websites
www.daleshighway.pwp.blueyonder.co.uk, www.settle-carlisle.co.uk
Maps
OS Landranger: 91, 98, 104
OS Explorer: 2, 19, 21, 31, 41, 288, 297
Publications, badges and certificates
Paperbacks
Dales High Way by Chris and Tony Grogan (Skyware Ltd) 2008. ISBN 9780955998706. 56pp. £6.99.
Walking Support Providers
Brigantes

Dales Traverse — DALT

N YORKS — 40km/25 miles

This route in Upper Wharfedale takes in Kettlewell, Cam Head, Buckden Pike, Litton and Mastiles Lane. Proceeds from sales of badges are donated to a local hospice.

Attributes
Challenging; Anytime Challenge; Moorland; Charity
Start and Finish
Kilnsey, N Yorks SD974679

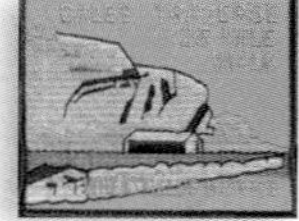

Maps
OS Landranger: 98
OS Explorer: 2, 30

Publications, badges and certificates
Looseleaf
Dales Traverse (Simon Townson) 2007. 1pp; A4. Free (+ 9 x 4 SAE). Free to download from LDWA website.
Badge & certificate
Dales Traverse (Simon Townson). £2.00 (+ 10 x 7 SAE).

Dales Way DALESW

CUMBRIA, N YORKS, W YORKS 126km/78 miles

The Way follows attractive dales through the Yorkshire and Howgill Fells, and the south-eastern part of the Lake District. From Ilkley it heads along Wharfedale passing Bolton Abbey, the Strid, Grassington and Buckden before crossing Cam Fell and the Pennine Way National Trail to descend to Dentdale. From here, the River Dee is followed to Sedbergh, then the Lune to the Crook of Lune. The Way crosses farmland to reach Burneside and the River Kent, which is traced for several miles before the path branches off to the finish. Link routes run from: Leeds (Leeds – Dales Way, 19 miles, on OS maps); Bradford/Shipley (Shipley – Dales Way, 8 miles, on OS maps) each described in the Gemmell-Speakman publication, also now with a Bradford – Shipley link, 3 miles, with an online description; and from Harrogate (Harrogate – Dales Way, 20 miles). The Saltaire Village World Heritage Site is at Shipley, a complete and well-preserved industrial village of the second half of the 19th century.

Attributes
River; Moorland; World Heritage Site
Start
Old Bridge, Ilkley, W Yorks SE111481
Finish
Bowness-on-Windermere, Cumbria SD402968
Waymark
Orange/green named discs/signposts with green hill graphic
Websites
www.dalesway.org.uk, www.bradford.gov.uk, www.saltairevillage.info
Maps ◈
OS Landranger: 96, 97, 98, 104
OS Explorer: 2, 7, 19, 30, 288, 289, 297, 298
Harvey Map (Stripmap)
Dales Way (Harvey Maps)
Publications, badges and certificates
Paperbacks
Dales Way: Complete Guide to the Trail by Terry Marsh (Cicerone Press) 2005. ISBN 9781852844646. 160pp; 116 x 172. £10.00.
Dales Way Companion by Paul Hannon (Hillside Publications) 2000. ISBN 9781870141536. 96pp; 175 x 115. £5.99 (+ 70p p&p). Includes details of link routes.
Dales Way Walk: Seven Glorious Days by Alistair Wallace (Jema Publications) 1997. ISBN 9781871468533. 96pp; A5. £5.99.
Booklets
Gemmell/Speakman Dales Way Route Guide by Arthur Gemmell, Colin Speakman (Dales Way Association) 2006. ISBN 9780906886724. 48pp; 188 x 114. £5.99 (+ 40p p&p). Cheques to Dales Way Association.
Dales Way: Handbook (includes accommodation details) (Dales Way Association) Annual. A5. £1.50 (incs p&p). By post from the Dales Way Association (Free to members).
Looseleaf
Harrogate Dales Way (RA Harrogate Group). 6pp; A5. £0.30 (+ A5 SAE).
Badge & certificate
Dales Way (Dales Way Association). £1.50 & £1.50 (incs p&p).
Walking Support Providers
Brigantes; Celtic; Contours; Discovery; HF; Instep; Knobbly Stick; Macs; Mickledore; Northwestwalks; Sherpa Van; Wycheway

Dearne Way DNW

S YORKS, W YORKS 48km/30 miles

A route following the River Dearne from its source to the confluence with the River Don, passing contrasting countryside including Bretton Country Park, Barnsley, canals and riverside.

Attributes
River; Canal
Start
Birds Edge, W Yorks SE201079
Finish
Mexborough, S Yorks SK478998
Waymark
Named discs with miners lamp logo
Maps ◈
OS Landranger: 110, 111
OS Explorer: 1, 278, 279, 288
Publications, badges and certificates
Leaflets
Dearne Way: Route Guide by Barnsley MBC (Countryside Team) (Barnsley MBC – Countryside Unit). Set of 8.

Denby Way DENW

S YORKS, W YORKS **80km/50 miles**

A circular route in an area to the west of the M1, bounded by the River Calder to the north and the River Don to the south, taking in Denby Dale, famous for its giant pie, Penistone, Silkstone, Bretton Park and Emley Moor.

Attributes
Moorland
Start and Finish
Denby Dale, W Yorks SE228084
Maps
OS Landranger: 110
OS Explorer: 278
Publications, badges and certificates
Folder
Walking in Pie Country (J K E Piggin) 1995. ISBN 9781898978022. 26pp; 210 x 147. £3.45 (incs p&p). Cheques to J.K.E. Piggin.
Certificate
Denby Way (J K E Piggin). Free (+ 9 x 6 SAE).

Doncastrian Way DONCW

S YORKS **53km/33 miles**

A route around the urban fringes of Doncaster across open fields and following river banks and green lanes and taking in the settlements of Barnby Dun and Dunsville before returning through Sprotbrough and along the River Don.

Attributes
River
Start and Finish
Doncaster, S Yorks SE566041
Waymark
Named signposts
Maps
OS Landranger: 111
OS Explorer: 279
Publications, badges and certificates
Leaflets
Doncastrian Way (LDWA Vermuyden Group). A5. Free (+ SAE).
Badge & certificate
Doncastrian Way (LDWA Vermuyden Group). £2.00 (+ A5 SAE).

Dunford Round DUNR

S YORKS **37km/23 miles**

The route crosses Thurlstone Moors and visits Dunford Bridge.

Attributes
Challenging; Anytime Challenge
Start and Finish
Flouch Inn, S Yorks SE197016
Maps
OS Landranger: 110
OS Explorer: 1
Publications, badges and certificates
Looseleaf
Dunford Round (Allen Pestell) 2007. £0.50 (+ 9 x 6 SAE).

Durham Coastal Footpath DUCP

DURHAM **18km/11 miles**

Passing through, or close to, Seaham Harbour, Dawdon, Easington, Danemouth and Blackhall, it traverses old mining areas. Reclamation projects following the pit closures, and the natural effects of the sea, have brought about improvements, with several Sites of Special Scientific Interest. Circular and other larger sculptures have been placed on the route.

Attributes
Coastal; Industrial History
Start
Seaham Hall Beach, Durham NZ422511
Finish
Crimdon Park, Durham NZ476384
Waymark
Coastal footpath logo
Websites
www.easington.gov.uk
Maps ◈
OS Landranger: 88, 93
OS Explorer: 308
Publications, badges and certificates
Booklets
Durham Heritage Coastal Footpath (Turning The Tide). 20pp; A5. Free (+ 9 x 6 SAE).

Durham Railway Paths DURWYP

DURHAM **92km/57 miles**

A network of former railway lines which have been reclaimed for use by walkers, horseriders and cyclists.

They include the Derwent Valley Walk (11 miles), Lanchester Valley (12 miles), Waskerley Way (7 miles), Deerness Valley (8 miles), Brandon-Bishop Auckland (9 miles), Auckland Walk (4 miles) and Tees Valley Railway Path (6 miles).

Attributes
Easy; Former Railway; Cycle Route;
Horse Ride (Multi User)
Start
Lydgetts Junction (common point), Durham NZ098493
Finish
Broom Park (common point), Durham NZ251415
Websites
www.durham.gov.uk
Maps ◈
OS Landranger: 87, 88, 92, 93
OS Explorer: 308, 316
Publications, badges and certificates
Pack
Railway Paths in County Durham (Durham County Council) 1997. 7 leaflets; A5. Free. Some data is out-of-date. Free (while stocks last). Will be replaced by website downloads.

East Riding Heritage Way ERHW

E YORKS, N YORKS **136km/85 miles**

The route consists of four linked walks, which can be done separately or all together: Beverley Twenty (on OS mapping and waymarked) – 20 miles from the Humber Bridge car park on the estuary over undulating farmland to Beverley Minster; Hutton Hike – 23 miles also with riverside paths and a nature reserve, on to Driffield; Rudston Roam – 21 miles with gentle field paths on to Bridlington; Headland Walk – 20 miles on chalk cliffs to Filey.

Attributes
Anytime Challenge; Heritage
Start
Humber Bridge Car Park, Hessle (Point), E Yorks TA026253
Finish
Filey Brigg, N Yorks TA130815
Waymark
Bridge/minster orange stickers for Beverley 20 only
Websites
http://beehive.thisishull.co.uk
Maps ◈
OS Landranger: 101, 106, 107
OS Explorer: 293, 295, 301
Publications, badges and certificates
Looseleaf
East Riding Heritage Way by Glen Hood (Glen Hood) 1993. 9pp; A4. Free (+ 2nd class Large Letter 250g postage).
Badge & certificate
East Riding Heritage Way (Glen Hood). £1.15 (+ SAE) & £0.15 (+ A5 SAE).
Badge (for each route)
East Riding Heritage Way (Glen Hood). £0.75 each (+ SAE).

East Thriding Treble Ten ETTTEN

E YORKS **48km/30 miles**

A figure-of-eight route over the southern chalk wolds of East Yorkshire, visiting Brantingham, South Cave and North Cave.

Attributes
Challenging; Anytime Challenge; Downland/Wolds
Start and Finish
Welton, E Yorks SE959272
Maps
OS Landranger: 106
OS Explorer: 293
Publications, badges and certificates
Looseleaf
East Thriding Treble Ten (Kim Peacock). Free (+ 9 x 4 SAE).
Badge
East Thriding Treble Ten (Kim Peacock). £1.00 (+ 9 x 6 SAE).

Ebor Way EBRW

N YORKS, W YORKS, YORK **119km/74 miles**

From Helmsley the route heads to Hovingham and then to Strensall, from where the River Foss is followed to York. After crossing the city it follows the banks of the Ouse to Tadcaster, where it turns west along the Wharfe valley to Wetherby and Harewood. It climbs the gritstone escarpment bounding Ilkley Moor to finish at Ilkley.

Attributes
Easy; River; Moorland
Start
Helmsley, N Yorks SE613838
Finish
Ilkley, W Yorks SE117476
Waymark
Cross, castle and ram on green disc
Maps ◈
OS Landranger: 100, 104, 105
OS Explorer: 26, 289, 290, 297, 300

Publications, badges and certificates
Folder
Ebor Way by J. K. E. Piggin (J K E Piggin) 2000. ISBN 9781872881003. 22pp; 204 x 117. £4.00 (incs p&p).

Eskdale Way ESKW

CLEVELAND, N YORKS 134km/83 miles

A meandering circuit of Eskdale taking in Glaisdale, Commondale, the Guisborough Moors, Kildale, Wheeldale, Goathland and Whitby.

Attributes
Moorland
Start and Finish
Whitby, N Yorks NZ900117
Maps
OS Landranger: 94
OS Explorer: 26, 27
Publications, badges and certificates
Folder
Eskdale Way (J K E Piggin) 1998. ISBN 9781898978039. 13 cards; 210 x 147. £3.45 (incs p&p).
Walking Support Providers
HF

Foss Walk FOS

N YORKS 45km/28 miles

The Walk follows footpaths along or near the River Foss, from its confluence with the Ouse in the historic city of York to its source at Pond Head, four miles from Easingwold and the finish.

Attributes
Easy; River
Start
York, N Yorks SE605511
Finish
Easingwold, N Yorks SE528695
Waymark
Named signposts and named arrows with frog logo
Maps ◈
OS Landranger: 100, 105
OS Explorer: 290, 299, 300
Publications, badges and certificates
Booklets
Foss Walk by Mark W. Jones (Dales Court Press) 1994. 16pp; 210 x 135. £2.45 (incs p&p).

Great North Forest Heritage Trail GNF

TYNE AND WEAR 105km/65 miles

The Trail is part of an initiative to improve the countryside in this former mining area and passes Pelton, Bournmoor, Hetton-le-Hole, the Penshaw Monument and Witherwack.

Attributes
Former Railway; Cycle Route; Industrial History
Start and Finish
Causey Arch, Tyne & Wear NZ204564
Waymark
Name & leaf
Maps ◈
OS Landranger: 88
OS Explorer: 307, 308, 316
Publications, badges and certificates
Booklets
Great Walks in the Great North Forest (Great North Forest). £4.99.

Gritstone Edge Walk GREW

DERBYS, S YORKS 43km/27 miles

A linear walk along the eastern edge of the Peak District, taking in Derwent, Stanage, Burbage, Froggatt, Baslow and Chatsworth Edges.

Attributes
Anytime Challenge; Moorland
Start
Flouch Inn, S Yorks SE197016
Finish
Baslow, Derbys SK256725
Maps
OS Landranger: 110, 119
OS Explorer: 1, 24
Publications, badges and certificates
Booklets
Peak District End to End Walks by John Merrill (John Merrill Foundation) 2006. ISBN 9780907496397. 52pp; A5. £5.95 (+ £1.00 p&p). Cheques to John Merrill Foundation.
Badge & certificate
Gritstone Edge Walk (John Merrill Foundation). £5.00 (incs p&p).

Hambleton Hillside Mosaic Walk HHMW

N YORKS 58km/36 miles

A walk along the western edge of the North York Moors, taking in cliff tops, woodlands and villages, and passing 23 mosaics along the way.

Attributes
Moorland
Start and Finish
Sutton Bank, N Yorks SE516831
Maps
OS Landranger: 100
OS Explorer: 26
Publications, badges and certificates
Paperbacks
Hambleton Hillside Mosaic Walk (North York Moors National Park) 1998. ISBN 9780907480693. 28pp; A5. £3.95 (+ £1.25 p&p).

Hambleton Hobble HAMH

N YORKS 52km/32 miles

A tough route with 2,500ft of ascent to the west of the North York Moors National Park, passing through Osmotherley, Arden, Scawton, Hawnby, Boltby and Silton.

Attributes
Challenging; Anytime Challenge; Moorland
Start and Finish
Hambleton Corner, Osmotherley, N Yorks SE461985
Websites
www.lykewakewalk.co.uk
Maps
OS Landranger: 100
OS Explorer: 26
Publications, badges and certificates
Leaflets
Hambleton Hobble (Lyke Wake Club). £0.25 (+ 9 x 4 SAE). Cheques to Lyke Wake Company Limited.
Badge
Hambleton Hobble (Lyke Wake Club). £2.00 (+ SAE). Cheques to Lyke Wake Company Limited.

Harden Hike HARH

W YORKS 35km/22 miles

The walk makes a complete circuit of Rombald's Moor, where you can get extensive views of Airedale and Wharfedale.

Attributes
Challenging; Anytime Challenge; Moorland
Start and Finish
Golden Fleece Inn, Harden, W Yorks SE085384
Maps
OS Landranger: 104
OS Explorer: 288, 297
Publications, badges and certificates
Looseleaf
Harden Hike (Peter Bashforth). Free (+ 9 x 4 SAE). Free to download from LDWA website.
Badge & certificate
Harden Hike (Peter Bashforth). £1.25 (+ SAE) & £0.25 (+ 9 x 6 SAE).

Harrogate & Knaresborough Heritage Trail HKHW

N YORKS 35km/22 miles

The route passes a wealth of historical buildings and sites in, and near to, one of the leading Spa and conference towns in the country.

Attributes
Anytime Challenge; Heritage
Start and Finish
Pannal Railway Station, near Harrogate, North Yorks SE306515
Maps
OS Landranger: 104
OS Explorer: 289
Publications, badges and certificates
Looseleaf
Harrogate & Knaresborough Heritage Trail by Michael Best, Victor Lokie (Michael Best). 4pp; A4. Free (+ A5 SAE). Free to download from LDWA website.
Badge & certificate
Harrogate & Knaresborough Heritage Trail by Michael Best, Victor Lokie (Michael Best). A5 certificate. £2.00 (+ A5 SAE).

Harrogate Ringway HGR

N YORKS **32km/20 miles**

A trail encircling the spa town at a radius of 3-4 miles, mostly on attractive country paths.

Attributes
Easy; River; Urban
Start and Finish
Pannal, N Yorks SE306516
Waymark
Named signposts
Maps ◈
OS Landranger: 104
OS Explorer: 289, 297, 298
Publications, badges and certificates
Folder
Harrogate Ringway (Harrogate Borough Council) 1997. 6pp; A4/3. £2.25.
Leaflets
Harrogate Ringway (RA Harrogate Group) 2002. 4pp; A5. £0.30 (+ 9 x 4 SAE).
Badge
Harrogate Ringway (RA Harrogate Group). £1.50 (+ SAE).

Heron Way HERW

S YORKS **48km/30 miles**

The Heron Way is a series of eight walks through pleasant countryside linking nature reserves, country parks, tourist sites, lovely villages and some of the best viewpoints around Doncaster. Both the start and finish are accessible via Doncaster's transport system.

Attributes
Easy
Start
Parrots Corner Park and Ride, Doncaster, S Yorks SK629994
Finish
Northern Park and Ride, Doncaster, S Yorks SE546064
Maps
OS Landranger: 111
OS Explorer: 278, 279
Publications, badges and certificates
Booklets
Heron Way by RA Doncaster (Doncaster Tourist Information Centre). A5. £2.00 (+A5 SAE). Cheques to Doncaster MBC.

Herriot Way HERRW

N YORKS **88km/55 miles**

A route taking in many of the locations referred to in the James Herriot books and based on Aysgarth and the Youth Hostels at Grinton, Keld and Hawes.

Attributes
Moorland; Literary
Start and Finish
Aysgarth Falls, Aysgarth, N Yorks SE012885
Maps
OS Landranger: 92, 98
OS Explorer: 30
Publications, badges and certificates
Booklets
Herriot Way: Map (Norman F. Scholes) 1999. ISBN 9780953035700. 208 x 140. £3.50 (incs p&p).
Walking Support Providers
Brigantes; Coast to Coast Holidays; Contours; Discovery; Footpath; HF; Sherpa Van

High Hunsley Circuit HHC

E YORKS **39km/24 miles**

A route which takes in wooded valleys of the south Wolds and visits the villages of Bishop Burton, Walkington, Skidby, Welton, Brantingham, South Cave and Newbald.

Attributes
Challenging; Anytime Challenge; Downland/Wolds
Start and Finish
Walkington, E Yorks SE999368
Waymark
Named signs/discs with HHC
Maps ◈
OS Landranger: 106, 107
OS Explorer: 293, 294
Publications, badges and certificates
Leaflets
High Hunsley Circular (RA Beverley Group). A4. Free (+ 9 x 4 SAE).
Badge
High Hunsley Circuit (RA Beverley Group). £1.50 (+ 6 x 4 SAE).

Holme Valley Circular Walk HVCW

W YORKS **39km/24 miles**

A walk along the heights around the Holme Valley, taking in Castle Hill, the villages of Farnley Tyas, Thurstonland, Hepworth, Netherthong and Honley. The scenery is varied with many viewpoints.

Attributes
Challenging; Moorland
Start and Finish
Berry Brow, W Yorks SE136137
Maps ◈
OS Landranger: 110
OS Explorer: 288, 1
Publications, badges and certificates
Paperbacks
Holme Valley Circular Walk by E. S. Boocock (Holmfirth Tourist Information Centre). 32pp; 135 x 200. £2.50 (+ 50p p&p).
Looseleaf
Holme Valley Circular Challenge Walk (Norman F. Scholes). Free (+ 9 x 4 SAE).
Badge & certificate
Holme Valley Circular Challenge Walk (Norman F. Scholes). £1.00 (+ 9 x 4 SAE).

Hope Valley Line Challenge HVLC

DERBYS, S YORKS **60km/37 miles**

This walk takes advantage of the Sheffield to Manchester Railway Line through the Hope Valley, the route crossing the Peak District and visiting Grindleford, Hathersage, Edale and Chinley.

Attributes
Easy; Anytime Challenge; Former Railway
Start
Dore Railway Station, S Yorks SK324813
Finish
New Mills, Railway Station, Derbys SJ997854
Maps
OS Landranger: 110
OS Explorer: 1, 24, 278
Publications, badges and certificates
Booklets
Train to Walk Vol 1 The Hope Valley Line by John Merrill (John Merrill Foundation) 2001. ISBN 9781903627075. 64pp; A5. £6.95 (+ £1.00 p&p). Cheques to John Merrill Foundation.
Walking Support Providers
Peaks

Hovingham Hobble HOVH

N YORKS **37km/23 miles**

An undulating route providing superb views of Castle Howard, the distant North York Moors across Ryedale, and visiting the unspoilt villages of Hovingham, Terrington and Bulmer.

Attributes
Challenging; Anytime Challenge; Heritage
Start and Finish
Hovingham, N Yorks SE667756
Maps
OS Landranger: 100
OS Explorer: 300
Publications, badges and certificates
Looseleaf
Hovingham Hobble by Ben Booth (Ben Booth) 2007. 4pp; A5. Free (+ 9 x 4 SAE). Free to download from LDWA website.
Badge & certificate
Hovingham Hobble (Ben Booth). £2.00 (+ 9 x 6 SAE).

Howden 20 H20

E YORKS **32km/20 miles**

The walk heads west along the bank of the River Ouse, then north along the Derwent valley via Asselby and Wressle to Bubwith before returning to Howden.

Attributes
Easy; Anytime Challenge; River
Start and Finish
Howden, E Yorks SE748283
Waymark
Standard arrows with H20
Maps ◈
OS Landranger: 105, 106
OS Explorer: 291
Publications, badges and certificates
Looseleaf
Howden 20 (Goole Rambling Club). Free (+ A4 SAE).
Badge & certificate
Howden 20 (Goole Rambling Club). £0.50 (+ A4 SAE). Cheques to Goole and District Rambling Club.

Wharram Percy is the most famous of the deserted villages in the Yorkshire Wolds

Howdenshire Way HOWH

E YORKS **27km/17 miles**

A route around the market town of Howden, passing from Eastrington to Saltmarshe, then along the River Ouse to Boothferry where it turns to Asselby and Newsholme.

Attributes
Challenging; Anytime Challenge; River
Start and Finish
Eastrington, E Yorks SE786298
Waymark
Standard arrows with white spot
Maps
OS Landranger: 105
OS Explorer: 291
Publications, badges and certificates
Looseleaf
Howdenshire Way (Don Sweeting). 5pp; A4. Free (+ A5 SAE).
Certificate
Badge & Certificate for Howdenshire Way (Don Sweeting). Free (+ SAE).

Humber Bridge Link Walk HUMBLW

E YORKS, LINCS **55km/34 miles**

This is a twin circuits walk based on Hessle and the Humber Bridge. The northern circuit route remains to the north of the Humber and links with the Wolds Way; the southern circuit crosses to the Lincolnshire Wolds, south of the river, where it links with the Viking Way.

Attributes
Challenging; Anytime Challenge; River; Downland/Wolds
Start and Finish
Hessle, E Yorks TA035256
Websites
http://beehive.thisishull.co.uk
Maps
OS Landranger: 106, 107, 112
OS Explorer: 281, 293
Publications, badges and certificates
Looseleaf
Humber Bridge Link Walk (LDWA East Yorkshire Group). 2pp; A4. Free (+ 9 x 4 SAE).
Badge & certificate
Humber Bridge Link Walk (Glen Hood). £2.00 (+ 9 x 6 SAE).

Inn Way... to the North York Moors IWTNYM

N YORKS **144km/89 miles**

A route visiting Hutton-le-Hole, Levisham, Egton Bridge, Rosedale Abbey and Hawnby, passing 31 traditional inns along the way.

Attributes
Challenging; Moorland
Start and Finish
Helmsley, N Yorks SE613838
Websites
www.innway.co.uk
Maps
OS Landranger: 94, 100
OS Explorer: 26, 27
Publications, badges and certificates
Paperbacks
Inn Way...to the North York Moors by Mark Reid (Inn Way Publications) 2006. ISBN 9781902001043. 189pp; A5. £8.95 (+ £1.00 p&p).
Badge & certificate
Inn Way...to the North York Moors (Inn Way Publications). £2.50 & £1.75 (both + 50p p&p).
Walking Support Providers
Brigantes

Inn Way... to the Yorkshire Dales IWTYD

N YORKS **122km/76 miles**

A walk taking in many Yorkshire Dales attractions, catering for overnight stops at Buckden, Askrigg, Reeth, West Burton, Kettlewell and Grassington. 26 traditional inns are passed along the way.

Attributes
River; Moorland
Start and Finish
Grassington, N Yorks SE003641
Websites
www.innway.co.uk
Maps
OS Landranger: 98
OS Explorer: 2, 30
Publications, badges and certificates
Paperbacks
Inn Way...to the Yorkshire Dales by Mark Reid (Inn Way Publications) 2002. ISBN 9781902001036. 146pp; A5. £8.95 (+ £1.00 p&p).

Badge & certificate
Inn Way...to the Yorkshire Dales (Inn Way Publications). £2.50 & £1.75 (both + 50p p&p).
Walking Support Providers
Brigantes

Jorvic Way JVW

N YORKS **104km/65 miles**

Low-level route around Greater York, the Way passes the sites of the former Healaugh Priory and the Battle of Marston Moor, Moor Monkton – the confluence of the Rivers Nidd and Ouse, and the Moorlands Nature Reserve.

Attributes
River; Heritage
Start and Finish
River Bridge, Tadcaster, N Yorks SE487435
Waymark
Named signs
Maps
OS Landranger: 105
OS Explorer: 290
Publications, badges and certificates
Folder
Walking in the Countryside around York (J K E Piggin). ISBN 9781898978008. 13pp; 210 x 147. £3.45 (incs p&p).
Certificate
Jorvic Way (J K E Piggin). Free (+ 9 x 6 SAE).

Kirklees Way KLW

W YORKS **118km/73 miles**

The Kirklees Way provides a challenging route encircling the district, taking in the best of the landscape, scenery, history and unusual features. It mixes the exposed moorland tops with the industrial towns in the valleys. Including the Upper Colne Valley, it crosses the Spen Valley to Oakwell Hall, Dewsbury, Clayton West and the Holme Valley to Marsden.

Attributes
Challenging; Moorland; Industrial History
Start and Finish
Scholes, W Yorks SE167259
Waymark
Blue discs with name in yellow
Maps ◈
OS Landranger: 104, 110
OS Explorer: 288, 289, 21, 1
Publications, badges and certificates
Booklets
Walk the Kirklees Way by Nigel Patrick, Peter Williamson (Kirklees Metropolitan Council). ISBN 9780903603331. £8.95 (+ p&p).
Paperbacks
Stroller's Guide to Walks along the Kirklees Way by C. Dexter Ellis (Holmfirth Tourist Information Centre) 1991. 40pp; A5. £3.40 (+ 50p p&p).

Knaresborough Round KRD

N YORKS **32km/20 miles**

A route passing through the Nidd Gorge and a succession of villages to the north and east of this historic town. It can be linked with the Harrogate Ringway to form a 36-mile route.

Attributes
Challenging; Anytime Challenge
Start and Finish
Knaresborough, N Yorks SE350565
Waymark
Named metal signposts (white/green)
Maps ◈
OS Landranger: 99, 104, 105
OS Explorer: 289, 297
Publications, badges and certificates
Leaflets
Knaresborough Round (RA Harrogate Group) 2005. 4pp; A5. £0.30 (+ SAE).
Badge
Knaresborough Round (RA Harrogate Group). £1.50 (+ SAE).

Lady Anne's Way LAW

CUMBRIA, N YORKS **161km/100 miles**

This walk is based on some of the routes taken by Lady Anne Clifford. The route takes in the valleys of Wharfedale and Wensleydale, the traverse of the high-level Lady Anne's Highway at Abbotside Fells, Mallerstang, Eden Valley, and the castles of Pendragon, Brough and Brougham Castle.

Attributes
Challenging; Moorland; Heritage
Start
Skipton, N Yorks SD990519
Finish
Penrith, Cumbria NY515305
Websites
www.ladyannesway.co.uk

Maps
OS Landranger: 90, 91, 98, 103, 104
OS Explorer: 2, 5, 19, 30
Publications, badges and certificates
Paperbacks
Lady Anne's Way by Sheila Gordon (Hillside Publications) 1995. ISBN 9781870141352. 96pp; 115 x 175. £6.99 (+ 70p p&p). Signed copies from author at £7.00 (inc p&p) – see route website.
Badge
Lady Anne's Way (Sheila Gordon). £2.25 (post free).
Walking Support Providers
Brigantes; Contours; Discovery; Sherpa Van

Lake Pickering Circuit LPKC

N YORKS **249km/155 miles**

The Circuit follows the higher ground around the edges of the Vale of Pickering where it is believed a great lake occupied the Vale at the end of the Ice Age. The route is made up of 36 separate, but inter-connecting, circular day walks and includes the Howardian and Tabular Hills, the North Sea coastal cliffs and the Yorkshire Wolds. The Vale of Pickering has a rich history of Christian witness and pilgrimage.

Attributes
Coastal; Downland/Wolds; Moorland; Pilgrimage
Start and Finish
Kirkham Priory, N Yorks SE735658
Maps
OS Landranger: 100, 101
OS Explorer: 26, 27, 300, 301
Publications, badges and certificates
Paperbacks
Exploring Lake Pickering by John Eckersley (John Eckersley) 2003. ISBN 9780953586226. 112pp; 248 x 170. £9.00 (+ £1.00 p&p). All proceeds to Christian Aid.

Langbaurgh Loop LNLP

CLEVELAND **61km/38 miles**

The route takes in coastland paths, high cliff edges, agricultural land, heather moors, pine forests and ancient woods. Good knowledge of map reading is required.

Attributes
Challenging; Anytime Challenge; Coastal; Moorland
Start and Finish
Saltburn-by-the-Sea, Cleveland NZ668216

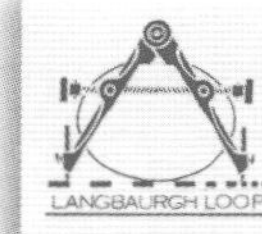

Waymark
Ellipse/callipers and name, in green
Maps
OS Landranger: 93, 94
OS Explorer: 26, 27
Publications, badges and certificates
Leaflets
Langbaurgh Loop (Langbaurgh Loop Recorder). A4/3. Free (+ 9 x 4 SAE).
Badge & certificate
Langbaurgh Loop (Langbaurgh Loop Recorder). £2.50 (+ SAE).

Lead Mining Trail LDMT

DURHAM **38km/24 miles**

A convoluted walk through the Durham moors and valleys, visiting lead mining sites, using the tracks of the old packhorse trails.

Attributes
Moorland; Industrial History
Start
Cowshill, Durham NY856407
Finish
Edmundbyers, Durham NZ018501
Waymark
Named discs
Maps
OS Landranger: 87
OS Explorer: 307
Publications, badges and certificates
Folder
Lead Mining Trail (Durham County Council) 1996. 3 leaflets; 125 x 210. £2.25 (+ 50p p&p).

Leeds Country Way LCW

W YORKS **100km/62 miles**

Encircling the city of Leeds it passes through some attractive countryside and villages especially on its north and eastern sides. The leaflets provide many options to walk the route, with four main 15-mile segments each broken into 5-mile parts. There are public transport connections using the many services around Leeds. From its start at Golden Acre Park the clockwise route visits the Harewood estate and Barwick-in-Elmet, goes via Garforth to the Aire riverside, then threads its way where possible through green corridors between Leeds and Wakefield, Dewsbury and Bradford, to return passing the airport.

Attributes
Easy; River; Canal
Start and Finish
Golden Acre Park, Leeds, W Yorks SE267417
Waymark
Yellow owl and letters LCW on olive green plaque
Websites
www.leeds.gov.uk
Maps ◈
OS Landranger: 104, 105
OS Explorer:
288, 289, 297
Publications, badges and certificates
Leaflets
Leeds Country Way (Leeds City Council) 2006. 4 leaflets, laminated, tearproof, in plastic folder; A3/4 (A5 folded). Free (+ 250g A4 large letter SAE). Also from local libraries/information centres.

Loaves & Fishes Walk LOAFW

N YORKS **37km/23 miles**

A route over limestone country in and around the Ribble Valley visiting Stainforth, Stainforth Foss (salmon may be seen here), Jubilee Cave and Langscar Gate. The walk takes its name from two hills: the Sugar Loaf and Rye Loaf.

Attributes
Challenging; Anytime Challenge; Moorland
Start and Finish
Settle, N Yorks SD820635
Maps
OS Landranger: 98
OS Explorer: 2
Publications, badges and certificates
Looseleaf
Loaves & Fishes Walk (Ian Parker). 1pp. Free (+ 9 x 4 SAE).
Badge & certificate
Loaves & Fishes Walk (Ian Parker). £2.00 (+ 9 x 6 SAE).

Lyke Wake Walk LYKEWW

N YORKS **64km/40 miles**

A classic traverse of the North York Moors, involving 5000ft of ascent, to be completed in 24 hours. It is coincident in parts with the Cleveland Way National Trail and the Coast to Coast route. The name derives from a lyke, the corpse; and the wake, watching over the corpse. In an effort to ease the use of the route the

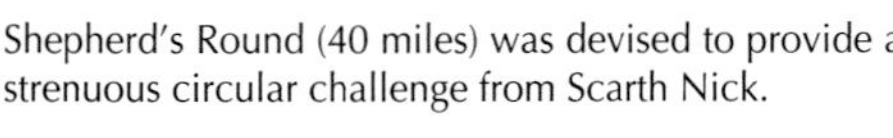

Shepherd's Round (40 miles) was devised to provide a strenuous circular challenge from Scarth Nick.

Attributes
Very Challenging; Anytime Challenge; Moorland
Start
Scarth Wood Moor, Osmotherley, N Yorks SE467992
Finish
Ravenscar, N Yorks NZ970013

Websites
www.lykewake.org, www.lykewakewalk.co.uk
Maps
OS Landranger: 93, 94, 100
OS Explorer: 26, 27
Publications, badges and certificates
Paperbacks
Lyke Wake Walk Guide by Brian Smailes (Illustrator) (Challenge Publications) 2007. ISBN 9781903568477. 56pp; 176 x 122. £4.50 (incs p&p). Cheques to Brian Smailes.
Three Peaks, Ten Tors by Ronald Turnbull (Cicerone Press) 2007. ISBN 9781852845018. 256pp; 170 x 120. £12.95.
Badge
Lyke Wake Walk (New Lyke Wake Walk Club) by Gerry Orchard (New Lyke Wake Club). £2.30 (incs p&p). Other souvenir merchandise available through website.
Lyke Wake Club (Lyke Wake Club). £2.00 (+ SAE).
Shepherd's Round (Lyke Wake Club). £2.00 (+ SAE).
Leaflets
Shepherd's Round (Lyke Wake Club). A4/3. £0.25 (+ 9 x 4 SAE). Cheques to Lyke Wake Company Limited.

Maltby Circular Walk MALTCW

S YORKS **24km/15 miles**

This walk through ancient woodlands and limestone gorges visits Hooton Levitt, Laughten-en-le-Morthern, Letwell, Firbeck, and other places with historical heritage interest.

Attributes
Heritage
Start and Finish
Roche Abbey, S Yorks SK545898
Maps
OS Landranger: 111
OS Explorer: 279
Publications, badges and certificates
Leaflets
Maltby Area Circular Walk (Rotherham Visitor Centre). A4/3. Free.

Manorlands Meander MM

W YORKS **29km/18 miles**

A contrasting route over Penistone Hill, through Oxenhope and passing the Hewenden reservoir and railway viaduct, and the waterfalls of Goitstock. Part of the South Pennines Twin Challenge, proceeds from sales are donated to the Manorlands Hospice.

Attributes
Challenging; Anytime Challenge; Lake/Reservoir; Moorland
Start and Finish
Haworth Tourist Information Centre, W Yorks SE030372
Maps
OS Landranger: 104
OS Explorer: 21
Publications, badges and certificates
Booklets
Manorlands Meander (Tony Wimbush). £2.00 (incs p&p). Cheques to W. A. Wimbush.
Badge & certificate
Manorlands Meander (Tony Wimbush). £1.50 (+ SAE). Cheques to W. A .Wimbush.

Millennium Way – Bradford MWBD

W YORKS **72km/45 miles**

A route within the Bradford Metropolitan boundary which visits many sites of interest including Bronte Falls, Whitewells and Shipley Glen. It also takes in Denholme, Oxenhope and Silsden as it passes through woodland, farmland and moorland. 16 shorter circular walks link with the Millennium Way enabling the route to be walked in shorter sections.

Attributes
Moorland
Start and Finish
Bracken Hall Countryside Centre, Shipley, W Yorks SE132390
Waymark
Named finger posts; named discs; yellow/blue arrows and 'MW'
Websites
www.homestead.com
Maps ◈
OS Landranger: 104, 103
OS Explorer: 288, 297, 21, 2
Publications, badges and certificates
Booklets
Bradford's Millennium Way (Bradford Millennium Way Project). 24pp; A5. £1.99 (+ 9 x 6 SAE) or £3.75 inc 16 shorter walks. Also from local TICs at Bradford, Haworth & Ilkley.

Millennium Way – York MWYK

N YORKS, YORK **37km/23 miles**

Linking the historic open strays of York and some of the best countryside around the city, the route crosses Hob Moor, and visits Knavesmire, Fulford Ings, Walmgate Stray, Monk Stray, Bootham Stray and Clifton Ings, providing an opportunity to view the lesser known historic sites of interest in the City.

Attributes
Easy; River; Heritage
Start and Finish
Lendal Bridge, York, N Yorks SE599519
Waymark
Named fingerposts/waymarks
Websites
www.york.gov.uk
Maps
OS Landranger: 105
OS Explorer: 290
Publications, badges and certificates
Folder
Millennium Way (York City Council). 5 leaflets; A5. £2.95 (+ 9 x 6 SAE).
Badge
Millennium Way – York (York City Council). £1.50 (+ 9 x 4 SAE).

Minster Way MINW

E YORKS, N YORKS **80km/50 miles**

Linking the two famous medieval Minsters at Beverley and York, the route crosses farmland and the hills of the Yorkshire Wolds. It follows the Yorkshire Wolds Way across Sylvan Dale before diverting to Millington, Bishop Wilton and Stamford Bridge. Here the River Derwent is followed before the Plain of York is crossed, using field and woodland paths, to meet and follow the River Ouse to York.

Attributes
Easy; River; Downland/Wolds; Heritage
Start
Beverley, E Yorks TA038393

Finish
York, N Yorks SE603522
Waymark
White stickers on standard waymarks plus named signposts
Websites
http://beehive.thisishull.co.uk
Maps ◈
OS Landranger: 105, 106, 107
OS Explorer: 290, 293, 294, 295
Publications, badges and certificates
Booklets
Minster Way (Ray Wallis) 2006. 46pp; A5. £4.00 (+ 2nd class Large Letter 250g postage). Cheques to R Wallis. Accommodation list available.
Badge
Minster Way (Ray Wallis). £1.70 (+ SAE). Cheques to R Wallis.

Myrtle Meander MYRM

W YORKS **40km/25 miles**

This walk, south of Bingley, combines rarely used paths with more popular routes. It visits Egypt, World's End, Queensbury and Haworth.

Attributes
Challenging; Anytime Challenge; Moorland
Start and Finish
Myrtle Park School, Bingley, W Yorks SE108387
Maps
OS Landranger: 104
OS Explorer: 288, 21
Publications, badges and certificates
Looseleaf
Myrtle Meander by Peter Bashforth (Peter Bashforth) 2007. 4pp; A4. Free (+ 9 x 4 SAE). Free to download from LDWA website.
Badge & certificate
Myrtle Meander (Peter Bashforth). £1.75 (+ SAE) & £0.25 (+ 9 x 6 SAE).

Newlands Way NEWLW

CLEVELAND, N YORKS, S YORKS, W YORKS
338km/210 miles

A route that takes in Leeds, Ilkley, Thirsk, Osmotherley, Robin Hood's Bay, Whitby and Middlesbrough, visiting six abbeys along the way. It is partly coincident with the Cleveland Way National Trail. Profits from sales are donated to a Religious Order for work in developing countries.

Attributes
Anytime Challenge; Moorland; Heritage; Religious
Start
Kirkstall Abbey, Leeds SE258362
Finish
Middlesbrough, Cleveland NZ499168
Maps
OS Landranger: 93, 99, 100, 104
OS Explorer: 288, 289, 306, 26, 27, 30
Publications, badges and certificates
Booklets
Newlands Way by C. M. J. Wright (Newlands School FCJ). ISBN 9780953603015. 128pp; 150 x 105. £5.00 (+ 80p p&p). Also available from C. M. J. Wright, St. Wilfrids RC College, Harton Lane, South Shields NE34 0PH.

Newtondale Trail NEWTT

N YORKS **32km/20 miles**

This walk links together the terminal stations of the North York Moors Railway, following Newton Dale northwards from Pickering across the moors to Grosmont. Some sections remain close to the Railway and others follow forest tracks and cross the open moors high above the valley. The waymarked circular Newtondale Horse Trail (35 miles) goes from Pickering on bridleways, providing alternatives to and from Grosmont.

Attributes
Moorland
Start
Pickering, N Yorks SE797842
Finish
Grosmont, N Yorks NZ828053
Websites
www.nymr.co.uk
Maps
OS Landranger: 94, 100
OS Explorer: 27
Publications, badges and certificates
Looseleaf
Newtondale Trail: Pickering to Grosmont by Peter Greenwood (Peter Greenwood). 2pp; A4. Free (+ SAE). Free to download from LDWA website.
Newtondale Trail: Grosmont to Pickering by Peter Greenwood (Peter Greenwood). 2pp; A4. Free (+ SAE).
Leaflets
Newtondale Trail: Pickering to Grosmont/'Train Time Table' (Peter Greenwood). A4/3. Free (+ 9 x 4 SAE).

Newtondale Trail: Grosmont to Pickering/'Train Time Table' (Peter Greenwood). A4/3. Free (+ 9 x 4 SAE).
Badge & certificate
Newtondale Trail (Peter Greenwood). £2.50 (+ 9 x 6 SAE).
Booklets
Newtondale Horse Trail (North York Moors National Park). ISBN 9780907480525. 32pp; 120 x 170. £3.95 (+ 95p p&p).

Nidd Vale Circuit NIDDVC

N YORKS **42km/26 miles**

Based mainly on Nidderdale the route takes in the River Cover and Caldbergh, and passes close to Roundhill Reservoir. Proceeds from the sale of badges and certificates are donated to a local hospice.

Attributes
Challenging; Anytime Challenge; Moorland
Start and Finish
Lofthouse, N Yorks SE101737
Maps
OS Landranger: 99
OS Explorer: 298
Publications, badges and certificates
Looseleaf
Nidd Vale Circuit (Simon Townson) 2007. 1pp; A4. Free (+ 9 x 4 SAE). Free to download from LDWA website.
Badge & certificate
Nidd Vale Circuit (Simon Townson). £2.00 (+ 13 x 9 SAE).

Nidd Valley Link NIDDVL

N YORKS **45km/28 miles**

A route connecting the Nidderdale Way at Hampsthwaite with the confluence of the rivers Nidd and Ouse near Nun Monkton, where a link to York is possible via the banks of the River Ouse (8 miles).

Attributes
Anytime Challenge; River
Start
Hampsthwaite, N Yorks SE258587
Finish
Nidd-Ouse Confluence, N Yorks SE513578
Maps
OS Landranger: 104, 105
OS Explorer: 289, 290, 297
Publications, badges and certificates
Looseleaf
Nidd Valley Link (John Eckersley) 1997. 3pp; A4. £1.00 (incs p&p).

Nidderdale Way NIDW

N YORKS **85km/53 miles**

The Way follows the northern side of the dale passing the gritstone outcrops of Brimham Rocks high above the dale, and the old lead mill at Smelthouses, before following paths close to the Nidd from Pateley Bridge to Lofthouse. Here the Way loops round the head of the valley to Scar House Reservoir. The route returns along the south side of the dale, looping away from the Nidd to visit Merryfield Mines and Heyshaw Moor.

Attributes
River
Start and Finish
Hampsthwaite, N Yorks SE259587
Waymark
Named signposts
Maps ◈
OS Landranger: 99, 104
OS Explorer: 298, 297, 30
Publications, badges and certificates
Paperbacks
Nidderdale Way by Paul Hannon (Hillside Publications) 1998. ISBN 9781870141642. 48pp; 175 x 115. £3.99 (+ 60p p&p).
Folder
Nidderdale Way by J. K. E. Piggin (J K E Piggin). ISBN 9781898978022. 14 cards; 204 x 117. £3.45 (incs p&p).
Badge & certificate
Nidderdale Way by Mike Warner (Mike Warner). £2.50 (+ A5 SAE).
Walking Support Providers
Contours

North Wolds Walk NWW

E YORKS **32km/20 miles**

An undulating route in the Yorkshire Wolds passing through the villages of Millington, Great Givendale, Bishop Wilton, Kirby Underdale and Thixendale.

Attributes
Challenging; Anytime Challenge; Downland/Wolds

Start and Finish
Millington Road End, near Fridaythorpe, E Yorks SE836567
Maps
OS Landranger: 100, 106
OS Explorer: 294, 300

Publications, badges and certificates
Looseleaf
North Wolds Walk (Ron Watson). A4. Free (+ 9 x 4 SAE). Free to download from LDWA website.
Badge
North Wolds Walk (Ron Watson). £1.50 (+ SAE).

North York Moors Wobble NYMW

N YORKS **51km/32 miles**

A route taking in Farndale, Rosedale Abbey, Rosedale Moor, Cropton, Appleton-le-Moors and Hutton-le-Hole, aimed at raising funds for a locally based search and rescue team.

Attributes
Challenging; Anytime Challenge; Moorland; Charity
Start and Finish
Gillamoor, N Yorks SE684901
Maps
OS Landranger: 100
OS Explorer: 26, 27
Publications, badges and certificates
Booklets
North York Moors Wobble (George Davies). 12pp. £5.00 (+ A4 SAE).
Certificate
North York Moors Wobble (George Davies). Free (+ A5 SAE).

North Yorkshire Moors Challenge Walk NYMCW

N YORKS **40km/25 miles**

A strenuous walk in the North York Moors National Park which includes high moorland.

Attributes
Challenging; Anytime Challenge; Moorland
Start and Finish
Goathland, N Yorks NZ838014
Maps
OS Landranger: 94
OS Explorer: 27
Publications, badges and certificates
Booklets
North Yorkshire Moors Challenge Walk by John Merrill (John Merrill Foundation). ISBN 9780907496366. 32pp; A5. £4.95 (+ £1.00 p&p). Cheques to John Merrill Foundation.
Badge & certificate
North York Moors Challenge Walk (John Merrill Foundation). £5.00 (incs p&p).

Otley Nine Leagues ONLJ

W YORKS **43km/27 miles**

A circular walk in the Wharfedale and Washburn valleys. The route passes through Pool-in-Wharfedale, Leathley, Timble, Denton, Middleton, Ilkley and Menston. There is over 3,500ft of ascent and good navigation skills are required in bad weather.

Attributes
Challenging; Anytime Challenge; Moorland

Start and Finish
Surprise View, Otley, W Yorks SE204441
Maps
OS Landranger: 104
OS Explorer: 279
Publications, badges and certificates
Looseleaf
Otley Nine Leagues by Derek Haller (Derek Haller) 2007. 3pp; A5. Free (+ A5 SAE). Free to download from LDWA website.
Badge & certificate
Otley Nine Leagues (Derek Haller). £2.00 (+ A5 SAE).

Peatlands Way PEATW

LINCS, S YORKS **80km/50 miles**

The route developed by the Humberhead Levels Green Tourism Forum links the historic settlements of Thorne, Crowle, Belton, Epworth, Haxey, Wroot, Kirk Bramwith and Sykehouse. It also crosses the Thorne and Hatfield Moors, part of the largest complex of lowland raised bogs in Britain, where a map and compass is essential.

Attributes
Easy; Canal; Heath; Geological
Start and Finish
Delves Fishponds, Thorne, South Yorkshire SE682132
Waymark
Nightjar on yellow background
Websites
www.thorne-moorends.gov.uk
Maps
OS Landranger: 111, 112
OS Explorer: 279, 280, 291
Publications, badges and certificates
Leaflets
Peatlands Way (Thorne Moorends Town Council). A4/3. Free. Downloadable route description.

Penistone Boundary Walk PNBW

S YORKS **25km/16 miles**

A route around the boundary of the town. The route is crossed by the Trans Pennine Trail and also by the main Barnsley – Huddersfield railway line which caters for easy access.

Attributes
Moorland
Start and Finish
Cubley Hall, Penistone, S Yorks SE246016
Waymark
Head profile of Penistone Sheep
Maps ◈
OS Landranger: 110
OS Explorer: 1, 278, 288
Publications, badges and certificates
Leaflets
Penistone Boundary Walk (Penistone Town Council). A3/4. Free (+ 9 x 4 SAE).

Penistone Line Trail PLT

S YORKS, W YORKS **97km/60 miles**

The varied landscape route is a station to station walk between Sheffield and Huddersfield. Between Sheffield and Barnsley the trail follows the rivers Don and Dearne, entering the upper Don Valley at Oxspring. It crosses into the Holme Valley, which joins the Colne Valley at Huddersfield.

Attributes
River; Urban
Start
Sheffield Railway Station, South Yorks SK358869
Finish
Huddersfield Railway Station, West Yorks SE143169
Maps
OS Landranger: 110, 111
OS Explorer: 1, 278, 288
Publications, badges and certificates
Booklets
Penistone Line Trail by Penistone Line Partnership (Penistone Line Partnership) 2003. ISBN 9780954479602. 44pp; 202 x 144. £4.95 (+ 55p p&p). Cheques to Penistone Line Partnership.

Penistone Loop-D-Loop PLDL

S YORKS **77km/48 miles**

Comprising four walks of between 9 and 15 miles taking the form of a 'D', each of which links with the next and visiting Flouch, Penistone and Wortley.

Attributes
Challenging; Anytime Challenge; Moorland
Start and Finish
Dunford Bridge, S Yorks SE157025
Maps
OS Landranger: 110
OS Explorer: 1
Publications, badges and certificates
Looseleaf
Penistone Loop-D-Loop (Allen Pestell). 1pp; A4. £0.50 (+ 9 x 6 SAE).

Rezzy Rush REZZR

N YORKS **64km/40 miles**

A route visiting four reservoirs in the Washburn Valley, four in Oak Beck Valley, and two in the Harrogate area. It is coincident in parts with the Harrogate – Dales Way link and the Harrogate Ringway. Proceeds from sales are donated to charitable causes.

Attributes
Very Challenging; Anytime Challenge; Lake/Reservoir; Moorland
Start and Finish
Valley Gardens, Harrogate, N Yorks SE298554
Maps
OS Landranger: 104
OS Explorer: 297
Publications, badges and certificates
Looseleaf
Rezzy Rush (John Eckersley). 6pp. £2.00 (incs p&p).

Ribskip Challenge RIBC

N YORKS **53km/33 miles**

Utilising the Settle – Carlisle Railway, and some lesser used paths, the route visits Pen-y-ghent, Attermire Scar, Otterburn and Gargrave.

Attributes
Very Challenging; Anytime Challenge; Moorland
Start
Ribblehead Railway Station, N Yorks SD766790

Finish
Skipton Railway Station, N Yorks SD989515
Maps
OS Landranger: 98, 104
OS Explorer: 2
Publications, badges and certificates
Looseleaf
Ribskip Challenge (Edwin and Julia Tum). 5pp; A4. Free (+ 9 x 4 SAE).
Badge & certificate
Ribskip Challenge (Edwin and Julia Tum). £3.00 (+ 9 x 4 SAE).

Ripon Rowel — RIPR

N YORKS — **80km/50 miles**

A route around the ancient city of Ripon, visiting villages, historic sites, wooded valleys, rivers, lakes and streams. The route includes Markenfield Hall, the romantic and magnificent Fountains Abbey, Studley Water Gardens and Park and the beautiful St Mary's Church. There are visits to the tranquil River Skell's Valley of the Seven Bridges and to Eavestone Lakes, Dallowgill, Ilton-Cum-Pot and the quaint Druids Temple.

Attributes
River; Moorland; World Heritage Site; Heritage
Start and Finish
Ripon, N Yorks SE313713
Waymark
Rowel logo – circular part of a spur
Maps ◈
OS Landranger: 99
OS Explorer: 298, 299, 302
Publications, badges and certificates
Booklets
Ripon Rowel Walk by Les Taylor (RA Ripon Group) 1996. 70pp; 210 x 145. £4.95 (+ 70p p&p). Cheques to The Ripon Rowel.
Badge
Ripon Rowel (RA Ripon Group). £1.50 (+ SAE). Cheques to The Ripon Rowel.

Rosedale Circuit — RSC

N YORKS — **61km/38 miles**

A strenuous route, with 4,000ft of ascent, through Rosedale, Farndale, Bransdale, Westerdale, Danby Dale, Great Fryup Dale and Glaisdale.

Attributes
Challenging; Anytime Challenge; Moorland; Industrial History
Start and Finish
Rosedale Abbey, N Yorks SE723959
Waymark
Letters R C in white
Maps
OS Landranger: 94, 100
OS Explorer: 26, 27
Publications, badges and certificates
Looseleaf
Rosedale Circuit (Kim Peacock). 2pp; A4. Free (+ 9 x 4 SAE). Includes list of grid references. Free to download from LDWA website.
Badge & certificate
Rosedale Circuit (Kim Peacock). £1.50 (+ 9 x 6 SAE). Cheques to East Yorkshire LDWA.

Rotherham Ring Route — RTRR

S YORKS — **80km/50 miles**

A circuit around the boundary of the Metropolitan Borough of Rotherham, mostly on rights of way across gently rolling rural landscapes, contrasting with townscapes, reservoirs, rivers and country parks. Rotherham had bell foundries in the 17th-19th centuries.

Attributes
Lake/Reservoir; Urban
Start and Finish
Templeborough Magna Centre, Rotherham, S Yorks SK408914
Waymark
Green bell and white arrow
Websites
www.syned-ramblers.org.uk
Maps
OS Landranger: 111
OS Explorer: 278, 279
Publications, badges and certificates
Leaflets
Rotherham Ring Route by RA Rotherham Metro Group (Rotherham Visitor Centre) 2004. 10 leaflets in plastic wallet. £2.00 (+£1.00 p&p). Cheques to Rotherham TIC. Describes the route anti-clockwise.
Badge
Rotherham Ring Route (Rotherham Visitor Centre). Prices on application. Red Badge for completion within 24 hours (with completion card), Green Badge if longer.

Rotherham Round Walk RTRW

S YORKS **40km/25 miles**

The route, a complete clockwise circuit, leaves the town through a wooded clough and soon enters attractive countryside round the Wentworth Estate in the north. It then goes through a short industrial section and semi urban area to the west, and more undulating rural country to the south, re-entering the town through Boston Park. There is a variety of terrain including one or two short steepish climbs but the walking is relatively easy.

Attributes
Easy; Urban
Start and Finish
Rotherham, S Yorks SK428928
Waymark
Named discs with Chantry Bridge logo
Websites
www.rotherhamrotary.org.uk
Maps ◈
OS Landranger: 110, 111, 120
OS Explorer: 278, 279
Publications, badges and certificates
Leaflets
Rotherham Roundwalk (Rotherham Visitor Centre). A4/3. Free.
Looseleaf
Route map (Rotherham Rotary). £1.00 (+ A5 SAE).
Badge & certificate
Rotherham Round Walk (Rotherham Rotary). £1.90 & £1.00 (+ A5 SAE).

Samaritan Way SAMW

CLEVELAND, N YORKS **64km/40 miles**

A strenuous route across the North York Moors, crossing Commondale, Great Fryup Dale, Glaisdale and Farndale Moors, returning via Westerdale, Baysdale and part of the Cleveland Way National Trail.

Attributes
Challenging; Anytime Challenge; Moorland
Start and Finish
Guisborough, Cleveland NZ615160
Maps
OS Landranger: 93, 94, 100
OS Explorer: 26, 27
Publications, badges and certificates
Looseleaf
Samaritan Way (Richard Pinkney). Free (+ 9 x 4 SAE).
Badge & certificate
Samaritan Way (Richard Pinkney). £2.25 & £0.25 (+ SAE).

Scarborough Rock Challenge SCARC

N YORKS **42km/26 miles**

A route taking in the East Yorkshire coast, Oliver's Mount, the moors, Hackness, Burniston and Scalby.

Attributes
Challenging; Anytime Challenge; Coastal
Start and Finish
Peasholm Park, Scarborough, N Yorks TA035897
Maps
OS Landranger: 101
OS Explorer: 27
Publications, badges and certificates
Looseleaf
Scarborough Rock Challenge Walk (Mike Ellis). A4. Free (+ 9 x 4 SAE).
Badge
Scarborough Rock Challenge (Mike Ellis). £1.00 (+ SAE).

Seahorse Saunter SEAHS

N YORKS **69km/43 miles**

The route, with 5500ft of ascent, crosses the North York Moors to the old Nordic settlement of Whitby. In poor weather conditions navigational skills are appropriate.

Attributes
Challenging; Anytime Challenge; Moorland
Start
Kilburn White Horse, N Yorks SE515812
Finish
Whitby, N Yorks NZ901113
Maps
OS Landranger: 94, 100
OS Explorer: 26, 27
Publications, badges and certificates
Looseleaf
Seahorse Saunter (Simon Townson) 2007. 1pp; A4. Free (+ 9 x 4 SAE). Free to download from LDWA website.
Badge & certificate
Seahorse Saunter (Simon Townson). £2.00 (+ 10 x 8 SAE).

Settle Scramble — SETTS

N YORKS — **40km/25 miles**

A route taking in Fountain's Fell, Helwith Bridge and Feizor.

Attributes
Challenging; Anytime Challenge; Moorland
Start and Finish
Settle, N Yorks SD821632
Maps
OS Landranger: 98
OS Explorer: 2
Publications, badges and certificates
Looseleaf
Settle Scramble (Ian Parker). A4. Free (+ 9 x 4 SAE).
Badge & certificate
Settle Scramble (Ian Parker). £2.00 (+ 9 x 6 SAE).

Silver Lincs Way — SLW

LINCS, NE LINCOLNSHIRE — **40km/25 miles**

Linking Grimsby and Louth this rural walk is in celebration of the Silver Jubilee of the Grimsby/Louth group of The Ramblers' Association.

Attributes
No significant attribute
Start
Scartho Village, Grimsby, NE Lincs TA265064
Finish
St James Church, Louth, Lincs TF327874
Maps
OS Landranger: 113
OS Explorer: 284
Publications, badges and certificates
Leaflets
Silver Lincs Way by Ted Johnson (RA Grimsby & Louth). Free (+ C5 SAE). Also linked Circular Walks leaflet.

Skipton Double Trigger — SDT

N YORKS — **35km/22 miles**

A circular walk, west of Skipton, visiting Sharp Haw. Flasby, Gargrave, East Marton, Thornton-in-Craven, Pinhaw Beacon, Tow Top, Burnt Hill and Carleton-in-Craven.

Attributes
Challenging; Anytime Challenge; Canal; Moorland
Start and Finish
Aireville Park, Skipton, N Yorks SD978519
Publications, badges and certificates
Looseleaf
Skipton Double Trigger by Ian Parker (Ian Parker) 2007. 3pp; A4. Free (+ A5 SAE). Free to download from LDWA website.
Badge & certificate
Skipton Double Trigger by Ian Parker (Ian Parker). A5. £2.00 (+ A5 SAE).

Skipton Saunter — SKIPS

N YORKS — **42km/26 miles**

A circular walk, north west of Skipton, visiting part of the Leeds & Liverpool Canal, Sharp Haw. Flasby, Weets Top, Airton, parts of the Pennine Way, Gargrave and Crag Wood.

Attributes
Challenging; Anytime Challenge; Moorland
Start and Finish
Aireville Park, Skipton, North Yorks SD978519
Maps
OS Landranger: 98, 103
OS Explorer: 2
Publications, badges and certificates
Looseleaf
Skipton Saunter by Ian Parker (Ian Parker) 2007. 1pp; A4. Free (+ A5 SAE). Free to download from LDWA website.
Badge & certificate
Skipton Saunter by Ian Parker (Ian Parker). A5. £2.00 (+ A5 SAE).

Skipton-Settle Link — SKIPSL

N YORKS — **32km/20 miles**

A walk linking two North Craven market towns and visiting the trig points on Sharp Haw and Weets Top.

Attributes a
Challenging; Anytime Challenge; Moorland
Start
Aireville Park, Skipton, N Yorks SD979518
Finish
Settle, N Yorks SD821632
Maps
OS Landranger: 98, 103
OS Explorer: 2

Publications, badges and certificates
Looseleaf
Skipton-Settle Link by Ian Parker (Ian Parker) 2007. 2pp; A4. Free (+ 9 x 4 SAE).
Badge & certificate
Skipton-Settle Link (Ian Parker). £2.00 & £0.50 (+ 9 x 6 SAE).

South Tyneside Heritage Trail STHT

TYNE AND WEAR **42km/26 miles**

From South Shields the route initially heads south along the coast to Whitburn then inland partly following the River Don west to reach the Tyne at Hebburn, returning via Jarrow. The Trail is fairly flat, much of it paved, and passes through most of the Borough's towns and villages. There is some interesting heritage and history explained on 32 panels en route. The 12-mile waymarked Bede's Way commemorates the Venerable Bede, early medieval Europe's greatest scholar, who lived here around 700AD. It follows the Don out of Jarrow to Boldon and finishes along the coast south of Whitburn, thus linking the twin Anglo Saxon monasteries of St Paul's in Jarrow and St Peter's at Wearmouth.

Attributes
Easy; Coastal; River; Urban; Heritage
Start and Finish
'Conversation Piece', South Shields, S Tyneside NZ366681
Waymark
Multi coloured motif on signed posts with name
Websites
www.visitsouthtyneside.co.uk
Maps
OS Landranger: 88
OS Explorer: 308, 316
Publications, badges and certificates
Leaflets
South Tyneside Heritage Trail (South Shields TIC) 2006. A3 (A5 folded). Free.
Bede's Way (South Shields TIC) 2006. A2 (A4/3 folded). Free.

Spen Way Heritage Trail SPWHT

W YORKS **34km/21 miles**

A circuit, and valley path extension, of the former borough of Spenborough and the Spen, a tributary of the River Calder. The Way concentrates on the history of this old textile manufacturing area, visiting Scholes, East Bierley and Gomersal through a varied mixture of urban areas, parkland and farmland.

Attributes
Urban; Heritage
Start and Finish
Royds Park, Cleckheaton, W Yorks SE199246
Waymark
Black letters SWHT combined on white squares
Maps ◈
OS Landranger: 104
OS Explorer: 288
Publications, badges and certificates
Booklets
Spen Way Heritage Trail (Rotary Club of Cleckheaton & District). 16pp; A5. £2.00 (+ 9 x 6 SAE).
Badge
Spen Way Heritage Trail (Rotary Club of Cleckheaton & District). £2.00 (+SAE). £2.00 (+SAE).

Sting in the Tail SIT

W YORKS **58km/36 miles**

A demanding route around the Wharfe and Washburn Valleys visiting Burley Woodhead, Cow and Calf Rocks, Windgate Nick, Bolton Abbey, Blubberhouses, Fewston Reservoir, Dobpark Bridge, Clifton, Otley and Otley Chevin.

Attributes
Challenging; Anytime Challenge
Start and Finish
Menston Village SE176433
Maps
OS Landranger: 104
OS Explorer: 297
Publications, badges and certificates
Looseleaf
Sting in Tail by Louise Mallinson (Louise Mallinson). 5pp; A4. Free (+ SAE). Free to download from LDWA website.

Swale Way SWALEW

CUMBRIA, N YORKS **124km/77 miles**

A route tracing the River Swale upstream from the confluence with the Ure near Boroughbridge to the Swale's origin in the head of Swaledale near Keld, at the meeting of Birkdale and Great Sleddale Becks, within the Yorkshire Dales National Park. Partly because of a lack of rights of way, the Way does not slavishly follow the river, in some places diverging, with the largest detour to visit the market town of Thirsk on Cod Beck, itself a Swale tributary. The fine and historic market town of Richmond upon Swale, with its castle ruins, is also en route.

Attributes
River
Start
Boroughbridge, N Yorks SE395670
Finish
Kirkby Stephen, Cumbria NY774087
or Keld, N Yorks NY892009
Maps
OS Landranger: 91, 92, 98, 99
OS Explorer: 299, 302, 304, 19, 30
Publications, badges and certificates
Booklets
Swale Way by John Brock (Richmondshire District Council) 1997. 16pp; A5. £1.30 (incs p&p). Cheques to Richmondshire District Council.
Walking Support Providers
Contours

Tan Hill to Kirkstone Inn — THKI

CUMBRIA, N YORKS — **72km/45 miles**

A demanding self-devised route in the Yorkshire Dales, across the Howgills and visiting Nine Standards, High Pike, High Seat, Wild Boar Fell, The Calf, Wind Scarth, Harter Fell, Mardale Ill Bell, Thornwaite Beacon, Stoney Cove Pike and Pike Howe. There is a time limit of 20 hours.

Attributes
Very Challenging; Anytime Challenge; Kanter; Moorland
Start
Tan Hill Inn, Richmond, N Yorks NY896067
Finish
Kirkstone Inn, Ambleside, Cumbria NY401080
Websites
www.gofar.org.uk
Maps
OS Landranger: 90, 91
OS Explorer: 7, 19
Publications, badges and certificates
Looseleaf and registration form with certificate
Over the Hill Club routes (Tony Wimbush). Free or download from website. Quality colour certificate: £1:50 with registration form.

Three Crags Walk — 3CRAGW

N YORKS, W YORKS — **25km/16 miles**

A linear and varied route across the Wharfedale Valley passing the crags of Almscliffe, Caley, and Cow & Calf. Good views can be seen along the ridge between Caley Crags and Ilkley.

Attributes
Easy; Anytime Challenge
Start
Weeton Station, N Yorks SE276476

Finish
Cow & Calf, Ilkley, W Yorks
SE130467
Maps
OS Landranger: 104
OS Explorer: 297
Publications, badges and certificates
Looseleaf
Three Crags Walk by Lower Wharfedale Ramblers Association (Peter Bayer). £0.50 (+ A5 SAE).
Badge
Three Crags Walk (Peter Bayer). £2.00 (+ SAE).

Three Moors Walk — TMW

N YORKS, W YORKS — **48km/30 miles**

A walk taking in The Chevin, Rombalds Moor and Round Hill (Langbar/Middleton Moor). Good navigational skills are required.

Attributes
Challenging; Anytime Challenge;
Moorland
Start and Finish
Otley, W Yorks SE203455
Maps
OS Landranger: 104
OS Explorer: 297
Publications, badges and certificates
Looseleaf
Three Moors Walk by Lower Wharfedale Ramblers Association (Peter Bayer). £0.50 (+ A5 SAE).
Badge
Three Moors Walk (Peter Bayer). £2.00 (+ SAE).

Three Peaks Walk (Yorkshire) TPWYOR

N YORKS **39km/24 miles**

This classic scenic walk, taking in the peaks of Pen-y-ghent (2,278ft), Whernside (2,416ft) and Ingleborough (2,376ft), involves over 5,000ft of ascent. A popular route, it has suffered from path erosion.

Attributes
Challenging; Anytime Challenge; Moorland
Start and Finish
Horton in Ribblesdale, N Yorks SD809725
Websites
www.3-peaks.co.uk
Maps
OS Landranger: 98
OS Explorer: 2
Harvey Map (Stripmap)
Yorkshire Dales: Three Peaks (Superwalker) (Map)
Map (Other)
Yorkshire Three Peaks, Sketch Map & Route Guide Walk (Map) (Challenge Publications)
Publications, badges and certificates
Paperbacks
Yorkshire Three Peaks Walk by Brian Smailes (Challenge Publications) 2008. ISBN 9781903568460. 52pp; 125 x 185. £4.50 (incs p&p). Includes pull-out sketch map.
Three Peaks, Ten Tors by Ronald Turnbull (Cicerone Press) 2007. ISBN 9781852845018. 256pp; 170 x 120. £12.95.
Leaflets
Three Peaks Yorkshire Dales: A Hill-Walker's Map & Guide by Altos Design Ltd (Pen-y-ghent Café) 1997. A4/3. £3.95 (+ 9 x 6 SAE).
Pen-y-Ghent Café Safety Service (Pen-y-ghent Café). A4/3. Free (+ 9 x 4 SAE).
Badge
Three Peaks Walk (Yorkshire) (Pen-y-ghent Café). Details from Pen-y-ghent Café.

Three Ridings on Foot TROF

CLEVELAND, E YORKS, N YORKS, S YORKS, W YORKS **706km/439 miles**

A route tracing the border of Yorkshire on rights of way and permissive paths through the moors of the Pennines, the northern Yorkshire Dales, the North York Moors and the coastline.

Attributes
Challenging; Moorland
Start and Finish
Bawtry, S Yorks SK652932
Maps
OS Landranger: 92, 93, 94, 98, 101, 103, 106, 107, 110, 111, 112
OS Explorer: 278, 279, 291, 292, 293, 295, 301, 304, 1, 2, 19, 21, 26, 27, 30, 41
Publications, badges and certificates
Paperbacks
Three Ridings on Foot by A. & G. Birch and others (P3 Publications) 1996. ISBN 9780952209843. 120pp; 200 x 103. £2.99 (+ £1.00 p&p).

Three Rivers Walk TRWK

N YORKS, W YORKS **40km/25 miles**

A walk from the Aire to the Wharfe at Ilkley and then via Denton to the River Washburn near Swinsty Hall before returning to the Wharfe at the finish.

Attributes
Challenging; Anytime Challenge; Moorland
Start
Market Clock, Shipley, W Yorks SE147375
Finish
Otley Jubilee Clock, W Yorks SE202455
Maps
OS Landranger: 104
OS Explorer: 288, 297
Publications, badges and certificates
Looseleaf
Three Rivers Walk by Lower Wharfedale Ramblers Association (Peter Bayer). £0.50 (+ A5 SAE).
Badge
Three Rivers Walk (Peter Bayer). £2.00 (+ SAE).

Todmorden Centenary Way TCW

W YORKS **31km/19 miles**

A route around Todmorden created to commemorate the centenary of the granting of Borough status, taking in moors, valleys, woods, reservoirs, villages and poignant ruins.

Attributes
Challenging; Lake/Reservoir; Moorland
Start and Finish
Todmorden, W Yorks SD936242
Waymark
Green disc with name in orange

Maps
OS Landranger: 103, 109
OS Explorer: 21
Publications, badges and certificates
Folder
Todmorden Centenary Way (Hebden Bridge Visitor and Canal Centre) 1996. A5. £1.95 (+ £1.00 p&p).

Trans Pennine Trail — TPT

CHESHIRE, DERBYS, E YORKS, GTR MAN, LANCS, MERSEYSIDE, N YORKS, S YORKS, W YORKS — 346km/215 miles

A multi-user trail, braided in parts, following former railway lines, canal towpaths and other waterside routes, and linking the urban areas of Hull, Doncaster, Barnsley, Greater Manchester and Merseyside. Much of the route is urban, but there are long rural stretches in the east and some sections in the attractive country around the Pennine and Manchester areas. Areas in the historic centre, and docklands, of the maritime mercantile City of Liverpool are recognised as a World Heritage Site named Liverpool Maritime Mercantile City. Many sections of the Trans Pennine Trail were badly affected by flooding in 2007 and 2008, most seriously in South Yorkshire. The whole Trail has been reopened with some sections flagged as passable with care or with diversion routes – see Trail website. There are spurs from the main Trail, from Selby to York, and from Barnsley to Wakefield/Leeds and Sheffield/Chesterfield. In parts it uses other longer established paths including the Longdendale Trail, the Dove Valley Trail (each 9 miles) and, from the west of Warrington to Liverpool, part of the waymarked Mersey Way (22 miles and on OS mapping). The total length of the Trail and spurs is some 350 miles. The section from Hull to Liverpool forms part of the E8 European Long Distance Path, see E-Routes (E8).

Attributes
Challenging; Former Railway; Coastal; River; Canal; Moorland
Start
Hornsea, E Yorks TA208479
Finish
Southport, Merseyside SD326174
Waymark
Named discs/posts with trail logo
Websites
www.transpenninetrail.org.uk, www.tameside.gov.uk, www.makingthemostofthemersey.com

Maps 
OS Landranger: 104, 105, 106, 107, 108, 109, 110, 111, 112, 119, 120
OS Explorer: 1, 30, 266, 268, 269, 275, 276, 277, 278, 279, 281, 285, 288, 289, 290, 291, 292, 293, 295
Publications, badges and certificates
Illustrated map guides
Trans Pennine Trail: Irish Sea – Pennines Map 1 by Trans Pennine Trail Project (Trans Pennine Trail Officer) 2001. ISBN 9780953227716. A2/4. £5.95 (+ 75p p&p). Cheques to Barnsley MBC.
Trans Pennine Trail: Derbyshire & Yorkshire – Central Map 2 by Trans Pennine Trail Project (Trans Pennine Trail Officer) 2007. ISBN 9780953227785. A2/4. £5.95 (+ 75p p&p). Cheques to Barnsley MBC.
Trans Pennine Trail: Yorkshire – North Sea Map 3 by Trans Pennine Trail Project (Trans Pennine Trail Officer) 2007. ISBN 9780953227792. A2/4. £5.95 (+ 75p p&p). Cheques to Barnsley MBC.
Booklets
Trans Pennine Trail: Accommodation & Visitor Guide by Trans Pennine Trail Project (Trans Pennine Trail Officer) 2005. ISBN 9781901464184. 112pp; 166 x 126. £6.95 (+ 75p p&p). Cheques to Barnsley MBC.
Pack
Trans Pennine Trail (Trans Pennine Trail Officer). 4 publications. £24.25.

Trans-Dales Trail – 1 — TRANDT1

N YORKS — 97km/60 miles

A scenic route crossing Ribblesdale, Littondale, Wharfedale and Nidderdale, taking in Brimham Rocks, Fountains Abbey, Ingleborough, Pateley Bridge and Studley Royal.

Attributes
Challenging; Anytime Challenge; Lake/Reservoir; Moorland; Heritage
Start
Ingleton, N Yorks SD695730
Finish
Ripon, N Yorks SE314711
Websites
dalestrails.co.uk
Maps
OS Landranger: 98, 99
OS Explorer: 298, 2, 30
Publications, badges and certificates
Paperbacks
Trans-Dales Trail 1 (Arnold Underwood) 1997. ISBN 9780952977100. 40pp; A5. £2.50 (incs p&p).

Trans-Dales Trail – 2 TRANDT2

DURHAM, N YORKS **97km/60 miles**

From Teesdale this tough trail takes in Arkengarthdale, Swaledale, Oxnop Scar, Wensleydale, Stake Moss, Wharfedale, Littondale, Cogar Scar, Malham and Gargrave.

Attributes
Challenging; Anytime Challenge; Lake/Reservoir; River; Canal
Start
Greta Bridge, Durham NZ086132
Finish
Skipton, N Yorks SD992521
Websites
www.dalestrails.co.uk
Maps
OS Landranger: 92, 98, 103
OS Explorer: 2, 30
Publications, badges and certificates
Paperbacks
Trans-Dales Trail 2 (Arnold Underwood) 1997. ISBN 9780952977117. 52pp; A5. £2.50 (incs p&p).

Trollers Trot TROLLT

N YORKS **43km/27 miles**

This tough walk, with 3750ft of ascent, visits Simons Seat, Trollers Ghyll, Burnsall, Linton Falls (Grassington), Winterburn Reservoir, Rylestone Church and Rylestone Fell.

Attributes
Challenging; Anytime Challenge; Moorland
Start and Finish
Bolton Abbey, N Yorks SE070539
Maps
OS Landranger: 98
OS Explorer: 2
Publications, badges and certificates
Leaflets
Trollers Trot by John Sparshatt (John Sparshatt) 2007. 4pp; A4. Free (+ A5 SAE). Free to download from LDWA website.
Badge & certificate
Trollers Trot by John Sparshatt (John Sparshatt) 2007. £2.00 (+ A4 SAE). Cheques to W Yorks LDWA.

Two Beacons Challenge TWOBCH

N YORKS, W YORKS **53km/33 miles**

This is an extension of the Wharfedale Washburn Challenge, visiting Addingham Moor and Beamsley Beacon.

Attributes
Challenging; Anytime Challenge; Moorland
Start and Finish
Recreation Ground, Menston, W Yorks SE175435
Maps
OS Landranger: 104
OS Explorer: 297
Publications, badges and certificates
Looseleaf
Two Beacons Challenge (Louise Mallinson). Free (+ 9 x 4 SAE). Free to download from LDWA website.
Badge & certificate
Two Beacons Challenge (Louise Mallinson). £1.50 (+ SAE).

Wadsworth Millennium Walk WADMW

W YORKS **34km/21 miles**

This scenic walk in the South Pennines follows as near to the Wadsworth Parish boundary as existing footpaths permit.

Attributes
Anytime Challenge; Moorland
Start and Finish
Hebden Bridge SD992272
Maps
OS Landranger: 103
OS Explorer: 21
Publications, badges and certificates
Badge & certificate
Wadsworth Millennium Walk by Dave Bell (Alan Crabtree) 2003. A5. £3.00.
Leaflets
Wadsworth Millennium Walk by Dave Bell (Alan Crabtree) 2003. 6pp; A4. Free (+ SAE).

Wakefield Way WFW

W YORKS **121km/75 miles**

A circular walking route around the Wakefield Metropolitan District, visiting Wintersett Reservoir,

Newmillerdam, Woolley, Bretton Hall, Bank Wood, Horbury Bridge, River Calder, Gawthorpe, Bottom Boat, Stanley Ferry, the Aire & Calder Navigation Canal, Pontefract Park and East Hardwick.

Attributes
River; Canal
Start and Finish
Wintersett Reservoir Visitor Centre, Wakefield, W Yorks SE374154
Maps
OS Landranger: 104, 105, 110, 111
OS Explorer: 278, 288, 289
Publications, badges and certificates
Book
Wakefield Way by Douglas Cossar (RA West Riding Area) 2005. ISBN 9781901184747. 96pp; 204 x 148. £5.99 (+ £1.00 p&p).

Walden Round — WALDR

N YORKS — 42km/26 miles

A route through Nidderdale, Coverdale, Waldendale and Wharfedale. There is a total ascent of over 4,500 feet.

Attributes
Challenging; Anytime Challenge; Moorland
Start and Finish
Kettlewell, N Yorks SD969723
Maps
OS Landranger: 98
OS Explorer: 30
Publications, badges and certificates
Looseleaf
Walden Round (LDWA Nidderdale Group) 2007. 3pp; A4. Free (+ 9 x 4 SAE). Free to download from LDWA website.
Badge & certificate
Walden Round (LDWA Nidderdale Group). £2.00 (+ 9 x 6 SAE). Cheques to LDWA Nidderdale Group.

Weardale Way — WEARW

DURHAM, TYNE AND WEAR — 124km/77 miles

A route following the River Wear from the sea, at the Lindesfarne Memorial, Roker, Sunderland, to the headwaters in the east Pennines, keeping as close as is possible to the river. After leaving the initially urban surroundings of Sunderland it visits Lumley Castle, Durham (where the Castle and Cathedral forms a World Heritage Site), Bishop Auckland and Stanhope. After Stanhope the Way makes a northward loop to Rookhope to take in part of a tributary, Rookhope Burn.

Attributes
Easy; River; Urban; World Heritage Site
Start
Lindesfarne Memorial, Marine Walk, Roker, Tyne and Wear NZ407590
Finish
Killhope Lead Mining Museum, near Cowshill, Upper Weardale, Tyne and Wear NY825431
Waymark
Named green discs
Websites
www.weardaleway.com
Maps ◈
OS Landranger: 87, 88, 91, 92, 93
OS Explorer: 31, 305, 307, 308
Publications, badges and certificates
Grid Reference List
Weardale Way: Grid Reference List (Walking Support). £2.50 + VAT. Available from Walking Support website.
Leaflets
River Wear Trail (Sunderland City Council) 2000. A2 folded. Free. Photocopies only available.
Walking Support Providers
Walking Support

Wharfedale Washburn Challenge — WWC

N YORKS, W YORKS — 40km/25 miles

The route visits Otley Chevin, Pool, Lindley Wood, Timble, Denton, Middleton, Cow and Calf at Ilkley, Burley Woodhead and Bleach Mill. Proceeds from sales go to Martin House Hospice.

Attributes
Challenging; Anytime Challenge; Moorland
Start and Finish
Recreation Ground, Menston, W Yorks SE175436
Maps
OS Landranger: 104
OS Explorer: 297
Publications, badges and certificates
Looseleaf
Wharfedale Washburn Challenge (Louise Mallinson). Free (+ 9 x 4 SAE). Free to download from LDWA website.
Badge & certificate
Wharfedale Washburn Challenge (Louise Mallinson). £1.50 (+ SAE).

Whitby Way — WHITW

N YORKS — **106km/66 miles**

The route meanders through the Vale of York and over the North York Moors visiting many pilgrimage places of interest and taking in Crayke, Coxwold, Helmsley, Kirkbymoorside, Egton and Sleights. Profits from sales are donated to Christian Aid.

Attributes
Moorland; Pilgrimage; Religious; Charity
Start
York Minster, N Yorks SE603522
Finish
Whitby Abbey, N Yorks NZ904113
Maps
OS Landranger: 94, 100, 105
OS Explorer: 290, 299, 26, 27
Publications, badges and certificates
Booklets
Whitby Way by Leslie Stanbridge (Mark Comer) 2000. ISBN 9781871125429. 36pp; A5. £4.50 (+ £1.00 p&p). Cheques to Christian Aid.

White Rose Challenge Walk — WRCW

CLEVELAND, N YORKS — **56km/35 miles**

A route linking the landmarks of the White Horse and Roseberry Topping, taking in Sneck Yate, Thimbleby Moor, Sheepwash, Clay Bank, Kildale and part of the Cleveland Way N.T.

Attributes
Challenging; Anytime Challenge; Moorland; Charity
Start
White Horse, Kildale, N Yorks SE514813
Finish
Newton under Roseberry, Cleveland NZ570128
Maps
OS Landranger: 93, 94, 100
OS Explorer: 26
Publications, badges and certificates
Booklets
White Rose Challenge Walk by Darryl Dawson (Connexions) 2003. ISBN 9780954493707. 32pp; 202 x 144. £4.99. Proceeds to White Rose Children's Charity. Also from TICs in the area.
Looseleaf
White Rose Walk (George E. Garbutt). 1pp; A4. Free (+ 9 x 4 SAE).
Badge & certificate
White Rose Walk (George E. Garbutt). £1.10 & £0.20 (+ 9 x 4 SAE).

Wilberforce Way — WILBW

E YORKS, HULL, YORK — **97km/60 miles**

The Wilberforce Way is a linear trail devised to mark the bicentenary of the 1807 Act of Parliament abolishing British involvement in the Transatlantic Slave Trade. The trail starts in Hull (where William Wilberforce was born), goes through Pocklington (where he went to school) and finishes in York (where he was declared M.P. for the County of Yorkshire). As well as visiting places of special importance in the struggle for human freedom and dignity, the walks include places of more general interest and some delightful Woldian landscapes.

Attributes
Heritage; Pilgrimage; Religious; Charity
Start
The Deep, Hull, E Yorks TA103283
Finish
York Minster, York SE603522
Waymark
Broken chain / name
Websites
www.wilberforceway.co.uk
Maps
OS Landranger: 105, 106, 107
OS Explorer: 293, 290, 294
Publications, badges and certificates
Paperbacks
Wilberforce Way by John Eckersley (John Eckersley) 2007. ISBN 9780953586240. 56pp; 248 x 170. £7.00 (+ £1.00 p&p). All proceeds to Christian Aid.
Leaflets
Wilberforce Way (Yorkshire and Humber Faiths Forum). 1pp; A3 (A5 folded). Free.

Yorkshire Dales Challenge Walk — YDCW

N YORKS — **37km/23 miles**

A walk through the National Park visiting Buckden Pike, Cray, Hubberholme, Beckermons, parts of the Dales Way in Langstrothdale, Littondale and Arncliffe.

Attributes
Challenging; Anytime Challenge; Moorland

Start and Finish
Kettlewell, N Yorks SD971724
Maps
OS Landranger: 98
OS Explorer: 30
Publications, badges and certificates
Booklets

Yorkshire Dales: Challenge Walk by John Merrill (John Merrill Foundation). ISBN 9780907496861. 32pp; A5. £4.50 (+ £1.00 p&p). Cheques to John Merrill Foundation.
Badge & certificate
Yorkshire Dales Challenge Walk (John Merrill Foundation). £5.00 (incs p&p).

Yorkshire Dales Top Ten YDTT

N YORKS **129km/80 miles**

A route which takes in the 10 highest peaks/fells in the Yorkshire Dales with over 22,000 feet of ascent. Included are: High Seat, Swarth Fell, Great Coum and Crag Hill.

Attributes
Very Challenging; Anytime Challenge; Moorland
Start and Finish
Hardraw, N Yorks SD867912
Maps
OS Landranger: 98
OS Explorer: 2, 19, 30
Publications, badges and certificates
Paperbacks
Yorkshire Dales: Top Ten by Brian Smailes (Challenge Publications) 1999. ISBN 9780952690054. 90pp; 125 x 185. £6.50 (incs p&p).

Yorkshire Ridings 200 Furlongs YR2F

N YORKS, W YORKS **40km/25 miles**

A delightful walk around the Nidderdale AONB visiting Almscliffe Crag, Beckwithshaw, Beaver Dyke Dam, Dobpark Bridge and Farnley. There is about 2,300ft of ascent.

Attributes
Challenging; Anytime Challenge
Start and Finish
Jubilee Clock, Otley, West Yorkshire SE202455
Maps
OS Landranger: 104
OS Explorer: 297
Publications, badges and certificates
Looseleaf
Yorkshire Ridings 200 Furlongs by Derek Haller (Derek Haller) 2007. 2pp; A4/3. Free (+ A5 SAE). Free to download from LDWA website.
Badge & certificate
Yorkshire Ridings 200 Furlongs by Derek Haller (Derek Haller). £2.00 (+ A5 SAE).

Yorkshire Water Way YWW

N YORKS, S YORKS, W YORKS **166km/103 miles**

Commissioned by Yorkshire Water the route visits many of the reservoirs in the Yorkshire Area. It goes through Yorkshire from the Dales to the Peak District tracing the rivers and reservoirs of the Pennines. The first volume describes a 41-mile walk from Kettlewell to Ilkley. From the wilds of Great Whernside and the source of the River Nidd, it passes through the beautiful eastern Yorkshire Dales following the rivers and reservoirs of Nidderdale and the Washburn Valley. The second four-day 62-mile section of the route takes the walker on from Ilkley through the valleys and across the Moorlands of the South Pennines, Bronte country, and Last of the Summer Wine country to the finishing point at Langsett in the Peak District. The whole 103 mile route from Kettlewell to Langsett involves some 15,300ft of ascent.

Attributes
Challenging; Lake/Reservoir; Moorland
Start
Kettlewell, North Yorks SD968723
Finish
Langsett Reservoir Visitor Centre, South Yorks SE212004
Websites
www.innway.co.uk
Maps
OS Landranger: 98, 99, 104, 110
OS Explorer: 1, 21, 288, 297
Publications, badges and certificates
Paperbacks
Yorkshire Water Way: Kettlewell to Ilkley (Vol. 1) by Mark Reid (Inn Way Publications) 2006. ISBN 9781902001142. 72pp; A5. £3.99.
Yorkshire Water Way: Ilkley to Langsett (Vol.2) by Mark Reid (Inn Way Publications) 2008. ISBN 9781902001159. 96pp; A5. £3.99.

EAST CENTRAL ENGLAND

Chrome Hill from the summit of Parkhouse Hill

KEY FACTS

Areas	Derbyshire, Lincolnshire, Nottinghamshire
National Parks	Peak District
Principal AONBs	Lincolnshire Wolds
World Heritage Sites	Derwent Valley Mills
E-Routes	E2 variants Dover – Stranraer, E2 variant Harwich – Stranraer
National Trails (England)	Pennine Way (part), Pennine Bridleway (part)
Walking Routes (trail miles)	67 main routes (3600 miles); 20 waymarked (1630 miles)
Resident population	3 million

DON'T MISS! TRAIL SECTIONS (CHALLENGING/REMOTE MARKED WITH *)

Pennine Way	Edale to Snake Pass, over moorland on Kinder Scout, (15km, 1100ft ascent, 200ft descent)
Derwent Valley Heritage Way	Ladybower reservoir to Baslow, river valley under Curbar, Froggatt, Baslow Edges, easy (18km, 700ft ascent)
Limestone Way	Bonsal to Tissington, across rolling White Peak limestone country (16km, 1500ft ascent)
Monsal Trail	Monsal Head to Bakewell, much on an old railway line in steep sided White Peak dales, easy (17km, 1000ft ascent)
Robin Hood Way	Elkersley to Creswell Crags, limestone crags, Welbeck Abbey, across Sherwood forests, past Clumber Lake (19km, 660ft ascent)
Trespass Trail	circular from New Mills Heritage Centre, on to Kinder Scout side, tracing the 1932 Mass Trespass, includes the Millennium Walkway (23km, 2391ft ascent)

Dove Dale from the summit of Thorpe Cloud

EAST CENTRAL ENGLAND

Back Tor on Derwent Edge, Derbyshire, passed on the Derwent Valley Skyline

For walkers the highlight of East Central England must be the Peak District National Park, with the landscapes of the northern gritstone Dark Peak – peat-covered hills reaching 2000ft on Kinder Scout with narrow 'cloughs' (valleys) – contrasting with the rolling southern limestone White Peak, cut by steep dales.

Geography

Reservoirs are a feature of the Dark Peak, which is drained by the Derwent and its tributaries south into the River Trent. The Trent itself then flows northwards across Nottinghamshire and along the Lincolnshire borders. These lowlands are fertile agricultural lands. Here coal measures were the original basis for the prosperity of the now densely populated, gently undulating areas in and around the Trent valley, forming the basis for past industries.

North of Nottingham are the forests of Sherwood with their conifer plantations. Towards the Lincolnshire coast are the rolling chalk Lincolnshire Wolds, falling away to the flat, cultivated coastal plain that offers fine wetland habitats for birds. The south of Lincolnshire comprises the often-wooded limestone-based Kesteven Plateau, while around The Wash are the fenlands, flat, low-lying terrain, rich agriculturally, with many straight, canalised drainage channels but sparse woodlands. The Wash itself is the UK's largest estuarine system, with extensive sandflats supporting migrating wildfowl. The Welland, Glen and Witham rivers drain into The Wash from Lincolnshire.

The Trails

Two related **National Trails** start in Derbyshire. From the Dark Peak, the Pennine Way National Trail heads north onto Kinder on its long journey along the central upland spine of England, while its new sister route, the multi-user Pennine Bridleway National Trail, designed specifically for horse riders and mountain bikers, runs parallel. The Trespass Trail follows in the footsteps of the 1932 Kinder Scout Mass trespassers, up onto Kinder Scout.

Routes following **landscape features** include the Limestone Way, a White Peak route through the heart of the Derbyshire limestone dales. One of Britain's main charity routes, Macmillan Way – Boston to Abbotsbury, raising funds for Macmillan Cancer Support, traces the oolitic limestone belt that soon starts to crop out in Rockingham Forest (in Northamptonshire). The Nev Cole Way passes

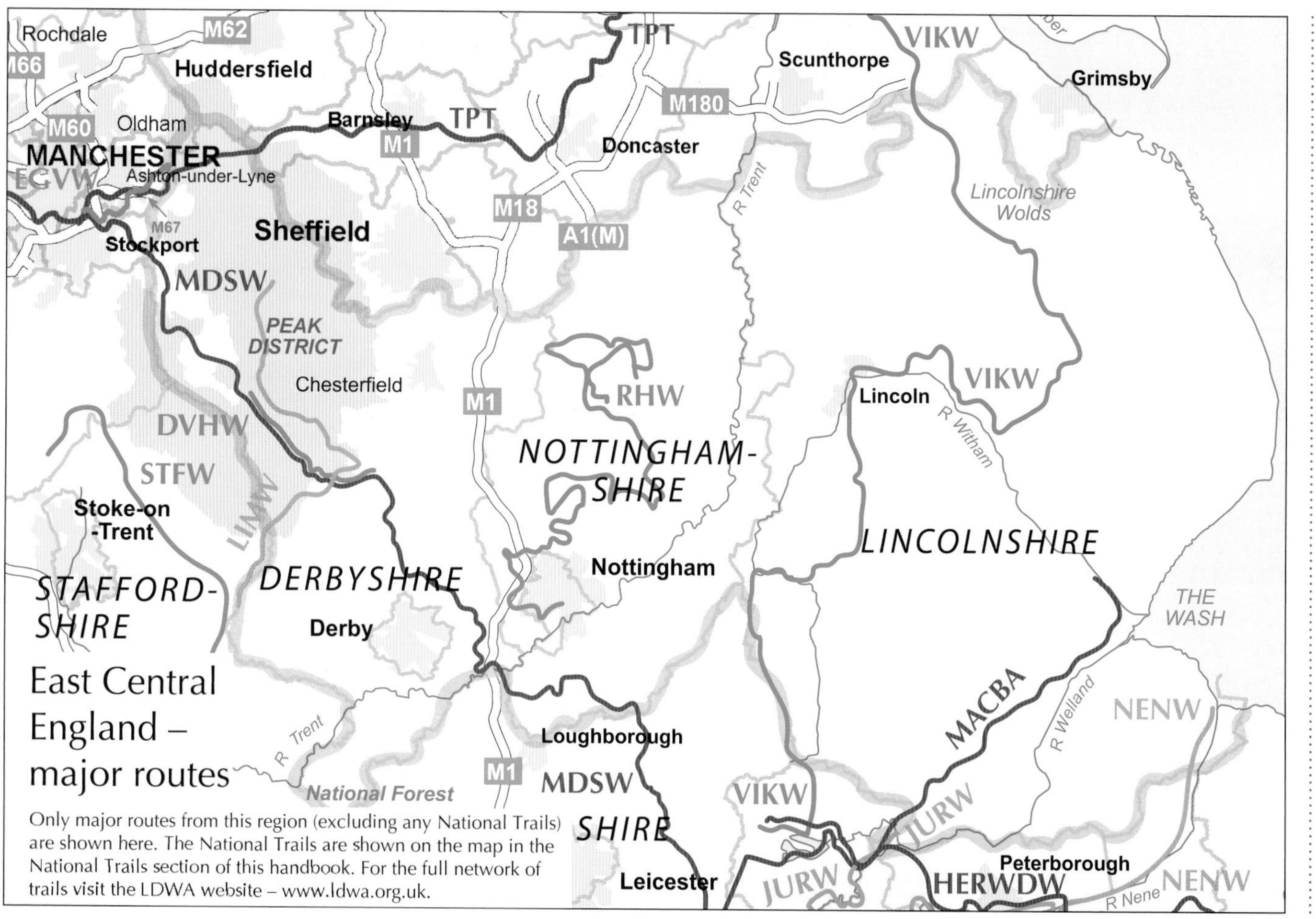

East Central England – major routes

Only major routes from this region (excluding any National Trails) are shown here. The National Trails are shown on the map in the National Trails section of this handbook. For the full network of trails visit the LDWA website – www.ldwa.org.uk.

from the Jurassic scarp overlooking the River Trent and visits the Lincolnshire Wolds. The Wanderlust Way is another Lincolnshire Wolds circuit. Tops of the North (Three Shire Head to Carlisle) is based on the county tops (old and new) of northern England. The long Inn Way... to the Peak District heads through the Peak District, taking in many 'edges' and passing 53 traditional country pubs.

Easy **canal towpath** walking is available on the Derby Canal Ring on the Derby, Erewash and Trent & Mersey canals. Fenland waterways are explored by the Brown Fen Waterway Trail (and its sister Black Fen Waterway Trail). The Cuckoo Way is on the 220-year old Chesterfield Canal, the 'Cuckoo Dyke'. Grantham Canal provides walks along this towpath. Other easy walking opportunities on former **railway lines** include the White Peak Trails that include the Monsal Trail.

There are **heritage** routes and numerous routes around **boroughs** and **towns**. The Robin Hood Way features areas of Nottingham associated with this legendary figure. The Danelaw Way links the two 'burghs' of the ancient Viking Danelaw, Lincoln and Stamford. The Viking Way crosses an area once occupied by Norse invaders. The Derbyshire Footpaths Preservation Society established the Centenary Way (Derbyshire) for its own centenary. The Bonnie Prince Charlie Walk celebrates the Ramblers' Diamond Jubilee and the Prince's 1745 walk. The Chesterfield Round Walk tours the town's outskirts and Dronfield's 2000 Rotary Walk was this town's millennium walking project. The Sheffield Country Walk tours around the outskirts of the city, the Gingerbread Way circuits the town of Grantham, and the Plogsland Round circuits the city of Lincoln. The Lindsey Loop links six market towns, visiting the hills of the Lincolnshire Wolds. The South Kesteven Round route circles around this district, while Spires and Steeples crosses North Kesteven discovering its artistic and historical heritage.

The Derwent Valley Heritage Way takes in a World Heritage Site in the Derwent Valley, birthplace of the water-powered system for making textiles. Circular Walks in the Derwent Valley also includes this Site, covering both sides of the valley.

There are 37 **Anytime Challenges**. Three authors provide two-thirds of these. John Merrill, who has lived in the Peak District, has 13 routes: the Peakland Way, a multi-day route through the National Park, the Dark Peak Challenge Walk, Derby Canal Ring, Happy Hiker Challenge Walk, Jennifer's Challenge Walk, Limestone Dale Walk, Limey Way, Limestone Dale Walk, Lincolnshire Wolds Black Death Challenge Walk, Little John Challenge Walk, Peak District High Level Route, Rivers Way and White Peak Challenge Walk. Ken Jones supplies seven more: Dam Long Walk, Dark Peak Snake, Dark Peak Stones, Derwent Valley Skyline, Kinder Dozen Challenge, Kinder Killer and Round the Reservoirs. Mike Warner adds another six: Beast of Bolsover, Derbyshire Derwent Mills and Hills Anytime Challenge Walk, Derbyshire Windmill Wander, Eleven Guide Stoops of Bradfield, Royal Shrovetide Challenge Walks and Sherwood Foresters Memorial Walk. Alan Edwards offers the High Peak Way and Pride of the Peak Walk and Martyn Bishop has the Bourne Blunder and Tennyson Twenty.

Also represented are Keith Bown with the three Three Feathers Walks, Vic Cox with the Bell Walk Major, David Firth with Ten Church Challenge, Bob Garlick has the Derbyshire Dawdle, David Irons provides the Dark Peak Boundary Walk, the LDWA Vermuyden Group offer the Vermuyden Way, Paul Pugh has the Longshaw Limber and Brian Smailes the Derbyshire Top Ten.

ROUTE CODES

DVHW	Derwent Valley Heritage Way	**MDSW**	Midshires Way
EGVW	Etherow–Goyt Valley Way	**NENW**	Nene Way
HERWDW	Hereward Way	**RHW**	Robin Hood Way
JURW	Jurassic Way	**STFW**	Staffordshire Way
LIMW	Limestone Way	**TPT**	Trans Pennine Trail
MACBA	Macmillan Way (Boston to Abbotsbury)	**VIKW**	Viking Way

Beast of Bolsover BOB

DERBYS **32km/20 miles**

In coal mining country it takes in Sutton Scarsdale Hall, Hardwick Hall, Bolsover Castle and the preserved pit-head buildings of Pleasley Colliery. It visits the villages of Heath, Palterton and Teversal, the setting for *Lady Chatterley's Lover*. A shorter, 14.5 miles, route is also available.

Attributes
Challenging; Anytime Challenge; Heritage; Industrial History
Start and Finish
Bolsover Castle, Bolsover, Derbys SK473705
Maps
OS Landranger: 120
OS Explorer: 269
Publications, badges and certificates
Looseleaf
Beast of Bolsover by Mike Warner (Mike Warner) 2003. A4. Free (+ A5 SAE with Large Letter 250g stamp).
Badge & certificate
Beast of Bolsover (Mike Warner). £4.00 (incs p&p). Cheques to Mike Warner.

Bell Walk Major BMJW

DERBYS, S YORKS **58km/36 miles**

The walk links the churches of Dronfield, Old Whittington, Norton, Dore, Hathersage, Totley and Holmesfield, all of which have bells. The route can be split into two Bell Minor routes of 22 or 14 miles, as explained in the route description.

Attributes
Challenging; Anytime Challenge; River; Moorland; Heritage; Industrial History; Religious
Start and Finish
Dronfield, Derbys SK353784
Maps
OS Landranger: 110, 119
OS Explorer: 269, 278, 1, 24
Publications, badges and certificates
Looseleaf
Bell Walk Major (Vic Cox). 4pp; A4. Free (+ 9 x 6 SAE).
Badge & certificate
Bell Walk Major (Vic Cox). £2.00 (+ 9 x 6 SAE). Cheques to St John the Baptist Church Bellringers.

Bonnie Prince Charlie Walk BPCW

DERBYS **28km/17 miles**

Devised to celebrate the RA Diamond Jubilee, the walk follows the general route taken by Prince Charles Edward Stuart on his march in 1745 from Ashbourne to Derby, through woods and farmland.

Attributes
Heritage; Monarchy
Start
Ashbourne, Derbys SK181467
Finish
Derby, Derbys SK353365
Waymark
Prince's head and name in gold on brown disc
Maps ◈
OS Landranger: 128
OS Explorer: 259
Publications, badges and certificates
Leaflets
Bonnie Prince Charlie Walk (John Pritchard-Jones) 1995. A5/4. Free (+ 9 x 4 SAE).

Bourne Blunder BBL

LINCS **32km/20 miles**

A route to the south of Grantham taking in a sculpture trail, the Grimsthorpe Castle Estate, an 11th century castle mound, and lakes at Holywell Hall.

Attributes
Easy; Anytime Challenge; Lake/Reservoir; Heritage
Start and Finish
Bourne Woods Car Park, Lincs TF077202
Maps
OS Landranger: 130
OS Explorer: 234, 248
Publications, badges and certificates
Looseleaf
Bourne Blunder (Martyn Bishop). Free (+ 9 x 4 SAE).
Badge & certificate
Bourne Blunder (Martyn Bishop). £2.00 (+ SAE). Cheques to Martyn Bishop.

Brown Fen Waterway Trail BRFWT

LINCS, SUFFOLK **108km/67 miles**

A route following the courses of various waterways visiting Surfleet, Spalding, Crowland and Donnington with a spur to Swainshead (10 miles) also described. See Black Fen Waterway Trail.

Attributes
Easy; River; Heath
Start and Finish
Boston, Lincs TF327441
Waymark
Named signs with land/water/plant life logo
Websites
www.visitthefens.co.uk
Maps
OS Landranger: 131
OS Explorer: 235, 248, 249, 261
Publications, badges and certificates
Leaflets
Explore the Fens Waterways: Walkers Guide to Black Fen and Brown Fen Waterway Trails (Spalding Tourist Information Centre). 1pp; A2 folded. Free (+ 9 x 4 SAE).

Centenary Way (Derbyshire) CWD

DERBYS **40km/25 miles**

An east to west walk devised by the Derbyshire Footpaths Preservation Society to commemorate their centenary, connecting Ilkeston with Ashbourne and visiting the lesser known but attractive villages of West Hallam, Duffield, Weston Underwood, Brailsford, Edmaston, Shirley and Osmaston. The Way links with the Bonnie Prince Charlie Walk at Ashbourne.

Attributes
Heritage
Start
Ilkeston, Derbys SK460418
Finish
Ashbourne, Derbys SK180470
Waymark
Named signs
Maps ◈
OS Landranger: 128, 129
OS Explorer: 259, 260
Publications, badges and certificates
Booklets
Centenary Way: Ilkeston to Ashbourne (Derbyshire Footpaths Preservation Society) 1994. 24pp; A5. £2.50 (incs p&p). Cheques to The Derbyshire Footpaths Preservation Society.

Chesterfield Round Walk CHRW

DERBYS **55km/34 miles**

This is a circular walk exploring the varied countryside surrounding the suburban fringes of Chesterfield. Described in a clockwise direction, can be split into six convenient sections between places served by public transport and with parking.

Attributes
Heritage
Start and Finish
Troway, Derbys SK412792
Websites
www.chesterfieldroundwalk.org.uk
Maps
OS Landranger: 119
OS Explorer: 269
Publications, badges and certificates
Leaflets (A1 folded)
Chesterfield Round Walk (RA Chesterfield & NE Derbyshire). 1pp; A5. £1.50 (+ 9 x 6 SAE). Cheques to Chesterfield & North East Derbyshire Ramblers Group.
Badge
Chesterfield Round Walk by RA Chesterfield and NE Derbyshire (RA Chesterfield & NE Derbyshire) 2008. £3.50 (+ SAE). Cheques to Chesterfield & North East Derbyshire Ramblers Group.

Circular Walks in the Derwent Valley CWDV

DERBY **85km/53 miles**

This interesting circular walk explores both sides of the Derwent Valley between Derby and Matlock. En route you will pass mills, canals, vantage points offering extensive views, historic houses, industrial housing and many picturesque villages. Part of the route also follows the River Derwent. Shorter walks are also possible by using the railway line that runs through the valley.

Attributes
World Heritage Site; Heritage; Industrial History
Start
Derby Station, Derbyshire SK361356
Finish
Matlock Station, Derbyshire SK295603
Maps
OS Landranger: 119, 128
OS Explorer: 24, 259

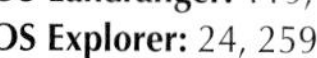

Publications, badges and certificates
Paperbacks
Circular Walks in the Derwent Valley by John Merrill (John Merrill Foundation). £5.95 (+ £1.00 p&p). Cheques to John Merrill Foundation.

Cuckoo Way CUCKW

DERBYS, NOTTS, S YORKS 74km/46 miles

A walk along the 220-years-old Chesterfield Canal, known locally as the Cuckoo Dyke. It ceased to be used commercially in the 1950s. Efforts are being made to restore the canal, but in some places the path is overgrown and occasionally difficult to find on the ground. The path passes through, or close to, Staveley, Worksop and Retford. Between Shaw Bridge (SK738920) and the finish it is coincident with the Trent Valley Way.

Attributes
Canal
Start
Chesterfield, Derbys SK388713
Finish
West Stockwith Lock, Notts SK784946
Waymark
Canal company plaque
Websites
www.chesterfield-canal-trust.org.uk
Maps ◈
OS Landranger: 112, 119, 120
OS Explorer: 269, 270, 271, 278, 279, 280
Stripmap
Chesterfield Canal and the River Trent (GEOprojects)
Publications, badges and certificates
Paperbacks
Chesterfield Canal: A Richlow Guide (Richlow Guides) 2006. ISBN 9780955260902. 40pp.

Dam Long Walk DAMLW

DERBYS 64km/40 miles

A circular walk around 32 dams and reservoirs surrounding Black Hill in the North Western section of the Dark Peak. Shorter variations of the route are possible by using sections of road.

Attributes
Very Challenging; Anytime Challenge; Moorland
Start and Finish
Crowden Youth Hostel, Derbys SK073994
Maps
OS Landranger: 110
OS Explorer: 1
Publications, badges and certificates
Booklets
Dam Long Walk (Ken Jones). A5. Free (+ A5 SAE).
Certificate
Dam Long Walk (Ken Jones). Free (+ 9 x 6 strengthened SAE).

Danelaw Way DANEW

LINCS, RUTLAND 96km/60 miles

This route links the two 'burghs' of the ancient Viking Danelaw, Lincoln and Stamford. Passing through peaceful Lincolnshire countryside, it takes in Ancaster, Corby Glen and a short section in Rutland associated with the poet John Clare. Minor variations, including a short circular route option from Ryhall, can extend the distance by 5 miles.

Attributes
Heritage; Literary
Start
Castle Square, Lincoln, Lincs SK976718
Finish
Golden Fleece, Sheepwash, Stamford, Lincs TF029071
Websites
www.lincscountyramblers.co.uk
Maps
OS Landranger: 121, 130, 141, 142
OS Explorer: 234, 247, 272
Publications, badges and certificates
Paperback (ring-bound)
Danelaw Way by Brett Collier (RA Lincoln) 2005. ISBN 9781901184761. 56pp; 202 x 144. £4.95 (+ 80p p&p). Cheques to Ramblers Association (Lincoln Group).
Badge (cloth)
Danelaw Way (Colin Smith). £1.25 (+ SAE). Cheques to Ramblers Association (Lincoln Group).

Dark Peak Boundary Walk DPBW

DERBYS, S YORKS, W YORKS 131km/81 miles

A circuit around the fringes of Kinder Scout, Bleaklow and Black Hill in the Peak District. The route passes Glossop, Marsden, Hathersage and Bradwell.

Attributes
Challenging; Anytime Challenge; Moorland
Start and Finish
Hayfield, Derbys SK037869
Maps
OS Landranger: 110
OS Explorer: 1, 21

Publications, badges and certificates
Looseleaf
Dark Peak Boundary Walk by Dave Irons (Dave Irons) 2007. 11pp; A4. £1.50 (incs p&p).
Walking Support Providers
Peaks

Dark Peak Challenge Walk DPCW

DERBYS 38km/24 miles

This high-level walk takes in Stanage Edge, Derwent Edge, Back Tor, Derwent Reservoir, Win Hill and Bamford. There is 3,300ft of ascent.

Attributes
Very Challenging; Anytime Challenge; Moorland
Start and Finish
Hathersage, Derbys SK232815
Maps
OS Landranger: 119
OS Explorer: 1
Publications, badges and certificates
Booklets
Dark Peak Challenge Walk by John Merrill (John Merrill Foundation). ISBN 9780907496663. 32pp; A5. £4.95 (+ £1.00 p&p). Cheques to John Merrill Foundation.
Badge & certificate
Dark Peak Challenge Walk (John Merrill Foundation). £5.00 (incs p&p).

Dark Peak Four County Tops DPK4CT

DERBYS, GTR MAN, S YORKS, W YORKS 69km/43 miles

A self-devised circuit linking the four county tops of Kinder Scout (Derbyshire), High Stones (South Yorkshire, just south of Margery Hill), Black Hill (West Yorkshire) and Black Chew Head (Greater Manchester), crossing Longdendale. There is a 21-hour limit with a series of optional 'times' for over 50s. Good navigation skills are required.

Attributes
Very Challenging; Anytime Challenge; Kanter; Moorland
Start and Finish
Bowden Bridge car park, Hayfield, Derbyshire SK049869
Websites
www.gofar.org.uk
Maps
OS Landranger: 110
OS Explorer: 1
Publications, badges and certificates
Looseleaf and registration form with certificate
Over the Hill Club routes (Tony Wimbush). Free or download from website. Quality colour certificate: £1.50 with registration form.

Dark Peak Snake DARPS

DERBYS 28km/17 miles

An interesting route over a wide variety of terrain and following the ridges and high ground encircling the Snake Road. It takes in Blackden Brook, Kinder Edges, Bleaklow, Alport Rid and Alport Castles. A shorter variation of 17 miles is possible by following the wooded Alport Valley. Good navigational skills are required.

Attributes
Challenging; Anytime Challenge; Moorland
Start and Finish
Snake Road, Derbyshire SK131895
Maps
OS Landranger: 110
OS Explorer: 1
Publications, badges and certificates
Booklets
Dark Peak Snake (Ken Jones). A5. Free (+ 9 x 6 SAE).
Certificate
Dark Peak Snake (Ken Jones). Free (+ 9 x 6 strengthened SAE).

Dark Peak Stones DARPST

DERBYS 32km/20 miles

A linear route which visits the most famous of the Derbyshire stone sculptures, where it is traditional to stand on the top of each stone in turn. Route extensions are also available.

Attributes
Challenging; Anytime Challenge; Moorland
Start
Snake Road Summit, Derbys SK088929
Finish
Ladybower Inn, Derbys SK205865
Maps
OS Landranger: 110
OS Explorer: 1
Publications, badges and certificates
Booklets
Dark Peak Stones (Ken Jones). 12pp; A5. Free (+ 9 x 6 SAE).
Certificate
Dark Peak Stones (Ken Jones). Free (+ 9 x 6 strengthened SAE).

Derby Canal Ring — DCR

DERBYS, NOTTS — **45km/28 miles**

A walk taking in the Derby, Erewash and Trent & Mersey canals. Diversions may be in operation at Shardlow so check the LDWA website for details.

Attributes
Easy; Anytime Challenge; Canal
Start and Finish
Railway Station, Derby SK362356
Maps
OS Landranger: 128
OS Explorer: 245, 259, 260
Publications, badges and certificates
Booklets
Walking the Derby Canal Ring by John Merrill (John Merrill Foundation) 1997. ISBN 9781874754282. 32pp; A5. £3.95 (+ £1.00 p&p). Cheques to John Merrill Foundation.
Badge & certificate
Derby Canal Ring (John Merrill Foundation). £5.00 (incs p&p).

Derbyshire Dawdle — DERD

DERBYS — **32km/20 miles**

A circuit around Matlock through varied countryside with absorbing views, charming villages, industrial heritage and other interesting features.

Attributes
Anytime Challenge; Canal; Heritage; Industrial History
Start and Finish
Layby on B5035, between Crich and Holloway, Derbyshire SK340552
Maps
OS Landranger: 119
OS Explorer: 24
Publications, badges and certificates
Looseleaf
Derbyshire Dawdle (Bob Garlick) 2008. 11pp; A4. £1.50 (incs p&p). Includes certificate.

Derbyshire Derwent Mills and Hills Anytime Challenge Walk — DDMHACW

DERBYS — **35km/22 miles**

A walk exploring part of the Derwent Valley, which is now a designated World Heritage Site.

Attributes
Challenging; Anytime Challenge; World Heritage Site; Heritage
Start and Finish
Matlock Station SK296602
Maps
OS Landranger: 119
OS Explorer: 24
Publications, badges and certificates
Looseleaf
Derbyshire Derwent Mills & Hills by Mike Warner (Mike Warner). A4 route description. Free. A5 SAE + two first class stamps.
Badge & certificate
Derbyshire Derwent Mills & Hills by Mike Warner (Mike Warner). A5. £4.00.

Derbyshire Top Ten — DERTT

DERBYS — **47km/29 miles**

A route visiting the ten highest peaks/moorland fells of Derbyshire, including Crowden Head, Edale Head (2087ft), Bleaklow Head and Hartshorn (1982ft).

Attributes
Challenging; Anytime Challenge; Moorland
Start and Finish
Edale car park, Derbys SK125853
Maps
OS Landranger: 110
OS Explorer: 1
Publications, badges and certificates
Paperbacks
Derbyshire Top Ten (Paperback) by Brian Smailes (Challenge Publications) 2001. ISBN 9781903568033. 48pp; 125 x 185. £3.95 (incs p&p).

Derbyshire Windmill Wander — DERWW

DERBYS — **39km/24 miles**

A walk between the only two complete windmills left in Derbyshire at Nether Heage and Dale Abbey.

Attributes
Challenging; Anytime Challenge
Start and Finish
Belper SK352475
Maps
OS Landranger: 128
OS Explorer: 259

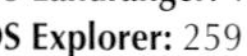

Publications, badges and certificates
Looseleaf
Windmill Wander by Mike Warner (Mike Warner). A4 route description. Free. A5 SAE + two first class stamps.

Derwent Valley Heritage Way DVHW

DERBYS **82km/51 miles**

A route that explores the beauty and heritage of Derbyshire's River Derwent. From the banks of Ladybower Reservoir it follows the River Derwent through the Peak District National Park via Chatsworth and the Derwent Valley Mills World Heritage Site until the Derwent joins the River Trent near Shardlow. En route Matlock, Belper and Derby are traversed keeping close to the river. The Derwent Valley between Matlock Bath and Derby is a World Heritage Site due to its importance as the birthplace of the water powered factory system for textile manufacture, a milestone in the industrial revolution.

Attributes
Lake/Reservoir; River; Urban; World Heritage Site; Heritage
Start
Ladybower Reservoir, Heatherdene, Derbys SK202858
Finish
Derwent Mouth, nr Shardlow, Derbys SK458308
Waymark
Purple disc with name in yellow
Websites
www.derwentvalleymills.org, www.nationalheritagecorridor.org.uk
Maps ◈
OS Landranger: 110, 119, 128, 129
OS Explorer: 1, 24, 259, 260, 269
Publications, badges and certificates
Paperbacks
Derwent Valley Heritage Way by Kevin Borman (Jarrold Publishing) 2003. ISBN 9780711729582. 96pp; 132 x 228. £11.99.
Leaflets
Derwent Valley Heritage Way (Derbyshire Dales District Council). A5. Free (+ A5 SAE).
Badge & certificate
Derwent Valley Heritage Way (Mike Warner). £5.00. Cheques to Derwent Valley Trust.
Walking Support Providers
Peaks

Derwent Valley Skyline DERVS

DERBYS **42km/26 miles**

This route, around the ridges encompassing the Derwent Valley, follows the popular Derwent Edges, tackling the remote and desolate Howden Edge to Bleaklow Stones, before reaching the finish. Good navigational skills are essential.

Attributes
Challenging; Anytime Challenge; Moorland
Start and Finish
Ladybower Reservoir SK197864
Maps
OS Landranger: 110
OS Explorer: 1
Publications, badges and certificates
Booklets
Derwent Valley Skyline (Ken Jones). A5. Free (+ 9 x 6 SAE).
Certificate
Derwent Valley Skyline by Ken Jones (Ken Jones). A5 or A4. Free (+ A5 or A4 strengthened SAE).

Dronfield 2000 Rotary Walk DR2RW

DERBYS **24km/15 miles**

Created as a Millennium project, the route is through woodland and farmland visiting Apperknowle and Holmesfield. There are links with the Sheffield Way.

Attributes
Easy; Forest/Woodland
Start and Finish
Coal Aston, Derby SK360797
Waymark
Yellow arrow on red, name on green ring, yellow edged disc
Maps
OS Landranger: 110, 119
OS Explorer: 269, 278, 24
Publications, badges and certificates
Leaflets
Dronfield 2000 Rotary Walk (Dronfield 2000 Rotary Walk). A2/3. £2.50 (incs p&p). Cheques to Dronfield 2000 Rotary Walk.

Eleven Guide Stoops of Bradfield — EGSB

DERBYS — **27km/17 miles**

The walk provides an opportunity to discover the gritstone Stoops (one of the earliest forms of signpost) of Derbyshire. The route has over 2000ft of ascent.

Attributes
Challenging; Anytime Challenge; Heritage
Start and Finish
Sands car park, Low Bradfield, Derbys SK263920
Maps
OS Landranger: 110
OS Explorer: 1
Publications, badges and certificates
Folder
Eleven Guide Stoops of Bradfield by Mike Warner (Mike Warner) 2005. 14pp, incs map; A4. Free (+ 2 x 1st or 2nd class stamps).
Badge & certificate
Eleven Guide Stoops of Bradfield (Mike Warner) 2005. £4.00 on completion of the walk. Cheques to Mike Warner.

Gingerbread Way — GINGW

LINCS — **40km/25 miles**

A route that circuits the town of Grantham. The name of the walk refers to the gingerbread biscuit, a local speciality.

Attributes
Challenging
Start and Finish
Londonthorpe, Grantham, Lincolnshire SK953379
Maps
OS Landranger: 130
OS Explorer: 247
Publications, badges and certificates
Leaflets
Gingerbread Way (RA Grantham). 8pp; A4. £1.20 (post free). Cheques to Grantham Ramblers.

Grantham Canal — GRANTC

LEICS, LINCS, NOTTS — **53km/33 miles**

A walk along the towpath of the Grantham Canal, which runs through the heart of the Vale of Belvoir; passing through many unspoilt villages and providing an opportunity to enjoy the East Midlands countryside.

Attributes
Easy; Canal
Start
Nottingham, Notts SK569392
Finish
Grantham, Lincs SK908355
Websites
www.granthamcanal.com
Maps
OS Landranger: 129, 130
OS Explorer: 246, 247, 260
Publications, badges and certificates
Paperbacks
Short Circular Walks on the Grantham Canal by John Merrill (John Merrill Foundation) 2004. £9.95. ISBN 9781903627563. 208 x 152.
Booklets
Romantic Canal alongside the Grantham by The Grantham Canal Partnership (Grantham Canal Partnership). £6.50. Cheques to Grantham Canal Restoration Society.

Happy Hiker Challenge Walk — HHCW

DERBYS — **42km/26 miles**

The route explores the quieter side of the White Peak, taking in the villages of Flagg, Earl Sterndale, Longnor and Pilsbury. It also involves over 2,000ft of ascent.

Attributes
Challenging; Anytime Challenge
Start and Finish
Car Park, Over Haddon, Derbys SK202665
Maps
OS Landranger: 119
OS Explorer: 24
Publications, badges and certificates
Booklets
Happy Hiker (White Peak) Challenge Walk by John Merrill (John Merrill Foundation) 2002. ISBN 9781903627297. 44pp. £5.50 (+ £1.00 p&p). Cheques to John Merrill Foundation.
Badge & certificate
Happy Hiker Challenge Walk by John Merrill (John Merrill Foundation). £5.00 (incs p&p).

High Peak 60 HP60

DERBYS **96km/60 miles**

This walk designed to celebrate the RA Diamond Jubilee takes you through a varied landscape that includes farmland, river valleys and bleak exposed moorland in the High Peak country, circuiting Glossop and taking in Castleton, Buxton and New Mills. There are a number of steep ascents.

Attributes
Challenging; Moorland
Start and Finish
New Mills, Derbys SJ998854
Maps
OS Landranger: 110, 119
OS Explorer: 1, 24
Publications, badges and certificates
Booklets
High Peak 60 by David Firth (David Frith) 2006. A5. £1.00 (+ A5 SAE).

High Peak Way HPW

DERBYS, S YORKS **48km/30 miles**

A walk with in excess of 7000ft of ascent, through Hope, Hathersage and along the Great Ridge between Mam Tor and Lose Hill. It is not recommended in adverse weather conditions.

Attributes
Very Challenging; Anytime Challenge; Moorland
Start
Chinley, Derbys SK038826
Finish
Padley, Derbys SK251788
Maps
OS Landranger: 109, 110, 119
OS Explorer: 1, 24
Publications, badges and certificates
Booklets
High Peak Way by Alan S. Edwards (Alan S. Edwards) 1993. 20pp. Free (+ A5 SAE).
Badge & certificate
High Peak Way (Alan S. Edwards). £2.25 (incs p&p).
Walking Support Providers
Peaks

Inn Way... to the Peak District IWTPD

DERBYS **135km/84 miles**

This is a long distance circular walk through the Peak District, taking in the edges of Kinder Scout, Hathersage, Baslow, Chatsworth Park, Stanton Moor, Youlgrave, Tideswell, Eyam, Castleton, the Great Ridge, Edale and Hayfield. In addition to the diverse and varied landscape of the Peak District the route passes 53 traditional country pubs.

Attributes
Challenging; Moorland
Start and Finish
Hayfield, Derbyshire SK035869
Websites
www.innway.co.uk
Maps
OS Explorer
1, 24
Publications, badges and certificates
Paperbacks
Inn Way...to the Peak District by Mark Reid (Inn Way Publications) 2007. ISBN 9781902001098. 216pp; A5. £8.95.
Walking Support Providers
Brigantes; Peaks

Jennifer's Challenge Walk JCW

DERBYS **37km/23 miles**

The walk takes in the villages of Brassington, Kniveton, Hognaston, Carsington, Middleton-by-Wirksworth and Bonsal, and visits churches, of which two are dedicated to St James.

Attributes
Challenging; Anytime Challenge; Religious
Start and Finish
Longcliffe, Derbyshire SK224558
Maps
OS Landranger: 119
OS Explorer: 24
Publications, badges and certificates
Paperbacks
Jennifer's Challenge Walk (John Merrill Foundation). ISBN 9781903627587. 56pp. £6.00 (+ £1.00 p&p).
Badge & certificate
Jennifer's Challenge Walk by John Merrill (John Merrill Foundation). £5.00 (incs p&p).

Kinder Dozen Challenge KINDDC

DERBYS **39km/24 miles**

A demanding route involving 10,000 feet of ascent to be completed in under 12 hours. It circumnavigates Kinder Scout and visits most of the plateau's famous features.

Attributes
Very Challenging; Anytime Challenge; Moorland; Mountain
Start and Finish
Nags Head, Edale, Derbys SK123860
Maps
OS Landranger: 110
OS Explorer: 1
Publications, badges and certificates
Booklets
Kinder Dozen (Ken Jones). 12pp; A5. Free (+ 9 x 6 SAE).
Certificate
Kinder Dozen Challenge (Ken Jones). Free (+ 9 x 6 strengthened SAE).

Kinder Killer KINDK

DERBYS **53km/33 miles**

A walk following the most attractive routes up, down and around Kinder's complex system of ridges and valleys, including some easy rock scrambles. Two shorter walks are also available.

Attributes
Very Challenging; Anytime Challenge; Moorland
Start and Finish
Nag's Head, Edale, Derbyshire SK123860
Maps
OS Landranger: 110
OS Explorer: 1
Publications, badges and certificates
Booklets
Kinder Killer by Ken Jones (Ken Jones) 2003. Free (+ A5 SAE).
Certificate
Kinder Killer by Ken Jones (Ken Jones). 12pp; A5. Free (+ A5 SAE).

Limestone Dale Walk LIMDW

DERBYS, S YORKS **39km/24 miles**

A route through the limestone dales of the White Peak to Ashbourne, via Cunning, Woo, Deep and Horseshoe Dales to Earl Sterndale; then Dovedale to Hartington, Milldale and Mapleton.

Attributes
Anytime Challenge; River
Start
Fairfield, Buxton, Derbys SK069741
Finish
Ashbourne, Derbys SK180468
Maps
OS Landranger: 119, 128
OS Explorer: 24
Publications, badges and certificates
Booklets
Peak District End to End Walks by John Merrill (John Merrill Foundation) 2006. ISBN 9780907496397. 52pp; A5. £5.95 (+ £1.00 p&p). Cheques to John Merrill Foundation.
Badge & certificate
Limestone Dale Walk (John Merrill Foundation). £5.00 (incs p&p).

Limestone Way LIMW

DERBYS, STAFFS **74km/46 miles**

A White Peak route through the heart of the Derbyshire limestone dales, heading south from Castleton through Peak Forest, Millar's Dale, Flagg, Monyash, Youlgreave, Winster, Matlock, Bonsall, Ible, Parwich, Tissington, Thorpe, crossing the Dove to Marten Hill, Lower Ellastone and finishing in the Dove valley at Rocester.

Attributes
River; Moorland
Start
Castleton, Derbys SK150829
Finish
Rocester, Staffs SK112392
Waymark
Derby Ram
Websites
www.visitpeakdistrict.com
Maps ◈
OS Landranger: 110, 119, 128
OS Explorer: 259, 1, 24
Publications, badges and certificates
Leaflets
Limestone Way (Derbyshire Dales District Council) 2007. 28pp; A5. £0.80 (+ A5 SAE).
Walking Support Providers
HF; Peaks

Limey Way LMYW

DERBYS 64km/40 miles

A meandering traverse of the limestone countryside of the White Peak area visiting twenty dales including Cave Dale, Monsal Dale, Deep Dale, Lathkill Dale and Dove Dale.

Attributes
Challenging; Anytime Challenge; Moorland
Start
Castleton, Derbys SK151828
Finish
Thorpe, Derbys SK157505
Maps
OS Landranger: 110, 119
OS Explorer: 24
Publications, badges and certificates
Booklets
Limey Way by John Merrill (John Merrill Foundation) 1989. ISBN 9780907496830. 48pp; A5. £4.50 (+ £1.00 p&p). Cheques to John Merrill Foundation.
Badge & certificate
Limey Way (John Merrill Foundation). £5.00 (incs p&p).

Lincolnshire Wolds Black Death Challenge Walk LWBDCW

LINCS 42km/26 miles

This scenic route links nine deserted medieval villages ravaged by the Black Plague. Visiting Kelstern, Donnington on Bain and Withcall, it is, in part, coincident with the Viking Way.

Attributes
Challenging; Anytime Challenge
Start and Finish
St James Church, Louth, Lincs TF326874
Maps
OS Landranger: 113, 122
OS Explorer: 282
Publications, badges and certificates
Booklets
Lincolnshire Wolds Black Death Challenge Walk by John Merrill (John Merrill Foundation) 2001. ISBN 9781903627198. 40pp; A5. £5.50 (+ £1.00 p&p). Cheques to John Merrill Foundation.
Badge & certificate
Lincolnshire Wolds Black Death Challenge Walk (John Merrill Foundation). £5.00 (incs p&p).

Lindsey Loop LINL

LINCS 153km/95 miles

A figure-of-eight loop over the rounded chalk hills of the Lincolnshire Wolds and through lowland farmland. It links the six market towns of Market Rasen, Spilsby, Alford, Caistor, Horncastle and Louth. *See* Towers Way.

Attributes
Easy; Downland/Wolds
Start and Finish
Market Rasen, Lincs TF111897
Websites
www.lincscountyramblers.co.uk
Maps
OS Landranger: 113, 121, 122
OS Explorer: 273, 274, 282, 283, 284
Publications, badges and certificates
Badge
Lindsey Loop (Colin Smith). £1.25 (+ SAE). Cheques to Ramblers Association (Lincoln Group).

Little John Challenge Walk LJCW

NOTTS 45km/28 miles

An interesting walk through Sherwood Forest, the heart of Robin Hood country, taking in Church Warsop, Cuckney, Cresswell Crags, Clumber Park, Bothamsall and Ollerton.

Attributes
Challenging; Anytime Challenge
Start and Finish
Edwinstowe, Notts SK626669
Maps
OS Landranger: 120
OS Explorer: 270
Publications, badges and certificates
Booklets
Little John Challenge Walk by John Merrill (John Merrill Foundation). ISBN 9780907496465. 32pp; A5. £4.50 (+ £1.00 p&p). Cheques to John Merrill Foundation.
Badge & certificate
Little John Challenge Walk (John Merrill Foundation). £5.00 (incs p&p).

Longshaw Limber LONGL

DERBYS **50km/31 miles**

A high level scenic and interesting route in the Peak District, taking in Stanage Edge, Win Hill, Curbar Edge and White Edge. It includes 5,600ft of ascent.

Attributes
Challenging; Anytime Challenge; Moorland
Start and Finish
Longshaw Estate Visitor Centre, Derbys SK266800
Websites
www.paulpugh.co.uk
Maps
OS Landranger: 110, 119
OS Explorer: 1, 24
Publications, badges and certificates
Booklets
Longshaw Limber (Paul Pugh). A5. Free (+ 9 x 6 SAE).
Badge & certificate
Longshaw Limber (Paul Pugh). £2.50 (+ 9 x 6 SAE).

Macmillan Way – Boston to Abbotsbury MACBA

DORSET, GLOS, LEICS, LINCS, NORTHANTS, OXON, RUTLAND, SOMERS, WARKS, WILTS **467km/290 miles**

A route devised to raise funds for Macmillan Cancer Support to which all proceeds are donated. It runs along sea banks and river banks, across the Lincolnshire fens via Stamford, eventually to Abbotsbury on the Dorset Coast. From the fens it follows, as near as possible, the course of the oolitic limestone belt, called 'Cotswold' stone in that area, but found in slightly varying form from South Yorkshire to Dorset.

Attributes
River; Geological; Charity
Start
Boston, Lincs TF327442
Finish
Abbotsbury, Dorset SY560845
Waymark
Green bow, walk name and 'Across Country for Cancer Care'. Both directions.
Websites
www.macmillanway.org
Maps 
OS Landranger: 130, 131, 141, 142, 151, 152, 162, 163, 172, 173, 183, 194
OS Explorer: 117, 129, 142, 143, 156, 168, 179, 191, 206, 207, 223, 233, 234, 235, 248, 249, 261, 15, 45
Publications, badges and certificates
Paperbacks
Macmillan Way: Guidebook by Peter Titchmarsh (Macmillan Way Association) 2000. ISBN 9780952685128. 128pp; 134 x 215. £9.75 (incs p&p).
Booklets
Macmillan Way: South to North Supplement by Peter Titchmarsh (Macmillan Way Association) 2000. 26pp; A4. £4.50 (incs p&p).
Macmillan Way: Planner & Accommodation Guide – Boston to Abbotsbury by Peter Titchmarsh (Macmillan Way Association). 12pp; A4. £3.00 (incs p&p).
Badge
Macmillan Way (Macmillan Way Association). £2.50 (incs p&p).
Leaflets
Macmillan Ways by Peter Titchmarsh (Macmillan Way Association) 2008. 1pp; A4 folded. Free.
Walking Support Providers
Westcountry

Nev Cole Way NEVCW

LINCS **93km/58 miles**

The way passes from the Jurassic scarp overlooking the River Trent, via the south bank of the Humber to Immingham and Grimsby. Here it turns inland into the gently sloping Lincolnshire Wolds, passing through several villages to Nettleton which provides a link with the Viking Way and which could be used to return north to Barton-upon-Humber.

Attributes
River; Downland/Wolds
Start
Burton upon Stather, Lincs SE870178
Finish
Nettleton, Lincs TA112001
Waymark
Named squares
Maps
OS Landranger: 112, 113
OS Explorer: 281, 284
Publications, badges and certificates
Booklets
Nev Cole Way (Wanderlust Rambling Club) 1991. ISBN 9780951109229. 32pp; 147 x 206. £1.50 (+ 50p SAE).

Badge & certificate
Nev Cole Way (Wanderlust Rambling Club). £2.00 (+ SAE) & £0.50 (+ 9 x 4 SAE).

Peak District High Level Route PDHLR

DERBYS, S YORKS, STAFFS **147km/91 miles**

This tough route around the Peak National Park takes in Dovedale, the Roaches, Shining Tor, Chinley Churn, the southern edge of Kinder, Ladybower reservoir, Stanage, Beeley and the Derwent Valley.

Attributes
Very Challenging; Anytime Challenge; Moorland
Start and Finish
Matlock, Derbys SK297601
Maps
OS Landranger: 110, 119
OS Explorer: 1, 24
Publications, badges and certificates
Booklets
Peak District High Level Route by John Merrill (John Merrill Foundation). ISBN 9780907496557. 60pp; A5. £5.95 (+ £1.00 p&p). Cheques to John Merrill Foundation.
Badge & certificate
Peak District High Level Route by John Merrill (John Merrill Foundation). £5.00 (incs p&p).
Walking Support Providers
Peaks

Peakland Way PEAKW

DERBYS **156km/97 miles**

This route through the National Park visits Ilam, Longnor, Blackwell, Mam Tor, Kinder Scout, Snake Pass and Tissington where it joins the Tissington Trail.

Attributes
Challenging; Anytime Challenge; Moorland
Start and Finish
Ashbourne, Derbys SK179469
Maps
OS Landranger: 110, 119
OS Explorer: 259, 1, 24
Publications, badges and certificates
Book (wire bound)
Peakland Way by John Merrill (John Merrill Foundation) 2006. ISBN 9781903627464. 88pp; A5. £8.95 (+ £1.00 p&p). Cheques to John Merrill Foundation.
Badge & certificate
Peakland Way (John Merrill Foundation). £5.00 (incs p&p).
Walking Support Providers
Peaks

Plogsland Round PLOGR

LINCS, NOTTS **76km/47 miles**

A walk around the city of Lincoln with the cathedral in view for much of the route. It links many villages following paths and green lanes across the flat, drained arable land and along the banks of the River Witham.

Attributes
Easy; River
Start and Finish
Fiskerton, Lincs TF058715
Websites
www.lincscountyramblers.co.uk
Maps
OS Landranger: 121
OS Explorer: 271, 272
Publications, badges and certificates
Badge
Plogsland Round (Colin Smith). £1.25 (+ SAE). Cheques to Ramblers Association (Lincoln Group).

Pride of the Peak Walk POTPW

DERBYS **48km/30 miles**

This scenic route takes in the villages of Sheldon. Litton, Hassop, Calver Sough, Froggatt, Baslow and Edensor as well as Monsal Viaduct, Cressbrook Mill and Chatsworth House. There is 5,000ft of ascent.

Attributes
Challenging; Anytime Challenge; Moorland; Heritage
Start and Finish
Bakewell, Derbys SK217685
Maps
OS Landranger: 119
OS Explorer: 24
Publications, badges and certificates
Booklets
Pride of the Peak Walk by Alan S. Edwards (Alan S. Edwards) 2005. 30pp; A5. £2.55 (incs p&p).
Badge & certificate
Pride of the Peak Walk (Alan S. Edwards). £2.75 (incs p&p).

Walking Support Providers
Contours

Rivers Way RIVWAY

DERBYS, STAFFS **69km/43 miles**

A meandering route that links five principal rivers – The Noe, Derwent, Wye, Dove and Manifold – and visits Hope, Grindleford, Baslow, Bakewell, Flagg, Hartington and Wetton.

Attributes
Anytime Challenge; River
Start
Edale, Derbys SK124853
Finish
Ilam, Derbys SK135509
Maps
OS Landranger: 119
OS Explorer: 1, 24
Publications, badges and certificates
Booklets
Rivers Way by John Merrill (John Merrill Foundation). ISBN 9780907496410. 36pp; A5. £4.95 (+ £1.00 p&p). Cheques to John Merrill Foundation.
Badge & certificate
Rivers Way (John Merrill Foundation). £5.00 (incs p&p).

Robin Hood Way RHW

NOTTS **172km/107 miles**

The Way features areas of Nottingham associated with the legendary figure of Robin Hood and his exploits, crossing lowland farmland and heathland, and visiting the great houses and parks of the Dukeries and forests, including Sherwood Forest. A new guidebook is planned by the Robin Hood Way Association in 2009.

Attributes
Forest/Woodland; Heath; Heritage
Start
Nottingham, Notts SK570395
Finish
Edwinstowe, Notts SK625669
Waymark
Bow and arrow, green on white
Websites
www.robinhoodway.co.uk
Maps ◈
OS Landranger: 120, 129
OS Explorer: 260, 270, 271
Publications, badges and certificates
Paperbacks
Robin Hood Walks by Nottingham Wayfarers (Nottinghamshire County Council) 1994. ISBN 9781871890020. 176pp; 192 x 133. £4.95 (incs p&p).

Round the Reservoirs RTR

DERBYS **48km/30 miles**

A circular tour around nine reservoirs in the Eastern Section of the Dark Peak. It combines many of the least frequented reservoirs, with a high level crossing over Howden via Cut Gate, before finishing in the Derwent Valley. Maximum interest is maintained through fine scenery and interesting architectural features.

Attributes
Challenging; Anytime Challenge; Lake/Reservoir; Moorland
Start and Finish
Fairholmes Visitor Centre, Derbys SK173894
Maps
OS Landranger: 110
OS Explorer: 1
Publications, badges and certificates
Booklets
Round the Reservoirs by Ken Jones (Ken Jones). A5. Free (+ A5 SAE).
Certificate
Round the Reservoirs (Ken Jones). Free (+ 9 x 6 strengthened SAE).

Royal Shrovetide Challenge Walks SHCW

DERBYS **31km/19 miles**

A route connected with football with goals at Sturston and Clifton. Visiting these two locations, the routes also take in Nether Sturston, Madge Hill, Tissington, Thorpe and Mayfield.

Attributes
Challenging; Anytime Challenge; Sport
Start and Finish
Ashbourne, Derbys SK184464
Waymark
Orange discs on longer route, green on shorter; orange/green on coincident parts
Maps
OS Landranger: 119, 128
OS Explorer: 259, 24

Publications, badges and certificates
Paperbacks (spiral/laminated)
Royal Shrovetide Challenge Walks (Mike Warner). 41pp; A5. £5.00 (incs p&p).
Badge & certificate
Royal Shrovetide Challenge Walk (Mike Warner). £2.00 & £1.00 (post free). Available for each walk.
Pack
Including guidebook, badges and certificates for both routes (Mike Warner). £7.50 (incs p&p).

Sheffield Country Walk SHCYW

DERBYS, S YORKS **85km/53 miles**

This varied route around the outskirts of the city passes many sites and buildings of archaeological, historical and industrial interest. It follows woodland and riverside paths, crossing undulating farmland and the open gritstone moorlands to the west of the city.

Attributes
Challenging; River; Moorland; Heritage; Industrial History
Start and Finish
Eckington, Derbys SK434798
Waymark
Yellow arrows and sheaf symbols
Maps ◈
OS Landranger: 110, 111, 120
OS Explorer: 269, 278, 1, 24
Publications, badges and certificates
Booklets
Sheffield Country Walk by John Harker (RA Sheffield) 1996. £4.50 (incs p&p).

Sherwood Foresters Memorial Walk SFMW

DERBYS **32km/20 miles**

A tour of War Memorials in the Matlock area associated with the Sherwood Foresters (now Worcestershire and Sherwood Foresters) Regiment.

Attributes
Anytime Challenge; Heritage; Military
Start and Finish
Matlock Bath Station, Derbyshire SK297585
Maps
OS Landranger: 119
OS Explorer: 24

Publications, badges and certificates
Looseleaf
Sherwood Foresters Memorial Walk: Route Description by Mike Warner (Mike Warner). A4. Free. Free (+ A5 SAE with Large Letter 250g stamp).
Badge & certificate
Sherwood Foresters Memorial Walk by Mike Warner (Mike Warner). £4.00 on completion of the walk. Cheques to Mike Warner.

South Kesteven Round SKESTR

LINCS **209km/130 miles**

An extended route around the district of South Kesteven in the southwest of Lincolnshire connecting the market towns of Grantham, Sleaford and Bourne visiting 42 villages and 21 pubs on route with an extra loop into Market Deeping

Attributes
No significant attribute
Start and Finish
Grantham TF327441
Maps
OS Landranger: 130
OS Explorer: 247
Publications, badges and certificates
Paperbacks
South Kesteven Round: A Continuous Walk Around South Kesteven by R. A. Brownlow (R A Brownlow) 2005. ISBN 9780955175206. 100pp. £7.50.

Spires and Steeples SPST

LINCS **40km/25 miles**

A route across North Kesteven discovering artistic and historical treasures. The name refers to church spires, landmarks for visitors and key to the rural sport of Steeple chasing. North Kesteven has a rich history and heritage intertwined with its characteristic landscape of flat fens and heath under wide and changing skies.

Attributes
Easy; Heritage; Religious
Start
Lincoln Catherdral, Lincs SK977719
Finish
St Denys Church, Sleaford, Lincs TF068459
Waymark
Green motif on white disc with black name

Websites
www.spiresandsteeples.com
Maps
OS Landranger: 121, 130
OS Explorer: 272
Publications, badges and certificates
Booklets
Spires and Steeples by Hugh Marrows (artsNK) 2008. 68pp; 99 x 210. Free. Or Sleaford TIC Tel: 01529 414 294.

Ten Church Challenge TENCC

DERBYS **34km/21 miles**

A circular route visiting ten chapels around the Black Brook, Goyt and Todd Brook valleys of the High Peak.

Attributes
Anytime Challenge; Religious
Start and Finish
Whaley Bridge, Derbys SK012811
Maps
OS Landranger: 110, 119
OS Explorer: 1, 24
Publications, badges and certificates
Booklets
Ten Church Challenge by David Firth (David Frith). A5. £1.00 (+ A5 SAE).
Certificate
Ten Church Challenge (David Frith). Free (+ 9 x 6 SAE & 2 x 2nd class stamps).

Tennyson Twenty TENNYT

LINCS **32km/20 miles**

This route through the Lincolnshire Wolds, circles the village of Somersby, birthplace of Alfred Lord Tennyson, and passes small isolated villages and deserted hamlets as well as nature reserves.

Attributes
Easy; Anytime Challenge; Downland/Wolds; Literary
Start and Finish
Hagworthingham, Lincs TF344696
Maps
OS Landranger: 122
OS Explorer: 273, 274
Publications, badges and certificates
Looseleaf
Tennyson Twenty (Martyn Bishop). Free (+ 9 x 4 SAE).
Badge & certificate
Tennyson Twenty (Martyn Bishop). £2.00 (+ SAE). Cheques to Martyn Bishop.

Three Feathers Walks TFW

DERBYS, N YORKS, S YORKS **Various**

A series of three circular walks, based on: Kettlewell, Yorkshire Dales (34 miles); Kilburn, North York Moors (30 miles); Yorkshire Bridge, Peak District (28 miles). To qualify for a badge, the routes must be completed within a calendar year.

Attributes
Challenging; Anytime Challenge; Moorland
Start and Finish
Various
Maps
OS Landranger: 98, 100, 110
OS Explorer: 1, 2, 26, 30
Publications, badges and certificates
Looseleaf
Three Feathers Walks by Keith Brown (Keith Bown) 2007. 2pp; A4. Free (+ A5 SAE). Free to download from LDWA website.
Badge
Three Feathers Walks (Keith Bown). £3.50 (+ SAE).

Tops of the North (Three Shire Head to Carlisle) TOPOTN

CUMBRIA, DERBYS, LANCS, W YORKS **370km/230 miles**

This high-level route is based on the county tops (old and new) of northern England. From Three Shire Head it takes in Kinder Scout, Black Hill, Pendle Hill, Arnside Knot, the Old Man of Coniston, and the Lakes Three-thousanders. It also takes in the South Lancs moors, the Forest of Bowland, Leighton Moss nature reserve, Morecambe Bay, Arthur Ransome country, Rossendale, and Carnforth Station on the way to its finish at Carlisle.

Attributes
Challenging; Moorland; Mountain
Start
Three Shire Heads, Buxton, Derbys SK009684
Finish
Carlisle, Cumbria NY395560
Websites
www.millracebooks.co.uk
Maps
OS Landranger: 85, 89, 90, 97, 102, 103, 109, 110, 119
OS Explorer: 1, 4, 5, 6, 7, 21, 24, 41

Publications, badges and certificates
Hardback
Tops of the North by Graham Wilson (Millrace Books) 2008. ISBN 9781902173269. 184pp; 170 x 120. £14.95.

Trespass Trail TRESPT

DERBYS 23km/14 miles

The idea of New Mills man and first chairman of Natural England, Sir Martin Doughty, whose father, Harold, witnessed the Mass Trespass, the route follows in the footsteps of the Kinder Scout Mass trespassers who fought for the Right to Roam on Britain's mountains and moors. Sir Martin Doughty, who died in 2009, will be remembered as a life-long advocate for British conservation and access.

Attributes
Easy; Moorland; Heritage
Start and Finish
New Mills Heritage Centre, Derbyshire SK000854
Websites
www.kindertrespass.com
Maps
OS Landranger: 110
OS Explorer: 1
Publications, badges and certificates
Booklets
Trespass Trail by Sir Martin Doughty, Roly Smith (New Mills Heritage and Information Centre) 2007. 8pp; A5. £1.00 (+ A5 SAE).

Vermuyden Way VERMW

LINCS 32km/20 miles

The walk follows an elongated circuit along the artificial watercourses of the Isle of Axleholme, which was drained by Cornelius Vermuyden during the 17th century.

Attributes
Easy; Anytime Challenge; Lake/ Reservoir; Industrial History
Start and Finish
Belton, N Lincs SE782054
Waymark
Letter VW on black discs
Maps
OS Landranger: 112
OS Explorer: 280
Publications, badges and certificates
Looseleaf
Vermuyden Way (LDWA Vermuyden Group). Free (+ 9 x 4 SAE).
Badge & certificate
Vermuyden Way (LDWA Vermuyden Group). £1.50 (+ 10 x 7 SAE).

Viking Way VIKW

LEICS, LINCS, RUTLAND 237km/147 miles

Crossing an area which was occupied by Norse invaders, from the banks of the River Humber it traverses the Lincolnshire Wolds to Caistor, then along the Bain valley to Horncastle. From here the Spa Trail is followed along the trackbed of a former railway to Woodhall Spa and along the Witham Valley, then over flat fenland to Lincoln. Turning along the limestone escarpment of Lincoln Cliff and over Lincoln Heath, the route of the prehistoric Sewstern Lane is traced to reach Woolsthorpe Locks on the Grantham Canal. Another section of Sewstern Lane is used to Thistleton, then field-paths and lanes past Greetham, Exton and Rutland Water. At Oakham it links with the Macmillan Way and the Hereward Way. See also E-Routes (E2).

Attributes
Former Railway; River; Downland/Wolds
Start
Barton-upon-Humber, Lincs TA028229
Finish
Oakham, Rutland SK857089

Waymark
Viking helmet on yellow disc
Websites
www.lincscountyramblers.co.uk
Maps ◈
OS Landranger: 106, 107, 112, 113, 121, 122, 130, 141
OS Explorer: 234, 247, 272, 273, 281, 282, 284
Publications, badges and certificates
Paperbacks
Viking Way (Lincolnshire County Council) 1997. ISBN 9781872375250. 64pp; 125 x 206. £2.50 (incs p&p).
Looseleaf
Viking Way: Factsheet – Accommodation, Transport etc. (Lincolnshire County Council) Annual. 24pp; A4. Free.
Badge
Viking Way (Colin Smith). £1.25 (+ SAE). Cheques to Ramblers Association (Lincoln Group).

Wanderlust Way WANDW

LINCS **32km/20 miles**

This Way is an elongated circuit passing through attractive small villages and across the woods and farmland of the undulating Lincolnshire Wolds, from where there are views across the mouth of the Humber Estuary.

Attributes
Downland/Wolds
Start and Finish
Bradley Woods, Lincs TA242059
Waymark
Yellow letters WW on green squares
Websites
www.nelincs.gov.uk
Maps
OS Landranger: 113
OS Explorer: 284
Publications, badges and certificates
Leaflets
Wanderlust Way (Alec Malkinson) 2001. A3/4. Free (+ 9 x 4 SAE).
Badge & certificate
Wanderlust Way (Alec Malkinson). £3.00 (+ A5 SAE). Cheques to A B Malkinson.

White Peak Challenge Walk WPCW

DERBYS **40km/25 miles**

A strenuous walk in the Peak National Park taking in Rowsley, Birchover, Youlgreave, Monyash, Flagg, Taddington and Great Longstone.

Attributes
Challenging; Anytime Challenge; Moorland
Start and Finish
Bakewell, Derbys SK217685
Maps
OS Landranger: 119
OS Explorer: 24
Publications, badges and certificates
Booklets
White Peak Challenge Walk by John Merrill (John Merrill Foundation) 2009. ISBN 9780907496779. 36pp; A5. £5.95 (+ £1.00 p&p).
Badge & certificate
White Peak Challenge Walk (John Merrill Foundation). £5.00 (incs p&p).

White Peak Trails WPT

DERBYS, STAFFS **Various**

Former railway lines providing useful links with many other routes through the White Peak area and which are open for use by walkers and cyclists. They are the High Peak Trail (18 miles) Cromford – Dowlow; Tissington Trail (13 miles) Ashbourne – Parsley Hay, where it connects with the High Peak Trail; Monsal Trail (9 miles) Wye Dale – Coombs Viaduct, Bakewell; Manifold Trail in Staffordshire (8 miles) Hulme End – Waterhouses. The High Peak Trail and the Manifold Trail are shown on the free 'Cycle Derbyshire' map available from Derbyshire County Council.

Attributes
Easy; Former Railway
Start
Various
Finish
Various
Waymark
Named posts
Maps ◈
OS Landranger: 119, 128
OS Explorer: 24
Publications, badges and certificates
Booklets
Walking the High Peak Trail by John Merrill (John Merrill Foundation) 2006. ISBN 9781903627655. 64pp. £6.95 (+ £1.00 p&p). Cheques to John Merrill Foundation.
Walking the Tissington Trail by John Merrill (John Merrill Foundation) 1993. ISBN 9781874754107. 32pp; 204 x 140. £4.95 (+ £1.00 p&p). Cheques to John Merrill Foundation.
Walking the Monsal Trail & Sett Valley Trails by John Merrill (John Merrill Foundation). ISBN 9781903627648. 64pp; A5. £5.95 (+ £1.00 p&p). Cheques to John Merrill Foundation.
Leaflets
Tissington & High Peak Trails (Peak District National Park) 1997. A4/3. Free (+ 9 x 4 SAE).
Peak National Park (Peak District National Park) 1997. A4/3. Free (+ 9 x 4 SAE).
Monsal Trail (Peak District National Park) 1996. A4/3. Free (+ 9 x 4 SAE).
Badge & certificate
Tissington Trail (John Merrill Foundation). £5.00 (incs p&p).
(Monsal Trail)
White Peak Trails (John Merrill Foundation). £5.00 (incs p&p).
DVD
Railway Walks with Julia Bradbury (Acorn UK) 2009. 175 minutes; Format: PAL. £16.99.

EAST OF ENGLAND

Small boats moored in a tidal creek close to Wells-next-the-Sea

KEY FACTS	
Areas	Bedfordshire, Buckinghamshire, Cambridgeshire, Essex, Hertfordshire, Leicestershire, Norfolk, Northamptonshire, Oxfordshire, Rutland, Suffolk
National Parks	The Broads
Principal AONBs	Norfolk Coast, Suffolk Coast & Heaths, Dedham Vale, The Chilterns (part)
World Heritage Sites	Blenheim Palace
Heritage Coast	North Norfolk, Suffolk
E-Routes	E2 variants: Dover – Stranraer, and Harwich – Stranraer
National Trails (England)	Peddars Way and Norfolk Coast Path, Ridgeway (part), Thames Path (part)
Walking Routes (trail miles)	81 main routes (4900 miles); 55 waymarked (3450 miles)
Resident population	9 million

DON'T MISS! TRAIL SECTIONS (CHALLENGING/REMOTE MARKED WITH *)	
Peddars Way	Castle Acre to North Pickenham, following part of the ancient Roman road across Norfolk, easy (12km, 350ft ascent)
North Norfolk Coast Path	Burnham Deepdale to Wells-next-the-Sea, coast path and beaches, easy (17km, 250ft ascent)
Hereward Way	Brandon to Harling Road Station, through the Brecks and Thetford Forest (25km, 770ft ascent)
Icknield Way Path	Ashley to Linton, part of the Cambridgeshire section (28km, 300ft ascent)
Ouse Valley Way	Bronham to Turvey, valley of the River Great Ouse (24km, 700ft ascent)
Stour Valley Path	Sudbury to Nayland, middle Stour valley (22km, 870ft ascent)
Suffolk Coast and Heaths Path	Dunwich to Kessingham, bird reserves – option to extend to Minsmere (28km, 430ft ascent)
Chiltern Way	Bovingdon Green to Stonor, Hambeldon Valley, Turville windmill, Stonor Park (18km, 430ft ascent)
Chiltern Way	Buckland Common to Dunstable Downs Visitor Centre, Grim's Ditch, Ashridge Park, Whipsnade/Tree Cathedral, downs ridge* (23km, 1300ft ascent)

Horsey Mill, near the Weavers Way, Norfolk Broads

EAST OF ENGLAND

Lea Valley Path canal walking

The East of England is an already populous area with a still-growing population, and an economy increasingly based on new technologies. Deposits of sands, gravels and till (boulder clay) left by the glaciers cover much of eastern England, and East Anglia, particularly, is a traditional agricultural heartland too, with rich soils, easily worked, in the vast fields of the flat fenlands and in the fertile lowlands further inland.

This is lowland England at its most characteristic, where the walker looking for less challenging routes can savour its gentle countryside, with languid rivers, miles of often-deserted, seemingly remote beaches, and wide estuaries with abundant bird-life. There are quintessentially English pastoral and riverside scenes, redolent of Constable's paintings – Flatford Mill is in the Stour valley in the Dedham Vale AONB. There are many picturesque villages, where reeds from the marshlands have found valuable uses roofing the pretty thatched cottages.

Geography

The coastline includes the eastern side of The Wash, and the Norfolk and Suffolk coasts, with their varied scenery of low cliffs, wide beaches and mobile shingle spits (the 'nesses' – Orford is Europe's second largest). Just inland, the Norfolk and Suffolk Broads is Britain's largest protected wetland and third largest inland waterway. It has national park status, but with its own legislation, giving equal status to navigation of the waterways, and to conservation and public enjoyment. The Wash is itself a large estuarine system, with the River Great Ouse and the Nene draining the flat fenlands, assisted by networks of man-made 'drains', that carve straight lines across the wide landscapes.

Further south, the Essex coast includes the estuaries of the Stour, Chelmer, Blackwater, Colne, Crouch and Roach, and the wide estuary of 'Old Father Thames' himself. Here are winding, shallow creeks, and mudflats. The East

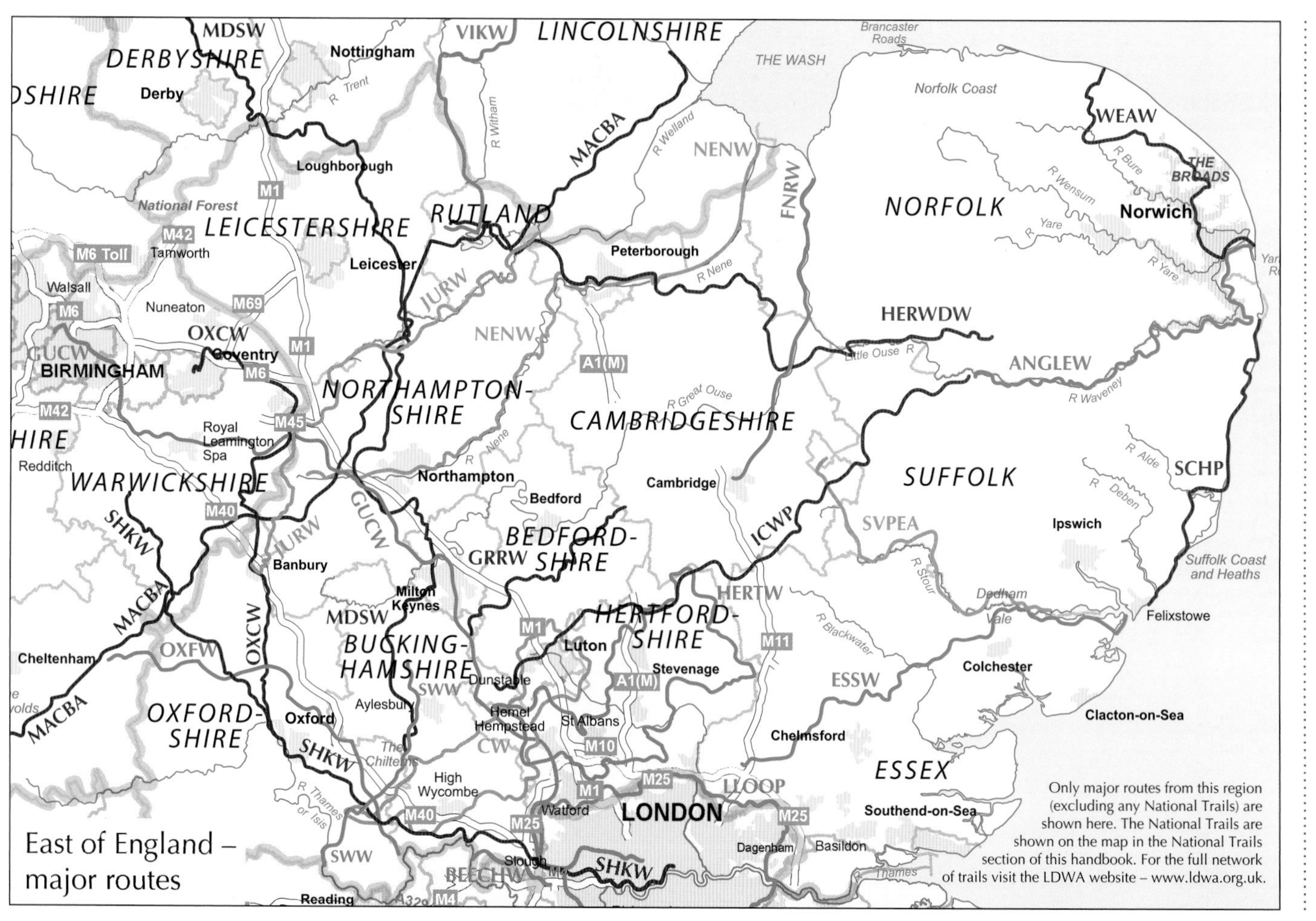

East of England – major routes

Only major routes from this region (excluding any National Trails) are shown here. The National Trails are shown on the map in the National Trails section of this handbook. For the full network of trails visit the LDWA website – www.ldwa.org.uk.

Chiltern beechwoods near Turville

Coast is an eroding shoreline, with sea-levels rising inexorably, and with its dune systems fed by crumbling cliffs. It all provides ideal habitats for bird-life, with some major RSPB reserves linked, or visited, by the many walking trails.

Towards the west are the Chiltern Hills, with this region's main downland areas. These provide miles of walking in beechwoods, with, in season, spring bluebells and golden autumnal colours. There are sharp slopes on the western scarps, and many long 'dry valleys', relics of a past era when this area was tundra on the southern edges of the great ice sheets. On longer walks, the undulating Chiltern terrain can be quite challenging.

In Oxfordshire Lambourn Downs is another prominent chalk ridge. There are other ridges and hills, notably the Greensand Ridge across Bedfordshire, and in Leicestershire the ancient hills of volcanic origin at Charnwood Forest that is part of the National Forest. Oxfordshire has the limestone Cotswold fringes around Wychwood. There are heathlands, such as the Brecklands, with its fine wind-blown sands, and pingos, shallow glacial hollows. In Rutland, Rutland Water is a major inland reservoir, circuited by easy trails.

The Trails

The region includes three **national trails** (see National Trails section). The Peddars Way & Norfolk Coast Path National Trail provides both inland and coastal walking. The Peddars Way is one of the links in a prehistoric route, often called the Greater Ridgeway, from The Wash to the Dorset Coast, and is a Romanised section of the prehistoric Icknield Way Path, itself one of the links in this ancient route. The Greater Ridgeway also includes the Ridgeway National Trail. The Thames Path National Trail also has a section through Oxfordshire.

The Angles Way, which includes waterside and heathland walking, was devised by the Ramblers, and together with the Peddars Way, Norfolk Coast Path and Weavers' Way, it forms the triangular 227-mile Around Norfolk Walk. The Angles were an ancient people who lived in East Anglia. Another tribe, the Iceni, is marked in the Iceni Way, and in Boudica's Way, remembering the Iceni's legendary warrior queen.

Among the **heritage** routes, two link Blenheim Park, a World Heritage Site of architectural importance: the Wychwood Way, a walk around the heart of the ancient forest of Wychwood, and the Oxfordshire Way. Two more routes were devised for, respectively, the Queen's Golden and Silver Jubilees: the Jubilee Way (Bernwood), on the boundary of an ancient Forest, and the Jubilee Way (Leicestershire). The North Bedfordshire Heritage Trail passes through 23 villages.

ROUTE CODES

Code	Route	Code	Route
ANGLEW	Angles Way	**MACBA**	Macmillan Way (Boston to Abbotsbury)
BEECHW	Beeches Way	**MDSW**	Midshires Way
CW	Chiltern Way	**NENW**	Nene Way
ESSW	Essex Way	**OXCW**	Oxford Canal Walk
FNRW	Fen Rivers Way	**OXFW**	Oxfordshire Way
GRRW	Greensand Ridge Walk	**SCHP**	Suffolk Coast and Heaths Path
GUCW	Grand Union Canal Walk	**SHKW**	Shakespeare's Way
HERTW	Hertfordshire Way	**SVPEA**	Stour Valley Path (East Anglia)
HERWDW	Hereward Way	**SWW**	Swan's Way
ICWP	Icknield Way Path	**VIKW**	Viking Way
JURW	Jurassic Way	**WEAW**	Weavers Way
LLOOP	London Loop		

The **Chiltern Hills** are the focus for the Chiltern Way which links many sites and characteristic landscapes in the Chiltern Hills Area of Outstanding Natural Beauty (AONB). The Chiltern Heritage Trail links the towns and parishes of Chiltern District. Both routes include much beech woodland, and woodlands also feature on the Beeches Way south of the Thames through the famous Burnham Beeches. The Swan's Way crosses the Vale of Aylesbury to meet the Ridgeway near Princes Risborough and then follows the chalk slopes of the Chilterns to the Thames at Goring. In Essex, the Forest Way (Essex) links Epping Forest and Hatfield Forest, across commons.

Routes following other **landscape** or **geological** features include the Greensand Ridge Walk, tracing the line of a greensand ridge, and passing Woburn Abbey. The Jurassic Way follows the band of Jurassic limestone along Northamptonshire's northern boundary. The Cotswold Round is a variant within the Macmillan Way's network of charity routes that generally follows the oolitic limestone belt across England.

The many **river** routes include the Black Fen Waterway Trail (and its Brown Fen sister), that explore fenland waterways, as does the Fen Rivers Way with the rivers Cam and Great Ouse. The Weavers' Way (Norfolk) runs in Broadland river valleys. The Ouse Valley Way is a source-to-sea route on one of England's longest rivers. The Peter Scott Walk remembers a noted local naturalist in going along the Great River Ouse to the Wash and on the sea wall. The Stour Valley Path (East Anglia) follows this river's valley downstream. The Tas Valley Way follows the Tas's course up to its source. The Kingfisher Way follows the River Ivel. The Mid Suffolk Footpath covers the Dove and Gipping valleys. The Nar Valley Way lies within the Nar's watershed.

The Nene Way in the Nene Valley includes canalised riverbank. The Colne Valley Path (Essex) and the Lambourn Valley Way follow these two river valleys. The Lea Valley Walk joins the Lea's source near Dunstable Downs to London's Docklands and its outflow into the Thames, passing the main 2012 Olympic Park. The broadly parallel New River Path traces a man-made channel, cut to bring clean water to London. The South Bucks Way follows the Rivers Misbourne and Colne to reach the Grand Union Canal. Shakespeare's Avon Way follows the River Avon's course, through the Bard's Stratford upon Avon.

Estuaries are explored by the Roach Valley Way, on the coastal margins of the Roach and Crouch. Linking Felixstowe to the Suffolk Coast and Heaths Path, the Stour and Orwell Walk also follows coast and heaths along the estuaries of the Orwell and the Stour, going around the Shotley peninsula. Coastal routes in Suffolk use riverside, forest and heathland paths to visit significant lowland habitats. The Suffolk Coast and Heaths Path itself runs along the Suffolk Heritage Coast, while the broadly parallel Sandlings Walk generally takes an inland line.

There are routes associated with **past heroes** and military battles. The long Nelson Way links locations associated with Horatio Nelson, between Norfolk and HMS Victory at Portsmouth. The Battlefields Trail links three significant battlefields in the heart of England. Byrhtnoth's Last Essex Visit is named after a Saxon hero. Other routes remember **historical** and **literary figures** or **fictional characters**. In Norfolk, Kett's Country Walk remembers Robert Kett, who led Kett's rebellion in 1549, while, in Bedfordshire and Hertfordshire, the John Bunyan Trail marks the Puritan Evangelist and author of the book *Pilgrim's Progress*. The Ivanhoe Way in Leicestershire includes Charnwood Forest, in the countryside of the famous novel by Sir Walter Scott, written in 1819 and set in 12th-century England.

Several routes make **county traverses**. The past Suffolk saint and king, St Edmund, is marked in the St Edmund Way route across the county. The Saffron Trail traverses the County of Essex from south-east to north-west. Cromer to the M11 follows historic lines of communication, and includes Norfolk Heritage Coast, Brecklands, and chalk hills (and to end, the M11!). The Cross Bucks Way is a west-to-east crossing of Buckinghamshire. Edgar Eastall's Church 'Fields' Way links Essex churches in eight settlements with names ending in 'field'. The Hereward Way is a Ramblers' jubilee route that links the Viking and Peddars Ways, across country associated with Hereward the Wake.

City, **town** and **borough circuits** abound: the Aylesbury Ring lies in the Vale of Aylesbury below the Chiltern ridge; the Stort Valley Way goes around Harlow; the Waveney Way circumnavigates Waveney District; the Kesgrave

Outer Ring encircles Kesgrave; the Leighton–Linslade Loop encircles Leighton Buzzard; the rural Mansell Way is never far from Braintree; the Oxford Green Belt Way is a CPRE jubilee route around Oxford marking the Green Belt's importance; and the Southend Millennium Walk, devised by the Ramblers, explores many aspects of Southend. County circuits include the Leicestershire Round, and two routes around the smaller counties – the Hertfordshire Way and the Rutland Round. The Three Shires Way is a bridleway route that includes the conjunction of the boundaries of 'Bucks, Beds and Northants', and it also makes a circuit of Graffham Water.

Other routes designed for a **range of users** include the very lengthy Midshires Way, linking the Ridgeway National Trail with the Trans Pennine Trail across the shires of Middle England. The Hanslope Circular Ride is in open north Buckinghamshire countryside.

Routes with a **railway** theme include the East Suffolk Line Walks that traverse unspoilt Suffolk countryside, using stations along the way. Marriott's Way goes along a former railway line, near to the River Wensum. The West Anglian Way makes use of the Cambridge to Liverpool Street railway line's stations.

There are 13 **Anytime Challenges** on offer. John Merrill, who has latterly made his home here, provides seven, exploring landscape, heritage and pilgrimage themes. These are the Belvoir Witches Challenge Walk, the Charnwood Forest Challenge Walk, the Epping Forest Challenge Walk, the Rutland Water Challenge Walk; and three with pilgrimage themes: St Alban's Way, the Walsingham Way – Ely to Walsingham and the Walsingham Way – King's Lynn to Walsingham. Through Bobbie Saeurzapf, LDWA Norfolk and Suffolk offers the Daffodil Dawdle, the Flower of Suffolk and the Poppyline Marathon (the Poppyline was a railway), all also available in challenge event formats. Adrian Moody offers the Chequers Challenge that passes the famous Chiltern political residence. And finally Derek Keeble provides two Essex routes – the Whamblab Extravaganza and Winstree Marathon.

The cliffs and shoreline approaching Sherringham on the Poppyline Marathon

Angles Way — ANGLEW

NORFOLK, SUFFOLK — 124km/77 miles

From Great Yarmouth the route goes by Breydon Water, along and near the River Waveney, passing around Oulton Broad, Beccles and Bungay, and Harleston and Diss, to its source, and then by the Little Ouse from its source very close by through heathland and marsh to Knettishall Heath in the Suffolk Brecks. Less than a mile onwards, west across the heath, the coincident start of the Peddars Way and finish of the Icknield Way Path are reached. The Angles Way was devised by the Ramblers, and together with the Peddars Way, Norfolk Coast Path and Weavers' Way, forms the 227-mile Around Norfolk Walk.

Attributes
Easy; Lake/Reservoir; River; Heath
Start
Vauxhall station, Great Yarmouth, Norfolk TG519081
Finish
Knettishall Heath, Suffolk TL955806
Waymark
Yellow disc with name and otter logo in green
Websites
www.discoversuffolk.org.uk,
www.countrysideaccess.norfolk.gov.uk
Maps ◈
OS Landranger: 134, 144, 156
OS Explorer: 230, 231, 40
Publications, badges and certificates
Paperbacks
Angles Way (includes accommodation & public transport details) by Sheila Smith (Editor) (RA Norfolk Area) 2005. ISBN 9781901184846. 28pp; 210 x 143. £2.70 (+ 30p p&p). Cheques to Ramblers Association (Norfolk Area).
Leaflets (with map)
Angles Way by Norfolk County Council (Norfolk County Council). A2 (A5 folded). £0.50 (+ SAE). Also available from TICs and some local Libraries.

Aylesbury Ring — AYLR

BUCKS, HERTS — 50km/31 miles

Originally created by the Aylesbury and District group of the Ramblers, the route is never more than 5 miles from the centre of Aylesbury, encompassing some of the remoter areas of the Vale and passing through Great Kimble, Dinton, Waddesdon, Hardwick, Rowsham, Hulcott and Aston Clinton. Much of the western route is coincident with the North Bucks Way.

Attributes
Easy
Start and Finish
Wendover, Bucks SP869078
Waymark
Aylesbury duck on named white disc
Websites
www.chilternsaonb.org
Maps ◈
OS Landranger: 165
OS Explorer: 181
Publications, badges and certificates
Leaflets
Aylesbury Ring (Buckinghamshire County Council) 1993. A4/3. £3.00. Available as a pack of 19 walks from BCC or local TICs.

Battlefields Trail — BATTW

NORTHANTS, OXON, WARKS — 32km/20 miles

It links three of England's most important battlefields. Edgehill (Warwickshire, 1642) was the first major action of the Civil War in England. Cropredy Bridge (Oxfordshire, 1644) was a Civil War battle where the king temporarily rescued the royalist cause from total destruction. Edgcote (Northamptonshire, 1469) was a significant but largely forgotten battle in the Wars of the Roses.

Attributes
Challenging; Heritage; Military; Monarchy
Start
Mill Lane, Chipping Warden, Northants SP499486
Finish
Kineton, Warks SP335510
Waymark
Black arrow in red/orange circle with name
Websites
www.battlefieldstrust.com
Maps
OS Landranger: 151
OS Explorer: 206
Publications, badges and certificates
Leaflets
Edgcote to Edgehill Battlefields Trail (Battlefields Trust) 2006. 1pp; A2 folded. Free. Route description, background to battles, OS mapping. Download from Trust website.

Beeches Way BEECHW

BUCKS, GTR LONDON **25km/16 miles**

Developed by the Iver and District Countryside Association, it connects the River Thames at Cookham with the Grand Union Canal at West Drayton, passing through several ancient woodlands now designated as SSSIs, including part of Burnham Beeches and the village of Stoke Poges.

Attributes
Easy
Start
Cookham, Bucks SU896854
Finish
West Drayton, Gtr London TQ057805
Waymark
Beechnut logo and name
Websites
www.buckscc.gov.uk
Maps ◈
OS Landranger: 175, 176
OS Explorer: 172
Publications, badges and certificates
Pack
Two packs: Chilterns & South Buckinghamshire Countryside Pack (Buckinghamshire County Council). £3.00 per pack or £5.00 for both. 19 recreational route leaflets covering the county from Marsworth to Marlow.

Belvoir Witches Challenge Walk BWCW

LEICS, LINCS **40km/25 miles**

A walk around the Vale of Belvoir, where 17th century witches were in residence, taking in Denton Reservoir, Belvoir Castle and part of the Grantham Canal.

Attributes
Challenging; Anytime Challenge; Canal
Start and Finish
Bottesford, Leics SK806392
Maps
OS Landranger: 129, 130
OS Explorer: 247
Publications, badges and certificates
Booklets
Belvoir Witches Challenge Walk by John Merrill (John Merrill Foundation) 2009. ISBN 9781903627594. 32pp; A5. £6.95 (+ £1.00 p&p). Cheques to John Merrill Foundation.
Badge & certificate
Belvoir Witches Challenge Walk (John Merrill Foundation). £5.00 (incs p&p).

Black Fen Waterway Trail BLFWT

CAMBS, NORFOLK **105km/65 miles**

A route following the courses of various waterways including the River Great Ouse and the Nene-Ouse Navigation Link passing through Downham Market, Littleport, Ely and Chatteris. Details of a loop to Flood's Ferry (10 miles) are included. See also Brown Fen Waterway Trail.

Attributes
Easy; River; Canal
Start and Finish
March, Cambs TL412976
Waymark
Named signs with land/water/plant life logo
Websites
www.visitthefens.co.uk
Maps
OS Landranger: 143
OS Explorer: 225, 226, 227, 228, 236
Publications, badges and certificates
Leaflets
Explore the Fens Waterways: Walkers Guide to Black Fen and Brown Fen Waterway Trails (Spalding Tourist Information Centre). 1pp; A2 folded. Free (+ 9 x 4 SAE).

Boudica's Way BOUW

NORFOLK **61km/38 miles**

Named after the legendary warrior Queen of the Iceni, the route incorporates a strong historical theme with links to Caistor Roman Town and Tasburgh Hill Fort. It connects Norfolk's county town Norwich and the market town of Diss on the Suffolk borders.

Attributes
Easy; Heritage; Military
Start
Railway Station, Norwich, Norfolk TG239083
Finish
Diss, Norfolk TM128797
Waymark
Sword on yellow & green named discs
Websites
www.south-norfolk.gov.uk

Maps ◈
OS Landranger: 134, 144, 156
OS Explorer: 230, 237, 40
Publications, badges and certificates
Folder
Boudica's Way (South Norfolk Council) 1999. 28pp; A5. £3.50 (incs p&p).

Byrhtnoth's Last Essex Visit BYLEV

ESSEX **79km/49 miles**

Named after a Saxon hero called Ealdoram Byrhtnoth the route takes in the river valleys of the Cam, the Pant, the Chelmer and the Blackwater; visiting Saffron Walden, Thaxted, Great Dunmow and Chelmsford en route to its finish at Maldon, where he fought some Viking raiders on 11 August 991.

Attributes
Heritage
Start
Great Chesterford, Essex TL502427
Finish
Maldon, Essex TL860054
Maps
OS Landranger: 154, 167, 168
OS Explorer: 183, 195, 209
Publications, badges and certificates
Booklets
Byrhtnoth's Last Essex Visit by Laurence S. Taylor (Derek Keeble) 2006. 18pp; A5. £2.50 (incs p&p). Cheques to Lexden St Leonard's Parish Church.
Folder
West Anglian Way (RA Cambridge Group). 6pp; A4. Route description and illustrative map. £3.00 (incs p&p). Cheques to Ramblers Association (Cambridge Group).

Charnwood Forest Challenge Walk CFCW

LEICS **40km/25 miles**

A walk in hill country to the north-east of Leicester passing Newton Lifford, Ulverscroft Priory, Bardon Hill, Mount St Bernard Abbey, Beacon Hill and Woodhouse Eaves.

Attributes
Challenging; Anytime Challenge
Start and Finish
Bradgate Park, Leics SK543114
Maps
OS Landranger: 129
OS Explorer: 246
Publications, badges and certificates
Booklets
Charnwood Forest Challenge Walk by John Merrill (John Merrill Foundation) 1992. ISBN 9780907496649. 32pp; A5. £4.50 (+ £1.00 p&p). Cheques to John Merrill Foundation.
Badge & certificate
Charnwood Forest Challenge Walk (John Merrill Foundation). £5.00 (incs p&p).

Chequers Challenge CHCH

BUCKS **34km/21 miles**

A route in the Chiltern Hills taking in the Chequers Estate, a section of the Ridgeway, Wendover Woods, and the County Tops of Buckinghamshire and Hertfordshire.

Attributes
Challenging; Anytime Challenge; Downland/Wolds
Start and Finish
Car Park, Tring High Street, Tring, Herts SP925115
Maps
OS Landranger: 165
OS Explorer: 181
Publications, badges and certificates
Looseleaf
Chequers Challenge by Adrian Moody (Adrian Moody). Free (+ SAE).
Badge & certificate
Chequers Challenge by Adrian Moody (Adrian Moody). £2.50 (+A4 SAE). Cheques to A P R Moody.

Chiltern Heritage Trail CHT

BUCKS **85km/53 miles**

The Heritage Trail offers walking and cycling options. The walking trail links the towns and parishes of Chiltern District and goes through scenic country and picturesque villages including Jordans, Chalfont St Giles and the Lee. Popular visitor attractions include the Chiltern Open Air Museum, Chenies Manor House and John Milton's Cottage. It is partly coincident with the South Bucks Way and meets the Chiltern Way at Chalfont St Giles.

Attributes
Cycle Route; Heritage
Start and Finish
Chesham Town Centre, Chesham, Bucks SP960017
Waymark
Named discs with beech leaf design

Websites
www.chiltern.gov.uk
Maps
OS Landranger: 165, 175
OS Explorer: 172, 181
Publications, badges and certificates
Booklets
Chiltern Heritage Trail by Barry Totterdell (Chiltern District Council) 2000. 32pp; A5. £2.99 (incs p&p).

Chiltern Way CW

BEDS, BUCKS, HERTS, LUTON, OXON **301km/187 miles**

The Way passes through some of the most attractive parts of the Chilterns, including the Bovingdon Plateau, the Chess valley, the Misbourne valley, Penn Country, the Hambleden valley, Stonor Park, Ewelme, Swyncombe Down, Bledlow Ridge, Hampden Country, Bulbourne valley and Dunstable Down. Based on an earlier unofficial route, the Chiltern Hundred, it was created by the Chiltern Society as its Millennium Project. Originally it took in all of the Chilterns from north to south across the Chilterns AONB, in a 125-miles circuit extending from Ewelme in the south west, Chorleywood in the south east and Sharpenhoe Clappers and Great Offley in the north east, visiting Chalfont St Giles, the edge of Marlow, Hambleden, Bix Bottom, Ewelme, the Ridgeway, Stokenchurch, Great Hampden, Aldbury, the Dunstable Downs, Sharpenhoe Clappers and Harpenden. Two extensions were added in 2003: the southern adds a loop of 50km (35 miles) from Bix Bottom via Mapledurham on the Thames and the northern extension 44km (27 miles) from Sharpenhoe Clappers via the Icknield Way and the outskirts of Hitchin. A short cut from Bix Bottom creates a 16km (10 miles) loop via Ewelme. The Chiltern Society's own footpath maps cover most of the route. A wildflower guide, with 18 shorter walks, to which Society members contributed expertise, is also listed.

Attributes
Forest/Woodland; River; Downland/Wolds
Start and Finish
Hemel Hempstead, Herts TL043059
Waymark
Name in green on white discs
Websites
www.chilternsociety.org.uk
Maps ◈
OS Landranger: 165, 166, 176, 175
OS Explorer: 159, 171, 172, 181, 182, 192, 193

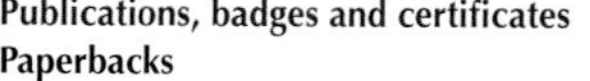

Publications, badges and certificates
Paperbacks
Chiltern Way & Chiltern Way Extensions: A Long-distance Circular Walk Round the Chilterns by Nick Moon (Chiltern Society Office) 2003. ISBN 9781903747339. 240pp; 204 x 148. £9.99. Chiltern Footpath Maps also sold by the Society, see Description.
Wild Flowers: And Where to Find Them in the Chilterns by Laurie Fallows, Gay Fallows (Frances Lincoln) 2007. ISBN 9780711227804. 160pp; 194 x 130. £7.99.

Colne Valley Path (Essex) COLVPE

ESSEX **35km/22 miles**

The route allows walkers to enjoy the views and delights of the Colne Valley taking in the historic village of Castle Hedingham, the great viaduct at Chappel, and Lexden Dyke near Colchester.

Attributes
River; Heritage
Start
Great Yedham, Essex TL760384
Finish
Balkerne Gate, Colchester, Essex TL999252
Websites
www.colnevalley.com
Maps
OS Landranger: 167, 168
OS Explorer: 184, 195
Publications, badges and certificates
Booklets
Colne Valley Path (River Colne Countryside Project) 2006. £3.50. Cheques to Braintree District Council.

Cotswold Round CTRD

BATH NES, GLOS, OXON, S GLOS, WARKS, WORCS **333km/207 miles**

A Macmillan Way variant, it comprises the Cross Cotswold Pathway (86 miles) from Banbury to Bath, a suggested turn north along the Cotswold Way National Trail to Chipping Campden, and then a return to Banbury by way of the Cotswold Link (21 miles). The Pathway is based largely on the Macmillan Way and the Link is coincident in parts with the Heart of England Way.

Attributes
Downland/Wolds; Charity
Start and Finish
Banbury Cross, Oxon SP453405

Waymark
Cotswold Way/Macmillan Way marks, these sections only
Maps
OS Landranger: 150, 151, 162, 163, 172, 173
OS Explorer: 155, 156, 167, 168, 179, 191, 206, 45
Publications, badges and certificates
Booklets
Macmillan Way: Cross Cotswold Pathway (Macmillan Way Association). 48pp. £4.00 (incs p&p).
Booklets
Cotswold Link by Macmillian Way Association (Macmillan Way Association). 12pp; A5. £1.75 (incs p&p).
Leaflets
Cotswold Accommodation Guide (Macmillan Way Association). 4pp; A5. £1.50 (incs p&p).
Walking Support Providers
Contours

Cromer to the M11 — CROM11

CAMBS, ESSEX, NORFOLK, SUFFOLK — **265km/165 miles**

Using established trails and ancient trackways, this walk takes in the Norfolk Heritage Coast, Breckland and the chalk hills of Cambridgeshire and north Essex.

Attributes
Coastal; Downland/Wolds
Start
Cromer, Norfolk TG219425
Finish
Audley End, Essex TL509372
Maps
OS Landranger: 132, 133, 144, 154, 155
OS Explorer: 195, 210, 226, 229, 236, 250, 251, 252
Publications, badges and certificates
Paperbacks
Treading Gently from Cromer to the M11 – Cromer to Wells-next-the-Sea by C. Andrews, D. Dear (Pathway Publishing) 1996. ISBN 9780952662815. 32pp; A5. £3.00 (incs p&p).
Treading Gently from Cromer to the M11 – Wells-next-the-Sea to Hunstanton by C. Andrews, D. Dear (Pathway Publishing) 1996. ISBN 9780952662822. 28pp; A5. £2.50 (incs p&p).
Treading Gently from Cromer to the M11 – Hunstanton to Thetford by C. Andrews, D. Dear (Pathway Publishing) 1996. ISBN 9780952662839. 32pp; A5. £3.00 (incs p&p).
Treading Gently from Cromer to the M11 – Thetford to M11 by C. Andrews, D. Dear (Pathway Publishing) 1997. ISBN 9780952662846. 28pp; A5. £3.00 (incs p&p).

Cross Bucks Way — CBUCKW

BEDS, BUCKS — **38km/24 miles**

A route mainly through agricultural land linking with the Oxfordshire Way at Stratton Audley, the North Bucks Way at Addington, the Swan's Way at Swanbourne and the Greensand Ridge Walk at Old Linslade.

Attributes
No significant attribute
Start
Stratton Audley, Bucks SP609260
Finish
Linslade, Beds SP912262

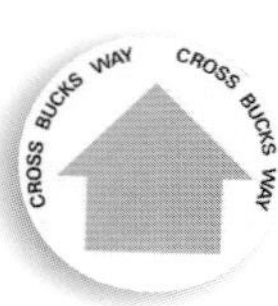

Waymark
Named standard waymarks
Websites
www.buckscc.gov.uk
Maps ◈
OS Landranger: 164, 165
OS Explorer: 192
Publications, badges and certificates
Pack
Pack 1: Vale of Aylesbury Countryside Pack (Buckinghamshire County Council). £3 per pack or £5 for both. 19 recreational routes from Westbury in the north to Stoke Mandeville and Bishopstone in the south.
Leaflets
Cross Bucks Way (Buckinghamshire County Council). A4/3. Free (+ SAE).

Daffodil Dawdle — DAFFD

CAMBS, SUFFOLK — **42km/26 miles**

A route between Newmarket and the River Stour, with an option for an 18 mile route. The walk is coincident in part with the Icknield Way Path and the Stour Valley Path (East Anglia).

Attributes
Challenging; Anytime Challenge
Start and Finish
Stetchworth, Cambs TL642583
Websites
www.notadog.org.uk
Maps
OS Landranger: 154
OS Explorer: 210
Publications, badges and certificates
Looseleaf
Daffodil Dawdle (Bobbie Sauerzapf) 2001. 2pp; A4. Free (+ SAE).

Badge & certificate

Daffodil Dawdle (Bobbie Sauerzapf). £1.50 (+ A4 SAE).

East Suffolk Line Walks ESLW

SUFFOLK **114km/71 miles**

The East Suffolk Line traverses some of the most delightful of Suffolk's unspoilt countryside. Stations along the way provide convenient starting and finishing points for exploring the surrounding area. The eleven walks covered can be joined up to make a long distance trail of over 70 miles. Some of the routes explore Suffolk rivers – the Alde, Deben and Fynn.

Attributes

Easy; River

Start

Ipswich Station, Suffolk TM156438

Finish

Lowestoft Station, Suffolk TM546929

Waymark

Windmill, church and sun graphic

Websites

www.eastsuffolklinewalks.co.uk

Maps

OS Explorer

40, 197, 212, 231

Publications, badges and certificates

Booklets

East Suffolk Line Walks (Station to Station Ipswich to Lowestoft) by Roger Wolfe (compiler) (East Suffolk Lines Community Rail Partnership). 28pp; A5. Free. Order online or download from website.

Edgar Eastall's Church 'Fields' Way EECFW

ESSEX **63km/39 miles**

This route links a number of churches in a cluster of eight settlements with names ending in 'field'. Using public transport the route can provide two linear walks of around 20 miles each from Bocking to Wethersfield and back. Longer circular options are also possible using part of Anita's Mucking Ugly Ways through Essex and the Mansell Way.

Attributes

Religious

Start and Finish

St Mary's Church, Panfield, Essex TL739254

Maps

OS Landranger: 155, 167

OS Explorer: 195

Publications, badges and certificates

Booklets

Edgar Eastall's Church 'Fields' Way by Magdalah Cooper with Roy Tover (Braintree & District Outdoor Pursuits) 2004. 24pp; A5. £1.00 (+ A5 SAE). Cheques to BDOPC. After cost, a donation is made to a charity of the club's choice.

Epping Forest Challenge Walk EPFOCW

ESSEX, GTR LONDON **34km/21 miles**

A delightful walk around Epping Forest starting at Waltham Abbey, where King Harold is reputedly buried and visiting places associated with Queen Boadicea.

Attributes

Challenging; Anytime Challenge

Start and Finish

Waltham Abbey, Essex TL382006

Maps

OS Landranger: 166

OS Explorer: 174

Publications, badges and certificates

Booklets

Epping Forest Challenge Walk by John Merrill (John Merrill Foundation) 2006. ISBN 9780955369100. 40pp; 215 x 140. £4.95 (+ £1.00 p&p). Cheques to John Merrill Foundation.

Badge & certificate

Epping Forest Challenge Walk (John Merrill Foundation) 2006. £5.00 (incs p&p).

Essex Way ESSW

ESSEX **130km/81 miles**

The Way heads across gently undulating agricultural land, passing through or near many attractive old villages including Willingdale, Pleshey, Coggeshall, Dedham, which has connections with the painter John Constable, and Manningtree where it takes to the Stour Estuary. To celebrate the 21st year of the Essex Way the Ridley Round (13-miles) was created which coincides for six miles. Beating the Bounds (Essex) is another circular walk (16 miles) and meets the Essex Way at Great Waltham. The John Ray Walk (9 miles) crosses the Essex Way between Braintree and Witham. See also E-Routes (E2).

Attributes

No significant attribute

Start
Theydon Bower Station, Epping, Essex TL461016
Finish
Harwich, Essex TM259324
Waymark
Red poppy and name on white disc

Websites
www.essexcc.gov.uk
Maps ◈
OS Landranger: 167, 168, 169
OS Explorer: 174, 183, 184, 195, 196, 197
Publications, badges and certificates
Booklets
Essex Way (includes free accommodation guide) (Contact Essex) 1994. ISBN 9781852810870. 32pp; A5. £3.00. Downloadable.
John Ray Walk (Essex County Council) 2000. ISBN 9781852812065. 24pp; 218 x 152. £3.00.
Leaflets
Beating the Bounds (Great Waltham Parish Council). A3/6. Free (+ 9 x 6 SAE).
Ridley Round (Great Waltham Parish Council). A3/3. Free (+ 9 x 6 SAE).
Badge (pin badge free with publication)
Essex Way (Contact Essex County Council). Free.

Fen Rivers Way — FNRW

CAMBS, NORFOLK — **80km/50 miles**

For much of the route, the Way follows the well-drained floodbanks of the rivers Cam and Great Ouse. At King's Lynn, there is a ferry link with the Peter Scott Walk (10 miles and on OS mapping but no publication) along the western edge of the Great River Ouse to the Wash and along the sea wall to the outfall of the River Nene. See also E-Routes (E2).

Attributes
Easy; Coastal; River
Start
Cambridge, Cambs TL449592
Finish
King's Lynn, Norfolk TF616199
Waymark
Eel logo and name on white disc
Websites
www.countrysideaccess.norfolk.gov.uk,
www.visitely.eastcambs.gov.uk,
www.cambridgeshire.gov.uk
Maps ◈
OS Landranger: 131, 132, 143, 154
OS Explorer: 209, 226, 228, 236, 250
Publications, badges and certificates
Booklets
Complete Fen Rivers Way and other walks (RA Cambridge Group) 2001. 49pp; A5. £4.50 (incs p&p). Cheques to RA Cambridge Group.
Leaflets
Fen Rivers Way: Cambridge to Ely Section (Cambridgeshire County Council) 1995. 36pp; A5. £2.00 (incs p&p).
Fen Rivers Way (Norfolk County Council). A5. £0.50 (+ SAE). Also available from TICs and some local Libraries.

Flower of Suffolk — FLOWS

SUFFOLK — **42km/26 miles**

A circular route (10 or 17 miles) using coastal and heathland paths. It is also an annual challenge event. See website for details.

Attributes
Challenging; Anytime Challenge; Coastal; Heath
Start and Finish
Walberswick, Suffolk TM498746
Websites
www.notadog.org.uk
Maps
OS Landranger: 156
OS Explorer: 212, 231
Publications, badges and certificates
Looseleaf
Flower of Suffolk (Bobbie Sauerzapf). 2pp. Free (+ 9 x 4 SAE).
Badge & certificate
Flower of Suffolk (Bobbie Sauerzapf). £1.50 (+ SAE).

Forest Way (Essex) — FWE

ESSEX — **40km/25 miles**

The Way links two forests and several open spaces in south-west Essex. From the edge of Epping Forest it runs north over farmland, from where there are views over the Lea valley, and crosses Latton and Harlow Commons to Hatfield Heath, Woodside Green and Hatfield Forest. At the end the walk meets with the waymarked Flitch Way (15 miles and on OS mapping) which follows the track of a former railway between Braintree and Bishops Stortford.

Attributes
Forest/Woodland
Start
Loughton Station, Essex TQ423956

Finish
Hatfield Forest Country Park, Takeley Street, Essex TL534213
Waymark
Tree and name on bright green disc/plaques
Websites
www.essexcc.gov.uk
Maps ◈
OS Landranger: 167, 177
OS Explorer: 174, 183, 194, 195
Publications, badges and certificates
Paperbacks
Forest Way (Essex County Council) 1996. ISBN 9781852810238. 14pp; A5. £2.50. Includes free accommodation guide.
Leaflets
Flitch Way (Essex County Council). 118 x 210. Free (+ SAE). Downloadable.

Greensand Ridge Walk GRRW

BEDS, BUCKS, CAMBS **64km/40 miles**

A route taking in woods and farmland along the dissected Greensand Ridge which rises from the clay vales on either side, passing Woburn Abbey and Ampthill Park where it connects with the John Bunyan Trail. At Leighton Buzzard, the Two Ridges Link (8 miles and included on OS mapping) provides a link via the Grand Union Canal to Ivinghoe Beacon and the Ridgeway National Trail/ Icknield Way Path. At Gamlingay, the waymarked Clopton Way (11 miles and on OS mapping) goes on to Wimpole Hall from whence the waymarked Wimpole Way (11 miles and on OS mapping) takes the walker to Cambridge. The waymarked Marston Vale Timberland Trail (14 miles) is a circular route coincident with the Greensand Ridge Walk between Ampthill Park and Lidlington.

Attributes
Downland/Wolds
Start
Linslade, Leighton Buzzard, Beds SP915251
Finish
Gamlingay, Cambs TL226533
Waymark
Letters GRW and deer emblem
Websites
www.greensandridgewalk.co.uk
Maps ◈
OS Landranger: 152, 153, 165
OS Explorer: 192, 193, 208
Publications, badges and certificates
Leaflets
Greensand Ridge Walk (Greensand Ridge Walk). A4/3. Free (+ A5 SAE). Available online.
Marston Vale Timberland Trail (Forest of Marston Vale) 2000. A4/3. Free (+ SAE).

Hanslope Circular Ride HCR

MILTON K **32km/20 miles**

The countryside of the Ouse and Tove Valleys gives extensive views across North Buckinghamshire and into Northants, with the distinctive spire of Hanslope Church the central feature. It includes a tour of the Saxon manors of Hanslope.

Attributes
Cycle Route; Horse Ride (Multi User)
Start and Finish
Great Linford, Milton K SP846424
Waymark
Named standard discs and posts – Circular Ride
Websites
www.milton-keynes.gov.uk
Maps ◈
OS Landranger: 152
OS Explorer: 192, 207
Publications, badges and certificates
Leaflets
Hanslope Circular Ride (Milton Keynes Council). Free (+ SAE).

Hereward Way HERWDW

CAMBS, LINCS, NORFOLK, NORTHANTS, PETERBORO, RUTLAND, SUFFOLK **177km/110 miles**

The Way links the Viking Way (at Oakham) with the Peddars Way near to Knettishall Heath. It passes through Stamford, Peterborough and Ely to reach the Brecklands heaths and forests at Brandon and Thetford. There are areas of flat open fenland. See also E-Routes (E2). The Torpel Way (11 miles from Peterborough to Stamford and included on OS mapping) provides an alternative option between those two locations – the route is to the north of the Hereward Way.

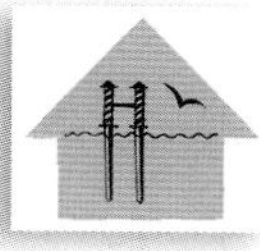

Attributes
River
Start
Oakham, Rutland SK861088

Ingham Church, Norfolk

Finish
Harling Road Station, Thetford, Norfolk TL977880
Waymark
Tiger face, named posts in Rutland; double sword logo in Cambs
Websites
www.visitely.eastcambs.gov.uk,
www.cp_ramblers.talktalk.net,
www.cambridgeshire.gov.uk
Maps ◈
OS Landranger: 141, 142, 143, 144
OS Explorer: 226, 227, 228, 229, 230, 234, 235
Publications, badges and certificates
Leaflets
Hereward Way: Oakham to Stamford (Oakham TIC). A4/3. Free.
Hereward Way: Peterborough to Ely (Cambridgeshire County Council) 2001. A5. £0.30 (+ A5 SAE).
Booklets
Country Walks around Peterborough – Volume 1 (includes Torpel Way) (Peterborough City Council). £2.50 (+ 9 x 6 SAE).
Walking Close to the Torpel Way by Clive Brown (Walking Pages Ltd). 24pp; 148 x 210. £2.00 (+ 95p p&p).

Hertfordshire Way HERTW

HERTS **267km/166 miles**

A route around one of the smallest counties visiting such as Codicote, St Albans, Tring, King's Langley, Cuffley and Bishop's Stortford through a variety of Hertfordshire scenery, mostly in open countryside but also through some of the more interesting and attractive villages. It includes the fringes of the Chilterns and Ashridge Forest, a National Trust estate. Hertford and St Albans, as the County Town and the main historic centre, are the only large towns on the route. There is an extension not shown on OS mapping of some 24 miles providing an alternative more easterly route from Cuffley to Hertford, going into the Lea and Ash valleys. This is described in the guidebook in two legs, from Cuffley to Broxbourne (12 miles) and Broxbourne to Hertford (12.5 miles), making some 190 miles of route in all. Although originally inspired by the Ramblers to celebrate the Ramblers' diamond jubilee in 1995, the Friends of The Hertfordshire Way is an autonomous group.

Attributes
Heritage
Start and Finish
Royston, Herts TL357403
Waymark
Name/head of deer

Maps ◈
OS Landranger: 153, 154, 165, 166, 167, 176
OS Explorer: 173, 174, 181, 182, 193, 194, 195, 209
Publications, badges and certificates
Paperbacks
Hertfordshire Way by Bert Richardson (Editor) (Book Castle) 2005. ISBN 9781903747612. 144pp; 148 x 204. £8.99.

Iceni Way ICEW

NORFOLK, SUFFOLK **129km/80 miles**

A route from Breckland to the Coast, taking in Thetford, Brandon, the Little Ouse, Brandon Creek, King's Lynn, Sandringham, the outskirts of Snettisham and Hunstanton where it links with the Norfolk Coast Path. The route also links with the Icknield and Nar Valley Ways.

Attributes
River
Start
Knettishall Heath, Suffolk TL943807
Finish
Hunstanton, Norfolk TF672412
Maps
OS Landranger: 132, 144
OS Explorer: 228, 229, 236, 250
Publications, badges and certificates
Booklets
Iceni Way (RA Norfolk Area) 2004. ISBN 9781901184648. 28pp; A5. £2.70 (+ 30p p&p).
Leaflets
Little Ouse Path (Brecks Countryside Project). A4/3. £2.00 (+ 50p p&p).

Icknield Way Path ICWP

BEDS, BUCKS, CAMBS, ESSEX, HERTS, LUTON, SUFFOLK **177km/110 miles**

One of the links in a prehistoric route, often called the Greater Ridgeway, from The Wash to the South Devon Coast. From the Ridgeway and using green lanes, farm and forestry tracks the Way follows, as far as is possible, the group of prehistoric trackways which form the Icknield Way along the chalk spine from the Chilterns to Norfolk. Many sights of archaeological interest are passed on the route through Luton, Baldock, Royston, Great Chesterford and Icklingham meeting the Peddars Way at the finish. An alternative route exists avoiding Dunstable and Luton. The Icknield Way Association Guide includes details of a link to Thetford from West Stow. See also E-Routes (E2). The waymarked Ridgeway

Link (7.5 miles and coincident with the Icknield Way Path on OS mapping) is a linking route from the Chilterns Gateway Visitor Centre near Dunstable to the finish of Ridgeway National Trail at Ivinghoe Beacon where there are no visitor facilites. The Link uses the route of the existing Icknield Way Path that has been upgraded to make it stile-free and steps have been added on a steep section.

Attributes
Forest/Woodland; Downland/Wolds; Heritage
Start
Ivinghoe Beacon, Bucks SP960168
Finish
Knettishall Heath, Suffolk TL944807
Waymark
Named disc with neolithic flint axe emblem
Websites
www.icknieldwaypath.co.uk, www.buckscc.gov.uk, www.cambridgeshire.gov.uk
Maps ◈
OS Landranger: 144, 153, 154, 155, 165, 166
OS Explorer: 181, 182, 193, 194, 195, 208, 209, 210, 226, 229, 230
Publications, badges and certificates
Paperbacks
Icknield Way Path (Icknield Way Association) 2006. ISBN 9780952181927. 70pp; 210 x 148. £8.50 (+ £1.50 p&p). 5th Edition, with route updates and additional 5 miles.
Greater Ridgeway: A walk from Lyme Regis to Hunstanton by Ray Quinlan (Cicerone Press) 2003. ISBN 9781852843465. 256pp; 172 x 116. £12.95.
Leaflets
Icknield Way: Walkers Route (Cambridgeshire County Council). A4/3. Free.
Ridgeway Link by Chilterns Conservation Board (Chilterns AONB) 2007. A4/3. Free. Download only from website, or free from local TICs/libraries.
Booklets
Accommodation List (Icknield Way Association). Free (+ SAE).
Badge
Icknield Way Path (Icknield Way Association). £1.30 (+ SAE).

Ivanhoe Way IVW

LEICS **56km/35 miles**

A route around the north-western area of the county including Charnwood Forest. The castle at Ashby and the surrounding countryside were the setting for the novel of the same name. The route links with the Leicestershire Round at Bagwith/Shakerstone.

Attributes
Literary
Start and Finish
Ashby-de-la-Zouch, Leics SK361165
Waymark
Named signs
Websites
www.leics.gov.uk
Maps ◈
OS Landranger: 128, 129, 140
OS Explorer: 232, 233, 245
Publications, badges and certificates
Leaflets
Ivanhoe Way (Leicestershire County Council) 2000. A5. £1.00. Cheques to Leicestershire County Council.

John Bunyan Trail JBUT

BEDS, HERTS **121km/75 miles**

The Trail was created by the Bedfordshire Group to celebrate the RA Diamond Jubilee and is dedicated to the memory of John Bunyan, the Puritan Evangelist and author of the book 'Pilgrim's Progress'. The route passes through a number of attractive villages and scenic countryside, taking in many places of historic interest connected with Bunyan. The waymarked Clay Way (11½ miles, map online) which follows the West Bedfordshire Clay Ridge is partly coincident with the Trail at Cranfield.

Attributes
Heritage; Literary; Religious
Start and Finish
Sundon Hills Country Park, Upper Sundon, Beds TL047286
Waymark
Silhouette of head and name on white disc
Websites
www.marstonvale.org
Maps ◈
OS Landranger: 153, 166
OS Explorer: 193, 208
Publications, badges and certificates
Leaflets
John Bunyan Trail: Section One (G. J. Edwards). A4/3. £0.60 (+ 1st class SAE).
John Bunyan Trail: Section Two (G. J. Edwards). A4/3. £0.60 (+ 1st class SAE).

Jubilee Way (Bernwood) JUBWBWD

BUCKS, OXON **98km/61 miles**

A celebration of the Queen's Golden Jubilee, a trail developed by the Bernwood Ancient Hunting Forest Project within the boundary of the ancient Forest that lies in Aylesbury Vale between Buckingham, Aylesbury, Thame and Oxford, and a chance to learn of its history. Starting from Brill, its historical administration centre, it crosses undulating rural terrain with a range of scenery and wildlife.

Attributes
Heritage
Start and Finish
Brill, Bucks SP656142
Waymark
Named arrows
Websites
www.buckscc.gov.uk, www.initiatives.smallwoods.org.uk
Maps
OS Landranger: 165
OS Explorer: 180, 181, 192
Publications, badges and certificates
Booklets
Bernwood Jubilee Way by Mark Bailey (Buckinghamshire County Council) 2002. 80pp (+ maps); 135 x 210. Free.

Jubilee Way (Leicestershire) JUBWL

LEICS, LINCS **34km/21 miles**

The Way, devised to mark the Queen's Silver Jubilee, connects the Leicestershire Round at Burrough Hall Country Park with the Viking Way at Woolsthorpe by following a meandering course, passing through Melton Mowbray and across pasture and woodland and past old ironstone workings near Eaton before climbing through woods to Belvoir castle from where there are fine views over the Vale of Belvoir. The waymarked Mowbray Way (9 miles and included on OS mapping) from Scalford on the Jubilee Way provides a second link to the Viking Way at Buckminster.

Attributes
Heritage
Start
Burrough Hall Country Park, Leics SK765116
Finish
Woolsthorpe by Belvoir, Lincs SK846336
Waymark
Orb, brown on yellow
Websites
www.leics.gov.uk
Maps ◈
OS Landranger: 129, 130
OS Explorer: 246, 247, 260
Publications, badges and certificates
Leaflets
Leicestershire Jubilee Way (Leicestershire County Council). A4/3. Free. Downloadable.
Mowbray Way (Leicestershire County Council) 2006. 12pp; A5. Free.

Jurassic Way JURW

LINCS, NORTHANTS, OXON, RUTLAND **142km/88 miles**

The Way follows the band of Jurassic Limestone that runs along the northern boundary of Northamptonshire going first along the Oxford Canal and then via Middleton Cheney and Woodford Halse to Braunston on the Grand Union Canal. Here it turns to pass between Market Harborough and Corby, following the Welland Valley to Rockingham with its castle.

Attributes
Canal; Downland/Wolds; Geological
Start
Banbury, Oxon SP460406
Finish
Stamford, Lincs TF041075
Waymark
Ammonite logo and name, black & white disc
Websites
www.explorenorthamptonshire.co.uk, www3.northamptonshire.gov.uk
Maps ◈
OS Landranger: 140, 141, 151, 152
OS Explorer: 191, 206, 222, 223, 224, 234
Publications, badges and certificates
Folder
Jurassic Way (Northamptonshire County Council) 1994. 3 leaflets; A4/3. £1.95 (+ 30p p&p). Northern Section not now available, Central and Southern still in print.

Kesgrave Outer Ring KESGOR

SUFFOLK **35km/22 miles**

A walk around Kesgrave via fields and woods and passing Martlesham Creek. The route is partly coincident with the Fynn Valley Walk (9 miles and named on OS mapping). It is the outer ring of a network of parish walks.

Attributes
No significant attribute
Start and Finish
Brendon Drive, Ipswich, Suffolk TM208448
Maps
OS Landranger: 169
OS Explorer: 197
Publications, badges and certificates
Folder
Parish Walks by Kesgrave Parish Council the Outer Ring and other walks (Kesgrave Town Council) 2008. Map and 9 leaflets; A5. £1.35 (incs p&p).
Leaflets
Fynn Valley Walk (Suffolk County Council). A4/3. £0.20 (+ 9 x 4 SAE).

Kett's Country Walk — KTCW

NORFOLK — **32km/20 miles**

A walk based on the 16th century activities of Robert Kett, who led Kett's rebellion in 1549, taking in a number of churches along a meandering route. The Norwich Riverside Walk links it to Marriott's Way.

Attributes
Heritage
Start
Cringleford, Norfolk TG200059
Finish
Wymondham, Norfolk TM109012
Waymark
Name in green on white disc
Websites
www.countrysideaccess.norfolk.gov.uk
Maps
OS Landranger: 134, 144
OS Explorer: 237
Publications, badges and certificates
Booklets
Kett's Country (Norfolk County Council) 1997. 12pp; A5. £0.50 (+ SAE).

Kingfisher Way — KFRW

BEDS, HERTS — **34km/21 miles**

The Way follows the course of the River Ivel from the source at Ivel Springs to where it meets the River Great Ouse, passing through the towns and villages of the Ivel Valley. The route links the Icknield Way path at Baldock with the Greensand Ridge Walk. The waymarked Navigator's Way (7 miles) based on Shefford and making use of the disused River Ivel Navigation, can be linked to the Kingfisher Way at Langford.

Attributes
River
Start
Baldock, Herts TL248342
Finish
Tempsford, Beds TL162535
Waymark
Name and/or Kingfisher profile in blue
Maps
OS Landranger: 153
OS Explorer: 193, 208
Publications, badges and certificates
Folder
Kingfisher Way (Ivel & Ouse Countryside Project). 4 leaflets. Free (+ 9 x 4 SAE).
Leaflets
Navigator's Way (Ivel & Ouse Countryside Project). Free (+ 9 x 4 SAE).

Lambourn Valley Way — LMVW

OXON, W BERKSHIRE — **35km/22 miles**

The Way runs from the Berkshire Downs near the Uffington White Horse to Newbury along the valley of the River Lambourn connecting the Ridgeway with the Kennet valley. The route passes through the villages of Lambourn, East Garston, Great Shefford and Boxford.

Attributes
River; Downland/Wolds
Start
Uffington Castle, Oxon SU292866
Finish
Newbury, W Berkshire SU472673
Waymark
Named discs and posts
Maps ◈
OS Landranger: 174
OS Explorer: 158, 170
Publications, badges and certificates
Leaflets
Lambourn Valley Way (West Berkshire District Council) 2001. A4/3. Free (+ SAE).

Lea Valley Walk LEAVP

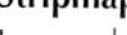

BEDS, ESSEX, HERTS, GTR LONDON, LUTON **85km/53 miles**

A route mainly on riverside paths, linking the source near the Icknield Way Path east of the Dunstable Downs to the London Docklands. It first follows the course of the river, which is variously spelt Lee and Lea, and then after a suburban diversion from the river at Welwyn, it takes the canalised navigations from Hertford, using wherever possible green waterside corridors. It passes the numerous reservoirs that line the Lea valley through North London. It incorporates the Upper Lea Valley Walk (9 miles and on OS mapping), the Cole Green Way west of Hertford, a multi-user trail including the route of a disused railway (leaflet PDF download is on the weblink), and the Lee Navigation towpath. The short Hertford Union Canal (c. 1.5km) links the River Lea Navigations and the Regent's Canal along the southern side of Victoria Park. En route towns traversed or passed to reach the London fringes are Luton, Harpenden, Wheathampstead, Welwyn/Hatfield, Hertford, Ware, Hoddesdon, Cheshunt and Waltham Abbey. In Greater London the Boroughs traversed are Enfield, Hackney, Haringey, Newham, Tower Hamlets and Waltham Forest. Within London the 13 miles of route is one of the Mayor of London's Strategic Walks – see the free leaflet listed below available from the Walk London weblink that also provides downloads. The Beane Valley Walk (14 miles) from Walkern, near Stevenage, provides a linear route along the gentle valley slopes of the River Beane to Hertford where it can be linked to the Lea Valley Walk. The Pymmes Brook Trail (10 miles and included on OS mapping) provides a link from the London Loop from Monken Hadley Common through Palmer's Green to the Lea Valley Walk at Pickett's Lock.

Attributes
Easy; Former Railway; River; Canal; Urban
Start
Leagrave, Beds TL061249
Finish
Bow Lock, Gtr London TQ383824
Waymark
Named discs with swan logo
Websites
www.leevalleypark.org.uk, www.walklondon.org.uk, www.leavalleywalk.org.uk, www.welhat.gov.uk
Maps
OS Landranger: 166, 176, 177
OS Explorer: 162, 173, 174, 182, 194, 193
Stripmap
Lee and Stort Navigations with East London Ring (GEOprojects)
Publications, badges and certificates
Paperbacks
Lea Valley Walk: From the Source to the Thames by Leigh Hatts (Cicerone Press) 2007. ISBN 9781852845223. 160pp; 174 x 117. £10.00 (+ £1.00 p&p). 2nd Edition.
Walking the River Lee Navigation: Walking from London to Hertford Via the River Lee Navigation (Canal Walks Series) by John Merrill (John Merrill Foundation) 2007. ISBN 9780955369186. 108pp. £9.95.
(plastic cover)
Short Circular Walks on the River Lee Navigation – Northern Volume by John Merrill (John Merrill Foundation) 2005. ISBN 9781903627686. 58pp; A5. £5.95. 10 – 5/6 Miles long circular walks on the River Lee Navigation, in Hertfordshire.
(spiral bound)
Short Circular Walks on the River Stort Navigation by John Merrill (John Merrill Foundation) 2006. ISBN 9781903627730. 92pp; A5. £8.95.
Booklets
Short Circular Walks on the River Lee Navigation – Southern Volume by John Merrill (John Merrill Foundation) 2006. ISBN 9781903627747. 77pp; A5. £6.95.
Leaflets
Lea Valley Walk: within London (Walk London – Strategic Walks Information Service) 2008. A2/8. Free (+ SAE). Downloads or order leaflets free from Walk London website.
Lea Valley Walks (Lee Valley Regional Park). On request from LVPA. Some leaflets downloadable from LVPA path weblink.
Beane Valley Walk (Hertfordshire County Council). A4/3. Free (+ SAE).
Pymmes Brook Trail (Barnet Council). A4/3. Free (+ SAE).
Pack
Alban Way, Cole Green Way, Ayot Greenway, Great North Way (Welwyn Hatfield Council). 5 leaflets in plastic wallet with activity map. Free.

Leicestershire Round LEICR

LEICS, RUTLAND **163km/101 miles**

A circuit of the county around Leicester within easy reach of the market towns of Oakham, Melton Mowbray, Hinkley, Loughborough, and Lutterworth, taking in Burrough Hill, Foxton Locks, High Cross, Bosworth and Charnwood Forest.

Attributes
Heritage
Start and Finish
Burrough Hill, Leics SK766115
Waymark
Circle of brown arrows on standard waymarks
Websites
www.leics.gov.uk
Maps ◈
OS Landranger: 129, 140, 141
OS Explorer: 222, 223, 232, 233, 234, 245, 246
Publications, badges and certificates
Paperbacks
Leicestershire Round (Leicestershire County Council) 1996. ISBN 9780850223903. 126pp; 116 x 170. £5.00 (+ £1.00 p&p). New edition in preparation.
Badge
Leicestershire Round (Leicestershire Footpath Association). £2.50 (+ SAE).

Leighton – Linslade Loop LEIGLL

BEDS **32km/20 miles**

A walk encircling Leighton Buzzard via woods, villages, fields and along a towpath. The walk connects with the Grand Union Canal Walk and the Greensand Ridge Walk.

Attributes
No significant attribute
Start and Finish
Stockgrove Country Park, Heath and Reach, Bedfordshire SP920294
Websites
http://jduxbury.users.btopenworld.com
Maps
OS Landranger: 165
OS Explorer: 192
Publications, badges and certificates
Leaflets
Leighton Buzzard Millennium Walks by RA Leighton Buzzard (RA Leighton Buzzard) 2000. Free (+ 2 x 1st class stamps). Also from Libraries, Countryside Parks and Tourist Information Centres in the region.

Mansell Way MANW

ESSEX **32km/20 miles**

Remembering Dennis Mansell, photographer, journalist and hill walker, it circuits around Braintree, visits the valleys of the Rivers Pant, Blackwater and Brain.

Attributes
River
Start and Finish
Braintree, Essex TL761228
Maps
OS Landranger: 167
OS Explorer: 195
Publications, badges and certificates
Booklets
Mansell Way by Edgar Eastall, John Spratling (Braintree & District Outdoor Pursuits) 1993. 18pp; A5. £1.00 (+ A5 SAE).

Marriott's Way MARW

NORFOLK **34km/21 miles**

A peaceful and secluded walk along a former railway line near to the River Wensum. At Hellesdon it can be linked with the Norwich Riverside Walk (5 miles; downloadable publication), and at Aylsham to the Bure Valley Path (9 miles and included on OS mapping; no publication) which, alongside the Bure Valley Railway, follows the River Bure through Coltishall to Wroxham. The Bickling Hall link path (1 mile; no publication), near Cawston can be used to connect with the Weavers' Way.

Attributes
Easy; Former Railway; Cycle Route
Start
Hellesdon Bridge, Norfolk TG197100
Finish
Aylsham, Norfolk TG195265
Websites
www.countrysideaccess.norfolk.gov.uk, www.visitnorwich.co.uk
Maps ◈
OS Landranger: 133, 134
OS Explorer: 237, 238, 252
Publications, badges and certificates
Leaflets
Marriott's Way (Norfolk County Council) 1996. A4/3. £0.50 (+ SAE). Also available from TICs and some local Libraries.

Mid Suffolk Footpath MSFP

SUFFOLK **32km/20 miles**

The footpath broadly follows the valleys of the rivers Dove and Gipping via Eye, Thorndon and Mendlesham. The start of the walk connects with the Angles Way whilst near the end of the route is the waymarked

Gipping Valley River Path (17 miles and on OS mapping – road link) which takes the walker on to Ipswich.

Attributes
River
Start
Hoxne, Suffolk TM184782
Finish
Stowmarket Greens Meadow, Suffolk TM042599
Waymark
Named discs with poppy logo
Websites
www.suffolk.gov.uk
Maps ◈
OS Landranger: 155, 156
OS Explorer: 211, 230
Publications, badges and certificates
Folder
Mid Suffolk Footpath (Mid Suffolk District Council) 1998. 5 leaflets; 229 x 127. £1.50 (incs p&p).

Midshires Way MDSW

BUCKS, DERBYS, GTR MAN, LEICS, MILTON K, NORTHANTS, NOTTS **362km/225 miles**

The Way, designed for multi-use, links the Ridgeway National Trail with the Trans Pennine Trail across the shires of Middle England. For the most part it follows bridleways and quiet lanes with, wherever possible, alternative waymarked footpath routes provided for walkers. In Derbyshire particularly, the bridleway development for other users has yet to be completed. The Brampton Valley Way (14 miles) is used between Boughton Crossing near Northampton and Little Bowden Crossing near Market Harborough. From Whaley Bridge in Derbyshire to Compstall in Greater Manchester the route is coincident with the Goyt Way (10 miles; see also E-Routes – E2). After this, part of the Etherow-Goyt Valley Way is used to the finish. All three Ways are named on OS mapping. The folder listed below has details of the whole route and it is also obtainable from the Leicestershire website which has maps of the Leicestershire section. Long Horse Bridge between Shardlow and Sawley has been dismantled. There are plans to rebuild this by summer 2009, and until it is replaced walkers cannot cross the Trent at this point and need to use the diversion.

Attributes
Horse Ride (Multi User)
Start
Bledlow, Bucks SP770012
Finish
Stockport, Gtr Man SJ893903
Waymark
Named discs with letters MW in linked acorn form
Websites
www.leics.gov.uk, www.leics.gov.uk
Maps ◈
OS Landranger: 109, 110, 119, 128, 129, 141, 152, 165
OS Explorer: 181, 192, 207, 223, 233, 245, 246, 259, 260, 268, 269, 277, 1, 24
Publications, badges and certificates
Paperbacks
Walking the Midshires Way: A Long-distance Walk Through Middle England by Ron Haydock, Bill Allen (Sigma Leisure) 2003. ISBN 9781850587781. 160pp. £6.95.
Folder
Midshires Way (Derbyshire County Council) 1994. 12pp; A5. £3.00 (+ £1.00 p&p). County sections from each Council: check price/availability with them.
Leaflets
Brampton Valley Way (Northamptonshire County Council) 1993. A4/3. £0.75 (+ 20p p&p).
Goyt Way (Derbyshire County Council). £0.10.

Nar Valley Way NARVW

NORFOLK **54km/34 miles**

A route contained almost entirely within the watershed of the River Nar, visiting many attractive villages and historical sites. The walk links with the Peddars Way at Castle Acre. An extension from Gressenhall into East Dereham is included.

Attributes
River
Start
King's Lynn, Norfolk TF616198
Finish
Gressenhall, Norfolk TF975169
Waymark
Named signposts & white named discs
Websites
www.countrysideaccess.norfolk.gov.uk, www.west-norfolk.gov.uk
Maps ◈
OS Landranger: 132, 143
OS Explorer: 236, 238, 250
Publications, badges and certificates
Booklets
Introduction to the Nar Valley Way by C. Andrews,

D. Dear (Pathway Publishing) 1999. ISBN 9780952662853. 36pp; 206 x 146. £3.00 (incs p&p).

Leaflets

Nar Valley Way (Norfolk County Council). A5. £0.50 (+ SAE). Also available from TICs and some local Libraries.

Nelson Way — NELW

ESSEX, HANTS, GTR LONDON, NORFOLK, SUFFOLK, SURREY — **682km/424 miles**

An historical walk linking locations associated with Horatio Nelson following a route from Burnham Thorpe in Norfolk. It takes in coastlines, rivers, broads, heathland, fields, forests, hills, villages, towns and cities.

Attributes

Coastal; River; Heath; Moorland; Heritage; Military

Start

Burnham Thorpe, Norfolk TF853414

Finish

HMS Victory, Portsmouth SU628006

Maps

OS Landranger: 132, 133, 134, 155, 156, 167, 168, 169, 177, 178, 186, 187, 196, 197

OS Explorer: 40, 119, 120, 133, 145, 146, 161, 162, 174, 183, 184, 195, 196, 197, 212, 231, 251, 252

Publications, badges and certificates

Paperbacks

Nelson Way by Les Ham (Trafford Publishing) 2002. ISBN 9781412054751. 212pp. £11.49 (+ £1.00 p&p).

Nene Way — NENW

CAMBS, LINCS, NORTHANTS, PETERBORO — **177km/110 miles**

A route along the Nene Valley including canalised riverbank passing through Northampton, Wellingborough, Oundle, Peterborough and Wisbech. See website below for route through Northamptonshire. At Badby, Northamptonshire, the waymarked Knightley Way (12 miles and included on OS mapping) visits Foxley, Farthingstone and Fawsley Park to end at Greens Norton at the end of the Grafton Way (see North Bucks Way). At Sutton Bridge there is a link with the Peter Scott Walk (10 miles and on OS mapping) that remembers the famous naturalist who lived at the lighthouse. At Wadenhoe, the linking Lyveden Way (10 miles) includes Fermyn Woods Country Park, Lyveden New Bield, an Elizabethan lodge and moated garden, and Wadenhoe.

Attributes

River; Canal

Start

Badby, Northants SP560588

Finish

Car Park opposite Guy's Head, Sutton Bridge, Lincs TF492255

Waymark

Named signposts

Websites

www.cambridgeshire.gov.uk, www3.northamptonshire.gov.uk

Maps ◈

OS Landranger: 131, 141, 142, 143, 152, 153

OS Explorer: 207, 223, 224, 227, 234, 235, 249, 206

Publications, badges and certificates

Leaflets

Nene Way: A Cambridgeshire Country Walk (Cambridgeshire County Council). A5. £0.30. Tel: 01223 717445.

Paperbacks

Wilderness Walks: Twelve Guided Wildlife Walks Along the North Norfolk Coast by David North (Larks Press) 1993. ISBN 9780948400193. 40pp; 204 x 144. £2.50.

Leaflets

Peter Scott Walk (Norfolk County Council). A4/3. Free (+ SAE).

Lyveden Way (Northamptonshire County Council). Free.

New River Path — NRP

HERTS, GTR LONDON — **45km/28 miles**

A walk along a man-made channel dug in the early 17th century to bring clean water into London following the channel as closely as possible, from open countryside with riverside paths, to the inner city streets. Here from the 'Castle' at Stoke Newington, it finishes with a 3-mile Heritage Section, on the historic but now truncated course through open spaces and on-street. This ends at the New River Head, an historic complex of installations and buildings mostly visible from Nautilus House garden, off Myddelton Passage, with a visitor information point (for its opening times see the Thames Water booklet). As well as the open channels, the New River runs in some straightened and piped sections. The riverside paths include permissive sections restricted to use by walkers, who must observe safety notices and any diversion when closures are required for operational reasons. In 1985 the New River was threatened with closure and the New River Action Group led those urging Thames Water to preserve the route as a long distance path, with the company making a substantial investment in the walking route including providing the route booklet. The New River is an important resource for leisure and wildlife.

Attributes
Easy; River; Heritage
Start
South bank of River Lea near Hertford, Herts TL340138
Finish
New River Head, Rosebery Avenue, Islington, Gtr London TQ314827
Waymark
Named posts/NR logo
Websites
www.newriver.free-online.co.uk, www.newriver.org.uk
Maps
OS Landranger: 166, 176, 177
OS Explorer: 173, 174, 194
Publications, badges and certificates
Booklets
New River Path (Thames Water). 28pp; A4/3. Free.
Paperbacks
Exploring the New River: Hertford to Stoke Newington by Michael Essex-Lopresti (Brewin Books Ltd) 1997. ISBN 9781858580685. 102pp; 148 x 209. £8.95 (+ £2.00 p&p).
Booklets
Historical walk along the New River : Stoke Newington to Islington by Mary Cosh (Islington Archaeology & History Society) 2001. ISBN 9780950753270. 32pp; A5. £4.99 (incs p&p).

North Bedfordshire Heritage Trail — NBHT

BEDS — **113km/70 miles**

The Trail passes through 23 villages including Bromham, Odell, Riseley, Wilden and Sandy, two country parks and by 30 public houses.

NORTH BEDFORDSHIRE HERITAGE TRAIL

Attributes
No significant attribute
Start and Finish
St Paul's Square, Bedford, Beds TL049497
Waymark
River, bridge, church in blue/white disc, not signed on fields
Maps
OS Landranger: 153
OS Explorer: 208
Publications, badges and certificates
Leaflets
North Bedfordshire Heritage Trail (G. J. Edwards). A4/3. Free (+ 9 x 4 SAE).

North Bucks Way — NBUW

BUCKS, MILTON K — **53km/33 miles**

Set up by the Ramblers Association in 1972, it is a walk from the Ridgeway at Chequers Nature Reserve to the county boundary at Pulpit Hill Nature Reserve, crossing the Vale of Aylesbury and taking in a number of villages. It connects with the Cross Bucks Way at Addington. At Wolverton the waymarked Grafton Way (13 miles and on OS mapping) leads to Greens Norton to join with the Knightley Way (see Nene Way). The Tramway Trail (6 miles) provides an alternative connection between Quainton and Waddesdon, the route taking to the Brill Tramway and the grounds of Waddesdon Manor. The Ouse Valley Walk (13 miles) follows the River Great Ouse between Buckingham and Milton Keynes and connects with the North Bucks Way at Iron Viaduct.

NORTH BUCKS WAY BUCKINGHAMSHIRE COUNTY COUNCIL BRIDLEWAY

Attributes
No significant attribute
Start
Pulpit Hill Nature Reserve, Great Kimble, Princes Risborough, Bucks SP830053
Finish
Wolverton, Milton Keynes, Bucks SP806413
Waymark
Named discs, with Bucks swan
Websites
www.milton-keynes.gov.uk, www.buckscc.gov.uk
Maps ◈
OS Landranger: 152, 165
OS Explorer: 181, 192, 207
Publications, badges and certificates
Leaflets
North Bucks Way (Buckinghamshire County Council). A4/3. Free (+ SAE).
Package
Pack 1: Vale of Aylesbury Countryside Pack (Buckinghamshire County Council). £3 per pack or £5 for both. 19 recreational routes from Westbury in the north to Stoke Mandeville and Bishopstone in the south.

Ouse Valley Way — OVW

BEDS, BUCKS, CAMBS, MILTON K, NORFOLK, NORTHANTS — **229km/142 miles**

A source-to-sea route on one of England's longest rivers, it follows the River Great Ouse on its meandering passage. It passes through Stowe Park to reach Buckingham, fringes north of Milton Keynes and Newport Pagnell, then heads via Emberton Country Park to Sharnbrook (with H E Bates connections), visits Bedford's Priory Park and passes a Danish Camp at Willingdon. It links St Neots, Huntingdon (Cromwell's birthplace), St Ives and Earith, and the Stretham Old Engine tells the story of the draining of the Fens. Before Ely, with its cathedral visible on the skyline, it meets the River Cam, and after Ely it runs in common with the Fen Rivers Way, crossing the Bedford Level to Downham Market and Kings Lynn, where the river finally flows out into the Wash. Rolling Buckinghamshire countryside gives way to open black-soiled fenland landscapes, now sunk metres below the elevated riverbanks. Stretches leave the river to avoid areas flood-prone in winter and there is some road walking, some alongside busy roads. A full route descriptions may be downloaded from the route's website. The former Ouse Valley Walk (13 miles) follows the River Great Ouse between Buckingham and Milton Keynes and connects with the North Bucks Way at Iron Viaduct.

Attributes
Easy; River; Canal; Heritage; Industrial History; Literary
Start
King's Head Pub, Syresham, Northants SP631415
Finish
Kings Lynn, Norfolk TF617198
Waymark
Named discs with two swans on water (Beds); swan, water and tree logo (Cambs)
Websites
www.ousevalleyway.org.uk, www.buckscc.gov.uk
Maps ◈
OS Landranger: 142, 143, 153, 154, 132, 152
OS Explorer: 208, 225, 236, 226, 207, 228, 206
Publications, badges and certificates
Booklets
Ouse Valley Way: Bedford to St Neots (Bedford Rural Communities Charity) 2004. A5. Free (+ A5 SAE).
Folder
Ouse Valley Way: Eaton Socon to Earith (Huntingdon District Council) 2000. 7 leaflets; A4/3. £3.00 (post free).
Certificate
Ouse Valley Way (Huntingdon District Council). Free (+ A4 SAE). For the 26 mile section in Huntingdonshire.

Oxford Green Belt Way — OGBW

OXON — **80km/50 miles**

A route by the Campaign to Protect Rural England (CPRE) Oxfordshire branch celebrating both its 75th anniversary and 50 years of Oxford's Green Belt, and marking the significance of the Green Belt in protecting the open countryside surrounding England's cities. The route has one mile for each year since the designation of Green Belts in 1956. It passes through some of Oxfordshire's most picturesque countryside and historic villages, and alongside delightful stretches of the River Thames near Abingdon and the Oxford Canal north of Oxford, and links four of Oxford's Park & Ride sites and is crossed by major bus routes.

Attributes
River
Start and Finish
Thornhill Park & Ride, Oxon SP565074
Waymark
Green edged disc with name and yellow arrow
Websites
www.greenbeltway.org.uk
Maps
OS Landranger: 164
OS Explorer: 180, 170
Publications, badges and certificates
Paperbacks
CPRE Oxford Green Belt Way by Gordon Garroway (CPRE Oxfordshire – Campaign to Protect Rural England) 2007. ISBN 9780955772306. 48pp. £5.00 (+ £1.00 p&p).
Leaflets
Oxford Green Belt Way (CPRE Oxfordshire – Campaign to Protect Rural England). Free (+ SAE).

Poppyline Marathon — POPM

NORFOLK — **42km/26 miles**

An undulating route in North Norfolk, partly coincident with the Norfolk Coast Path, in an area traversed by the North Norfolk Railway, known locally as the Poppyline.

Attributes
Challenging; Anytime Challenge; Former Railway; Coastal
Start and Finish
Sheringham, Norfolk TG159430
Websites
www.notadog.org.uk
Maps
OS Landranger: 133
OS Explorer: 251, 252
Publications, badges and certificates
Looseleaf
Poppyline Marathon (Bobbie Sauerzapf) 1997. 2pp; A4. Free (+ SAE).

Badge & certificate
Poppyline Marathon (Bobbie Sauerzapf). £1.50 (+ A4 SAE).

Roach Valley Way ROAVW

ESSEX **37km/23 miles**

A route around south-east Essex which takes in a variety of landscapes including the ancient woodlands of Hockley and the coastal margins of the Roach and Crouch estuaries.

Attributes
Easy; Coastal; River
Start and Finish
Rochford, Essex TQ873905
Waymark
Blue/yellow river scene & name
Maps ◈
OS Landranger: 168, 178
OS Explorer: 175, 176
Publications, badges and certificates
Booklets
Roach Valley Way (Essex County Council) 1997. ISBN 9781852811495. 16pp; A5. £2.50.

Rutland Round RUTR

RUTLAND **104km/65 miles**

A circular walk round the county of Rutland, always inside, or on the border. In five sections, it can be started at any point and travelled in either direction. Diversions are made to visit Rutland Water and the County town of Oakham.

Attributes
Lake/Reservoir
Start and Finish
Rutland County Museum, Oakham, Rutland SK863086
Waymark
Green and yellow named signs, acorn and CPRE logo
Maps
OS Landranger: 130, 141
OS Explorer: 234, 247
Publications, badges and certificates
Paperbacks
Rutland Round by John Williams (Cordee Ltd) 2000. ISBN 9781871890440. 48pp; 210 x 138. £4.99.

Rutland Water Challenge Walk RWCW

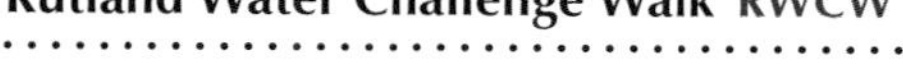

RUTLAND **38km/24 miles**

A route around the largest man-made reservoir in Europe.

Attributes
Easy; Anytime Challenge; Lake/Reservoir
Start and Finish
Rutland Water, Rutland SK935083
Maps
OS Landranger: 141
OS Explorer: 234
Publications, badges and certificates
Booklets
Rutland Water Challenge Walk by John Merrill (John Merrill Foundation). ISBN 9780907496885. 36pp; A5. £4.50 (+ £1.00 p&p). Cheques to John Merrill Foundation.
Badge & certificate
Rutland Water Challenge Walk (John Merrill Foundation). £5.00 (incs p&p).

Saffron Trail SAFFRT

ESSEX **116km/72 miles**

The route traverses the County of Essex from south-east to north-west crossing the Essex Way at Great Waltham. After the coast at Haddleigh Country Park the route turns inland, initially urban, but later in open countryside. The River Crouch is reached at Hullbridge and it is followed to Battlesbridge, associated with the battle of Ashingdon in 1016. The Chelmer is followed to the confluence with the River Cam, which in turn is followed through Chelmsford to Great Dunmow, then in undulating countryside to the finish.

Attributes
Easy; Coastal; River; Urban
Start
Southend on Sea, Essex TQ883851
Finish
Saffron Walden, Essex TL537386
Waymark
Crocus
Websites
www.essexarearamblers.co.uk
Maps
OS Landranger: 167, 178
OS Explorer: 175, 183, 195

Publications, badges and certificates
Booklets
Saffron Trail by David Hitchman (Redbridge Ramblers) 2009. 40pp. £3.50 (incs p&p).

Sandlings Walk SANDLW

SUFFOLK 89km/55 miles

The route encompasses lowland habitats using riverside, forest and heathland paths. It passes through Martlesham Heath, Woodbridge, Rendlesham Forest, Snape and Sizewell. At its start at Southwold, it connects with the Suffolk Coast and Heaths Path that continues north up the coast to Lowestoft. See Suffolk Coast and Heaths Path – together these routes provide for a number of shorter circular options.

Attributes
Coastal; River; Heath
Start
Southwold, Suffolk TM512768
Finish
Rushmere Heath, Ipswich, Suffolk TM197453
Waymark
Stylised nightjar logo
Websites
www.suffolkcoastandheaths.org, www.rspb.org.uk
Maps ◈
OS Landranger: 156, 169
OS Explorer: 197, 212, 231
Publications, badges and certificates
Folder
Sandlings Walk by Suffolk Coast & Heaths Project (Suffolk Coast and Heaths Project) 2001. 11 laminated leaflets. £4.75 (+ £1.00 p&p). Cheques to Suffolk County Council.
Paperbacks
Sandlings Walks: 20 Circular Walks Around the Suffolk Coast & Heaths by Simon Malone (Larks Press) 2007. ISBN 9781904006381. 104pp; 206 x 144. £6.50.

Shakespeare's Avon Way SHAW

GLOS, NORTHANTS, WARKS, WORCS 142km/88 miles

It follows the course of the River Avon as closely as possible using existing public footpaths, bridleways and a few minor roads, from its source at Naseby to its confluence with the Severn at Tewkesbury, passing through Warwick, Stratford upon Avon and Evesham. Naseby, Tewkesbury and Evesham were the sites of decisive battles. Tewkesbury, Pershore and Evesham have historic abbeys and Warwick and Kenilworth castles. Bredon Hill, visible from the later stages of the path, is visited by a detour. The 'Walking with William Shakespeare' book below provides shorter walks linked with extracts from Shakespeare's works, and covers Warwickshire and London. The River Avon book covers the river not the path.

Attributes
River; Literary; Charity
Start
Source of Avon, near Naseby, Northants SP688781
Finish
Severn/Avon confluence, Tewkesbury, Glos SO888331
Waymark
White arrow with Shakespeare's head and river symbol on green disc with name
Websites
www.shakespearesavonway.org
Maps
OS Landranger: 140, 141, 150, 151
OS Explorer: 190, 205, 221, 222, 223
Publications, badges and certificates
Paperbacks
Shakespeare's Avon Way (Shakespeare's Avon Way Association). 56pp. £6.25 (incs p&p). Available from SAWA website.
Walking with William Shakespeare by Anne-Marie Edwards (Jones Books) 2005. ISBN 9780976353904. 224pp; 212 x 140. £9.95.
River Avon: A Journey Following the River from Tewkesbury to Its Source by John Bradford (Hunt End Books) 2006. ISBN 9780954981310. 172pp; 232 x 212. £12.95.
Booklets
Shakespeare's Avon Way: The Upstream Supplement (Shakespeare's Avon Way Association). £4.75 (post free). Available from SAWA website.
Shakespeare's Avon Way: Planner (Shakespeare's Avon Way Association). £3.25 (incs p&p). Available from SAWA website.

South Bucks Way SBUW

BUCKS 37km/23 miles

From the Ridgeway the route descends through woodland to the source of the River Misbourne which it follows through Amersham to Denham where it joins the River Colne and ends on the towpath of the Grand Union Canal.

Attributes
River; Canal; Downland/Wolds

Start
Coombe Hill, Bucks SP849067
Finish
Denham, Bucks TQ053862
Waymark
Standard waymark with name and swan logo
Websites
www.buckscc.gov.uk
Maps ◈
OS Landranger: 165, 175, 176
OS Explorer: 172, 181
Publications, badges and certificates
Leaflets
South Bucks Way (Buckinghamshire County Council). A4/3. Free (+ SAE).

Southend Millennium Walk SNDMW

ESSEX, SOUTHEND **39km/24 miles**

Devised by the Ramblers Association, it covers all aspects of the town from the famous Golden Mile featuring the longest pier in the world, the surrounding golden sands to the beautiful countryside that surrounds the town.

Attributes
Easy; Coastal
Start and Finish
Southend Leisure Centre, Southend TQ898875
Waymark
Named discs
Maps
OS Landranger: 178
OS Explorer: 175
Publications, badges and certificates
Booklets
Ramblers' Millennium Walk Around Southend-on-Sea by David Hitchman (Southend Borough Council) 2000. 16pp; A5. £1.00 (+ A5 SAE).

St Alban's Way STALBW

ESSEX, HERTS **40km/25 miles**

Across the gentle Hertfordshire landscape, it links two major pilgrimage centres and Abbey churches: Waltham Abbey (Augustinian) and The Cathedral and Abbey Church of St Alban (Benedictine). The route also visits the 14th-century church at North Nymms.

Attributes
Anytime Challenge; Heritage; Pilgrimage
Start
Waltham Abbey, Essex TL382006
Finish
St Albans Cathedral, St Albans, Herts TL145070
Maps
OS Landranger: 166
OS Explorer: 174, 182
Publications, badges and certificates
Booklets
St Alban's Way by John Merrill (John Merrill Foundation) 2006. ISBN 9780955369131. 48pp. £5.95 (+ £1.00 p&p). Cheques to John Merrill Foundation.
Badge & certificate
St Alban's Way (John Merrill Foundation) 2006. £5.00 (incs p&p).

St Edmund Way STEDW

ESSEX, SUFFOLK **127km/79 miles**

A route across Suffolk, using the Stour Valley Path (East Anglia) to Sudbury and Long Melford and then going via Lavenham and Little Welnetham to Bury St Edmunds, burial place of the martyr King Edmund slain by the Danes in 869, along the waymarked Lark Valley Path to the Icknield Way Path at West Stow before striking over the Brecks to Thetford and the Hereward Way. Marked on OS maps but no current publication.

Attributes
River
Start
Manningtree, Essex TM094322
Finish
Brandon, Suffolk TL784866
Maps ◈
OS Landranger: 144, 155, 168, 169
OS Explorer: 184, 196, 211, 229
Publications, badges and certificates
Leaflets
Lark Valley Path (Brecks Countryside Project) 1997. A4/3. £0.20 (+ SAE).

Stort Valley Way STORTVW

ESSEX, HERTS **45km/28 miles**

A circuit around Harlow, the River Stort Navigation is followed to Sawbridgeworth from where the villages of Sheering, Matching, Magdalen Laver and Epping Green are visited. A relatively low level walk, never more than 400ft above sea level, and only 1200ft of ascent.

Attributes
River
Start and Finish
Roydon, Essex TL406105
Waymark
Dragonfly on green and yellow named discs
Maps ◈
OS Landranger: 166, 167
OS Explorer: 174, 183, 194
Publications, badges and certificates
Leaflets
Stort Valley Way (Epping Forest Countrycare) 1996. A4/3. Free (+ SAE).

Stour and Orwell Walk S&OW

SUFFOLK **67km/42 miles**

The walk is an extension west from Felixstowe to the Suffolk Coast and Heaths Path and follows the coast and heaths along the estuaries of the Orwell and the Stour, going around the Shotley peninsula to Cattawade, providing links with the Essex Way (at Manningtree, across the river) and the Stour Valley Path (East Anglia) (at Cattawade). On OS mapping, Landranger maps show the Stour and Orwell Path combined while Explorer maps name them both.

Attributes
Coastal; River; Heath
Start
Felixstowe, Suffolk TM324363
Finish
Cattawade, Suffolk TM101333
Waymark
Named signs
Websites
www.suffolkcoastandheaths.org
Maps ◈
OS Landranger: 169
OS Explorer: 197
Publications, badges and certificates
Folder
Stour & Orwell Walk by Annette Lea (Suffolk Coast and Heaths Project). 5 map cards. £4.00 (+ £1.00 p&p). Cheques to Suffolk County Council (includes accommodation list).

Stour Valley Path (East Anglia) SVPEA

CAMBS, ESSEX, SUFFOLK **96km/60 miles**

The Path follows the river valley downstream and links the Icknield Way path, which it crosses at Stetchworth, with Sudbury and the Essex Way at Manningtree passing through some of the most attractive country in East Anglia, including Constable country towards the end around East Bergholt. It provides part of the E2 E-Route. The waymarked Bury to Clare Walk (19 miles and on OS mapping) provides a link from the Path at Clare Castle to Bury St Edmunds (see St Edmund Way).

Attributes
River
Start
Newmarket, Suffolk TL646636
Finish
Cattawade, Suffolk TM101332

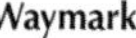

Waymark
Named discs and posts with stylised river and dragonfly logo
Websites
www.dedhamvalestourvalley.org
Maps ◈
OS Landranger: 154, 155, 168, 169
OS Explorer: 184, 195, 196, 197, 210, 226
Publications, badges and certificates
Folder
Stour Valley Path (Suffolk County Council) 2001. 10 route cards; A5. £3.50 (incs p&p). With accommodation and public transport details.
Leaflets
Bury to Clare Walk (St Edmundsbury Borough Council). A5. £0.20 (post free).

Suffolk Coast and Heaths Path SCHP

SUFFOLK **80km/50 miles**

The Path follows rights of way and permissive paths along the Suffolk Heritage Coast north from Felixstowe on river and sea walls and across marsh, heath, foreshore and low cliffs and via the foot ferry to Bawdsey. It then follows the river wall along the large shingle spit of Orford Ness to meet the River Alde at Snape Maltings and regain the coast at the festival town of Aldeburgh and from there it follows the coast to Lowestoft Harbour. The Sandlings Walk takes a route generally inland from the Suffolk Coast and Heaths Path that runs broadly parallel, particularly south of Snape towards Ipswich where the Sandlings route snakes across the inland heaths and forests, while the Path returns to the coast. Between Snape and Southwold the two routes meet and cross several times. Near Dunwich both routes skirt the RSPB Minsmere Nature Reserve (link below), the Path here going along the coast and the Walk inland. These intersections provide for a number of circular options for shorter walks.

Attributes
Coastal; Heath
Start
Felixstowe, Suffolk TM313349
Finish
Lowestoft, Suffolk TM548926
Waymark
Small named yellow and purple markers (being replaced by Suffolk Coast Path)
Websites
www.suffolkcoastandheaths.org, www.rspb.org.uk
Maps ◈
OS Landranger: 134, 156, 169
OS Explorer: 197, 212, 231, 40
Publications, badges and certificates
Folder
Suffolk Coast & Heaths Path (Suffolk Coast and Heaths Project) 2000. 8 water-resistant maps; A5. £4.00 (+ £1.00 p&p). Cheques to Suffolk County Council (includes transport booklet).
Paperbacks
Sandlings Walks: 20 Circular Walks Around the Suffolk Coast & Heaths by Simon Malone (Larks Press) 2007. ISBN 9781904006381. 104pp; 206 x 144. £6.50.

Swan's Way — SWW

BUCKS, MILTON K, NORTHANTS, OXON — **106km/66 miles**

From the Northants border the route crosses the Vale of Aylesbury to meet the Ridgeway near Princes Risborough and then follows the chalk slopes of the Chilterns to the Thames at Goring. There is a link with the Cross Bucks Way at Swanbourne. The Judge's Ride (16 miles), coincident for short sections with the Swan's Way and the Ridgeway, provides a link to Stoke Row, the location of the Maharajah's Well.

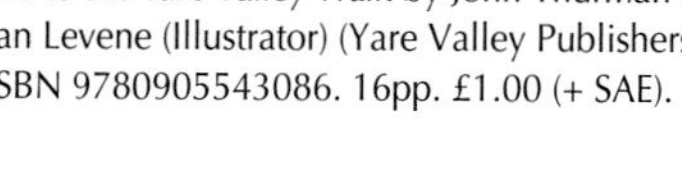

Attributes
Horse Ride (Multi User); Downland/ Wolds
Start
Salcey Forest, Milton K SP810509
Finish
Goring-on-Thames, Oxon SU601808
Waymark
Swan's head in horseshoe on named discs
Websites
www.buckscc.gov.uk
Maps ◈
OS Landranger: 152, 164, 165, 174, 175
OS Explorer: 171, 181, 192, 207
Publications, badges and certificates
Leaflets
Swan's Way (Buckinghamshire County Council). A4/3. Free (+ SAE).
Judge's Ride (Oxfordshire County Council). A4/3. £0.40 (+ SAE). Downloadable.

Tas Valley Way — TASVW

NORFOLK — **42km/26 miles**

The Way goes through Intwood, Swardeston, Mulbarton and Hapton and then follows the course of the River Tas to the source near to New Buckenham, with 16 churches and towns or villages en route. At Cringleford there are links with the Ketts Country Walk and Yare Valley Walk (7 miles), the latter following the valley of the River Yare and returning along the wooded southern slopes. The linking waymarked Upper Tas Valley Walk (19 miles and on OS mapping) starts at Hethersett, heading to the source.

Attributes
River
Start
Cringleford, Norfolk TG200059
Finish
Attleborough, Norfolk TM045952
Waymark
Named yellow discs

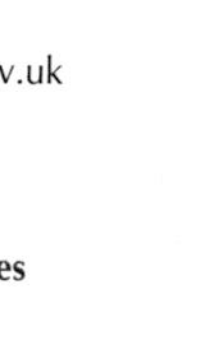

Websites
www.countrysideaccess.norfolk.gov.uk
Maps
OS Landranger: 134, 144
OS Explorer: 237
Publications, badges and certificates
Leaflets
Tas Valley Way (Norfolk County Council). A5. £0.50 (+ SAE).
Booklets
Guide to the Yare Valley Walk by John Thurman (Editor), Ian Levene (Illustrator) (Yare Valley Publishers) 2004. ISBN 9780905543086. 16pp. £1.00 (+ SAE).

Three Shires Way 3SHW

BEDS, CAMBS, MILTON K, NORTHANTS 79km/49 miles

A bridleway running through quiet rural landscape and remnants of ancient woodland. Linking with the Swan's Way at the start, it takes in the county boundaries of Bucks, Beds and Northants at Threeshire Wood. The original Grafham Water Circular Ride, around the reservoir (12.4 miles) has now been added to the route at the finish to make the total distance 49 miles.

Attributes
Horse Ride (Multi User); Lake/Reservoir
Start
Tathall End, Milton K SP820468
Finish
Grafham Water, Cambs TL144697
Waymark
Triple-linked horseshoes
Websites
www.visitely.eastcambs.gov.uk, www.cambridgeshire.gov.uk
Maps ◈
OS Landranger: 152, 153
OS Explorer: 207, 224, 225
Publications, badges and certificates
Leaflets
Three Shires Way (Cambridgeshire County Council) 1990. A4/3. Free.
Grafham Water Circular Ride (Anglian Water Leisure). Free.

Walsingham Way – Ely to Walsingham WALSW

CAMBS, NORFOLK, SUFFOLK 117km/73 miles

First in a series of three pilgrimage walks to Walsingham. The route, via the fens, takes in Brandon, Swaffham, and Rougham.

Attributes
Easy; Anytime Challenge; Lake/Reservoir; Pilgrimage; Religious
Start
TIC, Ely, Cambs TL538802
Finish
Slipper Chapel, Little Walsingham, Norfolk TF934369
Maps
OS Landranger: 132, 143
OS Explorer: 228, 229, 236, 238, 251
Publications, badges and certificates
Booklets
Walsingham Way: King's Lynn to Walsingham (John Merrill Foundation). ISBN 9781903627419. £5.95 (+ £1.00 p&p). Cheques to John Merrill Foundation.
Pilgrim Way Series
Walsingham Way: Ely to Walsingham by John Merrill (John Merrill Foundation) 2003. ISBN 9781903627334. 56pp; 145 x 210. £6.95 (+ £1.00 p&p). Cheques to John Merrill Foundation.
Walsingham Way: London to Walsingham (John Merrill Foundation). ISBN 9781903627334. £6.95 (+ £1.00 p&p). Cheques to John Merrill Foundation.
Badge & certificate
Walsingham Way (John Merrill Foundation). £5.00 (incs p&p).

Walsingham Way – King's Lynn to Walsingham WWKLTW

NORFOLK 56km/35 miles

Second in a series of three pilgrimages to Walsingham, the route takes in North Wootton, Castle Rising, West Newton, Great Bircham, Docking, Stanhoe and North Creake.

Attributes
Easy; Anytime Challenge; Pilgrimage; Religious
Start
King's Lynn, Norfolk TF620200
Finish
Slipper Chapel, Little Walsingham, Norfolk TF934369
Maps
OS Landranger: 132
OS Explorer: 250, 251
Publications, badges and certificates
Booklets
Walsingham Way: King's Lynn to Walsingham (John Merrill Foundation). ISBN 9781903627419. £5.95 (+ £1.00 p&p). Cheques to John Merrill Foundation.
Badge & certificate
Walsingham Way (John Merrill Foundation). £5.00 (incs p&p).

Waveney Way WVW

SUFFOLK 116km/72 miles

A walk around the boundary of Waveney District, completed in 2000 for the Waveney Ramblers' silver anniversary. It coincides with the Angles Way between Lowestoft and Bungay and has stretches of the coast and the valleys of the Blyth and Waveney rivers.

Attributes
Easy; Coastal; River
Start and Finish
Ness Point, Lowestoft, Suffolk TM554931
Maps
OS Landranger: 134, 156
OS Explorer: 231, 40
Publications, badges and certificates
Booklets
Waveney Way (R.A. Waveney) 2000. 24pp; A5. £2.70 (+ 50p p&p). Cheques to Ramblers Association (Waveney).

Weavers' Way (Norfolk) WEAVW

NORFOLK **90km/56 miles**

Use is made of public footpaths, disused railway line and some minor roads in passing through very varied scenery, from the mixed farmland and woodland of the north to the extensive, traditional grazing marshes of the Broadland river valleys, with fine flint churches, several large country houses, and many wind-pumps. Parts of the Paston Way (18 miles and included on OS mapping) which visits 16 churches and villages over a meandering and convoluted route in north-east Norfolk can be used in linking Cromer with North Walsham.

Attributes
Former Railway; River
Start
Cromer, Norfolk TG218424
Finish
Great Yarmouth, Norfolk TG531075
Waymark
Named discs with route logo
Websites
www.countrysideaccess.norfolk.gov.uk
Maps ◈
OS Landranger: 133, 134
OS Explorer: 40, 238, 252
Publications, badges and certificates
Paperbacks
Langton's Guide to the Weavers Way & Angles Way by Andrew Durham (Andrew Durham) 1995. ISBN 9781899242016. 144pp; 210 x 130. £6.95 (incs p&p).
Booklets
Peddars Way & North Norfolk Coast Path with the Weavers Way Guide by Ian Mitchell (Editor), Sheila Smith (Editor) (RA Norfolk Area) 2006. ISBN 9781906494148. 28pp; A5. £3.70 (incs p&p). Cheques to Ramblers Association (Norfolk Area). Includes accommodation list.
Paston Way (Norfolk County Council) 1996. 12pp; A5. £0.50p (+ SAE). Also available from TICs and some local Libraries.
Leaflets
Weavers' Way (Norfolk County Council) 1997. A5. £0.50p (+ SAE). Also available from TICs and some local Libraries.

West Anglian Way WAW

CAMBS, ESSEX, HERTS **103km/64 miles**

A linear route devised to make use of the Cambridge to Liverpool Street railway line stations. The route connects with stations at Whittlesford, Newport, Bishop's Stortford, Harlow, Broxbourne and Cheshunt. There are links with the Fen Rivers Way, which runs between Cambridge and King's Lynn, and to Byrhtnoth's Last Essex Visit.

Attributes
Easy
Start
Cambridge, Cambs TL462573
Finish
Waltham Abbey, Essex TL365003
Maps
OS Landranger: 154, 166, 167
OS Explorer: 174, 194, 195, 209
Publications, badges and certificates
Folder
West Anglian Way (RA Cambridge Group). 6pp with route description and illustrative map; A4. £3.00 (incs p&p). Cheques to Ramblers Association (Cambridge Group).

Whamblab Extravaganza WHAME

ESSEX **35km/22 miles**

This walk takes its name from the initial letters of the eight Roding parishes and churches that it links along the way.

Attributes
Anytime Challenge
Start and Finish
Margaret Roding, Essex TL599120
Maps
OS Landranger: 167
OS Explorer: 183
Publications, badges and certificates
Booklets
Whamblab Extravaganza by Megdalah Cooper (Derek

Keeble). £2.50 (incs p&p) £4.50 incs Winstree Marathon. Cheques to Derek Keeble.

Winstree Marathon WINM

ESSEX **42km/26 miles**

An exploration of the old Winstree Hundred south of Colchester, passing Abberton Reservoir, the Colne valley seawall, the Roman River valley nature reserve and Layer de la Haye.

Attributes
Challenging; Anytime Challenge; Lake/Reservoir
Start and Finish
Tiptree, Essex TL892167
Maps
OS Landranger: 168
OS Explorer: 184
Publications, badges and certificates
Booklets
Winstree Marathon by Laurence S. Taylor (Derek Keeble). £2.50 (incs p&p). Cheques to Derek Keeble (£4.50 incs Whamblab Extravaganza).

Wychwood Way WYCHW

OXON **60km/37 miles**

A walk around the heart of the ancient forest of Wychwood. From Woodstock the route passes through Stonesfield, Chadlington, Ascott-under-Wychwood, Leafield, Ramsden, North Leigh, East End and Combe to return to the start. The Way goes through Blenheim Park (a World Heritage Site of architectural importance), and also uses the Roman Road of Akeman Street and the ancient Saltway. It is partly coincident with the Oxfordshire Way.

Attributes
World Heritage Site; Heritage
Start and Finish
Market Street, Woodstock, Oxon SP444167
Waymark
Named discs with oak tree
Websites
www.wychwoodproject.org
Maps ◈
OS Landranger:164
OS Explorer: 180, 191
Publications, badges and certificates
Booklets
Wychwood Way by Alan Spicer, Mary Webb (Oxfordshire County Council) 2002. ISBN 9780953973101. 44pp; 128 x 210. £4.95 (+ 35p p&p). Order form on Oxfordshire CC website.

Ceredigion Coast Path between Aberystwyth and Llanrhystud

WALES

KEY FACTS	
Areas	Monmouthshire, Glamorgan (11 unitaries), Carmarthenshire, Pembrokeshire, Ceredigion, Gwynedd, Isle of Anglesey, Conwy, Denbighshire, Flintshire, Wrexham, Powys
National Parks	Brecon Beacons, Pembrokeshire Coast, Snowdonia
Principal AONBs	Anglesey, Clwydian Range, Gower, Lleyn, Wye Valley (part)
World Heritage Sites	Castles and Town Walls of King Edward in Gwynedd (Beaumaris on Anglesey, Conwy, Caernarfon and Harlech castles, and the towns of Conwy and Caernarfon); the Blaenavon Industrial Landscape
Heritage Coast	Conwy: Great Orme; Gwynedd: Lleyn; Isle of Anglesey: Aberffraw Bay, Holyhead Mountain, North Anglesey; Ceredigion; Pembrokeshire: Dinas Head, St Bride's Bay, St David's Pennisula, South Pembrokeshire, Marloes and Dale; South Wales: Gower, Glamorgan
National Walking Trails (Wales)	Glyndwr's Way/Llwybr Glyndwr, Pembrokeshire Coast Path, Offa's Dyke Path (part)
Walking Routes (trail miles)	62 main routes (4330 miles); 32 waymarked (2267 miles)
Resident population	3 million

DON'T MISS! TRAIL SECTIONS (CHALLENGING/REMOTE MARKED WITH *)	
Pembrokeshire Coast Path	Newport to St Dogmaels*, excellent cliff-top walking, spectacular views, rocky bays, Cemmaes Head (24km, 4000ft ascent)
Pembrokeshire Coast Path	Newgale Sands to Whitesands Bay, sandy beaches, St David's peninsula, views of Ramsey Island (27 km, 2600ft ascent)
Cambrian Way	Abergavenny to Capel-y-Ffin*, good ridge walk, Sugar Loaf, Bal Mawr, Chwarel-y-fan, views of Vale of Ewyas and Grwyne Forest (22km, 3450ft ascent)
Gower Way	Gowerton to Rhosilli, mining history, fine bays and beaches just off route, Gower peninsula and Worm's Head (31km, 1700ft ascent)
Beacons Way (Brecon)	Craig-y-Nos to Llanddeusant*, Dan-yr-Ogof show caves, Caradog's Church, Fan Hir, Fan Brycheiniof, Bannau Sir Gaer (or low level alternative) (16km, 2820ft ascent)
St Illtyd's Walk	Pembrey Country Park to Hendy, Pembrey Mountain, views of the Gower peninsula and Carmarthen Bay, Stradey woods (32km, 2500ft ascent)
Wye Valley Walk	Rhayader to Builth Wells, old Mid-Wales railway, the infant River Wye (26km, 1970ft ascent)
Dee Valley Walk	Llangollen to Corwen, steep-sided valleys under Llantysilio Mountain and Moel Ferna (24kms)
Offa's Dyke Path	Chirk Mill to Llangollen, Chirk Castle ruins, rivers Ceiriog and Dee, Pont-cysyllte viaduct, Panorama Walk, Castell Dinas Bran and detour descent to Llangollen (16km 1950ft ascent)
Glwndwr's Way	Llanidloes to Afon Biga, lead mining area, history of Rebecca Riots, Garth Hill, Llyn Clywedog dam and reservoir (16km, 2150ft ascent)
Snowdon Challenge Walk	circular from Pontllyfni, to the top and back by contrasting routes* (48km, 5000ft of ascent)
Lleyn Peninsula Coastal Path	Aberdaron to Abersoch, pilgrim's route to Bardsey, Norman history, King Arthur connections, Porth Ysgo, Hell's Mouth Bay (23km, 1800ft ascent)

Snowdonia welcome sign

WALES

Pen Y Fan, on the Cambrian and Beacons Ways

Wales offers a wide scenic range from the rugged peaks of Snowdonia in the north across the central mountains and moorlands to the angular Brecons Beacons in the south. There is a fine coastline with some superb long and unspoilt beaches, while an ancient earthwork, Offa's Dyke, traces much of the English border. There are many rivers and lakes, and a rich heritage, both human – with Wales' famous sons – and industrial – in the remains of its past mineral and coal industries.

With such a wealth of walking opportunities it is not suprising that Wales includes three National Trails, Offa's Dyke Path, Glyndwr's Way/Llwybr Glyndwr and the Pembrokeshire Coast Path, in all some 500 miles of quality walking along rivers, across hills and on the coastline (see National Trails section). As a border route, Offa's Dyke Path is shared with England.

Geology

The Welsh mountains perhaps provide the highlights for the walker. Snowdonia National Park in the north-west is a dramatic landscape of hard volcanic rocks cut by past glaciers to leave soaring peaks and sharp edges, with quiet cwms and lakes below, and there is much evidence of slate and mineral industries. In the south there is a long broken band of Devonian Old Red Sandstone whose north-facing ridgeline forms the flat-topped peaks of the Black Mountain, the Brecon Beacons and the Black Mountains, again hewn out by the ice. North of this is the moorland mass of Mynydd Epynt and the huge expanse of the Cambrian Mountains, a series of dissected plateaus covering much of central Wales, with its watershed where the Severn and Wye rise quite close to the western coasts of Cardigan Bay.

In the north east of Wales the Clwydian and the Berwyn ranges, separated by the Dee valley, arc around towards central Wales. Between the Clwydians and Snowdonia is another moorland mass, Mynydd Hiraethog. South of the Beacons are the valleys of South Wales Valleys with their intervening ridges providing plenty of ridge-walking opportunities. These finally drop away to the populous coastal lands of the Vale of Glamorgan and the sea.

The Trails

Wales offers splendid upland and mountain walking, nowhere more than in Snowdonia, where

Wales – major routes

Only major routes from this region (excluding any National Trails) are shown here. The National Trails are shown on the map in the National Trails section of this handbook. For the full network of trails visit the LDWA website – www.ldwa.org.uk.

Lleyn Peninsula – south west tip

rather than waymarked trails, there are many enthusiasts' routes, as befits the challenging terrain. The other major mountain ranges have much to offer. Tony Drake's major Cambrian Way traverses many of the main Welsh upland ranges in its epic journey of some 274 miles between Cardiff and Conwy, truly one for the mountain connoisseur. The Beacons Way (Brecon) is the main official trail of this National Park, traversing its three ranges, the Black Mountains, Brecon Beacons and the Black Mountain. The Clwydian Way circles through the Clwydian Range while the North Berwyn Way traverses it. The Pererindod Melangell is a linear walk on the Berwyn's fringes.

In South Wales the many **ridgelines** between the vales provide good walking with distant views. In Caerphilly the Rhymney Valley Ridgeway Walk circles above this valley. The Taff Ely Ridgeway Walk follows another line of hills in Rhondda and Caerphilly. The multi-user Taff Trail uses old railway lines, canals and forest tracks between Cardiff and the Brecons. Other routes in South Wales provide ridge walking or elevated viewpoints; these include the Sirhowy Valley Ridgeway Walk, Ogwr Ridgeway Walk, Coed Morgannwg Way and the Sky to Sea Walks.

Much of the varied, and often spectacular, Welsh **coastline** beyond the more populous south

ROUTE CODES

BREABRW	Beacons Way (Brecon)	**PERMEL**	Pererindod Melangell
CLWYDW	Clwydian Way	**RVRW**	Rhymney Valley Ridgeway Walk
CMW	Cambrian Way	**SEVW**	Severn Way
GLOUCS	Gloucestershire Way	**SVRW**	Sirhowy Valley Ridgeway Walk
GOWW	Gower Way	**TBRW**	Taff Ely Ridgeway Walk
MAELW	Maelor Way	**VMHT**	Valeways Millennium Heritage Trail
NWP	North Wales Path	**WYEVW**	Wye Valley Walk

now has a promoted coastal path. Starting from the tidal limits of the Dee estuary there is the Dee Way to Prestatyn, followed by the North Wales Path to Bangor. Offshore the Isle of Anglesey has its Anglesey Coast Path. Back on the mainland the Lleyn Peninsula Coast Path continues via Caernarfon to Portmadoc where the Meirionnydd Coast Walk heads, via Harlech, to Aberdyfi. This section links King Edward's four castles and town walls that make up the World Heritage Site.

Continuing across the Dyfi estuary the Ceredigion Coast Path covers the county's coastline from Borth all the way to Cardigan, where the Pembrokeshire Coast Path goes around St David's Head to Amroth. These coastal trails together total some 520 miles of walking. In South Wales several routes include sections on or near the coast – the St Illtyd's Walk near Llanelli, the Gower Way to Worm's Head, and on its circuit of the Vale of Glamorgan the Valeways Millennium Heritage Trail takes in the Glamorgan Heritage Coast.

The major Welsh **rivers** provide some excellent, sometimes quite challenging, riverside routes. The Wye Valley Walk links Chepstow, close to the confluence with the Severn, to the source high on the access moorland of Plynlimon. Nearby, the Severn's source is the start of the Severn Way itself on its 210-mile journey to the sea. The Dee Way traces the Dee from its wide estuary to its moorland origins high above Llyn Tegid, with the separate Dee Valley Way providing for alternatives between Llangollen and Corwen. The Usk Valley Walk follows the Usk from Caerleon upstream and high into the Brecons.

Some easy walking, around reservoirs on Denbighshire's **moors**, is included in the Brenig Trail and the Alwen Trail. There is more moorland

Berriew aqueduct/ Shropshire Union Montgomery canal pathway

Rhossili Down, view north, on the Gower Way (David Hunt)

walking nearby; on Conwy's Hiraethog Trail, and on the network of the Mynydd Hiraethog & Denbigh Moors Footpath.

Among the **themed routes**, in this land of music, the Ann Griffiths Walk in Powys is named after a prolific and influential 18th-century hymn writer; while St Illtyd's Walk in South Wales has a religious theme – remembering Illtyd, an early saint held in high veneration in Wales. St Winefride's Way is a pilgrim's trail in North Wales. The Cistercian Way links the Cistercian abbey sites in a long 650-mile journey making a full circuit of the country.

Wales' 'famous sons' include the renowned author and poet Dylan Thomas. The Dylan Thomas Trail visits places near his home on the Cardigan coast and locations that inspired *Under Milk Wood*. The explorer famous for meeting Dr Livingstone is remembered in the HM Stanley Trail in Denbighshire. While not quite in the same league, the Mal Evans Way remembers a respected Ceredigion Rambler.

Industrial history is covered by the Iron Mountain Trail visiting the Blaenavon Industrial Landscape World Heritage Site, marking the town's early leading role in the UK's iron and coal industries. The Four Valleys Path visits the slate mining valleys of north Gwynedd, while the Gower Way includes an historic former mining area. In Wrexham, Mines, Moorland and Mountains includes old mining sites.

Historic **boundaries** and **ancient routes** provide themes for the Gower Way as it crosses the past lordship of Gower, while the Landsker Borderlands Trail explores the rural area on the Pembrokeshire/Carmarthenshire border – Landsker being an old Norse word for frontier. The Sarn Helen follows an old Roman route across west Wales, while Wat's Dyke Heritage Trail follows a linear earthwork in the Welsh Marches, paralleling the Offa's Dyke Path, that has a similar theme. Remembering past border skirmishes the Three Castles Walk links border castles in Monmouthshire. Circuits of towns or administrative areas provide the themes for the Bridgend Circular Walk and the Torfaen Trail.

Two **long routes** start in Wales, but most of their length is in England. The Gloucestershire Way starts in Chepstow, as does the Great English Walk, which begins its 620-mile journey to Berwick-upon-Tweed there. The Wysis Way links Offa's Dyke Path at Monmouth and the Thames Path in Gloucestershire.

Three routes mainly aimed at **horseriders** are shared with walkers. The Radnor Forest Ride is mainly in Powys, as are the Llwybr Ceiriog Trail and the Epynt Way, where the MoD welcomes walkers, horse riders and cyclists to a circuit of the wild Mynydd Epynt plateau both also in Powys.

Enthusiast's routes abound with some demanding terrain on offer. There are 17, almost all rated very challenging. Ten walk developers are represented. David Irons provides Around Idris, Around the Carneddau, and Around the Rhinogs, each circuiting its named range. He also offers the Snowdonia Challenges, a group of three comprising: the Heart of Snowdonia 24 Peaks Circuit that climbs 24 peaks with 20,000ft of ascent, the Snowdonia Five Ranges Round visiting the highest summit in each principal mountain range in Central Snowdonia, and the Welsh 1000m Peaks Marathon that includes the Carneddau's tops and Snowdon.

Tony Hill offers the Carneddau Challenge Walk and the Glyderau Challenge Walk, while Richard Hill provides the Black Mountains Traverse Challenge which does 'just what it says on the tin'. Derek Fisher provides the Brecon Beacons Traverse that includes the Black Mountains. Offa's Hyke is a charity challenge from Michael Skuse that aims to help a children's hospice. Gerry Jackson offers the Taith Torfaen that climbs Blorenge, Coity Mountains and other Torfaen hills.

Snowdonia is well represented with yet another five challenges, John Merrill has the Snowdon Challenge Walk, to the top and back by different routes. The Snowdonia Round links YHA youth hostels and includes several summits. Ed Dalton has the Snowdonia 24-hour Circuit including the horseshoe, the Glyders, Carneddau and Moel Siabod, as well as the Snowdonia Panoramic Walk on the Carneddau, Snowdon and along the Nantlle ridge. Both Ed Dalton and Peter Travis offer the Welsh 3000s, crossing the main Snowdonia summits with some exposed scrambling, and if that challenge is still not enough, the Welsh 3000s Double Crossing (28 summits) certainly should be!

Anglesey Coast Path ACP

ANGLESEY **195km/121 miles**

A long distance route that follows much of the island's coastline. It falls within a designated Area of Outstanding Natural Beauty (AONB) which covers 95% of the coast. It passes through landscape that includes a mixture of farmland, coastal heath, dunes, salt-marsh, foreshore, cliffs, a National Nature Reserve and a few small pockets of woodland. The route primarily caters for walkers, however cyclists and horse riders can also enjoy certain sections.

Attributes
Easy; Coastal
Start and Finish
St Cybi's Church, Holyhead, Isle of Anglesey SH247826
Waymark
Gull on island outline with name
Websites
www.islandofchoice.com
Maps
OS Landranger: 114
OS Explorer: 262, 263
Publications, badges and certificates
Paperbacks
Isle of Anglesey Coastal Path by Carl Rogers (Northern Eye Books Limited (Mara)) 2006. ISBN 9781902512136. 288pp; 204 x 136. £9.99 (+ £2.00 p&p). In English and Welsh.
Island of Anglesey Coast Path (Mike Salter) 2007. 21pp; OS map size. £2.50 (+ 50p p&p). Only available direct from Author Tel: 01684 565211.
Booklets
Walking the Isle of Anglesey Coastline by John Merrill (John Merrill Foundation). ISBN 9781874754138. 60pp; A5. £6.95 (+ £1.00 p&p). Cheques to John Merrill Foundation.
Hardback
All Around Anglesey by Terry Beggs (Gomer Press) 2007. ISBN 9781843237150. 244 x 224. £19.99.
Badge & certificate
Anglesey Coast Path (John Merrill Foundation). £5.00 (incs p&p).
Illustrated map guide
Guide to Isle of Anglesey Coastal Path (Llanfairpwll Tourist Information Centre). £1.99.
Walking Support Providers
Anglesey; Byways; Celtic; Explore Britain; Footpath

Around Idris ARI

GWYNEDD **39km/24 miles**

A circuit of the Cadair Idris mountain range using good, well-marked footpaths. The scenic route takes in Llynnau Cregennen, Ffordd dhu, and Tyn-y-ddol (Mary Jones Cottage).

Attributes
Very Challenging; Anytime Challenge; Moorland; Mountain
Start and Finish
Minffordd Car Park, Gwynedd SH732116
Maps
OS Landranger: 124
OS Explorer: 18, 23
Publications, badges and certificates
Looseleaf
Around Idris by Dave Irons (Dave Irons) 2001. 4pp; A4. £1.00 (incs p&p).

Around the Carneddau ARC

CONWY **64km/40 miles**

A circuit around the edge of the Carneddau visiting the lakes of Llyn Crafnant, Llyn Cowlyd, Melynnllyn and Llyn Dulyn. It follows the Roman Road to Bont Newydd, visits Aber Falls then traverses Moel Wnion to Gerlan before skirting Llyn Ogwen.

Attributes
Very Challenging; Anytime Challenge; Moorland; Mountain
Start and Finish
Capel Curig, Conwy SH721581
Maps
OS Landranger: 115
OS Explorer: 17
Publications, badges and certificates
Looseleaf
Around the Carneddau (Dave Irons) 1994. 5pp; A4. £1.00 (incs p&p).
Paperbacks
Ridges of Snowdonia by Steve Ashton (Cicerone Press) 2005. ISBN 9781852843502. 172 x 116. £12.00.

Around the Rhinogs ARR

GWYNEDD **61km/38 miles**

A remote and arduous circular walk exploring the fascinating and varied Rhinogs countryside. Although no summits are taken in, it is essential that anybody undertaking this walk should be fit, well equipped, and have good map reading and compass skills before tackling the roughest and wildest mountain range in Snowdonia.

Attributes
Very Challenging; Anytime Challenge; Moorland; Mountain
Start and Finish
Trawsfynydd, Gwynedd SH707355
Maps
OS Landranger: 124
OS Explorer: 23
Publications, badges and certificates
Looseleaf
Around the Rhinogs by Dave Irons (Dave Irons) 2001. 5pp; A4. £1.00 (incs p&p).

Beacons Way (Brecon) BEABRW

CARMS, MONS, POWYS **161km/100 miles**

The Beacons Way is the official trail of the Brecon Beacons National Park Authority in Wales, passing east-west through major ranges of the Black Mountains, the Brecon Beacons and the Black Mountain. The Brecon Beacons National Park is a significant protected landscape with some of the most spectacular upland scenery in Britain. The route involves remote and rugged terrain and some 8500ft of ascent and is designed for experienced walkers. As well as reaching many of the major peaks, including Fan y Big, Pen y Fan, Fan Llia, Fan Hir, Fan Foel and Twyn Swnd, there are glacial lakes, ancient standing stones, churches and fine mountain views. It traverses the Brecon Beacons between the Holy Mountain, Abergavenny and Llangadog. The route takes in Llanthony, Crickhowell, Llangynidir, Craig Cerrig-gleisiad, Craig-y-nos, Llanddeusant, and Carreg Cennen before its finish at Llangadog. It can be completed over eight consecutive days or explored as a series of linear walks. The route, mainly through open country, has very little lane or road walking. Some of the route is in common with the Cambrian Way but with easier alternatives. The website provides 'Hints and Tips' and posts corrections and route diversions.

Attributes
Challenging; Moorland; Mountain
Start
Abergavenny, Mons SO301141
Finish
Llangadog, Carms SN699286
Waymark
Beacons and river with name
Websites
www.breconbeaconsparksociety.org, www.tourism.powys.gov.uk
Maps ◈
OS Landranger: 160, 161
OS Explorer: 12, 13
Publications, badges and certificates
Paperbacks
Beacons Way: The Holy Mountain to Bethlehem by John Sansom, Arwel Michael (Brecon Beacons Park Society) 2005. ISBN 9781902302355. 144pp; 208 x 134. £12.00.
Walking Support Providers
Celtic; Drover; Marches Walks

Black Mountains Traverse Challenge BMTC

HEREFS, POWYS **38km/24 miles**

A demanding undulating route across the Black Mountain ridge taking in the highest peaks and lowest valley points, with some 6500ft of ascent on a self-devised route, mostly off-track. It can be walked in either direction.

Attributes
Very Challenging; Anytime Challenge; Moorland; Mountain
Start
Llangorse Church, Powys SO135276
Finish
Craswell, Herefs SO278361
Maps
OS Landranger: 161
OS Explorer: 13
Publications, badges and certificates
Looseleaf
Black Mountains Traverse Challenge (Richard Hill) 1990. 2pp. Free (+ 9 x 6 SAE).
Certificate
Black Mountains Traverse Challenge (Richard Hill) 1990. £5.00 (+ 10 x 8 SAE). Cheques to R Hill on completion with brief walk account.

Brecon Beacons Traverse BBT

CARMS, MONS, POWYS **142km/88 miles**

A tough 24 hour route through the wild regions of Carmarthen Fan, Forest Fawr, Brecon Beacons and the Black Mountains. It includes over 20,000ft of ascent. A list of grid references is available from the website below.

Attributes
Very Challenging; Anytime Challenge; Moorland; Mountain
Start
Pen Rhiw-Wen, Carms SN732184
Finish
Llanthony Abbey, Mons SO289278
Websites
www.gofar.org.uk
Maps
OS Landranger: 160, 161
OS Explorer: 12, 13
Publications, badges and certificates
Looseleaf (and maps)
Brecon Beacons Traverse (Derek G. Fisher). 18pp; A4. £2.50 (+ 50p p&p).
Certificate
Brecon Beacons Traverse (Derek G. Fisher). £0.50 (incs p&p). Available for completions under 24 hours.

Brenig Trail — BRT

CONWY, DENBIGHS — 16km/10 miles

The route circumnavigates Llyn Brenig along the edge of the shoreline with one noticeable climb. Part of this trail runs along a B Road. The reservoir is one of the largest areas of water in Wales. The walk can be extended by continuing on the Two Lakes Trail onto the Mynydd Hiraethog, and around the Alwen Reservoir on the waymarked Alwen Trail (8 miles).

Attributes
Lake/Reservoir; Heritage
Start and Finish
Visitor Centre, Llyn Brenig, Denbighshire SH967547
Websites
www.hiraethog.org.uk, www.aboutbritain.com
Maps
OS Landranger: 116
OS Explorer: 264
Publications, badges and certificates
Leaflets
Brenig Trail (Llyn Brenig Reservoir and Visitor Centre). Free.
Alwen Trail (Llyn Brenig Reservoir and Visitor Centre). Free. The Visitor Centre Tel: 01490 420 463.

Bridgend Circular Walk — BRICW

BRIDGEND — 32km/20 miles

This relatively flat walk links towns and villages within an approximate 3-mile radius of the town of Bridgend. The route, although mainly in rural surroundings, does cross the M4 twice. It is described in a clockwise direction and visits Laleston, Sarn, Hendre, Treoes, Corntown, Llampha and St Brides Major. Near the start there is an opportunity to visit Ogmore Castle. Links to other routes nearby are described in the leaflets.

Attributes
Easy
Start and Finish
Merthyr Mawr car park, Bridgend SS883774
Waymark
Curled blue arrows encircled by name (English/Welsh)
Websites
www.bridgend.gov.uk
Maps
OS Landranger: 170
OS Explorer: 151
Publications, badges and certificates
Leaflets (set of 3)
Bridgend Circular Walk (Bridgend Tourist Information Centre) 2004. 3 leaflets; A4/3. Free.

Cambrian Way — CMW

CAERPHILLY, CARDIFF, CARMS, CEREDIGION, CONWY, GWYNEDD, MONS, POWYS, TORFAEN — 441km/274 miles

Described as the Mountain Connoisseur's Walk, this route through upland Wales involves 61,540ft of ascent and requires much stamina to complete. It is a tough, high-level route which should not be underestimated. Navigational skills are of paramount importance. From the start, it follows a meandering northerly route over the Black Mountains, Brecon Beacons, Carmarthen Fan, Plynlimon, Cadair Idris, the Rhinogs, the Snowdon massif and the Carneddau to reach the north coast. In places there are route options. Tony Drake pioneered the route, and his guide, reprinted in 2008, includes a comprehensive accommodation and services list. Explorer maps 151 and 214 cover only small sections.

Attributes
Very Challenging; Moorland; Mountain
Start
Cardiff ST180765
Finish
Conwy, Conwy SH783775
Websites
www.cambrianway.org.uk

Maps
OS Landranger: 115, 124, 135, 147, 160, 161, 171
OS Explorer: 12, 13, 17, 18, 23, 151, 152, 187, 213, 214, 215
Publications, badges and certificates
Paperbacks
Cambrian Way: The Mountain Connoisseur's Walk by A. J. Drake (Cordee Ltd) 2008. ISBN 9780950958057. 96pp; 210 x 128. £6.50 (+ £1.50 p&p).
Accommodation list (with updates)
Cambrian Way (A. J. Drake). £0.50 (+ SAE).
Walking Support Providers
Celtic; HF

Carneddau Challenge Walk CCW

CONWY, GWYNEDD **32km/20 miles**

A route from sea level to the summit of Carnedd Llewelyn, with 4750ft of ascent.

Attributes
Challenging; Anytime Challenge; Mountain
Start and Finish
Aber-Ogwen, Gwynedd SH613721
Maps
OS Landranger: 115
OS Explorer: 17
Publications, badges and certificates
Booklets
Carneddau Challenge Walk by Tony Hill (John Merrill Foundation) 1996. ISBN 9781874754466. 32pp; A5. £4.50 (+ £1.00 p&p). Cheques to John Merrill Foundation.
Badge & certificate
Carneddau Challenge Walk (John Merrill Foundation). £5.00 (incs p&p).

Ceredigion Coast Path CERCP

CEREDIGION **100km/62 miles**

This attractive route, strenuous in parts, extends along the entire coastline of Ceredigion. From Cardigan in the south, where it links with the Pembrokeshire Coast Path, it visits the resorts of Aberporth, Llangrannog, New Quay – where it links with the Dylan Thomas Trail, Aberaeron, Aberystwyth and Borth. Along the way you will see two 13th century castles, two prehistoric forts, delightful old harbours and six medieval churches. From its finish at Ynyslas it is possible to use local paths to link up with Glyndwr's Way just south of Machynlleth. Local Ramblers' volunteers were key to the route's construction. Walkers should note that the section between Cardigan and Mwnt could be unavailable: see the website for an alternative route.

Attributes
Challenging; Coastal
Start
Cardigan, Ceredigion SN177458
Finish
Ynyslas, Borth, Ceredigion SN605925
Waymark
Coast and sea graphic
Websites
www.ceredigioncoastpath.org.uk
Maps
OS Landranger: 135, 145, 146
OS Explorer: 198, 199, 213
Publications, badges and certificates
Guidebook
Ceredigion Coast Path by Gerald Morgan (Ceredigion Tourism Service) 2008. 240pp. £10.00 (+ £1.00 p&p). Also from local TICs.
Paperbacks
Ceredigion Coast Path by Mike Salter (Mike Salter) 2007. 21pp; OS map size. £2.50 (+ 50p p&p). Only available direct from Author Tel: 01684 565211.

Cistercian Way (Wales) CISW

CAERPHILLY, CARMS, CEREDIGION, CONWY, DENBIGHS, GWYNEDD, MONS, NEATH PT, PEMBROKES, POWYS, RHONDDA CT, TORFAEN **1046km/650 miles**

A walk into the heart of Wales exploring the great abbeys of the Cistercian order, the little churches of the Welsh hills, the geology of the Pembrokeshire coast, Stone Age burial mounds, medieval castles, sheep-farms, picturesque landscaped gardens, and the industrial heritage of the nineteenth and twentieth centuries.

Attributes
Challenging; Moorland; Mountain; Heritage; Geological; Industrial History; Monarchy; Religious
Start and Finish
Llantarnam, Cwmbran, Torfaen ST311929
Websites
http://cistercian-way.newport.ac.uk
Maps
OS Landranger: 115, 116, 117, 124, 125, 126, 135, 136, 145, 146, 147, 158, 159, 161, 162, 170, 171

OS Explorer: 13, 14, 17, 18, 23, 36, 152, 165, 166, 177, 178, 185, 187, 188, 199, 200, 213, 214, 215, 240, 256, 264, 265
Publications, badges and certificates
Route notes (online only)
Cistercian Way (Dr Madeleine Gray).

Clwydian Way — CLWYDW

CONWY, DENBIGHS, FLINTS — 196km/122 miles

First developed by North Wales Ramblers, this circular route intertwines with Offa's Dyke Path National Trail as it takes the Clwydian Range south to Llangollen. Here it turns west along the Llantysilio Range to Corwen, passing through some of North Wales' finest countryside, a haven for wildlife. The return to the start is via Clocaenog Forest and Llyn Brenig. The route takes in the historic towns of Llangollen, Corwen, Ruthin (nearby), St. Asaph and Rhuddlan (nearby). It also has links with a number of other long distance paths. Prestatyn is well served by bus and rail connections. From Llyn Brenig, an alternative more northerly moorland route up over Mynydd Hiraethog and through Llansannan has spectacular views of the mountains of Snowdonia. It returns to the main route via Denbigh. By using link paths it is also possible to create three other circular routes: South 88 miles, West 54 miles and North 42 miles.

Attributes
Challenging; Lake/Reservoir; River; Moorland; Mountain
Start and Finish
Prestatyn, Denbighs SJ061838
Waymark
Buzzard and name on white disc
Websites
www.clwydianway.co.uk
Maps ◈
OS Landranger: 116, 117, 125
OS Explorer: 18, 255, 256, 264, 265
Publications, badges and certificates
Paperbacks
Clwydian Way by David Hollett (RA North Wales Area) 2000. ISBN 9781901184365. 88pp; 239 x 165. £7.50 (incs p&p). Cheques to Ramblers Association (North Wales Area).

Coed Morgannwg Way — COEDMW

MERTHYR T, NEATH PT, RHONDDA CT — 58km/36 miles

The Coed Morgannwg Way, most of which is on Forestry Commission land, follows ancient tracks of Celtic origin. It crosses part of the Coed Morgannwg, a complex of four upland forests visiting the Dare Valley and Craig y Llyn, which at 1,968ft (600 metres) is the highest point on the route. After ascending several more viewpoints you reach Afan Argoed Country Park, from where the route follows less elevated paths and passes a number of archaeological remains from prehistoric to industrial times. On a clear day the Brecon Beacons and the Bristol Channel can be seen. Near to Bodvic Stone, the Way links with the Ogwr Ridgeway Walk and there is a link with the Taff Trail at the finish.

Attributes
Challenging; Forest/Woodland; Moorland; Mountain; Heritage
Start
Gethin Woodland Park, Merthyr T SO052033
Finish
Margam, Neath PT SS806864
Waymark
White footprint on brown background
Websites
www.bridgend.gov.uk
Maps ◈
OS Landranger: 170
OS Explorer: 165, 166
Publications, badges and certificates
Booklets
Coed Morgannwg Way (Neath & Port Talbot County Borough Council) 1995. 10pp; A5. £1.00 (+ 50p p&p).

Dee Way — DEW

CHESHIRE, DENBIGHS, FLINTS, GWYNEDD, WREXHAM — 204km/127 miles

The main Dee Way traces the River Dee (Afon Dyfrdwy) upstream from Connah's Quay, on the shores of the Dee Estuary, to the source high on Dduallt above Llyn Tegid in Snowdonia National Park. It passes the historic Roman city of Chester and goes through a succession of attractive towns and villages: Aldford; border communities of Farndon, Bangor-on-Dee, Overton and Chirk; then Llangollen, Carrog, Corwen, Llandrillo, Y Bala and Llanuwchllyn. Borderland flood plains lead from the tidal limit at Chester weir. There are broad wooded valleys and steep-sided valleys between Llantysilio Mountain and Moel Ferna (Berwyns). En route are castles, old churches, ancient bridges, and canal and railway engineering. The long tidal estuary, with its mudflats, salt-marshes, sand dunes and low cliffs, is renowned for its bird-life. In addition to the continuous long-distance walk, the guidebook includes a 57½-mile estuary walk between Hoylake and Prestatyn; a 14-mile upland circuit of Llyn Tegid, Wales' largest natural lake; plus 23 day walks. The waymarked Dee Valley Way runs for 15 miles between Llangollen and Corwen.

Attributes
Forest/Woodland; Coastal; Lake/Reservoir; River; Canal; Moorland; Urban; Heritage; Industrial History
Start
Prestatyn SJ060837
Finish
Dee source on Dduallt, Gwynedd SH813275
Websites
www.thedeeway.com, www.deevalleywalks.com
Maps
OS Landranger: 117, 125, 116, 108, 126
OS Explorer: 18, 23, 240, 255, 256, 257, 264, 265, 266
Publications, badges and certificates
Paperbacks
Dee Way by David Berry (Kittiwake) 2009. ISBN 9781902302669. 120pp; A5. £8.95.
Booklets
Dee Valley Way (Denbighshire County Council). Free.
Walking Support Providers
Contours

Dylan Thomas Trail — DYLTT

CEREDIGION — **40km/25 miles**

Taking in some of the places that inspired some of his best writing, including *Under Milk Wood*, the route goes through Red Kite country to Talsarn, then follows the Aeron valley to Aberaeron, where it turns south along the heritage coast of Cardigan Bay. The guidebook contains two short extensions and other short diversions.

Attributes
Forest/Woodland; Coastal; River; Literary
Start
Central Hotel, Llanon, Ceredigion SN515671
Finish
Towyn Road, New Quay, Ceredigion SN389601
Maps
OS Landranger: 145, 146
OS Explorer: 198, 199
Publications, badges and certificates
Paperbacks
Dylan Thomas Trail by David N. Thomas (Y Lolfa) 2002. ISBN 9780862436094. 144pp; 148 x 210. £6.95.
Walking Support Providers
Celtic

Epynt Way — EPTW

POWYS — **90km/56 miles**

A circular bridleway, normally open to walkers, horse riders and cyclists, around the boundary of the Ministry of Defence's Sennybridge Training Area (SENTA). This is a danger area, on Mynydd Epynt, where any temporary safety restrictions must be strictly observed. Mynydd Epynt is a wild plateau, between the Brecon Beacons in the South and the Cambrian Mountains in the North, famous as the breeding ground for Welsh Cobs. The name Epynt originated from an ancient expression meaning "haunt of horse".

Attributes
Horse Ride (Multi User); Moorland; Military
Start and Finish
Pentre Dolan Honddu, Builth Wells, Powys SN992438
Waymark
Stylised white cob horse head and name on green disc
Websites
www.defence-estates.mod.uk, www.tourism.powys.gov.uk
Maps
OS Landranger: 147, 160
OS Explorer: 188
Publications, badges and certificates
Leaflets (online)
Epynt Way (Epynt Way Development Officer). Free. Downloadable from website.

Four Valleys Path — 4VP

GWYNEDD — **31km/19 miles**

A route through the hills and former slate mining valleys of north Gwynedd, including the Nantlle, Gwyrfai, Padarn and Ogwen valleys. It skirts the Snowdonia National Park boundary between Penygroes and Bethesda, passes through Llanberis, near the Snowdon mountain railway, and takes in many small villages.

Attributes
Moorland; Industrial History
Start
Penygroes, Gwynedd SH470531
Finish
Bethesda, Gwynedd SH620669
Waymark
Mountain, water, bootprint, name in blue, white disc
Websites
www.gwynedd.gov.uk
Maps
OS Landranger: 115
OS Explorer: 17
Publications, badges and certificates
Leaflets
Four Valleys Path (Gwynedd County Council). Free. Downloadable sectional leaflets in PDF format.

Gloucestershire Way GLOUCSW

GLOS, MONS **151km/94 miles**

A route through the Forest of Dean, the Severn Plain and Cotswolds linking the Wye Valley Walk and Offa's Dyke Path National Trail to the Severn, Cotswold, Oxfordshire and Heart of England Ways. The guide also provides details of a link from Tewksbury to the Worcestershire Way.

Attributes
No significant attribute
Start
Chepstow Castle, Mons ST534941
Finish
Tewkesbury, Glos SO891324
Waymark
Gloucester Cathedral, river, tree topped hill, name on yellow disc
Websites
www.countryside-matters.co.uk
Maps ◈
OS Landranger: 150, 162, 163, 172
OS Explorer: 167, 179, 190, 14, 45
Publications, badges and certificates
Paperbacks
Gloucestershire Way: Forest and Vale and High Blue Hill (Paperback) by Gerry Stewart (Countryside Matters) 1996. ISBN 9780952787006. 128pp; 210 x 140. £5.95 (incs p&p).
Leaflets
Walking the Gloucestershire Way (Gloucestershire County Council) 2000. A4/3. Free.

Glyderau Challenge Walk GCW

CONWY, GWYNEDD **26km/16 miles**

A tough traverse of the Glyderau with 6,500ft of ascent. Some scrambling is involved – mountaineering equipment may be required for a winter crossing.

Attributes
Very Challenging; Anytime Challenge; Moorland; Mountain
Start
Capel Curig, Conwy SH720580
Finish
Bethesda, Gwynedd SH625670
Maps
OS Landranger: 115
OS Explorer: 17
Publications, badges and certificates
Booklets
Glyderau Challenge Walk by Tony Hill (John Merrill Foundation). ISBN 9781841730059. 32pp; A5. £4.95 (+ 75p p&p). Cheques to John Merrill Foundation.
Badge & certificate
Glyderau Challenge Walk (John Merrill Foundation). £5.00 (incs p&p).

Gower Way GOWW

SWANSEA **56km/35 miles**

The Gower Society's Millennium route across the ancient lordship of Gower, including some permissive paths and roads. Surrounded by 5,000 years of history, from Bronze Age dolmens and Iron Age forts to Norman castles and churches, it crosses Cefn Bryn to end with fine coastal views of Worms Head. The central section has evidence of an historic industrial and mining area, now largely cleared.

Attributes
Forest/Woodland; Moorland; Heritage; Industrial History
Start
Penlle'r Castell, Gower, Swansea SN665096
Finish
Rhossili, Gower, Swansea SS402874
Waymark
Green edged disc/name. Marked stones (1km intervals)
Websites
www.gowersociety.org.uk

Maps ◈
OS Landranger: 159
OS Explorer: 164, 178
Publications, badges and certificates
Leaflets
Gower Way by Gower Society (Gower Society). 3 leaflets. £0.75 each (+60p p&p for 1, 2 or 3 leaflets).

Great English Walk GEW

MONS, NORTHUMBERLAND, NUMEROUS **1003km/623 miles**

A trek across England from south-east Wales to north-east England. The route takes in the Forest of Dean, the Malvern hills, the Cheshire Plain, the Peak District, parts of the Yorkshire Dales, Allendale and the Northumbrian towns of Rothbury and Wooler.

Attributes
Challenging; Moorland
Start
Chepstow, Monmouth ST535942
Finish
Berwick-upon-Tweed, Northumberland NT996533
Maps
OS Landranger: 75, 80, 81, 87, 92, 99, 103, 104, 110, 117, 118, 119, 126, 138, 149, 150, 162
OS Explorer: 1, 14, 16, 21, 24, 30, 31, 42, 43, 190, 204, 217, 218, 241, 257, 267, 268, 297, 298, 302, 307, 339, 346
Publications, badges and certificates
Paperbacks
Great English Walk – Volume One: Chepstow to Hathersage by Margaret Nightingale, Brian Nightingale (Nightingale Publications) 1996. ISBN 9780952949015. 192pp; 210 x 148. £7.95.
Great English Walk – Volume Two: Hathersage to Berwick-upon-Tweed by Margaret Nightingale, Brian Nightingale (Nightingale Publications) 1997. ISBN 9780952949022. 192pp; 210 x 148. £7.95. Both volumes together – £15.00.

H M Stanley Trail HMST

DENBIGHS **26km/16 miles**

The walk, which marks the centenary of Stanley's death in 1904, links Denbigh, Tremeirchion and St Asaph, three of the key places in his life. The route takes in the Vale of Clwyd, the western edge of the Clwydian Hills and Y Graig. It commemorates Henry Morton Stanley, soldier, journalist and explorer, most famous for his meeting with Dr Livingstone – 'Dr Livingstone I presume...'.

Attributes
River; Moorland
Start and Finish
Denbigh Castle, Denbighshire SJ051657
Websites
www.visitdenbigh.co.uk
Maps
OS Landranger: 116
OS Explorer: 264, 265
Publications, badges and certificates
Paperbacks
Denbighshire People and Places: H M Stanley Walks by David Berry (Denbigh Library). £2.00 (+ 50p p&p). Denbigh Library Tel: 01745 816313.
Stanley: The Impossible Life of Africa's Greatest Explorer by Tim Jeal (Faber & Faber) 2008. ISBN 9780571221035. 592pp; 196 x 122. £9.99.
Livingstone (Yale University Press) 2001. ISBN 9780300091021. 448pp; 192 x 126. £11.99.

Hiraethog Trail HIRT

CONWY **53km/33 miles**

This interesting and scenic trail links the villages of Pentrefoelas, Cerrigydrudion, Llanfihangel Glyn Myfr and Llanrhaeadr using public footpaths, quiet lanes and country roads.

Attributes
Forest/Woodland; Moorland
Start and Finish
Pentrefoelas, Conwy SH873515
Websites
www.hiraethog.org.uk
Maps
OS Landranger: 116
OS Explorer: 264
Publications, badges and certificates
Pack
Hiraethog Trail by Conway County Borough Council (Llyn Brenig Reservoir and Visitor Centre). £1.00 (incs p&p). Cheques to Conwy County Borough Council.

Iron Mountain Trail IMT

TORFAEN **19km/12 miles**

The route consists of two walks which combine to make a figure-of-eight circuit of the major sites of the Blaenavon Industrial Landscape World Heritage Site, with other linking routes as extensions. From the mid 18th Century Blaenavon's people played a leading role in the United Kingdom's iron and coal industries, also playing a key part in the Industrial Revolution.

Attributes
Moorland; World Heritage Site; Heritage; Industrial History
Start and Finish
Pen-fford-goch Pond Car Park, Blaenavon, Torfaen SO253108
Websites
www.world-heritage-blaenavon.org.uk
Maps
OS Landranger: 161
OS Explorer: 13
Publications, badges and certificates
Leaflets
Blaenavon Walks Pack including Iron Mountain Trail (Visit Wales). Free.

Landsker Borderlands Trail LBT

CARMS, PEMBROKES 96km/60 miles

Landsker is an old Norse word for frontier. The route explores the rural area on the Pembrokeshire/Carmarthenshire border from Llanboidy and Efailwen in the north, via Canaston Bridge on the Daugleddau, to Landshipping and Lawrenny in the south, returning via Reynalton and Ludchurch. The leaflet does not include a full route description but the route is on OS maps and waymarked.

Attributes
Coastal
Start and Finish
Canaston Bridge, Pembrokes SN067152
Waymark
Named disc with Celtic design for logo
Websites
www.planed.org.uk
Maps ◈
OS Landranger: 145, 157, 158
OS Explorer: 177, 185, 35, 36
Publications, badges and certificates
Leaflets
Landsker Borderlands Trail by PLANED Community Project (PLANED) 2001. 24pp; A4. Free.
Walking Support Providers
Greenways; Walka-Longway

Lleyn Peninsula Coastal Path LLCP

GWYNEDD 135km/84 miles

The walk follows in the footsteps of early pilgrims heading to the tiny island of Bardsey, hence a number of small churches are passed along the way. The route, although mainly coastal, does turn inland on occasions where the higher ground provides good views of the peninsula. Along the north coast, the section from Llanwnda to Penygroes is part of the Lon Eifion route (12 miles from Caernarfon to Bryncir). From Aberdaron it may be possible to cross to Bardsey. Between Pwllheli and Porthmadoc, on the south coast, there is an opportunity to visit the village of Llanystumdwy, childhood home of David Lloyd George. At Porthmadoc the Path links to the Meirionnydd Coast Walk.

Attributes
Coastal; Pilgrimage
Start
Caernafon Castle, Gwynedd SH477626
Finish
High Street, Portmadoc, Gwynedd SH570385
Waymark
Route name in blue ring with map
Websites
www.gwynedd.gov.uk, www.visitsnowdonia.info
Maps
OS Landranger: 114, 115, 123, 124
OS Explorer: 17, 18, 253, 254, 263
Publications, badges and certificates
Paperbacks
Lleyn Peninsula Coastal Path by John Cantrell (Cicerone Press) 2006. ISBN 9781852844790. 224pp; 115 x 175. £10.00.
Brochure
Lleyn Peninsula Coast Path (Gwynedd County Council) 2006. Free. From Pwllheli TIC.
Leaflets
Gwynedd Recreational Routes: Lon Eifion and other routes (Pwllheli TIC). Free.

Llwybr Ceiriog Trail LCT

DENBIGHS, POWYS, SHROPS, WREXHAM 37km/23 miles

The Trail, developed primarily for horse riders, crosses some rugged terrain. It crosses the River Ceiriog at Pandy and Castle Mill and is coincident with Offa's Dyke Path National Trail in the Bronygarth/Craignant area. The waymarked Upper Ceiriog Trail (14 miles and on OS mapping) takes in Llanarmon Dyffryn Ceiriog and provides a loop to the west of Pandy.

Attributes
Horse Ride (Multi User); Moorland
Start and Finish
Spring Hill Farm, Pandy, Powys
SJ210344
Waymark
Stirrup/'Llwybr Ceiriog Trail' in black on white background
Maps ◈
OS Landranger: 117, 125, 126
OS Explorer: 240, 255, 256
Publications, badges and certificates
Leaflets
Ceiriog Trail (Llangollen Tourist Information Centre). A4/3. £1.00 (+ £1.00 p&p).
Upper Ceiriog Trail (Llangollen Tourist Information Centre). A4/3. £1.00 (+ £1.00 p&p).

Mal Evans Way – Borth to Devil's Bridge MEWBDB

CEREDIGION **29km/18 miles**

The walk remembers Mal Evans of the Ramblers. It offers some fine scenery and passes through some old mining areas to join Ystumtuen, which is on the route of the Cambrian Way, and reaches the sea at Borth. It also has links with the Dyfi Valley Way and the Cardigan Bay Coast Walk

Attributes
Industrial History
Start
Borth, Ceredigion SN608907
Finish
Devil's Bridge, Ceredigion SN739768
Websites
http://tourism.ceredigion.gov.uk
Maps
OS Landranger: 135
OS Explorer: 213
Publications, badges and certificates
Leaflets
Mal Evans Way: Borth to Devil's Bridge by Mal Evans (Ceredigion County Council) 2007. 12pp; A5. £0.40 (+A5 SAE).

Meirionnydd Coast Walk MEICW

GWYNEDD **116km/72 miles**

This walk takes in standing stones, stone circles and holy wells, and visits Barmouth and Harlech. At Barmouth Railway Bridge pedestrians pay a toll. It has links with the Dyfi Valley Way, the Cambrian Way and the Lleyn Peninsula Coastal Path.

Attributes
Coastal; Heritage; Religious
Start
Aberdyfi Railway Station SN607961
Finish
Porthmadog Railway Station SH566392
Maps
OS Landranger: 124, 135
OS Explorer: 18, 23
Publications, badges and certificates
Paperbacks
Meirionnydd Coast Walk by Laurence Main (Gwasg Carreg Gwalch) 2001. ISBN 9780863816666. 115pp; 123 x 184. £4.50 (+ £1.50 p&p).

Mines, Moorland & Mountain MMM

WREXHAM **24km/15 miles**

The walk goes up the Clywedog Valley and onto the heather moorland above, where there is a choice of three routes of varying lengths, each having good viewpoints. The longest route includes 700m of ascent around Esclusham Mountain, passing old lead mines, limestone quarries, a 'long house', and a stone cross marking the scene of a WW2 plane crash.

Attributes
Challenging; Heritage; Industrial History
Start and Finish
Nant Mill Visitor Centre, Coedpoeth, Wrexham SJ289501
Websites
www.wrexham.gov.uk
Maps
OS Landranger: 117
OS Explorer: 256
Publications, badges and certificates
Looseleaf
Mines, Moorland & Mountain (Wrexham Tourist Information Centre) 2007. 8pp; A4. £1.00 (+ p&p).

Mynydd Hiraethog & Denbigh Moors Footpath MHDMF

CONWY, DENBIGHS **64km/40 miles**

This route covers an extensive footpath network in the rural south-east of the County Borough (around Pentrefoelas and Cerrigydrudion), and extends into Denbighshire. The network consists of a linear 40 mile route, together with six shorter circular routes which can each be walked individually. The leaflet pack consists of a set of ten maps together with some information about the area (including accommodation and services).

Attributes
Moorland
Start
Pentrefoelas, Conwy SH874514
Finish
Llanrhaeadr, Denbighs SJ082635
Waymark
Named green discs with wall and tree design
Websites
www.conwy.gov.uk
Maps
OS Landranger: 116
OS Explorer: 264, 18
Publications, badges and certificates
Looseleaf (in plastic wallet)
Mynydd Hiraethog & Denbigh Moors Footpath Network (Conwy County Borough Council) 2000. ISBN 9781840470048. 28pp; A5. £1.00 (incs p&p). Cheques to Conway CBC.

North Berwyn Way NBERW

DENBIGHS **24km/15 miles**

A linear trail that climbs and traverses the wild North Berwyn Mountains to the south of the River Dee. It is a challenging route for experienced walkers and it is essential to be properly equipped. The route is split into five sections that start and finish at easily accessible points. It crosses a major area of upland heath – high heather moorland – passing the walk's highest point (Moel Fferna, 630m, though not the highest point in the Berwyns), across a landscape used for centuries for slate quarrying and grouse shooting and more recently forestry. It can be combined with the Dee Valley Way to form a circular walk of some 30 miles, or using the link paths shown, there are shorter options. Details of both walks (schematic maps) are available online.

Attributes
Challenging; Moorland
Start
Llangollen, Denbighshire SJ214420
Finish
Corwen, Denbighshire SJ080435
Waymark
Heather moor/blue river graphic and name on white disc
Websites
www.deevalleywalks.com
Maps
OS Landranger: 117, 125
OS Explorer: 255
Publications, badges and certificates
Booklets
North Berwyn Way (Llangollen Tourist Information Centre) 2007. 24pp; A5. Free. In English and Welsh.

North Wales Path NWP

CONWY, DENBIGHS, GWYNEDD **96km/60 miles**

This partly coastal route has significant stretches that allow the walker to explore some of the hilly hinterland. However, most of the larger resorts situated along the North Wales coastline are accessible. It links with the Offa's Dyke Path National Trail, and the Clwydian Way, at Prestatyn.

Attributes
Coastal; Moorland
Start
Bangor, Gwynedd SH592726
Finish
Prestatyn, Denbighs SJ060837
Waymark
Named discs with stylised hills and sea
Maps ◈
OS Landranger: 114, 115, 116
OS Explorer: 263, 264, 265, 17
Publications, badges and certificates
Paperbacks
North Wales Path & Ten Selected Walks by David Slater, Dave Worrall (Gwasg Carreg Gwalch) 1999. ISBN 9780863815461. 120pp; 183 x 123. £4.50 (+ £1.50 p&p).
Folder
North Wales Path (Conwy County Borough Council) 1997. 16pp; A5. £1.00 (incs p&p). Cheques to Conway CBC.
Walking Support Providers
Celtic; HF

Offa's Hyke **OFFAH**

DENBIGHS, FLINTS **32km/20 miles**

A tough walk on and around the Clwydian Hills, with some 4000ft of ascent. It is coincident with parts of the Offa's Dyke Path National Trail. Profits from sales go to Hope House Childrens Hospice. This walk should not be underestimated. Good navigation skills are required.

Attributes
Very Challenging; Anytime Challenge; Moorland; Charity
Start and Finish
Bwlch Penbarra, Denbighs SJ161605
Maps
OS Landranger: 116
OS Explorer: 265
Publications, badges and certificates
Looseleaf
Offa's Hyke (Michael Skuse). 1pp; A4. Free (+ SAE). Updated May 2008.
Badge & certificate
Offa's Hyke (Michael Skuse). £3.00 (+ A5 SAE).

Pererindod Melangell **PERMEL**

POWYS **24km/15 miles**

On the eastern fringes of the Cambrian/Berwyn mountains, it traces an undulating route between the Vyrnwy and Tanat Valleys, trodden in centuries past by pilgrims, quarrymen and drovers. At Llanwyddyn, there are facilities based around Lake Vyrnwy. St Melangell's Church is named after a saint, who is said to have hidden a hare under her robes so it could escape being killed by a prince and his huntsmen. He was so impressed with her godliness that he gave her the valley, where she established an abbey.

Attributes
Challenging; Moorland
Start
Pont Llogel, Powys SJ032154
Finish
Llangynog, Powys SJ053261
Waymark
Saint and hare, with name on green/blue disc
Websites
www.tourism.powys.gov.uk
Maps ◈
OS Landranger: 125
OS Explorer: 239
Publications, badges and certificates
Booklets
Pererindod Melangell Walk (Powys County Council). £3.25. Cheques to Powys County Council.

Radnor Forest Ride **RDFR**

POWYS, SHROPS **113km/70 miles**

A multi-user route along bridleways, byways and quiet lanes, passing through some of the most beautiful upland scenery in Wales. It links with the Three Rivers Ride at the Brecon Beacons National Park Visitors Centre, the Jack Mytton Way in Shropshire, and provides access to the Epynt Way.

Attributes
Challenging; Horse Ride (Multi User); Moorland
Start
Beacons National Park Visitor Centre, nr Libanus, Powys SN977262
Finish
Lloyney, Powys SO244759
Websites
www.ride-uk.org.uk
Maps
OS Landranger: 148, 160
OS Explorer: 12, 188, 200, 201
Publications, badges and certificates
Leaflets (with accommodation list)
Radnor Forest Ride by British Horse Society (British Horse Society). Free. £2 donation requested. Cheques to British Horse Society.

Rhymney Valley Ridgeway Walk **RVRW**

CAERPHILLY **45km/28 miles**

Winding its way across the hills encircling the unique and often spectacular scenery of the Rhymney Valley, this walk follows quiet countryside paths and lanes, where steep beech woodlands merge into panoramic mountain tops. Mynydd Machen is the highest point. It links with the Taff-Ely Ridgeway Walk at Caerphilly Common, and in the east is partly coincident with the Sirhowy Valley Walk. The Northern Rhymney Valley Ridgeway Walk (12 miles) links with the main circular walk at Gelligaer and finishes at Bryn Bach Park.

Attributes
Moorland
Start and Finish
Penallta Community Park ST130951

Waymark
Hill/river logo
Websites
www.caerphilly.gov.uk
Maps ◈
OS Landranger: 161, 171
OS Explorer: 151, 152, 166
Publications, badges and certificates
Route notes (4 A4 waterproof route maps folded in card cover)
Rhymney Valley Ridgeway Walk (Caerphilly County Borough Council) 2006. 120 x 150. Free.
Leaflets
Northern Rhymney Valley Ridgeway Walk (Caerphilly County Borough Council) 1998. A3 folded. Free.

Sarn Helen SARNH

CARMS, CEREDIGION, CONWY, GWYNEDD 258km/160 miles

This is an old Roman route through West Wales, connecting places linked with Roman interest. From the Roman fort at Caerhun the route heads along the edge of Snowdonia to the Swallow Falls, Dolwyddelan, skirts Blaunau Ffestiniog to Trawsfynydd, and continues to Dolgellau and Machynlleth. After crossing the Rheidol valley, the route becomes less wild and more agricultural to reach Bronant, Lampeter, and Carmarthen. Navigational skills are esssential on the northern part of the route.

Attributes
Challenging; Cycle Route; Moorland; Heritage
Start
Conwy, Conwy SH783775
Finish
Carmarthen, Carms SN400210
Websites
http://mbruk.co.uk
Maps
OS Landranger: 115, 124, 135, 146, 159
OS Explorer: 177, 185, 186, 199, 213, 17, 18
Publications, badges and certificates
Booklets
Sarn Helen Trail: Mountain Bike Route Companion Packs (MTB-Wales.com) 1998. ISBN 9781902891033. 43pp. Available from MTB-Wales website.

Severn Way SEVW

BRISTOL, GLOS, POWYS, SHROPS, S GLOS, WORCS 338km/210 miles

A route along the entire Severn Valley, from the source to the sea. Starting on the wild Plynlimon plateau in Mid-Wales, the route takes in Hafren Forest, Llanidloes, Newtown, Welshpool, Shrewsbury and Ironbridge before heading south through Worcester, Tewkesbury and Gloucester to reach Severn Beach, it then links along the Avon into Bristol City Centre. There are links with a number of other long distance paths, and Shakespeare's Avon Way provides a promoted route along the River Avon.

Attributes
River; Moorland
Start
Plynlimon, Powys SN822899
Finish
Bristol City Centre, Bristol ST585727
Waymark
Severn Trow logo and named posts
Websites
www.severnway.com, www.tourism.powys.gov.uk
Maps ◈
OS Landranger: 126, 127, 136, 137, 138, 150, 162, 172
OS Explorer: 14, 154, 155, 167, 179, 190, 204, 214, 215, 216, 217, 218, 219, 240, 241, 242
Publications, badges and certificates
Paperbacks (spiral bound)
Severn Way: the Longest Riverside Walk in Britain (Official Guide) by Severn Way Partnership (Environment Agency) 1999. ISBN 9781902999005. 103pp; A5. £6.95 (incs p&p).
Leaflets (set of four describing the route in Powys)
Severn Way (Powys County Council). Free.
Walking Support Providers
Bobs

Sirhowy Valley Ridgeway Walk SVRW

BLAENAU G, CAERPHILLY, NEWPORT 42km/26 miles

From the built-up fringes of Newport to the mountain ridges of Mynydd Machen and Mynydd Manmoel, the route passes lowland and upland farms; woodlands and riverside parks; many sites of historical interest, including an Iron Age hill fort, an old mill and a canal centre. The Walk links with the waymarked Ebbw Valley Walk (16 miles from Wattsville to Ebbw Vale and on OS mapping) near Cwm. The circular waymarked Raven Walk

(12 miles and on OS mapping) uses part of the Sirhowy Valley Walk near Ynysddu.

Attributes
Challenging; River; Moorland; Mountain; Heritage
Start
Tredegar House, Newport ST290850
Finish
Aneurin Bevan Memorial, Tredegar SO150106
Waymark
Named standard discs
Websites
www.walking.visitwales.com, www.caerphilly.gov.uk
Maps ◈
OS Landranger: 161, 171
OS Explorer: 152, 166, 13
Publications, badges and certificates
Leaflets
Sirhowy Valley Walk (Caerphilly County Borough Council). A3 folded. Free.
Raven Walk by Islwyn Access Network (Caerphilly County Borough Council) 1995. A4. Free.

Sky to Sea SKTSEA

BRIDGEND, GLAMORGAN, RHONDDA CT **56km/35 miles**

This walk offers two routes, called Sky to Sea through the Vale (19 miles) and Sky to Sea over the Bwlch (16 miles), linking the mountains to the sea, taking in the spectacular countryside of West Glamorgan Heritage Coast. There are links with many other long distance routes in South Wales.

Attributes
Moorland; Mountain
Start
Dare Valley Country Park, Rhondda CT SN983026
Finish
Gileston, Glamorgan SS956675
Waymark
Waves and blue cloud logo
Maps
OS Landranger: 170
OS Explorer: 151, 166
Publications, badges and certificates
Leaflets
Sky to Sea: Over the Bwlch Walk by Glamorgan County Council (Bridgend Tourist Information Centre). Free.
Sky to Sea: Through the Vale (Bridgend Tourist Information Centre). Free.

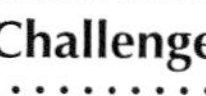

Snowdon Challenge Walk SNOWCW

GWYNEDD **48km/30 miles**

A tough walk, with 5,000ft of ascent, to the top of Snowdon and back. From Caernarfon Bay it climbs via the Ranger Path and descends via the Rhyd-ddu path.

Attributes
Very Challenging; Anytime Challenge; Moorland; Mountain
Start and Finish
Pontllyfni, Gwynedd SH435526
Maps
OS Landranger: 115
OS Explorer: 17
Publications, badges and certificates
Booklets
Snowdon Challenge Walk by John Merrill (John Merrill Foundation). ISBN 9780907496793. 40pp; A5. £4.50 (+ £1.00 p&p). Cheques to John Merrill Foundation.
Badge & certificate
Snowdon Challenge Walk (John Merrill Foundation). £5.00 (incs p&p).

Snowdonia 24hr Circuit SNOW24C

CONWY, GWYNEDD **72km/45 miles**

A tough rollercoaster circuit of approximately 16,500ft of ascent which includes the Snowdon Horseshoe, Glyders, Carneddau and Moel Siabod massifs.

Attributes
Very Challenging; Anytime Challenge; Moorland; Mountain
Start and Finish
Capel Curig, Conwy SH721583
Maps
OS Landranger: 115
OS Explorer: 17
Publications, badges and certificates
Looseleaf
Snowdonia 24hr Circuit (Ed Dalton). 1pp; foolscap. Free (+ 9 x 4 SAE).
Certificate
Snowdonia 24hr Circuit (Ed Dalton). Free (+ 9 x 6 SAE).
Paperbacks
Ridges of Snowdonia by Steve Ashton (Cicerone Press) 2005. ISBN 9781852843502. 172 x 116. £12.00.

Snowdonia Challenges — SNC

CONWY, GWYNEDD — **Various**

These comprise three routes: the Heart of Snowdonia 24 hour Circuit (50 miles & 20,000ft of ascent); the Snowdonia Five Ranges Round (40 miles & 12,500ft of ascent) and the Welsh 1000m Peaks Marathon (26 miles & 9,050ft of ascent).

Attributes
Very Challenging; Anytime Challenge; Moorland; Mountain
Start
Various
Finish
Various
Maps
OS Landranger: 115
OS Explorer: 17, 18
Publications, badges and certificates
Looseleaf
Three Snowdonia Challenge Walks by Dave Irons (Dave Irons) 1994. 14pp; A4. £2.00 (incs p&p).
Certificate
Snowdonia Challenges by Dave Irons (Dave Irons). Free (+ A4 SAE).

Snowdonia Panoramic Walk — SNOWPW

GWYNEDD — **48km/30 miles**

A strenuous walk with about 12,500ft of ascent over ridge paths of Snowdonia, taking in the summits of Carnedd Llewellyn, Snowdon, and the seven peaks of the Nantlle Ridge.

Attributes
Very Challenging; Anytime Challenge; Moorland; Mountain
Start
Abergwyngregyn, Gwynedd SH662720
Finish
Nebo, Gwynedd SH479505
Maps
OS Landranger: 115
OS Explorer: 17
Publications, badges and certificates
Booklets
Snowdonia Panoramic Walk (Ed Dalton) 1987. 8pp; A4. £1.50 (+ 9 x 6 SAE).

Paperbacks
Ridges of Snowdonia by Steve Ashton (Cicerone Press) 2005. ISBN 9781852843502. 172 x 116. £12.00.

Snowdonia Round — SNOWR

CONWY, GWYNEDD — **103km/64 miles**

A route visiting the youth hostels at Idwal Cottage, Pen-y-Pass, Bryn Gwynant and Lledr Valley, taking in Drum, Glyder Fawr, Snowdon and Dulwyddelan.

Attributes
Very Challenging; Anytime Challenge; Moorland; Mountain
Start and Finish
Conwy Youth Hostel, Conwy SH774773
Maps
OS Landranger: 115
OS Explorer: 17
Publications, badges and certificates
Looseleaf
Snowdonia Round Route Notes (YHA Northern Region). £1.00 (incs p&p).

St Illtyd's Walk — STILLTW

CARMS, NEATH PT, SWANSEA — **103km/64 miles**

This is a walk across varied terrain, including sands, canals, woodlands and gentle hills. The route crosses four rivers, the Loughor, Tawe, Neath and Afan. It links with the Coed Morgannwg Way at Margam, giving access to the Rhymney Valley Ridgeway Walk and Taff Trail. St Illtyd flourished in the latter part of the fifth and beginning of the sixth century, and was held in high veneration in Wales.

Attributes
Canal; Religious
Start
Pembrey Country Park, Carms SN403000
Finish
Margam Country Park, Neath PT SS806862
Waymark
Black turreted tower on named discs
Maps ◈
OS Landranger: 159, 160, 170
OS Explorer: 164, 165, 166, 178, 12
Publications, badges and certificates
Booklets
St Illtyd's Walk by G. Colin Davies (Carmarthenshire

County Council). 30pp; A5. £2.00 (+ 30p p&p). Cheques to Carmarthenshire CC.

Taff Ely Ridgeway Walk/ Ffordd y Bryniau — TBRW

CAERPHILLY, CARDIFF, RHONDDA CT — **34km/21 miles**

Using footpaths, bridleways and lanes, the Walk follows a line of hills running from Mynydd Maendy in the west, to Caerphilly Common in the east. The route passes through forestry and visits Llantrisant, and Caerau ancient hill fort. There are links with the Rhymney Valley Ridgeway Walk at Caerphilly Common; the Taff Trail near to Taff's Well; and the waymarked Ogwr Ridgeway Walk (13 miles and on OS mapping) at the start. The latter joins the Coed Morgannwg Way.

Attributes
Challenging; Forest/Woodland; Moorland; Heritage
Start
Mynydd Maendy, Rhondda CT SS977861
Finish
Caerphilly Common, Caerphilly ST153856
Waymark
Yellow/black named discs with hills motif
Websites
www.bridgend.gov.uk
Maps ◈
OS Landranger: 170, 171
OS Explorer: 151
Publications, badges and certificates
Leaflets
Taff Ely Ridgeway Walk/Ffordd y Bryniau (Cardiff County Council). A4/3. Free.
Ogwr Ridgeway Walk (Bridgend Tourist Information Centre) 1991. A4/3. Free.

Taff Trail — TAFFT

CARDIFF, MERTHYR T, POWYS, RHONDDA CT — **88km/55 miles**

The Trail, used by walkers and cyclists, runs mostly along converted railway lines but also uses former canal towpaths and forestry tracks. It runs along the Taff valley to Llandaff, Pontypridd and Merthyr Tydfil. From here the main route circles to the east of the Brecon Beacons via Talybont and Pencelli to Brecon. An alternative route via Neuadd Reservoir creates a circular walk between Merthyr and Brecon. At Gethin Woodland Park, near Merthyr, the Trail links with the Coed Morgannwg Way.

Attributes
Former Railway; Cycle Route; Forest/ Woodland; Lake/Reservoir; River; Canal
Start
Cardiff ST192745
Finish
Brecon, Powys SO045285
Waymark
Stylised viaduct in black on arrow
Websites
www.tafftrail.org, www.sustrans.org.uk, www.tourism.powys.gov.uk
Maps ◈
OS Landranger: 160, 161, 170, 171
OS Explorer: 151, 166, 12, 13
Publications, badges and certificates
Leaflets
Taff Trail for Walkers & Cyclists (Merthyr Tydfil TIC) 1995. 4pp; A4/3. Free.
Walking Support Providers
Drover

Taith Torfaen — TAITOR

BLAENAU G, CAERPHILLY, MONS, TORFAEN — **80km/50 miles**

Two loops, forming a figure-of-eight walk, take in Blorenge Mountain and Coity Mountain in the north and Twmbarlwm, Mynydd Machen, Islwyn and the Torfaen Hills in the south.

Attributes
Challenging; Anytime Challenge; Moorland
Start and Finish
Pontypool Leisure Centre, Torfaen SO285007
Maps
OS Landranger: 161, 171
OS Explorer: 152, 13
Publications, badges and certificates
Looseleaf
Taith Torfaen (Gerry Jackson). 6pp; A4. Free (+ 9 x 6 SAE).
Badge & certificate
Taith Torfaen (Gerry Jackson). £2.00 & £0.50 (+ SAE).

Torfaen Trail TFT

TORFAEN **56km/35 miles**

This scenic figure of eight route, with 5,200ft of ascent, takes in the whole of Torfaen, from Cwnbran in the south, through Pontypool, to Bleanavon in the north.

Attributes
Challenging; Forest/Woodland; Moorland; Mountain
Start and Finish
Main Leisure Centre, Pontypool, Torfaen SO285007
Maps
OS Landranger: 161, 171
OS Explorer: 13, 152
Publications, badges and certificates
Booklets (includes set of nine Leaflets)
Torfaen Trail (Torfaen County Borough). Free.

Usk Valley Walk USKVW

MONS, NEWPORT, POWYS **77km/48 miles**

Using riverside, field and woodland paths, and some minor roads, the Walk follows the Usk valley upstream past the historic market town of Usk, to Abergavenny. Here it takes to the Monmouthshire and Brecon Canal towpath which it follows to Brecon. Mainly an easy walk, there are two climbs: to the Kemeys Ridge, north of Caerleon, and to Glanusk Park, west of Crickhowell.

Attributes
Easy; River; Canal
Start
Caerleon, Newport ST341903
Finish
Brecon, Powys SO043286
Waymark
Named yellow arrows
Websites
www.monmouthshire.gov.uk, www.uskvalleywalk.org.uk, www.tourism.powys.gov.uk
Maps ◈
OS Landranger: 160, 161, 171
OS Explorer: 12, 13, 152
Publications, badges and certificates
Booklets
Usk Valley Walk (Monmouthshire County Council) 2003. £6.95 (+ 50p p&p).
Walking Support Providers
Contours; Drover; HF; Marches Walks

Valeways Millennium Heritage Trail VMHT

GLAMORGAN **105km/65 miles**

A circular route around the Vale of Glamorgan through landscapes of historical and scenic interest. With inland and coastal sections, it visits Barry, Rhoose, Llanblethian, Llantwit Major, Monknash, St Bride's Major and Llanharry. The 14-mile Glamorgan Heritage Coast provides a coastal route with rocky and sandy beaches, sand dunes and cliffs.

Attributes
Coastal; Heritage
Start
Museum of Welsh Life, St Fagans, Glamorgan ST119770
Finish
Peterston-super-Ely, Glamorgan ST081762
Waymark
White discs with letter M and name in arrow (replacing purple discs)
Websites
www.valeways.org.uk
Maps ◈
OS Landranger: 170, 171
OS Explorer: 151
Publications, badges and certificates
Folder
Valeways Millennium Heritage Trail (Valeways) 2005. ISBN 9780955056505. 36pp; A5. £8.49 (incs p&p). Includes 8 A3/4 sectional route leaflets (including Glamorgan HT).

Wat's Dyke Heritage Trail WDHT

FLINTS, POWYS, SHROPS **98km/61 miles**

Wat's Dyke is a 40-mile earthwork running through the northern Welsh Marches which runs through pastoral countryside close to the Welsh border, generally parallel to Offa's Dyke, sometimes very close but always within three miles. The route includes Oswestry, Overton, Wrexham, Caergwrie, New Brighton and Rhosesmar.

Attributes
Heritage
Start
Llanymynech, Powys SJ266209
Finish
Basingwerk Abbey, Holywell, Powys SJ194774

Waymark
Black band on named white disc with castle/well motif
Websites
www.watsdykeway.org, www.maesbury.org
Maps
OS Landranger: 116, 117, 126
OS Explorer: 240, 256, 265
Publications, badges and certificates
Paperbacks
Wat's Dyke Way Heritage Trail (Mold Bookshop) 2008. ISBN 9780955962509. 128pp. £5.95 (+ £1.95 p&p). Available from website.

Welsh 3000s — W3000S

CONWY, GWYNEDD — **47km/29 miles**

A crossing of the 15 Snowdonian summits over 3,000ft, taking in the Carneddau, the Glyders and the Snowdon Massif. It involves 12,000ft of ascent with some exposed scrambling. If that challenge is not enough the Welsh 3000s Double Crossing (28 summits) is also available.

Attributes
Challenging; Anytime Challenge; Moorland; Mountain
Start
Snowdon summit, Gwynedd SH609544
Finish
Foel Fras summit, Conwy SH697682
Maps
OS Landranger: 115
OS Explorer: 17
Publications, badges and certificates
Paperbacks
Welsh Three Thousand Foot Challenges by Ron Clayton, Ronald Turnbull (Grey Stone Books) 1997. ISBN 9780951599662. 128pp; 175 x 115. £6.95.
Ridges of Snowdonia by Steve Ashton (Cicerone Press) 2005. ISBN 9781852843502. 172 x 116. £12.00.
Three Peaks, Ten Tors by Ronald Turnbull (Cicerone Press) 2007. ISBN 9781852845018. 256pp; 170 x 120. £12.95.
Looseleafs
Welsh 3000s Double Crossing (Peter Travis). 3pp; A4. Free (+ 9 x 4 SAE).
Welsh 3000s Double Crossing (Ed Dalton). 1pp; foolscap. Free (+ 9 x 4 SAE).
Certificates
Welsh 3000s (Peter Travis). £1.25 each (incs p&p). For single or double crossing.
(double crossing)
Welsh 3000s (Ed Dalton). £2.00 (incs p&p).
Hardback
Macc & the Art of Long Distance Walking by Graham Wilson (Millrace Books) 2007. ISBN 9781902173245. 192pp; 172 x 124. £13.95.
Walking Support Providers
Aengus

Wye Valley Walk — WYEVW

GLOS, HEREFS, MONS, POWYS — **222km/138 miles**

A walk following the banks of the river for most of its length but including some hill climbing. The route passes Lovers Leap and Tintern Abbey and several vantage points are visited before crossing over to the other bank at Redbrook to reach Monmouth. From here it meanders on past English Bicknor, Welsh Bicknor and Goodrich Castle before heading across country to Ross-on-Wye and Hereford. Through cider orchards, parkland and farmland, the Walk continues via Bredwardine, Merbach Hill, Hay-on-Wye, Builth Wells, Newbridge and Rhayader. It then heads towards the source of the Wye on the slopes of Plynlimon, eventually turning to meet the Severn Way in Hafren Forest. This can then be followed east to reach transport at Llanlidloes.

Attributes
Forest/Woodland; River; Moorland; Heritage
Start
Chepstow Castle, Mons ST533942
Finish
Rhyd-y-Benwch Car park, Hafren Forest, Powys SN857869
Waymark
Leaping salmon on named disc
Websites
www.wyevalleywalk.org, www.tourism.powys.gov.uk
Maps ◈
OS Landranger: 136, 147, 148, 149, 161, 162
OS Explorer: 188, 189, 200, 201, 202, 214, 13, 14
Publications, badges and certificates
Paperbacks
Wye Valley Walk: Official Route Guide 2nd Edn (Powys County Council) 2003. ISBN 9780954339906. 128pp; A5. £7.95 (+ £1.05 p&p). Incs 42 maps. Spiral bound. With free Accommodation/Transport Guide (26pp) Cheques to Powys County Council.
Leaflets
Wye Valley Walk – Source to Rhayader (Powys County Council). Free. Available from Tourism Section, Powys County Council.
Walking Support Providers
Celtic; Contours; Drover; Marches Walks; Wycheway

Wysis Way — WYSW

GLOS, MONS — **88km/55 miles**

Linking Offa's Dyke Path National Trail at Monmouth to the beginning of the Thames Path National Trail in Gloucestershire, this walk crosses the distinctive areas of the Forest of Dean, the Severn Vale and the Cotswolds. It also links with the Three Choirs Way and other long distance paths.

Attributes
River; Downland/Wolds
Start
Monmouth, Mons SO510130
Finish
Kemble, Glos ST985975
Waymark
Cathedral & rivers graphic, name, 'Offa's Dyke to Thames Path' on orange disc
Websites
www.countryside-matters.co.uk
Maps ◈
OS Landranger: 162, 163
OS Explorer: 14, 168, 179
Publications, badges and certificates
Paperbacks
Wysis Way: Offa's Dyke to the Thames Path by Gerry Stewart, Genny Proctor (Countryside Matters) 1998. ISBN 9780952787013. 80pp; A5. £5.95 (incs p&p).

SCOTLAND

The River Spey, flanked by banks of bleached cobbles, passes below Ordiquish

KEY FACTS

Areas	Aberdeenshire, Angus, Argyll & Bute, Ayrshire, Clackmannanshire, Dumbartonshire, Dumfries & Galloway, Western Isles, Fife, Strathclyde including Glasgow, Highland, Lothian including Edinburgh, Moray, Orkney & Shetland, Perth & Kinross, Renfrewshire, Scottish Borders, Stirling
National Parks	Cairngorms, Loch Lomond & The Trossachs
Principal National Scenic Areas	Western Isles: St Kilda, (South Lewis, Harris & North Uist), South Uist Machair, Orkney: Hoy and West Mainland, Shetland: Herma Ness, Fethaland, Esha Ness, Muckle Roe, SW Mainland, Foula, Fair Isle, Highland: NW Sutherland, Kyle of Tongue, Assynt-Coigach, Webster Ross, Trotternish, Cuillin Hills, Glen Affric, Kintail, Knoydart, Dornoch Firth, Glen Strathfarrar, The Small Isles, (Morar, Moidart & Ardnamurchan), Loch Shiel, Lynn of Lorn, Loch na Keal, Ben Nevis and Glencoe, Argyll and Bute: Knapdale, Jura, (Scarba, Lunga and the Garvellachs), The Kyles of Bute, Perth and Kinross: Loch Rannoch and Glen Lyon, Loch Tummel, River Tay (Dunkeld), River Earn (Comrie to St Fillans), Aberdeenshire: Deeside and Lochnager, Ayrshire: North Arran, Dumfries and Galloway: Fleet Valley, East Stewartby Coast, Nith Estuary, Scottish Borders: Upper Tweeddale, Eidon & Leaderfoot
World Heritage Sites	Old and New Towns of Edinburgh, Heart of Neolithic Orkney, New Lanark, St Kilda
E-Routes	E2 variants Dover – Stranraer, E2 variant Harwich – Stranraer
National Trails (Scotland)	Great Glen Way, Speyside Way, West Highland Way, Southern Upland Way, Pennine Way (a very small part)
Walking Routes (trail miles)	31 main routes (2300 miles); 18 waymarked (1170 miles)
Resident population	5 million

DON'T MISS! TRAIL SECTIONS (CHALLENGING/REMOTE MARKED WITH *)

Clyde Walkway	Crossford (or longer options) to New Lanark, mostly easy, riverside walking by the Clyde to a World Heritage industrial village and up to the Falls of Clyde (15km, 1000ft ascent).
Ayrshire Coastal Path	Maidens to Dunure, shorelines, Turnberry Open Championship Golf Course, views of Ailsa Craig (23km)
John Muir Way	Dunglass to Dunbar, on cliffs and shorelines in Muir's footsteps to his birthplace and museum (16km), options to JM Country Park
Cowal Way	Clachan Strachur to Arrochar, passing Cnoc Coinnich* (27km, 4000ft ascent), peak bagging options on this and the Cobbler*
West Highland Way – 1	Kinlochleven to Fort William along the Old Military Road and through Nevis Forest (24km, 2419ft ascent)
West Highland Way – 2	Inversnaid to Crianlarich along the banks of Loch Lomond and through the Trossachs National Park and Glen Falloch (21km, 2041ft ascent)
Speyside Way	Cromdale to Cragganmore via riverside and Tom-an-uiard Wood (17km, 1251ft ascent)
Great Glen Way	Invermoriston to Lewiston via the densely forested slopes alongside Loch Ness. Look out for the 'monster' (21km, 1970ft ascent).
Southern Upland Way	Castle Kennedy to Dranigower Bridge with views of the White and Black Lochs, Castle Kennedy, Loups of Barnshagen (waterfall) and Glenwhan Moor (15km, 883ft ascent)

REFERENCE SOURCES INCLUDING MANY REGIONAL ROUTES

Scottish Hill Tracks (Scottish Rights of Way and Access Society, 2004, 191pp, ISBN: 978-0954673505, £16) describes some 350 Scottish routes. Its map of Scotland graphically illustrates the wealth of long distance cross-country walks across the hills and moors.

SCOTLAND

Geographically, Scotland divides essentially into three areas, with each boundary aligned very roughly south west to north east. Heading north from the English borders these are: the Southern Uplands, the Central Lowlands and, furthest north, the Highlands and Islands.

Geography and geology

The Southern Uplands are agricultural plains, and rolling hills rising to about 2700ft (815m). These rounded hills had their origins in sediments laid down in a former ocean. The Central Lowlands lie between the two main Firths – estuaries – of the Clyde and the Forth, and between Glasgow and Edinburgh. They are home to most of Scotland's population, its major industries and its commercial centres.

The Lowlands are the remains of a rift valley, such as we see now in East Africa, where tectonic forces began to pull Scotland apart. There were volcanoes here, now eroded to the hills that pepper the landscape, such as Arthur's Seat in Edinburgh.

Separated from the Lowlands by the geological fracture of the Highland Boundary Fault between Helensburgh and Stonehaven, the Highlands and Islands form the remaining and largest part of Scotland's land area, about half. Here can be found Scotland's most dramatic and rugged landscapes – mountain ranges of schist, granite, quartzite, and sandstone, remote peaks whose summits have a hostile, arctic climate, Scotland's two national parks, and also much of its commercial forestry. The main population centres are on the coast, at Aberdeen and Inverness.

Another fault splits the Highlands; this is the Great Glen fault with its line of lochs including Loch Ness. South of the Glen are the great mountain massifs of the Cairngorm, Ben Nevis – Britain's highest summit at 4406ft (1343m) – and the peaks around Glen Coe. These are the remains of long-past igneous intrusions and volcanoes. North of the Glen there are peaks of reddish sandstones, of gneiss, and on Skye are the distinctive Black Cuillins, peaks of volcanic gabbro.

Scotland has seen many glaciations, the ice wearing down the mountains and carving out the corries and the loch basins. Scotland's west and east coasts strongly contrast. Long sea lochs

Blackrock Cottage and Buachaille Etive Mór on the approach to Kingshouse, West Highland Way

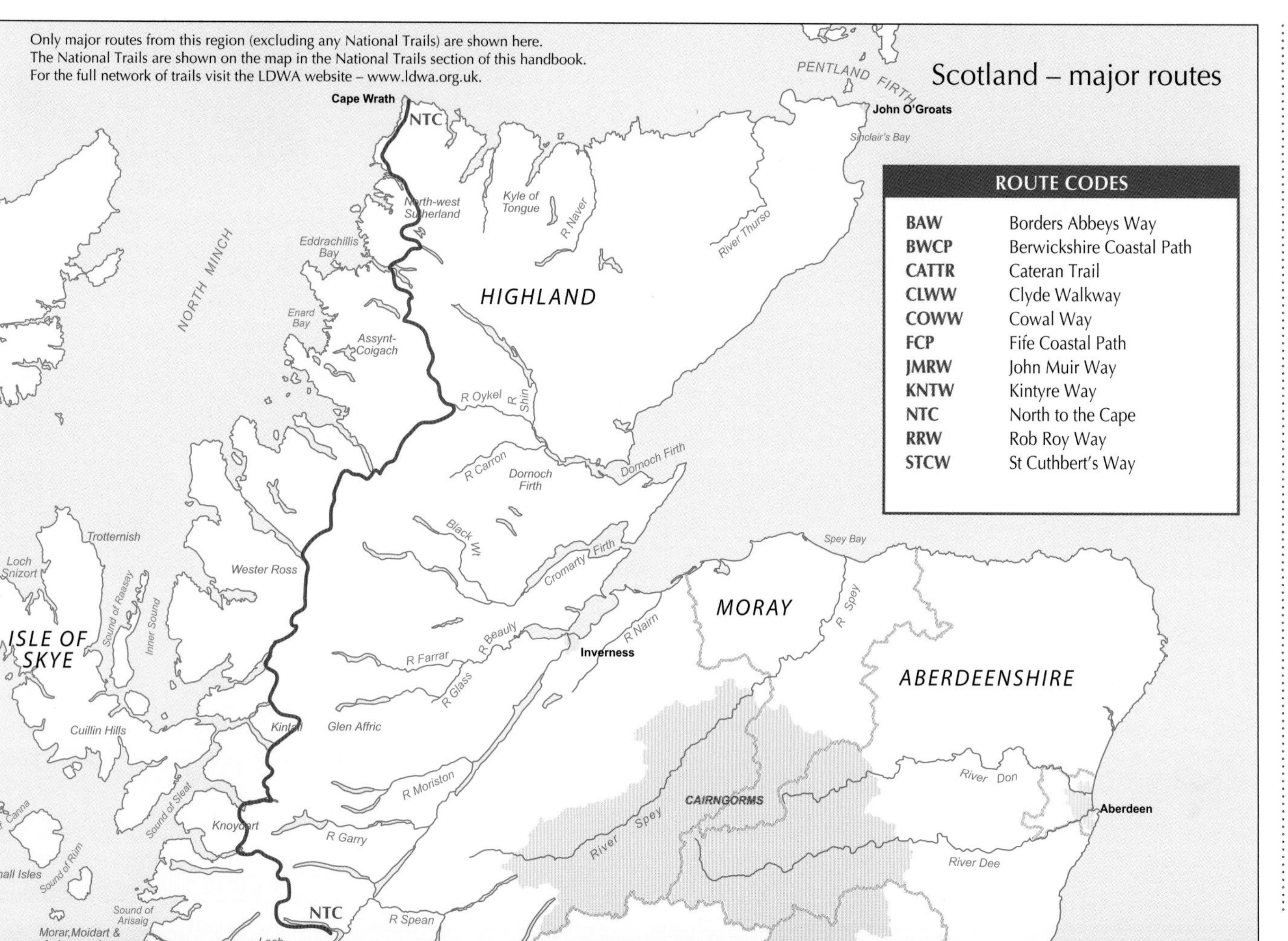
Only major routes from this region (excluding any National Trails) are shown here.
The National Trails are shown on the map in the National Trails section of this handbook.
For the full network of trails visit the LDWA website – www.ldwa.org.uk.
Scotland – major routes
ROUTE CODES
BAW Borders Abbeys Way
BWCP Berwickshire Coastal Path
CATTR Cateran Trail
CLWW Clyde Walkway
COWW Cowal Way
FCP Fife Coastal Path
JMRW John Muir Way
KNTW Kintyre Way
NTC North to the Cape
RRW Rob Roy Way
STCW St Cuthbert's Way
PENTLAND FIRTH
John O'Groats
Sinclair's Bay
Cape Wrath
NTC
North-west Sutherland
Kyle of Tongue
R Naver
River Thurso
HIGHLAND
NORTH MINCH
Eddrachillis Bay
Enard Bay
Assynt-Coigach
R Oykel
R Shin
R Carron
Dornoch Firth
Dornoch Firth
Black Wt
Cromarty Firth
Spey Bay
Trotternish
Loch Snizort
Wester Ross
MORAY
R Spey
R Nairn
Inverness
ISLE OF SKYE
Sound of Raasay
Inner Sound
R Beauly
R Farrar
R Glass
ABERDEENSHIRE
Cuillin Hills
Kintail
Glen Affric
R Moriston
River Don
CAIRNGORMS
River Spey
Aberdeen
Sound of Sleat
Knoydart
R Garry
River Dee
Small Isles
Sound of Rum
Sound of Arisaig
NTC
R Spean
Morar, Moidart &

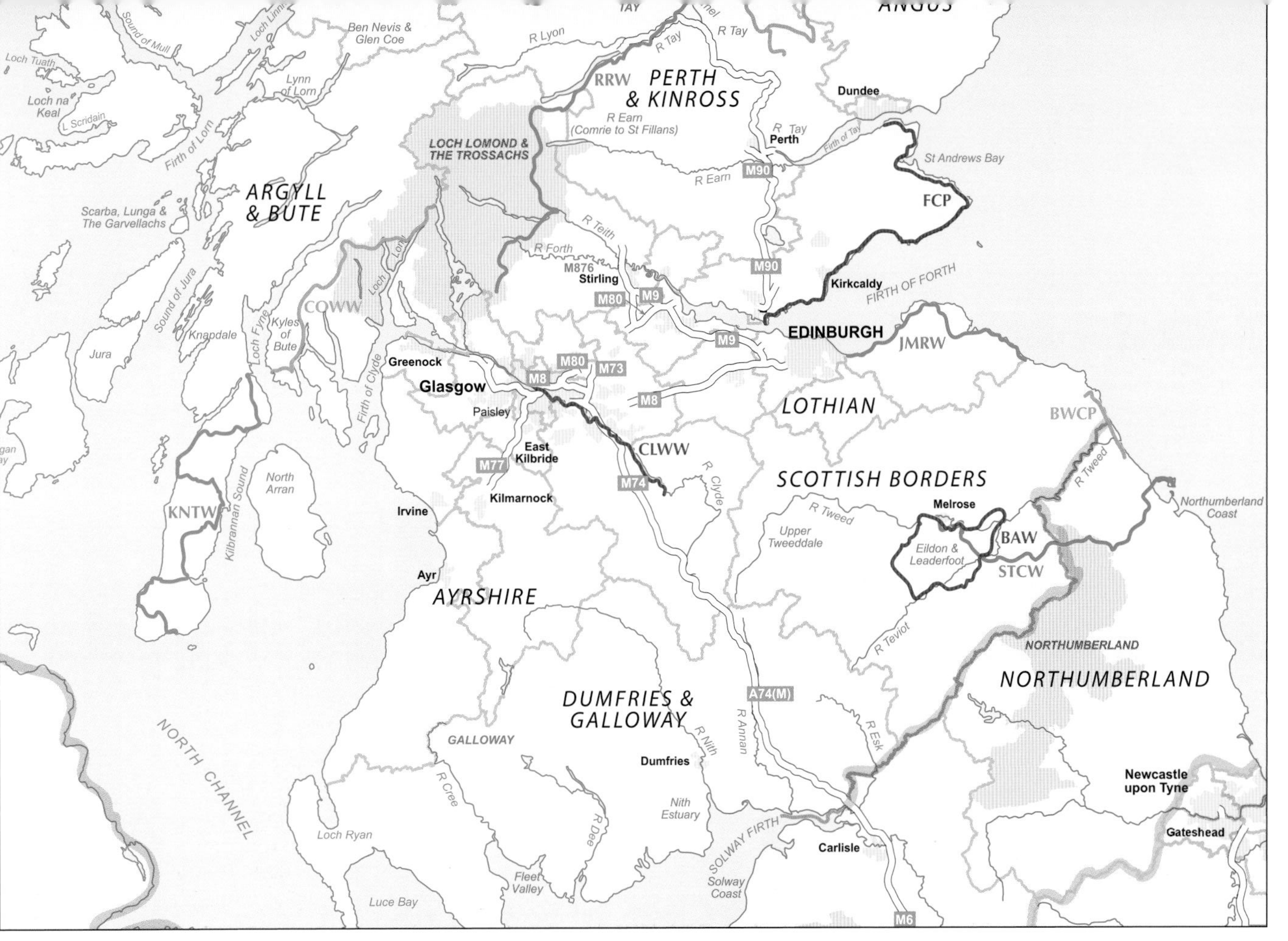
Sound of Mull
Ben Nevis & Glen Coe
R Lyon
R Tay
R Tay
Loch Tuath
Loch na Keal
L Scridain
Lynn of Lorn
Firth of Lorn
RRW
PERTH & KINROSS
R Earn (Comrie to St Fillans)
Dundee
R Tay
Perth
Firth of Tay
St Andrews Bay
LOCH LOMOND & THE TROSSACHS
M90
R Earn
FCP
ARGYLL & BUTE
Scarba, Lunga & The Garvellachs
R Teith
R Forth
M876
Stirling
M90
Kirkcaldy
FIRTH OF FORTH
Sound of Jura
Loch Long
COWW
M80
M9
Knapdale
Loch Fyne
Kyles of Bute
M9
EDINBURGH
JMRW
Jura
Greenock
M80
M73
Firth of Clyde
M8
Glasgow
M8
Paisley
LOTHIAN
BWCP
CLWW
East Kilbride
M77
North Arran
R Clyde
M74
SCOTTISH BORDERS
R Tweed
Kilbrannan Sound
Kilmarnock
Melrose
Northumberland Coast
KNTW
Irvine
R Tweed
Upper Tweeddale
Eildon & Leaderfoot
BAW
STCW
Ayr
AYRSHIRE
R Teviot
NORTHUMBERLAND
NORTHUMBERLAND
DUMFRIES & GALLOWAY
A74(M)
NORTH CHANNEL
GALLOWAY
R Nith
R Annan
R Esk
Dumfries
Newcastle upon Tyne
R Cree
Nith Estuary
Gateshead
Loch Ryan
R Dee
SOLWAY FIRTH
Carlisle
Fleet Valley
Solway Coast
Luce Bay
M6

The Southern Upland Way crosses open ground between two forests near Ettrick Head

indent the west coast, separating the peninsulas that reach out far towards the Atlantic swells and that are often broken into island strings. Further offshore are many more islands – Scotland has almost 800, with only about 130 inhabited, the main groups being the Orkneys and Shetlands. The east coast is smoother, but indented by the Firths of Forth, Tay, Moray and Dornoch.

Walking in Scotland

With this scenic variety, Scotland offers the walker a wide choice of walking styles, from easy lowland walks to backpacking epics across its beautiful, wild and remote hills. While there are many options for trailwalkers wanting to follow an established and perhaps marked route, they do not yet reflect Scotland's potential.

Scotland has about a third of Britain's land area but a much lower density of trails, and there are very good reasons for this. Apart from its relatively small population, which leads to less local demand for trails and not having the resources to create them, the key is in Scotland's access traditions and in its undoubted attractions for the peakbagger.

Access in Scotland has long been founded on a tolerance of walkers by landowners – permitting generally free access subject to sensible restrictions during the stalking and shooting seasons – rather than on a complex rights of way network in the remoter areas. With ever growing demands from walkers, more recently in 2003/4 the combination of the Land Reform Act and the Scottish Access Code has provided statutory access rights for outdoor activities over most of Scotland's open ground. Walkers, however, should still carefully respect these codes and take advice before setting out away from the established trails.

Scotland is also famous for its Munros (the 284 Scottish mountains over 3000ft) with Munro-bagging a major draw for the hillwalker keen to attempt these challenging and occasionally untracked peaks. This combination of the Munros and of good statutory access has lessened the pressures for trailwalkers' routes. However, the increasing pressure from walking tourists, and the growing realisation of the economic and health benefits of a well-connected system of promoted trails, is now leading to new walks being developed to build upon the prime routes already available.

However, for the competent navigator with time to plan their own excursions, there is a fine network of hill paths in Scotland that can be combined into all manner of other long distance expeditions. *Scottish Hill Tracks*, from the Scottish Rights of Way and Access Society, describes some 350 routes in all areas from the Cheviots to the

Highlands. The Society has long been working to improve countryside access, recording known rights of way and many other routes, and in partnership with Scottish Natural Heritage it maintains the National Catalogue of Rights of Way.

Scotland does have four of its own **Long Distance Routes**, its national trails, in total providing over 450 miles of quality walking. These are the Great Glen Way, Southern Upland Way, Speyside Way and the West Highland Way, covered in the National Trails section and briefly below. Also, from England, the Pennine Way edges briefly across the border to its finish in Scotland.

Scotland's **coastline** now has a promoted walking route along a significant part. On the east coast there are three UK sections of the developing North Sea Trail (see E-Routes section), comprising the planned Moray Firth Trail that so far has the Moray Coastal Path section open; further south is the Fife Coastal Path that links the Firths of Forth and Tay; and on the East Lothian coast is the John Muir Way. On the west coast Ayrshire now has its own Ayrshire Coastal Path with famous golf courses en route. Apart from these mainland coastal routes, several of Scotland's wealth of offshore islands offer promoted routes. Off the west coast the island of Arran has its Arran Coastal Way. On the Shetlands the various Shetland Walks provide a range of coastal options as well as inland walking. The Skye Trail covers both coast and moorland, and the West Island Way circuits Bute. Two recent trails explore peninsulas along the west coast: the Kintyre Way snakes across Kintyre, with its famous Mull and exposed Atlantic coast. Just across Loch Fyne from Tarbert is the Cowal Way extending as far as Loch Lomond and linking to the West Highland Way. These three routes together with the Great Glen Way now provide an almost continuous traverse across much of Scotland. The Lochaber Walks series explores Highland areas to the west of Loch Linnhe.

River valley routes include the Clyde Walkway and the Kelvin Walkway that links to the start of the West Highland Way, both setting out from Glasgow, a city well endowed with other shorter urban walking trails. Ayrshire's River Ayr Way is almost complete, and on the Falkirk/West Lothian border the River Avon Heritage Trail has its first section open. The Speyside Way follows this famous salmon river, from the Grampians through Strathspey, with some easy walking using disused railways. A newer route nearby, the Dava Way, provides more railway walking.

One route takes in a World Heritage Site: the Clyde Walkway visits the historic village of New Lanark. The Edinburgh to Glasgow Canals Walk starts very close to another Site, the Old and New Towns of Edinburgh.

Figures from Scotland's history abound. The iconic environmental campaigner and a son of Dunbar, more famous for his pioneering conservation work in the US, is remembered in the John Muir Way. In the border counties there are Ways dedicated to the authors John Buchan and Sir Walter Scott. Two routes with less worthy associations are the Rob Roy Way (Rob Roy Macgregor was Scotland's most notorious outlaw) from Drymen, linking with the West Highland Way, and that heads east to Pitlochry. West of Pitlochry the Cateran Trail follows in the footsteps of past cattle rustlers – the caterans. The lengthy Famous Highland Drove Walk traces Skye cattle drovers' routes across Scotland to Crieff. On a much more **religious** note, two routes in the English borders, the Border Abbeys Way and the St Cuthbert's Way, remember in turn the founding of these great abbeys and a past saint.

As the country of the Munro-bagger, Scotland perhaps does not need many **Anytime Challenges** and so far we only list one, the Moffat Mountain Marathon, a remote and demanding route in the Galloway Hills from Alan Castle, an LDWA member who looks after the LDWA's Hillwalkers and National Trails Registers. The Three Peaks of Great Britain is a challenge to climb the highest summit in each UK mainland country and is included here as it often starts with Ben Nevis. The Coast to Coast – Scotland is a kanter with self-devised routes linking Oban and St Andrews, in the spirit of the annual TGO challenge.

For those attempting Land's End to John O'Groats, **end-to-end** options across Scotland are of interest. We include the Central Scottish Way, an old route providing an easterly variant linking the West Highland and Pennine Ways. In the west, a new Annandale Way is being developed from Moffat to Gretna, following the valley of the Annan. If Moffat were linked to Lanark it would open a western corridor, via the Clyde's Walkways and the West Highland Way, from the English border all the way to Inverness.

Arran Coastal Way ARCW

ARRAN **105km/65 miles**

This walk encircles the island, mainly at or near sea-level with two excursions inland, one rising to 2050ft over the shoulder of Goat Fell, the island's highest mountain (2867ft). It is suggested that the route be walked anti-clockwise. It visits the villages of Sannox, Lochranza, Pirnmill, Blackwaterfoot, Lagg and Whiting Bay, from where an inland loop takes in Glenashdale Falls and Iron Age Fort, dropping to Lamlash and returning at sea-level via Corriegills Point to Brodick. Accommodation is available in most of these villages. Some sections can be impassable at high tide, but can be avoided using roads.

Attributes
Challenging; Coastal
Start and Finish
Ferry Terminal, Brodick, Isle of Arran, North Ayrshire NS022359
Websites
www.coastalway.co.uk
Maps
OS Landranger: 69
OS Explorer: 361
Publications, badges and certificates
Paperbacks
Walking in the Isle of Arran by Paddy Dillon (Cicerone Press) 2008. ISBN 9781852844783. 256pp; 172 x 118. £12.95.
(spiral bound)
Arran Coastal Way by Jacquetta Megarry (Rucksack Readers) 2008. ISBN 9781898481287. 64pp + 4pp map flap; 145 x 210. £10.99.
Booklets
Guide to the Coastal Way (Coastal Way Books). 24pp. £7.00 (incs p&p).
Walking Support Providers
Absolute Escapes; Arran; Celtic; Contours; Macs

Ayrshire Coastal Path AYRCP

N AYRSHIRE, S AYRSHIRE **161km/100 miles**

Created by the Rotary Club of Ayr it heads along Scotland's south west coast, providing views of the granite plug of Ailsa Craig and to Arran, using cliff-top tracks, old turnpike roads, and rough and sandy beaches, past ruined castles and small fishing villages – and the Open Championship golf course at Turnberry. From Ayr northwards, the going is much gentler along sandy beaches past Prestwick – the birthplace of Open championship golf – and its successor, Royal Troon. There are plans to link the Ayrshire Coastal path to the Southern Upland Way and to link from Skelmorlie to the Erskine Bridge and Forth and Clyde Canal, thence to the West Highland Way, so enabling a walk from Eyemouth to Inverness via Stranraer and the Ayrshire coast.

Attributes
Challenging; Coastal; Heritage; Sport
Start
Glenapp Kirk, Ballantrae, South Ayrshire NX074746
Finish
Skelmorlie, North Ayrshire NS193685
Waymark
Coastal scene in green on white disc
Websites
www.ayrshirecoastalpath.org
Maps
OS Landranger: 63, 70, 76
OS Explorer: 317, 326, 333, 341
Publications, badges and certificates
Paperbacks
Ayrshire Coastal Path: The Official Guide Book by James Begg (James Begg) 2008. ISBN 9780955906305. 160pp. £12.00 (+ £1.00 p&p). From Ayrshire Coastal Path website, local bookshops & Tourist Offices in Ayrshire.

Borders Abbeys Way BAW

BORDERS **105km/65 miles**

Passing the sites and ruins of 12th Century Abbeys in the Scottish Borderlands, it is steeped in 12th century history: the time when the Border Abbeys were first established and granted their Royal Charters. The monks selected prime locations, next to the River Tweed and Teviot for their salmon fishing, and in the fertile plains below the Eildon Hills. From Kelso the Way visits Jedburgh, Hawick, Selkirk and Melrose, before returning to Kelso via Dryburgh Abbey.

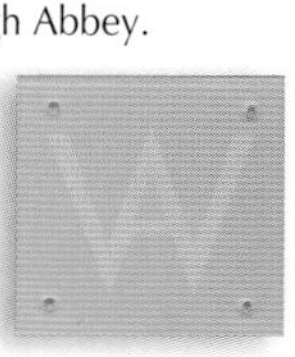

Attributes
Moorland; Heritage; Religious
Start and Finish
Kelso Abbey, Borders NT727337
Waymark
AW symbol on yellow square
Maps ◈
OS Landranger: 73, 74, 79, 80
OS Explorer: 331, 338, 339, 16
Publications, badges and certificates
Leaflets
Borders Abbeys Way (Jedburgh Tourist Information

Centre). 9 x 4 inches. Set of 5. Free (+ 9 x 4 SAE).
Borders Abbeys Way (Jedburgh Tourist Information Centre). Free.

Grid Reference List

Borders Abbeys Way: Grid Reference List (Walking Support) 2007. £2.50 + VAT. Available from Walking Support website.

Walking Support Providers

Contours; Footpath; Walking Support

Cateran Trail CATTR

ANGUS, PERTH **103km/64 miles**

A circular route based on Bridge of Cally, with a spur to and from Blairgowrie, it follows in the footsteps of the cattle rustlers – caterans – through the Perthshire Glens passing close to Kirkmichael, Enochdhu, Spittal of Glenshee, Cray and Alyth. It uses very minor roads, tracks and paths and includes some high level walking. The route has been improved with an 8-mile off-road section replacing the road slog from Dalnaglar to Kirkton of Glenisla and covered in an upgrade card for the guidebook. The Trail can be completed comfortably within 4-5 days, and there are options to link with the Rob Roy Way, and for a weekend Minitrail.

Attributes

Challenging; Moorland

Start and Finish

Blairgowrie, Perth and Kinross NO178454

Waymark

Red heart on white disc with name

Websites

www.caterantrail.org, www.perthshire.co.uk

Maps ◈

OS Landranger: 43, 44, 52, 53
OS Explorer: 380, 381, 387, 388

Publications, badges and certificates

Paperbacks

Explore the Cateran Trail by Chic Leven, Ken Roberts (Perth & Kinross Countryside Trust) 2008. A5. £9.99. From Blairgowrie TIC.

(spiral/laminated)

Cateran Trail by Jacquetta Megarry (Rucksack Readers) 2004. ISBN 9781898481218. 64pp + 4pp map flap; 145 x 210. £10.99. With upgrade card with detailed directions and mapping.

Leaflets

Cateran Trail (Perth & Kinross Countryside Trust) 2009. A4/3. Free. Includes accommodation/services.

Walking Support Providers

Contours; Easyways; Macs; Make Tracks

Central Scottish Way CTSW

E DUNBARTON, EDINBURGH, GLASGOW, MIDLOTHIAN, N LANARK, NORTHUMBERLAND, BORDERS, W LOTHIAN **235km/146 miles**

An old route providing a link from Scotland to England across the Scottish Borders and so useful as an easterly option for LEJOG. Commencing from the start of the West Highland Way it takes in part of the Glasgow Walkways/Cycleways, the Union Canal and the Forth & Clyde Canal to Edinburgh, then heads south to meet the Southern Upland Way at Lauder and goes via Dere Street to meet the Pennine Way at Black Halls just north of Byrness.

Attributes

Canal; Urban

Start

Easter Carbeth, Strathbane, Stirling NS534796

Finish

Low Byrness, Northum NT779015

Maps

OS Landranger: 64, 65, 66, 72, 73, 74, 80
OS Explorer: 16, 338, 342, 345, 348, 349, 350

Publications, badges and certificates

Hardback

Walking the Central Scottish Way by Erl B. Wilkie (Mainstream Publishing Co Ltd) 1996. ISBN 9781851587476. 176pp; 220 x 130. £9.99. Secondhand copies online.

Leaflets

Fit for Life: Glasgow Walkways (Glasgow City Council) 2000. 1pp; A1 (A4 folded). Free.

Clyde Walkway CLWW

GLASGOW, N LANARK, S LANARK **60km/37 miles**

A multi-user route nearly completed, following the course of the River Clyde from the centre of Glasgow through Hamilton, Strathclyde Park and Lanark. It passes the attractions of Bothwell Castle and woods, the David Livingstone Centre, Strathclyde Country Park, the Palace Grounds and Mausoleum at Hamilton, and the Barons Haugh Nature Reserve, to end at the spectacular Falls of Clyde, just up-river from the UNESCO World Heritage village of New Lanark with its historic cotton mills. Reaching the Falls of Clyde it passes Corra Linn and the path ends at the upper Bonnington Linn falls. The book *River Clyde – from The Source to The Sea* provides background and history and also details

12 simple walks. In Glasgow, the Walkway links in to the numerous pathways of the City, including the Kelvin Walkway (9 miles and on OS mapping), a waterside walk that heads north of the city to meet the West Highland Way using three watercourses, of the Allender, Kelvin and Clyde, to form a 'green link' from the countryside to Glasgow's many parks and places of interest. The Trailblazer West Highland Way guide includes this Walkway between the city-centre and the official start of the West Highland Way.

Attributes
Easy; Cycle Route; Horse Ride (Multi User); River; Urban; World Heritage Site; Industrial History
Start
Central Glasgow NS563655
Finish
Falls of Clyde, New Lanark, South Lanarkshire NS882408
Waymark
Fish logo in blue with name
Websites
www.northlan.gov.uk, www.newlanark.org
Maps ◈
OS Landranger: 64, 65, 71, 72
OS Explorer: 335, 342, 343
Publications, badges and certificates
Paperbacks
West Highland Way by Charlie Loram (Trailblazer Publications) 2006. ISBN 9781873756904. 192pp; 120 x 180. £9.99.
Walking in Clydesdale by Paul Lamarra (Tinto Press) 2002. ISBN 9780954228507. 120pp; 206 x 146. £7.95.
Livingstone (Yale University Press) 2001. ISBN 9780300091021. 448pp; 192 x 126. £11.99.
Leaflets
Clyde Walkway (Glasgow City Council) 2005. 6 leaflets. Free.
Fit for Life: Glasgow Walkways (Glasgow City Council) 2000. 1pp; A1 (A4 folded). Free.
Hardback
River Clyde: From the Source to the Sea by Keith Fergus (Breedon Books Publishing Co Ltd) 2008. ISBN 9781859836668. 192pp; 228 x 228. £16.99.

Coast to Coast – Scotland CTCSCO

ARGYLL AND BUTE, FIFE, PERTH, STIRLING **206km/128 miles**

In keeping with the spirit of the annual TGO Challenge which allows participants to plan their own routes within broad limits, the route takes a line through Tyndrum, Crianlarich, St Fillans and passes the Hopetoun Monument. Various alternatives can be planned.

Attributes
Challenging; Kanter; Moorland
Start
Oban, Argyll and Bute NM858299
Finish
St Andrews, Fife NO514168
Maps
OS Landranger: 49, 50, 51, 57, 58, 59
OS Explorer: 359, 365, 368, 369, 370, 371, 377, 384, 392
Publications, badges and certificates
Paperbacks
Scottish Coast to Coast by Brian Smailes (Challenge Publications) 2000. ISBN 9780952690085. 64pp; 125 x 185. £6.50 (incs p&p).
Walking Support Providers
Easyways; Transcotland

Cowal Way COWW

ARGYLL AND BUTE **92km/57 miles**

The Cowal Peninsula lies west of Glasgow but within easy reach, offering moorland scenery, deep glens and narrow sea lochs typical of the West Coast and is rich in history, heritage and wildlife. The Cowal Way crosses the Cowal Peninsula from south-west to north-east, beginning at Portavadie, Loch Fyne and heading via Loch Goil and Loch Long to the west shore of Loch Lomond at Inveruglas, linking the villages of Tighnabruaich, Glendaruel, Strachur, Lochgoilhead and Arrochar. It runs through remote and rugged countryside, with fine views over Bute and the Firth of Clyde, with a mixture of lochside and woodland walking, rough paths and some quiet roads. The Cobbler can be climbed as an excursion. Ferry links to the Kintyre Way and a seasonal Loch Lomond ferry link to the West Highland Way, and thence to the Great Glen Way, open up a walk from the Mull of Kintyre all the way to Inverness.

Attributes
Challenging; Forest/Woodland; Lake/Reservoir; River; Moorland; Heritage
Start
Portavadie, Argyll and Bute NR929698
Finish
Inveruglas, Argyll and Bute NN322099
Waymark
Peninsulas graphic and name
Websites
www.rucsacs.com
Maps ◈
OS Landranger: 55, 56, 62, 63
OS Explorer: 362, 363, 364

Publications, badges and certificates
Paperbacks
Cowal Way with Isle of Bute by Michael Kaufman and James McLuckie (Rucksack Readers) 2009. ISBN 9781898481324. 64pp + 3pp maps; 145 x 210. £10.99. With Bute map showing the West Island Way.
Walking Support Providers
Argyll

Edinburgh to Glasgow Canals Walk EGCW

E DUNBARTON, EDINBURGH, FALKIRK, GLASGOW, N LANARK, W DUNBARTON, W LOTHIAN **108km/67 miles**

A route following wherever possible the towpaths of the Union and Forth & Clyde Canals from Edinburgh through Ratho, Broxburn, Linlithgow, Falkirk and Bonnybridge. Near the start point is the World Heritage Site of the Old and New Towns of Edinburgh. In Glasgow the route links in to the city's numerous pathways and cycleways providing access to the start of the West Highland Way at Milngavie and also the Clyde Walkway. The first part of the River Avon Heritage Trail (9 miles) extends along the River Avon between Avonbridge and Linlithgow. The River Avon flows over weirs and waterfalls and in narrow gorges. The disused Westfield Viaduct dominates an early section of the route. Closer to the finish are Muiravonside Country Park and the Avon Aqueduct that takes the Union Canal over the river and finally the railway viaduct where the Trail ends under one of its stone pillars on the south side of the river. The full Trail is planned to provide a route along the whole length of the River Avon from Slamannan in the Heart of Central Scotland to the shores of the River Forth at Grangemouth.

Attributes
Canal; Urban; World Heritage Site
Start
Haymarket Station, Edinburgh NT239731
Finish
Old Kilpatrick, West Dunbartonshire NS448736
Maps
OS Landranger: 64, 65, 66
OS Explorer: 342, 347, 348, 349, 350
Stripmap
Forth & Clyde and Union Canals with the Crinan Canal (GEOprojects)
Publications, badges and certificates
Leaflets
Fit for Life: Glasgow Walkways (Glasgow City Council) 2000. 1pp; A1 (A4 folded). Free.
River Avon Heritage Trail (Central Scotland Forest Trust) 2007. A3/8. Free. Free download on website on path webpage.

Famous Highland Drove Walk FHDW

HIGHLANDS, PERTH **290km/180 miles**

A walk tracing one of the routes taken by the cattle drovers from Skye; through seven mountain ranges, along riversides, quiet glens and wild mountain passes, to the mart at Crieff, Perthshire.

Attributes
Challenging; Moorland
Start
Glenbrittle, Highland NG409225
Finish
Crieff, Perth NN863218
Maps
OS Landranger: 32, 33, 34, 41, 50, 51, 52, 57, 58
OS Explorer: 368, 378, 392, 377, 384
Publications, badges and certificates
Paperbacks
Famous Highland Drove Walk by Irvine Butterfield (Grey Stone Books) 1996. ISBN 9780951599655. 128pp; A5. £9.95.

Fife Coastal Path FCP

FIFE **129km/80 miles**

The Fife Coast Path (now part of the North Sea Trail) keeps faithfully to the shore between the Forth Road Bridge and Newport on Tay. It includes numerous castles, fishing villages, remarkable rock formations, caves and long sandy beaches. The coast is a haven for bird life and flora. Apart from the exposed Elie Chainwalk, carved steps with chains, at Kincraig Point, the walking is easy, though times of high tide are best avoided in some places as the walk uses the foreshore.

Attributes
Coastal
Start
North Queensferry, Fife NT123808
Finish
Newport-on-Tay, Fife NO425287
Waymark
Sea, beach, land graphic
Websites
www.fifecoastalpath.net, www.fifecoastalpath.co.uk

Maps ◈
OS Landranger: 54, 59, 65, 66
OS Explorer: 350, 367, 370, 371, 380
Publications, badges and certificates
Hardback
Along the Fife Coastal Path by Hamish Brown (Mercat Press) 2004. ISBN 9781841830575. 176pp; 216 x 136. £12.99.
Leaflets
Fife Coastal Path: North Queensferry to Tay Bridge (Visit Scotland – Fife). 4 leaflets. Free (+ 9 x 4 SAE).
Illustrated map guide
Fife Costal Path Footprint (Footprint) 2004. ISBN 9781871149708. 202 x 122. £4.95.
Grid Reference List
Fife Coastal Path: Grid Reference List (Walking Support). £2.50 + VAT. Available from Walking Support website.
Walking Support Providers
Contours; Easyways; Explore Britain; FCP; Walking Support

Gordon Way — GORDW

ABERDEENSHIRE — **18km/11 miles**

From Bennachie this trail in Eastern Aberdeenshire partly follows the old peat extraction routes on the Bennachie forests. You walk the length of Bennachie and then continue west to Suie Car Park and take in forests, farmland and moorlands across several hills. Currently the available publication covers the route to Suie car park, with the intention to extend to Rhynie in due course.

Attributes
Forest/Woodland; Moorland
Start
Bennachie Centre, near Inverurie, Aberdeenshire NJ700217
Finish
Suie Car Park, Aberdeenshire NJ547231
Waymark
Hexagonal logo with letters GW
Websites
www.forestry.gov.uk
Maps ◈
OS Landranger: 37, 38
OS Explorer: 420, 421
Publications, badges and certificates
Leaflets
Bennachie & The Gordon Way (Bennachie Project) 1996. A4/3. £0.75 (+ 9 x 4 SAE). Downloadable map online.

John Buchan Way — JBW

BORDERS — **23km/14 miles**

An undulating walk mainly on hill tracks with over 2500ft of ascent crossing the upper Tweed valley linking Peebles to Broughton (with bus return option). It is named after John Buchan, the famous writer whose family is strongly linked with the area and who wrote fondly of this part of the Scottish Borders. It visits Broughton Hills, Stobo, The Glack and Cademuir Hill.

Attributes
Challenging; River; Moorland; Literary
Start
Broughton, Borders NT114356
Finish
Peebles, Borders NT251404
Waymark
Stylised book with 'JBW' on cover
Maps
OS Landranger: 72, 73
OS Explorer: 336, 337
Publications, badges and certificates
Leaflets
John Buchan Way (Visit Scottish Borders). Free. From TICs in the Borders area.

John Muir Way — JMRW

E LOTHIAN — **72km/45 miles**

A coastal path from Musselburgh (close to Edinburgh) to the East Lothian border near Cocksburnpath, essentially linking the capital with the Southern Upland Way. Not to be confused with the John Muir Trail in California, which is a very different matter, and while hardly itself a wilderness experience, the John Muir Way honours one of the County's most famous sons born in Dunbar, the iconic writer on the natural world and later American conservation campaigner and founder of the Sierra Club who was a prime-mover in the establishment of the USA's National Park system. The Way offers generally easy walking including in the John Muir Country Park (1,760 acres managed by East Lothian Council on the western side of Dunbar). Dunbar has a memorial to Muir and an exhibition at his birthplace. The Way includes much of East Lothian's varied coastline, with beaches, cliffs, sandstone arches and dunes, and the lowland below the Lammermuir Hills, with rivers, waterfalls and woods. There is ruined Dunbar castle, salt pans at Prestonpans, and many harbours and fishing ports. A short walking link leads to Cockburnspath, where the Southern Upland Way ends, and from the westernmost end of the John Muir Way at Fisherrow Harbour in Musselburgh, roadside pavements reach the City of Edinburgh's Waterfront Promenade. The John Muir Way forms part of NORTRAIL – the North Sea Coastal Path Project.

Attributes
Coastal; Heritage
Start
Fisherrow Harbour, Musselburgh, East Lothian NT334729
Finish
County Boundary, near Cocksburnpath, East Lothian NT769722
Waymark
Named signs
Websites
www.eastlothian.gov.uk, www.visiteastlothian.org, www.jmt.org
Maps ◈
OS Landranger: 66, 67
OS Explorer: 351
Publications, badges and certificates
Leaflets
John Muir Way (East Lothian Council) 2006. 6 leaflets; A4/3. Free. Downloadable.
Booklets
John Muir Way: 14 Short Walks (East Lothian Council). 32pp; A5. Free. Short walks based around the John Muir Way.
Hardback
Muir and More by Ronald Turnbull (Millrace Books) 2008. ISBN 9781902173276. 192. £14.95. Covers John Muir Way and Trail, but not a trailguide.

Kintyre Way — KINTW

ARGYLL AND BUTE — **144km/89 miles**

More island than mainland, the unexplored Kintyre Peninsula boasts hidden coves, deserted beaches along the wild atlantic coast, tiny fishing communities, and gentle hills. The Way criss-crosses the peninsula: the full walk is 103 miles with all options and 89 miles direct. Additional spurs link to Bellochuntuy and Peninver. Most of the trail is on forestry land, with road connections, and two interesting beach sections. The bulbous end of Kintyre features some of the most spectacular scenery on the peninsula and includes the famous Mull of Kintyre, just off the route but accessible, the nearest Britain gets to Ireland just 12 miles away. The east coast is gentler than the west, sheltered from Atlantic winds with fine views to Arran. The west coast is among the most exposed stretches, with rocky shorelines and deserted sandy beaches pounded by Atlantic breakers. The 2008 edition (A1/) of Explorer 356 shows the correct routings.

Attributes
Forest/Woodland; Coastal; Moorland
Start
Tarbert harbour, Argyll and Bute NR864686
Finish
Dunaverty Bay, Southend, Argyll and Bute NR688075
Waymark
Route name and coastal graphic
Websites
www.kintyreway.com, http://walking.visitscotland.com
Maps ◈
OS Landranger: 62, 68
OS Explorer: 356, 357
Publications, badges and certificates
Paperbacks
Kintyre Way by Jacquetta Megarry (Rucksack Readers) 2007. Spiral bound and laminated. ISBN 9781898481294. 64pp + 4pp map flap; 145 x 210. £10.99.
Leaflets
Kintyre Way (Tarbert TIC) 2006. A4/3. Free. Also from TICs in Lochgilphead & Campbeltown.
Walking Support Providers
Absolute Escapes; Easyways; Macs

Lochaber Walks — LOCHBW

HIGHLANDS — **Various**

A series of ten cross-country walks in Morvern, Sunart, Ardgour and Lochaber, areas to the west of Loch Linnhe. The distances are between 7 and 17 miles and some walks can be connected. The start points include Drimnin, Strontian, Polloch, Kinlochan and Glenfinnan.

Attributes
Moorland
Start
Various
Finish
Various
Waymark
Scotways signs/named posts
Websites
www.scotways.com
Maps
OS Landranger: 40, 41, 47, 49
OS Explorer: 374, 384, 390, 392, 391

A walker approaches Over Phawhope Bothy at the head of the Ettrick Valley

Publications, badges and certificates
Leaflets
Lochaber Walks (Scottish Rights of Way and Access Society). 8 leaflets; A4/3. Free (+ 2 x 1st class stamps).

Moffat Mountain Marathon MOFMM

DUMFRIES & GALLOWAY, BORDERS 53km/33 miles

An isolated, self-navigated, demanding walk over mainly trackless and remote terrain in high mountain country with ascent/descent of some 2300m (7500ft) over the Moffat Hills in the heart of the Scottish Southern Uplands. It includes the ascent of two Corbetts (Scottish hills above 2500ft with at least a 500ft drop on all sides), ten Donalds (2000ft + hills in the Scottish 'Lowlands') and two Donald Deweys (500m–609m Scottish hills with a drop on all sides of at least 30m). A list of grid references may be downloaded: the route is a 'kanter' joining these.

Attributes
Very Challenging; Anytime Challenge; Kanter; Moorland; Mountain
Start and Finish
Moffat main car park, Moffat, Dumfries and Galloway NT084049
Maps
OS Landranger: 78, 79
OS Explorer: 330
Publications, badges and certificates
Route notes (online only)
Moffat Mountain Marathon (Alan Castle) 2008. 2pp; A4. Free. Downloadable from LDWA website.

Moray Firth Trail MFT

ABERDEENSHIRE, HIGHLANDS, MORAY 80km/50 miles

The Moray Firth Trail is part of the North Sea Trail and explores around 470 miles of coastline from the northern tip of the UK near to John O'Groats to the fertile lowlands of the Moray. The waymarked 'Moray Coast Trail' some 50 miles between Forres/Findhorn and Cullen on the south shore of the Firth – is the first local section to be officially signposted. This traverses the fine coast of Moray with its rugged cliffs, caves and sheltered coves, fishing harbours and sweeping sands.

Attributes
Coastal
Start
Railway Station, Forres, Moray NJ029589
Finish
The Square, Cullen, Moray NJ512671
Waymark
Bird and name
Websites
www.morayfirth.org, www.morayways.org.uk
Maps
OS Landranger: 27, 28
OS Explorer: 422, 424
Publications, badges and certificates
Leaflets
Moray Coastal Trail (Moray District Council) 2007. 2pp; A3/8. Free. Free to download only.

North to the Cape NTC

HIGHLANDS 349km/217 miles

A backpacking trekking route through the West Highlands for the experienced walker. Taking 2-3 weeks, it crosses wild land of Scotland's northwest coast including Morar, Knoydart, Applecross, Torridon and Assynt on its way to the Cape. It visits Lochs Arkaig, Hourn, Duich, Carron, Maree, Broom, Assynt and More before finishing on the coastline.

Attributes
Very Challenging; Forest/Woodland; Coastal; Lake/Reservoir; Moorland; Mountain
Start
Fort William, Highland NN094751
Finish
Cape Wrath, Highland NC258747
Maps
OS Landranger: 9, 15, 16, 19, 20, 25, 33, 40, 41
OS Explorer: 391, 392, 398, 399, 413, 414, 429, 433, 435, 436, 439, 440, 442, 445, 446
Publications, badges and certificates
Paperbacks
North to the Cape by Denis Brook, Phil Hinchliffe (Cicerone Press) 1999. ISBN 9781852842857. 207pp; 116 x 176. £11.99.
Walking Support Providers
Aberchalder

River Ayr Way RAYW

E AYRSHIRE, S AYRSHIRE 66km/41 miles

Scotland's first source to the sea path, it heads from east to west over moorland, through sandstone gorges and on rich farmland. A section between Mauchline and Failford is still under development.

Attributes
River
Start
Glenbuck, East Ayrshire NS753287
Finish
Ayr, South Ayrshire NS334225
Websites
www.theriverayrway.org
Maps
OS Landranger: 70, 71
OS Explorer: 326, 327, 328
Publications, badges and certificates
Paperbacks
River Ayr Way (East Ayrshire Council) 2006. ISBN 9780951812846. 120pp; 208 x 108. £3.99.

Rob Roy Way RRW

PERTH, STIRLING **127km/79 miles**

This walk follows the tracks and paths used by Rob Roy Macgregor in the 17th and 18th centuries as he worked, fought, and lived the life of Scotland's most notorious outlaw. Starting at Drymen, where it links with the West Highland Way, the route takes in Aberfoyle, Callander, Strathyre, Killin, Ardtalnaig, Aberfeldy before finishing at Pitlochry. You also walk alongside Loch Venachar, Loch Lubnaig and Loch Tay and pass Ben Ledi, Ben Lawers and Ben Chonzie.

Attributes
Former Railway; Lake/Reservoir; River
Start
Drymen, Stirlingshire NS474886
Finish
Pitlochry, Perthshire NN940584
Websites
www.robroyway.com
Maps
OS Landranger: 51, 52, 57
OS Explorer: 347, 365, 378, 379, 386
Publications, badges and certificates
Paperbacks
Rob Roy Way by Jacquetta Megarry (Rucksack Readers) 2006. ISBN 9781898481263. 64pp + 5pp map flap; 145 x 215. £10.99. 2nd revised edition.
Leaflets
Lowland Highland Trail by Sustrans (Callander TIC). Free. Cycle route. Also from Tyndrum TIC Tel: 08707 200 626.
Grid Reference List
Rob Roy Way: Grid Reference List (Walking Support). £2.50 + VAT. Available from Walking Support website.
Walking Support Providers
Absolute Escapes; Bike & Hike; Celtic; Contours; Easyways; Let's Go Walking!; Macs; Transcotland; Walking Support

Shetland Walks SHETLW

SHETLAND **Various**

A series of extensive long distance routes along the coastlines of the islands of Shetland, namely Yell (101 miles), Unst (63 miles), Fetlar (31 miles), Northmavine (125 miles), Westside (162 miles), South Mainland (78 miles), and Eastside. The walks are covered in a series of seven books by Peter Guy. A series of 15 shorter walks of up to 6.5 miles (10.5km) on the islands is available as a free booklet that may also be downloaded from the link below.

Attributes
Challenging; Coastal
Start
Various
Finish
Various
Websites
www.walkshetland.com
Maps
OS Landranger: 1, 2, 3, 4
OS Explorer: 466, 467, 468, 469, 470
Publications, badges and certificates
Paperbacks
Walking on the Orkney and Shetland Isles by Graham Uney (Cicerone Press) 2009. ISBN 9781852845728. 224pp; 172 x 116. £12.95.
Walking the Coastline of Shetland: 1 – Island of Yell by Peter Guy (Shetland Times Bookshop) 1996. ISBN 9781898852186. 96pp; A5. £6.95 (+ £1.05 p&p).
Walking the Coastline of Shetland: 2 – Unst by Peter Guy (Shetland Times Bookshop) 2002. ISBN 9781898852766. 96pp; 206 x 148. £9.99 (+ £1.50 p&p).
Walking the Coastline of Shetland: 3 – Island of Fetlar by Peter Guy (Shetland Times Bookshop) 1991. ISBN 9780951584514. 70pp; A5. £4.99 (+ 75p p&p).
Walking the Coastline of Shetland: 4 – Northmavine by Peter Guy (Shetland Times Bookshop) 1993. ISBN 9780952002604. 112pp; A5. £9.99 (+ £1.50 p&p).
Walking the Coastline of Shetland: 5 – Westside by Peter Guy (Shetland Times Bookshop) 1995. ISBN 9781898852063. 96pp; A5. £9.99 (+ £1.50 p&p).
Walking the Coastline of Shetland: 6 – South Mainland by Peter Guy (Shetland Times Bookshop) 2000. ISBN 9781898852643. 112pp; A5. £8.99 (+ £1.35 p&p).

Walking the Coastline of Shetland: 7 – Eastside by Peter Guy (Shetland Times Bookshop) 2004. ISBN 9781904746010. 144pp; 206 x 148. £9.99 (+ £1.50 p&p).

Booklets

Shetland Walking Guide (VisitShetland) 2007. 38pp; A4. Free. Downloadable.

Sir Walter Scott Way SRWSW

DUMFRIES & GALLOWAY, BORDERS **148km/92 miles**

A cross-country walk between Moffat in South Central Scotland and Cockburnspath on the South East Scottish Coastline and mostly coincident with the Southern Upland Way. It runs through lowland valleys, by lochs and reservoirs, alongside the River Tweed and its tributaries, over several Corbetts and through communities steeped in history and which also have connections with Sir Walter Scott, one of Scotland's greatest writers.

Attributes

Lake/Reservoir; River; Moorland

Start

Moffat, Dumfries and Galloway NT085052

Finish

Cockburnspath, Borders NT774711

Websites

www.sirwalterscottway.com

Maps

OS Landranger: 67, 73, 74, 78, 79

OS Explorer: 330, 337, 338, 339, 346

Publications, badges and certificates

Paperbacks

Southern Upland Way: Recreational Path Guides by Anthony Burton (Aurum Press) 1997. ISBN 9781854104557. 168pp; 210 x 130. £12.99.

Southern Upland Way: Official Guide by Roger Smith (Mercat Press) 2005. ISBN 9781841830773. 218pp; 218 x 136. £17.99.

(PVC)

Southern Upland Way: Scotland's Coast to Coast Trail by Alan Castle (Cicerone Press) 2007. ISBN 9781852844097. 224pp; 172 x 116. £12.00.

Certificate

Sir Walter Scott Way (Walking Support). A4. Free.

Walking Support Providers

Walking Support

Skye Trail SKYET

HIGHLANDS **120km/75 miles**

A route from south to north along the longest length of the island visiting both east and west coasts and traversing mountain and moorland regions.

Attributes

Moorland; Mountain

Start

Armadale, Highland NG640038

Finish

Duntulm, Highland NG408742

Maps

OS Landranger: 23, 32

OS Explorer: 408, 410, 411, 412

Publications, badges and certificates

Paperbacks

A Long Walk on the Isle of Skye by David Paterson (Peak Publishing Ltd) 2005. ISBN 9780952190899. 144pp; 259 x 224. £14.95 (+ £2.00 p&p).

St Cuthbert's Way STCW

NORTHUMBERLAND, BORDERS **101km/63 miles**

The Way was inspired by the life of St Cuthbert, who began his ministry at Melrose in 650 AD, eventually becoming the Bishop of Lindisfarne. The route provides a link over the Cheviot Hills between the Southern Upland Way (at Melrose) and the Pennine Way National Trail (at Kirk Yetholm) with the Northumbrian Coastline path. *See* also E-Routes (E2).

Attributes

Challenging; Moorland; Heritage; Religious

Start

Melrose Abbey, Borders NT548341

Finish

Lindisfarne, Northumberland NU126418

Waymark

Celtic Cross on named disc

Websites

www.stcuthbertsway.net

Maps ◈

OS Landranger: 73, 74, 75

OS Explorer: 16, 338, 339, 340

Harvey Map (Stripmap)

St Cuthbert's Way (Harvey Maps)

Publications, badges and certificates

Paperbacks

St Cuthbert's Way: Official Guide by Roger Smith, Ron

Shaw (Mercat Press) 1997. ISBN 9780114957629. 96pp; 220 x 135. £6.99 (online).

St Cuthbert's Way: Pilgrims' Companion by Mary Low (Wild Goose Publications). ISBN 9781901557220. 222pp; A5. £9.99. Not a guide book: complements 'Official Guide' with history/other information.

Southern Upland Way & St Cuthbert's Way by Mike Salter (Mike Salter) 2007. 47pp; OS map size. £3.95 (+ 50p p&p). Only available direct from author.

Leaflets

St Cuthbert's Way (Visit Scottish Borders). Free. Includes accommodation/facilities details.

Certificate

St Cuthbert's Way (Berwick-upon-Tweed Tourist Information Centre). £1.00 (+ SAE).

Badge

St Cuthbert's Way (Visit Scottish Borders). £2.00 (+ SAE).

Grid Reference List

St Cuthbert's Way: Grid Reference List by Walking Support (Walking Support). £2.50 + VAT. Available from Walking Support website.

Walking Support Providers

Absolute Escapes; Bobs; CarryLite; Celtic; Contours; Discovery; Easyways; Footpath; HF; Instep; Macs; Make Tracks; Ramblers; Sherpa Van; Walking Support

Three Peaks of Great Britain — TPGB

CUMBRIA, GWYNEDD, HIGHLANDS — **42km/26 miles**

A popular challenge for charity fundraisers, it can have adverse environmental and other impacts, especially when undertaken by large numbers of participants. It is a misnomer that the challenge of climbing the highest peaks of Scotland, England and Wales, Ben Nevis, Scafell Pike and Snowdon respectively, has to be completed within 24 hours. Heed should always be taken of the inconvenience often caused to the residents in the affected areas and of the real dangers for vehicle occupants when travelling between the peak bases. The Institute of Fundraising provides guidelines for this challenge and organisers may find the LDWA's Guidelines for Events booklet useful. The other publications cover routes to the mountain tops and between them by public transport or by road, and safety advice, and are appropriate for individual walkers. Cicerone's guide, *Three Peaks, Ten Tors*, also provides the challenge of accomplishing the peaks by public transport.

Attributes

Very Challenging; Moorland; Mountain

Start

Car Park, Glen Nevis Youth Hostel, Highland NN128718

Finish

Car Park, Pen-y-pass Youth Hostel, Gwynedd SH647556

Websites

www.institute-of-fundraising.org.uk

Maps

OS Landranger: 41, 90, 115

OS Explorer: 4, 6, 17, 392

Publications, badges and certificates

Booklets

Outdoor Fundraising in the UK (Institute of Fundraising). 9pp; A4. Free to download from IoF website. Page 8 covers the Three Peaks of Great Britain.

Paperbacks

National 3 Peaks Walk by Brian Smailes (Challenge Publications) 2009. ISBN 9781903568538. 96pp; 125 x 185. £6.95 (incs p&p). Covers Slieve Donald (NI) – fourth peak.

Three Peaks, Ten Tors by Ronald Turnbull (Cicerone Press) 2007. ISBN 9781852845018. 256pp; 170 x 120. £12.95.

Badge & certificate

Three Peaks of Great Britain (Challenge Publications). £3.30 & £1.20 (both incs p&p). On hammered ivory paper.

West Island Way — WIW

ARGYLL AND BUTE — **48km/30 miles**

A route on the Isle of Bute embracing a variety of landscapes including seashore, moorland, farmland and forest. It passes St Blane's Chapel, the abandoned townships in Glen More and the outskirts of Rothesay. There is minimal road-walking.

Attributes

Coastal; Moorland

Start

Kilchattan Bay, Argyll and Bute NS107546

Finish

Kames Bay, Argyll and Bute NS069674

Waymark

Named signs

Maps

OS Landranger: 63

OS Explorer: 362

Publications, badges and certificates

Illustrated map guide

West Island Way: Map & Guide (Footprint) 2001. ISBN 9781871149517. 122 x 204. £2.50 (+ 25p p&p).

Paperbacks

Cowal Way with Isle of Bute by Michael Kaufman and James McLuckie (Rucksack Readers) 2009. ISBN 9781898481324. 64pp + 3pp maps; 145 x 210. £10.99. With Bute map showing the West Island Way.

NORTHERN IRELAND

Brandy Pad, under the castles, off the Mourne Way

KEY FACTS	
Areas	The Six Counties (Antrim, Armagh, Down, Fermanagh, Londonderry and Tyrone)
Principal AONBs	Antrim Coast and Glens, Causeway Coast, Lagan Valley, Lecale Coast, Mourne, Binevenagh, Ring of Gullion, Sperrin, Strangford Lough, Erne Lakeland (under designation), Fermanagh Caveland (under designation)
World Heritage Sites	Causeway Coast
National Trails (N Ireland Waymarked Ways)	Nine Waymarked Ways totalling 260 miles: Antrim Hills Way, Carleton Trail, Causeway Coast Way, Central Sperrins Way, Lecale Way, Moyle Way, Newry Canal Way, Ring of Gullion Way, Silabh Beagh Way
Walking Routes (trail miles)	11 main routes (314 miles); all waymarked, plus overlapping Ulster Way (585 miles) (not currently promoted)
Resident population	1,750,000

DON'T MISS! TRAIL SECTIONS (CHALLENGING/REMOTE MARKED WITH *)	
Causeway Coast Way	Carrick-a-Rede to Portballintrae, Giant's Causeway World Heritage Site, remarkable geology, spectacular coastal scenery, summer bus link (24km)
Ring of Gullion Way	Jonesborough to Meigh under Slieve Gullion, exploring a volcanic ring-dyke (25km approx)
Newcastle Challenge Trail	circular from Newcastle, forest parks, Dundrum Bays and beaches (44km)
Antrim Hills Way	Glenarm to Slemish Mountain, in the footsteps of St Patrick over rugged hills* (35km), much shorter options from Glenhead village (A36)

REFERENCE SOURCES INCLUDING MANY REGIONAL ROUTES

Walk Northern Ireland (brochure) (Countryside Access and Activities Network), free and downloadable. Well-produced general introduction, including pointers to many shorter walks.

Waymarked Ways of Northern Ireland (Countryside Access and Activities Network) 2006. Complete package (plastic pouch or presentation box): 9 route guides. £6.50 plastic or £6.99 boxed (inc p&p). Cheques payable to Countryside Recreation NI.

A Story Through Time – Formation of the Scenic Landscapes of Ireland – North by Patrick McKeever (Landscapes from Stone) 1999. €6.50. Useful guide to the geology and landforms of the north of Ireland for the non-geologist. Separate companion map sold.

Guidance Notes on the Law, Practices and Procedure: Guide to Public Rights of Way and Access to the Countryside (Northern Ireland Environment & Heritage Service) 2006, downloadable from www.ehsni.gov.uk.

Mourne Wall, west ridge of Slieve Commedagh

NORTHERN IRELAND

Newcastle, Mountains of Mourne

The 'Six Counties' of Northern Ireland, although only about six per cent of the UK's land area, offer great variety for the walker, in landscapes forged by fire and ice, on mountains rising to almost 3000ft, and along its lengthy and scenic coastline.

The Trails

The Province's varied two billion-year **geological past** has created some remarkable landform features that provide the themes for several of its promoted routes. On its journey around the Antrim shores the Causeway Coast Way visits the world-famous Causeway Coast, celebrated as a World Heritage Site. The Ring of Gullion Way takes its theme from the ring of hills that are the relic of a volcanic 'ring dyke', the finest such feature in the British Isles, that extends a little into the Republic, where subsidence around a circular fault, under the weight of lavas, created this ring of hills around the central mass of Slieve Gullion.

The Sliabh Beagh Way also reaches briefly into the Republic, in Monaghan, to cross the Drumlin Belts that extend much further south into Cavan. Drumlins are glacial features, numerous small rounded elongated hills of glacial clay, often called a 'basket-of-eggs topography'. Much of Armagh and Down shares this landscape. (The name drumlin is of Celtic origin, while Cavan means 'the hollow' and Monaghan 'the place of little hills'.) The Central Sperrins Way heads through the Sperrin range, where broad, rounded summits were formed by the erosion of former higher peaks by the glaciers that blanketed them in the last ice age, creating at the same time the beautiful valleys of Glenelly and Ownkillew that this trail encounters.

For **peakbaggers**, the Moyle Way heading from the Antrim coast, provides a challenge in ascending Slieveannora and boggy Trostan. The Six Counties offer more challenges for the determined day-walker and we include the Newcastle Challenge Trail, a 28-mile route around the Mourne Area of Outstanding Natural Beauty (AONB) and the Dundrum Bays.

Ireland's **famous sons** are marked by the Lecale Way that follows in the footsteps of St Patrick from his landing place on Strangford Loch, offering views to the Mourne Mountains, while the Antrim Hills Way climbs from the coast

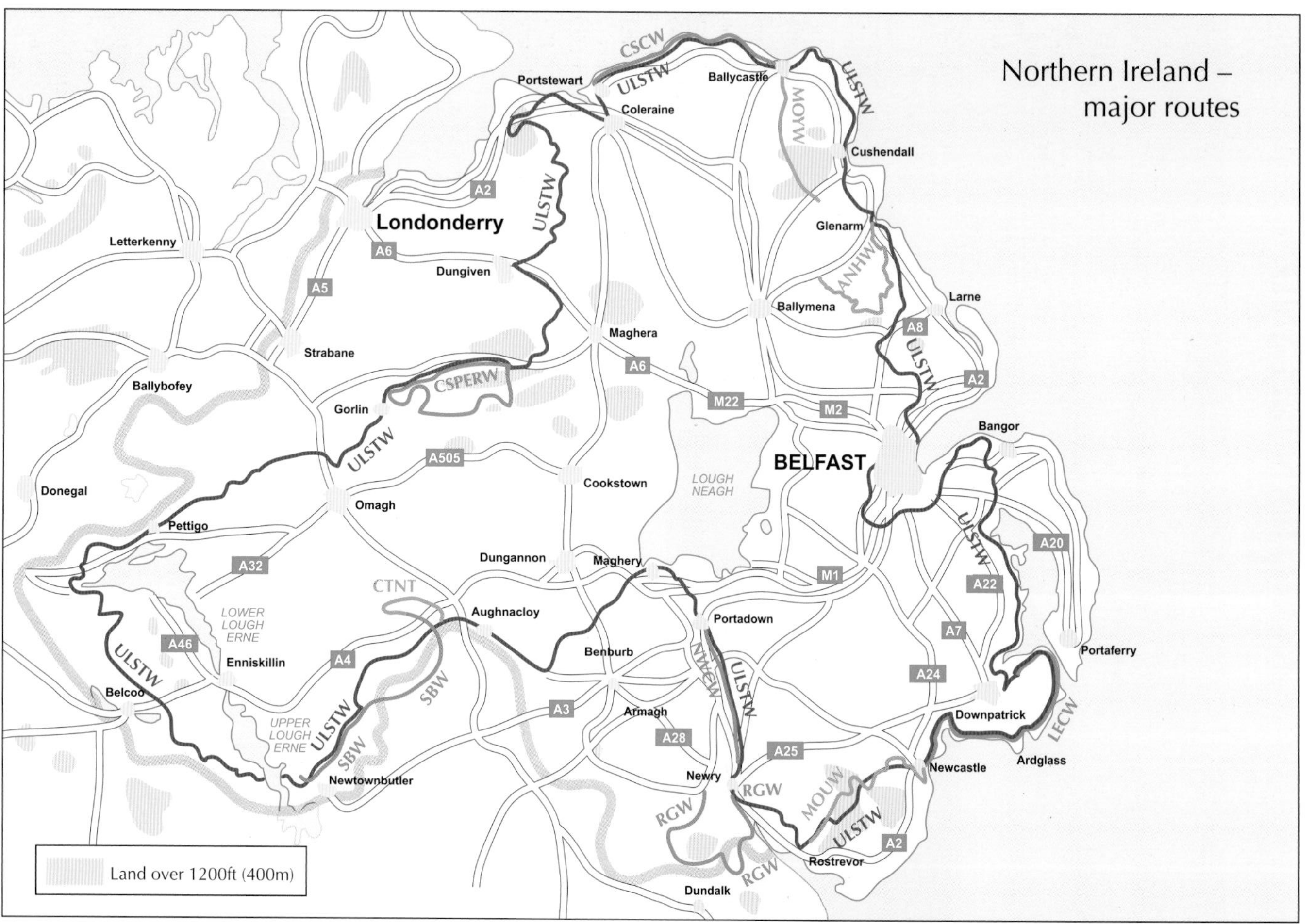
Northern Ireland – major routes
CSCW
Portstewart
ULSTW
Ballycastle
ULSTW
Coleraine
MOYW
Cushendall
A2
Londonderry
ULSTW
Letterkenny
Glenarm
A6
Dungiven
ANHW
A5
Larne
Ballymena
A8
Strabane
Maghera
ULSTW
A6
A2
Ballybofey
CSPERW
M22
M2
Gorlin
Bangor
ULSTW
A505
BELFAST
Donegal
Cookstown
LOUGH NEAGH
Omagh
Pettigo
ULSTW
A20
A32
Dungannon
Maghery
M1
CTNT
A22
Aughnacloy
Portadown
LOWER LOUGH ERNE
A7
A46
Portaferry
Enniskillin
A4
Benburb
NWCW
ULSTW
A24
ULSTW
SBW
Belcoo
A3
Armagh
Downpatrick
LECW
UPPER LOUGH ERNE
ULSTW
A28
SBW
A25
Newcastle
Ardglass
Newtownbutler
Newry
RGW
MOUW
RGW
ULSTW
A2
Rostrevor
RGW
Dundalk
Land over 1200ft (400m)

Portbraddon, Causeway Coast Path

through the glens to the hallowed mountain of Slemish, another volcanic plug, where legend has it that St Patrick herded swine as a boy. The 19th-century poet and author, William Carleton, is remembered in the Carleton Trail, taking in the attractive landscapes of the Clogher Valley, passing Lough More. The Mourne Way traverses the foothills of this eroded mountain range whose origins are also volcanic.

For those looking for easy **towpaths**, and **industrial heritage**, the Newry Canal Way along the UK's first summit-level canal fits the bill.

The limited range of promoted quality routes reflects the access traditions in the Province. Northern Ireland currently has nine promoted **Waymarked Ways**, walking routes spread across Northern Ireland and accredited by the Northern Ireland Countryside Access and Activities Network (CAAN), an umbrella organisation. Ranging in length from 20 to 35 miles, the aim of these Waymarked Ways is to open up the countryside to the people of Northern Ireland and tourists alike. The CAAN website, www.walkni.com, provides excellent information in an attractive format, identifies the Quality Walks and provides useful access updates.

While for now the Waymarked Ways arguably provide the pick of Northern Ireland's longer trails, the future of the Province's best hope for a true major Ulster 'national trail', the 'Ulster Way', remains unclear and it is not currently being promoted. A long route encircling the Province, and subsuming most of the Waymarked Ways with linking sections, the experienced walker should still be able to negotiate most of it using the recommended book by Paddy Dillon.

ROUTE CODES	
ANHW	Antrim Hills Way
CTNT	Carleton Trail
CSCW	Causeway Coast Way
SCPERW	Central Sperrins Way
LECW	Lecale Way
MOUW	Mourne Way
MOYW	Moyle Way
NWCW	Newry Canal Way
RGW	Ring of Gullion Way
SBW	Sliabh Beagh Way
ULSTW	Ulster Way

Access in Northern Ireland

Northern Ireland has very few public rights of way. In many areas walkers can only enjoy the open countryside, and venture 'off-road', because of the goodwill and tolerance of landowners. There is no presumption of access and no equivalent of 'right to roam' as in, say, England, and there are no National Parks that could provide large areas of access.

There are different attitudes to access and property rights and, with the large proportion of small owner-occupied farm holdings, many landowners are concerned about their liabilities and legal responsibilities were there to be public access to their land. There is a framework in place under which new paths may be developed but this involves the creation of new rights of way or the negotiation of new permissive access agreements. (See the Guidance Notes listed in the Key Facts box.) This makes it difficult to extend the network of promoted routes where users expect a guarantee of access.

There are many public country and urban parks and much of Northern Ireland's public land is accessible, such as Water Service and Forest Service land. Land owned by the National Trust covers some 120 miles of coastline and 40 square miles of countryside including parts of the Mournes such as Slieve Donard, the Province's highest mountain. The Woodland Trust provides some accessible woodlands.

These access issues led many early walking routes to use significant on-road sections, now increasingly trafficked and less pleasant for walkers. They make the development of a comprehensive network of long distance off-road routes difficult. The Province has relatively few, although there are many other excellent shorter walking opportunities. The attempts to establish the Ulster Way as a circuit around the Province – including most of the Waymarked Ways both on the coast and inland – produced a route with some undoubted quality sections but linked by significant road walking.

The potential benefits of extending the path network for use both by the local population and to attract walking tourism, and to generate economic value is being recognised, as is the need to provide confidence for path users that promoted routes will be open and will be well maintained. Isolated cases of denial of access have a disproportionate effect on confidence. The Northern Ireland Countryside Access and Activities Network (CAAN) has taken the lead by identifying and promoting the best short, medium and long distance walking routes in the Province. In partnership with Environment and Heritage Service and the Northern Ireland Tourist Board it has developed a Quality Walks 'stamp' awarded to routes that meet its standards. The assessment includes visitor facilities, signage, the proportions of off-road and on-road walking and scenic quality.

Portbraddon from White Park Bay, Causeway Coast Path

Antrim Hills Way ANHW

ANTRIM **35km/22 miles**

A scenic walking trail in the Antrim Coast and Glens AONB taking the walker among the Glens of Antrim across Black Hill and Scawt Hill, a volcanic plug, over fields and moorland, from the historic village of Glenarm to end at a second volcanic plug, Slemish Mountain, with its connections with St Patrick, where there is an access road and car park below. Slemish is said to be where the boy-slave herded swine for his master Miluic in the 5th Century and it has long been a place of pilgrimage on St Patrick's Day (17 March). The walk has extensive inland views across the Mountains of Antrim. From the coastline Scotland can be seen on clear days. An open upland route, it can be wet underfoot and is exposed to the weather.

Attributes
Challenging; NI Quality Walk; Coastal; Moorland; Religious
Start
Glenarm, Antrim D309154
Finish
Slemish, Antrim D311153
Waymark
Quality Walks fern logo
Websites
www.walkni.com, www.ccght.org
Maps
OS (NI) Discoverer
9 (Ordnance Survey of Northern Ireland)
OS (NI) Activity Map
Glens of Antrim (Ordnance Survey of Northern Ireland)
Publications, badges and certificates
Leaflets
Antrim Hills Way (Countryside Access and Activities Network) 2006. £1.00 (incs p&p). Cheques to Countryside Recreation NI.

Carleton Trail CTNT

TYRONE **48km/30 miles**

This route is associated with the 19th Century poet and author, William Carleton. It follows lanes and forest tracks and passes Lough More with views of the Clogher Valley, this is mostly on-road. It connects with the Sliabh Beagh Way at Clogher.

Attributes
NI Quality Walk; Lake/Reservoir; Literary
Start and Finish
Clogher Rural Centre, Tyrone H537516
Waymark
Quality Walks fern logo
Websites
www.walkni.com
Maps ◈
OS (NI) Discoverer
18 (Ordnance Survey of Northern Ireland)
Publications, badges and certificates
Leaflets
Carleton Trail (Countryside Access and Activities Network). £1.00 (incs p&p). Cheques to Countryside Recreation NI.

Causeway Coast Way CSCW

ANTRIM **53km/33 miles**

The Way offers a great variety of coastal scenery within the Causeway Coast and Glens AONB, passing sandy beaches, rocky bays, high cliffs, resorts and villages. Sites of interest include the Giant's Causeway, the ruins of Dunluce, the exposed Carrick-a-Rede rope bridge and Dunserverick and Kenbane Castles. The remarkable Giant's Causeway is a World Heritage Site. Its basalt columns were formed 65 million years ago by cooling volcanic lava. The Way connects with the Moyle Way at Ballycastle.

Attributes
Challenging; NI Quality Walk; Coastal; World Heritage Site; Geological
Start
Portstewart, Coleraine J812367
Finish
Ballycastle, Moyle D114406
Waymark
Quality Walks fern logo
Websites
www.walkni.com, www.giantscausewayofficialguide.com
Maps ◈
OS (NI) Discoverer
4, 5 (Ordnance Survey of Northern Ireland)
Publications, badges and certificates
Leaflets
Causeway Coast Waymarked Way (Countryside Access and Activities Network). £1.00 (incs p&p).
Paperbacks
Companion to the Causeway Coast Way: A Comprehensive Guide to the Walk from Portstewart to Ballycastle by Philip S. Watson (Blackstaff Press) 2004. Spiral bound. ISBN 9780856407581. 128pp; 208 x 168. £9.99.

Central Sperrins Way CSPERW

TYRONE **48km/30 miles**

The route goes through one of the largest uplands in Ireland. Within the Sperrins AONB, the gentle rounded contours of the Sperrin Hills are followed, through villages using country lanes, over open moorland, and along green lanes and farm tracks. It includes the Gap (Barnes), an ice-age cut; views of Coneyglen; Glenelly; the Owenkillew Valley, an SSSI, and it goes around Mullaghbane.

Attributes
NI Quality Walk; Moorland
Start and Finish
Barnes Car Park, Glenelly Valley, Tyrone H552905
Waymark
Quality Walks fern logo
Websites
www.walkni.com
Maps ◈
OS (NI) Discoverer
13 (Ordnance Survey of Northern Ireland)
OS (NI) Activity Map
Sperrins (Ordnance Survey of Northern Ireland)
Publications, badges and certificates
Leaflets
Illustrated Guide to the Central Sperrins Way (Countryside Access and Activities Network). £1.00 (incs p&p).

Lecale Way LECW

DOWN **64km/40 miles**

The Way follows in the footsteps of St Partick, from his landing place on the shores of Strangford Lough – the largest sea lough in the British Isles – around the rocky coastline of the Irish Sea. Within the Lecale AONB there are views not only of Strangford Lough but of the Mourne Mountains and Murlough Bay. The route includes attractive Killough and Tyrella Beach. The old railway line that forms the coastal path near Dundrum, and sand dunes near Newcastle complete the route. There are significant road sections.

Attributes
NI Quality Walk; Coastal; Religious
Start
Raholp, Down J533474
Finish
Newcastle, Down J376310
Waymark
Quality Walks fern logo
Websites
www.walkni.com
Maps ◈
OS (NI) Discoverer
21, 29 (Ordnance Survey of Northern Ireland)
OS (NI) Activity Map
Strangford (Ordnance Survey of Northern Ireland)
Publications, badges and certificates
Leaflets
Lecale Way (Countryside Access and Activities Network). £1.00 (incs p&p).

Mourne Way MOUW

DOWN **42km/26 miles**

This route is almost entirely off road, traversing the foothills of the Mourne Mountains from Newcastle on the Irish Sea to Rostrevor on Carlingford Lough. The Mourne AONB is a unique, largely granite, landscape shaped by ice and man, with fine views of coast, sea and countryside.

Attributes
NI Quality Walk; Moorland
Start
Newcastle Tourist Information Centre, Down J376309
Finish
Kilbroney Park, Rostrevor, Down J185180
Waymark
Quality Walks fern logo
Websites
www.walkni.com
Maps
OS (NI) Discoverer
29 (Ordnance Survey of Northern Ireland)
OS (NI) Activity Map
Mournes (Ordnance Survey of Northern Ireland)
Publications, badges and certificates
Leaflets
Mourne Way (Countryside Access and Activities Network) 2007. 2pp; A4. Free.
Paperbacks
Mournes Walks by Paddy Dillon (O'Brien Press Limited) 2009. ISBN 9781847171412. 160pp; 192 x 130. £7.99.

Moyle Way MOYW

ANTRIM **32km/20 miles**

The Way starts on the coast, heads around the forested slopes of Knocklayd, and follows the River Glenshesk upstream. An ascent of Slieveanorra is followed by the boggy shoulder of Trostan. It connects with the

Causeway Coast Path at Ballycastle. The route ends at Glenariff Forest Park where there is a visitor centre, a cafe, a shop and a number of waymarked walks. The Way is mostly off-road and signage is being improved. Some areas of commercial forestry and game-bird shooting lie on the route.

Attributes
Challenging; NI Quality Walk; Forest/Woodland; Moorland
Start
Ballycastle, Moyle D114406
Finish
Glenariff Forest Park, Moyle D185215
Waymark
Quality Walks fern logo
Websites
www.walkni.com
Maps
OS (NI) Discoverer
5, 9 (Ordnance Survey of Northern Ireland)
Publications, badges and certificates
Leaflets
Moyle Way (Countryside Access and Activities Network). £1.00 (incs p&p). Cheques to Countryside Recreation NI.
Walking Support Providers
Irish Cycle Tours

Newcastle Challenge Trail (Northern Ireland) NEWCW

DOWN **45km/28 miles**

A long-distance walking route through the Mourne AONB with fine views out over the Irish Sea and across the Mourne Mountains. The route includes Tollymore and Castlewellan Forest Parks, Maghera village, a shoreline walk around the Murlogh National Nature Reserve, and finally along Dundrum Inner and Dundrum Outer Bays.

Attributes
Challenging; Forest/Woodland; Coastal; Moorland
Start and Finish
Newcastle TIC, Newcastle, NI J377309
Waymark
Name/Mourne Heritage Trust symbol on posts/brown signs
Websites
www.walkni.com, www.downdc.gov.uk
Maps
OS (NI) Discoverer
29 (Ordnance Survey of Northern Ireland)
OS (NI) Activity Map
Mournes, Slieve Croob Outdoor Pursuits Map (Ordnance Survey of Northern Ireland)
Publications, badges and certificates
Leaflets
Newcastle Challenge Trail (Northern Ireland) (Down District Council). Free. Tel: Countryside Development 028 4461 0800; downloadable.

Newry Canal Way NWCW

ARMAGH **32km/20 miles**

Mostly off-road, the Way follows the towpath of the now disused canal that was the first summit-level canal in the United Kingdom. It passes 13 lock gates and the villages of Scarva, Poyntzpass and Jerrettspass.

Attributes
Easy; NI Quality Walk; Cycle Route; Canal
Start
Shillington's Quay, Portadown, Armagh J014539
Finish
Newry Town Hall, Newry, Armagh J041505
Waymark
Quality Walks fern logo
Websites
www.walkni.com
Maps ◈
OS (NI) Discoverer
20, 29 (Ordnance Survey of Northern Ireland)
Publications, badges and certificates
Leaflets
Illustrated Guide to the Newry Canal Way (Countryside Access and Activities Network). £1.00 (incs p&p).

Ring of Gullion Way RGW

ARMAGH, LOUTH (ROI) **58km/36 miles**

This route follows a natural geological formation known as a volcanic ring-dyke, this being one of the best examples in the British Isles. It goes through the Ring of Gullion AONB, with abundant views of Slieve Gullion, the ring-dyke itself, Carlingford Lough and the Mourne Mountains. Use is made of forestry and grass tracks and rugged open hillsides, but there are some significant road sections.

Attributes
NI Quality Walk; Forest/Woodland; Moorland; Geological
Start
Newry, Armagh J084257

Finish
Derrymore House, Bessbrook, Armagh J057277
Waymark
Quality Walks fern logo
Websites
www.walkni.com
Maps ◈
OS (NI) Discoverer
29, 28 (Ordnance Survey of Northern Ireland)
Publications, badges and certificates
Leaflets
Ring of Gullion (Countryside Access and Activities Network). £1.00 (incs p&p). Cheques to Countryside Recreation NI.

Sliabh Beagh Way — SBW

FERMANAGH, MONAGHAN (ROI), TYRONE — **48km/30 miles**

This route takes in lakes and valleys; the Sliabh Beagh Mountain near to the summit; the drumlin fields of Monaghan, and glacial features. Use is made of forest tracks, country lanes and rugged open countryside. Some parts may not be accessible, please check with the relevant Council before undertaking this walk. Upgrading is planned to lead to a relaunch in 2009. It connects with the Carleton Trail at Clogher.

Attributes
Challenging; NI Quality Walk; Lake/Reservoir; Mountain
Start
St Partrick's Chair and Well in Glen of Altadaven, Tyrone J598497
Finish
Donagh, Fermanagh J399299
Waymark
Quality Walks fern logo
Websites
www.walkni.com
Maps ◈
OS (NI) Discoverer
18, 19, 27 (Ordnance Survey of Northern Ireland)
Publications, badges and certificates
Leaflets
Sliabh Beagh Walking Route (Countryside Access and Activities Network).

Ulster Way — ULSTW

BELFAST, NUMEROUS — **941km/585 miles**

The Ulster Way essentially encircles the Province by linking the Waymarked Ways and using other paths and road sections. It has links with trails in the Republic of Ireland, including a 69-mile spur traversing mountainous country in County Donegal. Most of the NI AONBs are visited with use made of paths, forestry tracks and minor lanes. While the Waymarked Ways arguably provide the pick of Northern Ireland's longer trails, the future of the Ulster Way remains unclear and it is not currently being promoted. There have been concerns with its link sections, route quality, its many road sections and with access issues. Some sections may be closed to the public. The Dillon book covers the route as it appears on OS mapping, while the Warner book is an account of a walk using an earlier version of the route.

Attributes
Challenging; Forest/Woodland; Coastal; Lake/Reservoir; Canal; Moorland; Mountain; World Heritage Site; Religious
Start and Finish
Belfast Castle, Belfast J290745
Waymark
Quality Walks fern logo on some sections
Websites
www.walkni.com, www.ulsterway.co.uk
Maps ◈
OS (NI) Discoverer
4, 5, 7, 8, 9, 12, 13, 15, 17, 18, 19, 21, 27, 29, 28 (Ordnance Survey of Northern Ireland)
OS (NI) Activity Map
Glens of Antrim, Lough Erne, Mournes, Slieve Croob Outdoor Pursuits Map, Sperrins, Strangford (Ordnance Survey of Northern Ireland)
Publications, badges and certificates
Paperbacks
Complete Ulster Way Walks by Paddy Dillon (O'Brien Press Limited) 1999. ISBN 9780862785895. 208pp; 130 x 198. £9.99.
Walking the Ulster Way: A Journal and a Guide by Alan Warner (Appletree Press Ltd) 2000. ISBN 9780862812270. 200pp; 145 x 206. £6.99.
Mournes Walks by Paddy Dillon (O'Brien Press Limited) 2009. ISBN 9781847171412. 160pp; 192 x 130. £7.99.

E-ROUTES

The lovely little fishing harbour of Staithes is associated with Captain Cook

KEY FACTS

Paths included in the E2, E8 and E9 routes in Britain

E2 (Eastern Variant: Dover – Stranraer)	North Downs Way National Trail, Dover to Guildford; Wey-South Path/ Wey Navigation, Guildford to Weybridge; Thames Path National Trail, Weybridge to Oxford; Oxford Canal, Oxford to Kirtlington; Oxfordshire Way, Kirtlington to Bourton on the Water; Heart of England Way, Bourton on the Water to Cannock Chase; Staffordshire Way, Cannock Chase to Rushton Spencer; Gritstone Trail, Rushton Spencer to Disley; Peak Forest Canal, Disley to Marple; Goyt Way, Marple to Compstall; Etherow/Goyt Valley Way, Compstall to Broadbottom; Tameside Trail, Broadbottom to Mossley; Oldham Way, Mossley to Standedge; Pennine Way National Trail, Standedge, via Middleton in Teesdale where the Central/Southern section joins, to Kirk Yetholm; St Cuthbert's Way, Kirk Yetholm to Melrose; Southern Upland Way, Melrose to Stranraer.
E2 (Central/Southern Variant: Harwich – Stranraer)	Essex Way, Harwich to Dedham; Stour Valley Path, Dedham (via link path) to Stetchworth; Icknield Way, Stetchworth to Linton; (Roman road link not included in the Handbook, Linton to Cambridge); Fen Rivers Way, Cambridge to Ely; Hereward Way, Ely to Rutland Water; Viking Way, Rutland Water to Barton-upon-Humber; (Humber Bridge, Barton-upon-Humber to Hessle); Yorkshire Wolds Way National Trail, Hessle to Filey; Cleveland Way National Trail, Filey to Guisborough; Tees Link, Guisborough to Middlesbrough; Teesdale Way, Middlesbrough to Middleton in Teesdale; joint section Pennine Way National Trail, Middleton in Teesdale to Kirk Yetholm; St Cuthbert's Way and Southern Upland Way (as above).
E8	Trans Pennine Trail, section from Hull to Liverpool
E9 Dover to Plymouth	Saxon Shore Way, Dover to Rye; 1066 Country Walk, Rye to Jevington; South Downs Way National Trail, Jevington to Queen Elizabeth Country Park (QECP); Staunton Way, QECP to Broadmarsh; Solent Way, Broadmarsh to Portsmouth. From Portsmouth there are mainland and Isle of Wight (IOW) variants: Mainland variant: Solent Way, Portsmouth to Lymington on Sea and Milford on Sea; (Local routes, signed as E9, on the Bournemouth Coast Path, Milford on Sea to Poole); Sandbanks Ferry, to Studland; South West Coast Path National Trail, Studland to Plymouth. IoW variant: Ferry, Portsmouth to Ryde; Isle of Wight Coastal Path (IoWCP), Ryde to Bembridge; Bembridge Trail, Bembridge to Newport; (Local route, Newport to Carisbrooke); Tennyson Trail, Carisbrooke to The Needles; IoWCP, Needles to Yarmouth; Ferry, Yarmouth to Lymington; then as the mainland variant to Plymouth.

E-ROUTES

The celebrated rock arch at Durdle Door is an iconic image on the Dorset Coast

Since the 1990s a number of supra-national European Long Distance Paths that cross several countries have been established. Three of these – E2, E8 and E9 – go through Britain, with both Ramblers and LDWA members involved in their development.

The **E2** runs from Galway to Nice. The 3030-mile (4850km) route currently starts in Stranraer, then goes through Southern Scotland, with variants through Eastern England and the Netherlands or Central and Southern England and Flanders to Antwerp, then Ardennes, Luxembourg, Vosges, Jura, Grande Traversée des Alpes (this is the well-known GR5) to Nice. The British section totals some 875 miles (1400km).

The **E8** is a 2740-mile (4390km) route from East Cork in Ireland to Istanbul, crossing England from Liverpool to Hull along the Trans-Pennine Trail via Stockport, Barnsley and Selby, about 190 miles (300km), then heading via Rotterdam, Aachen, Regensburg, Vienna, Bratislava, through Southern Bulgaria to the Turkish Border.

The **E9**, the European Coast Path from France to Estonia, with a planned length of some 3100 miles (5000km), runs along the South Coast of England from Dover to Plymouth, about 450 miles (720km). Sir John Johnson (LDWA President) and Jan Havelka (ERA President) officially opened this latest E-route in the UK in 2002 at Poole, Dorset.

In Britain, the E-Routes simply comprise linked sections of existing LDPs, shown on OS mapping, but not usually marked in their own right. The constituent paths forming the British sections of these E-routes are listed in the box and details may be reached through the LDPs section of the LDWA website: www.ldwa.org.uk. Details of these and many other E-routes in other European countries may be viewed through the website of the European Ramblers Association (ERA): www.era-ewv-ferp.org. Many European countries have their own national LDP networks, some highly structured, and summaries are included on this ERA website.

A woodland path fringed with garlic-scented ramsons high on Box Hill, Surrey

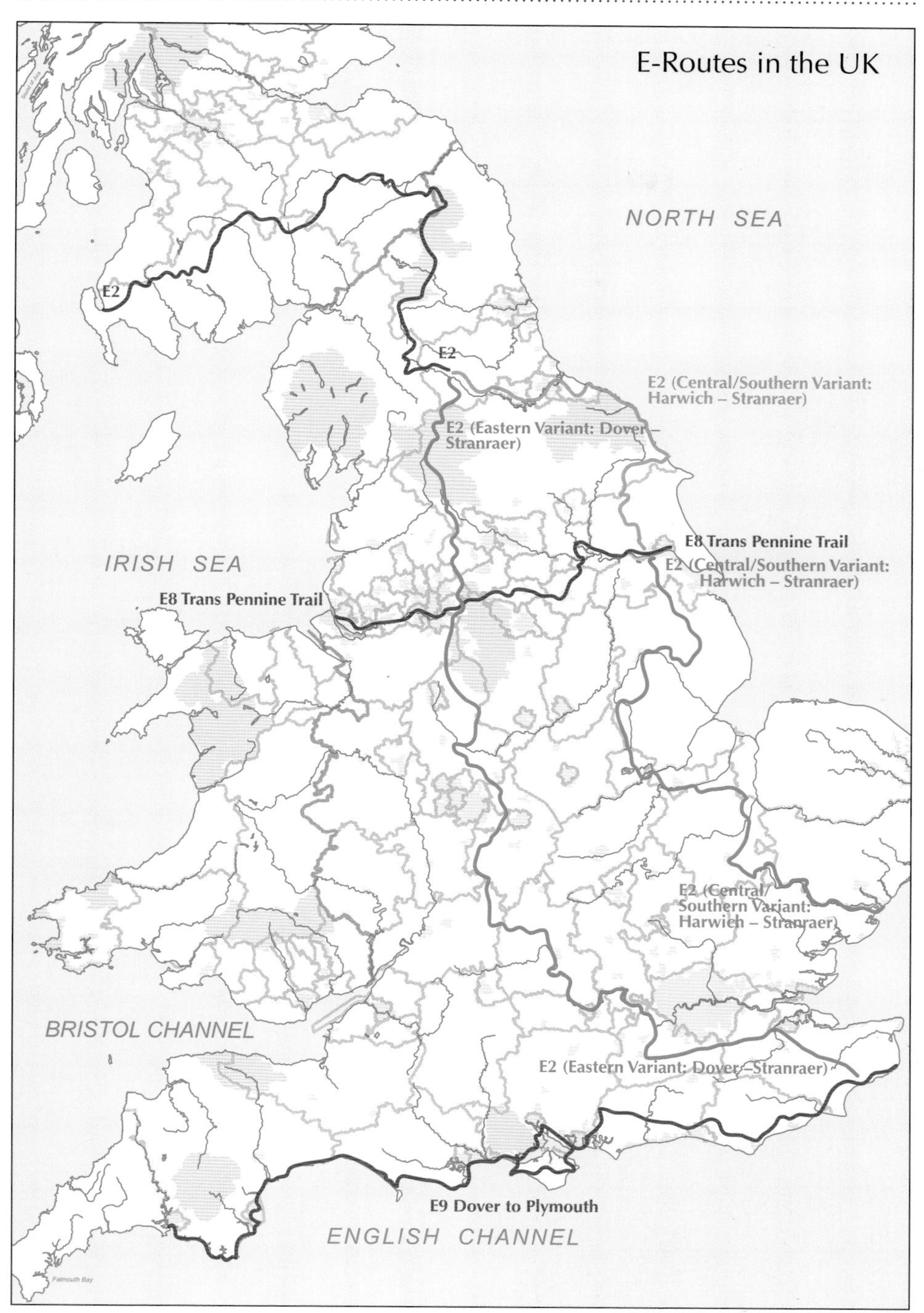
E-Routes in the UK
NORTH SEA
IRISH SEA
BRISTOL CHANNEL
ENGLISH CHANNEL
E2
E2
E2 (Central/Southern Variant: Harwich – Stranraer)
E2 (Eastern Variant: Dover – Stranraer)
E8 Trans Pennine Trail
E2 (Central/Southern Variant: Harwich – Stranraer)
E8 Trans Pennine Trail
E2 (Central/ Southern Variant: Harwich – Stranraer)
E2 (Eastern Variant: Dover–Stranraer)
E9 Dover to Plymouth

A separate recent pan-European initiative is the **North Sea Trail** (NORTRAIL), that aims to provide a trail around the North Sea coastline of the countries that border it, regenerating a network of landscapes and pathways, and linking footpaths and sites in recreational areas of these coastal countries. When complete it will pass through Norway, Sweden, Germany, Denmark, Netherlands, England and Scotland, making a total distance of just under 3100 miles (5000km). Up-to-date information on the full Trail is online at www.northseatrail.co.uk.

In Britain, six existing paths form sections of the North Sea Trail but do not yet provide an unbroken walk. Furthest north is the Moray Firth Trail running into the Aberdeenshire coast walk, part of which, the Moray Coast Trail, is now designated, then the Fife Coastal Path and the coast of East Lothian, where the recent John Muir Way is signed. In England the Northumberland Coastal Path and the coastal section of the Cleveland Way National Trail in North Yorkshire complete the picture. Details of each route are in the relevant regional sections.

Looking back along the cliff coast path from Skinningrove to Hunt Cliff, Cleveland Way

LISTINGS

Hardraw Force can be visited after leaving Hawes (Pennine Way)

TOP 100 TRAILS BY DISTANCE

	km	m
Land's End to John O'Groats	1368	850
Cistercian Way (Wales)	1046	650
South West Coast Path National Trail	1014	630
Great English Walk	1003	623
Monarch's Way	990	615
Ulster Way	941	585
Three Ridings on Foot	706	439
Nelson Way	682	424
Orange Way	563	350
Pennine Bridleway National Trail	558	347
Hope House Way	539	335
Land's End Trail	480	298
Macmillan Way – Boston to Abbotsbury	467	290
Greenwich Meridian Trail	444	276
Cambrian Way	441	274
Pennine Way National Trail	404	251
Walking the Riversides of Sussex	404	251
Seven Shires Way	377	234
Tops of the North (Three Shire Head to Carlisle)	370	230
Midshires Way	362	225
North to the Cape	349	217
Trans Pennine Trail	346	215
Southern Upland Way	343	213
Ravenber Way	338	210
Newlands Way	338	210
Severn Way	338	210
Cotswold Round	333	207
Walking the Castles of Kent	311	193
Bay to Bay Walks	307	191
Wainwright's Remote Lakeland	306	190
Chiltern Way	301	187
Pembrokeshire Coast Path National Trail	299	186
Thames Path National Trail	296	184
Coast to Coast (Wainwright)	294	183
Cumbria Coastal Way	293	182
Round Dorset Walk	291	181
Tarka Trail	291	181
Walking the Castles of Sussex	291	181
Famous Highland Drove Walk	290	180
Kent Coastline Walk	286	178
Offa's Dyke Path National Trail	284	176
Hertfordshire Way	267	166
Lake to Lake Walk	267	166
Cromer to the M11	265	165
Saxon Shore Way	262	163
Sarn Helen	258	160
North Downs Way National Trail	250	155
Lake Pickering Circuit	249	155
Herefordshire Trail	248	154
Reiver's Way	242	150

	km	m
London Loop	241	150
Birmingham and Aberystwyth Walk	238	148
Viking Way	237	147
Central Scottish Way	235	146
Shakespeare's Way	235	146
Grand Union Canal Walk	234	145
Ouse Valley Way	229	142
Shropshire Way	224	139
Wye Valley Walk	222	138
Wessex Ridgeway	221	137
Glyndwr's Way/Llwybr Glyndwr National Trail	217	135
South Kesteven Round	209	130
Elan Valley Way	206	128
Coast to Coast – Scotland	206	128
Dee Way	204	127
Clwydian Way	196	122
Anglesey Coast Path	195	121
One Week Coast to Coast Trek	193	120
Berwick Borough Boundary Walk	193	120
Wye to the Thames	192	119
Abbey Trail	187	116
Shropshire Cakes and Ale Trail	177	110
Nene Way	177	110
Hereward Way	177	110
Cleveland Way National Trail	177	110
Icknield Way Path	177	110
Geopark Way	175	109
Greensand Way	173	107
Abbott's Hike	172	107
Robin Hood Way	172	107
Hadrian's Coastal Route	169	105
Lakeland Tour	167	104
Abbeys Amble	166	103
Samaritans Way South West, Bristol to Lynton	166	103
Yorkshire Water Way	166	103
Wainwright Memorial Walk	164	102
Cotswold Way National Trail	164	102
Three Downs Link	164	102
Macmillan Way West – Castle Cary to Barnstaple	164	102
Heart of England Way	163	101
Leicestershire Round	163	101
Three Choirs Way	161	100
Lady Anne's Way	161	100
Trans Pennine Way	161	100
South Downs Way National Trail	161	100
Ayrshire Coastal Path	161	100
Chairman's Walk	161	100
Trent & Mersey Canal Walk	161	100
Navigation Way	161	100
Beacons Way (Brecon)	161	100

INDEX OF TRAILS

H

I

S

DIRECTORY OF SUPPLIERS

WSP: Walking Support Provider (holiday company and/or baggage carrying service that covers one or more routes in this handbook).

A

A Coventry Way Association, 106 Oxendon Way, COVENTRY, CV3 2GR; Tel 024 7645 5251; www.acoventryway.org.uk

Abbott, Peter, 5 Hillstone Close, Greenmount, BURY, Lancashire, BL8 4EZ; Tel 01204 885979

Aberchalder Baggage Transfer (WSP), Calderburn Cottage, Aberchalder Estate, INVERGARRY, PH35 4HN; Tel 01809 501411; www.greatglenway.com

Abingdon Information, Old Abbey House, Abbey Close, ABINGDON, OX14 3JD; Tel 01235 522711

About Argyll Walking Holidays (WSP), Letters Lodge South, STRATHLACHAN, Argyll, PA27 8BZ; Tel 01369 860272,; www.aboutargyll.co.uk

Absolute Escapes Ltd (WSP), 27/10 Maxwell Street, EDINBURGH, EH10 5HT; Tel 0131 447 2570; www.absoluteescapes.com

Acorn UK, 16 Welmar Mews, 154 Clapham Park Road, LONDON, SW4 7DD; Tel 0845 123 2312; www.acornmediauk.com

Alnwick Tourist Information Centre, 2 The Shambles, ALNWICK, NE66 1TN; Tel 01665 511333; www.visitnorthumberland.com

AMS Scotland Ltd (WSP), 22 Redhills View, Lennoxtown, GLASGOW, G66 7BL; Tel 01360 312 840; www.amsscotland.co.uk

Andrews, Nigel, 59 Pensfield Park, BRISTOL, BS10 6LE

Anglesey Walking Holidays (WSP), Tel 01248 713611; www.angleseywalkingholidays.com

Anglian Water Leisure, Customer Services, PO Box 770, LINCOLN, LN5 7WX; Tel 01480 812154; www.anglianwaterleisure.co.uk

Anquet Maps, Adam House, 7-10 Adam Street, The Strand, LONDON WC2N 6AA Tel: 0800 033 7030, sales@anquet.co.uk, www.anquet.co.uk

Appletree Press Ltd, The Old Potato Station, 14 Howard Street South, BELFAST, BT7 1AP; Tel 02890 243074; www.appletree.ie

Aqua3 (Hope Digital), Parsons Lane, Hope, Hope Valley, Derbyshire S33 6RB Tel: 01433 621779, www.aqua3.com

Archard, Richard, 57 Countess Road, AMESBURY, Wiltshire, SP4 7AS; Tel 01980 623341; www.btinternet.com

Arnside/Silverdale AONB and Countryside Management Service, The Old Station Building, Arnside, CARNFORTH, LA5 0HG; Tel 01524 761034

Arran Coastal Way Baggage Co (WSP), Tel 01770 302334; www.coastalway.co.uk

Arran Coastal Way Support Group, 8 Sheean Drive, Brodick, ISLE OF ARRAN, KA27 8DH; Tel 01770 302539

artsNK, The Hub, 3rd Floor, Navigation Wharfe, Carre Street, SLEAFORD, NG34 7TW; Tel 01529 410595

Ashburton Tourist Information Centre, Town Hall, North Street, ASHBURTON, Devon, TQ13 7QQ; Tel 01364 654123

Ashton, Jim, 19 Leslie Avenue, BURY, Lancashire, BL9 8DL

Ashworth, A. T., 22 Laneside, Haworth Road, Wilsden, BRADFORD, West Yorkshire, BD15 0LH; Tel 01535 272055

Aurum Press, 25 Bedford Avenue, LONDON, WC1B 3AT; Tel 020 7637 3225; www.aurumpress.co.uk

B

Backpackers Club, memsec@backpackersclub.co.uk, www.backpackersclub.co.uk

Backpackers Press, 2 Rockview Cottages, MATLOCK BATH, DE4 3PG Tel: 01629 580427, DaveDalley@aol.com, www.independenthostelguide.co.uk

Bag Tag (WSP), SHANKLIN, Isle of Wight, PO37 6QW; Tel 01983 861559; www.bagtagiow.co.uk

Barnet Council, Greenspaces Development Section, Barnet LB, North London Business Park, Building 4, Oakleigh Road South, LONDON, N11 1NP; Tel 020 8359 7823; www.barnet.gov.uk

Barnsley MBC – Countryside Unit, Barnsley MBC, Town Hall, BARNSLEY, South Yorkshire, S70 2TA; Tel 01226 770770

Barnsley Metropolitan Borough Council, Town Hall, BARNSLEY, South Yorkshire, S70 2TA; Tel 01226 772696; www.barnsley.gov.uk

Barrie Blenkinship, Long Laithes, Blencarn, PENRITH, Cumbria, CA10 1TX; Tel 01768 88649

Barrow Tourist Information Centre, Forum 28, Duke Street, BARROW IN FURNESS, Cumbria, LA14 1HU; Tel 01229 876505; www.barrowtourism.co.uk

Bashforth, Peter, 23 Effingham Road, Harden, BINGLEY, West Yorkshire, BD16 1LQ; Tel 01535 273271

Basingstoke Canal Authority, Canal Centre, Mytchett Place Road, MYTCHETT, Surrey, GU16 6DD; Tel 01252 370073; www.basingstoke-canal.co.uk

Bath & North East Somerset Council, Transportation, Access and Waste Management, Floor 2, Riverside South, Temple Street, Keynsham, BRISTOL, BS31 1LA; Tel 01225 394041; www.bathnes.gov.uk

Battle & Bexhill Tourist Information Centre, Battle Abbey Gatehouse, High Street, BATTLE, East Sussex, TN33 9AQ; Tel 01424 773721; www.1066country.com

Battlefields Trust, Meadow Cottage, 33 High Green, Brooke, NORWICH, NR15 1HR; Tel 01508 558145; www.battlefieldstrust.com

Bayer, Peter, 23a Lyon Road, Eastburn, KEIGHLEY, West Yorkshire, BD20 0UY

Bedford Rural Communities Charity, The Smithy, The Village, Old Warden, BIGGLESWADE, Beds, SG18 9HQ; Tel 01767 626465; www.ivelvalley.co.uk

Begg, James, 19a Ewenfield Road, AYR, Ayrshire, KA7 2QF; Tel 01292 269195

Bennachie Project, Bennachie Centre, Essons Car Park, Chapel Garioch, By INVERURIE, Aberdeenshire, AB51 5HX; Tel 01467 681470

Berwick-upon-Tweed Tourist Information Centre, 106 Marygate, BERWICK-UPON-TWEED, Northumberland, TD15 1BN; Tel 01289 330733; www.berwick-upon-tweed.gov.uk

Best of Bodmin Moor, Lower Trengale Farm, LISKEARD, Cornwall, PL14 6HF

Best, Michael, Flat 6, Tewit Well House, Tewit Well Road, HARROGATE, North Yorkshire, HG2 8JG

Bexley Council, Bexley – TIC, Hall Place Visitor Centre, Hall Place, Bourne Road, BEXLEY, DA5 1PQ; Tel 020 8308 7784; www.bexley.gov.uk

Bike and Hike Services (WSP), 25 Ledi Court, CALLANDER, Perthshire, FK17 8EX; Tel 01877 339788; www.bikeandhike.co.uk

Birmingham City Council, Transportation Strategy, 1 Lancaster Circus, Queensway, BIRMINGHAM, B4 7DQ; Tel 0121 303 7454

Bishop, Martyn, 32 Elmwood Avenue, BOSTON, Lincolnshire, PE21 7RU; Tel 01205 369653

Blackburn with Darwen Borough Council, Witton Country Park Visitor Centre, Preston Old Road, BLACKBURN, Lancashire, BB2 2TP; Tel 01254 55423; www.blackburn.gov.uk

Blackstaff Press, Sydenham Business Park, 4c Heron Wharf, BELFAST, BT3 9LE; Tel 0845 1200 386; www.blackstaffpress.com

Blackwater Valley Countryside Partnership, Ash Lock Cottage, Government Road, ALDERSHOT, Hampshire, GU11 2PS; Tel 01252 331353; www.blackwater-valley.org.uk

Bob Garlick, Highview, 39 North Street, Huthwaite, SUTTON-IN-ASHFIELD, Nottingham, NG17 2PE

Bobs Walking Holidays (WSP), 40 Spring Hill, Kingswood, BRISTOL, BS15 1XT; walkingholidays.uk.com

Bollin Valley Partnership, County Offices, Chapel Lane, WILMSLOW, Cheshire, SK9 1PU; Tel 01625 534790; www.bollinvalley.org.uk

Book Castle, 12 Church Street, DUNSTABLE, Beds, LU5 4RU; Tel 01582 605670; www.book-castle.co.uk

Book Guild Publishing Ltd, Pavilion View, 19 New Road, BRIGHTON, BN1 1UF; Tel 01273 720900; www.bookguild.co.uk

Booth, Ben, 19 Rawcliffe Drive, Clifton, YORK, YO30 6NT

Bottomley, Alec, 8 Ringwood Mount, LEEDS, West Yorkshire, LS14 1AL

Bound, Terry, 3 Alpha Street, Heavitree, EXETER, Devon, EX1 2SP; Tel 01392 435303

Bown, Keith, ROTHERHAM, South Yorkshire, S66 1UE; Tel 01709 543126

Bracknell Tourist Information Centre, The Look Out, Nine Mile Ride, BRACKNELL, Berks, RG12 7QW; Tel 01344 354400

Bradford Millennium Way Project, 10 Laburnum Grove, Cross Roads, KEIGHLEY, West Yorkshire, BD22 9EP; www.homestead.com

Braintree & District Outdoor Pursuits, c/o 3 Beaufort Gardens, BRAINTREE, Essex, CM7 9JY; Tel 01376 325125

Brecks Countryside Project, Kings House, Kings Street, THETFORD, Norfolk, IP24 2AP; Tel 01842 765400; www.brecks.org

Brecon Beacons Park Society, Walking Wales, 3 Glantwymyn Village Workshops, MACHYNLLETH, SY20 8LY; Tel 01650 511314; www.breconbeaconsparksociety.org

Breedon Books Publishing Co Ltd, 3 The Parker Centre, Mansfield Road, DERBY, DE21 4SZ; Tel 01332 384235; www.breedonbooks.co.uk

Brewin Books Ltd, Doric House, 56 Alcester Road, STUDLEY, Warks, B80 7LG; Tel 01527 854228; www.brewinbooks.com

Bridgend Tourist Information Centre, Bridgend Tourist Information Centre, Bridgend Designer Outlet, The Derwen, BRIDGEND, CF32 9SU; Tel 01656 654906; www.bridgend.gov.uk

Brigantes Accommodation & Baggage Courier Service (WSP), Rookery Cottage, Rookery Cottage, SKIPTON, N. Yorkshire, BD23 4BX; Tel 01729 830463; www.brigantesenglishwalks.com

Bristol Tourist Information Centre, Harbourside, BRISTOL, BS1 5DB; Tel 0906 711 2191

British Horse Society, Stoneleigh Deer Park, KENILWORTH, Warwickshire, CV8 2XZ; Tel 08701 202244; www.bhs.org.uk

British Waterways, Customer Services, Willow Grange, Church Road, WATFORD, Hertfordshire, WD1 3QA; Tel 01923 226422; www.british-waterways.org

British Waterways – Fazeley, Mather Road, NEWARK, Nottinghamshire, NG10 3AE; Tel 01827 252000; www.britishwaterways.co.uk

British Waterways – Tamworth, Peel's Wharf, Lichfield Street, Fazeley, TAMWORTH, Staffordshire, B78 3QZ; Tel 01827 252000; www.britishwaterways.co.uk

British Waterways – Tring, 510-524 Elder House, Elder Gate, MILTON KEYNES, MK9 1BW; Tel 01908 302509; www.britishwaterways.co.uk

Bromley Countryside Ranger Service, High Elms Country Park, Shire Lane, FARNBOROUGH, Kent, BR6 7JH; Tel 01689 862815; www.bromley.gov.uk

Bromsgrove Ramblers, 13 Victoria Road, BROMSGROVE, B61 0DW

Broom, Gary, 3 Ramshorn Close, Galmington, TAUNTON, Somerset, TA1 5DP; Tel 01823 283212

Brown, Bill, The Mill House, South Street, Wilton, SALISBURY, Wiltshire, SP2 0JX; Tel 01722 744274

Brownlow, R.A., The Old Farmhouse, 4 Glen Road, Castle Bytham, GRANTHAM, Lincolnshire, NG53 4RJ

Buckinghamshire County Council, Rights of Way and Access, County Hall, AYLESBURY, Buckinghamshire, HP20 1UY; Tel 01296 387679; www.buckscc.gov.uk

Butler, Graham, 1 Leaside Court, Lower Luton Road, HARPENDEN, AL5 5BX

Buttle, Paul, 18 Brewery Lane, KESWICK, Cumbria, CA12 5LJ; Tel 017687 75669

Byways Breaks (WSP), 25 Mayville Road, LIVERPOOL, L18 0HG; Tel 0151 722 8050; www.byways-breaks.co.uk

C

C-N-Do Scotland (WSP), Unit 33, Stirling Enterprise Park, Springbank Road, STIRLING, FK7 7RP; Tel 01786 445703; www.cndoscotland.com

Caerphilly County Borough Council, Countryside and Landscape Service, Council Offices, Pontllanfraith, BLACKWOOD, NP12 2YW; Tel 01495 235312; www.caerphilly.gov.uk

Calderdale Way Association, 16 Trenance Gardens, Greetland, HALIFAX, HX8 8NN; Tel 01422 373832

Caledonia Hilltreks (WSP), 61 Macaulay Drive, Craigiebuckler, ABERDEEN, AB15 8FL; Tel 01224 326925; www.caledoniahilltreks.com

Callander TIC, Rob Roy & Trossachs Visitor Centre, Ancaster Square, CALLENDER, FK17 8ED; Tel 08707 200628; www.visitscottishheartlands.com

Cambridgeshire County Council, Countryside Access Team, Box ET1009, Babbage House, Castle Park, CAMBRIDGE, CB3 0AT; Tel 01223 717445

Cardiff County Council, Natural Environment, Room 230, County Hall, Atlantic Wharf, CARDIFF, CF10 4UW; Tel 029 2087 3230; www.cardiff.gov.uk

Carlisle City Council, Green Spaces, Bousteads Grassing, CARLISLE, CA2 5LG

Carmarthenshire County Council, Visitor Centre, Pembrey Country Park, PEMBREY, Carms, SA16 0EJ; Tel 01554 833913; www.carmarthenshire.gov.uk

Carr, Geoffrey, Fern Cottage, Cardigan Lane, Manor Road, OSSETT, West Yorkshire, WF5 0LT

Carrs Breadmaker, Old Croft, Stanwix, CARLISLE, CA3 9BA; www.carrsbreadmaker.info

CarryLite (WSP), Tel 01434 634448; www.carrylite.com

Castle, Alan, Corehead House, Annanwater, MOFATT, Dumfries & Galloway, DG10 9LT

Celtic Trails (WSP), P.O.Box 11, CHEPSTOW, NP16 6DZ; Tel 01291 689774; www.celtrail.com

Central Scotland Forest Trust, Hillhouseridge, Shottskirk Road, SHOTTS, Lanarkshire, ML7 4JS; Tel 01501 822015; www.csft.org.uk

Ceredigion County Council, Penmorfa, ABERAERON, SA46 0PA; Tel 01545 570602

Ceredigion Tourism Service, Lisburne House, Terrace Road, ABERYSTWYTH, Ceredigion, SY23 2AG; Tel 01970 612125

Challenge Publications, 7 Earlsmere Drive, Ardsley, BARNSLEY, South Yorkshire, S71 5HH; Tel 01226 217695; www.chall-pub.co.uk

Chelwood Publications, 189A Leckhampton Road, CHELTENHAM, GL53 0AD

Cherwell District Council, Leisure Services Department, Bodicote House, Bodicote, BANBURY, Oxon, OX15 4AA; Tel 01295 259855; www.cherwell-dc.gov.uk

Cheshire County Council, Public Rights of Way Section, Goldsmith House, Hamilton Place, CHESTER, CH1 1SE; Tel 01244 603237; www.cheshire.gov.uk

Chesterfield Canal Trust, 197 Chatsworth Road, Brampton, CHESTERFIELD, S40 2BA; Tel 01246 273 055; www.chesterfield-canal-trust.org.uk

Chesterton, Keith, 'Firle', Chestnut Avenue, GUILDFORD, Surrey, GU2 4HD; Tel 01483 563392

Chiltern District Council, Council Offices, King George V Road, AMERSHAM, Buckinghamshire, HP6 5AW; Tel 01494 729000

Chiltern Society Office, White Hill Centre, White Hill, CHESHAM, Bucks, HP5 1AG; Tel 01494 771250; www.chilternsociety.org.uk

Chilterns AONB, The Lodge, Station Road, CHINNOR, Oxon, OX39 4HA; Tel 01844 355500; www.chilternsaonb.org

Cicerone Press, 2 Police Square, MILNTHORPE, Cumbria, LA7 7PY; Tel 01539 562069; www.cicerone.co.uk

Ciritis, Anton, 80 Willowfield Crescent, HALIFAX, West Yorkshire, HX2 7JW

Cleobury Mortimer Footpath Association, Brookside, Eagle Lane, Cleobury Mortimer, KIDDERINSTER, DY14 8RA

Coast to Coast Guides, Castle Hill Bookshop, 1 Castle Hill, RICHMOND, North Yorkshire, DL10 4QP; Tel 01748 824243; www.coasttocoastguides.co.uk

Coast to Coast Holidays (WSP), 60 Durham Road, REDCAR, Cleveland, TS10 3RY; Tel 01642 489173 Mobile: 07802 358457; www.coasttocoast-holidays.co.uk

Coast to Coast Packhorse Limited (WSP), Chestnut House, Crosby Garrett, KIRKBY STEPHEN, Cumbria, CA17 4PR; Tel 017683 71777; www.c2cpackhorse.co.uk

Coastal Way Books, Lochranza, ISLE OF ARRAN, KA27 8HL

Collins, Stephen J., 51 Russell Gardens, SIPSON, Middlesex, UB7 0LR; Tel 020 8759 1134; redgoblin.infinites.net

Comer, Mark, 171 Burton Stone Lane, YORK, YO30 6DG; Tel 01904 656295; www.cawalks.co.uk

Connexions, Willoughby House, Saint Mary's Road, TICKHILL, S Yorks, DN11 9JQ; Tel 01302 759696; www.connexions.uk.net

Constable and Robinson Ltd, 3 The Lanchesters, 162 Fulham Palace Road, LONDON, W6 9ER; Tel 020 8741 3663; www.constablerobinson.com

Contact Essex, County Hall, Market Road, CHELMSFORD, CM1 1QH; Tel 0845 7430 430; www.essexcc.gov.uk

Contours Walking Holidays (WSP), Gramyre, 3 Berrier Road, GREYSTOKE, Cumbria, CA11 OUB; Tel 01768 480451; www.contours.co.uk

Conwy County Borough Council, Countryside Service, Planning Department, Civic Offices, COLWYN BAY, LL29 8AR; Tel 01492 575460; www.conwy.gov.uk

Cooper, Mick, 8 Hazebrouck Drive, Baildon, SHIPLEY, W Yorkshire, BD17 5PE; Tel 01274 585089

Cordee Ltd, 11 Jacknell Road, Dodwells Bridge Industrial Estate, HINCKLEY, LE10 3BS; Tel 01455 611 185; www.cordee.co.uk

Cornwall County Council, Transportation & Estates, County Hall, TRURO, Cornwall, TR1 3AY; Tel 01208 73441; www.cornwall.gov.uk

Cotswold District Council, Bourton-on-the-Water Tourist Information Centre, Victoria Street, BOURTON-ON-THE-WATER, Gloucestershire, GL54 2BU; Tel 01451 820211

Cotswold Line Promotion Group, 4 Sandford Rise, CHARLBURY, Oxon, OX7 3SZ; www.clpg.co.uk

Cotswold Walking Holidays Ltd (WSP), 5 Tebbit Mews, Winchcombe Street, CHELTENHAM, GL52 2NF; Tel 01242 518888; www.cotswoldwalks.com

Countryside Access and Activities Network, The Stableyard, Barnett's Demesne, Malone Road, BELFAST, BT9 5PB; Tel 028 9030 3930; www.countrysiderecreation.com

Countryside Books, 2 Highfield Avenue, NEWBURY, Berkshire, RG14 5DS; Tel 01635 43816; www.countrysidebooks.co.uk

Countryside Council for Wales, Plas Penrhos, Penrhos Road, BANGOR, Gwynedd, LL57 2LQ; Tel 0248 585500; www.ccw.gov.uk

Countryside Matters, 15 Orchard Road, Alderton, TEWKESBURY, Gloucestershire, GL20 8NS; Tel 01242 620598; www.countryside-matters.co.uk

Cox, Vic, 36 Elwood Road, Bradway, SHEFFIELD, S17 4RH; Tel 0114 2368598

CPRE Oxfordshire – Campaign to Protect Rural England, Punches Barn, Waterperry Road, HOLTON, OX33 1PP; Tel 01865 874780; www.greenbeltway.org.uk

Crabtree, Alan, 10 Feversham Grange, HALIFAX, West Yorkshire, HX3 0NG; Tel 01422 368981

Crowood Press, The Stable Block, Crowood Lane, Ramsbury, MARLBOROUGH, Wiltshire, SN8 2HR; Tel 01672 520320

D

Dales Court Press, 25 Clifton Dale, YORK, YO30 6LJ; Tel 01904 338107; www.dalescourtpress.co.uk

Dales Way Association, c/o David Smith, Dalegarth, Moorfield Road, ILKLEY, West Yorkshire, LS29 8BL; Tel 01943 601761; www.dalesway.org.uk

Dalesman Publishing Co Ltd, The Water Mill, Broughton Hall, SKIPTON, North Yorkshire, BD23 3AE; Tel 01756 701033; www.dalesman.co.uk

Dalton, Ed, Mountain View, Fachell, Hermon, BODORGAN, Anglesey, LL62 5LL; Tel 01407 840600

Darlington Borough Council, Rights of Way Section, Development & Environment, Town Hall, DARLINGTON, DL1 5QT; Tel 01325 388637; www.darlington.gov.uk

Dartmoor Towns Ltd, Dartmoor Way, c/o Trail Venture, 7 North Street, ASHBURTON, Devon, TQ13 7QJ; Tel 0870 2411817; www.dartmoorway.org.uk

Dash4it (Dash (South West) Limited, Unit 2, Barncoose Industrial Estate, REDRUTH, Cornwall TR15 3RQ Tel: 0845 634 62 66, admin@dash4it.co.uk, www.dash4it.co.uk

Dava Way Association, The Hub, 20 Tolbooth Street, FORRES, Moray, IV36 1PH; www.davaway.org.uk

Davies, George, 33 Fir Tree Road, Fernhill Heath, WORCESTER, WR3 8RE; Tel 01905 451959

Denbigh Library, Hall Square, DENBIGH, LL16 3NU; Tel 01745 816313

Denbighshire County Council, Countryside Services, Loggerheads Country Park, near MOLD, Denbighshire, CH7 5LH; Tel 01352 810614; www.denbighshire.gov.uk

Derbyshire County Council, Middleton Top Visitor Centre, Wirksworth, MATLOCK, Derbyshire, DE4 4LS; Tel 01629 823204

Derbyshire Dales District Council, c/o Matlock Tourist Information Centre, Crown Square, MATLOCK, Derbyshire, DE4 3AT; Tel 01629 583 388; www.visitpeakdistrict.com

Derbyshire Footpaths Preservation Society, c/o Mrs K. Hodgkinson, 3 Crabtree Close, Allestree, DERBY, DE22 2SW

Devon County Council, Tourist Information Service, PO Box 55, BARNSTAPLE, Devon, EX32 8YR; Tel 01392 382084; www.devon.gov.uk

Discovery Travel (WSP), Opsa House, 5a High Ousegate, YORK, YO1 8ZZ; Tel 01904 632226; www.discoverytravel.co.uk

Diss Tourist Information Centre, Mere Street, DISS, Norfolk, IP22 3AG; Tel 01379 650523

Doncaster Tourist Information Centre, 38-40 High Street, DONCASTER, DN1 1DE; Tel 01302 734309; www.visitdoncaster.co.uk

Dorset County Council, Environmental Services Directorate, County Hall, Colliton Park, DORCHESTER, DT1 1XJ; Tel 01305 224214; www.dorsetforyou.com

Down District Council, c/o The Downpatrick Tourist Information Centre, The Saint Patrick Centre, 53A Market Street, DOWNPATRICK, Northern Ireland, BT30 6LZ; Tel 028 4461 2233; www.downdc.gov.uk

Downlands Project, Omnibus Building, Lesbourne Road, REIGATE, Surrey, RH2 7JA

Drake, A. J., 2 Beech Lodge, 67 The Park, CHELTENHAM, Gloucestershire, GL 50 2RX; Tel 01242 232131; www.cambrianway.org.uk

Dronfield 2000 Rotary Walk, Mill House, Unstone, DRONFIELD, Derbyshire, S18 4DD; Tel 01246 414970

Drover Holidays (WSP), Pemberton Minor, St Johns Place, HAY ON WYE, HR3 5BN; Tel 01497 821134; www.droverholidays.co.uk

Dumfries and Galloway Council, Countryside Ranger Service, Environment and Infrastructure, Rae Street, DUMFRIES, DG1 2JD; Tel 01387 260184; www.southernuplandway.gov.uk

Durham County Council, Countryside Group, Environment Dept, County Hall, DURHAM, DH1 5UQ; Tel 0191 3834144; www.durham.gov.uk

Durham, Andrew, Orchard House, 69 Common Road, Western Colville, CAMBRIDGE, CB1 5NS

E

East Lothian Council, North Berwick Tourist Information Centre, Quality Street, NORTH BERWICK, EH39 4HJ; Tel 01620 827671; www.eastlothian.gov.uk

East Ayrshire Council, The Gatehouse, Dean Castle Country Park, Dean Road, KILMARNOCK, KA3 1XB

East Suffolk Lines Community Rail Partnership, 12 Kemps Lane, BECCLES, Suffolk, NR34 9XA; Tel 01502 716961; www.eastsuffolklinewalks.co.uk

Easterhurst Publications Ltd, 19 Wells Avenue, Feniton, HONITON, EX14 3DR; Tel 01404 850470

Eastleigh Ramblers, 2 Pavillion Close, Fair Oak, EASTLEIGH, Hampshire, SO50 7PS

Easyways (WSP), Room 32, Haypark Business Centre, Marchmont Avenue, POLMONT, FK2 0NZ; Tel 1324 714132; www.easyways.com

Eckersley, John, The Vicarage, School Lane, Heslington, YORK, YO10 5EE; Tel 01904 410389

Edwards, Alan S., 6 Brittain Road, Cheddleton, LEEK, Staffordshire, ST13 7EH; Tel 01538 360357

Edwards, G. J., 10 Howard Close, Haynes, BEDFORD, MK45 3QH; Tel 01234 381508

Ellis, Mike, 74 Nelson Road, HULL, East Yorkshire, HU5 5HN; Tel 01482 505105

Elstead Maps (UK) Ltd, The Threshing Barn, Woodhayes, Luppitt, HONITON, Devon EX14 4TP Tel: 01483 898 099, www.elstead.co.uk

Encounter Cornwall (WSP), Woodlands, Lerryn, nr LOSTWITHIELl, Cornwall, PL22 0PY; Tel 01208 871066; encountercornwall.com

Engel, Carole E., 10 Brookfield, Penistone Road, Kirkburton, HUDDERSFIELD, West Yorkshire, HD8 0PE; Tel 01484 606850

Environment Agency, Recreation Dept, Hafren House, Welshpool Road, Shelton, SHREWSBURY, SY3 8BB; Tel 01743 272828

Epping Forest Countrycare, Planning Services, Civic Offices, High Street, EPPING, Essex, CM16 4BZ; Tel 01992 788203

Epynt Way Development Officer, c/o ATE Wales, Sennybridge Camp, BRECON, LD3 8PN; Tel 01874 635511

Essex County Council, Great Notley Country Park, Great Notley, BRAINTREE, Essex, CM77 7FS; Tel 01376 340262; www.essexcc.gov.uk

European Ramblers Association (ERA), Generalsekretariat, Wilhelmshoher Allee 157-159, D-34121 KASSELl, Germany, www.era-ewv-ferp.org

Expedition North, Dowbiggin, SEDBERGH, Cumbria, LA10 5LS; Tel 01539 620436

Explore Britain (WSP), Tel 01740 650900; www.xplorebritain.com

Eye Books, Colemore Farm,, Colemore Green, BRIDGNORTH, Shropshire, WV16 4ST; Tel 0845 450 8870

F

Faber & Faber, UK Sales Department, 3 Queen Square, LONDON, WC1N 3AU; Tel 020 7465 0045; www.faber.co.uk

Famedram Publishing Ltd, P O Box 3, ELLON, AB41 9EA; Tel 01651 842429

FCP Holidays (WSP), 2 Glebe Park, PITTENWEEM, KY10 2NA; Tel 01333 451451; www.walkingfifecoastalpath.com

Fen Rivers Way Working Group, 123 Birdwood Road, CAMBRIDGE, CB1 3TB

Fields, Kenneth, 574 Darwen Road, Egerton, BOLTON, BL7 9RU; Tel 01204 303706

Fisher, Derek G., 8 Highcroft Road, NEWPORT, Mons, NP9 5EG; Tel 01633 211316

Foot, A. G., Coombe House, Brithem Bottom, CULLOMPTON, Devon, EX15 1ND; Tel 01884 33077

Footpath Holidays (WSP), 16 Norton Bavant, Nr WARMINSTER, Wiltshire, BA12 7BB; Tel 01985 840049; www.footpath-holidays.com

Footprint, Stirling Surveys, Unit 87, Stirling Enterprise Park, STIRLING, FK7 7RP; Tel 01786 479866; www.stirlingsurveys.co.uk

Footprints of Sussex (WSP), Pear Tree Cottage, Jarvis Lane, STEYNING, West Sussex, BN44 3GL; Tel 01903 813381; www.footprintsofsussex.co.uk

Forest Enterprise North Yorkshire, Outgang Road, PICKERING, North Yorkshire, YO18 7EL; Tel 01751 472771; www.forestry.gov.uk

Forest of Avon, Ashton Court Visitors Centre, Ashton Court Estate, Long Ashton, BRISTOL, BS41 9JN; Tel 0117 953 2141; www.forestofavon.org.uk

Forest of Marston Vale, The Forest Centre, Station Road, MARSTON MORETAINE, Bedfordshire, MK43 0PR; Tel 01234 767037; www.marstonvale.org

Forest of Mercia, Chasewater Country Park, Pool Road, BROWNHILLS, Staffordshire, WS8 7NL; Tel 01543 370737; forestofmercia.org.uk

Forest of Rossendale Bridleways Association, 2 Baxenden House, Baxenden Fold, ACCRINGTON, BB5 2RU; www.forba.org.uk

Fox, Richard, 35 Mountside, GUILDFORD, Surrey, GU2 4JD; www.thefoxway.com

Fractal Press, Low Mill Cottages, GRASSINGTON, North Yorkshire, BD23 5BX; Tel 01756 752000; www.bay2bay.co.uk

Frances Lincoln, Distribution: Bookpoint Ltd, 130 Milton Park, ABINGDON, Oxon, OX14 4SB; Tel 01235 400 400; www.franceslincoln.com

Friends of Ridgeway, c/o Ian Ritchie, The Limes, Oxford Street, RAMSBURY, Wiltshire, SN8 2PS; Tel 01672 520090; www.ridgewayfriends.org.uk

Friends of the Hertfordshire Way, 53 Green Drift, ROYSTON, Herts, SG8 5BX; Tel 01763 244509; www.fhw.org.uk

Friends of the Trans Pennine Trail, c/o Richard Haynes, 32 Dalebrook Court, SHEFFIELD, S10 3PQ; Tel 0114 230 5358

Frith, David, 13 New Road, Whaley Bridge, HIGH PEAK, SK23 7JG; Tel 01663 732706

G

Garbutt, George E., 17 Kingsclere, Huntington, YORK, YO32 9SF; Tel 01904 768508

Garmin Europe Ltd, Hounsdown Business Park, SOUTHAMPTON, Hampshire SO40 9LR Tel: 023 8052 4000, www.garmin.com

Geographer's A-Z Map Company, www.a-zmaps.co.uk

GEOprojects, 8 Southern Court, South Street, READING, Berkshire, RG1 4QS; Tel 0118 939 3567; www.geoprojects.net

Glasgow City Council, Land Services, Richmond Exchange, 20 Cadogan Street, GLASGOW, G2 7AD; Tel 0141 287 9039

Gloucestershire County Council, Tourism Office, Environment Department, Shire Hall, GLOUCESTER, GL1 2TH; Tel 01452 425535; www.gloscc.gov.uk

Gomer Press, Wind Street, LLANDYSUL, Ceredigion, SA44 4QL; Tel 01559 362371; www.gomer.co.uk

Goole Rambling Club, c/o Wendy Wales, 29 Mount Pleasant Road, GOOLE, East Yorkshire, DN14 6LH; Tel 01405 764640

Gordano Footpath Group, c/o Jim Dyer, 3 Harmony Drive, Portishead, BRISTOL, BS20 8DH; Tel 01275 843829; www.gordano-footpath-group.org.uk

Gordon, Sheila, Haymeads, The Mains, Giggleswick, SETTLE, North Yorkshire, BD24 0AX; Tel 01729 824638

Gower Society, Swansea Museum, Victoria Road, SWANSEA, SA1 1SN

Grantham Canal Partnership, www.granthamcanal.com

Grantham Ramblers, 36 Huntley Avenue, GRANTHAM, NG31 7JJ; Tel 01476 402701

Gray, Dr Madeleine, Tel 01633 432 675; cistercian-way.newport.ac.uk

Great Glen Baggage Transfer (WSP), The Old Post Office, INVERMORISTON, Inverness shire, IV63 7YA; Tel 01320 351322; www.greatglenbaggagetransfer.co.uk

Great Glen Travel (WSP), Lismore, INVERGARRY, PH35 4HG; Tel 01809 501222; www.greatglentravel.com

Great North Forest, The Greenhouse, Greencroft Park, Annfield Plain, STANLEY, Durham, DH9 7XN; Tel 01207 524888

Great Waltham Parish Council, c/o 17 Cherry Garden Road, Great Waltham, CHELMSFORD, Essex, CM3 1DH

Green Branch Press, Laurel Cottage, Queen Street, Chedworth, CHELTENHAM, Gloucestershire, GL54 4AG; Tel 01285 720154; www.greenbranch.co.uk

Greensand Ridge Walk, Countryside Access Services, Bedfordshire County Council, County Hall, Cauldwell Street, BEDFORD, MK42 9AP; www.greensandridgewalk.co.uk

Greenways Holidays (WSP), The Old School, Station Road, NARBETH, Pembrokeshire, SA67 7DU; Tel 01834 862107; www.greenwaysholidays.com

Greenwood, Peter, 53 Wrenthorpe Road, WAKEFIELD, West Yorkshire, WF2 0LP; Tel 01924 366642

Grey Stone Books, c/o Cordee Ltd., 3a DeMonfort Street, LEICESTER, LE1 7HD; www.cordee.co.uk

Griffiths, Margaret, 288 Turton Road, Bradshaw, BOLTON, Lancashire, BL2 3EF; Tel 01204 301420

Groundwork Thames Valley, Colne Valley Park Centre, Denham Court Drive, Denham, UXBRIDGE, Middlesex, UB9 5PG; Tel 01895 832662; www.colnevalleypark.org.uk

Guidepost, 37 Normanton Lane, KETWORTH, Nottinghamshire, NG12 5HB Tel: 0115 937 7449, www.guidepost.com

Gwasg Carreg Gwalch, 12 Lard yr Orsaf, Llanrwst, DYFFRYN, Conwy, LL26 0EH; Tel 01492 642031; www.carreg-gwalch.co.uk

Gwynedd County Council, Economic Development & Planning Dept, Council Offices, Shirehall Street, CAERNARFON, Gwynedd, LL55 1SH; Tel 01286 672255; www.gwynedd.gov.uk

H

Hadrian's Wall Heritage, East Peter Field, Dipton Mill Road, Hexham, NEWCASTLE UPON TYNE, NE46 2JT; Tel 01434 322002; www.nationaltrail.co.uk

Hadrian's Wall Heritage Ltd, East Peterel Field, Dipton Mill Road, HEXHAM, Northumberland, NE46 2JT; Tel 01434 609700; www.hadrians-wall.org

Haller, Derek, 21 Sunnydale Crescent, OTLEY, West Yorkshire, LS21 3LU; Tel 01943 462801

Halsgrove Press, Halsgrove House, Ryelands Industrial Estate, Bagley Road, WELLINGTON, Somerset, TA21 0PZ; Tel 01823 653777; www.halsgrove.co.uk

Hampshire County Council, Countryside Services, Mottisfont Court, High Street, WINCHESTER, Hants, SO23 8ZB; Tel 01962 846970; www3.hants.gov.uk

Harrogate Borough Council, c/o Tourist Information, Royal Baths Assembly Rooms, Crescent Road, HARROGATE, North Yorkshire, HG1 2RR; Tel 01423 537300

Harvey Maps, 12-22 Main Street, DOUNE, Perthshire, FK16 6BJ; Tel 01786 841202; www.harveymaps.co.uk

Haworth Tourist Information Centre, 2–4 West Lane, HAWORTH, West Yorkshire, BD22 8EF; Tel 01535 642329

Headley, Trevor, 18 Hillcrest Road, ORMSKIRK, L39 1NH; Tel 01695 574346

Heap, Hilda & Graham, 30 Dunvan Close, LEWES, E Sussex, BN7 2EY

Heart of England Way Association, Longchamp, Newhouse Farm, Barnes Lea End Lane, Hopwood, BIRMINGHAM, B48 7AX; Tel 0121 743 3367; www.heartofenglandway.org

Hebden Bridge Visitor and Canal Centre, Butlers Wharf, New Road, HEBDEN BRIDGE, HX7 8AF; Tel 01422 843831; www.calderdale.gov.uk

Hereford Ramblers, 98 Gorsty Lane, HEREFORD, HR1 1UN

Herefordshire & Worcestershire Earth Heritage Trust, University of Worcester, Henwick Grove, WORCESTER, WR2 6AJ; Tel 01905 855184; www.EarthHeritageTrust.org

Hertfordshire County Council, Countryside Management Service (East), Little Samuels Farm, Widford Road, HUNSDON, Herts, SG12 8NN; Tel 01462 459395; enquire.hertscc.gov.uk

HF Holidays (WSP), Catalyst House, 720 Centennial Court, Centennial Park, ELSTREE, Hertfordshire, WD6 3SY; Tel 0845 470 8558; www.hfholidays.co.uk

Hill, Richard, 5/6 Blorenge Terrace, Llanfoist, ABERGAVENNY, Mons, NP7 9NP; Tel 0779 292 7818

Hillingdon LB, Central Library, 14/15 High Street, UXBRIDGE, Middlesex, UB8 1HD; Tel 01895 250456

Hillside Publications, 12 Broadlands, Shann Park, KEIGHLEY, West Yorkshire, BD20 6HX; Tel 01535 681505; www.datechcs.co.uk

Hobnob Press, PO Box 1838, East Knoyle, SALISBURY, Wiltshire, SP3 6FA

Hollingworth Lake Visitor Centre, Rakewood Road, Littleborough, ROCHDALE, OL15 0AQ; Tel 01706 373421; www.rochdale.gov.uk

Holmfirth Tourist Information Centre, 49–51 Huddersfield Road, HOLMFIRTH, West Yorkshire, HD9 3JP; Tel 01484 222444

Hood, Glen, 329 Kingston Road, Willerby, HULL, HU10 6PY; Tel 01482 659780

Hope House Hospices, Nant Lane, Morda, OSWESTRY, SY10 9BX; Tel 01691 671671; www.hopehouse.org.uk

Hostelling International, 22–32 Donegal Road, BELFAST, BT12 5JN Tel: 028 9032 4733, info@hini.org.uk, www.hini.org.uk

Hunt End Books, 66 Enfield Road, REDDITCH, B97 5NH; Tel 01527 542516

Huntingdon District Council, Pathfinder House, St Mary's Street, HUNTINGDON, Cambridgeshire, PE29 3TN; Tel 01480 388588; www.huntsdc.gov.uk

I

Icknield Way Association, 1 Edgeborough Close, Kentford, NEWMARKET, CB8 8QY; www.icknieldwaypath.co.uk

Inn Way Publications, 102 Leeds Road, HARROGATE, North Yorkshire, HG2 8HB; Tel 01423 871750; www.innway.co.uk

Instep Walking Holidays, 35 Cokeham Road, LANCING, West Sussex, BN15 0AE; Tel 01903 766475; www.instephols.co.uk

Institute of Fundraising, Park Place, 12 Lawn Lane, LONDON, SW8 1UD; Tel 020 7840 1000; www.institute-of-fundraising.org.uk

Irish Cycle Tours (WSP), 28 The Anchorage, TRALEE, Co. Kerry, Ireland; Tel +353 66 7128733; www.irishcycletours.com

Irons, Dave, 57 Reservoir Road, Selly Oak, BIRMINGHAM, B29 6ST; Tel 0121 472 4995

Island 2000 Trust, Cowes Waterfront, Venture Quays, Castle Street, EAST COWES, Isle of Wight, PO30 5YS; Tel 01983 822118; www.island2000.org.uk

Isle of Man Department of Tourism & Leisure, Tourist Information Centre, St. Andrew's House, DOUGLAS, Isle of Man, IM1 2PX; Tel 01624 686801; www.visitisleofman.com

Isle of Wight Tourism, Mail Order Department, Westridge Centre, Brading Road, RYDE, Isle of Wight, PO33 1QS; Tel 01983 813813; www.islandbreaks.co.uk

Islington Archaeology & History Society, 8 Wynyatt Street, LONDON, EC1V 7HU; Tel 020 7833 1541

Ivel & Ouse Countryside Project, The Smithy, The Village, Old Warden, BIGGLESWADE, Beds, SG18 9HQ; Tel 01767 626326

J

Jackson, Gerry, 15 Edgehill, Llanfrechfa, CWMBRAN, Gwent, NP44 8UA; Tel 01633 482175

Jarrold Publishing, Whitefriars, NORWICH, NR3 1TR; Tel 01264 409217; www.totalwalking.co.uk

Jedburgh Tourist Information Centre, Murrays Green, JEDBURGH, Roxburghshire, TD8 6BE; Tel 01835 863688; www.scotborders.gov.uk

Jema Publications, 40 Ashley Lane, Moulton, NORTHAMPTON, NN3 7TJ; Tel 01604 644380

John Merrill Foundation, 32, Holmesdale, WALTHAM CROSS, Herts, EN8 8QY; Tel 01992 762776; www.johnmerrillwalkguides.com

Johnson, David, 1 The Hollies, Stainforth, SETTLE, North Yorkshire, BD24 9PQ

Jones Books, Gazelle Book Services Limited, White Cross Mills, Hightown, LANCASTER, LA1 4XS; Tel 01524 6876; www.gazellebookservices.co.uk

Jones, Ken, Longview, 163 Long Line, SHEFFIELD, S11 7TX

Jowett, Jack, 58 Queens Walk, CLEVELEYS, Lancashire, FY5 1JW; Tel 01253 853039

Jubilee Walkway Trust, Tel 07801 334 915; www.jubileewalkway.org.uk

K

Keeble, Derek, 9 Shelley Road, COLCHESTER, Essex, CO3 4JN

Kennet District Council, Devizes Visitor Centre, Cromwell House, Market Place, DEVIZES, Wilts, SN10 1JG; Tel 01380 734669; www.kennet.gov.uk

Kent County Council, Explore Kent, Kent County Council, Invicta House, County Hall, MAIDSTONE, Kent, ME14 1XX; Tel 08458 247 600; www.kent.gov.uk

Kent High Weald Project, Conservation Centre, Bedgebury Pinetum, Bedgebury Road, GOUDHURST, Kent, TN17 2SJ; Tel 01580 212972

Kerr, Marjorie, 9 Heathlands Avenue, West Parley, WIMBORNE, Dorset, BH22 8RW; Tel 01202 573192

Kesgrave Town Council, Ferguson Way, Kesgrave, IPSWICH, Suffolk, IP5 2FZ; Tel 01473 625179; www.kesgrave.org.uk

KIng, Jill, 112 Harlsey Road, Hartburn, STOCKTON-ON-TEES, TS18 5DA; Tel 01642 645789

Kingdom of Fife, St Andrews Tourist Information Centre, 70 Market Street, ST ANDREWS, Fife, KY16 9NU; Tel 01592 750066

Kirkby Stephen Tourist Information Centre, Market Street, KIRKBY STEPHEN, Cumbria, CA17 4QN; Tel 017683 71199; www.visiteden.co.uk

Kirklees Metropolitan Council, 3 Albion Street, HUDDERSFIELD, West Yorkshire, HD1 2NW; Tel 01484 223200; www.kirklees.gov.uk

Kirkpatrick, Ian & Caroline, 6 Tor View, Horrabridge, YELVERTON, Devon, PL20 7RE; Tel 01822 853123; www.ian.kirkpatrick2.btinternet.co.uk

Kittiwake, 3 Glantwymyn Village Workshops, Cemmaes Road, MACHYNLLETH, Montgomeryshire, SY20 8LY; Tel 01650 511314; www.kittiwake-books.com

Knobbly Stick (WSP), 5 Whitbarrow Close, KENDAL, Cumbria, LA9 6RR; Tel 01539 737576; www.knobblystick.com

L

Lancashire County Council, Countryside Section, P O Box 9, Guild House, Cross Street, PRESTON, Lancashire, PR1 8RD; Tel 01772 264709; www.lancashire.gov.uk

Lancaster City Council, Lancaster Tourism, 29 Castle Hill, LANCASTER, LA1 1YN; Tel 01524 32878; www.lancaster.gov.uk

Land's End to John O'Groats Association, 18 Coberley Ave, Davyhulme, MANCHESTER, M41 8QE; www.landsendjohnogroats.com

Landfall Publications, Penpol, Devoran, TRURO, TR3 6NR; Tel 01872 862581

Landscape Heritage, Thornhill, 47 Sandon Road, Cresswell, STOKE-ON-TRENT, Staffordshire, ST11 9RB; Tel 01782 398545; www.landscapeheritage.co.uk

Langbaurgh Loop Recorder, Bywood, Victoria Terrace, SALTBURN-BY-THE-SEA, Cleveland, TS12 1JE; Tel 01287 623443

Larks Press, Ordnance Farmhouse, Guist Bottom, DEREHAM, NR20 5PF; Tel 01328 829207

LDWA Calderdale Group, 80,Willowfield Crescent, HALIFAX, West Yorkshire, HX2 7JW; Tel 01422 380320

LDWA Cleveland Group, c/o Albert Bowes, 22 Highfield Crescent, Hartburn, STOCKTON-ON-TEES, TS18 5HJ; Tel 01642 645280

LDWA Cumbria Group, 4 Irthing Park, BRAMPTON, Cumbria, CA8 1EB; Tel 016977 42133; www.ldwa.org.uk

LDWA East Lancs, 3 Hillside Walk, ROCHDALE, Lancashire, OL12 6EB; Tel 01706 351525

LDWA East Yorkshire Group, Glen Hood, 329 Kingston Road, Willerby, HULL, East Yorkshire, HU10 6PY; Tel 01430 423860; beehive.thisishull.co.uk

LDWA Nidderdale Group, Walden Round Recorder, 24 Harlow Park Road, HARROGATE, HG2 0AN

LDWA Northumbria Group, 8 Handley Cross, CONSETT, DH8 6TZ; Tel 01207 563869; www.walknortheast.org.uk

LDWA Vermuyden Group, c/o Frank Lawson, 74 Tatenhill Gardens, Cantley, DONCASTER, South Yorkshire, DN4 6TL; Tel 01302 534079; www.ldwa.org.uk

LDWA West Lancashire Group, c/o Robert Waller, 33 Hazelmere Road, Fulwood, PRESTON, Lancashire, PR2 9UL; Tel 01772 862113

Ledbury TIC, The Masters House, St Katherines, LEDBURY, Herefordshire, HR8 1EA; Tel 01531 636147

Lee Valley Regional Park, Lea Valley Regional Park Information Service, Myddelton House, Bulls Cross, ENFIELD, EN2 9HG; Tel 08456 770 600; www.leevalleypark.org.uk

Leeds City Council, Parks & Countryside, Farnley Hall, Farnley Lane, LEEDS, LS12 5HA; Tel 0113 395 7400; www.leeds.gov.uk

Leicestershire County Council, Community Services Dept, County Hall, GLENFIELD, Leics, LE3 8TE; Tel 0116 305 8160; www.leics.gov.uk

Leicestershire Footpath Association, Gamekeepers Lodge, 11 London Road, GREAT GLEN, Leicestershire, LE8 0DJ; Tel 0116 2592932; beehive.thisisleicestershire.co.uk

Leominster TIC, 1 Corn Square, LEOMINSTER, HR6 8LR; Tel 01568 616460

Let's Go Walking! Ltd (WSP), 4 Victoria Cottages, NORTH TAWTON, Devon, EX20 2DF; Tel 01837 880075; www.letsgobiking.com

Libris Press, 16A St John's Road, ST HELIER, Jersey, JE2 3LD; Tel 01534 780488; www.ex-librisbooks.co.uk

Lincolnshire County Council, Office Services, County Offices, Newland, LINCOLN, LN1 1DN; Tel 01522 782070

Llanfairpwll Tourist Information Centre, Tel 01248 713177

Llangollen Tourist Information Centre, Castle St, LLANGOLLEN, Denbighshire, LL20 8NU; Tel 01978 860828; www.llangollen.org.uk

Llyn Brenig Reservoir and Visitor Centre, Cerrigydrudion, CORWEN, Conway, LL21 9TT; Tel 01490 420463; www.dwrcymru.com

Lower Mole Project, 2 West Park Farmhouse, Horton Country Park, Horton Lane, EPSOM, Surrey, KT19 8PL; Tel 01732 743783; www.countryside-management.org.uk

Lyke Wake Club, P O Box 24, NORTHALLERTON, North Yorkshire, DL6 3HZ

M

Machynlleth Tourist Information Centre, Canolfan Owain Glyndwr's, Heol Maengwyn, MACHYNLLETH, Powys, SY20 8EE; Tel 01654 702401

Macmillan Way Association, Newlands, School Lane, Stretton-on-Dunsmore, STRETTON-ON-DUNSMORE, Warwickshire, CV23 9NB; Tel 02476 545 858; www.macmillanway.org

Macs Adventure (WSP), Unit 510, 355 Byres Road, GLASGOW, G12 8QZ; Tel 0141 248 2323; www.macsadventure.com

Maidstone Borough Council, Maidstone Town Hall Visitor Information Centre, Town Hall, High Street, MAIDSTONE, Kent, ME14 1TF; Tel 01622 602169; www.tour-maidstone.com

Mainstream Publishing Co Ltd, 7 Albany Street, EDINBURGH, EH1 3UG; Tel 0131 557 2959; www.mainstreampublishing.com

Make Tracks Walking Holidays (WSP), 26 Forbes Road, EDINBURGH, EH10 4ED; Tel 0131 229 6844; www.maketracks.net

Malkinson, Alec, 2 Southern Walk, Scartho, GRIMSBY, DN33 2PG; Tel 01472 825612

Mallinson, Louise, 17 Prod Lane, BAILDON, West Yorkshire, BD17 5BN; Tel 01274 584658

Malpress, Andy, 10 Kilnfield Road, Rudgwick, HORSHAM, West Sussex, RH12 3EL; Tel 01403 823825

Map and Compass, 62 Watkins Square, Llanishen, CARDIFF CF14 5FL Tel: 0844 504 9898, www.mapandcompass.co.uk

Marches Walks Limited (WSP), Footsteps, Cwmbach, GLASBURY-ON-WYE, Powys, HR3 5LT; Tel 01497 847149; www.marches-walks.co.uk

MC Publications, The Schoolhouse, New Road, CROOK, County Durham, DL15 8QX; Tel 01388 811747

Memory-Map Europe, Unit 3-4 Mars House, Calleva Park, ALDERMASTON, RG7 8LA; Tel 0870 744 6414; www.memory-map.co.uk

Mendip Hills AONB Service, Charterhouse Centre, Blagdon, BRISTOL, BS40 7XR; Tel 01761 462338; www.mendiphillsaonb.org.uk

Mercat Press, 10 Coates Crescent, EDINBURGH, EH3 7AL; Tel 0131 225 9774; www.mercatpress.com

Meridian Books, Sales Office, 8 Hartside Close, Lutley, HALESOWEN, West Midlands, B63 1HP; www.bestwalks.com

Mersey Valley Partnership, The Coach House, Norton Priory, Tudor Road, Manor Park, RUNCORN, WA7 1SX; Tel 01928 573346; www.merseyvalley.org.uk

Merthyr Tydfil TIC, 14a Glebeland Street, MERTHYR TYDFIL, CF47 8AU; Tel 01685 379884

Mickledore Travel Ltd (WSP), 14 Manor Park, KESWICK, Cumbria, CA12 4AA; Tel 017687 72335; www.mickledore.co.uk

Mid Cheshire Footpath Society, c/o Mrs Marian Harris (Hon Sec), 1 Church Rise, Sandiway, NORTHWICH, CW8 2WE; Tel 01606 883815; www.mcfs.org.uk

Mid Suffolk District Council, Countryside Section, 131 High Street, NEEDHAM MARKET, Suffolk, IP6 8DL; Tel 01449 720711

Millrace Books, 2a Leafield Road, Disley, STOCKPORT, Cheshire, SK12 2JF; Tel 01663 765 080; www.millracebooks.co.uk

Milton Keynes Council, Rights of Way Section, Landscape Division, Environmental Directorate, PO Box 113, Civic Offices, 1 Saxon Gate East, MILTON KEYNES, MK9 3HN; Tel 01908 691691; www.mkweb.co.uk

Mind Technology Limited, P O Box 15, Hoylake, WIRRAL, CH48 1QQ; Tel 0151 625 3264; www.footpaths.connectfree.co.uk

Mold Bookshop, 33 High Street, MOLD, Flintshire, CH7 1BQ; Tel 01352 759879; www.moldbookshop.co.uk

Monarch's Way Association, 15 Alison Road, Lapal, HALESOWEN, West Midlands, B62 0AT; Tel 0121 6022458; www.monarchsway.50megs.com

Monmouthshire County Council, County Hall, CWMBRAN, Gwent, NP44 2XH; Tel 01633 644644

Moody, Adrian, 2 Poplar Close, AYLESBURY, Bucks, HP20 1XW; Tel 01296 395146

Moray District Council, Dept of Technical and Leisure Services, High Street, ELGIN, IV30 1BX; Tel 01343 543451

Moxon, Mark, www.landsendjohnogroats.info

Mozaic, 17 Main Road, WINDERMERE, Cumbria, LA23 1DX; Tel 015394 44085; www.windermere-way.co.uk

MTB-Wales.com, www.mtb-wales.com

N

National Map Centre, 22-24 Caxton Street, Westminster, LONDON, SW1H 0QU Tel: 020 7222 2466, info@mapsnmc.co.uk, www.mapsnmc.co.uk

National Trust: River Wey & Godalming Navigations, Dapdune Wharf, Wharf Road, GUILDFORD, GU1 4RR; Tel 01483 531667

Natural England, PO Box 1995, WETHERBY, West Yorkshire, LS23 7XX; Tel 0870 120 6466; www.naturalengland.org.uk

Neath & Port Talbot County Borough Council, Afan Argoed Countryside Centre, Afon Forest Park, PORT TALBOT, SA13 3HG; Tel 01639 850564

Needham, John, 23 Woodland Crescent, Hilton Park, PRESTWICH, M25 8WQ

New Lyke Wake Club, 4 Cavendish Grove, Hull Road, YORK, North Yorkshire, YO10 3ND; www.lykewake.org

New Mills Heritage and Information Centre, Rock Mill Lane, New Mill, HIGH PEAK, SK22 3BN; Tel 01663 746904; www.newmillsheritage.com

New River Action Group, c/o Mrs Frances Mussett (Chair), 24 Lavender Road, ENFIELD, EN2 0ST; Tel 020 8363 7187; www.newriver.free-online.co.uk

Newlands School FCJ, Saltersgill Avenue, MIDDLESBOROUGH, TS4 3JW; Tel 01642 825311

Nightingale Publications, 23 Grange Road, BIDDULPH, Staffordshire Moorlands, ST8 7SB

Ninebanks Youth Hostel, Orchard House, Mohope, Ninebanks, HEXHAM, Northumberland, NE47 8DQ; Tel 01434 345288

Norfolk County Council, Planning & Transportation, County Hall, Martineau Lane, NORWICH, NR1 2SG; Tel 01603 222769; www.countrysideaccess.norfolk.gov.uk

North Downs Way National Trail Officer, Officer Environment and Waste, Kent County Council, Invicta House, County Hall, MAIDSTONE, Kent, ME14 1XX; Tel 01622 221525; www.nationaltrail.co.uk

North West Kent Countryside Project, Mead Crescent, Mead Road, DARTFORD, DA1 2SH; Tel 01322 294727

North York Moors National Park, Information Service, The Old Vicarage, Bondgate, HELMSLEY, North Yorkshire, YO62 5BP; Tel 01439 770657; www.moors.uk.net

North-West Frontiers Ltd (WSP), Viewfield, STRATHPEFFER, Ross-shire, IV14 9DS; Tel 01997 421474; www.nwfrontiers.com

Northamptonshire County Council, Countryside Services, P O Box 163, County Hall, NORTHAMPTON, NN1 1AX; Tel 01604 237227

Northern Eye Books Limited (Mara), 22 Crosland Terrace, HELSBY, WA6 9LY; Tel 01829 770309; www.northerneyebooks.com

Northumberland County Council, Countryside Section, Technical Services, County Hall, MORPETH, Northumberland, NE61 2EF; Tel 01670 533000; www.northumberland.co.uk

Northwestwalks (WSP), 16 Langham Road, Standish, WIGAN, WN6 0TF; Tel 01257 424889; www.north-west-walks.co.uk

Nottinghamshire County Council, Rights of Way Section, Trent Bridge House, Fox Road, West Bridgford, NOTTINGHAM, NG2 6BJ; Tel 0115 9774483

NPI Media Group, Dukesbridge House, 23 Duke Street, READING, RG1 4SA

O

O'Brien Press Limited, 12 Terenure Road East, Rathgar, DUBLIN 6, Ireland; Tel 00 353 1 4923333; www.obrien.ie

Oakham TIC, Flores House, 34 High Street, OAKHAM, Rutland, LE15 6AL; Tel 01572 724329

Offa's Dyke Association, Offa's Dyke Centre, West Street, KNIGHTON, Powys, LD7 1EN; Tel 01547 528753; www.offasdyke.demon.co.uk

Oldham Metropolitan Borough Council, Countryside Service, Strinesdale Centre, Holgate Street, Waterhead, OLDHAM, OL4 2JW; Tel 0161 620 8202

Orchard Trails (WSP), 5 Orchard Way, Horsmonden, TONBRIDGE, Kent, TN12 8JX; Tel 01892 722680; www.btinternet.com

Ordnance Survey, Romsey Road, SOUTHAMPTON, SO16 4GU; Tel 08456 050505; www.ordnancesurvey.co.uk

Ordnance Survey of Northern Ireland, Colby House, Stranmillis Court, Malone Lower, BELFAST, BT9 5BJ; Tel 028 9025 5755; www.osni.gov.uk

Ottakars, 118 The High Street, NEWPORT, Isle of Wight, PO30 1TP; Tel 01983 527927

Oxfordshire County Council, Cultural Service, Countryside Service, Holton, OXFORD, OX33 1QQ; Tel 01865 810226; www.oxfordshire.gov.uk

P

P3 Publications, 13 Beaver Road, CARLISLE, Cumbria, CA2 7PS; Tel 01228 543302; www.p3publications.com

Palatine Books, Carnegie House, Chatsworth Road, LANCASTER, LA1 4SL; Tel 01524 840111; www.palatinebooks.com

Pamplin, Elizabeth, Little Critchmere, Manor Crescent, HASLEMERE, Surrey, GU27 2PB; Tel 01428 651158

Parker, Ian, 4 Raikeswood Drive, SKIPTON, North Yorkshire, BD23 1LY

Pathway Publishing, 16 Parkhill, Middleton, KING'S LYNN, Norfolk, PE32 1RJ; Tel 01553 840554

Peacock, Kim, 18 St Andrews Road, WHITBY, North Yorkshire, YO21 1LJ; Tel 01947 821906

Peak District National Park, Aldern House, Baslow Road, BAKEWELL, Derbyshire, DE45 1AE; Tel 01629 816200; www.peakdistrict.gov.uk

Peak National Park Information Centre, The Moorland Centre, Fieldhead, Edale, HOPE VALLEY, S33 7ZA; Tel 01433 670207

Peak Publishing Ltd, Camus Bhan, Invercoe, GLENCOE, Argyll, PH49 4HP; Tel 01855 811475

Peddars Way National Trail Office, The Old Courthouse, Baron's Close, FAKENHAM, Norfolk, NR21 8BE; Tel 01328 850530; www.nationaltrail.co.uk

Pembrokeshire Coast National Park, Llanion Park, PEMBROKE DOCK, Pembrokeshire, SA72 6DY; Tel 0845 3457275; www.pembrokeshirecoast.org.uk

Pen-y-ghent Cafe, HORTON-IN-RIBBLESDALE, North Yorkshire, BD24 0HE; Tel 01729 860333

Pendle Borough Council, Regeneration Unit, FREEPOST, NELSON, BB9 9ZY; Tel 01282 661985; www.pendle.gov.uk

Pengwern Books, 23 Princess Street, SHREWSBURY, Shropshire, SY1 1LW; Tel 01743 369165; www.pengwernbooks.co.uk

Peninsula Press, Rock House, Maddacombe Road, Kingskerswell, NEWTON ABBOT, TQ12 5LF

Penistone Line Partnership, St Johns Community Centre, Church Street, Penistone, SHEFFIELD, South Yorkshire, S36 6AR; Tel 01226 761782; www.penline.co.uk

Penistone Town Council, Town Clerk's Office, St John's Community Centre, Church Street, PENISTONE, S36 9AR; Tel 01226 370088

Pennine Way Association, c/o Chris Sainty, 29 Springfield Park Avenue, CHELMSFORD, Essex, CM2 6EL; Tel 01245 256772

Pennine Way Project Officer, Natural England, Block 2, Government Buildings, Otley Road, Lawnswood, LEEDS, LS16 5QT; Tel 0113 230 3750

Per-Rambulations, c/o Larkshill, Cranston Road, EAST GRINSTEAD, West Sussex, RH19 3HL; Tel 01342 315786; www.per-rambulations.co.uk

Perks, Eric, Selbhome, 10 Cordle Marsh Road, BEWDLEY, Worcestershire, DY12 1EW; Tel 01299 404216

Perth & Kinross Countryside Trust, Pullar House, 35 Kinnoull Street, PERTH, PH1 5GD; Tel 01738 475255; www.caterantrail.org

Pestell, Allen, 8 Sledbrook Crescent, Crowedge, SHEFFIELD, S36 4HD; Tel 01226 765042

Petefield, Mark, Eden Outdoors, 43 Market Street, KIRKBY STEPHEN, Cumbria, CA17 4QN; Tel 01768 372 431

Peterborough City Council, Planning Services, Bridge House, Town Bridge, PETERBOROUGH, PE1 1HB; Tel 01733 453472

Petersfield TIC, County Library, 27 The Square, PETERSFIELD, Hampshire, GU32 3HH; Tel 01730 268829; www.easthants.gov.uk

Pierrepoint Press, 2 Southwell Riverside, Bridgnorth, WV16 4AS; Tel 01746 768 956; www.bobbibby.co.uk

Piggin, J K E, 37 Hazel Garth, Stockton Lane, YORK, YO31 1HR; Tel 01904 412917

Pinkney, Richard, 11 Pine Road, Ormesby, MIDDLESBROUGH, TS7 9DH; Tel 01642 319 840

PLANED, The Old School, Station Road, NARBETH, Pembrokeshire, SA67 7DU; Tel 01834 860965; www.planed.org.uk

Plymouth City Council, Tourist Information Centre, Plymouth Mayflower, Plymouth, 3–5 The Barbican, PLYMOUTH, PL1 2LS; Tel 01752 306330; www.plymouth.gov.uk

Pocket Mountains, 6 Church Wynd, Bo'ness, WEST LOTHIAN, EH1 0AN; Tel 01506 500404; www.pocketmountains.com

Powys County Council, Tourism Section, Neuadd Brycheiniog, Cambrian Way, BRECON, Powys, LD3 7HR; www.powys.gov.uk

Preston, R., The Chantry, Wilkes Walk, TRURO, Cornwall, TR1 2UF; Tel 01872 262334

Pritchard-Jones, John, 2 Sycamore Close, Etwall, DERBY, DE65 6JS; Tel 01283 732642

Pugh, Paul, 3 Harlech Mead, SHEFFIELD, South Yorkshire, S10 4NT; Tel 0114 230 2182

Purbeck Information & Heritage Centre, South Street, WAREHAM, Dorset, BH20 4LU; Tel 01929 552740

Pwllheli TIC, Station Square, PWLLHELI, LL53 5HG; Tel 01758 613000

Q

Quantock Hills AONB Team, Quantock Hills Office, Castle Street, Nether Stowey, BRIDGWATER, Somerset, TA5 1LN; www.quantockhills.com

R

RA Berwick on Tweed, 5 Quay Walls, BERWICK ON TWEED, Northumberland, TD15 1HB; Tel 01289 309891

RA Beverley Group, c/o Dennis Parker, 20 St. Matthew's Court, BEVERLEY, East Yorkshire, HU17 8JH; Tel 01482 861988

RA Cambridge Group, 52 Maids Causeway, CAMBRIDGE, CB5 8DD; Tel 01223 560033; web.ukonline.co.uk

RA Chesterfield & NE Derbyshire, 11 Haleswoth Close, Bolsover, CHESTERFIELD, Derbyshire, S40 3LW; www.chesterfieldroundwalk.org.uk

RA Clitheroe Group, 22 Claremont Avenue, CLITHEROE, Lancashire, BB7 1JN; Tel 01200 423881

RA Dorset, 19 Shaston Crescent, DORCHESTER, Dorset, DT1 2EB; Tel 01305 263759

RA East Berkshire Group, P O Box 1357, MAIDENHEAD, Berks, SL6 7FP; Tel 0118 969 2878; www.eastberksramblers.org

RA East Yorkshire & Derwent Area, c/o Mrs Sheila M. Smith, 65 Ormonde Avenue, Beresford Avenue, Beverley High Road, HULL, HU6 7LT

RA Gloucester, c/o John Street, The Knoll, Critty Craft Lane, Churchdown, GLOUCESTER, GL3 2LJ; Tel 01452 855211

RA Gloucestershire Area, c/o Elizabeth Bell, Holly Tree House, Evenlode, MORETON-IN-MARSH, GL56 0NT

RA Godalming and Haslemere, c/o Kate Colley, 6 Hill Court, HASLEMERE, Surrey, GU27 2BD; Tel 01428 651369

RA Grimsby & Louth, 50 Gayton Road, CLEETHORPES, North East Lincolnshire, DN35 0HN; Tel 01472 509396

RA Harrogate Group, c/o Delia Wells, 20 Pannal Ash Grove, HARROGATE, North Yorkshire, HG2 0HZ

RA Isle of Wight, Merry Meeting, Ryde House Drive, Binstead Road, RYDE, Isle of Wight, PO33 3NF; Tel 01983 564909

RA Leighton Buzzard, John Hartley, 57 The Paddocks, LEIGHTON BUZZARD, Bedfordshire, LU7 2SX; Tel 01525 383595

RA Lincoln, c/o Colin & Miriam Smith, 2 Belgravia Close, LINCOLN, LN6 0QJ; Tel 01522 682479; www.lincscountyramblers.co.uk

RA Manchester Area, 31 Wyverne Road, MANCHESTER, M21 0ZW

RA Meon Group, 19 New Road, FAREHAM, Hampshire, PO16 7SR

RA New Forest Group, 9 Pine Close, Dibden Purlieu, SOUTHAMPTON, Hants, SO45 4AT; Tel 02380 846353; www.newforestramblers.org.uk

RA Norfolk Area, c/o Sheila Smith, Caldcleugh, Cake Street, Old Buckenham, ATTLEBOROUGH, Norfolk, NR17 1RU; Tel 01953 861094

RA North East Lancashire Area, c/o Mrs Sue Baxendale, 101 Blackburn Road, Clayton le Moors, ACCRINGTON, Lancashire, BB5 5JT

RA North Wales Area, PO Box 139, LLANFAIRPWLLGYWNGYLL, LL61 6WR

RA Northumbria, 8 Beaufort Avenue, NEXHAM, NE46 1JD

RA Richmond, 59 Gerard Road, Barnes, LONDON, SW13 9QH

RA Ripon Group, 10 Pine Walk, RIPON, North Yorkshire, HG4 2LW; Tel 01765 600 013

RA Sheffield, c/o John Harker, 317 Prince of Wales Road, SHEFFIELD, S2 1FJ; Tel 07929 051 978

RA Sussex Area, Cobbetts, Burnt Oak Road, High Hurstwood, UCKFIELD, Sussex, TN22 4AE; www.sussex-ramblers.org.uk

RA Waveney, c/o Miss Brenda Le Grys, 1 Church Close, REDENHALL, Norfolk, IP20 9TS; Tel 01502 717415

RA West Berkshire, 38 Kipling Close, THATCHAM, Berks, RG18 3AY; Tel 01635 826046

RA West Riding Area, 11 Woodroyd Avenue, Honley, HOLMFIRTH, West Yorkshire, HD9 6LG; www.ramblersyorkshire.org

Radburn, Peter, 31 Hillcrest Avenue, Chandler's Ford, EASTLEIGH, Hampshire, SO53 2JS; Tel 01703 263584

Ramblers Countrywide Holidays (WSP), Box 43, WELWYN GARDEN CITY, Hets, AL8 6PQ; Tel 01707 320226; www.ramblersholidays.co.uk

Ramsgate Tourist Information Centre, 17 Albert Court, York Street, RAMSGATE, Kent, CT11 9DN; Tel 08702 646111; www.kent.gov.uk

Reardon Publishing, PO Box 919, CHELTENHAM, Gloucestershire, GL50 9AN; Tel 01242 231800; www.reardon.co.uk

Redbridge Ramblers, 16 Windsor Road, LONDON, E11 3QU; Tel 020 8989 5116

Redcar & Cleveland Borough Council, Countryside Section, Redcar & Cleveland House, P O Box 86, Kirkleatham Street, REDCAR, TS10 1XX; Tel 01642 444187

Reigate and Banstead Borough Council, Town Hall, Castlefield Road, REIGATE, Surrey, RH2 0SH; Tel 01737 276045

Ribble Valley Borough Council, Tourist Information Centre, Ribble Valley Borough Council Offices, Church Walk, CLITHEROE, Lancs, BB7 2RA; Tel 01200 425566; www.ribblevalley.gov.uk

Richlow Guides, P.O. BOX 3994, SHEFFIELD, S25 9AZ; www.richlow.co.uk

Richmond, Brian, 31 Dartmouth Street, BARROW-IN-FURNESS, Cumbria, LA14 3AS

Richmondshire District Council, Tourist Information Centre, Friary Gardens, Victoria Road, RICHMOND, North Yorkshire, DL10 4AJ; Tel 01748 825994; www.yorkshiredales.org.uk

Ridgeway National Trail Officer, Environment & Economy Division, Holton, OXFORD, OX33 1QQ; Tel 01865 810224; www.nationaltrail.co.uk

River Colne Countryside Project, c/o Colchester Borough Council, PO Box 889, Town Hall, COLCHESTER, Essex, CO1 1FL; Tel 07702 918980; www.colnevalley.com

Robin Hood Way Association, www.robinhoodway.co.uk

Rochdale Pioneers Museum, 31 Toad Lane, ROCHDALE, OL12 0NU; Tel 01706 524920; museum.co-op.ac.uk

Romney Marsh Countryside Project, Romney Marsh Day Centre, Rolfe Lane, NEW ROMNEY, TN28 8JR; Tel 01797 367934; www.rmcp.co.uk

Rosalinde Downing, St Bega's Way, Langside, Bassenthwaite, KESWICK, Cumbria, CA12 4QH; www.stbegasway.org.uk

Rossendale Borough Council, c/o Tourist Information Centre, 41-45 Kay Street, Rawtenstall, ROSSENDALE, Lancashire, BB4 7LS; Tel 01706 226590

Rotary Club of Cleckheaton & District, c/o 2 Turnsteads Avenue, CLECKHEATON, West Yorkshire, BD19 3AJ; Tel 01274 877528

Rotary Club of Nuneaton, c/o Chris Mountford, 242 The Long Shoot, NUNEATON, Warwickshire, CV11 6JN; Tel 024 763 29392

Rotary Club of Westhoughton, Brookfield, Peel Street, Peel Street, Westhoughton, BOLTON, BL5 3SP; Tel 01942 891079; www.westhoughton-rotary.org

Rotherham Rotary, 11 The Green, Whiston, ROTHERHAM, S60 4JD; Tel 01709 372 442; www.rotherhamrotary.org.uk

Rotherham Visitor Centre, Central Library & Arts Centre, 40 Bridgegate, ROTHERHAM, S60 1PQ; Tel 01709 835 904; www.rotherham.gov.uk

Rucksack Readers, Landrick Lodge, DUNBLANE, FK15 0HY; Tel 01786 824696; rucsacs.com

Rye Bay Countryside Service, 111B High Street, RYE, East Sussex, TN31 7JF; Tel 01797 226488; www.ryebay.demon.co.uk

S

S B Publications, 14 Bishopstone Road, SEAFORD, West Sussex, BN25 2UB; Tel 01323 893498; http:/www.sbpublications.co.uk

Salter, Mike, Folly Cottage, 151 West Malvern Road, MALVERN, Worcs, WR14 4AY; Tel 01684 565211

Samaritans Way SW, 6 Mervyn Road, BRISTOL, BS7 9EL

Satmap, 4 Fountain House, Cleeve Road, Leatherhead, Surrey, KT22 7LX; Tel 0845 873 0101; www.satmap.com

Sauerzapf, Bobbie, 71b Plumstead Road, Thorpe End, NORWICH, Norfolk, NR13 5AJ; www.notadog.org.uk

Sayer, Ann, 29 Twickenham Road, TEDDINGTON, Middlesex, TW11 8AQ; Tel 020 8977 9495

Scholes, Norman F., Danelea, 4, Laburnum Avenue, Robin Hood's Bay, WHITBY, North Yorkshire, YO22 4RR; Tel 01947 880534

Scottish Borders Tourist Board, Tel 0870 608 0404; www.scot-borders.co.uk

Scottish Rights of Way and Access Society, 24 Annandale Street, EDINBURGH, EH7 4AN; Tel 0131 558 1222; www.scotways.com

Scottish Youth Hostels Association, 7 Glebe Crescent, STIRLING, FK8 2JA Tel: 01786 891400, www.syha.org.uk

SE London Green Chain Project, P O Box 22119, LONDON, SE18 6WY; Tel 020 8921 5028; www.greenchain.com

Sefton Metropolitan Borough Council, Southport Tourist Information Office, 112 Lord Street, SOUTHPORT, PR8 1NY; Tel 01704 533333; www.visitsouthport.com

Shakespeare's Avon Way Association, Newlands, School Lane, Stretton-on-Dunsmore, RUGBY, Warwickshire, CV23 9NB; Tel 02476 545858; www.shakespearesavonway.org

Shakespeare's Way Association, Newlands, School Lane, STRETTON-ON-DUNSMORE, Warwickshire, CV35 0PG; Tel 02476 545858; www.shakespearesway.org

Shepherd's Walks (WSP), 2 The Stone Barn, Kirkwhelpington, NEWCASTLE UPON TYNE, NE19 2PE; Tel 01830 540453; shepherdswalks.skedaddle.co.uk

Sherpa Van Project (WSP), 29 The Green, RICHMOND, North Yorkshire, DL10 4RG; Tel 0871 520 0124; www.sherpavan.com

Shetland Times Bookshop, 71/79 Commercial Street, LERWICK, Shetland, ZE1 0AJ; Tel 01595 695531

Shire Publications, Cromwell House, Church Street, Princes Risborough, AYLESBURY, Buckinghamshire, HP27 9AA; Tel 01844 344301; www.shirebooks.co.uk

Shropshire County Council, Countryside Service, The Shirehall, Abbey Foregate, SHREWSBURY, SY2 6ND; Tel 01743 255061; www.shropshire.gov.uk

Sidebottom, Joyce, 8 Mill Lane, Horwich, BOLTON, BL6 6AT; Tel 01204 692762

Sigma Leisure, 1 South Oak Lane, WILMSLOW, Cheshire, SK9 6AR; Tel 01625 531035; www.sigmapress.co.uk

Skuse, Michael, Caenant, Llangynhafal, RUTHIN, Denbighshire, LL15 1RU; Tel 01824 702973

Skyware Ltd, 48 Albert Ave, SHIPLEY, BD18 4NT; www.skyware.co.uk

Smith, Colin, 2 Belgravia Close, Forest Park, LINCOLN, LN6 0QJ; Tel 01522 682479

Socratic Walker's Club, 39 Thornton Crescent, Old Coulsdon, CROYDON, CR5 1LG; Tel 01737 552292

Solway Coast Heritage Centre, Solway Coast Heritage Centre, Liddell Street, SILLOTH ON SOLWAY, Cumbria, CA7 4DD; Tel 016973 33055

South Downs Way National Trail Officer, Queen Elizabeth Country Park, Gravel Hill, HORNDEAN, Hampshire, PO8 0QE; Tel 023 9259 7618; www.nationaltrail.co.uk

South Gloucestershire Council, Public Rights of Way Team, Civic Centre, High Street, Kingswood, BRISTOL, BS15 9TR; Tel 01454 868686; www.southglos.gov.uk

South Lakeland District Council, Cultural & Economy Group Services Department, South Lakeland House, Lowther Street, KENDAL, Cumbria, LA9 4DL; Tel 01539 733333; www.southlakeland.gov.uk

South Norfolk Council, South Norfolk House, Swan Lane, LONG STRATTON, Norfolk, NR15 2XE; Tel 01508 533945; www.south-norfolk.gov.uk

South Shields TIC, Museum and Gallery, Ocean Road, SOUTH SHIELDS, NE33 2HZ; Tel 0191 454 6612; www.visitsouthtyneside.co.uk

South West Coast Path Association, Bowker House, Lee Mill Bridge, IVYBRIDGE, Devon, PL21 9EF; Tel 01752 896237; www.swcp.org.uk

South West Coast Path Team, Devon County Council, Matford Lane Offices, County Hall, EXETER, Devon, EX2 4QW; Tel 01392 383560; www.southwestcoastpath.com

Southend Borough Council, Leisure Development Officer, Leisure Services Department, Civic Centre, Victoria Avenue, SOUTHEND ON SEA, SS2 6ER; Tel 01702 215612

Southern Upland Way (WSP), 26 Main Street, Dalry, CASTLE DOUGLAS, Scotland, DG7 3UW; Tel 0870 835 8448; www.southernuplandway.com

Spalding Tourist Information Centre, South Holland Centre, Market Place, SPALDING, Lincolnshire, PE11 1SS; Tel 01775 725 468

Sparshatt, John, 30A Sandholme Drive, Burley-in-Wharfedale, ILKLEY, West Yorkshire, LS29 7RQ; Tel 01943 864613

Speyside Way Ranger Service, Speyside Way Visitor Centre, Broomfield Square, ABERLOUR, Banffshire, AB38 9QP; Tel 01340 881266

Squibb, Frank, 4 Basset Place, FALMOUTH, Cornwall, TR11 2SS; Tel 01326 317534

St Edmundsbury Borough Council, c/o Bury St Edmunds Tourist Information Centre, 6 Angel Hill, BURY ST EDMUNDS, Suffolk, IP33 1UZ; Tel 01284 764667

Stanfords 12/14 Long Acre, LONDON, WC2E 9LP Tel: 020 7836 1321, customer.services@stanfords.co.uk, www.stanfords.co.uk

Staffordshire County Council, Environment & Counytryside Unit, Development Services Directorate, Riverway, STAFFORD, ST16 3TJ; Tel 01785 277264; www.staffordshire.gov.uk

Step by Step Walking Holidays (WSP), 11 Queens Road, SHANKLIN, Isle of Wight, PO37 6AW; Tel 01983 862403; www.step-by-step.co.uk

Stockport Metropolitan Borough Council, Staircase House, 30 Market Place, STOCKPORT; Tel 0161 474 4444; www.stockport.gov.uk

Striding Edge Limited, Crag House Farm, WASDALE, Cumbria, CA19 1UT; Tel 0800 027 2527 (mail order); www.stridingedge.com

Suffolk Coast and Heaths Project, Dock Lane, Melton, WOODBRIDGE, Suffolk, IP12 1PE; Tel 01394 384948; www.suffolkcoastandheaths.org

Suffolk County Council, Countryside Officer, Countryside Service, Environment and Transport, 8 Russell Road, Endeavour House, IPSWICH, Suffolk, IP1 2BX; Tel 01473 265106; www.suffolkcc.gov.uk

Sunderland City Council, c/o Tourist Information Centre, 50 Fawcett Street, SUNDERLAND, SR1 1RF; Tel 0191 553 2000; www.visitsunderland.com

Surrey County Council, Environment Department, County Hall, Penryth Road, KINGSTON UPON THAMES, Surrey, KT1 2DN; Tel 020 8541 9944

Sussex Downs Joint Commitee HQ, Victorian Barn, Victorian Business Centre, Chanctonbury House, Ford Lane, Ford, Nr ARUNDEL, West Sussex, BN18 0EF; Tel 01243 558700; www.southdownsonline.org

Sussex Downs Joint Commitee Northern Area Office, South Downs Joint Committee, Midhurst Depot, Bepton Road, MIDHURST, West Sussex, GU29 9QX; Tel 01730 817945; www.southdowns.gov.uk

Sutton London Borough, Leisure Stop, Central Library, St Nicholas Way, SUTTON, Surrey, SM1 1EA; Tel 020 8770 4444

Sweeting, Don, The Levels, Portington Road, Eastrington, GOOLE, DN14 7QE; Tel 01430 410641

T

Tameside Countryside Warden Service, Chief Wardens Office, Park Bridge Visitor Centre, The Stables, Park Bridge, ASHTON-UNDER-LYNE, OL6 8AQ; Tel 0161 330 9613; www.tameside.gov.uk

Tarbert TIC, Harbour Street, TARBERT, Argyll and Bute, PA29 6UD; Tel 08707 200624

Tattersall, Max, 79 Ormerod Road, BURNLEY, Lancashire, BB11 2RU; Tel 01282 422756

Taunton Deane Borough Council, The Library, Paul Street, TAUNTON, Somerset, TA1 3XZ; Tel 01823 336344

Taunton TIC, Paul Street, TAUNTON, TA1 3XZ; Tel 01823 336344

Taylor, Sam R., 13 Dixon Street, Lees, OLDHAM, Lancashire, OL4 3NG

Tees Forest, Stewart Park, The Grove, MIDDLESBROUGH, TS7 8AR; Tel 01642 300716; www.teesforest.org.uk

Telford & Wrekin Countryside Service, Stirchley Grange, TELFORD, TF3 1DY; Tel 01952 384611; www.telford.gov.uk

Tempus Publishing Ltd, The Mill, Brimscombe Port, STROUD, GL5 2QG; Tel 01453 883300; www.thehistorypress.co.uk

Thames Path National Trail Officer, Environment and Economy, Holton, OXFORD, OX33 1QQ; Tel 01865 810224

Thames Water, Customer Services, PO Box 436, SWINDON, Wiltshire, SN38 1TU; Tel 08459 200800; www.thameswateruk.co.uk

The Map Shop, 15 High Street, UPTON UPON SEVERN, Worcestershire, WR8 0HJ Tel: 0800 0854080, www.themapshop.co.uk

Thomas, Norman, 13 Buckingham Avenue, Horwich, BOLTON, Lancashire, BL6 6NR; Tel 01204 691206

Thorne Moorends Town Council, Assembly Rooms, Fieldside, Thorne, DONCASTER, DN8 4AE

Thurstaston Visitor Centre, Wirral Country Park, Station Road, Thurstaston, WIRRAL, Merseyside, L61 0HN; Tel 0151 648 4371; www.wirral.gov.uk

Tinto Press, P.O. Box 9420, LANARK, Lanarkshire, ML11 7YL; Tel 01555 663145

Tony's Taxis (WSP), Maes Dewi, ST. DAVIDS, Pembrokeshire, SA62 6PA; Tel 01437 720931; www.tonystaxis.net

Torbay Coast & Countryside Trust, Cockington Court, Cockington, TORQUAY, Devon, TQ2 6XA; Tel 01803 606035; www.countryside-trust.org.uk

Torfaen County Borough, Civic Centre, PONTYPOOL, NP4 6YB; Tel 01633 648066; www.world-heritage-blaenavon.org.uk

Townson, Simon, 15 First Avenue, Starbeck, HARROGATE, North Yorkshire, HG2 7PA

Tracklogs, www.tracklogs.co.uk

Trafford Publishing, www.trafford.com

Trailblazer Publications, The Old Manse, Tower Road, HINDHEAD, Surrey, GU26 6SU; www.trailblazer-guides.com

Trailguides Ltd, 35 Carmel Road South, DARLINGTON, Co. Durham, DL3 8DQ; Tel 01325 283170; www.trailguides.co.uk

Trans Pennine Trail Officer, Trans Pennine Trail Office, Neighbourhood Services, PO Box 605, BARNSLEY, S70 9FF; Tel 01226 772574; www.transpenninetrail.org.uk

Transcotland (WSP), 5 Dunkeld Road, ABERFELDY, Perthshire, PH15 2EB; Tel 01887 820848; www.transcotland.com

Travel-Lite (WSP), The Iron Chef, 5 Mugdock Road, Milngavie, GLASGOW, G62 8PD; Tel 0141 956 7890; www.travel-lite-uk.com

Travis, Peter, 23 Kingsway East, Westlands, NEWCASTLE-UNDER-LYME, Staffordshire, ST5 3PY; Tel 01782 612985

Trek-Inn Holidays Limited (WSP), PO Box 7486, BRAINTREE, Essex, CM77 8WB; Tel 07005 803364; www.trek-inn.com

Trident Maps, 70 High Street, Houghton Regis, DUNSTABLE LU5 5BJ Tel: 01582 867211, maps@tridentmaps.co.uk

Tum, Edwin and Julia, High Manley, Manley Street, BRIGHOUSE, West Yorkshire, HD6 1TE; Tel 01484 400227

Turning The Tide, c/o Environmental and Technical Services Dept, County Hall, DURHAM, DH1 5UQ; Tel 0191 383 4640

TV walks.com, Bonza TV Ltd., 12 Swainson Road, LONDON, W3 7XB; Tel 0208 746 7300; www.tvwalks.com

Two Moors Way Association, 63 Higher Combe Drive, TEIGNMOUTH, Devon, TQ14 9NL

U

UK Exploratory (WSP), 9 Copperfield Street, WIGAN, WN1 2DZ; Tel 01942 826270; www.alpineexploratory.com

Ulverston TIC, Coronation Hall, County Square, ULVERSTON, Cumbria, LA12 7LZ; Tel 01229 587120

Underwood, Arnold, 41 The Orchards, LEVEN, East Yorkshire, HU17 5QA; Tel 01964 543883

V

Valeways, Unit 7, Barry Community Enterprise Centre, Skomer Road, BARRY, Glamorgan, CF62 9DA; Tel 01446 749000; www.valeways.org.uk

Vanguards Rambling Club, 3 Harlington Road, BEXLEYHEATH, DA7 4AS; Tel 020 8301 3829

Virtual Book Company, Old Mill Business Centre, WEST LOOE, Cornwall, PL13 2AE; Tel 0845 052 1867; www.virtualbookcompany.co.uk

Visit Burnley, Burnley Tourist Information Centre, Burnley Bus Station, Croft Street, BURNLEY, BB11 2EF; Tel 01282 664421; www.visitburnley.com

Visit Scottish Borders, Customer Service Centre, Shepherd's Mill, Whinfield Road, SELKIRK, TD7 5DT; Tel 0870 6080404; www.visitscottishborders.com

Visit Wales, Tel 08701 211251; www.walking.visitwales.com

VisitShetland, Market Cross, Lerwick, SHETLAND, ZE1 0LU; Tel 01595 693434; www.walkshetland.com

W

W & A Enterprises Ltd, c/o 24 Griffiths Avenue, LANCING, West Sussex, BN15 0HW; Tel 01403 752403; www.weyandarun.co.uk

Walk Awhile (WSP), Montgreenan, St Catherine's Drive, FAVERSHAM, Kent, ME13 8QL; Tel 01227 752762; www.walkawhile.co.uk

Walk London – Strategic Walks Information Service, Guildhall, PO BOX 270, LONDON, EC2P 2EJ; Tel 0870 240 6094; www.walklondon.org.uk

Walka-Longway (WSP), Bwthyn Clofer, Wiston, HAVERFORDWEST, Pembrokeshire, SA62 4PT; Tel 01437 769344; www.walka-longway.co.uk

Walkers Bags (WSP), Unit 3A, Townfoot Industrial Estate, BRAMPTON, Cumbria, CA8 1SW; Tel 0870 9905549; www.walkersbags.co.uk

Walking Distance (Maps) Ltd, Bargate Centre, York Buildings, SOUTHAMPTON, SO14 1HF; Tel 0906 682 2001; www.hamblevalley.com

Walking Pages Ltd, www.walkingpages.co.uk

Walking Support, 2 Wembley Terrace, MELROSE, Scotish Borders, TD6 9QR; Tel 01896 822079; www.walkingsupport.co.uk

Walkways, 67 Cliffe Way, WARWICK, CV34 5JG; Tel 01926 776363; www.walkwaysquercus.co.uk

Wallis, Ray, 75 Ancaster Avenue, KINGSTON-UPON-HULL, HU5 4QR; Tel 01482 341596

Wandering Aengus Treks (WSP), Fellside End, Fellside, Cumbria; Tel +44 (0)16974 78443; www.wanderingaengustreks.com

Wanderlust Rambling Club, 1 Chapel Road, Tetney, GRIMSBY, Lincolnshire, DN36 5JF

Wandle Industrial Museum, The Vestry Hall Annexe, London Road, MITCHAM, Surrey, CR4 3UD; Tel 020 8648 0127

Warner, Mike, Redland House, Clifton Cross, Clifton, ASHBOURNE, Derbyshire, DE6 2GJ; Tel 01335 344005

Watson, Ron, 33 Sutherland Avenue, Endike Lane, HULL, HU6 7UG; Tel 01482 804182

Wealden District Council, Regeneration, Freepost SEA10959, CROWBOROUGH, East Sussex, TN6 1BR; Tel 01273 481637; www.wealden.gov.uk

Welwyn Hatfield Council, Pedal Point, Transportation Unit, Welwyn Hatfield Council, The Campus, WELWYN GARDEN CITY, AL8 6AE; Tel 01707 357551; www.welhat.gov.uk

West Berkshire District Council, Countryside and Environment, Council Offices, Faraday Road, NEWBURY, Berks, RG14 2AF; Tel 01635 519808

West Highland Way Ranger, Balmaha Visitor Centre, Balmaha, GLASGOW, G63 0JQ; Tel 01389 722100

West Sussex County Council, The Grange, Tower Street, CHICHESTER, West Sussex, PO19 1RH; Tel 01243 777544; www.westsussex.gov.uk

Westcountry Walking Holidays (WSP), Tel 0845 094 3848; www.westcountry-walking-holidays.com

Weston-super-Mare Heritage Centre, 3–6 Wadham Street, WESTON SUPER MARE, Somerset, BS23 1JY; Tel 01934 412144

White Cliffs Countryside Project, 6 Cambridge Terrace, DOVER, Kent, CT16 1TT; Tel 01304 241806

Whittet Books, South House, Yatesbury Manor, YATESBURY, SN11 8YE; Tel 01672 539004; www.whittetbooks.com

Wild Goose Publications, Iona Community, 4th Floor, Savoy House, 140 Sauchiehall Street, GLASGOW, G2 3DH; Tel 0141 332 6292; www.iona.org.uk

Wilderness Scotland (WSP), 3a St Vincent Street, EDINBURGH, EH3 6SW; Tel 0131 625 6635; www.wildernessscotland.com

Wilkins, D. E., 21 Lane Ings, Marsden, HUDDERSFIELD, HD7 6JP; Tel 01484 844845

Wimbush, Tony, 10 Beaufort Grove, BRADFORD, BD2 4LJ; Tel 01274 636907

Winchester City Council, City Offices, Colebrook Street, WINCHESTER, Hampshire, SO23 9LJ; Tel 01962 840222

Worcestershire County Council, Countryside Service, PO Box 373, County Hall, Spetchley Road, WORCESTER, WR5 2XG; Tel 01905 763763; www.worcestershire.gov.uk

Wrexham Tourist Information Centre, Lambpit Street, WREXHAM, LL11 1AY; Tel 01978 292015

Wright, David, Inglenook Cottage, Rudge, FROME, Somerset, BA11 2QG; Tel 01373 830795

Wychavon District Council, Civic Centre, Queen Elizabeth Drive, PERSHORE, Worcestershire, WR10 1PT; Tel 01386 565373 X366; wychavon.whub.org.uk

Wycheway Country Walks (WSP), 39 Sandpiper Crescent, MALVERN, WR14 1UY; Tel 01886 833828; www.wychewaycountrywalks.co.uk

Wyreside Ecology Centre, Wyre Estuary Country Park, River Road, Stanah, THORNTON, Lancashire, FY5 5LR; Tel 01253 857890

Y

Y Lolfa, TALYBONT, Ceredigion, SY24 5AP; Tel 01970 832304; www.ylolfa.com

Yale University Press, 47 Bedford Square, LONDON, WC1B 3DP; Tel 020 7079 4900; yalepress.yale.edu

Yare Valley Publishers, 20 Bluebell Road, NORWICH, NR4 7LF

Yatton Ramblers, 26 Moorside, Yatton, BRISTOL, BS49 4RL; Tel 01934 832164

Yeovil Heritage and Visitor Information Centre, South Somerset District Council, Hendford, YEOVIL, Somerset, BA20 1UN; Tel 01935 845946

YHA Northern Region, PO Box 67, MATLOCK, Derbyshire, DE4 3YX; Tel 01629 592600; www.yha.org.uk

York City Council, PROW, 9 St Leonard's Place, YORK, YO1 7ET; www.york.gov.uk

Yorkshire and Humber Faiths Forum, Joseph's Well, Hanover Walk, LEEDS, LS3 1AB; Tel 0113 245 6444; www.yorkshireandhumberfaiths.org.uk

Yorkshire Wolds Way Project, c/o North York Moors National Park, The Old Vicarage, Bondgate, HELMSLEY, North Yorkshire; Tel 01439 770657

Young, Ken, 14 Wilton Orchard, TAUNTON, Somerset, TA1 3SA; Tel 01823 323147

Youth Hostels Association, Trevelyan House, Dimple Road, MATLOCK, Derbyshire, DE4 3YH Tel: 01629 592600, www.yha.org.uk

LONG DISTANCE WALKERS' ASSOCIATION

The Long Distance Walkers' Association (LDWA) has pioneered the communication of information on the LDP network in the UK since its formation in 1972. With over 150 routes developed by 1980, it published its first comprehensive directory, the *Long Distance Walkers' Handbook*, edited by one of its founders, Barbara Blatchford, with a further six more fully updated editions up to 2002, by which time the network had grown to almost 640 routes.

The LDWA is a users' association, rather than a campaigning organisation. It aims to 'further the interests of those who enjoy long distance walking', with a particular emphasis on non-competitive walking in rural, mountainous and moorland areas. As well as covering long distance paths, it promotes 'challenge walks' – cross-country walks undertaken by many walkers on the same occasion aiming to complete a route within a given time limit, sometimes based on an LDP. Its challenge walks range up to 100 miles.

Since 1985 the LDWA has been recognised by Sport England (formerly the Sports Council) as the governing body for long distance walking. The LDWA has over 6000 members and 40 local groups across Britain, each with programmes of regular walks. Its members' magazine, *Strider*, produced three times a year, covers all aspects of long distance walking, including path updates and features, listings and reports of challenge walks, and its local groups' programmes. Similar listings are available on its public website and non-members are welcome on most of these social walks and events. The LDWA maintains a public 'National Trails Register' open to anyone completing several National Trails, with an attractive range of certificates up to 'diamond' standard for those achieving all of the British Trails. It also maintains a 'Hillwalkers' Register' of those who have completed ascents of hills in various categories.

New members can join online at www.ldwa.org.uk

or write to The LDWA Membership Secretary
7 Shetland Way, Radcliffe
Manchester M26 4UH

or email **membership@ldwa.org.uk**.

The annual subscription for 2010 is £13 for individuals and £20 for families.

www.ldwa.org.uk

LISTING OF CICERONE GUIDES

BACKPACKING AND CHALLENGE WALKING
Backpacker's Britain:
Vol 1 – Northern England
Vol 2 – Wales
Vol 3 – Northern Scotland
Vol 4 – Central & Southern Scottish Highlands
End to End Trail
The National Trails
The UK Trailwalker's Handbook
Three Peaks, Ten Tors

BRITISH CYCLING
Border Country Cycle Routes
Cumbria Cycle Way
Lancashire Cycle Way
Lands End to John O'Groats
Rural Rides:
No 1 – West Surrey
No 2 – East Surrey
South Lakeland Cycle Rides

PEAK DISTRICT AND DERBYSHIRE
High Peak Walks
Historic Walks in Derbyshire
The Star Family Walks – The Peak District & South Yorkshire
White Peak Walks:
The Northern Dales
The Southern Dales

SUMMIT COLLECTIONS
Europe's High Points
Mountains of England & Wales:
Vol 1 – Wales
Vol 2 – England
Ridges of England, Wales & Ireland
The Relative Hills of Britain

IRELAND
Irish Coast to Coast Walk
Irish Coastal Walks
Mountains of Ireland

THE ISLE OF MAN
Isle of Man Coastal Path
Walking on the Isle of Man

LAKE DISTRICT AND MORECAMBE BAY
Atlas of the English Lakes
Coniston Copper Mines
Cumbria Coastal Way
Cumbria Way and Allerdale Ramble
Great Mountain Days in the Lake District
Lake District Anglers' Guide
Lake District Winter Climbs
Lakeland Fellranger:
The Central Fells
The Mid-Western Fells
The Near-Eastern Fells
The Southern Fells
Roads and Tracks of the Lake District
Rocky Rambler's Wild Walks
Scrambles in the Lake District:
Vol 1 – Northern Lakes
Vol 2 – Southern Lakes
Short Walks in Lakeland:
Book 1 – South Lakeland
Book 2 – North Lakeland
Book 3 – West Lakeland
Tarns of Lakeland:
Vol 1 – West
Vol 2 – East
Tour of the Lake District
Walks in Silverdale and Arnside

NORTHERN ENGLAND
LONG-DISTANCE TRAILS
Dales Way
Hadrian's Wall Path
Northern Coast to Coast Walk
Pennine Way
Reivers Way
Teesdale Way

NORTH-WEST ENGLAND
OUTSIDE THE LAKE DISTRICT
Family Walks in the Forest of Bowland
Historic Walks in Cheshire
Ribble Way
Walking in the Forest of Bowland and Pendle
Walking in Lancashire
Walks in Lancashire Witch Country
Walks in Ribble Country

PENNINES AND NORTH-EAST ENGLAND
Cleveland Way and Yorkshire Wolds Way
Historic Walks in North Yorkshire
North York Moors
The Canoeist's Guide to the North-East
The Spirit of Hadrian's Wall
Yorkshire Dales – North and East
Yorkshire Dales – South and West
Walking in County Durham
Walking in Northumberland
Walking in the North Pennines
Walking in the South Pennines
Walks in Dales Country
Walks in the Yorkshire Dales
Walking on the West Pennine Moors
Walks on the North York Moors: Books 1 and 2
Waterfall Walks – Teesdale and High Pennines
Yorkshire Dales Angler's Guide

SCOTLAND
Ben Nevis and Glen Coe
Border Country
Border Pubs and Inns
Central Highlands
Great Glen Way
Isle of Skye
North to the Cape
Lowther Hills
Pentland Hills
Scotland's Far North
Scotland's Far West
Scotland's Mountain Ridges
Scottish Glens:
2 – Atholl Glens
3 – Glens of Rannoch
4 – Glens of Trossach
5 – Glens of Argyll
6 – The Great Glen
Scrambles in Lochaber
Southern Upland Way
Walking in the Cairngorms
Walking in the Hebrides
Walking in the Ochils, Campsie Fells and Lomond Hills
Walking Loch Lomond and the Trossachs
Walking on the Isle of Arran
Walking on the Orkney and Shetland Isles
Walking the Galloway Hills
Walking the Munros:
Vol 1 – Southern, Central and Western
Vol 2 – Northern and Cairngorms
West Highland Way
Winter Climbs – Ben Nevis and Glencoe
Winter Climbs in the Cairngorms

SOUTHERN ENGLAND
Channel Island Walks
Exmoor and the Quantocks
Greater Ridgeway
Lea Valley Walk
London – The Definitive Walking Guide
North Downs Way
South Downs Way
South West Coast Path
Thames Path
Walker's Guide to the Isle of Wight
Walking in Bedfordshire
Walking in Berkshire
Walking in Buckinghamshire
Walking in Kent
Walking in Somerset
Walking in Sussex
Walking in the Isles of Scilly
Walking in the Thames Valley
Walking on Dartmoor

WALES AND THE WELSH BORDERS
Ascent of Snowdon
Glyndwr's Way
Hillwalking in Snowdonia
Hillwalking in Wales:
Vols 1 and 2
Lleyn Peninsula Coastal Path
Offa's Dyke Path
Pembrokeshire Coastal Path
Ridges of Snowdonia
Scrambles in Snowdonia
Shropshire Hills
Spirit Paths of Wales
Walking in Pembrokeshire
Welsh Winter Climbs

AFRICA
Climbing in the Moroccan Anti-Atlas
Kilimanjaro – A Complete Trekker's Guide
Trekking in the Atlas Mountains

THE ALPS
100 Hut Walks in the Alps
Across the Eastern Alps: The E5
Alpine Points of View
Alpine Ski Mountaineering:
Vol 1 – Western Alps
Vol 2 – Central & Eastern Alps
Chamonix to Zermatt
Snowshoeing: Techniques and Routes in the Western Alps
Tour of Mont Blanc
Tour of Monte Rosa
Tour of the Matterhorn
Walking in the Alps

EASTERN EUROPE
High Tatras
Mountains of Romania
Walking in Hungary

FRANCE, BELGIUM AND LUXEMBOURG
Cathar Way
Écrins National Park
GR5 Trail
GR20: Corsica
Mont Blanc Walks
Robert Louis Stevenson Trail
Selected Rock Climbs in Belgium and Luxembourg
Tour of the Oisans: The GR54
Tour of the Queyras
Tour of the Vanoise
Trekking in the Vosges and Jura
Vanoise Ski Touring
Walking in Provence
Walking in the Cathar Region
Walking in the Cevennes
Walking in the Dordogne
Walking in the Haute Savoie:
Vol 1 – North
Vol 2 – South
Walking in the Languedoc
Walking in the Tarentaise and Beaufortain Alps
Walking the French Gorges
Walking on Corsica
Walks in Volcano Country

FRANCE AND SPAIN
Canyoning in Southern Europe
Way of St James – France
Way of St James – Spain

GERMANY AND AUSTRIA
Germany's Romantic Road
King Ludwig Way
Klettersteig – Scrambles in Northern Limestone Alps
Trekking in the Stubai Alps
Trekking in the Zillertal Alps
Walking in Austria
Walking in the Bavarian Alps
Walking in the Harz Mountains
Walking in the Salzkammergut
Walking the River Rhine Trail

HIMALAYA
Annapurna: A Trekker's Guide
Bhutan
Everest: A Trekker's Guide
Garhwal & Kumaon: A Trekker's and Visitor's Guide
Kangchenjunga: A Trekker's Guide
Langtang with Gosainkund and Helambu: A Trekker's Guide
Manaslu: A Trekker's Guide
Mount Kailash Trek

ITALY
Central Apennines of Italy
Gran Paradiso
Italian Rock
Shorter Walks in the Dolomites
Through the Italian Alps: The GTA
Trekking in the Apennines
Treks in the Dolomites
Via Ferratas of the Italian Dolomites:
Vols 1 and 2
Walking in Sicily
Walking in the Central Italian Alps
Walking in the Dolomites
Walking in Tuscany

MEDITERRANEAN
High Mountains of Crete
Jordan – Walks, Treks, Caves, Climbs and Canyons
Mountains of Greece
The Ala Dag (Turkey)
Treks and Climbs Wadi Rum, Jordan
Walking in Malta
Western Crete

NORTH AMERICA
Grand Canyon with Bryce and Zion Canyons
John Muir Trail
Walking in British Columbia

THE PYRENEES
GR10 Trail: Through the French Pyrenees
Mountains of Andorra
Rock Climbs in the Pyrenees
Pyrenees – World's Mountain Range Guide
The Pyrenean Haute Route
Through the Spanish Pyrenees: GR11
Walks and Climbs in the Pyrenees

SCANDINAVIA
Pilgrim Road to Nidaros (St Olav's Way)
Walking in Norway

SLOVENIA, CROATIA AND MONTENEGRO
Julian Alps of Slovenia
Mountains of Montenegro
Trekking in Slovenia
Walking in Croatia

SOUTH AMERICA
Aconcagua

SPAIN AND PORTUGAL
Costa Blanca Walks:
Vol 1 – West
Vol 2 – East
Mountains of Central Spain
Picos de Europa
Via de la Plata (Seville to Santiago)
Walking in Madeira
Walking in Mallorca
Walking in the Algarve
Walking in the Canary Islands:
Vol 1 – West
Vol 2 – East
Walking in the Cordillera Cantabrica
Walking in the Sierra Nevada
Walking the GR7 in Andalucia

SWITZERLAND
Alpine Pass Route
Bernese Alps
Central Switzerland
Tour of the Jungfrau Region
Walking in the Valais
Walking in Ticino
Walks in the Engadine

INTERNATIONAL CYCLING
Cycle Touring in France
Cycle Touring in Spain
Cycle Touring in Switzerland
Cycling in the French Alps
Cycling the Canal du Midi
Cycling the River Loire – The Way of St Martin
Danube Cycle Way
Way of St James – Le Puy to Santiago

MINI GUIDES
Avalanche!
First Aid and Wilderness Medicine
Navigating with GPS
Navigation
Snow

TECHNIQUES AND EDUCATION
Beyond Adventure
Book of the Bivvy
Map and Compass
Mountain Weather
Moveable Feasts
Outdoor Photography
Rock Climbing
Snow and Ice
Sport Climbing
The Adventure Alternative
The Hillwalker's Guide to Mountaineering
The Hillwalker's Manual

For full and up-to-date information on our ever-expanding list of guides, please visit our website: **www.cicerone.co.uk**.